War and Revolution
in Yugoslavia, 1941-1945

THE CHETNIKS

JOZO TOMASEVICH

STANFORD UNIVERSITY PRESS
STANFORD, CALIFORNIA
1975

Stanford University Press
Stanford, California
© 1975 by the Board of Trustees of the
Leland Stanford Junior University
Printed in the United States of America
ISBN 0-8047-0857-6
LC 73-89862

Published with the assistance of
The Andrew W. Mellon Foundation

Preface

————◄•••►————

This is the first of three projected volumes dealing with the war and revolution in Yugoslavia during the period 1941–45. I originally planned
a one-volume history of the period, but the manuscript grew too large
and its complexity too great, and its splitting into several volumes became imperative. Since a purely chronological splitting would not have
alleviated the problem of complexity, I have elected to make separate
studies of the three main internal forces of the period: the Serbian
Chetniks, the Croatian Ustashas and other open collaborators, and the
Yugoslav Partisans. These forces fought against one another because
they followed different political principles, and because they differed
fundamentally on the problem of the continuation and nature of the
state of Yugoslavia as such.

In pursuit of their differing objectives, the Chetniks, the Partisans,
and the various collaborationist forces developed their specific military
and political strategies and sought the aid of mightier warring powers
as best suited their goals. The Great Powers, at the same time, made or
tried to make use of these contending groups to promote their own interests. And so the wartime situation in Yugoslavia became an un-
believable imbroglio.

In Part I of this volume I have given the historical background of
Yugoslavia up to the time of the Axis invasion in April 1941 and the
collapse of the country, showing the forces responsible for the establishment of the state in 1918 as well as the problems that beset it in the
interwar period and lay beneath the enmity of the opposing groups that
emerged during the occupation. This, in fact, is the introduction for
the entire three-volume study. Parts II and III concentrate on the story
of the Chetniks and their leader, General Mihailović. I have necessarily
had to say a good deal at one time or another about collaborationist

forces and the Partisans, but I have reserved the bulk of my material on these subjects for the future volumes.

In setting forth the complex story of the Chetniks, I have made extensive use of books, collections of documents, and articles in learned journals and newspapers originating in almost a dozen countries. But by far the most important source of information for this study has been the microfilmed German and Italian wartime documents made available through the United States National Archives, together with some German microfilmed documents that I obtained from British, West German, and Yugoslav authorities and individuals. These are all duly noted in the Bibliography. For reasons of convenience and economy, I have translated into English all quotations from published materials, microfilmed documents, and unpublished documents, as well as the titles of all articles in less familiar foreign languages, but all sources have been fully identified so that persons interested in further study of this material can find it without difficulty.

In the course of gathering information, and especially in four trips to Yugoslavia between 1963, when I began my work, and 1972, I have talked with many scores of persons, including Marshal Tito, about their wartime experiences and their opinions on various issues. I have talked at length with many Yugoslav historians specializing in the Yugoslav National Liberation War and Revolution. And I have corresponded with a number of persons in Yugoslavia and other countries regarding various issues connected with my study. To all these persons I express my heartfelt appreciation; some specific acknowledgments are made in the notes.

Although over the years I have assembled a large private library, I was greatly helped by the rich library resources of the Hoover Institution at Stanford University, the Library of San Francisco State University, and the Library of the University of California at Berkeley. To the staffs of all these institutions I express my sincere thanks. I am grateful also for books and other published materials lent me by a number of other scholars in the field and by several other persons who collect published materials on Yugoslavia or its component nations. I am also grateful for having had the opportunity to consult unpublished archival materials in the United States, Yugoslavia, and Great Britain. On numerous occasions in the course of writing this study I have used sources —documents, correspondence, interviews—which, for a variety of reasons, I am not free to identify. I have scrutinized information from such sources as carefully as I have information from identified sources, and I have used it only when in my judgment it carries as much weight. A great deal of pertinent material—politically or otherwise sensitive Yugoslav documents, Soviet materials, operational intelligence reports—may not soon, or ever, become available for scholarly inspection. In the circumstances the scholar's task can only be to get as near as possible to the truth.

There are two close friends whom I want to thank specifically for their unflagging interest in the study and the help they have given me: Professor Wayne S. Vucinich of the Department of History of Stanford University and Colonel Vojmir Kljaković of the Institute of Military History in Belgrade. Both of them, as well as another friend, Professor Bariša Krekić of the Department of History of the University of California at Los Angeles, read the entire manuscript in an earlier draft and made many valuable comments.

I am grateful to the preliminary editors of the first several chapters of my manuscript, Jesse M. Phillips and my daughter Neda Ann, and to Dave Pauly for the preparation of the maps. A feeling of most heartfelt gratitude goes to Shirley Taylor, who took the burden of editing in the early stages and carried it with understanding, extreme care, and great patience to the final copy for the press. From June 1965, when I presented a few chapters of an early draft of the study to Stanford University Press, through the long evolution of the project from a one-volume to a three-volume affair, I have had the friendly support and expert counsel of their Editor, J. G. Bell, on the overall organization and innumerable details of the study, and it gives me great pleasure to thank him here.

With the exception of a research leave for the spring semester of 1969 from San Francisco State University and some typing help by the University's typing service, all costs involved in completing this study have been borne by the Tomasevich household. For this, and for their understanding, patience, and steady support, it is to all the members of my family, and in particular to my wife Neda, that I owe the greatest debt of gratitude.

JOZO TOMASEVICH

Palo Alto, California
October 1974

Contents

PART ONE

The Coming of the War

CHAPTER ONE

Yugoslavia Between the Wars

HISTORICAL BACKGROUND

At the beginning of the nineteenth century the territorial and national components of modern Yugoslavia were parts of the multinational Ottoman and Habsburg empires. Gradually, first the Ottoman and much later the Habsburg empire began to lose strength; at the same time, under the influence of traditional forces and of ideas of nationalism and democracy, the movement for independence grew among the Slavs and other peoples within their borders. Serbia and Montenegro achieved their independence from the Ottoman Empire in the course of the nineteenth century, and during the Balkan Wars of 1912–13 they liberated the South Slav areas that were still ruled by the Turks. After the fall of Austria-Hungary at the end of the First World War, Serbia and Montenegro formed a common South Slav state with the Croats, Slovenes, and Serbs who had formerly been under Habsburg rule. During the century of gradual liberation and unification, the South Slavs were able to make considerable progress in political, cultural, and economic affairs, but they still lagged markedly behind the states of western and central Europe. In 1918, the least advanced areas were those that had remained under Ottoman rule until 1878 (Bosnia and Herzegovina) or until 1913 (Sandjak and Macedonia).

The territorial formation of the new Yugoslav state during the period 1913–19 is indicated on Map 1. The unification of the South Slavs into one state at the end of the First World War brought together five different though closely related peoples (Serbs, Croats, Slovenes, Macedonians, and Montenegrins), living in eight historically relatively well-defined areas (Serbia proper, Macedonia, Vojvodina, Bosnia and Herzegovina, Croatia-Slavonia, Dalmatia, Slovenia, and Montenegro), belonging to three main religious denominations (Serbian Orthodox, Roman Catholic, and Moslem), speaking three closely related yet different languages (Serbo-Croatian, Slovene, and Macedonian), and using two scripts (Latin and Cyrillic).

These five nations had never before been united in one state, and their political, cultural, and socioeconomic pasts varied greatly.[1] During the Middle Ages, both the Serbs and the Croats had well-developed states. The Croats lost theirs in 1102, when they concluded an agreement with the Hungarian kingdom. This connection lasted until 1918. From 1526 to 1918 both the Hungarians and the Croats were ruled by the Habsburg dynasty. From 1868 to 1918 Croatia formed an autonomous part of the Hungarian half of the Dual Monarchy. The Serbian medieval state was conquered by the Turks over a period of about ninety years, beginning with the Battle of the Maritsa River in 1371 and ending with the fall of the despotate of Smederevo in 1459. In medieval times there were in the Montenegrin area several states generally considered Serbian. Montenegro fell to the Turks in 1499, but certain isolated and economically and strategically unimportant areas were never fully subdued and up to the establishment of the modern Montenegrin state in the 1850's the inhabitants of these areas lived on as associations of clans.

The Bosnian medieval state, whose conquest by the Turks was completed in 1463, included both Croats and Serbs. For most of its existence it was controlled by the Bogomils, a heretical Christian church, who strongly opposed the encroachments both of Catholic Croatia and Hungary and of Orthodox Byzantium and Serbia, and most of whom eventually embraced Islam. Most of the Moslems of Bosnia and Herzegovina, in 1971 about one and a half million, are descendants of the Bogomils.

The Slovenes also had some early medieval principalities, but their lands fell under the control of the Germanic states early and they remained associated with Austria until 1918. In Macedonia, too, there were medieval states, but the area, originally under Byzantium, shifted periodically from Serbian to Bulgarian control and back again; it came earliest under Turkish rule and remained so until 1913.

In the late eighteenth century the South Slav peoples felt the first stirrings of a sense of national identity and a desire for national independence and unification. Among the Serbs, Croats, and Slovenes national identity in the modern sense of the word was completely developed during the first half of the nineteenth century under the influence of modern ideas of nationalism and democracy coming from the West. Among the Montenegrins there was a duality of feeling, as there is still, some considering themselves a part of the Serbian people, others considering themselves a separate people though closely related to the Serbs. Among the Macedonians, whose territory was vigorously claimed by the Serbs, the Bulgarians, and the Greeks as an integral part of their

---

[1] For a review of the history of the South Slavs from the time of their arrival in the Balkans in the early Middle Ages until 1918, see my book *Peasants, Politics, and Economic Change in Yugoslavia,* pp. 3–232; Ćorović, *Istorija Jugoslavije*; and Grafenauer et al., *Istorija naroda Jugoslavije,* 2 vols., which cover only the developments until the end of the eighteenth century. For complete authors' names, titles, and publication data on all works and on published and unpublished (microfilmed or not) collections of documents cited in the notes, see the Bibliography, pp. 475–92.

Map 1. Territorial formation of Yugoslavia, 1913–1919

states, there gradually developed a sense of being a distinct nationality with no allegiance to any of the claimants. This conviction received great impetus during the Second World War, and today there is a fully developed Macedonian nation, with its own literary language and national feeling, existing as a separate socialist republic within Yugoslavia.

During the first half of the nineteenth century there also developed in Croatia the idea of South Slav cultural and political unity, an idea that was to become the ideology of Yugoslav supranationalism. Unity seemed logical in several ways. All the South Slav peoples had a common racial background. The Croats and the Serbs spoke variants of the same language and lived together in many areas. Individually, the South Slav peoples, especially those living in the Austro-Hungarian Monarchy, were too weak to oppose with full success the political, cultural, and economic pressures coming from the Austrians and Hungarians. Their best hope seemed to lie in uniting with other South Slavs in one state.

From Croatia the Yugoslav supranationalist ideology spread to a certain extent among the other South Slav peoples. Owing to their varying conditions and aspirations their interpretations of it differed, but they all agreed that the Serbs, Croats, and Slovenes were essentially branches of the same Yugoslav nation and could hope to achieve full political liberation and unification in one Yugoslav state in which the feeling of mutual belonging would gradually supplant the feeling of Serb, Croat, and Slovene national separateness. Yugoslavism had two basic sources. One was the desire to preserve national identity and acquire strength through unity in the struggle against the multinational Habsburg Empire in which they were threatened with Germanization and Magyarization and in which they were treated as second-class citizens. The other was the example of other European peoples still living in many states, primarily the Germans and the Italians. This integral Yugoslavism was never widespread among the masses, but it had many adherents among the intellectuals in most South Slav nations and was an important ideological force behind the formation of the Yugoslav state in 1918.[2]

Like many political ideologies, the Yugoslav ideology was long on idealism and short on specific reasoning, and the new Yugoslav state experienced great internal political difficulties from the moment of its inception. With the Habsburg threat gone and independence achieved, new problems rose to the fore. Faced with the narrower nationalist proclivities of individual South Slav nations, the concept of Yugoslav supranationalism proved totally inadequate. The greatest blow came when the Serbian establishment began using the ideology as a cloak for its own hegemony in the new state; as a result, the whole idea of integral Yugoslavism lost credit during the interwar period.

The South Slav peoples differ greatly in numbers. Since Yugoslavia between the wars was completely under Serbian domination and did not recognize either a Montenegrin or a Macedonian nation, claiming that both of these peoples were Serbs, the best figures for our purposes are from postwar census data (Table 1). As the table shows, the two chief South Slav peoples were the Serbs and the Croats, followed by the Slovenes, the Macedonians, the Moslems who refused to declare themselves either as Serbs or as Croats,[3] and finally the Montenegrins. Among "other

[2] For interwar Yugoslavia and the history of its various component parts see the bibliography (to 1954) in *Peasants, Politics, and Economic Change in Yugoslavia*, pp. 703–26. Some of the newer studies on Yugoslavia during the interwar period are Lederer, *Yugoslavia at the Paris Peace Conference: A Study in Frontiermaking*; Hoptner, *Yugoslavia in Crisis, 1934–1941*; Valev, Slavin, and Udaljcov, eds., *Istoriia Iugoslavii*, II, 7–184; Čulinović, *Jugoslavija izmedju dva rata*; Kukoleča, *Analiza privrede Jugoslavije pred Drugi svetski rat*; and Stajić, *Nacionalni dohodak Jugoslavije 1923–1939 u stalnim i tekućim cenama*. Of the literature published by the Yugoslav political exiles, see especially Pavelić, *Dr. Ante Trumbić: Problemi hrvatsko-srpskih odnosa*; Maček, *In the Struggle for Freedom*; Stojadinović, *Ni rat ni pakt: Jugoslavija izmedju dva rata*; Jareb, *Pola stoljeća hrvatske politike*; and Ostović, *The Truth About Yugoslavia*.

[3] The Moslems of South Slav origin, i.e. the Moslems of Bosnia and Herzegovina, were at liberty in the 1948 census to declare themselves as Serbs, Croats, or undecided. In round numbers, 89 percent declared themselves as undecided, 8 percent as Serbs, and 3 percent as Croats. In the late 1960's the Moslems of Bosnia and Herzegovina officially acquired a status identical to that of a separate nation.

TABLE 1

The National Composition of Yugoslavia as of March 15, 1948

Slavic peoples	Population	Percent of total	Non-Slav minorities	Population	Percent of total
Serbs	6,547,117	41.51%	Albanians	750,431	4.76%
Croats	3,784,353	23.99	Hungarians	496,492	3.15
Slovenes	1,415,432	8.98	Vlakhs	102,953	0.65
Macedonians	810,126	5.13	Turks	97,954	0.62
Montenegrins	425,703	2.70	Italians	79,575	0.50
Moslems, undecided	808,921	5.13	Gypsies	72,736	0.46
Other Slavs	240,990	1.53	Romanians	64,095	0.41
			Germans	55,337	0.35
			Others	19,883	0.13
TOTAL	14,032,642	88.97%		1,739,456	11.03%

SOURCE: Yugoslavia, *Statistički godišnjak FNRJ 1954* (Statistical Yearbook of the Federal People's Republic of Yugoslavia, 1954), Belgrade, 1954, p. 60.

Slavs" the largest group were the Slovaks and the Bulgarians. In addition, as a consequence of the peace treaties following the First World War, between 500,000 and 600,000 Croats and Slovenes living in Istria, the Julian March, Rijeka (Fiume), Zadar (Zara), and various Adriatic islands were allotted to Italy.[4] About 65,000 Carinthian Slovenes remained under Austria after 1918.

Non-Slavs make up a greater minority population in Yugoslavia than in any other European country except the Soviet Union. The most numerous are the Albanians, concentrated in the Kosovo region (about 30 percent of all Albanians live in Yugoslavia), and the Hungarians, living almost exclusively in Vojvodina. During the interwar period, to these two large minorities was added a third, the Germans living mostly in Vojvodina, Srijem, Slavonia, and Slovenia. In the 1930's they numbered around 550,000, but in 1948, after voluntary withdrawal with the retreating German armies in the closing stages of the war and then expulsion by the new government, they had dwindled to a tenth that number.

Added to the multinational character of Yugoslavia, the fact that most of the large minority population lived in border areas made the country extremely fragile from a political point of view during the interwar period. Large minorities are a potential source of trouble if they are subjected to political, cultural, and economic restrictions not imposed on the majority, or if their homelands are ready and able to exploit them for revisionist or expansionist purposes. Both conditions obtained in Yugoslavia.

Turning to the religious sphere, the census figures of 1931 show that roughly 48 percent were of the Serbian Orthodox faith (Serbs, Mace-

[4] These regions, except for a small part of the Julian March, were incorporated into the new Yugoslavia in 1945 and 1953.

donians, Montenegrins, and various minorities in areas populated mostly by Serbs), 37 percent were Roman Catholics (mainly Croats and Slovenes), 11 percent were Moslems (the Slavic Moslems of Bosnia and Herzegovina, and the Albanian and Turkish minorities), and fewer than 4 percent were Protestants or Jews. In the 1953 census the proportions were essentially the same: 48 percent Orthodox, 36 percent Catholic, 14 percent Moslem, and 2 percent all others.[5] Since religious ties greatly influenced the sense of national belonging of the various South Slav peoples, and since relations between the different churches were characterized by suspicion and intolerance (both for general historical reasons and for specific recent ones), the religious diversity of the country was yet another of its many problems.

GOVERNMENT AND POLITICS, 1918–1939

Having suffered in captivity for many centuries and, in the case of Serbs and Montenegrins, having experienced only a relatively short period of modern statehood, the South Slav peoples when united in 1918 were above all eager to preserve their national independence, their national character and heritage, and their national aspirations. Logically, the new state should have been organized on a federal principle so as to allow each of the peoples its free development so far as may have been compatible with the ultimate goal of strengthening the bonds between them. Instead, the new Yugoslav state of 1918 was organized on rigidly centralistic lines. Given Serbia's forty-odd years of virtual independence and another forty years of fully independent existence, its distinguished record in the Balkan Wars of 1912–13 and the First World War in which it was on the Allied side, and the fact that the Serbs were by far the largest of the nationalities, Serbian predominance in the new state was a foregone conclusion. The majority of non-Serb South Slavs probably soon came to feel that they had merely exchanged one form of foreign rule—by the Austrians, the Hungarians, or the Turks—for another, though milder, one. Thus from the very start the unsolved national question, particularly as it related to the Croats and Macedonians, poisoned the life of the new state and undermined its foundations.

In both domestic and foreign policies, the new multinational and multireligious Yugoslav state, now with more than 12 million people, was run by the Serbian ruling elite little differently from the pre-1918 Balkan Serbian kingdom—a small country, nationally and religiously homogeneous, without marked regional differences in the level of economic and cultural development, and with only 3.5 million people.[6] For

[5] Yugoslavia, Information Service, *The Church in the Federal People's Republic of Yugoslavia,* p. 3.
[6] For a concise presentation of the political developments and problems of Yugoslavia between the wars see Vucinich, "Interwar Yugoslavia," and for a discussion of the complex nationality problems between 1918 and the early 1960's see his "Nationalism and Communism."

many years, indeed, the leaders of the old Serbian state were the dominant political figures in the new Yugoslav state, which the Serbian establishment treated essentially as an expanded Serbia.

The Constitution of 1921, passed by the Serbian parties in the Constituent Assembly with the help of a few purchased votes of the Macedonian and Bosnian Moslems and a small Slovene splinter party, not only made Serbian hegemony constitutionally possible but also effectively stifled a potentially constructive political life in the new country.[7] Even during the parliamentary period, up to 1929, Alexander (Regent, and after August 16, 1921, King) wielded great power over the actions of Serbian politicians and political parties. For the sake of appearances a few Croats and Slovenes were always included in the cabinet, but the office of Prime Minister and the important ministries, such as Foreign Affairs, Army and Navy, Interior (Police), and Justice, were nearly always held by Serbs.

In the defense of their power, the Serbian ruling circles used a combination of sham legality and intimidation, turning to their purposes the centralistic constitutions, the gerrymandering of electoral districts, and after October 1929 also of banovinal (regional) boundaries, the enactment of severe laws on the protection of the realm, the total control of the military and the police force, and censorship of the press. Dissent was dangerous, even in parliament. On June 20, 1928, in the midst of a parliamentary debate, one of the deputies of the Radical Party (a former president of one of the extremist Chetnik associations), Puniša Račić, pulled out a revolver and shot five members of the Croatian Peasant Party, killing two on the spot, because they dared to denounce corruption in the government.[8]

On January 6, 1929, King Alexander abolished the Constitution of 1921, outlawed all political parties, and introduced his personal regime, naming General Petar Živković, the Comander of the Royal Guard, as Prime Minister.[9] His rule was ensured by the army—an exclusively Serbian-run institution over which he had gained control by eliminating the dissident part of the army leadership at the Salonika trial during the First World War—and by the Belgrade political and economic cliques.[10]

---

[7] In the voting on June 28, 1921, there were 223 votes in favor of the Constitution; 196 votes either were against it or belonged to members who did not participate in the work of the Constituent Assembly, e.g. the Croatian Peasant Party. The members of the Constituent Assembly who voted in favor of the Constitution represented, owing to gerrymandering of electoral districts, less than half of the total popular vote cast. After the adoption of the Constitution, the Constituent Assembly (*Ustavotvorna skupština*) declared itself a regular parliament (*Narodna skupština*).

[8] One of the three men wounded, Stjepan Radić, the party leader, died about six weeks later. On the background and political associations of Puniša Račić see Šehić, pp. 83–91. See also Chapter 5, pp. 118–19.

[9] The cabinet posts were held either by old Serbian, Croatian, and Slovene party politicians enjoying royal confidence, or by technicians.

[10] The Karadjordjević dynasty was returned to the Serbian throne in 1903 by a group of officers headed by Dragutin T. Dimitrijević-Apis after they had killed the last scion of the Obrenović dynasty, King Alexander. In 1911 Apis helped to organize the secret society Unification or Death, popularly known as the Black Hand, whose goal was the unification of all South Slavs; this society

Alexander justified the change on the grounds that the constant bicker-ings and disagreements among the political parties were endangering the existence of the state. In 1931, having come to think that it would be easier to rule with some semblance of political parties than without them, Alexander granted a new constitution that fully safeguarded his extraordinary personal prerogatives and powers while also allowing a very limited amount of party activity.

Alexander was assassinated in Marseilles on October 9, 1934, on his arrival for a state visit to France. His assassin was a member of the In-ternal Macedonian Revolutionary Organization, but the action was or-ganized by the Croatian terrorist organization Ustasha, led by Dr. Ante Pavelić, which operated from bases in Italy and Hungary.[11] Alexander was succeeded by his son King Peter II, but since he was a minor, a coun-cil of three regents, headed by Alexander's cousin Prince Paul, acted for the king. Prince Paul—in practice the only decision-making regent—was determined to protect the constitution and the nature of the regime so as to transmit it to Peter exactly as his father had left it. His dictatorial rule proved to be much milder than Alexander's and the external and domestic conditions forced him to make some revisions in the political organization of the country (which in fact meant a change in the 1931 constitution), but the Serbian hegemony remained almost as secure as before.

It was true enough, as the King had said in 1929, that the chief po-litical parties, including those in opposition—notably the Croatian Peas-ant Party, the Independent Democratic Party, the Serbian Agrarian Party, very often the Slovene People's Party and the Yugoslav Moslem Organization, and during the 1930's large segments of the (Serbian) Dem-ocratic and the Radical parties—seemed always in disagreement. No Yugoslav bourgeois or peasant political party had an all-Yugoslav pro-gram or following. Practically all parties were not only regional but backward-looking, so that even if they had found a way of uniting it is doubtful whether they could have dealt effectively with Yugoslavia's problems. By law, the minimum age for members of the National As-

---

was directly implicated in the assassination of Archduke Franz Ferdinand at Sarajevo in 1914. After the Balkan Wars, Apis (who in the meantime had become Chief of Military Intelligence) and his friends quarreled with the government on policies to be pursued in the newly liberated areas in the south. These differences continued even after the exodus of the Serbian army to the Greek island of Corfu in 1915 and its later transfer to Salonika. When in 1916 it appeared that Serbia might have to conclude a separate peace with the Central Powers, it was thought that Apis would stand in the way. Thus for a whole series of reasons it was thought best to remove him. Certain incidents were engineered and Apis and several others were accused of having attempted to assas-sinate Regent Alexander and Prime Minister Nikola Pašić and of plotting to overthrow the dynasty and introduce a military dictatorship. In a military trial at Salonika in 1917 Apis and two others were sentenced to death and later executed, many were imprisoned, and about forty officers were retired. In a retrial conducted in 1953 at Belgrade Apis and his friends were rehabilitated post-humously. See Milan Ž. Živanović, pp. 178–84 and *passim*.

[11] Vladeta Milićević, *Der Königsmord von Marseille*. More about the Ustasha organization will be said in Chapter 4.

sembly was thirty years, and for senators, forty. Since there was almost no political activity at the local level, there was no training ground for political leadership. Party leaders were mostly old, and youthful membership was not encouraged. This was true even in the well-established Croatian Peasant Party.[12]

Only on a few occasions during the 1930's did the opposition parties arrive at an agreement for combined action to counter the government party coalition. Thus in the elections of May 1935 and December 1938 several opposition parties jointly supported a single electoral list as a way of meeting the election requirements imposed by the 1931 constitution, which demanded for each electoral list a minimum of sixty signatures in more than half of all the counties in at least two-thirds of the nine *banovine*. For the most part, the opposition parties agreed only on what they were against, not what they were for.

A particularly interesting party, in the light of subsequent developments, was the Communist Party of Yugoslavia. It was established in 1919 by a merger of the Social Democratic parties that existed prior to 1914 in various areas consolidated into the state of Yugoslavia. As in other European countries, the "left" elements separated in 1919 and formed the Communist Party of Yugoslavia as a section of the Communist International. In the November 1920 elections for the Constituent Assembly, the Communist Party obtained 12.3 percent of the total vote cast and 13.8 percent of all representatives elected. It had even greater success in the elections for local government in Serbia and Croatia, especially in urban centers, including Zagreb and Belgrade.[13] In fact, the Communists won a plurality of votes cast in Belgrade and thus were entitled to control the city government, but the central government intervened and prevented them from assuming that control. The party fomented strikes in many parts of the country, including an effective one against the state railways, and spread propaganda against the existing government and social order. Alarmed at what had happened in Russia and Hungary, the Yugoslav government at the end of December 1920 issued a special decree drastically reducing the activity of the Communist Party, its trade union organizations, and its press. In June 1921 a party member attempted to assassinate Prince Regent Alexander, and

---

[12] When the Croatian Peasant Party participated in the government between August 1939 and April 1941 and had almost full control of autonomous Croatia, it sponsored a law for the elections to the *Sabor* (Croatian diet) which set the voting age at twenty-four. The voting age for the Yugoslav National Assembly was twenty-one, but Dr. Maček, the head of the CPP, thought that was too young for political responsibilities such as voting. Maček, pp. 200–201.

Many Yugoslav politicians mentioned in this book are referred to as "Dr." This is in agreement with the custom in Yugoslavia, and in many other European countries, by which all persons who have acquired a doctoral degree in medicine, law, humanities, or the social and natural sciences use the title with their name. Many politicians in prewar Yugoslavia had this title because they had acquired a Doctor of Jurisprudence degree, either at home or abroad in years prior to the Second World War.

[13] Hasanagić, ed., pp. 18–20, 38–40.

in July another member assassinated former Minister of the Interior Milorad Drašković, the author of the December 1920 decree. The government responded by outlawing the party altogether in August 1921, and the mandates of the Communist deputies were annulled by the parliament. The party went underground, where it continued to operate on a limited scale despite police harassment.

The underground Communist Party was not at all a cohesive political group. Its leaders were too doctrinaire to achieve a satisfactory understanding of Yugoslavia's political and economic situation, and they could not agree on what strategy and tactics to follow. The membership was infiltrated by police agents, and one by one the leaders were imprisoned, forced to flee the country, or killed.[14] By 1932 the party had dwindled to a few hundred members. During most of the interwar period the Central Committee operated from abroad. Both the Communist International and the Soviet authorities deplored the party's perennial factionalism; its leaders were repeatedly changed and practically all the members of the Central Committee in the mid-1930's perished in Stalin's purges of 1936 and 1937. Finally, in 1937, prospects for improving conditions in the party brightened when the Comintern installed Josip Broz—later known as Marshal Tito—as party chief with full power to appoint the remainder of the new leadership, who then set about rebuilding the party.[15]

ECONOMIC AND SOCIAL PROBLEMS, 1918–1939

Along with its disordered domestic politics, the Yugoslav state in the period between the wars had many problems of an economic and social nature, some of them common to other countries in the Balkan area, some uniquely Yugoslavian. Simply stated, these problems were the following: (1) a rising population overall, but widely differing rates of growth among the various South Slav peoples and religious groups; (2) economic underdevelopment together with a largely rural economy that was increasingly incapable of supporting a growing population; (3) complex relationships with other countries, in which political and economic interests were often incompatible; (4) extensive foreign interests in industry and mining; and, (5), the growing tendency toward statism, which had a direct political and economic significance.

In the years 1921 to 1939 the population of Yugoslavia increased from 12,149,000 to an estimated 15,703,000. For the period, this represented one of the highest growth rates in Europe, even though the annual rate

---

[14] For the texts of the principal laws and decrees directed against the Communists and their application in interwar Yugoslavia see Ribar, *Stara Jugoslavija i komunizam*. See also Hasanagić, pp. 47–56, 201–30.

[15] For the thinking of the CPY leadership during the late 1930's about the solution of the national question in Yugoslavia, see Kardelj (writing under the pseudonym Sperans), *Razvoj slovenskega narodnega vprašanja*, pp. 205–55.

was actually on the decline—falling from an average of 14.8 per thousand per annum during the period 1921–25 to an average of 11.7 per thousand during the period 1936–39. Both the birthrate and the death rate fell. The latter fell partly because of a reduction in the high rate of infant mortality (during the period 1936–38 it still averaged 141 per thousand live births). Life expectancy in 1931 was estimated at 46.5 years for males and 49.5 years for females.[16]

A leading Yugoslav demographer has calculated that the population of what today comprises Yugoslavia roughly doubled between 1880 and 1957. In the present territory of Slovenia the population increased 1.4 times; in Croatia, 1.6 times; in Serbia, 2.2 times; in Macedonia and Montenegro, 2.3 times; and in Bosnia and Herzegovina, 2.5 times.[17] In general, the increases were most rapid in the poor and backward regions, and the imbalance in the rates of population growth only added to the tension that already existed between the various national and religious groups. Especially important was the considerably higher rate of growth of the Serbian (Orthodox) than of the Croatian (Roman Catholic) population.

There was some shifting of population, especially in the years immediately following the First World War, when people from mountainous areas, mostly Serbs and Montenegrins, moved into Vojvodina, Srijem, Slavonia, Macedonia, and the Kosovo region to take over land made available by the agrarian reform. This colonization had a definite political aspect in that it was intended to strengthen the Serbian element in the respective areas. Some permanent emigration of the Turkish element from Macedonia to Turkey also occurred. There were, as well, relatively large shifts of population, primarily of young people, from rural areas into the cities and towns in search of work and education.

The movement away from rural areas to the towns was a long-established trend. But while the proportion of those engaged in agriculture and forestry declined slightly, the actual number of those so engaged rose steadily along with the population. The effects of the increase in terms of the peasant can be shown dramatically. Let us assume, as a generally acceptable norm under Yugoslav conditions of peasant farming, an agricultural population of 80 persons per 100 hectares of cultivated land (here defined as including arable land, gardens, orchards, and vineyards but excluding permanent meadowland and pastures) or about five hectares per average peasant family. In 1921 Yugoslavia already had 135 agricultural persons per 100 hectares of cultivated land—making it the most agriculturally overpopulated country of eastern and southeastern Europe. In the next ten years, despite an increase in cultivated

16 Tomasevich, *Peasants*, pp. 287–307.
17 Macura, pp. 7–8.

land which was more than compensated for by an increase in agricultural population, this ratio grew to 140, and in 1938 it reached an estimated 144, or according to the above standard a "surplus" agricultural population of 44.4 percent.[18] Moreover, a worsening of the ratio of agricultural population to livestock numbers occurred between the wars, which had unfavorable consequences for crop yields and the nutrition of the peasants. Finally, since emigration overseas was greatly restricted during the 1920's and became practically impossible during the 1930's because of the Depression, and since job opportunities outside of agriculture were growing very slowly, the bulk of the burgeoning rural population had to remain on the land, where its frustrations—exacerbated by political oppression, low income, unfavorable terms of trade between agricultural and industrial products, exorbitant interest rates, and crushing taxes—made it a potentially explosive force.

By the mid-1930's it was generally agreed that a solution, or even a marked amelioration, of the problem of agricultural overpopulation could not be found within agriculture alone—as was formerly believed, especially by the peasant parties—but required a massive, long-term industrialization effort. Unfortunately, conditions for mounting such an effort could scarcely have been worse. Per capita income in Yugoslavia in the 1930's was almost the lowest in Europe; for 1938 it has been estimated at 3,100 dinars, or roughly $70. From this basic fact arose the well-known vicious circle of underdevelopment. Low income meant low consumption and low savings; low savings meant low investment; low investment meant low income, and so on, without hope of change if things were left to themselves. The low per capita income in Yugoslavia was primarily a consequence of the poor productivity of the economy, which resulted from two factors: the paucity of natural resources and man-made means of production in comparison with the size of the population, and the low productivity of labor.

Other indicators, quantitative and qualitative, reflect the state of economic underdevelopment. In 1931, for example, 76.5 percent of the population derived their livelihood from agriculture and only 11 percent from industry, mining, and handicrafts. Between 1926 and 1939 (in 1938 prices) 46 percent of the national income was derived from agriculture, while 18.9 percent was derived from industry, and 35.1 percent from other activities.[19]

Furthermore, most of the farming was at the subsistence or quasi-subsistence level. About 80 percent of arable land was planted to cereals, mostly corn (maize), used chiefly for direct human consumption. Only

[18] Tomasevich, *Peasants*, pp. 322, 324. Moore, pp. 63–64, considers that during the 1930's the percentage of redundant population in Yugoslav agriculture, on the basis of norms different from ours, was as high as 61.5 percent.
[19] Stajić, "Real National Income of Yugoslavia During the Periods 1926–1939 and 1947–1956," p. 19.

about 14 percent of all protein consumption came from animal food products. Animal husbandry was managed along very primitive lines, and the performance of animal draft power was unsatisfactory in many areas. Just before the outbreak of the Second World War, there were in Yugoslavia only about 2,300 tractors, primarily in the area of Vojvodina where the farm technology was on a much higher level than in the rest of the country. Wooden plows were still much in use in areas south of the Danube and Sava rivers. Almost no artificial fertilizers were applied, and chemical pesticides were used only in vineyards and in certain areas also in orchards.

Internal trade organization was poorly developed. There was no national money and capital market, and the country's financial institutions were generally primitive. Social overhead capital was inadequately developed. Life expectancy remained short, as we have seen, and infant mortality high; high also were morbidity rates from tuberculosis, malaria, and nutritional diseases. In 1921, of all persons above the age of ten at least 51.5 percent were illiterate; a high additional percentage were semiliterate. The differences in literacy between areas were striking, ranging from 8.8 percent illiterate in Slovenia to 83.8 percent in Macedonia.[20]

Not surprisingly, the development of the economy varied a great deal from one region to another, in part because of the differences in natural resources but also because of differences in historical background and population growth. Since we have no figures for per capita income and per capita reproducible wealth between the wars on a regional basis, we must make do with 1953 figures (Table 2).[21] As the table shows, the level of per capita income in Slovenia was almost twice the national average; in Montenegro, Macedonia, and Bosnia and Herzegovina it was considerably below the national figure. Unfortunately, per capita income data are not available for the components of the People's Republic of Serbia, but the per capita wealth figures indicate the unevenness of the economic development: Serbia proper was twenty points below the national average in per capita reproducible wealth, the Autonomous Region Vojvodina was seventeen points above the national average, and the Albanian-populated Autonomous Region Kosovo-Metohia (now Kosovo), which has the highest rate of population growth in the country, was less than half the average.

Between the wars Yugoslavia badly lacked entrepreneurial talent.

20 Tomasevich, *Peasants*, p. 198.
21 These figures should be taken only as indicating orders of magnitude for 1953, because reproducible wealth was differently affected in different areas during the Second World War, investment activity between 1946 and 1953 differed greatly between various areas, and relative prices in 1953 departed considerably from the interwar price structure. The 1953 figures do, however, convey a fairly dependable picture of regional differences in the level of economic development between the wars.

TABLE 2

Distribution of Population, Per Capita Income, and Per Capita Reproducible Wealth, People's Republics, Yugoslavia, 1953

Area (PR—People's Republic AR—Autonomous Region)	Population (March 31, 1953) Percent of total	Per capita income (1953) Percent of national average	Per capita repro- ducible wealth (end of 1953) Percent of national average
FPR Yugoslavia	100.0%	100%	100%
PR Serbia	41.3	90	85
Serbia proper	26.4	—	80
AR Vojvodina	10.1	—	117
AR Kosovo-Metohia	4.8	—	45
PR Croatia	23.1	113	126
PR Slovenia	8.6	188	185
PR Bosnia and Herzegovina	16.8	80	80
PR Macedonia	7.7	71	62
PR Montenegro	2.5	61	74

SOURCES: For the population, Yugoslavia, *Statistički godišnjak FNRJ 1956* (Statistical Yearbook FPRY, 1956), Belgrade, 1956, p. 51. For per capita income, Yugoslavia, *Narodni dohodak 1952–1956* (National income, 1952–1956), Statistical Bulletin No. 115, Belgrade, 1958, p. 10. The Yugoslav concept of national income differs from the one used in the West in that it does not include the value of what Marxists call the economically unproductive services, such as state activity; this fact does not affect the above series in any appreciable fashion.

For per capita reproducible wealth, Ivo Vinski, *Procjena nacionalnog bogatstva po područjima Jugoslavije* (An Estimate of the National Wealth of Yugoslavia by Regions), Zagreb, 1959, p. 33. Vinski presents national wealth data both in undepreciated and depreciated figures. The undepreciated series is used here, but differences between the two series are not very pronounced. The undepreciated figures have a greater economic significance as indicators of produtive capacity.

People with capital to spare tended to invest it in trading activities or in urban real estate, which required little entrepreneurial or managerial capacity. Long-term investments in industrial activity attracted few, in good part because of the small demand for industrial products. (The textile industry, with its low capital-output ratio and sizable domestic market, was an exception.) The shortage of savings and of native entrepreneurial talent led to large-scale importation of foreign capital and managerial personnel, as well as to widespread government activity in the economy. The government sought to stimulate economic growth not only by such classic measures as a protective tariff and tax subsidies, but also by directly developing state-owned industrial plants and investing in transportation, public utilities, schools, and public health facilities, which in turn indirectly encouraged the development of privately owned enterprises.

Despite government efforts, the growth of the economy was so sluggish that it barely surpassed the rapid increase in the population.[22] The

[22] Stajić estimates that between 1926 and 1939 the per capita income of the population as a whole (in 1938 prices) rose by 0.73 percent annually ("Real National Income," pp. 21–26). Vinski's estimate for the period 1920–39, based on 1953 prices, is an annual rise of 1.70 percent ("National Product and Fixed Assets," pp. 206–11). The difference is due to the use of different base years and different relative prices. As we have seen, population rose on the average by 1.48 percent annually in the period 1921–25, and by 1.17 percent annually in the period 1936–39.

onslaught of the Great Depression, though it affected all branches of the Yugoslav economy, was especially felt in agriculture and the banking system, and to such an extent that recovery was delayed long after the trough of the depression had been left behind in many other countries. The sharp recovery that occurred after 1936 was largely the result of improved economic conditions abroad, in which the military preparations of various European countries, notably Germany, had a great share.

Amid the power relationships and conflicts of interwar Europe, the situation of Yugoslavia was precarious. From its inception the country was exposed to the revisionist and expansionist pressures of Italy, Bulgaria, and Hungary; after the advent of the Nazi government, Germany's political and economic pressures were an added threat. Each of these foreign states was in close contact with one or more extremist political groups within Yugoslavia, groups that were ready and willing to use foreign support to defeat their domestic enemies. The old Internal Macedonian Revolutionary Organization became a tool of both Bulgaria and Italy. The Croatian terrorist organization Ustasha was used by Italy, Hungary, and Germany; the German minority by Germany; and the Albanian minority by Albania and, after 1939, by Italy. In addition, the Communist Party of Yugoslavia was throughout the interwar period a tool of the Soviet Union and the Comintern. From 1923 to 1935, the party advocated not only the overthrow of the Yugoslav government but also the breaking up of the Yugoslav state into separate national Communist republics.

Yugoslavia's chief diplomatic ties between the wars were initially with France, and with Czechoslovakia and Romania in the Little Entente; that is, it was part of the French system of postwar alliances. In 1934, with Greece, Romania, and Turkey it formed the Balkan Entente. Of these five countries only Czechoslovakia had strong economic ties with Yugoslavia; Greece, Romania, and Turkey, all similar in economic structure to Yugoslavia, were not so much partners as competitors. What is worse, Yugoslavia's strongest economic ties were with countries with which it had little or no political sympathy—Italy, Austria, and Germany. The problem is dramatically illustrated by Table 3.

After the ascendancy of Nazi Germany in Europe and the eclipse of France, around 1935, Yugoslavia under the leadership of Prince Paul and Prime Minister Milan Stojadinović began to follow a foreign policy that was formally neutralist but gradually became quite friendly toward the Axis powers. The hardships forced on the country by the League of Nations' economic sanctions against Italy after its invasion of Ethiopia made a stronger economic orientation toward Germany inevitable, and with it a turn toward closer political ties. The absorption of Austria into the Reich and the breaking up of Czechoslovakia finally put Yugoslavia

TABLE 3

Yugoslavia's Exports and Imports by Country, 1931–35

(Percent of total)

Country	Exports to	Imports from
France	2.4%	4.5%
Great Britain	3.3	8.6
United States	2.7	5.3
Czechoslovakia	12.8	14.3
Austria	17.9	13.8
Germany	14.1	16.0
Italy	21.4	12.9
Greece	4.2	1.3
Romania	0.6	2.2
Turkey	0.1	0.1
Soviet Union	0.0	0.1

SOURCE: Yugoslavia, Ministry of Finance, Customs Section, *Statistique du commerce extérieur*, Belgrade, published annually 1931–35. Yugoslav exports consisted mostly of agricultural products and raw materials, such as timber and nonferrous metals; imports were mainly of textile raw materials, machinery, appliances, chemicals, pharmaceuticals, and fuels, including coke. For more information, see Jozo Tomasevich, "Foreign Economic Relations, 1918–1941," in Robert J. Kerner, ed., *Yugoslavia* (Berkeley and Los Angeles, 1949), pp. 169–214.

economically at the mercy of Germany; as in other instances, this economic advantage was used by the Germans to prepare the ground for political and/or military conquest.

Most large business enterprises in Yugoslavia between the wars—factories, mines, banks, insurance companies, and the like—were owned, controlled, and managed by foreigners. Before 1918, when more than half of Yugoslavia's territory was part of the Austro-Hungarian Empire, Austrian and Hungarian investors had dominated all capitalist branches of the economy in these parts. Most of their investments were "nationalized" after the First World War, but this nationalization was only formal and foreign owners continued to control these now nominally Yugoslav companies. In the mid-1920's, after the currency was de facto stabilized and public finances were put in order, foreign capital started to come in on an increasing scale, both directly and indirectly through foreign-owned commercial banks. To encourage this trend the government granted foreign-owned companies advantages in regard to taxes, duty-free importation of capital goods, transfer of profits, and the like.

At the end of 1937, the percentage of foreign ownership in the total share capital of corporations operating in Yugoslavia was as follows: electric power, 83 percent; chemicals and petroleum, 69.9 percent; mining, 69.2 percent; insurance, 38 percent; cement, bauxite, and glass, 37 percent; metallurgy, 32.7 percent; timber, 28.8 percent; sugar refining, 24 percent; textiles, 22.7 percent; hotels, 21 percent; flour milling, 19 percent; banking, 9 percent. One-fourth of the total foreign investment, taking share capital and foreign credits as a base, were French-owned. British interests held 17.4 percent, followed by the United States, 15 percent; Germany (including Austrian and Czechoslovakian participation), 11.1 percent; Italy, 9.5 percent; Belgium, 7.4 percent; Switzerland, 5.9 percent; and several smaller participants.[23] In addition, many companies whose share capital was predominantly Yugoslav were effectively controlled by foreign interests owing to their dependence on contracts with large foreign customers or foreign short-term credit or their participation in international cartels. In all foreign-controlled companies foreigners held the key positions; they were also common in lower-level managerial positions and in highly skilled jobs at the production level. But despite the high costs of imported capital and managerial talent, profits were usually extremely high because of tariff protection, the cartelization of industry, and especially the low wages resulting from the fact that Yugoslavia had a huge surplus of unskilled labor and no effective labor unions.

Between 1922 and 1931 Yugoslavia floated a number of foreign loans to finance budget deficits, railroad building and similar undertakings, and the stabilization of the currency. After 1931, because of the breakdown in the international capital movements, foreign loans to Yugoslavia were much smaller and were earmarked exclusively for the building of railroads, bridges, and similar installations of social overhead capital.

In the late 1930's Yugoslav public opinion turned decisively against foreign investment in the country. People were indignant at reports of the high profits and special privileges of foreign-controlled companies, and increasingly suspicious of foreign influence on domestic political affairs. The French and British were accused of helping to maintain the political status quo (i.e. the exclusive dominance of the Serbian establishment). The Germans were watched with growing apprehension, especially after they took control of large investments formerly held by Austria and Czechoslovakia. There can be no doubt, however, that during the interwar period the role of foreign capital in the economic development of Yugoslavia was exceedingly important, although the price for its contribution was very high.

Generally taken, the scant supply of private savings and entrepreneurial talent in Yugoslavia was responsible not only for the large-scale foreign investment and the importation of entrepreneurs and highly skilled labor, but also for the role of the state as investor and manager in many sectors of the economy that were left to private initiative in ad-

[23] Based on Rozenberg and Kostić, pp. 94–231. The participation is given according to the holders of shares actually represented in shareholders' meetings. See also Tomasevich, "Foreign Economic Relations," pp. 185–95.

vanced capitalist countries. Only the state, with its taxing capacity, could supply as a debtor the necessary collateral and safety for large-scale, long-term loans to finance railroad construction, river shipping, and the development of telegraph and telephone service; only the central or local governments could use tax revenues to finance schools, public utilities, and local transportation. Moreover, the necessity of pledging certain relatively safe and ample government tax sources to foreign creditors led to government ownership and monopolies in the production and sale of several mass-consumption items, notably tobacco, cigarette paper, matches, and salt.

In the educational and cultural fields, the state established and financed all schools (except the few belonging to religious denominations), all legitimate theaters, opera houses, museums, and galleries, and some publishing houses. Most of the facilities for the production of arms, ammunition, and naval craft were state-owned. The central and local governments also had a share of the country's banking in their hands, both supplementing and competing with private banks. By means of sequestration and nationalization after the First World War, the Yugoslav state had also acquired ownership of certain industrial enterprises, including coal mines, lumber production facilities, iron ore mines and foundries, sugar factories, and state farms.

With the onset of bilateralism in international trade and the appearance of large blocked balances abroad, especially in Germany, the government decided to invest in new facilities for producing steel, copper, and aluminum. The machinery for these installations was chiefly bought in Germany with blocked balances, and internal financing was arranged with the help of state banks. The Germans, with foresight, favored the expansion of these production facilities in strategic materials because they knew that in the event of war they would be able to bring them under their control.

The development of facilities for producing certain strategic materials, and armaments themselves, undoubtedly was a stimulus to Yugoslavia's industrial development. However, the fact that between the wars the Yugoslav military budget absorbed about 30 percent of all central government expenditures (5 to 7 percent of national income) leaves little room for doubt that large-scale spending for national defense was one of the things that impeded the growth both of agriculture and of the economy as a whole.

As a result of all these developments, the government became overwhelmingly the most important employer in the economy after agriculture. Patronage accordingly became a paramount political and economic concern of all political parties, and its control by the Serbian establishment added one more divisive issue to the national and religious differences that continued to plague and embitter the peoples of Yugoslavia.

In perspective, the problems of Yugoslavia between the wars were a continuation of, and a variation on, a situation that had existed since the arrival of the South Slav peoples in the Balkans—that crossroads of religious, cultural, political, military, and economic imperialisms. The South Slav nations and the new Yugoslavia had the misfortune to sit astride the lines that had at one time or another separated the Byzantine and Western Roman empires, the Eastern Orthodox and the Roman Catholic churches, the Cyrillic and the Latin scripts, the Byzantine and the Western European civilizations, the Moslem and the Christian religions, and the realms of predominantly despotic and of predominantly democratic rule. Moreover, the Balkans have been in recent centuries the area where the Great Powers of Europe have collided in their imperialist drives, using parcels of territory as tokens in settling their accounts.

Under such outside influences, the South Slav peoples have shifted between various worlds, trying now with more and now with less success to synthesize these pressures and achieve a way of life of their own. By 1939 those pressures had once again reached a peak as war broke out between the Western democracies and the Axis. Once again Yugoslavia and the Balkans were caught in the maelstrom.

CHAPTER TWO

On the Eve of War

After the decline of French predominance in the Danube Basin, which had been established through the peace treaties and other treaties following the First World War, and the emergence of Nazi Germany as the leading, and recklessly expansionist, power in Europe, Yugoslavia tried to maintain a neutralist position between the Western democracies and the Nazi-Fascist bloc. It succeeded in doing so for several years.[1] But during the later part of the Stojadinović premiership, political and economic pressures forced Yugoslavia closer and closer to the Axis side. The occupation of Austria and then the dismemberment and partial occupation of Czechoslovakia were events that made a successful stand against German pressure even less possible. These rapid changes in the political map of Europe, first by Hitler and then by Mussolini with the occupation of Albania in April 1939, ushered in a new phase in both the domestic and the foreign policies of Yugoslavia. The purely military aspects of the new situation in which Yugoslavia found itself will be discussed in the following chapter.

THE CVETKOVIĆ-MAČEK AGREEMENT

With Italy's occupation of Albania it became clear that Yugoslavia could probably not save itself from being drawn into the full-scale war that almost certainly lay ahead. Its geographical position in the center of the strategically important Balkan area made it a likely place of conflict as well as an object of territorial aims on the part of the revisionist powers. The question of national solidarity, so long neglected, now seemed vital, for if war came, the dissatisfied non-Serb peoples, especially the Croats, could cause the country a great deal of trouble. Practically from the beginning of his rule, Prince Regent Paul made repeated

[1] For a detailed, well-documented analysis of Yugoslav foreign policy during this period see Hoptner, *Yugoslavia in Crisis, 1934–1941.*

overtures to the head of the Croatian Peasant Party, Dr. Vladko Maček, in hopes of starting the discussion of the thorny Croatian question. At the request of the Regent, Prime Minister Stojadinović and Maček met once in January 1937, but the Prime Minister was unwilling to come face to face with the real issues. Partly because of his failure to achieve any progress toward the solution of the Croatian problem and partly because of Stojadinović's growing pro-Axis attitude, Prince Paul removed him from office in February 1939 and replaced him with Dragiša Cvetković, one of Stojadinović's former ministers, charging him specifically with the task of reaching an agreement with the Croats. The efforts of the new Prime Minister, Dr. Maček, and a group of experts took the better part of six months, but finally on August 26, 1939, an agreement (*sporazum*) between Cvetković and Maček and with the blessings of Prince Paul was concluded.[2]

The opening paragraph of the Cvetković-Maček Agreement contained the statement: "Yugoslavia is the best guarantee of the independence and progress of Serbs, Croats, and Slovenes." This was an important declaration of principle by the Croatian Peasant Party, which was at that time the undoubted representative of the Croatian people, reaffirming its acceptance of the Yugoslav state. This declaration was followed by a list of specific points of agreement: that a new government would be established, including the representatives of the Croatian Peasant Party; that a Banovina Croatia would be created by consolidating the areas of the existing banovine of Sava and Primorje, to which would be added certain counties in Slavonia, Dalmatia, and Bosnia and Herzegovina that presently lay within other banovine. In Banovina Croatia as in all parts of the country the political equality of Serbs, Croats, and Slovenes was to be guaranteed, including their equality in regard to employment in public service. All religious denominations were declared to be equal. To guarantee equal civil and political rights to all citizens, a new constitution was to be worked out and adopted. Within the Croatian region, administration in the fields of agriculture, trade, industry, forests and mines, judiciary, police (except gendarmerie), education, public health, public works, social welfare, and to some extent finance was to be transferred to the jurisdiction of Banovina Croatia. All other matters—that is, national security, defense, foreign affairs, finance, banking, and legislation and administration in all fields of general interest—would be left to the central government. Banovina Croatia was to have its own *sabor* (diet), and the head of the banovinal government was to be the *ban*

---

[2] Maček, pp. 177–95; Cvetković, "The Meaning, Character, and Consequences of the Serbo-Croatian Agreement." The best and most complete study of the August 26 agreement is Boban, *Sporazum Cvetković-Maček*. Especially interesting in his discussion, pp. 218–80, of the attitudes toward the Agreement of various Yugoslav political groups and parties not directly allied with Cvetković or Maček.

(governor), through whom the King was to carry out the executive powers in Croatia. The Ban was responsible to the King and the Sabor. All the laws and decrees pertaining to Banovina Croatia were to be signed by the King and countersigned by the Ban, including the decree on relieving the Ban of his position. The Banovina was to have its own budget, and sufficient financial means were to be assured it for the performance of its functions.

Finally, the Agreement stipulated that laws leading toward the democratization of the country would be passed and that this whole new arrangement was to be only of a temporary nature until a new constituent assembly should approve a new constitution. The Cvetković-Maček Agreement was thus not intended as anything more than a first step in the solution of the Croatian question, leading to a full-scale constitutional reorganization of the country. Dr. Maček and his party apparently were under the impression that the permanent constitutional reform would considerably increase Croatia's autonomy.[3] However, Prime Minister Cvetković had engaged a group of legal experts who drafted a plan for the establishment of a Serbian federal unit, with its seat at Skopje, which would include all the rest of the country except Slovenia.[4] Slovenia was to form a third federal unit, but since the population of that region was homogeneous, the existing Banovina Drava would simply become Banovina Slovenia, although it would have a somewhat enlarged jurisdiction.

The more separatist inclined Croats were not satisfied with the Agreement, and many Serbs were also unhappy, though for the opposite reason that it gave too much power to the Croats. And a great many people were against the division of Bosnia and Herzegovina—since there were those who claimed that the entire province was Croatian, and others, greater in number, who claimed that it was Serbian, and still others who thought that it should not be divided at all but should be allowed to lead a special political life of its own as a separate federal unit within the Yugoslav state. A further weakness in the Agreement was that it contained no provisions for and did not allude to any future provisions for a Macedonian or a Montenegrin federal unit. In other words, the Agreement, even as a temporary solution, fell far short of coming to grips with all aspects of the national problem in Yugoslavia.

The Cvetković-Maček Agreement was put into effect by means of a decree, based on Article 116 of the Constitution of 1931,[5] establishing a

---

[3] See in this respect Boban, pp. 281–319, 421–24.

[4] According to Boban, p. 314, this plan was worked out without the participation or the consent of the Croatian Peasant Party and it stipulated certain provisions to which the CPP was openly opposed. For the draft of this plan see *ibid.*, pp. 412–18.

[5] Article 116 of the Constitution of 1931 read as follows: "In the case of war, mobilization, disorders and rebellion, which would put in jeopardy public order and security of the state or when public interest is endangered to that extent, the King can, in this exceptional case, order by a ukase that, temporarily, extraordinary, absolutely necessary measures can be undertaken in the entire Kingdom or in any of its parts independently of the constitutional and legal provisions."

Banovina Croatia, and a new government was immediately formed in which Cvetković remained as Prime Minister and Maček became Vice-Premier. Dr. Ivan Šubašić, a deputy of the Croatian Peasant Party, known for his strong pro-dynastic and pro-Yugoslav leanings, was named Ban of Banovina Croatia. The outbreak of war in Europe just a few days after the conclusion of the Agreement permanently postponed the implementation of certain of its provisions, including electoral reform and the passage of a new constitution. But the Agreement granted the Croats a considerable degree of autonomy on a broad front. Among other things the Croatian Peasant Party strengthened its paramilitary organizations, the Peasant Guards (*Seljačka zaštita*) in rural areas and the Civic Guards (*Gradjanska zaštita*) in the cities; and in Zagreb the Civic Guards were declared an auxiliary police force.

Even under the most ideal conditions, the changes brought about by the Cvetković-Maček Agreement could not immediately have eradicated the ill effects of two decades of Serbian hegemony and crude centralism and one decade of royal dictatorship. Unfortunately, as everyone realized, the concessions made to the Croats by the Serbian establishment were not granted out of any love for federalism, but solely for the purpose of trying to unify and strengthen the country should it get involved in war. (Maček in fact reduced some of his demands after he was informed by his representative abroad, Dr. Juraj Krnjević, that war was imminent.)[6] Nor could national cohesion and solidarity, which had been effectively stifled during the preceding twenty years by the shortsighted policies of the Serbian establishment, spring alive in these anxious days when the country was under heavy political, psychological, and economic pressures, both domestic and international. The Agreement was essentially an emergency political measure, intended as a concession to Croatian political forces in hopes of strengthening internal political structure. But it was too late to achieve this. It could not have achieved this objective even if it had been formulated—as in fact it was not—to the satisfaction of the overwhelming majorities of both Croats and Serbs. Thus, Yugoslavia was still woefully ill prepared to face any major crisis, let alone a war against tremendous odds.

GROWING ECONOMIC DIFFICULTIES

No one in Yugoslavia, or in any part of the Balkans, could feel optimistic about the future in September 1939. Not only were the countries of southeastern Europe weak politically and militarily, but economically they were completely at the mercy of the Axis powers, especially Germany. They were isolated geographically, far removed from the Western democracies, which had in any case no strong economic ties with them, and politically they were bound in numerous ways to the Axis powers.

[6] Maček, pp. 191–92.

In some, there were strong pro-Nazi or pro-Fascist political groups and parties, and in some, including Yugoslavia, there were large German minorities which were ready to do all they could to advance the Nazi cause. The Western democracies' lack of strong interest in the Balkan countries and their unwillingness to come to their aid by substantially increasing their purchases of agricultural and livestock products contributed greatly in pushing these states into the hands of the Reich. In the period 1936–39 Germany took 28.3 percent of Yugoslavia's exports and supplied 34.8 percent of its imports; for the same period the French participation was 2.8 and 2.3 percent, respectively, and the British 8.4 and 7.5 percent. With the inclusion of Austria and the Czech Protectorate, Germany accounted for more than 50 percent of Yugoslavia's export and import trade. Furthermore, for the Yugoslav businessman, access to Germany and Italy was easy, cheap, and secure, whereas access to markets in western Europe was expensive and potentially hazardous. After September 1939 Yugoslavia had little choice but to yield to increased pressures for larger exports of food and raw materials, particularly nonferrous metals, to Germany and Italy, but at the same time it found it more and more difficult to import such necessary items as textile raw materials, petroleum products, and coke.[7]

Immediately after the outbreak of the war the government undertook several wide-ranging emergency measures in an effort to head off an economic crisis. It imposed restrictions on the withdrawal of bank deposits from both private and state banks to avoid runs by depositors, and as the flurry of hoarding and speculative price increases gained momentum, it enacted measures against speculation. When these proved inadequate, direct controls were laid down, regulating exports and imports, allocating supplies of raw materials, and establishing ceiling prices on flour, edible oils, and oil seeds, and (as of June 1940) on a broad list of imported commodities (rice, coffee, tea, raw cotton and cotton yarn, rubber and rubber products, hides, leather, tin, petroleum products, and so on). Special regulations controlled the sale of petroleum products, others set priorities for government purchases of coal, and still others dealt with the allocation of production of nonferrous metals for domestic consumption and especially for export. To help curb home consumption and leave a larger surplus of meat for export to the Axis countries, the government in May 1940 introduced two meatless days a week. The banking system was subjected to still further controls and various taxes were increased.[8]

[7] For statistics on Yugoslav trade between the outbreak of war in September 1939 and the invasion of the country in April 1941, especially with England, Germany, and France, see Djordjević, pp. 67–72, 174–91, 233–37.

[8] For the texts of all these regulations one has to consult the official gazette, *Službene novine Kraljevine Jugoslavije*. But the sequence and the gist of these measures can also be seen in the résumés given in Yugoslavia, National Bank, *L'activité économique en Yougoslavie*, published

Several new state agencies were established to help with the administration of emergency measures, beginning in September 1939 with a
Food Administration that was charged with the study and improvement
of nutrition, the stockpiling of food, and in general with the direction
of food policies. In March 1940 a special Foreign Trade Administration
was established, and in May of the same year a Government Council for
Defense Economy was created for the purpose of coordinating, so far as
possible, the policy directives on civilian and military supply requirements. In January 1941 a separate Ministry of Supply was created. But
none of these measures and new governmental agencies did much to
solve the mounting difficulties of foreign trade and the supply of food
and basic raw materials, or to prevent hoarding, speculative and other
price increases, and the wane of confidence in the banking system.

In May 1939, several months before the outbreak of war, the Yugoslav
government had taken the precaution of ordering the National Bank
of Yugoslavia to transfer the major part of its gold reserves to England;
these were subsequently, in the sum of \$47 million, deposited in the
Federal Reserve Bank of New York.[9] In the country, banknote circulation, the chief means of payment, had already risen from 6.6 billion
dinars at the end of December 1938 to 8.0 billion dinars at the end of
August 1939, but until the outbreak of war there had been no sign of
inflation—in fact, the general price index (1926 = 100) fell during the
eight-month period from 77.5 to 76.8. But beginning in September 1939
both banknote circulation and prices began to rise steeply.

By a special decree issued in September 1939 the government was empowered to discount with the National Bank special "national defense
bonds." This move proved to be the most important inflationary force
during the next year and a half: by the end of 1940 the discounted
amount of these bonds had risen to 6.9 billion dinars and had helped
to swell the banknote circulation to 13.8 billion. In the same period,
moreover, the demand deposit liabilities of the National Bank rose from
1.35 billion dinars (which was somewhat below normal) to 3.5 billion
dinars. Meanwhile, inflationary pressure was fed not only by the increase
in money supply but also by an increased velocity of circulation of
money (due to an anticipation of further price rises) and by shortages
of all kinds of goods. As a consequence of all this, the general price index
rose from 76.8 in August 1939 to 90.9 in December 1939, to 143.9 in
December 1940, and to 155.3 in February 1941. The most pronounced
rise occurred in food products of vegetable origin: from 75.7 in August

monthly in Belgrade until January 1941. Reports on many of these measures sent on by German
officials in Belgrade to their superiors may be seen in the collection of documents issued by Yugoslavia, Vojnoistorijski institut, *Aprilski rat 1941—Zbornik dokumenata*, pp. 358–59, 430–31, 464–65,
and *passim* (hereafter cited as *Aprilski rat 1941*). See also Hoptner, pp. 159–61.

[9] Hoptner, p. 156.

1939 to 90.7 in December 1939, to 195.6 in December 1940, and to 213.7 in February 1941. Because of a price freeze on the chief items of import in mid-1940, the prices of export goods rose more than prices of import goods. In spite of all controls, the cost of living in Belgrade rose from 81.7 in August 1939 to 141.3 in February 1941.[10]

GERMAN ADVANCES IN SOUTHEASTERN EUROPE

The conditions under which Yugoslavia functioned from September 1939 until it was invaded in April 1941 made inevitable the drift of its economic and financial conditions from bad to worse. Besides the increasing domestic economic and financial dislocations and the mounting political pressures, both internal and external, the conquest of France and the control of practically all of continental Europe to the Soviet borders by the Nazi-Fascist bloc, the incapacity of England to render effective assistance while in mortal danger at home and in its Mediterranean possessions, and the nonbelligerence of the United States made any reliance on the West at that time and for immediate purposes quite illusory.

Militarily, Yugoslavia's situation was precarious. The Italian occupation of Albania in 1939 had forced the country into a strategic vise between the Italian forces in Albania and the German and Italian forces in the northwest and north, putting into jeopardy most of the traditional military planning which was based on secure access to Salonika. A year later the fall of Yugoslavia's traditional ally France—whose military thinking had greatly influenced the Yugoslav General Staff—dashed all hopes of a French-British opening of a Salonika front after the fashion of the gambit that had worked so successfully in the First World War. In this new situation it was natural for Yugoslavia, notwithstanding its nonrecognition of the Soviet Union all these years, to try to find some support in Russia as a power traditionally interested in the Balkans and desirous of preventing German (or earlier Austro-Hungarian) predominance in that part of Europe.[11] In July 1940, following a treaty of commerce and navigation concluded the preceding May, Yugoslavia and the Soviet Union established diplomatic relations. The move proved popular in Yugoslavia, owing to the traditional ties linking Serbia and Montenegro with Russia, but it could be of little practical value, since the far-distant Soviet Union was itself desperately trying to avoid difficulties with Germany in order to gain time to strengthen its defenses against a German attack. As late as March 13, 1941, the Yugoslav govern-

---

[10] *L'activité économique en Yougoslavie*, March 1940, pp. 1, 14; May 1940, pp. 1, 12; January 1941, pp. 1, 7.

[11] At least some Yugoslav military authorities seem to have thought that the establishment of diplomatic relations with the Soviet Union might tend to ease the pressure from Germany. Cvetković, "Yugoslavia and the Development of the International Situation Between the Wars," esp. p. 20

ment still had hopes of concluding a Soviet-Yugoslav military alliance, but when the Yugoslav envoy in Moscow failed to act on the orders he received, the matter was not further pursued by Prince Paul during the remaining two weeks of his rule.[12]

The first critical moves toward an invasion of Yugoslav territory came not from Germany, which seemed most threatening, but from Italy, and Yugoslavia was apparently not fully aware of the danger at the time. In September 1940, according to the Deputy Chief of Staff of the Italian Army, General Mario Roatta, "all available forces in northern Italy gathered at the Yugoslav frontier between Tarvisio and Fiume: two armies in the front line, and a third army in reserve. Altogether there were thirty-seven divisions, eighty-five groups of medium-caliber artillery, and all the special formations, with corresponding services and supplies."[13] The Italians requested permission from the Germans to send a part of their troops and supplies over Reich (formerly Austrian) territory, so that they might invade Yugoslavia from the north through Austria as well as from their own border, but the Germans refused the request, saying that the Führer "wanted peace on the German southern frontier, since otherwise an excuse might be given to the British to establish themselves with their Air Force in Yugoslavia."[14] This answer forced Mussolini to reconsider, and "at the end of September he decided not to go ahead with the invasion, but rather ordered the demobilization of 600,000 reservists."[15] The generals agreed with Mussolini about giving up the invasion, but they disagreed on the demobilization. Nonetheless, it was partly carried out, and in this weakened military position, and this time without consulting Hitler about his plans, on October 28, 1940, Mussolini struck out from Albania against Greece.[16]

The Italian invasion of Greece was a terrible shock for the Yugoslavs, for it threatened to isolate Yugoslavia completely from the friendly world by closing off all access to Salonika. Immediately after the news was received in Belgrade, a meeting was held between Prince Regent Paul, Prime Minister Cvetković, Foreign Minister Aleksandar Cincar-Marković, Minister of the Army and Navy General Milan Nedić, the Chief of General Staff General Petar V. Kosić, and the Minister of the Royal Court Milan Antić. Nothing decisive resulted from the meeting, unless (as there is reason to believe) General Nedić was asked on that

[12] Kljaković, "Memoirs of General Simović and Documents, 1939–1942," *Politika*, Sept. 9, 1970. This serialized study in 96 installments by the Yugoslav military historian Colonel Vojmir Kljaković appeared in the Belgrade daily *Politika* between August 21 and November 24, 1970; it consists partly of Simović's memoirs and partly of documents, with comments by Kljaković.

[13] Roatta, p. 117. For a Serbo-Croatian translation of the directive of the Italian Supreme Command for the planned Operation "E" see *Aprilski rat 1941*, pp. 765–68. See also Rossi, pp. 72–75.

[14] Von Rintelen, p. 105.

[15] Roatta, p. 118.

[16] It seems that because of the opposition of the Italian General Staff, only about 300,000 reservists were demobilized. "But it was at this moment; the most critical and the most unforeseen, that the government chose to start war against Greece." *Ibid.*, p. 119.

occasion by Prince Paul to order the General Staff to prepare a contingency plan for a possible attack on the left flank of the Italian forces in Greece if it should appear that they were about to take Salonika.[17] Furthermore, it seems that General Nedić took the discussions at this meeting as reason for presenting his views on the military situation that was facing the country. In a long memorandum of November 1 addressed to Prince Paul and the government, by way of introduction, Nedić emphasized (1) that it was impossible and unwise to continue to follow a policy of neutrality, (2) that Yugoslavia was about to be fully encircled by enemy countries and that when this was accomplished it would have to lay down its arms if called upon to do so, and (3) that the Yugoslav army was weak and unprepared to face a strong enemy with modern armaments.[18] The chief issue facing the country, he said, was "Whether we want to go along with Germany and Italy or against them? If we want to go with them, we must definitely give up any contact and flirting with England." British aid to Greece could not be effective and could not save it. As for Yugoslavia, he said, "We are all alone. Nobody can seriously help us even with the best of will." If Yugoslavia wished to continue the present (neutralist) policy, it would be necessary to mobilize all its forces and rush to the aid of Greece in order to save Salonika from the Italians and prevent, together with the Greeks, the encirclement of Yugoslavia. But such a move would, in his opinion, bring on a combined attack on Yugoslavia by Germany, Italy, Hungary, Romania, and Bulgaria, followed by immediate defeat and dismemberment of the country. A defense pact with the Soviet Union might be considered, but in view of Russia's weak military position, caught as it was between Germany and Japan (and also for several other reasons), he concluded that no aid could be expected from that quarter. There remained only a third course: joining the Axis without further delay. He based his conclusion on his strong belief that Germany would win the war and that, barring a civil war, it would for a long time retain control of the European continent. He further thought that if Yugoslavia were to join the Axis immediately, Germany would protect it against its greedy neighbors. Even in that case, he thought that at the end of the war some revision of frontiers at Yugoslavia's expense would be unavoidable. Finally he made it clear that Prince Paul and the government would have to decide what policy they wanted to follow in the future and give him the decision "in writing," so that he as the cabinet member responsible for military affairs could go ahead with the necessary plans.

[17] See, e.g., Hoptner, pp. 183–87. He analyzes this episode on the basis of the minutes of the meetings held under the chairmanship of Prince Paul on October 28 and 31, and November 1, 1940. Hoptner, however, lacked one essential document, Nedić's November 1 memorandum to Prince Paul and the government. See also Čulinović, *Dvadeset sedmi mart*, pp. 85–100.

[18] For a German translation of the text of the memorandum see Microcopy No. T–501, Roll 251, Frames 368–71.

Although Prince Paul was hopeful of continuing the policy of neutrality, he and his political and military advisers were fully aware of the dangers for Yugoslavia if the Italians and Bulgarians linked forces at Salonika and thus completed the encirclement of the country. Formal discussions of this problem with Italy were considered out of the question,[19] and Nedić had made it clear that any independent Yugoslav moves on Salonika would precipitate intervention by Germany and its allies. Accordingly, he ordered Nedić to instruct the Yugoslav military attaché in Berlin, Colonel Vladimir Vauhnik, to try to find out from the German military authorities what the German reaction would be to Yugoslav moves in the direction of Salonika. On November 6, however, Prince Paul abruptly dismissed Nedić from his post, apparently having seen the impossibility of following his advice, and replaced him with a rather docile seventy-year-old retired general, Petar Pešić, who would be less inclined to question the Regent's ideas. Vauhnik's attempts in Berlin to sound out German opinion on what their reaction would be to a Yugoslav move on Salonika failed to elicit any response, and when General Nedić left the government, Vauhnik let the matter die.[20]

It would appear that the high-level discussions on October 28 and the succeeding days became known to the Italians and Germans, both of whom had excellent intelligence sources in the Yugoslav military, and the Italians undoubtedly also learned of Vauhnik's inquiries in Berlin. Perhaps as a warning, on November 5 Italian planes attacked the Yugoslav town of Bitola near the Greek border, dropping seventy-three bombs and killing ten and wounding twenty-three civilians.[21]

Notwithstanding its strong professions of complete neutrality, Yugoslavia apparently did what it could to aid its beleaguered neighbor to the south, if only to help it keep going and prevent the capture of Salonika by the Italians. According to Cvetković, the Yugoslav government secretly turned over to the Greeks various supplies from the military stores located in garrisons near the Greek frontier, and, by looking the other way, gave its approval to privately organized unauthorized exports of horses and of ammunition (especially grenades and fuses) from the Vistad armaments works (with plants at Valjevo and Višegrad) to Greece.[22] The reports of such exports are confirmed by Hoptner's inter-

[19] But some informal discussions were attempted; see below, p. 35.

[20] United States, Department of State, *Documents on German Foreign Policy, 1918–1945*, Series D, Vol. XI, p. 525 (hereafter cited as *DGFP*). See also Hoptner, pp. 183–86.

[21] General Simović says in his memoirs that Nedić submitted his memorandum to Prince Paul on November 5, after the Italians had bombed Bitola, and that in it he advocated the occupation of Salonika. See Kljaković, in *Politika*, Aug. 31, 1970. But the occupation of Salonika was not the alternative Nedić proposed, and sounding German opinion on the problem through Vauhnik seems to have been done on Prince Paul's suggestion. On the bombing of Bitola see also *Aprilski rat 1941*, pp. 890–91, 894–900.

[22] Cvetković, "Yugoslavia and the Development of the International Situation Between the Wars," pp. 16–18. In 1951–52 a bitter argument was waged between Cvetković and Radoje Knežević, who figured prominently in the revolt of March 27, 1941. the latter accusing Prince Paul

views with the former director of the Vistad works, Nikola Stanković, and by a letter from the Greek envoy in Belgrade at that time, R. Bibica-Rosettis, to Prince Paul in which Bibica-Rosettis states that the Yugoslavs supplied Greece with many tons of armaments and all the horses they needed.[23] I can find no confirmation of Cvetković's claim that the Yugoslavs shifted certain troops to the Albanian border area, causing the Italians to relax their pressure upon the Greeks, but it is true that the Yugoslav government ordered the reactivation (in fact mobilization) of its troops in Macedonia and parts of Serbia, which may have had some influence on Italian troop shifts.[24] It is also true that the Yugoslavs refused, on grounds of neutrality, to allow the Italians to transport a thousand trucks across Yugoslav territory from Germany to Albania. That refusal cost them—on Italian insistence—the delivery from Germany of 327 diverse aircraft engines (mostly from captured Polish, Belgian, and French stocks), as well as the construction materials for 40 German-designed aircraft and 50 finished German aircraft, even though these had been ordered and at least partly paid for.[25]

Italy still had hostile designs against the Yugoslav state, but Italy was not now the principal threat. The threat was of course Hitler, and the development of the Yugoslav situation during late 1940 and early 1941 has to be considered in the light of Hitler's plans. Having determined in July 1940 to invade the Soviet Union the following spring, he had to secure his right flank in the Balkans. No doubt he would have preferred to accomplish this by diplomatic, psychological, and military pressures as had been done in several of his earlier conquests, rather than by warfare, but Hitler's plans for southeastern Europe were complicated by the independent actions of his partner Mussolini. The Greeks, after some early Italian successes, rallied and began driving the Italians out of their country and the whole Italian campaign bogged down.[26] This turn of events exposed the weakness of the junior Axis partner and forced the German hand. Hitler now had to intervene in Greece, in

---

and Cvetković of having had secret plans to conclude a military alliance with Germany and to seize Salonika at the time when Greece was in mortal struggle with Italy. Knežević's attack was made in an article entitled "Prince Paul, Hitler, and Salonika," in *International Affairs*, January 1951, pp. 38–44, subsequently reprinted in *Poruka*, No. 2–3, pp. 3–6. Cvetković issued two strong denials: "Regarding the Article of Radoje Knežević About the 25th and the 27th of March" and "The 'Proofs' of Radoje Knežević," both in *Dokumenti o Jugoslaviji* (No. 1, pp. 11–22; No. 2, pp. 14–22). Cvetković not only denied that Yugoslavia ever contemplated seizing Salonika but declared that "Prince Paul and the Yugoslav government at that time had nothing to do with the famous question of Salonika" (see his first article, p. 15). Although this assertion was not at all true, as will be seen from many documents referred to below, there is no doubt that Knežević, whose facts were partly correct, was chiefly interested in blackening Prince Paul's record and, by contrast, improving the record of the putschists.

[23] Hoptner, pp. 191–92; the Bibica-Rosettis letter is in Hoptner's files.

[24] *Aprilski rat 1941*, pp. 875–89. But the Italian bombing of Bitola had the effect of dampening Yugoslavia's thoughts about a move toward Salonika.

[25] *DGFP*, Series D, Vol. XI, pp. 643–44, 803–4, 810–11. Earlier, Yugoslavia had placed orders for other military supplies totaling 41 million reichsmarks, but because of German needs most of these contracts had been canceled by mutual agreement. *Ibid.*, p. 644.

[26] The best Italian study of the ill-fated Italian campaign against Greece is Cervi, *Storia della guerra di Grecia*. For the Greek side see Papagos, *The Battle of Greece, 1940–1941*.

order to rescue his partner and prevent the British from establishing themselves with their air force and landing troops on the Greek mainland. In the overall scheme of Hitler's plans, he must on no account allow the British to establish a firm position on the Greek mainland, from which their air force could threaten the harbors and transportation facilities in southern Italy and the Balkans and, even more importantly, the Romanian oil fields, which were the chief source of oil for the Axis war machine. On November 12, 1940, Hitler issued his Directive No. 18, incorporating his objectives in the Mediterranean area. Among other things this directive ordered preparations for the occupation of Greece north of the Aegean Sea and entering by way of Bulgaria. The main objective of this move was to acquire air bases from which to attack British air bases in the eastern Mediterranean, especially those within bombing range of the Romanian oil fields.[27] At a meeting with the Italian Foreign Minister Count Galeazzo Ciano on November 18 and again in a letter to Mussolini of November 20, Hitler criticized the Italian attack on Greece. He outlined the Axis problems in the Mediterranean and the Balkans, pointing out to Mussolini that the Italian difficulties in Greece made German diplomatic initiatives in the Balkans more difficult, and he promised Mussolini that he would "do everything that may be of relief to you in the present situation." But, he said: "it is impossible to conduct a war in the Balkans before March. Any threatening pressure on Yugoslavia would therefore be useless, since the Serbian General Staff is well aware of the impossibility of actually carrying out such a threat before March. Yugoslavia must therefore, if at all possible, be won over by other ways and means."[28]

In his answer to Hitler of November 22, Mussolini apologized for not having informed him ahead of time about his action against Greece and explained Italian difficulties there. As far as Yugoslavia was concerned, Mussolini said: "I am ready to guarantee the present boundaries of Yugoslavia and to recognize Yugoslavia's right to Salonika, on the following conditions: (*a*) that Yugoslavia adhere to the Tripartite Pact; (*b*) that she demilitarize the Adriatic; (*c*) that her military intervention be agreed on; in other words, that it occur only after Greece has received an initial blow from Italy." Furthermore, Mussolini wrote: "By this letter I am therefore giving you my agreement with whatever you wish to do in order to reach this goal as quickly as possible."[29]

In another message to Mussolini, on December 5, Hitler informed him that he had given assurance to Romania that it would be protected against all threats and that he had given orders "to begin preparations

[27] *DGFP*, Series D, Vol. XI, pp. 527–31.
[28] For a German record of the Hitler-Ciano discussions see *ibid.*, pp. 606–10; for the text of Hitler's letter to Mussolini see *ibid.*, pp. 639–43.
[29] *Ibid.*, pp. 671–72.

for a possible advance of German units through Bulgaria toward Salonika."[30] On December 13 Hitler issued his Directive No. 24 for Operation Marita for the conquest of Greece.

In addition to securing the German right flank for the forthcoming operations against the Soviet Union by rescuing Mussolini in Greece and knocking out the British troops that had already landed there, Hitler's objectives in southeastern Europe were to complete the strategic encirclement of Yugoslavia so that it would have no choice but to accept German proposals to join the Tripartite Pact, and to frighten Turkey into continued neutrality. In other words, Hitler proposed to get on his side peacefully, or eliminate by force of arms, Hungary, Romania, Bulgaria, Yugoslavia, and Greece. Except for Greece, he foresaw no particular difficulties. Hungary and Romania were put under full control by the peaceful entry of German troops during October and November 1940 and they promptly joined the Tripartite Pact—Hungary on November 20 and Romania on November 23. Membership in the Berlin-Rome-Tokyo Axis was for small nations a test of loyalty to the Axis and to its plans for the "new order in Europe."[31] At the same time Hitler ordered several territorial adjustments in favor of Hungary and Bulgaria at the expense of Romania and greatly strengthened the position of the *Volksdeutsche* and to a certain extent also of the pro-Nazi political parties in these states. Hand in hand with this went further economic subjugation of all three countries to Germany.

After the entry of German troops into Romania, Hitler proceeded with the softening up of Bulgaria, and at the end of February 1941 Bulgaria, too, agreed to join the Tripartite Pact and open its frontiers to the Nazi armies. Thus by early March 1941, Hitler's armies were on the northern frontiers of Greece and Operation Marita could be sprung at any moment. His armies were also on all the northern and eastern frontiers of Yugoslavia. From the point of view of Yugoslav-German relations, the entry of German troops into Bulgaria meant that the diplomatic, economic, and now also military noose around the neck of Yugoslavia was being tightened to the point of strangulation.

YUGOSLAVIA JOINS THE TRIPARTITE PACT

While these actions with regard to the other countries in southeastern Europe were under way, Hitler was applying ever more intensive diplomatic, political, and psychological pressure on the Yugoslav government.[32] The Yugoslavs, fearful of Germany's designs, looked desperately

---

[30] *Ibid.*, pp. 789–91.

[31] The Tripartite Pact was concluded by Germany, Italy, and Japan on September 27, 1940. For a succinct presentation of the diplomatic and military advance of Nazi Germany in southeastern Europe see Wiskemann, "The Subjugation of South-eastern Europe, June 1940 to June 1941."

[32] For the sequence of events leading to the accession of Yugoslavia to the Tripartite Pact see Hoptner, pp. 202–43; Čulinović, *Dvadeset sedmi mart*, pp. 13–222; Terzić, pp. 99–126; Pavelić, "Yugoslavia and the Tripartite Pact." See also Gregorić, pp. 92–157.

for other alternatives—engaging in some informal discussions with Italy (using a Belgrade lawyer who otherwise acted as legal counsel for the Italian Legation, Dr. Vladislav Stakić, as go-between)[33] and exploring the possibility of obtaining effective aid from Great Britain, especially, and to some extent also from the Soviet Union and the United States. But the center of gravity was German plans and Yugoslav relations with Germany. The Germans made their first move late in November 1940 when they asked the Yugoslav Foreign Minister, Cincar-Marković, to come to Germany to meet with Foreign Minister Joachim von Ribbentrop. The meeting took place in greatest secrecy on November 27, and the following day Cincar-Marković talked with Hitler. These talks marked the start of direct German diplomatic pressure on Yugoslavia to move to the Axis side by joining the Tripartite Pact. Salonika was dangled as bait.[34]

Little more than a week after Cincar-Marković's return from Germany, on December 7, the Yugoslav government informed the German Envoy in Belgrade, Viktor von Heeren, that Yugoslavia was willing to discuss the signing of a nonaggression pact with Germany and Italy on the basis of the Yugoslav-Italian Agreement of March 25, 1937.[35] During the next three and a half months representatives of Yugoslavia and Germany (the latter acting for Italy as well) tried to reach an agreement on the nature of the pact that Yugoslavia was to sign and on what special notes would accompany the protocol of signature. Yugoslavia was doing all it could to prolong the bargaining process, hoping somehow to find an alternative to joining the Axis. In the meantime—on December 30, 1940—the British government offered to Greece to establish an air force base at Salonika, and informed both Yugoslavia and Turkey about this offer. Prince Paul thought that the move would be a grave mistake and that British action would be strong enough to provoke a German invasion of the Balkan states and not sufficient to prevent such an invasion from taking place. This view was shared by the Greeks as well.[36] The sending of British forces to Greece remained under discussion, and early in March—that is, after the Germans entered Bulgaria—British troops started to disembark on the Greek mainland.

It was clear to the Yugoslav government that neither Great Britain nor the Soviet Union could give sufficient immediate support to counterbalance German pressure. Even less could support be expected from the United States. Colonel William J. Donovan visited Belgrade as a special

[33] Stakić visited Rome once in November 1940 and twice in February 1941 and had extensive talks with Mussolini and Ciano; Stakić, pp. 80–117.

[34] For the report on the invitation extended to Cincar-Marković see *DGFP*, Series D, Vol. XI, p. 692, and for the subjects of discussion with Hitler as recorded by German officials, see *ibid.*, pp. 728–35. The record of the conversation between Cincar-Marković and von Ribbentrop was apparently lost.

[35] For the communication of the Yugoslav government to the German Envoy stating this willingness see *ibid.*, pp. 805–9.

[36] Woodward, I, 519–20.

representative of Secretary of the Navy Frank Knox on January 23–25, 1941, seeking to bolster the Yugoslavs to resist German pressure; he favored the British plan of opening a Balkan front, but he did not offer any immediate American aid.[37]

The next summons from the Germans came in mid-February, this time to both Prime Minister Cvetković and Foreign Minister Cincar-Marković. While the Germans were promising that all Yugoslav interests would be safeguarded and, in fact, strengthened, they also repeatedly pointed out that no one was in a position to withstand the continued advance of German arms in Europe. According to the paraphrased record of conversations, Hitler at one point told Cvetković that "For Yugoslavia a unique, historic occasion had arrived to fix her place in Europe definitely for all time. She now had to take a clear position regarding the new order in Europe, and that, to be sure, in her very own interest; that is, to take her place in the order envisaged by Germany and Italy by immediate accession to the Tripartite Pact."[38] He still offered Salonika as bait, but it was clear that he allowed no room for refusal when he urged the Yugoslavs to choose "immediate accession" to the Tripartite Pact. This was still short of an outright ultimatum—but the ultimatum was not long in coming. Finally, Prince Paul was summoned to a secret meeting at Berchtesgaden on March 4, at which Hitler reiterated much of what he had told Cvetković. He repeated the promise to grant Yugoslavia control of Salonika after the war if Yugoslavia secured its claim in time by joining the Axis, but there could be no delay: it was in Yugoslavia's interest to "make this decision within the next fortnight."[39] Still the Yugoslavs tried to put off signing, continuing to press the Germans for concessions. Most particularly, they wanted written declarations from Germany and Italy ensuring Yugoslav independence and the inviolability of Yugoslav territory including no movement of Axis troops across Yugoslav territory, along with a promise that there would be no request for military assistance from Yugoslavia.

The Yugoslav government, like other European governments before, was terrified by thoughts of the devastating force of the German war machine and of the political and police savagery of the Nazi system. For some months, since the Italian attack on Greece at the end of October, Yugoslavia had been faced with the dilemma: either join the Axis, or be crushed by the Axis military machine.

The Germans were not exaggerating the urgency of settling affairs

[37] Hoptner, p. 205; Woodward, I, 528–29.

[38] For German records of conversations with Cvetković see *DGFP*, Series D, Vol. XII, pp. 79–96; the quotation is from p. 95. For Cvetković's recollections of the meeting see his article "Conversations at Berchtesgaden"; see also Cvetković, "Yugoslavia and the Development of the International Situation."

[39] For the German record of the March 4 conversations between Prince Paul and Hitler see *DGFP*, Series D, Vol. XII, pp. 230–31.

with the Yugoslavs. May 12 had been set for the invasion of the Soviet Union, and before that date they had to crush Greece, whose forces had early in March been strengthened by a British expeditionary force of about 50,000 men, as well as secure the Yugoslav area in one way or another. Both Great Britain and the United States were keeping a close eye on Yugoslavia and the general situation in the Balkans, and the British were using all the pressure at their disposal to prevent Yugoslavia from caving in under German pressure. The British dispatched during these months of crisis some top military men to Belgrade, and other military and diplomatic representatives met with Yugoslav military representatives in Greece to discuss the problems facing Yugoslavia and possible British aid. They also greatly strengthened their intelligence and special operations detail in Belgrade (operatives of the British SOE or Special Operations Executive)[40] in an effort to counteract German pressure and, if necessary, to give support to groups opposed to the Yugoslav government and its drift toward joining the Axis.[41] It is interesting to note that, just as Hitler was trying to bribe Yugoslavia to join the Axis by promising it the Greek port of Salonika, the British were promising Yugoslavia a rectification of borders toward Italy if it stayed out of the Axis and joined the British.[42]

After sending an expeditionary force to Greece, the British were in no position to offer military aid to Yugoslavia, but they had plenty of moral encouragement and advice to give and they were prepared to use every possible means to keep Yugoslavia from joining the Axis. One suggestion, conveyed through the delegate of the Yugoslav General Staff, Major Milisav Perišić, who on March 8 attended a conference of British and Greek functionaries in Athens, was that Yugoslavia should invade

[40] The chief of the SOE detail in Belgrade was Tom S. Masterson, who had successfully managed the sabotaging of oil fields in Romania during the First World War. He was assisted by Julius Hanau, a British businessman resident in Belgrade from the end of the First World War; S. W. Bailey, a mining engineer formerly connected with the British-owned Trepča Mines, Ltd.; Duane T. (Bill) Hudson, a South African-born mining engineer who had also been associated with a British-owned mining enterprise in Serbia; and several others including the more academically oriented Hugh Seton-Watson and Julian Amery. A few months before the invasion of Yugoslavia the detail was reinforced by one of the top operatives of the SOE, George Taylor, an Australian by birth. See Sweet-Escott, pp. 21–22, 55, 60–64, and *passim*. At the time of the Yugoslav collapse in mid-April 1941 most of these men moved toward the Adriatic coast to be evacuated by British submarines, but instead they were caught by the Italian forces and taken to Italy. As diplomats they were soon released, and subsequently played important roles during the war either as key men in the SOE sections dealing with Yugoslav matters or as liaison officers with the Chetniks in the field. On the establishment and general objectives of the SOE see also Dalton, pp. 366–84. Of course, in addition to the SOE operatives in Yugoslavia prior to the invasion there were also a large number of regular intelligence operatives.

[41] One of the plans of the SOE and the British Intelligence Service in Yugoslavia called for the sabotaging of the Iron Gate waterway on the Danube either by the sinking of barges or by landslides. Both the Yugoslav and the German intelligence services were aware of the plan and under German pressure one of the British operatives, Julius Hanau, was arrested and subsequently deported. *Aprilski rat 1941*, pp. 505–6, 519–21.

[42] According to Phyllis Auty's review of British Foreign Office documents of 1941 with regard to Yugoslav matters, the British cabinet authorized Foreign Secretary Eden on February 27, 1941, "to hint to Prince Paul that if Yugoslavia came in on the side of the Allies she could expect frontier rectifications as regards Istria." See p. 3 of her unpublished paper, "Some Aspects of British-Yugoslav Relations in 1941," read at the Belgrade symposium on "The Uprising in Yugoslavia in 1941 and Europe," held in November 1971.

Italian-held Albania; such an action, besides making communications
with the Adriatic safer, would relieve some of the pressure on the Greeks
and release some Greek troops and all the British troops to fight the
Germans, and would make possible the appropriation of large stores of
Italian arms in Albania.[43] The Yugoslavs, certain that Germany would
retaliate by invading their country at once, ignored the suggestion. The
same suggestion among others was taken up by Foreign Secretary Anthony Eden in a letter to Prince Paul on March 17, again without favorable response.[44] This was the last British attempt to keep Prince Paul
from going over to the Axis side. But, as will presently be shown, British
diplomatic, intelligence, and special operations services, with some
American support, continued to operate full force in Belgrade, with
some far-reaching consequences.

For weeks, it had been evident that Yugoslavia could no longer postpone joining the Tripartite Pact. Since Prince Paul and his top advisers
were opposed to what they regarded as useless military resistance in defense of the country's neutrality, there seemed no way out. On March 6
the Crown Council agreed that Yugoslavia would sign if all its conditions were met, but the decision was kept secret.[45] A few days later Prince
Paul and the General Staff received a detailed message from Colonel
Vauhnik in Berlin informing them that Germany was preparing to
attack the Soviet Union very soon.[46] This news ought to have made it
clear to the Yugoslavs that Hitler would brook no delays in the Balkans,
but for some reason it had the opposite effect of encouraging the Yugoslavs to conjure new excuses. By March 19, however, the Germans had
met all Yugoslav counterproposals in regard to special open and secret
clauses to accompany the protocol of Yugoslav adherence to the Tripartite Pact, as well as the way in which some of them were to be published, and there were no more pretexts possible. At a meeting of the
Crown Council the next day, and then of the cabinet a few hours later,
it was decided that the fateful time had come. Three members of the
seventeen-member cabinet refused to agree, and the government itself
was so reluctant that it would not tell the Germans when it would sign
the Pact.[47]

[43] Eden, p. 255; Hoptner, pp. 224–25; and especially Kljaković, in *Politika*, Sept. 7 and 8,
1970, where he reproduces parts of minutes kept by Perišić during this meeting. See also Churchill's
message to Roosevelt of March 10, 1941, in United States, Department of State, *Foreign Relations
of the United States—Diplomatic Papers 1941*, II, 951–52 (hereafter cited as *FRUS 1941*). Some
anti-Fascist Italian army officers were also suggesting to the Yugoslav government, through confidential channels, that it should concentrate its military effort on throwing the Italian Army out
of Albania—so as to put an end to Mussolini and restore the power of the monarchy. See Vladeta
Milićević, pp. 101–2.
[44] Eden, pp. 257–59.
[45] Kljaković, in *Politika*, Sept. 6, 1970.
[46] See an article by Vauhnik entitled "Ten Years Since the Dismemberment of Yugoslavia,"
reproduced in part in *Dokumenti o Jugoslaviji*, No. 2, pp. 23–26. Colonel Vauhnik was a very
capable intelligence officer who was able to secure highly secret German military information. For
some details see Hoptner, pp. 231–33.
[47] Hoptner, pp. 233, 238.

It was then that the British played their first strong card by prevailing on one of their friends in the cabinet who had voted against joining the Axis to submit his resignation. Such an action might possibly send the whole cabinet down, and it ought at least to delay the signing.[48] The gambit failed. New ministers were appointed, and the government continued in office. The Germans apparently took the resignations as a cue to issue a deadline for a definite decision: midnight of March 23.[49] In spite of a last-minute telegram from Prime Minister Churchill on March 22 to Cvetković urging resistance to Germany,[50] the Yugoslav government, after additional meetings of the Crown Council and the cabinet, late on the evening of March 23 informed the German Envoy that on the following day it was sending its representatives, Prime Minister Cvetković and Foreign Minister Cincar-Marković, to Vienna and that they would sign the protocol of the adherence of Yugoslavia to the Tripartite Pact on March 25.[51] Prince Paul, in the meantime, told his foreign minister to inform the leaders of the Serbian opposition parties that the government was joining the Pact, but that it had negotiated various extenuating clauses that would become part of the documents on the adherence of Yugoslavia to the Pact. But these leaders were still against signing, as was also the Patriarch of the Serbian Orthodox Church, Gavrilo.[52] Pešić, the Minister of Army and Navy, and Kosić, the Chief of General Staff, were in favor of signing, as apparently were also the commanders of the seven armies in the field, who, according to some sources, had been consulted during the preceding weeks and were quickly informed of the final decision.[53] Prince Paul himself explained the decision to General Simović, the Commander of the Air Force and a former Chief of General Staff, who was a staunch pro-Westerner and very much opposed to the Pact and on several previous occasions had so expressed himself to Prince Paul. Simović was dismayed at the news and warned Prince Paul that if the government went ahead with its decision there would be a people's revolt and a mutiny in the Belgrade garrison and that the army would be on the side of the people. He told Prince Paul that as senior officer in the Belgrade garrison he had called a meeting of the garrison commanders to discuss the situation and that

---

[48] Actually three ministers resigned from the cabinet: Dr. Srdjan Budisavljević, Minister of the Interior, Dr. Branko Čubrilović, Minister of Agriculture, and Dr. Mihailo Konstantinović, Minister Without Portfolio, but only the first two resignations were made public. Neither British nor Yugoslav sources have ever revealed which of the three cooperated so closely with the British. See Eden, p. 62; Kljaković, in *Politika*, Sept. 9, 1970; Hoptner, p. 238. It was Budisavljević.

[49] Hoptner, p. 239.

[50] Churchill, *The Second World War*, III, 159–60.

[51] Hoptner, p. 240.

[52] *Ibid.*, pp. 237–38.

[53] Apparently on Prince Paul's own orders. *Ibid.*, p. 237. In this respect see especially the statement of the former Minister of the Royal Court, Milan Antić, before the Dinić Commission (a commission established by General Nedić, the head of the Serbian puppet government, at the request of the German occupation authorities to investigate the responsibility for the revolt of March 27, 1941) in *Dokumenti o Jugoslaviji*, No. 10, p. 4.

he would inform the Minister of the Army and Navy about the result.[54] The cabinet, when told of Simović's threats, discounted them completely.[55]

The Yugoslav government kept its word and on March 25 in Vienna Cvetković and Cincar-Marković signed the protocol making Yugoslavia a member of the Tripartite Pact. It was an act of surrender, but under the circumstances it must have seemed to Prince Paul and his ministers, as well as to most Yugoslav politicians and generals, a lesser evil than hopeless armed resistance. There can be no doubt that Prince Paul and his government were both ideologically and politically opposed to the Axis and did all they could to postpone the fateful signing, but without hope of effective military aid from abroad they could hold out no longer. The four months of negotiation had, at any rate, resulted in sufficient concessions to make the joining somewhat more palatable than it would otherwise have been. Four notes accompanied the protocol: the first two were to be published with the announcement of the Yugoslav accession to the Pact, and the last two were to be kept secret. The essential part of the first note stated: "the German Government confirms its decision to respect at all times the sovereignty and the territorial integrity of Yugoslavia." The chief part of the second note said: "the Axis Powers will not address the demand to Yugoslavia that she permit the passage or transportation of troops through Yugoslav territory." (This second note was not published verbatim but in a paraphrased formulation agreed upon by all signatory powers.) The two secret notes contained additional understandings between Yugoslavia and the Axis Powers. The first of these notes stated: "Germany and Italy, taking into account the military situation assure the Yugoslav Government that they will not, of their own accord, make any demand for military assistance. Should the Yugoslav Government at any time consider it to be in its own interest to participate in the military operations of the Powers of the Tripartite Pact, it will be left up to the Yugoslav Government to make the necessary military agreements for this with the Powers of the Tripartite Pact." The second secret note contained this essential paragraph: "In the new settlement of the frontiers in the Balkans the interests of Yugoslavia in a territorial connection with the Aegean Sea, through the extension of her sovereignty to the city and harbor of Salonika, are to be taken into account."[56] There was no assurance that additional obligations might not be imposed at some future date, as Hitler's plans for southeastern Europe changed in the course of the war. Nevertheless,

[54] Kljaković, in *Politika*, Sept. 11, 1970.
[55] Hoptner, pp. 239–40.
[56] For the full texts of the drafts of these notes see *DGFP*, Series D, Vol. XII, pp. 312–15, and for the Yugoslav-German written and verbal exchanges on the occasion of the signature of the protocol of the Yugoslav joining of the Tripartite Pact see *ibid.*, pp. 353–57. See also Hoptner, pp. 240–41, 303–5; Čulinović, *Dvadeset sedmi mart*, pp. 197–211.

Prince Paul, the Cvetković government, and the leadership of the Yugoslav military forces—with some notable exceptions—considered that joining the Pact, with the clauses that the government managed to secure, would preserve peace as well as the territorial integrity of the state at least for some time. It also offered the possibility of eventually switching to the Allied side when circumstances were more favorable.

It is very hard to say anything specific on the reaction of the broad strata of the Yugoslav population to the signing of the Tripartite Pact. What is definitely known is that there were many people, especially in Serbia, who, though quite aware of the danger of military destruction for refusing to sign or repudiating the signature, preferred war and occupation to surrender because they believed in the final victory of England and wanted Yugoslavia to be on the winning side at the end of the war. But most probably a large proportion of the population, in Serbia and especially in other areas, accepted the signing as the lesser of the two evils, just as Prince Paul and his government did.

Those who opposed Yugoslavia's entry into the Axis alliance included a large part of the Serbian-dominated officer corps, especially the lower ranks; a good many of the Serbian political leaders both within Serbia and in areas outside Serbia; leaders of the Serbian Orthodox Church; the leaders and a large portion of the membership of such Serbian organizations as the Serbian Cultural Club, the National Defense (*Narodna odbrana*), the Chetnik Association, and the Reserve Officers Association; a large part of the population of Serbia as well as parts of the population in other regions of Yugoslavia; and the liberals and Communists throughout the country. In the last days before the Pact was signed, even as the Prime Minister and Foreign Minister were in Vienna, most of these groups declared their opposition quite openly. Mass street demonstrations took place in Kragujevac, Belgrade, Split, Sušak, Ljubljana, and elsewhere. In all these demonstrations, members and supporters of the Communist Party of Yugoslavia were much in evidence and perhaps for the first time in many years people at large became aware of the party's readiness to play a leading role in those perilous times.

Within the Serbian-controlled army and the Serbian opposition political parties, hostility to the Pact had two closely related domestic political aspects. One of these was opposition to Prince Regent Paul, who had shown great tolerance toward the Croats and had been instrumental in bringing about the Cvetković-Maček Agreement of August 1939. Prince Paul was a somewhat effete British-educated intellectual who kept aloof from the Serbian political and economic elite and was, it was thought, much more interested in the arts and humanities than in politics. It did not help that during the two final and crucial years of his rule his Prime Minister, Cvetković, and the second pillar of the cabinet,

Dr. Maček, were men of only mediocre stature. The opposition was also directed against the policy embodied in the Cvetković-Maček Agreement itself, which many Serbs thought was too great a concession to the Croats and therefore a danger to the state. The extent of Serbian displeasure was not exactly a secret: as early as October 25, 1940, the German Legation in Belgrade reported to Berlin that there was growing opposition to Prince Paul and the Cvetković-Maček government among the generals and the Serbian nationalist forces and that rumors were circulating about the possibility of a putsch.[57] There were apparently several groups of officers, some of them including civilians as well, who considered the overthrow of the Prince Paul regime (some as early as 1938); but there was no plotting involving all the groups, and none of them can be taken as the forerunner of the group of generals and middle-ranking officers who planned and executed the revolt of March 27.[58]

Another force of no small importance in Belgrade in these extremely difficult days of March 1941 was the British diplomatic, intelligence, and special operations services, which were doing all they could to prevent Yugoslavia from joining the Tripartite Pact and, if these efforts failed, were prepared to undertake any measures, including giving assistance to a coup so that the new government would reverse the decision of its predecessor.[59] The United States also exercised, through diplomatic channels and direct messages of President Roosevelt to Prince Paul, some pressure upon the Yugoslavs to resist German advances, but this pressure was much less intense than that of the British.[60] For at least seven months the British had speculated on a revolt of some sort. On July 25, 1940, the British Envoy in Belgrade, Ronald Campbell, reported that there was a possibility of one, with the leadership coming from the Serbian patriotic organization National Defense, coinciding with a revolt by the Agrarian Party in Bulgaria, to be executed at a time when the British could give support from the Middle East. But Campbell considered that a premature revolt might do more harm than good to British interests in the Balkans and he ordered his staff not to encourage it. The Foreign Office agreed, but thought that at a later date the scheme might prove important. There was, however, one constraint on its possible use, namely, that no violence be used against Prince Paul.[61]

Prince Paul, with his pro-British sympathies and close ties with the Greek and British royal families, was the logical person for the British to appeal to, but his main concern during these months was to obtain immediate and sufficient aid to resist the Germans, and that was pre-

[57] *DGFP*, Series D. Vol. XI, p. 396.
[58] Čulinović, *Dvadeset sedmi mart*, pp. 248–52.
[59] Hoptner, pp. 241–43, 275.
[60] For American diplomatic maneuvers in Belgrade at this time see *FRUS 1941*, II, 937–84.
[61] For Campbell's telegram from Belgrade and the reaction in London see Auty, Ms. pp. 4–6.

cisely what the British could not give, nor promise to give in the near future. Consequently, when toward the end of 1940 it appeared that Prince Paul and his government were drifting irretrievably toward the Axis, the British decided that they must try another approach and begin applying pressure on some of the groups that opposed Prince Paul, though without relaxing the pressure on the Regent. If they could help to bring about the overthrow of the government, Yugoslavia might still be kept out of the Axis fold. Exchanges between Campbell and the British Foreign Office suggest that the British representatives in Belgrade worked so closely with some of the leading plotters that they were able to influence the actual timing of the coup. Campbell, in a telegram on March 21, requested advice from the Foreign Office whether at the time Yugoslavia signed the Tripartite Pact he should break off relations with the Yugoslav government and thus precipitate a coup. The first reply from the Foreign Office told Campbell to stay at his post and remain cautious about the coup, but on the following day Eden advised Campbell that he "should bear in mind that rather than allow Yugoslavia to slip by stages into German orbit, we are prepared to risk precipitating German attack." On March 24, after Campbell sent word that Hitler had given an ultimatum to the Yugoslavs to join the Axis, Eden authorized Campbell to use any means at his disposal to make public opinion and leaders understand the realities of the moment and to take any measures, even a coup d'état, to change the government.[62] The day after the Yugoslav representatives in Vienna signed the protocol joining the Pact, that is on March 26, a member of the British cabinet with many connections in Belgrade, Leopold S. Amery, sent an impassioned appeal over the BBC to the Yugoslavs, but especially to the Serbs, urging them to save their national honor by repudiating the action of the government.[63]

THE REVOLT OF MARCH 27, 1941

It was under these conditions that a group of air force and army officers, on the night of March 26–27 successfully overthrew the regime of Prince Paul and Prime Minister Cvetković. Although the plan for revolt apparently had been under discussion for months, the final phases seem to have been prepared with some haste, with the assistance, in both phases, of British representatives in Belgrade.

The planners and executors of this revolt were a group of pro-Western officers from the Air Force Headquarters at Zemun near Belgrade and from the army and Royal Guards units in Belgrade. Officers of the general rank came only from the air force, while from the army and the Royal Guards only officers of the middle ranks were involved. It has

[62] Eden, pp. 262–64.
[63] Hoptner, pp. 241–42.

been indisputably established who the various officers were who directed
the specific tasks involved, but there exist contradicting claims as to who
was actually in control of the overall plan—that is, who made the decision to undertake a revolt, when the revolt was to take place, and who
was to execute the various tasks of taking over the centers of power in
Belgrade (the various command posts and units, the centers of civilian
administration and police power, the units of the Royal Guards, the
Belgrade radio station, and so on). The contradictory claims to the
overall leadership of the revolt came from the commander of the air
force, General Dušan Simović, and from Simović's deputy, Brigadier
General Bora Mirković, and to some extent also so far as the execution
of the revolt was concerned from some of the lower-ranking officers,
notably Major Živan Knežević.

General Mirković began claiming sole credit as soon as the revolt was
completed,[64] and the matter became one of the elements in the factionalism that plagued the exile government in London during the war years.
King Peter, in a speech before a group of British dignitaries on December 17, 1941, gave credit for the revolt to the "younger and middle ranks
[of officers] of the Yugoslav army,"[65] pointedly omitting mention of both
General Simović and General Mirković. Nothing more was said publicly
until a decade later when, on the tenth anniversary of the revolt, Mirković told a group in London that he was the sole planner. He had, he said,
planned for several years for the army to take a greater role in the political life of the country and had quite a number of generals in mind
as helpers, but had reached no understanding with any of them until
he confided in General Simović, who accepted his idea. "Only after I
had informed General Simović about my idea and he had accepted it
did I make the decision to undertake the planned revolt. I made the decision myself, and I also carried out the whole organization. I made the
decision as to when the revolt had to take place."[66]

General Simović kept his silence, saving his side of the story for a
posthumous statement. In the statement published after his death in
1962 he placed his claims squarely opposite Mirković's. It was he
who "stood in the center of the whole undertaking" and had remon-
strated with Prince Paul and the Prime Minister. He had also talked
with the Patriarch of the Serbian Orthodox Church and with several
politicians and apprised them of the opposition of the armed forces to
the Tripartite Pact, and it was he who "personally engaged his assistant,
Brigadier General Bora Mirković, for the action" and put him in contact

[64] Kljaković, in *Politika*, Sept. 20, 1970.

[65] A section of the speech containing these words is quoted by Radoje Knežević, in his article in
Poruka, No. 53–54, p. 32. Radoje Knežević, Major Živan's brother, was Minister of the Royal
Court in the exile government and may very well have ghostwritten the King's speech.

[66] From General Mirković's speech as quoted in *Dokumenti o Jugoslaviji*, No. 2, p. 37. Hoptner,
p. 252, says: "Mirković probably began to give form to his plans for a *coup* around the time of
the signing of the Italo-Yugoslav pact of 1937."

with other officers, among them Major Knežević. The statement continues, using the third person: "On March 26 in the afternoon General Simović made the decision for the execution of the *coup d'état* in the night from 26th to 27th of March, and at 5.00 p.m. issued the order to Bora Mirković that the action should start at one o'clock after midnight on 26th to 27th." The statement ends as follows:

(1) I was doing only my duty just as all other participants in the March action and I do not ask for any higher recognition than those who exposed their lives in carrying out the action. (2) The opinion that Bora Mirković was the leader I cannot accept, and I consider that it is a mistake to stress his role above the role of other direct participants in the action of March 27. (3) Stressing the role of Živan Knežević and his brother Radoje above the role of others, especially above the role of Colonel Stojan Zdravković, is not appropriate.[67]

Simović's statement is firm, but Mirković (who reasserted his claim in another statement)[68] is the more credible of the two generals and his story has been corroborated from several sides, both Allied and Axis. An intelligence report of the German Twelfth Army, dated March 31, 1941, points out the weakness of the Simović government, noting that Simović "was too wise to take an anti-Axis course and too weak to ask from the people and perhaps the officer corps a policy [of cooperation] with Germany and Italy," and then goes on to say: "General Mirković, the man really responsible for the revolution, has contacted the German military attaché and stated that the new government will stand by the Tripartite Pact. The military attaché has not given any reply."[69] Prime Minister Churchill, who was certainly in a position to know a great deal about what had gone on in Belgrade, gave credit to Mirković and to the Knežević brothers.[70] According to a reliable source, there exists a memorandum written by Mirković himself a few days after the revolt and found in the Air Force Command which states that on the afternoon of March 26 he was visited by T. G. Mapplebeck—a long-time operative of the British Intelligence Service in Belgrade—who told him that the coup had to be executed within the next forty-eight hours. Mirković answered that it would be carried out on time. Neither Mirković, nor Simović, nor any of the other leaders of the revolt, however, ever made any public reference to any part that the British services played in the coup.

But if General Mirković was the chief planner of the revolt, why did

---

[67] Simović, "Explanation of the Role of Leading Personalities in the *coup d'état* of March 27, 1941." Captain Dragiša Ristić, Simović's aide during the upheaval, supports Simović's claim. See his *Yugoslavia's Revolution of 1941*, esp. pp. 84–94.

[68] Mirković's statement first appeared in the Oct. 22, 1962, issue of *Klic Triglava*, a periodical published by Slovene political exiles in London. Since this predates the publication of Simović's statement, Mirković must have had knowledge of its contents prior to publication. It was later quoted, almost in full, by Kljaković, in *Politika*, Sept. 19 and 20, 1970, and in its entirety as an appendix to the Serbo-Croatian translation of the already often quoted book of J. B. Hoptner, published in Belgrade, 1964, pp. 424–29.

[69] Microcopy No. T-312, Roll 470, Frames 8,059,270–71.

[70] Churchill, *The Second World War*, III, 161.

he not choose to head the new government? It is somewhat puzzling, but one must assume that he realized that as a brigadier general, with no national reputation and in a rank-conscious milieu, he would no doubt have had trouble getting higher-ranking generals to serve under him and getting the Serbian and especially non-Serbian politicians to serve in the cabinet. In these circumstances, the logical move was to ally himself with a man of the highest military rank and national reputation and of unquestioned pro-Western views. All these qualifications were fulfilled by his chief, General Simović, a known pro-Westerner who had consistently opposed Yugoslavia's joining the Tripartite Pact, and who was, furthermore, sympathetic to the idea of revolt.

Under General Mirković's overall command and supervision, the important tasks of leading the various units that were to take over the military, governmental, and police establishment in Belgrade and the air force facilities at Zemun were assigned to middle-ranking officers from the air force, the army, and the Royal Guards. At the appointed time, in the early hours of the morning, the plan was smoothly put into motion. Colonel Dragutin Savić (Air Force) seized command of the Zemun air force base; Colonel Dragutin Dimić (Army) took control of the two bridges over the Sava River between Zemun and Belgrade; Colonel Stjepan Burazović (probably the only Croat among the leading members of the revolt), Mirković's deputy in the Air Force Command, took over the City Administration, the Police Directorate, and the Belgrade radio station; Major Živan Knežević (Royal Guards) took over the area in which the buildings of various ministries and of the General Staff were located; Colonel Stojan Zdravković (Royal Guards) took over the Royal Court; Lt. Colonel Miodrag Lozić took control of the main post office in Belgrade; and still other officers took control of other units such as the barracks of the Royal Guards and the Automotive Command. Within a few hours it was all done and the regime of Prince Paul had been overthrown. Only one life was lost, and that by accident.[71]

It seems to be well established that the conspirators had made certain in advance of the support of many key officers in garrisons throughout the country, although with few exceptions only officers who were Serbs were taken into confidence.[72] Some senior officers who were supporting the government of Prince Paul, for example General Petar V. Kosić, the Chief of General Staff, tried to induce those units of the Royal Guards that did not originally participate in the coup to resist the putschists but quickly abandoned the effort as being hopeless.[73] Once the garrisons

---

[71] For descriptions of the revolt in English see Hoptner and Ristić. The standard Yugoslav work on the subject is Čulinović, *Dvadeset sedmi mart*, esp. pp. 268–76; but see also Kljakavić, in *Politika*, Sept. 12–20, and 27, 1970; Milovanović, *Vojni puč i 27 mart*, pp. 29–33; and Terzić, pp. 17–30.

[72] Hoptner, p. 256.

[73] See the Dinić Commission report, *Dokumenti o Jugoslaviji*, No. 10, p. 16.

were considered secure, the revolt leaders deposed the Regency Council headed by Prince Paul and proclaimed King Peter (who was not yet eighteen years old) as having reached his majority and as having assumed full powers. A junior officer with a voice resembling King Peter's went on the air with a "proclamation to the people" that came as a surprise to the king himself. General Simović immediately took over the government and as Prime Minister and Chief of General Staff ordered Prince Paul into exile in Greece and imprisoned (temporarily) a few politicians and generals.

The Serbian opposition political parties and patriotic groups and the Serbian Orthodox Church, all of which had opposed the Prince Paul government and were against the signing of the Tripartite Pact, received the news of the coup enthusiastically. In Belgrade and other Serbian cities and in many cities in other regions throughout Yugoslavia there were mass street demonstrations, some of them perhaps staged, many of them undoubtedly spontaneous, and these all worked together to spread the mood of successful revolt. In many of these demonstrations the Communist Party certainly had a part, though it had nothing whatever to do, directly or indirectly, with the revolt itself. What the reaction was to the revolt among the great mass of the Serbian people—especially the Serbian peasantry—is not known, but since it presaged war, we can assume that it caused a great deal of concern. This can also be safely said of the majority of population in non-Serbian areas.

For a brief time, the overthrow of the government and the demonstrations in support of the pro-Allied officers electrified the subjugated countries of Europe and struck a spark that was visible throughout the world. On the day of the coup Churchill declared that "early this morning the Yugoslav nation found its soul." But the moment of exultation was to have a bitter denouement. The significance of the revolt was that the accession of Yugoslavia to the Tripartite Pact was put in doubt and that it thereby set into motion a series of events of fateful consequences.

THE UNSOLVABLE TASKS

Forming a new government of national unity, which the conditions required, was the first task facing the successful rebel officers. It took several days to persuade Dr. Maček, the head of the Croatian Peasant Party—the leading non-Serbian party in the country—to accept a post in the cabinet. To his way of thinking, the revolt had been a purely Serbian affair directed not only against Prince Paul but against the Cvetković-Maček Agreement and he was reluctant to have any part in the new government. But his participation was a matter of the utmost importance as showing the full commitment of his party.[74] Although neither Maček

[74] Boban, p. 359.

nor Simović in his memoirs states that Maček put any conditions to his entering the government, there is no doubt that he did so. They were: first, that the agreement of August 26, 1939, on Croatian autonomy be recognized and some of the powers of Banovina Croatia, especially in regard to the control over gendarmerie and police, be enlarged; second, that the new government fully accept the commitments assumed by Yugoslavia when it joined the Tripartite Pact on March 25 in Vienna; and third, that one leading Serb and one leading Croat temporarily assume the role of regents. The first two conditions were fully met,[75] but since King Peter had already been pronounced as being of age, it was hardly possible to impose a new regency. One additional point was agreed upon by the leaders of the Croatian Peasant Party when they met in Zagreb on April 1 to discuss the question of Maček's joining the Simović cabinet: it was decided that in the event of war and a decision of the government to go into exile, Maček would resign as vice-premier and return to Zagreb and his post would be taken by the secretary of the party, Dr. Juraj Krnjević.[76] Whether Maček informed Simović or not about this constraint when he met him in Belgrade three days later is not known.

In entering the Simović government as First Vice-Premier, Dr. Maček, who was a confirmed pacifist, undoubtedly believed that he was helping to preserve the peace and the territorial integrity of the country.[77] But it appears that at the very first meeting of the cabinet on the afternoon of April 5, he realized that this was a forlorn hope. Regarding this meeting Maček says in his memoirs: "Then Simović began to speak. His speech had no political content whatsoever and consisted entirely of patriotic phrases and national slogans. It became plain that Simović wanted to enter the war at all cost."[78] According to a Slovak diplomat who knew Maček well and talked to him after that meeting, Maček realized that his efforts to preserve peace had failed, that he and his policies had failed, and that he was just a broken old man.[79]

In the end the government was composed of leading representatives of all the significant political parties, making it in terms of personalities included by far the "strongest" Yugoslav cabinet of the entire interwar period. The outlawed Communist Party of Yugoslavia was, of course, not represented, nor was there any relaxation of anti-Communist measures, the new government being in this way no different from the old, and also wishing to avoid an obvious affront to Hitler. But in fact the

[75] *Ibid.*, pp. 363, 371.
[76] *Ibid.*, pp. 366, 373. Krnjević had spent the years 1929–39 in exile.
[77] For the text of Maček's press statement see *Poruka*, No. 2–3, p. 7, as reprinted from *Obzor*, Zagreb, April 4, 1941.
[78] Maček, p. 223.
[79] For the full message of the German chargé d'affaires to his Foreign Ministry based on a communication from the Slovak diplomat, see Boban, p. 371.

government was extremely disunited and therefore weak. Judging from their statements and performance, the members of the Simović cabinet divided into two sharply different groups of opinion on the basic problem facing the government—war or peace with Germany—with a good third of the cabinet members in between. Besides Prime Minister Simović (who was also Chief of General Staff) and General Bogoljub Ilić, the Minister of the Army and Navy, there were several politicians who were strongly opposed to the Axis; these included Srdjan Budisavljević (Interior) and Sava Kosanović (Supply), both members of the Independent Democratic Party, a general Yugoslav party dominated by Serbs from Croatia; Branko Čubrilović (Agriculture), a Bosnian member of the Serbian Agrarian Party; and Radoje Knežević (Minister of the Royal Court), a member of the almost exclusively Serbian Democratic Party. At the other extreme were those members of the cabinet who sincerely wanted to maintain the obligations that Yugoslavia had entered on March 25 when it joined the Tripartite Pact and were looking for additional guarantees, hoping in this manner to preserve peace and the territorial integrity of the country. Besides Maček, the First Vice-Premier, this group included four other members of the Croatian Peasant Party: Ivan Andres (Trade and Industry), Josip Torbar (Posts and Telegraphs), Juraj Šutej (Finance), and Bariša Smoljan (Minister Without Portfolio); Momčilo Ninčić (Foreign Affairs), a member of the almost exclusively Serbian Radical Party; Džafer Kulenović (Forests and Mines), of the Yugoslav Moslem Organization, the party of Bosnian Moslems; and two members of the Slovene People's Party, a Slovene party controlled by the Catholic Church, Fran Kulovec (Construction) and Miha Krek (Minister Without Portfolio). The remaining seven members of the cabinet were in between, some of them leaning more toward the first and others toward the second group. These were: Slobodan Jovanović (Second Vice-Premier), outside parties; Milan Grol (Social Welfare and Public Health) and Boža Marković (Justice), both of the Democratic Party; Miloš Trifunović (Education), Radical Party; Bogoljub Jevtić (Transportation) and Jovo Banjanin (Minister Without Portfolio), members of the mostly Serbian Yugoslav National Party; and Marko Daković (Minister Without Portfolio), a retired Montenegrin politician.

Clearly, the officers who executed the revolt were not prepared to assume sole responsibility for the fate of the country and therefore insisted on Simović's forming a government with wide party political participation. This more than anything else is proof that the officers did not have any long-range plans, much less a detailed political program. The wide political representation in the new cabinet necessarily made unity of thinking and purpose impossible. But in their action of overthrowing

Prince Paul's regime and thus by implication negating Yugoslavia's adherence to the Tripartite Pact, they seemingly reflected the political desires of large segments of the army, the Serbian opposition political groups, religious and cultural forces, and the Serbian people, as well as a certain proportion of non-Serbs throughout the country. Those who stood resolutely behind the new government were all committed emotionally to the slogan, "Rather war than the pact; rather death than slavery," which was chanted in the streets of Belgrade and many other cities on the day of the revolt. But this was a slogan, not a program by which a country could be governed in time of peril. The dilemma that faced the government has been aptly described by Colonel Kljaković in his comments accompanying General Simović's memoirs:

> Not even two days after the execution of the coup, it became clear to the Simović government that the new friends (Great Britain and the United States) were unable to do anything efficacious in favor of Yugoslavia, while on the other hand the provoked rejected allies (Germany and Italy) possessed great strength. Between these two poles the government was unable to find a solution of its own. Now each of its acts was carefully weighed in order not to cause reproach on either side, and this became the essence of its foreign policy.[80]

Especially interesting, of course, is the question of what the new government obtained from the British in terms of aid after its leaders followed the British advice to overthrow the government that signed the Tripartite Pact. The answer is, nothing—except praise, advice, and promises. That, in fact, had already been decided upon by the British, as Eden had made clear in a message to Campbell in Belgrade on March 24. Eden had just given Campbell a free hand to help overthrow the government of Prince Paul. But later on the same day he informed him that it would not be possible to deliver to the Yugoslavs any weapons now in the hands of the British troops; nor would it be possible for the Yugoslavs to use these weapons without previous training, and that furthermore there was no other source of arms available.[81] Churchill on April 4, in his first communication to Simović, informed him about the massive movement of German troops toward Yugoslavia and gave him the already standard advice: "The one supreme stroke for victory and safety is to win a decisive forestalling victory in Albania, and collect the masses of equipment that would fall into your hands."[82]

General Simović's government declared itself prepared to accept all international obligations of the former government, including the accession to the Tripartite Pact, provided that the national interests of Yugoslavia were safeguarded. This declaration was not made only to Dr. Maček in order to bring him into the new cabinet as Vice-Premier; it was

[80] Kljaković, in *Politika*, Sept. 25, 1970.
[81] Eden, p. 264.
[82] Churchill, *The Second World War*, III, 174.

made also by the chief actor of the revolt, General Mirković, to the German military attaché in Belgrade, and, most emphatically, by Foreign Minister Ninčić in a statement handed to Viktor von Heeren, the German Envoy in Belgrade, on March 30 (and sent for information to all the Yugoslav legations abroad):

The present Royal Yugoslav Government remains true to the principle of respect for international treaties which have been concluded, among which the Protocol signed on the 25th of this month at Vienna belongs. It will insist in the most determined fashion on not being drawn into the present conflict. Its chief attention will be devoted to the maintenance of good and friendly relations with its neighbors the German Reich and the kingdom of Italy.

The Royal Government is particularly interested in the manner of applying the Protocol mentioned; in connection with this it is mindful of safeguarding all the essential interests of the Yugoslav State and people.[83]

Ninčić was of course acting with the direction and approval of Prime Minister Simović, and had (according to my sources) received a memorandum from Simović stating that Yugoslavia should not show any pro-British sympathies but should follow a sort of neutrality; that Yugoslavia would in fact protect the left flank of the Italians in Albania and the right flank of the Germans in Bulgaria, and should, furthermore, occupy Salonika in order to prevent anti-German forces from landing there.

Nonetheless, the new government wanted additional assurances from the Germans, and it therefore tried to initiate new talks—not only in Belgrade but also in Budapest (with the German representatives who were expected to attend the funeral of the Hungarian Prime Minister Paul Teleki) and after that in Berlin—and also sought, rather naïvely, to ask Mussolini, no friend to Yugoslavia, to mediate for them with Hitler. Yugoslav representatives for these talks were designated and were scheduled to leave for their assignments on April 6 or 7.

Meanwhile, the new government continued the Cvetković policy of strengthening the armed forces by speeding up the "activation" of the reserves. (It did not want, at first, to call a general mobilization, thinking that this would give additional offense to Hitler, which it was striving to avoid.) Some rather ineffectual attempts were made to shift food and other military supplies from the more exposed areas in the northern plains to the less accessible mountainous areas in the center of the country. Belgrade, Zagreb, and Ljubljana were declared open cities in the

---

[83] *DGFP*, Series D, Vol. XII, pp. 421–22. When von Heeren returned to his office from the visit to the Foreign Minister, he found a message from Berlin instructing him and other personnel of the legation to avoid any contacts with Yugoslav officials. The Germans never answered Ninčić's note. Von Heeren was called to Berlin to report and the chargé d'affaires was ordered to maintain utmost reserve toward the Yugoslav authorities. *Ibid.*, pp. 422–23. On April 2 the Germans ordered the immediate evacuation of all but a few officials from their legation in Belgrade. At the same time the chargé d'affaires was advised to suggest to the diplomats of other friendly nations in Belgrade that they send most of their personnel home or to a neutral country. *Ibid.*, pp. 431–32. The meaning of all these moves was obvious: the German attack on Yugoslavia was only days away.

event of war. Also following its predecessor, the government made a last effort to improve its position by further strengthening relations with the Soviet Union, and to this end a treaty of friendship and nonaggression was signed in Moscow on the night of April 5–6. This was, however, an almost meaningless diplomatic move, which could have no real effect on the existing situation.

In retrospect it is clear that the new regime had neither the time to consolidate its political hold on the country, nor the time and the resources to prepare the country politically, psychologically, militarily, and economically to undertake any sustained military resistance. It had no illusions about the state the country was in, nor of its chances of successfully opposing an invasion by the Axis powers. Thus while trying to stiffen its military defenses without arousing Hitler's wrath, it also tried to inaugurate new discussions with the Germans in the hope of getting further guarantees of its sovereignty and national independence. But if any kind of new agreement was to be reached with the Axis, both sides had to be willing to negotiate. Hitler's main concern now was the time schedule of the planned attack upon the Soviet Union, and he had neither the time nor the will to negotiate with the Yugoslavs, the more so as he considered the coup as a personal affront and an affront to the Third Reich. He therefore issued a directive (No. 25) on March 27, some hours after the news of the revolt was received, ordering the invasion of Yugoslavia at the earliest possible time: "The military putsch in Yugoslavia has changed the political situation in the Balkans. Even if Yugoslavia at first should give declarations of loyalty, she must be considered as a foe and therefore must be destroyed as quickly as possible."[84]

That the revolt of March 27 was an important but controversial event in Yugoslav history is attested by the way in which it was and still is viewed. It is pointed to as a source of pride by the most outspoken Serbian nationalists and representatives of a large portion of the former ruling groups. The supporters of a policy of accommodation with the Axis maintain that, had it not occurred, Yugoslavia would have been able to remain neutral and by doing so would have escaped invasion and many other consequences of the Second World War, or could have come into the war at a convenient time and with small sacrifices. The leadership of the Communist Party of Yugoslavia has had this to say about it:

The first revolutionary breakthrough of the old political system took place on March 27, 1941. The putsch of the pro-Western part of the bourgeoisie and high military against the entry of Yugoslavia into the Hitler bloc was surpassed by the feelings and movements of the national masses, because the growing revolutionary democratic pressure, which was materializing under the leadership

[84] *Ibid.*, pp. 395–96.

of the Communist Party, did not allow the putsch to remain within the limits in which its promoters tried to keep it. The Communist Party succeeded in further developing it in the direction of a deeper revolutionary movement.[85]

Regardless of how the revolt is interpreted by its initiators and supporters, by those against whose policies it was originally directed, or by those who profited most from it, there is no question of its tremendous immediate effect, and no question that it was, indeed, the starting point of the ultimately successful Communist revolution. As will be shown in the next chapter, it also had caused a fateful delay in the German invasion of the Soviet Union, a fact of considerable importance for the eventual victory of the Allies over the Axis powers.

[85] Communist Party of Yugoslavia, *VII kongres Saveza komunista Jugoslavije*, p. 991. See also Kardelj, "Ten Years of People's Revolution," pp. 55–59.

CHAPTER THREE

Invasion and Collapse

As we have seen, the coup of March 27 had come as a complete surprise to the Germans. German diplomats and agents in Belgrade were well aware that part of the Yugoslav officer corps and certain Serbian political, church, and cultural circles were dissatisfied with Prince Paul's policy toward the Axis and with the Cvetković-Maček government in general. But they discounted the likelihood of a coup, not believing that a small, politically softened, economically weak, disunited, and almost completely surrounded country would embark on a course of policy amounting to state suicide. When the unexpected happened, Hitler was so outraged by the action of the Serbs that he was determined to brush aside any possible declarations of loyalty by the new government in Belgrade and to make all preparations for destroying Yugoslavia militarily and as a state.

In the conference that took place in Hitler's office on the afternoon of March 27, the broad objectives of the forthcoming military operations against Yugoslavia were made clear:

Politically, it is especially important that the blow against Yugoslavia be carried out with inexorable severity and that the military destruction be carried out in a lightning-like operation. In this way Turkey would presumably be sufficiently deterred and the subsequent campaign against Greece would be influenced in a favorable way. It is to be expected that the Croats will take our side when we attack. They will be assured of political treatment (autonomy later on) in accordance with this. The war against Yugoslavia presumably will be very popular in Italy, Hungary, and Bulgaria, as these states are to be promised territorial acquisitions: the Adriatic coast for Italy, the Banat for Hungary, and Macedonia for Bulgaria.[1]

---

[1] Minutes of the conference, in *DGFP*, Series D, Vol. XII, pp. 372–75. "The Banat" here obviously refers to what the Yugoslavs called Vojvodina, consisting of the Yugoslav portion of the Banat, Bačka, and Baranja. Since the Romanians threatened to invade the Yugoslav part of the Banat if it were assigned to Hungary, Hitler included it as part of occupied Serbia and turned its administration over to the local German minority.

Hitler's order for the military destruction and political dismemberment of Yugoslavia was contained in Directive No. 25, issued after the
March 27 meeting. In Directive No. 26, issued on April 3, Hitler outlined the roles to be played in the Yugoslav campaign by Hungary, Romania, and Bulgaria. Only Hungary was to take part in the actual invasion; Romania was simply to secure its borders against Yugoslavia and
the Soviet Union, and Bulgaria was supposed to shift a large portion of
its troops to the frontier toward Turkey. In order to ensure the operational unity of the campaign, Hitler retained for himself the task of coordinating Hungarian and Italian participation, though he decided to
do it in such a way that the heads of the two states would appear before
their peoples and armed forces as "sovereign military leaders." Hitler
explained to Mussolini the whole plan for the attack on Yugoslavia in
a letter of April 5, in which he also gave him some operational pointers.[2]

THE YUGOSLAV DEFENSE PLANS

Like the general staffs of other countries, the Yugoslav General Staff
had prepared several war plans during the 1930's, and as time went on
and the strategic situation of the country changed, these plans were
modified accordingly. The first basic revision in the Yugoslav plans apparently was made as a result of the absorbing of Austria by Germany in
March 1938; the revised plan was signed by General Milutin Dj. Nedić
(brother of Milan), the Chief of General Staff, on September 17, 1938.[3]
A few weeks later Nedić was replaced by General Dušan T. Simović, and
under Simović's guidance a new war plan, Plan S (S standing for *sjever*
or North), was prepared, based on the assumption that attack would
come from Italy, Germany, and Hungary, and that the Germans would
attack also from the western frontier of Hungary.[4] According to this
plan about 60 percent of all Yugoslav forces were to be deployed on the
western and northern borders to take care of the initial defense, partly
in the front lines and partly in the established fortifications; the remaining 40 percent were to be held in reserve. Because a successful and
prolonged defense of these borders was considered impossible, the plan
foresaw a gradual and orderly withdrawal of all forces in a southeasterly
direction through the mountainous center of the country toward Greece,
where strong Allied armies would presumably be in control. The most
important considerations were to prevent a piecemeal breaking up and
loss of the armed forces and to keep open the lines of supply and the
withdrawal route.

[2] For the text of Directive No. 25 see *ibid.*, pp. 395–96, for that of Directive No. 26 see *ibid.*,
pp. 440–42; and for the text of Hitler's letter to Mussolini see *ibid.*, pp. 475–78.
[3] *Aprilski rat 1941*, pp. 38–40.
[4] Kljaković, in *Politika*, Aug. 21 and 22, 1970; Yugoslavia, Vojnoistorijski institut, *Drugi svetski
rat (Pregled ratnih operacija)*, I, 416–17 (hereafter cited as *Drugi svetski rat*). On the Yugoslav
war plans see also Terzić, pp. 309–24.

With the Italian occupation of Albania in April 1939, Yugoslavia's strategic position was radically altered, for the Italian presence in Albania, in itself a threat, also jeopardized Yugoslav access to Salonika, which had always been a basic part of Yugoslavia's war plans. At the beginning of January 1940 Prince Paul removed General Simović from the position of Chief of the General Staff and replaced him with General Petar V. Kosić. Because of changed conditions and somewhat different views on strategy, War Plan S was abandoned and during the early months of 1940 a new War Plan, R-40, was prepared.[5] This plan took into account the presence of the Italian forces in Albania and included several new features, but it followed Plan S in calling for an initial defense of the western and northern borders and a gradual withdrawal of all forces in a southeasterly direction toward Greece. The new features included a swift and strong attack upon the Italian base Zadar (Zara), on the Dalmatian coast, so as to reduce the threat from that area to the center of the country; the holding of the front against Albania; active reconnaissance toward Romania, and a concentric attack upon Bulgaria by all members of the Balkan Entente if Bulgaria should attack any member country. Forces committed to operations on the frontiers were to be increased to about 70 percent of the total.

But Plan R-40, too, was soon overtaken by the rapidly moving events, and in February 1941 Plan R-41 was worked out, taking into account the presence of German troops in Hungary and Romania and the likelihood of their entering Bulgaria. Plan R-41 was intended to provide a cordon defense of the entire land border of Yugoslavia, nearly 3,000 kilometers in all (about 1,860 miles), excluding only the Albanian border, where combined Greek-Yugoslav offensive action was anticipated in order to eliminate the Italian army in Albania and thus protect the withdrawal toward Greece. There was to be heavy troop concentration near the Bulgarian border, especially in the area of Yugoslav Macedonia, for protection of the Skopje-Salonika communication line and the withdrawal route. Unwisely, the ratio of reserves to total front-line effectives was even further reduced, to about one to seven. For one reason or another, however, Plan R-41 was not sent to the army commanders in the field until March 31. This left little time for reshuffling the armed forces in the days immediately preceding the invasion, and for all practical purposes the earlier Plan R-40 was still the operative plan in April 1941.[6]

All these plans assumed that attack would come from the Axis powers and that Yugoslavia would be allied with the Western democracies; they were defensive in character, the Yugoslav objective being to save as much as possible of its military manpower and to be on the winning, Allied,

[5] *Drugi svetski rat*, I, 416–17; Kljaković, in *Politika*, Aug. 25, 1970, according to a written deposition of General Kosić made after the war.
[6] *Drugi svetski rat*, I, 417, 421–22, 435–36. See also Kljaković, in *Politika*, Oct. 1 and 4, 1970.

side in the end. The initial defense of the frontiers and the use of frontier fortifications and of several partly prepared secondary lines of defense would permit gradual withdrawal to the mountainous center of the country, where protracted defense was thought possible. The route to Greece was to be kept open as a supply line and, if necessary, as an escape route; withdrawing to Greece, the Yugoslav army could link forces with the Greek army and other Allied armies, and later on, helped by Allied troops and supplies, it could return and free Yugoslavia from the enemy. Except that the retreat was made through Albania and that the Serbian troops were then shifted to the Salonika front this had been Serbian experience in the First World War, and it was on that experience that the plans of the 1930's were made.

For the kind of war fought by the Serbian army in 1914–15 and assuming the absence of enemy air forces and armored and motorized troops, these plans would have been theoretically feasible. But for the conditions of 1941 they were hopelessly inadequate. Against an enemy using the blitzkrieg technique based on the employment of huge air, armored, and motorized forces attacking the country from all sides at once, these plans were practically useless and invited speedy disaster.

Yugoslav war plans envisaged an army, when fully mobilized, of about 1,200,000 men in operative units and about 500,000 (those of the ages 41–50) in noncombat services.[7] During 1939–40 there were repeated but ineffectual periodic activations (euphemism for mobilization) of the reserves, called for the purpose of testing the effectiveness of the mobilization plans, for strengthening the contingents already under arms and giving further training, and also, in some instances, as a way of raising manpower for work on fortifications.[8] But there were numerous abuses in the matter of who was called up, when, and for how long, and the budget was inadequate to carry out the program in a satisfactory way or with sufficient logistic support. Moreover, it proved impossible to activate more than a small proportion of motor vehicles and draft animals. Thus the total effect of the activation policy on the fighting efficiency of the Yugoslav forces was negligible.[9]

The size and makeup of the fully mobilized wartime army were projected as follows:

The Supreme Command Staff; the staffs of the three groups of armies; the staffs of seven armies with certain elements outside the divisional formations; 28 in-

[7] *Drugi svetski rat*, I, 417.
[8] *Ibid.*, p. 433.
[9] A very unfavorable contemporary appraisal of the policy of periodic activation of reserves was given by Minister of the Army and Navy General Nedić in his memorandum of November 1, 1940, to Prince Paul and the cabinet. On the poor training of reserve officers at that time see a letter of such an officer apparently written in May 1939 in *Aprilski rat 1941*, pp. 236–41. Since the war, criticism of the policy has been expressed by Dr. Maček in his book *In the Struggle for Freedom*, pp. 196–98; and by General Živko Stanisavljević in a letter to *Politika*, Sept. 11, 1970 (in connection with the publication of Simović's memoirs by Colonel Kljaković).

fantry divisions; three cavalry divisions; one cavalry guards brigade; three mountain detachments (each consisting of a mountain regiment and an artillery battalion); 16 combined detachments (each consisting of one to three infantry regiments and one to three artillery battalions); 16 regiments in frontier fortifications; two fortress commands (Bay of Kotor and Šibenik); the Air Force command with its units and installations; the Navy command with its units and installations; special units outside the armies; four regiments of motorized artillery; two battalions of tanks; one battalion of signal troops; three regiments of railroad troops; six automobile battalions; the Rear Areas command of the Supreme Command with its units and installations; the commands of six army areas, 16 divisional areas, and 49 military districts; troops for the protection and securing of frontiers and for the securing of the interior areas, consisting of 48 infantry regiments in the strength of two to five battalions with some artillery, and including also gendarmerie and regular frontier troops; and the territorial Anti-aircraft Defense command with its units and installations.[10]

In addition to the above, the Yugoslav military organization from April 1940 on also included a special Guerrilla Operations Command (*Četnička komanda*), which had its own command staff and was supposed to have seven battalions of troops. This force may have been intended for use against domestic fifth-column activity as well as for guerrilla operations. At the beginning of April 1941 only six of the seven battalions were organized, and they were attached to the army commands (that is, one battalion to an army) rather than being under separate command.[11]

Two of the fundamental weaknesses of the pre-1941 Yugoslav army were its system of very large units and its dependence on animal draft power (often oxen) and pack animals for transportation; they were responsible for the low speed and lack of maneuverability of the Yugoslav forces, particularly of large formations. Thus the wartime complement of an infantry division was set at 26,000 to 27,000 men, and that of a cavalry division at 6,000 to 7,000 men.[12] And according to plan, the army when fully mobilized would have had about 900,000 draft and pack animals.[13] Furthermore, the experience of periodic activation of troops, draft animals, and vehicles had shown that the maintenance of animals and vehicles cost twice as much as the maintenance of activated men. The Yugoslav military were fully aware of these weaknesses and in June 1940 began a study directed toward streamlining and cutting the size of army formations and reducing the dependence on animal draft power,

[10] *Drugi svetski rat*, I, 418. For detailed information on the peacetime organization of the army see *ibid.*, pp. 74–77, and the article "Yugoslav Army [Old Yugoslavia]," *Vojna enciklopedija*, IV, 235–55.

[11] *Vojna enciklopedija*, II, 321, and IV, 252. Hagen (p. 243) confuses names: it was not Colonel Draža Mihailović who was the chief of the Guerrilla Operations Command but Divisional General Mihailo Mihailović (who as of July 1965 was still alive and living in Belgrade). See also Terzić, p. 696. For some time, under pressure from Vice-Premier Maček, the name of the command was Storming Operations Command (*Jurišna komanda*), a total misnomer. The original name was restored in April 1941.

[12] *Drugi svetski rat*, I, 75–76.

[13] *Ibid.*, p. 417.

but except for the motorization of four artillery regiments practically nothing else had been accomplished in this direction by the time the country was invaded.[14]

An even more serious problem was the inadequate supply of arms (especially automatic and special purpose weapons, which accounted for the low firepower of Yugoslav units) and other military supplies, and the practically total inability of replenishing these arms and supplies. The arms of the infantry and artillery troops—the main force of the Yugoslav army—consisted in terms of origin and age of three main segments: (a) heavy arms, including heavy machine guns, left over from the First World War, many of which were obsolete and in poor condition; (b) some heavy arms and some light arms, such as light machine guns, which had been imported during the interwar period from Czechoslovakia and to a lesser extent from France; and (c) light arms, consisting of about 1,000,000 Mauser rifles and 20,000 submachine guns, partly imported but mostly produced at home under foreign license. Only these light arms were in sufficient supply and up to date. The reservist troops were armed with Austrian rifles of First World War vintage.

Of about 7,000 pieces of artillery, about 4,000 pieces were relatively modern, including about 800 antitank guns. There were also about 1,900 modern mortars and about 250 antiaircraft guns. All these arms were imported, from different sources, which meant that the various models of arms often were without proper ammunition or lacked proper repair and maintenance facilities. After the outbreak of the war in Europe on September 1, 1939, it became much more difficult and in many cases impossible to replenish the arms originating abroad. Furthermore, at the beginning of April 1941 the Yugoslav army had on hand supplies of ammunition for only 75 days for infantry arms, 100 days for artillery, and for only two to seven days for the antiaircraft guns.[15] The army had 110 tanks, 60 of which were unusable five-ton machines of First World War vintage and 50 of which were modern ten-tonners bought in Belgium in 1940.[16] There were only a few tank crews, none of them well trained. For antitank operations, training was negligible.

The 459 aircraft of the Yugoslav Air Force were also of assorted manufacture—British, French, German, Italian, and Yugoslav—and not even for the Yugoslav planes was there any chance of securing spare parts and replacements. The total force consisted of 125 fighters (38 of them obsolete), 173 bombers, and 161 reconnaissance aircraft (about 150 obsolete).[17]

Yugoslavia's navy was modest. It consisted of one obsolete small

[14] *Aprilski rat 1941*, pp. 715–17.
[15] *Drugi svetski rat*, I, 431. See also *Vojna enciklopedija*, IV, 250–52.
[16] *Drugi svetski rat*, I, 432.
[17] *Vojna enciklopedija*, IV, 248. *Drugi svetski rat*, I, 422–25, gives somewhat lower figures, but since the first-quoted source is of a later date, I use its data.

cruiser, four modern destroyers, four old torpedo boats and eight large and two small motor topedo boats, four submarines, eleven minelayers, a dozen or so auxiliary vessels, and four river monitors that operated on the Danube.[18] The navy had also about 150 seaplanes, most of them obsolete.[19] The basic objective of the naval defense plan was to contain a possible Italian amphibious landing for twenty-four to forty-eight hours, the time needed for land forces to reach the coast and begin operations against the bridgehead.[20]

The basic reason for Yugoslavia's lack of modern arms was the underdeveloped economy. The low per capita income and small industrial base made it impossible either to produce a sufficient amount of modern arms at home or to import them. In 1938, the per capita income was estimated at 3,100 dinars or about $70. Compare this with the cost of imported arms, in November 1938: light tanks (12 to 15 tons), 2,500,000 dinars; heavy tanks (20 to 25 tons), 5,000,000 dinars; heavy trucks, 90,000 dinars; 150 mm. howitzers (M 36), 3,500,000 dinars; fighter planes (apparently without armaments), 1,750,000 dinars; bombers (apparently without armaments), 4,500,000 dinars.[21] The contrast between the extremely low per capita income and these high armaments prices reveals the absurdity of the situation in which economically underdeveloped countries like Yugoslavia have found themselves when they have tried to develop a modern army, or even to carry out a partial modernization of their armed forces. Or take steel production as an indicator of economic and thereby also of military strength. In 1938 Yugoslavia produced around 230,000 tons of steel, of which about one-third was produced in mills in border areas or not far distant from the border.[22] That same year, German steel production was about 22.6 million tons,[23] and in the next three years, as Germany brought under its control the steel production capacity of Austria, Czechoslovakia, Poland, France, Belgium, Luxembourg, Holland, Denmark, and Norway, the total production at the disposal of Germany increased enormously, while that of Yugoslavia rose scarcely at all.

Yugoslav military authorities were painfully aware of the small economic potential of their country, of the smallness of their armaments

[18] One of the extreme illustrations of the diversity of Yugoslavia's foreign arms suppliers is indicated by the destroyer S.S. *Dubrovnik*. This ship was built in England; her main guns came from Czechoslovakia, the antiaircraft guns from Sweden, the torpedo installations from England, the gunnery equipment from the Netherlands, and the radio equipment from Belgium. *Drugi svetski rat*, I, 431; see also *Vojna enciklopedija*, IV, 241–43.

[19] *Vojna enciklopedija*, IV, 248.

[20] According to a personal communication from former Commander Zenon V. Adamich of the Yugoslav Royal Navy, who worked on these plans in the Yugoslav Admiralty.

[21] For the prices of various arms see the report of the General Staff to the Minister of the Army and Navy of November 20, 1938, dealing with the unpreparedness of Yugoslavia's armed forces and the need for increasing its armaments and supplies as well as for expanding the country's military industry, in *Aprilski rat 1941*, pp. 68–95, esp. pp. 85–90.

[22] *Ibid.*, pp. 49–50; Yugoslavia, *Statistički godišnjak FNRJ 1954*, p. 157.

[23] For data on German steel production see Germany, Länderrat des Amerikanischen Besatzungsgebiets, *Statistisches Handbuch von Deutschland, 1928–1944*, pp. 8–9, 288, 600.

and ammunition supplies, and of the lack of other necessary military goods such as clothing, shoes, medical supplies, vehicles, and food reserves.[24] In 1938 they started frantically trying to improve their domestic production for military purposes, but the time was too short and the means too meager to work miracles. Yugoslavia continued to buy foreign arms, but after war broke out and its neutralist position raised doubts both on the part of the Axis powers and on the part of Great Britain, these imports became more and more difficult and sometime in 1940 became only a trickle.[25]

On the eve of invasion, clothing and footwear were available for only two-thirds or so of the potential front-line troops and only partially for other troops; some other essential supplies were available for only a third of the front-line troops; medical and sanitary supplies were available for only a few weeks, and supplies of food for men and feed for livestock were available for only about two months.[26] In all cases there was little or no possibility of replenishment.

In the months just preceding the invasion, Yugoslavia was able to import from the United States about 1,000 trucks for military purposes, but practically all heavy armaments and supply trains were still dependent on animal draft power.[27] By way of illustration: German troops and supplies could move in one hour the same distance as Yugoslav troops and supplies moved in twenty-four hours. It should be noted, too, that Yugoslavia, with negligible domestic oil production, was almost completely dependent upon oil imports, some of which came from countries like Romania that were now under German control; imports by sea could easily be cut off by the Italian navy. The reserves available in the country, assuming that storage and refining facilities were not bombed, were reportedly sufficient for two to three months of operations.[28]

Since 1937 the Yugoslavs had been spending fairly large sums of money on the fortification of their frontiers, first toward Italy and then toward Germany (Austria) and Hungary. On the frontier toward Romania, Bulgaria, and Albania, fortification works on a large scale were to have been started late in March 1941, notwithstanding the lesson of the Maginot Line, but at the time of the invasion, fortifications had been completed only on the western and northwestern frontiers. These were much less elaborate than those of Czechoslovakia, for example, toward Germany, and consisted mainly of pillboxes, antitank barriers, and wire bar-

---

[24] See especially the report of the Yugoslav General Staff of Nov. 20, 1938, cited in note 21.

[25] For a list of arms and military supplies that Yugoslavia wanted to import or buy at home dated March 20, 1939, see *Aprilski rat 1941*, pp. 152–60. The chief suppliers of arms were to be Germany and Italy, but after war broke out both Axis countries greatly reduced their deliveries. For aircraft and arms procurement from Great Britain between 1935 and March 1941 see Vinaver, pp. 77–92. On the general problem of military industry and procurement of arms and military supplies from domestic and foreign sources see also Terzić, pp. 290–97, esp. p. 297.

[26] Terzić, pp. 277–78.

[27] *Drugi svetski rat*, I, 432.

[28] Terzić, p. 274.

riers against infantry.[29] A very small amount of construction of fortifications on the right banks of the Danube, Sava, and Una rivers for purposes of defense in depth had also been started.[30] Ironically, when the invasion came, the main thrust was on the Bulgarian frontier, which under war plans S and R-40 had not been regarded as a point of great danger and was practically without any fortifications at all.[31]

It has been pointed out that all Yugoslav war plans between 1938 and 1941 took into account the possibility of withdrawing to Greece in the case of need and leaning on powerful Allied armies there. It was, at the same time, in the British and Greek interest to help Yugoslavia resist any hostile attack. In order to assist the Greeks a British expeditionary force had begun landing at Piraeus on March 7.[32] On March 8, as we have mentioned in the previous chapter, the Yugoslavs sent Major Perišić of the General Staff to Greece to inform the British Commander in the Middle East, General Henry Maitland Wilson, that the Yugoslavs would resist if attacked by the Germans, and to inquire whether or not they could count on some specific forms of military support by British troops in case the Yugoslavs had to withdraw a large part of their troops to Greece. The British and Greek commanders were greatly disappointed that all Yugoslav plans were of a defensive nature and urged a change toward an offensive approach, particularly in regard to the Italian forces in Albania. The Yugoslav authorities concluded that they could not expect any help from the British in Greece. After the coup in Belgrade the British continued to press the Yugoslavs to coordinate their plans with those of the British and Greek forces, but they met with an unexpected lack of response. The new Yugoslav government refused to let Foreign Secretary Eden visit Belgrade, fearing that it would be considered a provocation by the Germans, and reluctantly consented to receive General Sir John G. Dill, the Chief of the Imperial General Staff, on condition he come in civilian clothes. Dill's talks with Simović on April 1 were almost completely fruitless: the Yugoslavs were not willing to take

---

[29] For discussions of fortifications by the leading Yugoslav military authorities, decisions to undertake them, costs, areas to be fortified, and progress of work see *Aprilski rat 1941*, pp. 99–123, 143–50, 223–32, 319–29, and *passim*.

[30] *Ibid.*, pp. 638–43, 649–50, 658, 700–704.

[31] *Drugi svetski rat*, I, 427–30; Terzić, pp. 303–9.

[32] The British had had a hard time deciding whether or not to send an expeditionary force to Greece. British military authorities in the Middle East, and Foreign Secretary Eden when he visited Athens, were optimistic about the success of such an operation and they recognized that the failure to help an ally in need would reflect unfavorably on the British image. Colonel William J. Donovan, who visited the Balkans and Turkey in January, was even more optimistic about the larger prospect of a British challenge to the Germans in the Balkans. The British finally sent about 62,000 men to Greece. From a military point of view the operation was clearly a blunder. By the end of April the Germans had reached the southernmost tip of the Peloponnesus and between May 20 and May 31 they conquered Crete through a masterful airborne invasion. From the expeditionary force in Greece the British succeeded in withdrawing about 50,000 men. British casualties from all causes, including prisoners, were about 12,000. In addition, 209 aircraft and about 8,000 trucks were lost. On Crete, British casualties were also heavy: 1,742 killed, 1,737 wounded, and 11,835 captured. See Playfair et al., II, 70–105, 121–51; Woodward, I, 525–36.

any action that would be objectionable to the Germans, and would only consent to send another officer to Greece for further talks. Thus on April 3 the Deputy Chief of General Staff General Radivoje Janković journeyed to Greece; but those talks, too, were fruitless. The actual weakness in the potential British-Greek-Yugoslav combination and, at least on the Yugoslav side, the overwhelming fear of the Germans prevented the formulation of any realistic plans for common action. The only agreement that was reached had to do with a combined Yugoslav-Greek attack on Italian forces in Albania—and this was not implemented when invasion came. None of the three parties was in a position to help the others, and the result was mutual disillusionment, and an easy victory for the Germans in Yugoslavia and Greece.[33]

The weaknesses of the Yugoslav army in manpower, armaments, transportation facilities, and supplies were compounded by lack of cohesion and unity of views and purpose among government leaders, leaders of the armed forces, and the population at large. The shortsighted policies, in both political and military affairs, of the Serbian-dominated regime during the preceding twenty-three years had left the country almost totally unprepared for any great external crisis. Briefly, just before and just after the March 27 coup, fighting resolution animated the spirits of a certain portion of the army and air force officers and the Serbian politicians, as well as the general public in Serbia and, to a very small extent, elsewhere in the country, but when the new government came face to face with reality, this spirit vanished. Once the invasion had started, most of the high-ranking army officers, convinced that resistance against Germany was hopeless, thought only of how to surrender most quickly and save lives, not how to resist and defend the country.

Fifth-column activity was seen as a real danger, owing to the dissatisfaction of various South Slav nations and national minorities, especially the *Volksdeutsche* in Vojvodina, but few steps had been taken to deal with it.[34] Although the leadership of the Croatian extremist organization Ustasha and three to four hundred of its most ardent followers were in exile, they had perhaps several times that number of sworn members and several tens of thousands of sympathizers in the country at the beginning of 1941, and were sure to get more should Yugoslavia get involved in war. There were also potential fifth columns among the pro-Bulgarian Macedonian population and the Albanian population in the Kosovo area. Yugoslav military authorities in the years preceding the invasion had been obsessed by the idea of the Communist danger in the country generally and in the armed forces in particular, but they also

[33] *Drugi svetski rat*, I, 435–521; Wilson, pp. 63–103, esp. pp. 72–75, 80–84, 100; Hoptner, pp. 274–75; Terzić, pp. 111–13, 145–50.
[34] See Todor Milicević, pp. 13–14.

closely followed developments among the national minorities and among the Croats and Macedonians.[35]

Finally, it should be stressed that because of the conventional or the First World War approach to warfare by the Yugoslav military establishment, relatively short service in the cadres, and the lack of modern arms both for training and use in combat, the training of all armed services was outmoded and poor.[36]

At the time of invasion, Yugoslavia had only about 700,000 men under arms, of whom more than 400,000 were poorly trained inductees of four weeks or less.[37] Most units were still in their assembly camps rather than in positions on or near the fronts where they were supposed to be deployed according to the plans. Not a single division was ready for action, though certain infantry and cavalry regiments and some pioneer units were. According to most authoritative sources, not one higher command staff, signal unit, artillery unit, frontier unit, rear area unit, medical unit, or supply unit was staffed and manned to its planned wartime strength, that is, fully mobilized, when the invasion came. Thus in several instances units that were ready or nearly ready but were dependent upon the support of other units could not be used to proper advantage.[38] A general mobilization had purposely not been called so as not to offend Hitler, and was not ordered until April 3. And when it was ordered, there were a good many men, and owners of livestock and animal-drawn and motor vehicles, who ignored the call, especially in certain areas not sympathetic to the regime.

THE AXIS ATTACK

Hitler's Directive No. 25, issued on the afternoon of March 27, had declared that Yugoslavia "must be destroyed as quickly as possible." Point 2 of the Directive outlined the basic strategy:

It is my intention to break into Yugoslavia in the general direction of Belgrade and southward by a concentric operation from the area of Rijeka-Graz on the one side and from the area around Sofia on the other and to give the Yugoslav armed forces an annihilating blow. In addition I intend to cut off the extreme southern part of Yugoslavia from the rest of the country and seize it as a base for the continuance of the German-Italian offensive against Greece.[39]

Hitler further postulated that "the domestic political tensions in Yugoslavia will be sharpened by political assurances to the Croats."[40] Among

---

[35] See e.g. various reports in *Aprilski rat 1941*, pp. 175–76, 252–60, 341–43, 382–83, 412–16, and *passim*.

[36] *Drugi svetski rat*, I, 433.

[37] According to a statement by General Kosić, Chief of General Staff from January 1940 until the coup, in Čulinović, *Slom stare Jugoslavije*, pp. 162–68. According to official data, about 600,000 men were under arms on the day of the coup (*Drugi svetski rat*, I, 434), but Terzić (p. 358) says that this number included some military units that were working on fortifications.

[38] *Drugi svetski rat*, I, 434; Terzić, p. 359; *Vojna enciklopedija*, IV, 254.

[39] For the complete text see *DGFP*, Series D, Vol. XII, pp. 395–96.

[40] This part of Hitler's strategy against Yugoslavia led later to the proclamation of the Independent State of Croatia, of which more will be said in Chapter 4.

the important details of the directive was the following: "As soon as sufficient forces stand ready and the weather situation permits, the ground organization of the Yugoslav Air Force and Belgrade are to be destroyed by continuous day and night attacks of the Luftwaffe."[41]

The Germans, with no prior plans to attack Yugoslavia and caught by surprise by the Belgrade coup, were forced to improvise: they had to devise an attack that would guarantee a rapid crushing of the Yugoslav forces and cause the least disruption to their own preparations for the invasion of Russia (Operation Barbarossa).[42] And since Hitler was uncertain what sort of resistance the Yugoslavs might put up, a strong, swift attack was all the more necessary. Troops of the German Twelfth Army were already poised in Bulgaria for the attack against Greece and a part of them could easily be used against Yugoslav Macedonia and Serbia, and parts of other large German units that were massing at various locations in Austria, Hungary, and Romania for use in Operation Barbarossa could be diverted temporarily for operations against Yugoslav forces in Slovenia, Croatia, Vojvodina, and Serbia. Not all these troops were battle-ready, however, owing to shortages of matériel. Consequently, "the forces to be committed in the Yugoslav campaign had to be gathered from the area between eastern Germany and southern France and, in certain cases, it was necessary to take special measures to speed up their preparation for commitment in combat."[43]

Altogether, the attacking forces consisted of 24 German divisions and about 1,500 German aircraft, 23 Italian divisions and about 670 Italian aircraft together with a considerable number of naval units, and five Hungarian divisions, totaling in all 52 divisions and about 2,200 aircraft. Of these, the German divisions were the best armed and best equipped, and constituted the backbone of the invasion force. About two-fifths of them were armored or fully motorized divisions with tremendous firepower and maneuverability, and they were led by veterans of campaigns in Poland, Norway, and France, men superbly trained, confident, resourceful, and under overall masterful leadership. They bore the brunt of such resistance as was offered.

The Yugoslav army, amounting to about thirty divisions, of which not one had its full complement of men and was ready for battle, or had taken up positions in the particular area foreseen by the war plans, was, by contrast, poorly trained, inexperienced in battle except for higher

---

[41] *DGFP*, Series D, Vol. XII, p. 395.

[42] The plan, Operation 25, was submitted to Hitler on March 29. It was hastily prepared and put together by the specialized departments of the German General Staff and the Operations Staff of the Wehrmacht. For the description of these preparations by a German officer who at that time was an adjutant in the Army General Staff see Mueller-Hillebrand, *The German Campaign in the Balkans, 1941—A Model of Crisis Planning*, pp. 17–34. For detailed deployment orders as issued by the Army High Command (OKH) on March 30, 1941, see Microcopy No. T-78, Roll 329, Frames 6,285,869–915. See also Germany, Wehrmacht, Oberkommando, *Kriegstagebuch des Oberkommandos der Wehrmacht (Wehrmachtführungsstab)*, I, 150, 368–70, 1181 (hereafter cited as *KTB/OKW/WFSt*); Greiner, pp. 280–82.

[43] Mueller-Hillebrand, *The German Campaign*, p. 73.

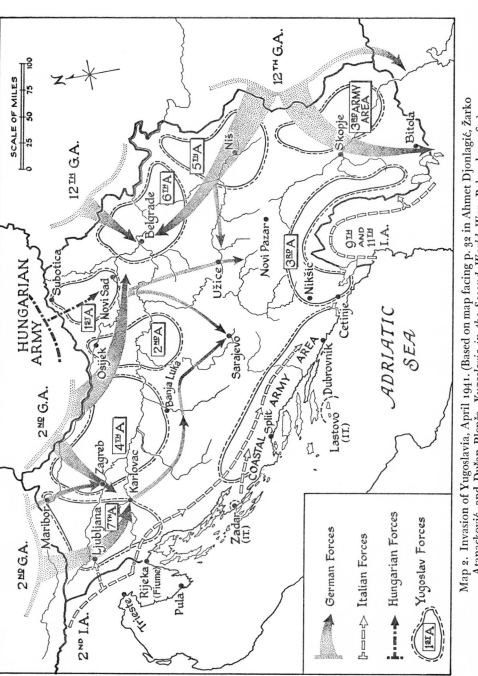

Map 2. Invasion of Yugoslavia, April 1941. (Based on map facing p. 32 in Ahmet Djonlagić, Žarko Atanacković, and Dušan Plenča, *Yugoslavia in the Second World War*, Belgrade, 1967.)

echelon officers who had been in the First World War, and marked by an utterly defeatist spirit among its top commanding officers. Furthermore, some of the largest army formations were put under the command of generals called back from retirement just a few days before the invasion.[44]

Map 2 shows the disposition of the Yugoslav defending forces and of the attacking armies, and the direction of the latter's advance. Most of the German Twelfth Army was deployed in Bulgaria but some of its units were in Romania; the Second Army was in position in Austria and western Hungary. The Italian Second Army was in Istria and to the north up to the Austrian frontier; the Italian Ninth and Eleventh armies were in Albania. The bulk of the Hungarian forces was concentrated in the area between the Danube and Tisa rivers.

The seven Yugoslav armies, divided into four groups of armies, were deployed in a cordon defense around the periphery of the country. The First Group of Armies was composed of the Seventh Army, deployed in Slovenia and northwestern Croatia and facing the Germans and the Italians, and the Fourth Army in northern Croatia to guard against German attack from western Hungary. The Second Group of Armies included the Second Army in Slavonia and Baranja and the First Army in Bačka. The Third Group of Armies consisted of the Third Army, which was to defend Montenegro, Kosovo, and western Macedonia against attack from Albania, and the forces of the Third Army Area, which were to defend Macedonia against attack from Bulgaria. The Fifth Army, deployed in southeastern and eastern Serbia, and the Sixth Army, deployed in southern Banat and central Serbia, were directly under the command of the Supreme Command and were to defend Serbia and Banat against attack from Bulgaria and Romania respectively. In addition, there was the rather weak Adriatic Coastal Force guarding against land attack by the Italians from Zadar and against attack by the Italian navy or by amphibious landings. All points of attack were thus guarded, but none of them strongly enough to withstand heavy assault. Furthermore, there were few troops in reserve, as we recall from the war plans, which had gradually increased the ratio of front-line to reserve troops until, under Plan R-41 and during the 1941 invasion, the ratio was about seven to one. Moreover, the reserves were poorly located, and their lack of mobility further reduced their usefulness.[45]

The day for the attack, first set as March 31, was postponed until April 6. The Yugoslav government, on April 2, was informed of the exact day by the Yugoslav military attaché in Berlin, Colonel Vauhnik, but did not take the warning seriously.[46] On April 6 the onslaught began with a

[44] Zelenika, p. 209.
[45] *Drugi svetski rat*, I, 444–45, 491.
[46] See Hoptner, pp. 281–83; Kljaković, in *Politika*, Oct. 3, 1970.

massive air attack on Belgrade and on all airfields and ground installations of the Yugoslav air force.[47] Simultaneously, land attacks by armored, motorized, and infantry units of the German Twelfth Army were
launched from southwestern Bulgaria against Yugoslav Macedonia.[48]
The powerful thrust into Macedonia enabled the Germans on April 7
to capture the city of Skopje, cutting the rail and highway links between
Yugoslavia and the Greek and British forces in Greece and thus delivering a fatal blow to the underlying principle of all Yugoslav war plans,
namely, to keep open the way to Salonika as a line of supply or possible
retreat. On April 8, German forces from Bulgaria penetrated into Serbia
and swept north toward Belgrade. Four days later these and other German forces coming from Romania reached Belgrade and took it without
opposition. Land attacks by units of the German Second Army from
western Hungary against Croatia and from Austria against Slovenia
had started on April 7, but these were only preparatory operations. The
Yugoslav Fourth Army, despite Ustasha fifth-column activity, offered
scattered resistance but on April 9 was forced to begin withdrawing
southward. The Seventh Army in Slovenia also began withdrawing. On
April 10, following earlier probing attacks and the establishment of
bridgeheads, German troops from western Hungary unleashed a devastating assault in northern Croatia, the area supposedly held by the
Fourth Army, and moved rapidly toward Zagreb. Late in the afternoon
German tanks began entering the city. German units advancing from
Austria through Slovenia had by then taken most of Slovenia, and on
April 11, at a point south of Zagreb, some of these units joined units
advancing from Hungary. Other German units from western Hungary
turned southeast through Slavonia with the objective of reaching Sarajevo in Bosnia—the approximate center of the country—and on
April 15 they joined with forces advancing from Zagreb. It was in the
neighborhood of Sarajevo that on April 15 the Germans captured the

[47] On the day of invasion the Yugoslavs asked the United States for arms. By the end of April
the United States had earmarked a small amount of arms from existing stock, but by then it was
too late. See Stettinius, p. 91.

[48] For the German accounts of the campaigns in the Balkans see Germany, Wehrmacht, Oberkommando, *Der Feldzug auf dem Balkan und die Rückeroberung der Cyrenaika*; *KTB/OKW/WFSt*, I,
375–82; Bathe and Glodschey, *Der Kampf um den Balkan*; Greiner, pp. 273–82, 286–87. Also United
States, Department of the Army, *The German Campaigns in the Balkans (Spring 1941)*, Department
of the Army Pamphlet No. 20–260. This pamphlet and various others were compiled from reports
written by German officers while American prisoners of war, essentially from memory rather than
on the basis of documentary evidence, although they made use of the diaries of Field Marshal Franz
Halder, situation maps, and interviews with other participants. For the Italian accounts see Italy,
Stato Maggiore del R. Esercito, *Bollettini della guerra*, pp. 229–39; Zanussi, I, 83–101; Roatta,
pp. 161–83.

Among the Yugoslav sources most important for documents is Yugoslavia, Vojnoistorijski
institut, *Zbornik dokumenata i podotaka o narodnooslobodilačkom ratu jugoslovenskih naroda*,
Tome II, Vol. 2, pp. 465–570 (herafter cited as *Zbornik DNOR*). For the discussion and analysis of
the April 1941 war the most important sources are *Drugi svetski rat*, I, 74–77, 393–493, esp. 446–
93; the works by Terzić, Krizman, and Zelenika; Čulinović, *Slom stare Jugoslavije*, pp. 145–347; and
the article "The April War," in *Vojna enciklopedija*, I, 185–89. For the views of a royal Yugoslav
general in exile, see Todor Milićević.

Yugoslav Supreme Command, which was in fact waiting to surrender. Throughout the entire campaign in Yugoslavia, when weather conditions allowed, the Germans used their air forces intensively for independent operations and in tactical support of ground forces. Although the Yugoslav air force was almost completely mobilized when the invasion came, and performed rather well against the enemy, the Germans acquired control of the air over Yugoslavia on the first day of the war.

The Italians started their air attacks against air force and naval units and installations and cities along the Adriatic coast on April 7 and continued them intermittently in the following days. They also let the Germans use their airfields for raids against the same targets. Operations of the Second Army troops were limited to sporadic artillery fire from the sixth to the eleventh, when the Italian troops launched their drive into Yugoslav territory. By then, the Yugoslav forces were already in the process of disintegration on all fronts and in all areas except on the Albanian front. Meeting practically no resistance on the front in Slovenia, Croatia, and Dalmatia, the Italians advanced rapidly. They entered Ljubljana on the twelfth while other parts of the Second Army advanced into Croatia and Dalmatia. Some Yugoslav forces penetrated into Albanian territory, where the Italian troops of the Ninth Army were deployed, but the Italians, who had broken the Yugoslav code, confused the Yugoslav higher commands on the Albanian front by sending them fake messages, so that even there the Yugoslavs scored no success.[49] This must have especially pleased Hitler, who had implored Mussolini to defend the Albanian front with all vigor.[50] On April 11 the Hungarian troops started their operations against Yugoslavia, in Bačka. They too, meeting practically no resistance, advanced rapidly toward their objectives in order to occupy or annex the respective areas, and a week later, on the nineteenth, Bulgarian troops moved into Yugoslavia in order to take over the areas assigned to them under Hitler's plan.

The German strategy in the invasion of Yugoslavia was simple: first, to produce a tremendous psychological shock by delivering a brutal air attack on Belgrade, by cutting the possible retreat route to Greece, and by making relentless attacks on the air fields and air force installations to neutralize this arm of Yugoslav defenses; next, to disrupt main communications by air attacks and to engage the Yugoslav land armies from several directions with greatly superior forces in order to slice the country into segments by powerful frontal and enveloping operations, which

[49] Janeković, pp. 27–46, esp. pp. 27–28. According to this source, the Italian military attaché in Belgrade had before the war thirty-four agents in the Yugoslav armed forces, of whom two were in the General Staff.
[50] *DGFP*, Series D, Vol. XII, p. 476, Hitler's letter to Mussolini of April 5, 1941.

would forestall resistance by the half-mobilized, poorly equipped, slow-moving, and poorly led Yugoslav forces; and then to destroy the Yugoslav armies piecemeal and eliminate them as organized fighting units. In fact all these operations were rolled into one and were carried out during the first five or six days of operations. Hitler's decision to deliver a swift, massive attack and bring Yugoslavia to its knees as quickly as possible could hardly have been more effective. Within days, the country had fallen.

THE MILITARY AND POLITICAL COLLAPSE

The military campaign of the Axis against Yugoslavia can be conveniently divided into two phases: the first decisive onslaught lasting from April 6 to April 10, and the second phase, April 11–17, including the capture of vital territory and ending in the surrender of the Yugoslav army.[51] The first phase included the massive offensives into Macedonia, Serbia, and the Banat, and finally on April 10 into northern Croatia and Slovenia, as a result of which Yugoslav defenses on all the principal fronts were broken. By April 10 the Yugoslav forces were in full disarray, surrendering or retreating in all areas except along the Albanian border. Seeing collapse on all fronts, the Yugoslav Supreme Command issued on that day its Operational Directive No. 120, ordering a general withdrawal of all troops to the mountainous interior where they might establish a strong line of defense and hold out until help arrived from the Western Allies. The Supreme Command also notified its troops by radio that wherever possible they should fight the enemy at their own initiative—though that was surely an idle hope, with the disintegration of the armed forces of the country so nearly complete.[52]

On the last day of the first phase, April 10, a few hours before German tanks rolled into Zagreb, the Croatian Ustashas with the guidance and assistance of German agents proclaimed the Independent State of Croatia. In Slovenia, on the first day of the war, the Slovene political parties (except the Communists) had established a Slovene National Council, and on April 11, following the events in Zagreb, the Council announced over Radio Ljubljana that it was the only sovereign authority representing the Slovene nation.[53] The next day the Council surrendered to the Italian army when it entered the city of Ljubljana.

On April 13, with the Axis armies advancing at their own pace on all fronts, Prime Minister Simović transferred the office of Chief of the Supreme Command (which he had held jointly with the premiership) to

[51] The chronology of the April War must be reconstructed on the basis of sparse Yugoslav documentary materials, published enemy materials, and the depositions of some high-ranking officers who were in command of various Yugoslav units at that time. See *Drugi svetski rat*, I, 7; Dedijer, "Sur l'armistice 'germano-yougoslave,'" esp. pp. 1–2.

[52] Terzić, pp. 505–7.

[53] For the developments in Slovenia see Saje, pp. 15–27.

General Danilo Kalafatović, and he gave him instructions to seek an armistice, further resistance being impossible "because of the developments in Croatia and Dalmatia."[54] By "developments in Croatia and Dalmatia" Simović meant the fifth-column work of the Ustashas and of some Croatian officers in the Yugoslav army, and of a part of the paramilitary organizations of the Croatian Peasant Party, but these were in fact of only minor significance militarily, like the activities of the Slovene politicians in Slovenia. They were hardly the cause of the complete breakdown, but they were a convenient excuse to explain what was in fact—as Simović himself later recognized—a total collapse of the Yugoslav armed forces on all fronts and the failure of the Yugoslav officers in the higher echelons—nearly all of them Serbs—to show any fighting initiative or determination against the enemy.[55]

The plight of the Yugoslav forces from the first day of the invasion and the immediate causes of their collapse are best characterized by the authoritative *Vojna enciklopedija* in its article on "The April War":

Three initial attacks determined the fate of the Yugoslav Army, on April 6 in Macedonia, April 8 in Serbia, and April 10 in Croatia. On all three occasions the Hitlerites breached the frontier defenses, pushed deep into the interior, and dislodged the Yugoslav defenses from their moorings. On the first day of the invasion War Plan R-41 was compromised; a day later, when the Germans had taken Skopje, it could no more be implemented.... After the breakthrough of the frontier defenses, the Yugoslav troops were soon outmaneuvered, broken up, surrounded, without contact with each other, without supplies, and without leadership.[56]

But however much the Yugoslav army was to blame for its lack of fighting zeal, it was simply no match for the Axis forces. The combined military strength of Germany and her allies was overwhelming, and the small army of Yugoslavia had no chance of successful defense. On the first day of the war the Yugoslav Supreme Command lost control of its armies in the field, and in most cases all contact with them. It continued to issue orders, but these were only formal, since they were not related to the real conditions in the field and could not be communicated to the armies, much less put into operation.[57]

On April 14 the King and his entourage, and on April 15 Prime Min-

---

[54] Simović apparently took this step on his own. For the text of his order to Kalafatović and other documents pertaining to the collapse of the armed forces and armistice see *Zbornik DNOR*, Tome II, Vol. 2, pp. 549–70; see also Čulinović, *Slom stare Jugoslavije*, pp. 281–309.

[55] Terzić's detailed presentation of the higher command personnel of the Yugoslav armed forces during the April War (pp. 691–98), from which the nationality of the commanders can be deduced almost without fail, shows that in addition to the posts of Chief of the Supreme Command and Minister of the Army and Navy, all the command posts above the level of the division were in the hands of Serbs. Of the thirty divisions, twenty-nine were commanded by Serbs, and of the twelve combined detachments eleven were commanded by Serbs. In the command posts of the air force the non-Serbs were fairly well represented and in the navy most of the command posts were held by non-Serbs.

[56] *Vojna enciklopedija*, I, 189.

[57] *Drugi svetski rat*, I, 491–92.

ister Simović and the cabinet, and practically all the main actors in the recent revolt, were flown out of the country from the airfield at Nikšić in Montenegro. Except for some fighting on the Albanian frontier by units that had not heard the news, the April War was over. Of the entire Yugoslav armed forces, only fragments escaped capture, and some of those only temporarily: a small part of the navy, consisting of a submarine and two motor torpedo boats, escaped to Egypt;[58] part of the air force, consisting of between sixty and seventy aircraft, were flown out of the country; and about 1,500 army soldiers escaped to Greece. The soldiers were subsequently taken prisoner by the Germans, and forty-four of the aircraft that were saved were shortly afterward destroyed by a German bombing attack on the Paramythia airfield near Ioannina in northwestern Greece; about twenty others were flown to Egypt.[59]

Both the Germans and the Italians were surprised by the swiftness of the Yugoslav collapse. They had expected the army or at least a part of the army to retreat after the initial reverses to the mountainous interior areas and fight hard as long as their ammunition and food held out.[60] Instead, as one German officer remarked, "from the German point of view the conquest of Yugoslavia was virtually a military parade."[61] General Roatta made the following comment in his memoirs: "We knew in fact very well that the Yugoslav army could not have held up against the forces of the Axis: but we thought that the enemy command, realizing that the struggle was lost, would still prefer to go down in glory ['morire in bellezza'] by attempting some brilliant sorties on some of our weak points, either on the front in the Alps or in Albania."[62]

Yugoslavia's mountainous terrain, ideally suited to guerrilla warfare, was indeed its one great military asset, but the Yugoslav army, aside from a few guerrilla units, had been trained only for conventional infantry and artillery warfare of the type used in the First World War. Nor would guerrilla warfare have been possible under the conditions existing in Yugoslavia at that time. General Terzić (a former royal Yugoslav officer who during the war became a Partisan general) has made the suggestion that the Yugoslav Supreme Command should have issued orders for a general people's guerrilla war in areas where fifth-column activity was not widespread, but his suggestion springs from the successes of the Partisans later on, which were achieved under quite different political and psychological circumstances from those that prevailed at the time of invasion and during the April War.[63]

[58] See Adamich, "The Royal Yugoslav Navy in World War II."
[59] Richards, I, 298.
[60] See the deployment orders for Operation 25 of March 30, 1941, as issued by the Army High Command (OKH), in Microcopy No. T-78, Roll 329, Frame 6,285,870.
[61] Von Mellenthin, p. 31.
[62] Roatta, p. 162.
[63] Terzić, pp. 506–7.

THE ARMISTICE OF APRIL 17, 1941

On April 17, two days after General Kalafatović and the staff of the Supreme Command were captured by the Germans at Sarajevo, the Yugoslavs and the Axis signed a formal agreement entitled "Directives for the Implementation of the Armistice Agreement of April 17, 1941." From a strictly legal point of view it was not a binding document. It was, as Article 1 specifically stated, not an armistice but an unconditional surrender—and Kalafatović had been empowered by Prime Minister Simović only to seek and sign an armistice. This lack of authority alone made the agreement an illegal document so far as Yugoslavia was concerned. Furthermore, the Yugoslav signators, General Radivoje Janković and Aleksandar Cincar-Marković, were acting as representatives of General Kalafatović, but Kalafatović, as a prisoner of war, was in fact legally incapable either of acting in the name of Yugoslavia or its armed forces or of authorizing a representative to do so (and Janković, too, was a prisoner of war).[64]

The document of April 17 provided for the surrender of all Yugoslav officers, noncommissioned officers, and men under arms; of all arms and ammunition, all military draft animals, all communications equipment and other military stores, of all army, navy, and air force facilities, and all transportation and shipping facilities; and of all documents, archives, plans, and other records of military significance. One especially important provision in the light of later developments was contained in the first paragraph of Point 14: "Military personnel are prohibited from leaving the country. Whoever should engage in armed struggle against the powers of the Axis will be considered a franc-tireur and dealt with accordingly." Consequently, during the occupation, the Axis generals always insisted that since Yugoslavia had surrendered unconditionally and signed the agreement of April 17, all the measures to suppress the armed resistance undertaken by the occupation armies were justified under this agreement and under the international law of war.

Although all officers and men of the Yugoslav army were forced to surrender with all their arms and stores, differentiation in treatment was applied. The German policy was to take as prisoners of war only Serbs and some Slovenes, and of the other nationalities only those known to be of strong pro-Yugoslav orientation. Thus, practically all Croats, as

---

[64] For the details of the negotiations see an article by one of the participants, Lt. Colonel Radmilo Trojanović, "The Negotiations for an Armistice with Germany on April 16 and 17, 1941," pp. 9–17. For the text of the "Directive" see *Zbornik DNOR*, Tome II, Vol. 2, pp. 559–62, or Čulinović, *Slom stare Jugoslavije*, pp. 303–5. General Janković was Deputy Chief of Staff of the Supreme Command, but Cincar-Marković, the former Minister of Foreign Affairs in the Cvetković government, had no official standing whatever. General Maximilian von Weichs, the commander of the German Second Army, and Colonel Luigi Bonfatti, the Italian military attaché in Belgrade, signed for the Axis. For more details on how the armistice agreement was concluded and its illegal character see Dedijer, "Sur l'armistice 'germano-yougoslave.' "

well as men from Macedonia (on the grounds that they were Bulgarians), those belonging to minorities, and most Montenegrins and Slovenes were not taken as prisoners of war, or if taken were soon released. The Italians followed much the same policy. Later on, Serbs from the territory of the Independent State of Croatia were also released if they so desired. For obvious reasons then, data on the number of prisoners of war are rather confusing. According to the earliest official German data, prisoners of war numbered 6,298 officers and 337,864 noncommissioned officers and men, all Serbs.[65] According to American sources that are based on captured German documents, the Germans took about 254,000 prisoners of war, not counting those who did not come from Serbia.[66] Terzić, writing later on the basis of fuller evidence, states that about 375,000 men were taken prisoner—about 30,000 of them by the Italians. After the release of various categories of men, including some sick ones, he estimates that finally there remained abroad as prisoners of war about 200,000 in Germany and 10,000 in Italy, of whom 90 percent were Serbs.[67] A still later German official source puts the number of Yugoslav prisoners of war in Germany as of June 21, 1941, including those who were released, or who fled or died, at 181,258. Of this total, 13,559 were officers.[68]

Owing to the destruction, capture, or loss of Yugoslav wartime documents, and to the general disorganization of the armed forces, there are no data, not even approximate estimates, on the number of Yugoslav officers and soldiers killed during the April War. The losses in the bombing of Belgrade were at first estimated at over 10,000 people, but the figure has been much reduced after careful postwar investigations. The combined loss of life from German bombings in April 1941 and Allied bombings between April and September 1944 was somewhat over 5,000; the loss due to German action in 1941 was somewhere between 3,000 and 4,000.[69] There are no Yugoslav estimates on deaths among the civilian population during the two-week war.

The "parade" nature of the invasion is clearly indicated by the extremely small losses on the German side: 151 killed, 392 wounded, and 15 missing in action. In its drive on Belgrade the XLIth Panzer Corps lost only one officer, the victim of a civilian sniper.[70]

The speed and manner of the collapse of the Yugoslav army and state in April 1941 seemed to imply that Yugoslavia would never recover or be capable of revival as anything looking even remotely like the political

[65] Germany, Oberkommando, *Der Feldzug auf dem Balkan*, p. 97.
[66] United States, Department of the Army, *The German Campaigns in the Balkans*, p. 64.
[67] Terzić, pp. 575–76.
[68] *KTB/OKW/WFSt*, I, 1106.
[69] Marjanović, *Srbija u narodnooslobodilačkoj borbi: Beograd*, pp. 300–304, 343. The purpose of the Allied bombings was to destroy communications facilities in Belgrade, but civilian casualties were heavy, especially in the strikes of April 16 and 17, 1944, when an estimated 1,160 were killed.
[70] *The German Campaigns in the Balkans*, p. 64.

and territorial entity that it was during the interwar period. Not only was the old political regime finished, but it seemed also that Yugoslavia as a state was finished.

WHO WAS RESPONSIBLE?

The question of responsibility for the failure of the Yugoslav state leadership and the royal army in April 1941 is still a controversial issue. The Serbian ruling elite, which had justified its hegemony during the interwar period on the grounds of Serbian state-building virtues, political acumen, and military valor, was clearly the group most immediately responsible for the ignominious defeat, and it at once tried to find scapegoats in the various fifth-column groups. At the same time, those who had long been the internal adversaries of Yugoslavia, primarily the Croatian Ustashas, tried to claim a much larger share of credit for the collapse than they deserved. Wartime writers and the writings of the Yugoslav political exiles after 1945 on the "War of April 1941" abound in recriminations and accusations, with all sides trying to shift responsibility—or to claim it. Even some recent writings continue the argument, and there are at least half a dozen conflicting interpretations.

Although General Simović blamed the "developments in Croatia and Dalmatia"—the fifth-column activity of the Croatian Ustashas and their sympathizers—for the collapse of the army and used these "developments" as a pretext for ordering General Kalafatović to conclude an armistice, Kalafatović himself admitted quite candidly that there had been a failure of the armies on all fronts, but especially in Croatia, Slovenia, and Dalmatia.[71] Both generals ignored the fatal areas of collapse— Yugoslav Macedonia, where the German forces cut the only link with and possible escape route toward Greece on the second day after the invasion, and eastern Serbia, where the defense lines disintegrated under the strong attack of German forces coming from Bulgaria and opened the road to Belgrade.

Simović repeated his accusations after he had escaped to Athens with the rest of the government (after some initial praise of Serb, Croat, and Slovene units),[72] but a week or so later, at the Tantura monastery near Jerusalem where the government was in temporary residence, he told the cabinet that it was the commanding generals who were responsible: "Almost all generals were against fighting. . . . When the generals wanted the armistice as soon as possible in order to return to their families, what could one expect from the rank and file."[73] And they were all Serbs.

[71] *Zbornik DNOR*, Tome II, Vol. 2, pp. 549–50, 553–54.
[72] Kljaković, in *Politika*, Oct. 23, 1970.
[73] Marić, p. 105. Marić is quoting from the minutes of the cabinet meeting which are deposited in the archives of the Institute of Military History in Belgrade. A statement to the same effect has been made by Branko Čubrilović (*Zapisi iz tudjine*, p. 26), Minister of Agriculture in the Simović cabinet, who was present at the meeting on April 28, 1941.

Nearly all the generals in leading command positions of the ground forces had advised the Cvetković government to accede to the Tripartite Pact because they believed that Yugoslavia could not withstand an Axis invasion, and it was Simović himself who brought General Milan Nedić back into the army and put him in command of the Third Group of Armies, charged with the defense of the vital area of Yugoslav Macedonia, the bridge to Salonika and Greece. Since Nedić had been removed as Minister of the Army and Navy for wanting to join the Axis and had not altered his views between November and April, his desire for a quick armistice was not at all surprising. It was almost a foregone conclusion that he and the other generals in command of ground forces after March 27 would favor as speedy a conclusion of an armistice as possible, using the ready-made argument that they were trying to prevent the unnecessary shedding of blood. But if General Simović understood what had happened, his judgment has been ignored by other exiled Serbian writers on the war, who do not like to cast an unfavorable light on the royal army as the foremost institution of the interwar Serbian-dominated regime. The standard explanation of the generals and politicians of the Great Serbia school is that old Yugoslavia disintegrated militarily because it was betrayed by the Croats—implying by this explanation that the war might otherwise have developed differently and that its outcome was by no means certain defeat.

The exile group of younger officers who took part in the March 27 coup and made up the so-called League of Majors later accused both Simović and his Minister of the Army and Navy, General Ilić, of poor leadership and cowardly surrender in April 1941.[74] It had to be the individual generals, not the army as a whole, because in carrying out the coup these officers claimed to have the support of the army, the Serbian people, and large segments of other peoples of Yugoslavia as well. The same group of officers also put the blame on Prince Regent Paul and the Cvetković government, for the surrender at Vienna and the military unpreparedness and general lack of leadership before March 27. Here again, the accusation is partly true, partly exaggerated. The Cvetković-Maček government, or Prince Paul as the principal decision-maker, can justly be accused of indecision and defeatism and eventual surrender to Axis pressure, but all these men were pro-Allied, not pro-Axis, and they sought an accommodation with the Axis as the only possible alternative under the existing conditions. They made their decisions in full consultation with the leaders of the armed forces, in the belief that they were in the best interests of the country. The leading generals under the Cvet-

---

[74] This accusation was made in the heat of the so-called Scandal of Cairo, to be discussed in Chapter 8. See especially the comments of Radoje L. Knežević in *Poruka*, Nos. 2–3, pp. 9–11, answering a charge made by General Vasilije Petković in *Iskra* (a Ljotić group emigré newspaper published in Munich), March 1, 1951, that the putschist government caused the war.

kovic-Maček government, Nedić, Pešić, and Kosić, were of course hope-lessly defeatist, but a large portion of the putschist government and most of its generals in command of the ground forces were also not much different in this respect.

Meeting charge with charge, former Prime Minister Cvetković and some of his ministers—while throwing part of the blame on the Croatian Ustasha fifth column—put the prime responsibility for the war and collapse upon the Simović government, primarily the officers behind it, following the reasoning that their reckless action in overthrowing the Cvetković government provoked Hitler and caused the invasion, which was followed inevitably by the collapse and disintegration of the country.[75] It was all very simple: had there been no coup, Yugoslavia could have stayed outside the conflict, because the Axis had undertaken in Vienna to respect its neutrality. Then, after the tide of the war changed and Germany began losing, Yugoslavia, whose sympathies were always with the Allies, could have entered the war on the Allied side, when it was ready, and thus been on the winning side when victory came and in a position to gather its share of the fruits. Except for the coup, there would have been no invasion, no collapse, no partition of the country, no Partisans, no civil war, and in the end no Communist victory and no Communist dictatorship after the war.

A similar interpretation of the collapse is given in the already quoted article by General Todor Milićević. Milićević is primarily concerned with opposing the thesis offered by some people that the Yugoslav army wanted war in 1941 and was therefore responsible for the collapse. He argues that if a really representative and therefore strong government had existed in Belgrade in March 1941 instead of the "unrepresentative" (presumably in the sense of Cvetković and his Serbian colleagues not being true representatives of the Serbian people) and weak Cvetković-Maček government, and if such a government had joined the Tripartite Pact and there had been no coup, Yugoslavia could have remained neutral. In his opinion, neither the people of Yugoslavia nor the "supreme military leadership" wanted war with the Germans under the existing conditions: "The war was, therefore, caused and desired by the government of March 27."[76] General Milićević's statement is yet another proof of the division that existed both within the leadership and within the officer corps of the Yugoslav army. Although most of the officers, especially those in the higher ranks, were extremely defeatist and capitulationist, there were some, mostly in the lower ranks, who were prepared to fight at whatever cost, and still others who were engaged in fifth-column work, for the Germans, the Italians, or the Ustashas. These

[75] See e.g. Cvetković's publication *Dokumenti o Jugoslaviji*, No. 1, p. 10; No. 2, pp. 27–33; No. 6, p. 31. See also Maček, p. 223.
[76] Todor Milićević, p. 47.

differences, both prior to and during the war, were of course, a reflection of differences in the body politic of Yugoslavia, on a wide range of political, national, economic, and ideological matters.

On the other side of the argument are the Croatian Ustashas and those persons who, for one reason or another, support the Ustasha position. They do not merely accept part of the responsibility for the collapse—they claim it. Their fifth-column activity and the Croatian armed rebellion, they say, by disarming or otherwise neutralizing the Fourth Army in northern Croatia and the Adriatic Division in northern Dalmatia, hastened the defeat of Yugoslavia by the Germans and Italians. Many Ustashas, during the war and in exile since then, have made such an assertion. Foreign Minister Mladen Lorković gave his detailed analysis in a speech to the Ustasha-convoked Croatian Diet on February 24, 1942:

On April 6, 1941, the war against Yugoslavia got under way. As early as April 7, certain detachments of Croatian soldiers, following the call of the Poglavnik [Pavelić] and the voice of their Croatian blood, rose against the Serbian officers and the Serbian army units. On April 8 and 9 such phenomena occurred more and more in various areas of Yugoslavia. On April 10 the Croatian units that were supposed to defend the frontier of Yugoslavia at the Drava River after disarming and taking hold of Serbian units met the liberating German army not only without putting up any defense, but with the greatest jubilation, just as that army was met with delirious jubilation on the afternoon of the same day in the capital city of Zagreb. When at this moment Marshal Slavko Kvaternik, in the name of the Poglavnik [title of the chief of the Ustasha movement, and later of the head of the Croatian puppet state], declared the re-creation of the Independent State of Croatia on the whole Croatian national area from the Mura, Drava, and Danube rivers to the Drina River and the Adriatic Sea, the general Croatian national revolution exploded, in the course of which the Croatian soldiers, Ustashas, as well as the Civic and Peasant Guards, in an unbelievably short time took power everywhere, disarmed and chased away the defeated units of the Serbian [i.e. Yugoslav] army, and awaited with enthusiasm the arrival of the allied German and Italian troops. With pride and deep satisfaction we can affirm the historical truth that the revolution of the Croatian people, which followed upon the proclamation and the call of the Poglavnik and was executed by the long-prepared Ustasha action, contributed considerably to the speedy collapse of Yugoslavia. Thereby the Croatian revolution shortened the shedding of blood and reduced the losses of the great allied [Axis] troops, which on the eastern frontiers of Serbia had already given a death blow to Yugoslavia.[77]

Lorković's claims contain some elements of truth. There is no question that Ustasha actions in the area of the Fourth Army, together with the actions of some Croat army officers who were working for the Axis or for the Ustashas, and the actions of the paramilitary organizations of the

[77] Independent State of Croatia, *Brzopisni zapisnici Prvog zasjedanja Hrvatskog državnog sabora u Nezavisnoj Državi Hrvatskoj godine 1942*, p. 20.

Croatian Peasant Party which, as Ustasha-infiltrated organizations, sided in April 1941 with the Ustashas, helped to disorganize and demoralize the front and the rear of the Yugoslav Fourth Army. The Ustashas especially mention the rebellion of April 8 in the 108th Regiment of the Slavonian Division stationed at Bjelovar, about forty miles due east of Zagreb, but this so-called rebellion amounted only to the troops' refusing to go to the front or deserting, and did not involve taking up arms against established Yugoslav authority. Far more important, it seems, was the treachery of a single Croat officer in the Yugoslav army, Colonel Franjo Nikolić, the Chief of Staff of the First Group of Armies, who went to Zagreb on the morning of April 10 with an offer of aid to Slavko Kvaternik, a retired former Austro-Hungarian colonel and confidant of Pavelić who was the principal military expert in the Ustasha organization in Zagreb. After coming to an agreement with Kvaternik, Nikolić returned to his post and announced that talks with the Germans for an armistice had started and that therefore there was no need for further action. He then ordered that some units of the Fourth Army be moved away from the vicinity of Zagreb, thus allowing Kvaternik to carry out the proclamation of the Independent State of Croatia without any danger.[78] There was also some Ustasha fifth-column activity in the rear of the Second Army in Slavonia, and some in the area of the Adriatic Division stationed around Knin in northern Dalmatia. It is worth noting, however, that Lorković states that the "death blow to Yugoslavia" was given "on the eastern frontiers of Serbia" (which apparently is intended to include also the eastern frontiers of Yugoslav Macedonia), where the forces of the Third Army Area and of the Third, Fifth, and Sixth armies collapsed under the full force of the German attack.

THE COMMUNISTS AND THE APRIL WAR

The Communist Party of Yugoslavia offered its own explanation of the military and political collapse of April 1941 in a document that was drawn up at a meeting of party leaders in Zagreb a month after the surrender.[79] This interpretation is the more important because of the leading role in Yugoslav affairs that the CPY was shortly to assume. The CPY of course had no stake in the old order and no love for the Axis, and furthermore its attitude was truly Yugoslav, so its views, while biased, were quite different from those of the previously mentioned groups or individuals. When the CPY began participating actively in the organiz-

---

[78] For Nikolić's actions see a report of General Vilko Begić, the Undersecretary in the Croatian Ministry of Armed Forces, of early November 1941, to General Edmund Glaise von Horstenau, the German Plenipotentiary General in Croatia, in Microcopy No. T-501, Roll 265, Frames 782–84. As a reward, Nikolić was accepted as of April 12, 1941, into the new Croatian General Staff with his Yugoslav army rank of colonel.

[79] "Conclusions of the April [*sic*] 1941 Consultation of the Communist Party of Yugoslavia in Zagreb," *Zbornik DNOR*, Tome II, Vol. 2, pp. 7–23.

ing of street demonstrations in cities throughout the country during the second half of March, it did so because it opposed Yugoslavia's approaching adherence to the Axis, and also because such activities were part of its systematic attempt to develop its political image as a patriotic force wholly committed to the defense of the country. It is in this light, as well as in the light of Communist ideology, that the "Conclusions" drawn up in May 1941 must be viewed—recognizing that they had specific political and propaganda objectives.

The underlying reason given by the CPY for the speedy military collapse was that the bourgeoisie (primarily the Serbian as the ruling bourgeoisie but also the others), failed to prepare the country for defense militarily, economically, and politically. To safeguard their class interests, a large part of the bourgeoisie put itself in the service of the enemy even before the invasion, as the open fifth-column activity and utter defeatism clearly proved. After the collapse each of the national bourgeois groups tried to put the blame on some other group, or tried to claim credit, as in the case of the Ustashas, if this better suited its political objectives. The Serbian bourgeoisie blamed the Croatian people for the disaster of April 1941, and the Croatian bourgeoisie blamed the Serbian people for the earlier suffering of the Croats—both in this way undermining the moral foundations of the Yugoslav state of the future. At all times, before, during, and after the military collapse, the bourgeoisie put class interest ahead of national interest and allied itself with the enemy against its own people.

The "Conclusions" also asserted that all Communists of military age who were in the ranks were determined to fight and that the Party line that the country must be defended met with sympathies and readiness to fight on the part of the soldiers, noncommissioned officers, and a part of the lower-echelon officers, but they were prevented from fighting by higher military and civilian leaders who either were engaged in active fifth-column work or were completely defeatist. The fifth column, the "Conclusions" charged, was rampant from the top of the military organization of the country to its bottom, but the higher ranks contained most of the real traitors:

It is clear to everyone today, because everyone is able to convince himself, that we Communists were completely right when we spoke and wrote about the destructive activity of the fifth column, when we spoke and wrote that the fifth column did not consist of *Frankovci* [Croatian extremists] and similar groups alone, but that it existed in the Cabinet, in the General Staff of the army, the state apparatus, the police, and the other government agencies. We had seen this and explained it to the people, but it was necessary to go through this difficult and bloody experience in order for the broadest strata of the people to see this with their own eyes. Our soldiers who went with plenty of élan to defend the independence of the peoples of Yugoslavia from the imperialist bandits soon realized with horror that at the highest echelons of the army blossomed treason and espionage, that all was systematically prepared, not for defense, but for defeat and capitulation ... and the complete collapse on all fronts was clear to everyone.[80]

The propaganda line in interpreting the Yugoslav happenings of March and April 1941 in terms of class-struggle and class-interest contradictions is very apparent here: play up the betrayed masses of common soldiers and lower-echelon officers, demonstrating to the masses of the people that only the Communist Party was the true defender of their interests and castigating the political and military leadership as the leaders of the class enemy, the bourgeoisie.

The true facts were not so clear cut. There were, as the CPY said, some Yugoslav military units and many individual officers and soldiers who were determined to fight, and did fight, including practically all of the air force, but the bulk of the troops did not want to fight, primarily because they had no real stake in the Yugoslav state as it existed during the interwar period. That state was an instrument of national oppression for all non-Serb nations of the country, and it failed to do anything of significance to meet the social and economic needs of the great mass of the people. None of its leaders were men whom the common people fully trusted, or felt compelled to follow; and indeed, none of the old leadership themselves had faith in the country when it had to be defended, or believed strongly in its resurrection after it collapsed and was partitioned.

The interpretation of the April defeat by the CPY also tends to ignore what was the most obvious reason for the speedy military collapse—the overwhelming superiority of the aggressors in military capability. To have recognized this fact would have weakened the propaganda line, and the propaganda element was of course a powerful political and psychological weapon against both the foreign enemy and the domestic opponents of the party and a means of arousing the masses and bringing them around to the CPY views.

From the advent of Hitler to power and especially after the Seventh Congress of the Comintern in August 1935, which raised the banner of the Popular Front against the rising fascist menace, and during and after the Spanish Civil War, the Yugoslav Communists, like Communists generally, had vehemently opposed the Nazis and the Italian Fascists and their expansionist plans—plans that were especially dangerous for Yugoslavia, lying directly in the path of the German and Italian drives into the Danube Basin and the Balkans. After Tito became Secretary General in 1937, the CPY started a process of rejuvenation so as to be ready for a future time of international crises and probable war—conditions

[80] *Ibid.*, p. 9. For the meaning of the term *Frankovci* see Chapter 4, n. 39.

which, according to Marxist doctrine, would be favorable to revolutionary activity and the seizure of power by Communist parties.[81] But as Marshal Tito told me in an interview on August 4, 1965, there was only a handful of Communists and they had an a-national reputation. It was therefore necessary to develop in the party members a sense of Yugoslav patriotism and a determination to defend the Yugoslav state against the rising fascist danger, for only in that case could they hope to take the leading role in the armed struggle against the enemy in the expected conditions of occupation, and acquire strength and support for that struggle and for their quest for power and revolutionary transformation of Yugoslavia into a Communist state.

As the possibility of war increased, the CPY faced the following urgent tasks. (1) It was necessary to improve the party's secret organization, the conspiratorial methods of work, and the morale of its members so that it could survive as a revolutionary organization under the possible invasion and occupation, when it would be exposed to even greater persecution than before. (2) The leading cadres must be prepared for the conditions that would exist during the war and occupation: there would be extreme danger if mistakes were made, but boundless opportunities if the old regime should collapse and the Communists should prove successful in organizing armed resistance, mobilizing the revolutionary energies of the Yugoslav masses, and channeling them politically. (3) The policy of the Popular Front was to be continued and ever stronger support of the masses was to be sought, because it was only with the mass support of non-Communists that the CPY could hope to achieve its objectives. (4) As a disciplined member of the Comintern, the CPY had to abide by all the policy turns of the Soviets, but this should not prevent it from strengthening itself and preparing for a possible Axis attack upon Yugoslavia. (5) So far as the foreign political orientation of the country was concerned, the CPY urged ever closer ties with the Soviet Union as the bulwark of peace, and in this regard a big change actually took place in official policy when Yugoslavia in July 1940 recognized the Soviet Union and established diplomatic relations with it in the hope of somewhat counteracting the increasing German influence upon Yugoslavia.[82]

The signing of the German-Soviet treaty of August 1939 put the CPY in an awkward position, which was reflected in its propaganda statements. From a clearly anti-fascist stand in accordance with the decisions

---

[81] See Tito, *Political Report of the Central Committee of the Communist Party of Yugoslavia* (1948), pp. 44–50.

[82] The conclusion of a treaty of friendship and nonaggression late at night on April 5, 1941, did nothing to improve Yugoslavia's military position. A month later (May 9) the Soviet Union, in order not to offend Hitler, recognized the subjugation of Yugoslavia and withdrew the diplomatic status of the Yugoslav legation in Moscow. After Russia itself was invaded, relations with the Yugoslav government, now in exile in London, were reestablished.

of the Seventh Congress of the Comintern, the party shifted to a stand of opposing imperialist wars in general and especially any lining up of Yugoslavia on the side of France and England in their war with Germany. It continued to advocate a change in the domestic government in the direction of Popular Front and a stronger orientation toward the Soviet Union. It was in accordance with this line that the Fifth Conference of the CPY at Zagreb in October 1940 formulated its statements and its policies, propagating the idea of the defense of the country against imperialist attackers.[83] At the same conference, the party leadership sharply criticized the propaganda line taken by the regional party organization in Montenegro in May 1940 when it advocated demobilization of soldiers, refusal of discipline, and even desertion from the military ranks. In fact, Chetnik sources have published excerpts from CPY leaflets in which men of military age were urged to ignore the call to the colors lest they be used as cannon fodder in the interest of British imperialists.[84]

But it is one thing to show the Yugoslav Communists as being against the government in 1940 and early 1941 and issuing propaganda material in one section of the country urging men in the reserve in May 1940 not to respond to the call to arms, and quite another thing to blame them for the collapse of the army as Živan Knežević did when he wrote: "Aside from the treachery of the Croatian Ustashi in the course of the war, the Communists, with their activities, stabbed in the back the Yugoslav Army which had come to grips with the Axis powers on April 6, 1941."[85] The Communists were too weak to have influenced the outcome of the invasion one way or another;[86] they could neither have hastened the collapse nor delayed it, much less could they have averted it. Knežević's accusation, made at a time when the Communists were proving their strength as a revolutionary resistance force, was a recognition of their new position as a formidable threat to the defenders of the old Serbian-dominated order.

From the Communist point of view the miserable performance and almost overnight collapse of the government and the army in April 1941

---

[83] For Tito's report to the Fifth Party Conference see *Communist* (English ed.), No. 1, pp. 49–89; and for the Resolution adopted by this conference see *Komunist* (Serbo-Croatian ed.), No. 1, pp. 101–22. For Tito's report of late May 1941 to the Comintern on conditions in Yugoslavia immediately before the invasion, on the course of the war and responsibility for the speedy collapse, and conditions under occupation during the first six weeks or so, see Tito, *Vojna djela*, I, 11–20. See also Trgo's paper, "The Communist Party of Yugoslavia and the Defense of the Country," delivered at a symposium at Split in October 1969, which deals specifically with the period 1935 through April 1941.

[84] For Tito's criticism of the propaganda line taken by the Montenegrin Communists see his report to the Fifth Conference in *Communist*, No. 1, pp. 69–70; for some excerpts from CPY leaflets and from some anti-French and anti-British Communist writings coming from a Chetnik source, see Vukašin Perović, pp. 72–75.

[85] Živan L. Knežević, *Why the Allies Abandoned the Yugoslav Army of General Mihailovich*, Part I, p. 17, from a memorandum delivered to the British government on June 2, 1943, which was prepared by Knežević in his official capacity as head of the Military Office of the Prime Minister.

[86] Tito, *Stvaranje i razvoj Jugoslovenske armije*, p. 47.

was the best thing that could have happened. All the power factors in
the country—the dynasty, the army, the police, and the bourgeois political parties, both Serbian and non-Serbian—were totally discredited and/
or disintegrated, leaving a huge political and psychological vacuum.,
The Communist Party, still practically intact, and not discredited because it had never had the opportunity to do anything that might have
discredited it, which knew what it wanted and dared to go after its objectives in spite of terrible odds, was the only dynamic and integrative
force embracing the whole country—and the only force capable of
mounting an armed struggle against the occupying armies and the
puppet regimes established by them, and later also against the Chetniks
as champions of the old order. As such an integrative force, it was in a
position to work out gradually a program of political and, at least by
implication, also of socioeconomic reforms that would attract steadily
growing support among all the peoples of Yugoslavia and, with them,
achieve victory.

Most of the CPY's effective propaganda came after the collapse, it is
true, rather than before, in part because of the very swiftness of the collapse. There were few actual Communists in the army, and in fact, members of the CPY in some army units in Croatia that rebelled under
Ustasha prodding stood by without doing anything and later were criticized by the party leadership. Aside from surviving the war and the partition of the country almost intact—a fact of the greatest importance—
the party also took advantage of the chaos by secreting a considerable
amount of arms and ammunition picked up from the disintegrating
army, thus acquiring a part of the arms wherewith to start the uprising
a few months later. The real change in image of the CPY in the public's
eye came later and gradually, as a result of tremendous effort and excellent leadership against the armies of occupation, the various quisling
forces, and the Chetniks, and aided indirectly by the politically shortsighted and extremely bloody measures of the occupying armies and
quisling regimes against all people who refused to accept their rule.
Especially important in this respect was the policy of the CPY, outlined
in the "Conclusions" of May 1941, which advocated unity and brother-
hood among all peoples of Yugoslavia as well as relentless struggle
against the foreign enemies and their domestic helpers as a matter of
sheer survival.

THE FUNDAMENTAL CAUSES OF THE COLLAPSE

But after all that has been said about certain internal factors that contributed to Yugoslavia's collapse in April 1941—fifth-column activities
by the Ustashas and others, defeatism among the political and military
leadership which resulted in a general lack of fighting morale, incom-

plete mobilization—we return inevitably to the primary cause of the defeat, which was simply Germany's overwhelming military strength. The aggressor in this war, even without its allies, was a tremendous industrial power which under Hitler had been arming feverishly and perfecting its military leadership and technology. In April 1941 it was at the peak of its strength. The defender was a small, poor, and weak country, with a peasant-based economy and an extremely limited potential for modern warfare. Germany was the second most important industrial power in the world, whereas Yugoslavia had only the rudimentary beginnings of industrial development. Germany in May 1939 (without Austria) had a population of 69.3 million against the 15.5 million Yugoslavs. In 1938 it had an average per capita national income of $480 as against $70 in Yugoslavia, and it produced 22.6 million metric tons of raw steel as against 230,000 metric tons, or only one percent, produced by Yugoslavia.

The difference in size and economic structure between the two countries was of course reflected in the number of troops that they could put in the field, and especially in the level of military technology and in the amount of arms that they could produce or otherwise acquire, and thus in the strategy and tactics that these arms made possible. Germany had already acquired more resources by conquering Poland and France, countries that were considerably larger and stronger than Yugoslavia, as well as the Low Countries, Denmark, and Norway. Against such a foe, totally isolated and without prospect of immediate aid from outside, Yugoslavia succumbed to paralyzing fear, which permeated not only all Yugoslav political and military agencies and decision-makers but also the broad masses of the population, dispelling any reasonable hope of defense along conventional lines. There simply did not exist the necessary geographical, economic, political, military, and psychological foundations for prolonged defense. Germany in 1941 had enormous amounts of modern arms at its disposal and could easily replenish them, and the German strategy and tactics of the blitzkrieg—the use of massive air strikes and speedy breakthroughs by strong armored and motorized units—had been tested and perfected. Against all this, the Yugoslav army—organized, trained, and led according to the strategic and tactical principles developed during the First World War, armed according to the economic power of a small peasant country, and at that only half-mobilized—had next to nothing in its favor, as was promptly demonstrated on the first day of combat in each of the three main areas of attack, Macedonia, southeastern Serbia, and the northern parts of Croatia and Slovenia. In terms of conventional warfare the confrontation of such unequal forces was grotesque.

The nature of the collapse, however, must be explained by something more than Germany's power. Yugoslavia was a divided country, which for more than twenty years had been ruled by Serbs who ignored the rights and needs of the other nations within the country. It had a government of the few, by the few, and for the few. Only a small minority of people had a genuine stake in Yugoslavia as it existed in 1941, and evidently even they felt that it was hardly worth fighting or dying for. Thus the purely military difficulties and inadequacies were compounded by divisiveness among the component nations and classes, general political, social, and economic dissatisfaction, and centrifugal political forces that were used by the country's neighbors.

From this point of view then, the Serbian ruling groups and the Serbian-controlled army must be held responsible for the way in which the collapse of April 1941 occurred. Defeat by Germany was inevitable under any circumstances, but had the country not been hopelessly divided, the collapse would have been purely military and not also, as it actually was, political and moral.

The rapid military collapse of the Yugoslav army in April 1941 was the consequence of the tremendous economic and military discrepancy between the adversaries. The political and moral disintegration of Yugoslavia in the process of military defeat—only the final phase of a development of long standing—was the consequence of the political regime of the interwar period, characterized by the Serbian hegemony and its most debilitating feature, the unsolved national problem in the state. Dissatisfaction over the national problem was compounded by the myriad of socioeconomic problems to which the regime—a narrow, rapacious political and economic elite—paid little or no attention. The chief dissatisfied social stratum was the peasantry, augmented by the nascent working class and a large part of the intelligentsia, to all of whom the old regime did not and could not open any hopeful perspectives. These groups did not consider the Yugoslav state of the interwar period worth preserving.

All other factors, including the fifth-column activity, were ancillary, having nominal effect on the speed and totality of the military collapse, and only small effect on the way in which the army and the state collapsed.

THE APRIL WAR AND ULTIMATE ALLIED VICTORY

A few words may be said about the effect of the Yugoslav invasion on Hitler's prosecution of the war and the ultimate victory of the Grand Alliance. The events in Yugoslavia that began with the coup of March 27 were a partial cause of what proved to be a fateful delay in Hitler's invasion of the Soviet Union. Originally that invasion, the beginning of Operation Barbarossa, had been set for May 12.[87] The first postponement

---

[87] Görlitz, ed., *General Feldmarschall Keitel: Verbrecher oder Offizier?*, p. 231.

of Barbarossa was made on March 27 during Hitler's conference with the leaders of the Wehrmacht following the coup in Belgrade. After a discussion of the new situation and the way in which Hitler had decided to deal with Yugoslavia, the minutes of the meeting say: "This plan [the invasion of Yugoslavia] presupposes that we speed up the schedule of all preparations and employ such strong forces that the Yugoslav collapse will take place within the shortest time. *In this connection, the beginning of Operation Barbarossa will have to be postponed up to 4 weeks.*"[88] Later on, the invasion was postponed again, and it actually started on June 22.

Many writers consider that this delay was responsible for the German failure to capture Moscow in the winter of 1941–42, and that it was here rather than at Stalingrad that the turning point of the war occurred. Thus DeWitt C. Poole, who led a group of American experts in a survey of how Nazi foreign policy was formulated, wrote: "Karl Ritter, who for some time represented the Foreign Office with the General Staff, told us with sober mien that the delay cost the Germans the winter battle before Moscow, and it was there the war was lost."[89]

A German admiral who has especially studied the Battle of Moscow and calls it, rather than the Battle of Stalingrad, the turning point of the Second World War, has stated that the military operations against Yugoslavia were the cause of the delay in the invasion of Russia and the consequent loss of valuable time, which, in conjunction with the extremely severe winter of 1941–42, made it impossible for the Germans to capture Moscow, a fact which proved fatal for the German war against Russia.[90] Two other factors, it is generally agreed, also played an important role in the German failure to capture Moscow: first, the bitter disagreements between Hitler and the leadership of the German Army about the strategy to be followed against Russia in the autumn of 1941, which caused delays in German operations, and second, the knowledge about the Japanese plans to attack the United States rather than the Soviet Union, acquired by excellent Soviet intelligence sources in Japan, which made it possible for the Russians to shift a large portion of their forces from the Far East for the strengthening of Moscow defenses. Weather conditions, too, were involved, for in the spring of 1941 in Poland and western Russia rivers were swollen from heavy runoff, meaning a postponement on that account alone of two or three weeks. Nevertheless, according to H. B. Mueller-Hillebrand, while in regard to man-

---

[88] *DGFP*, Series D, Vol. XII, p. 374. Italics as in the original.

[89] Poole, p. 150.

[90] Assmann, *Deutsche Schicksalsjahre*, pp. 255–86. Colonel General Alfred Jodl, the Chief of the Wehrmacht Operations Staff, made much the same point on May 15, 1945: ". . . the Führer and the General Staff saw clearly when the catastrophe of the winter 41–42 came (partly because of the immense severity of that winter) that from this culmination point in the beginning of the year 1942 no victory could be achieved." See *KTB/OKW/WFSt*, Vol. IV, Part 2 (1945), p. 1503.

power and matériel supplies, the Balkan operations, because of their speedy execution and complete success, had no appreciable effect on Barbarossa, they did contribute to its delay "at the most three weeks."[91] And these three weeks were extremely significant. Thus, from the point of view of the total war effort against the Axis, the Belgrade coup and the invasion of Yugoslavia which it made necessary worked in a very important, if indirect, way toward the final victory over the Axis.

[91] Mueller-Hillebrand, *Der Zusammenhang zwischen dem deutschen Balkanfeldzug und der Invasion in Russland*, pp. 22-25.

CHAPTER FOUR

Partition and Occupation

————◆•••◆————

It is an acknowledged rule of international law of war that after the defeat and subjugation of a country in war, its territory stays under formal military occupation until the conclusion of peace treaties. But as with most of the other rules of laws of war and occupation, Hitler disregarded that rule when it came to Yugoslavia.[1] The partition of Yugoslavia between the two Axis powers and among their various satellites, as well as the establishment of a puppet Independent State of Croatia, was decided, in part, prior to the invasion and in part during the course of the war, though the final settlement was not determined until after the conquest. The main outlines were decided upon almost solely by Hitler himself.[2]

Hitler had a number of territorial concerns in Yugoslavia. For one thing, he wanted to round out the territory of the Reich by annexing or otherwise incorporating areas inhabited either by Germans or by people who according to German ideas of the 1930's were amenable to speedy Germanization. He also wanted to reward good service by satisfying the territorial aspirations both of Italy and of his minor partners, Hungary and Bulgaria. The Croatian Ustashas, too, could be rewarded with territory to create an "independent" state. By making these payoffs, Hitler could preserve valuable support and at the same time reaffirm "Germany's special economic interests in the former Yugoslav State."[3] Thus, all arrangements with his partners on the division of Yugoslav territory

[1] According to Oppenheim and Lauterpacht, 7th ed., II, 448–49, during the active period of hostilities in the Second World War, Germany "became guilty, in particular with regard to the territories occupied in Eastern Europe, of unprecedented violation of practically all the laws of belligerent occupation."

[2] For Hitler's basic plan of April 12, 1941, for the partition of Yugoslavia see International Military Tribunal, *Trial of the Major War Criminals Before the International Military Tribunal, Nuremberg,* XXVII, 60–62. This plan was implemented by Foreign Ministers von Ribbentrop and Ciano in their meeting of April 20–22, 1941, in Vienna. See *DGFP,* Series D, Vol. XII, pp. 606–10 and, esp., pp. 630–32. See also Tudjman, *Okupacija i revolucija,* pp. 69–80; Hory and Broszat, pp. 39–57.

[3] *DGFP,* Series D, Vol. XII, p. 632.

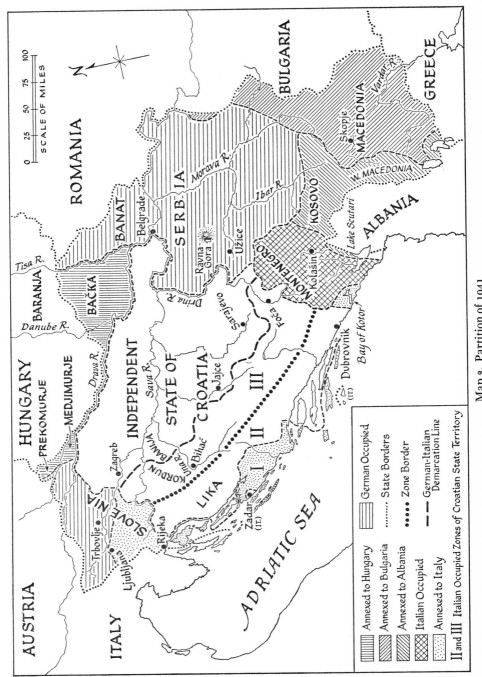

Map 3. Partition of 1941

included special clauses protecting or formally or informally establishing German control over important economic resources in the territory assigned to them, at least for the duration of the war.

By far the most troublesome matter in the division of Yugoslavia between Germany and Italy was that of the Independent State of Croatia. Only a few years earlier, in 1938–39, German statesmen had professed to have only economic, not political, interests in Yugoslavia; they seemed to agree that Yugoslavia lay properly within the Italian zone of interest.[4] During 1940 and the first months of 1941, however, the German attitude changed. Yugoslavia now seemed tremendously important politically because it lay in an area strategically of great significance for Germany's plans in southeastern Europe and in Russia. On the basis of these new considerations, the Germans decided to recognize Italy only as a junior partner in regard to Yugoslav spoils, but they continued to declare that the Italians would play the controlling political role in Croatia.

THE PARTITIONING

Following Hitler's decisions of April 12 and the German-Italian discussion in Vienna on April 20–22, Yugoslavia was partitioned among the parties concerned: the Axis partners, their satellites Hungary, Bulgaria, and (for the Italian account) Albania, and the newly established Croatian puppet state. The Croatian state was split approximately in half by a Line of Demarcation into a German zone and an Italian zone, which, from the point of view of the Axis, were virtually occupation zones. The Line of Demarcation actually started in Slovenia and continued beyond the Croatian state territory in a southeasterly direction to the juncture of the German, Italian (i.e. Albanian), and Bulgarian zones of occupation (or annexation). As shown in Map 3, Germany occupied the greater part of Slovenia, excluding the city of Ljubljana but including the northwestern areas of the province to the Italian border and the entire area extending northward from a line about ten to fifteen kilometers from the right bank of the Sava River and east to the new Croatian and Hungarian borders. Germany drew this line in Slovenia entirely on its own without consulting Italy. Italy had to be satisfied with what was left. Originally Germany intended to annex this area to the Reich, but the plan was never carried out formally—perhaps because the denationalization of the Slovenes, who made up 96.4 percent of the total population, and the planned large-scale deportations of Slovene population, were never accomplished.[5] Italy annexed the remainder of Slovenia, calling it the Province of Ljubljana. It was extremely disappointed at losing to Germany those parts of Slovenia through which the

---

[4] *Ciano's Diary 1939–43*, pp. 49, 52 and *passim*; Hory and Broszat, pp. 31–33.
[5] Herzog, pp. 45–46. For more details see Harriman, "Slovenia as an Outpost of the Third Reich."

railroad to Zagreb ran and the area in which the Trbovlje (Trifail) coal mines were located.[6]

In size, however, Italy's other annexations were not insignificant. Italy took part of the Croatian territory in the hinterland of Rijeka (Fiume); a strip of land running along much of the eastern Adriatic coast, together with most of the Adriatic islands; and the whole area of the Bay of Kotor. In addition, it occupied all of Montenegro, which was supposed to be made into a separate kingdom, attached to Italy as a vassal state. Albania annexed—for the account of Italy—the western part of Macedonia, most of the Kosovo region, and a small strip of Montenegro near Lake Scutari—that is, all the areas in which Albanians made up a majority or a large proportion of the population. Bulgaria was allowed to annex the greater part of Macedonia, part of Serbia, and a small part of the Kosovo region;[7] Hungary was allowed to annex Bačka, Baranja, the Croatian area of Medjimurje, and the Slovene area of Prekomurje.[8]

Serbia, essentially in its pre-1912 limits but including a section of the Kosovo region and the Banat, was occupied by German troops outright and put under a system of military government, but the Banat was administered by the local *Volksdeutsche*. Of the total population of 640,000 in the Banat, the *Volksdeutsche* accounted for about 120,000, or 18.7 percent.[9] Serbia proper was administered by the German army of occupation, first with the help of a group of Serbian administrators (commissioners), and from August 29, 1941, with the help of a quisling government headed by General Milan Nedić, the former Yugoslav Minister of the Army and Navy. By special agreements between the Germans and Bulgarians, the Bulgarian troops were invited, in two successive steps, to occupy a large part of Serbia and thus to relieve some of the German troops for service elsewhere. But the control remained in German hands.

Finally, from the territory of Croatia-Slavonia (minus Medjimurje, a small area north of Rijeka, and some north Adriatic islands), together with that part of Dalmatia not annexed by Italy and the whole territory of Bosnia and Herzegovina, was created the Independent State of Croatia. Its frontiers with Germany were regulated by the German-Croatian Treaty of May 13, 1941, and with Italy by the Italian-Croatian Treaty of May 18, 1941; its border toward Serbia, put at the Drina River, was "settled" by a unilateral Croatian decree which was first cleared with and later formally acknowledged by Germany; the border toward Montenegro was settled by a special Italian-Croatian Treaty of October 27,

---

[6] Mikuž, I, 37–45, 52–68.

[7] This was done not by a special proclamation or a similar act of government, but simply by extending Bulgarian legislation and governmental organization to these areas. Čulinović, *Okupatorska podjela Jugoslavije*, pp. 602–5.

[8] A special objective of the Hungarians, namely, an arrangement whereby the Croats and Italians would grant them special rights for an outlet on the Adriatic Sea at Rijeka, was, however, never realized. See *DGFP*, Series D, Vol. XII, pp. 574–77, 586.

[9] Marjanović, *Ustanak i narodnooslobodilački pokret u Srbiji 1941*, p. 23 (hereafter cited as Marjanović, *Ustanak 1941*).

1941.[10] So drawn, the borders of the Croatian puppet state took in a Serbian population that represented about one-third of the total population, spread over some 65 to 75 percent of the territory. Like the Yugoslavia of the interwar period (and that of the postwar period), but to a lesser degree, the short-lived Independent State of Croatia was a multinational and multireligious state. Unwisely, as time proved, the Ustasha regime chose not to recognize the legitimacy of existence of this large Serbian population, putting it outside the law, and in its actions toward it during the course of the Second World War it achieved a most inhuman and horrible record.

In terms of territory and population, Yugoslavia (which at the end of March 1941 had an area of 247,542 square kilometers and an estimated 15.97 million people)[11] was divided in the following manner:[12]

	Area (sq. km.)	Population (approx.)
Slovenia, part occupied by Germany	9,620	775,000
Slovenia, part annexed by Italy	5,242	380,000
Other territory annexed by Italy	5,381	380,000
Montenegro and areas annexed to Albania	28,000	1,230,000
Areas annexed by Bulgaria	28,250	1,260,000
Serbia, occupied by Germany	51,100	3,810,000
The Banat, occupied by Germany	9,776	640,000
Areas annexed by Hungary	11,601	1,145,000
Independent State of Croatia	98,572	6,300,000

The continued presence in the Independent State of Croatia of both German and Italian troops, although they were stationed and operating in different areas, made it necessary to regulate their mutual relations, since these inevitably influenced their respective relations with the Ustasha state. The territorial aspect of the problem was only temporarily solved by von Ribbentrop and Ciano in Vienna, as Helmuth Greiner points out:

Because an agreement [on the partition of Croatia for occupation purposes] could not be achieved, because the Italians presented enormous territorial claims and actually claimed predominance in all of Croatia, which after the arrival of German troops in Zagreb was proclaimed by the Croatian leader Dr. Pavelić [actually his representative, Colonel Kvaternik] as a separate, independent state, [the ministers] limited themselves for the start to the establishment of a Line of Demarcation between the Italian and the German occupation zones.[13]

---

[10] For the treaties here mentioned see Independent State of Croatia, Ministry of Foreign Affairs, *Medjunarodni ugovori 1941*, pp. 24–28 for the treaty with Germany, pp. 49–59 for the treaties with Italy (there were concluded at the same time several other treaties between Italy and Croatia, which are discussed below), pp. 83–86 for the decree regarding the border toward Serbia, and pp. 305–6 for the treaty with Italy regarding the border with Montenegro.

[11] This figure was obtained by projecting 1937–38 annual banovinal growth rates.

[12] As quoted in Marjanović, *Ustanak 1941*, pp. 22–23. These are German estimates for May 1, 1941, but there is no indication whether they are simple projections based on population growth during the 1930's or (less likely) estimates of the actual population in various areas as of May 1, 1941.

[13] Greiner, p. 286.

The general direction of the Line of Demarcation was, of course, Hitler's decision, but since drawing the line involved questions of troop withdrawals and transfers, communications between the military commands, railway and road communications, and above all vital mineral resources, military, foreign political, and economic agencies also played a part. The two foreign ministers put the finishing touches on decisions made by Hitler and the military, and regulated other issues, such as the control of economic resources. The virtual occupation of the Independent State of Croatia by both Germany and Italy led to a great deal of rivalry between the two Axis partners later on, and in particular severely hampered military actions against the armed resistance that gradually developed within the puppet state.

In both Germany and Italy, military and political leaders were sharply divided on the question of the partitioning and occupation of Yugoslavia. Military leaders in both countries apparently favored outright occupation of the whole of Yugoslavia, taking the position that puppet states anywhere greatly complicate the role of the military by reducing its influence and freedom of action. In Germany, Foreign Minister von Ribbentrop strongly favored a puppet state of Croatia, perhaps on the theory that with a puppet regime he would have a certain influence in Zagreb through his representative, the envoy, which would not be the case if a simple regime of military occupation were established. Presumably, von Ribbentrop was supported by Hitler, who systematically tried to divide authority among his subordinates and in this particular instance wanted also to satisfy the pressing need of his partner, Mussolini, to announce some "victories" to his people. In Italy, it was primarily Mussolini who favored the immediate division of the territorial spoils and thus establishment of the puppet state, in which Italy would supposedly have full predominance.

Quite soon after the proclamation of the Independent State of Croatia, the Ustasha regime of Ante Pavelić began a systematic persecution of its Serbian population. This persecution directly provoked the first outbursts of armed resistance in Herzegovina late in June, but this was a local and spontaneous manifestation and not a part of a well-planned uprising. In July, following the German attack on the Soviet Union on June 22 and the call on the European Communist parties by Stalin and the Comintern to engage in armed resistance and sabotage against the Germans as a way of drawing some of the pressure off Russia, the Communist Party of Yugoslavia began more or less simultaneously in various parts of the country a systematic armed uprising against both the occupation troops and quisling authorities and troops. In most areas the resistance forces were mixed, consisting for the first five to six months of both Communists and their sympathizers and Serbian nationalist groups, but in Serbia the Communist and Serbian nationalist or Chetnik forces were separate from the beginning.

The nature of the occupation or quisling regime in the several parts of dismembered and occupied Yugoslavia had a great effect on the growth of resistance in its various forms, and for that reason a brief description of the system of control of the major areas (omitting the areas annexed by Bulgaria and Hungary, which played only a minor role in the Chetnik movement), especially through the first year of occupation, is a necessary preliminary to an examination of the Chetnik movement of Draža Mihailović. The specific conditions in Montenegro and Slovenia will be left for discussion in Chapter 7.

GERMAN SYSTEMS OF CONTROL

Serbia proper, approximately within its pre-1912 frontiers, the only area of dismembered Yugoslavia in which an outright German military government was established, was extremely valuable to the Reich for several reasons. Its transportation lines—the Danube River and the Serbian railroads—connected central Europe with Bulgaria to the east and, to the south, with Greece and ultimately North Africa, and it had a rich supply of strategically important nonferrous metals which Germany needed for its war industry. With such assets to protect, the Germans had to maintain law and order, and of course they also wanted to run the country at the least expense. A Serbian puppet government (of which more will be said later) was established to help in this task.

The German military government in Serbia was established by an order of the Chief of the German Army High Command (OKH), Field Marshal Walther von Brauchitsch, of April 20, 1941. This order, effective on April 22 and implemented by a series of others, established the office of the Military Commander in Serbia as the chief of the occupation regime. He was subordinate to the Quartermaster General of the Army High Command and, as long as the German Second Army was in the field in Serbia, also to the commanding officer of that army, and he carried out his executive powers in the name of both.[14] According to the brief (*Dienstanweisung*) for the Military Commander in Serbia of April 17, his main duties were the safeguarding of the railroad line between Belgrade and Salonika and the Danube shipping route, the execution of the economic orders issued by Reichsmarshal Hermann Göring as the Plenipotentiary for the Four Year Plan, and the establishment and maintenance of law and order.[15]

A special order of the Army High Command of April 23 specified in

[14] Microcopy No. T-501, Roll 264, Frame 421.
[15] *Ibid.*, Frames 427–28. Among the important early tasks were also the guarding of Yugoslav prisoners of war still in Serbian territory and the protection of military booty captured from the Yugoslav army.

more detail the duties and the powers of the Military Commander in Serbia. His immediate command was divided into a military staff and an administrative staff. To organize his command he was assigned staff personnel for four area and about ten district commands; four battalions for local defense (*Landesschützen*), the troops to be distributed among the four area commands; one group of secret field police, and other personnel for supervising the administration and organizing and carrying out the economic exploitation of the country. He had no combat or garrisoning troops under his command and his responsibility was specifically limited to the maintenance of law and order "only as far as it could be established and assured by administrative orders, legislation, and law enforcement."[16]

The first Military Commander in Serbia was Air Force General Helmuth Förster. He was replaced in June 1941 by Antiaircraft Artillery General Ludwig von Schröder. Schröder died about a month later from injuries suffered in a plane crash, and for the rest of the summer the post was held by Air Force General Heinrich Danckelmann.[17]

In June, for garrisoning purposes in Serbia the Germans brought in the Higher Command for Special Purposes LXV consisting of four understrength divisions under the command of General of Artillery Paul Bader. (This was very briefly under the jurisdiction of the Second Army until all parts of that army were shifted to the Russian front; thereafter it fell under the authority of the Armed Forces Commander in Southeast Europe.) Three of the four garrisoning divisions—the 704th, 714th, and 717th—were deployed in occupied Serbia; the 718th was in the adjacent parts of the Croatian puppet state. General Bader's position was parallel with rather than subordinate to that of the Military Commander in Serbia. The latter as territorial commander could order Bader to undertake military operations in the event of an uprising, but he could not act as Bader's military superior.[18]

The presence of several occupying armies—that is, German, Italian, and Bulgarian—in areas acquired by the Axis powers in the Balkans and the existence of different occupation regimes in various areas under German control, made it necessary for all the German forces in the Balkans to be put under a unified command. This was established by Hitler in his Directive No. 31 of June 9, 1941. By this directive, Field Marshal Wilhelm List, the Commander in Chief of the German Troops in the Balkans (the command post which up to May 17 was known as Commander in Chief of the Twelfth Army), was redesignated Armed Forces Commander in Southeast Europe (*Wehrmachtbefehlshaber im Südost-*

[16] *Ibid.*, Roll 249, Frames 1046–48, esp. Frame 1046.
[17] Stambolić, "The Occupation of Serbia in 1941," p. 50. This article (1953) is the earliest systematic Yugoslav study of the German occupation of Serbia. See also Višnjić, "The German Occupation System in Serbia in 1941."
[18] Stambolić, pp. 55–56.

en), directly subordinate to Hitler. List's headquarters continued to be in Salonika, but his jurisdiction extended over the military commanders in Serbia, the Salonika-Aegean area, and southern Greece, as well as General Bader in Serbia. This meant that he had the responsibility for security and defense of the entire area specified and the maintaining of liaison between the German forces in the area and their allies, primarily the Italians.[19] This command organization remained in effect, with two changes of commander, until December 31, 1942.

After the uprisings broke out in July 1941, the local gendarmerie and the small *Landesschützen* and German police forces who were charged with maintaining law and order in Serbia found themselves quite unable to cope with their task. In mid-August, as the disorder grew, General Bader as head of the Higher Command for Special Purposes LXV was put in charge.[20] The three garrisoning divisions at his disposal had been somewhat strengthened since June, partly by artillery units using heavy arms captured from the Yugoslavs, but they were still small and weak, with many overage soldiers, poor armament, and no motorized transportation, even though the various units were deployed over large areas.[21] They were divisions designed for service in peaceful rear areas and were not strong enough to reestablish order in Serbia. On September 4 the 125th Infantry Regiment, reinforced with an artillery unit, was sent in from Greece. By now the uprising was growing rapidly, and after further consultations at Belgrade, at Marshal List's headquarters in Salonika, and at Hitler's headquarters, stern measures were undertaken to put it down.

In Directive No. 31a of September 16 Hitler ordered Marshal List to crush the uprising in Serbia, saying that the chief objective was "first to secure the communication lines and the enterprises important for the German war economy and then in a wider sense to reestablish order in the whole area by the application of sharpest means."[22] The same directive shifted General Franz Böhme, the commanding general of the XVIIIth Army Corps in Greece, to Serbia—giving him the title of Plenipotentiary Commanding General—to take charge of all German troops in Serbia and all operations against the rebels; it also promised to send to Serbia one or, if necessary, two regular divisions. Of far-reaching importance, also on September 16 the Armed Forces High Command (OKW) issued Hitler's order on the suppression of the "Communist

[19] Hubatsch, ed., *Hitlers Weisungen für die Kriegführung 1939–1945*, pp. 117–19, 122–25 (hereafter cited as *Hitlers Weisungen*). The Italians had one liaison unit in Salonika and another with the German command posts in Belgrade. See Microcopy No. T-501, Roll 247, Frame 1047.

[20] See Bader's order on the "Combating of the Communist Bands" of August 13, 1941, Microcopy No. T-501, Roll 246, Frames 78–80.

[21] Document No. NOKW-1898, a 190-page version of a longer report prepared by Ernst Wisshaupt, a military archivist, for the Chief of Staff of the Commander in Chief in Southeast Europe, and entitled "Die Bekämpfung der Aufstandsbewegung im Südostraum," Part I, June 1941–August 1942, p. 6.

[22] *Hitlers Weisungen*, p. 128.

Armed Resistance Movements in the Occupied Areas," which was to serve as the formal basis for much of the German military and police activity against the armed uprising in Yugoslav territory, especially in Serbia, during the next two years, particularly in regard to mass reprisals against the civilian population.

General Böhme took over his new command on September 19. Shortly thereafter General Danckelmann was relieved of his post, apparently for having misread the seriousness of the uprising, and General Böhme took over also as head of the occupation regime in Serbia. Also around September 20 the 342nd Infantry Division began arriving from France and a few days later was engaged in operations in the northwestern part of Serbia. A detachment of the 100th Tank Brigade was also transferred to Serbia, and early in November another division, the 113th Infantry, was brought in from Russia.[23] The combined efforts of these forces and the Serbian quisling troops broke the resistance: by early December the uprising in Serbia had been almost completely subdued and General Böhme and the staff of the XVIIIth Army Corps were shifted to Finland. With their departure, General Bader took over the duties of the Plenipotentiary Commanding General in Serbia; two months later (February 2, 1942) his powers were further strengthened when, following an order of the Armed Forces High Command, the three-pronged military command establishment in Serbia, consisting of the Plenipotentiary Commanding General in Serbia, the Military Commander in Serbia, and the Higher Command for Special Purposes LXV, was consolidated into the single office of the Commanding General in Serbia. In that capacity, General Bader was subordinate to the Armed Forces Commander in Southeast Europe.[24]

With the quelling of the uprising in Serbia, the Germans had withdrawn the army units sent in from outside for that task, and starting in January 1942 they began to make use of Bulgarian troops for occupation duty in Serbia as a way of further cutting back on their own troop commitments. In two successive extensions of the area occupied by Bulgarian troops, most of the territory of Serbia was brought under Bulgarian control, though these troops were themselves, of course, acting under overall German command and for German interests.[25]

In the Independent State of Croatia, which was acknowledged by Germany to be a sovereign state, the Germans had no formal power to introduce a military occupation government as in Serbia, but in time they

[23] *Wisshaupt*, pp. 42, 51–52, 62, 66–67; *Zbornik DNOR*, Tome I, Vol. 1, pp. 450–52, 622–23, and *passim*.
[24] *Zbornik DNOR*, Tome I, Vol. 1, p. 626; Microcopy No. T-501, Roll 247, Frame 940.
[25] For a discussion of the presence of Bulgarian occupation troops in Serbia during the Second World War see Vojin Popović, "The Bulgarian Army in Occupied Serbia, 1941–1944."

established in an informal way a large degree of control over the government of the puppet state. On April 15, 1941, five days after the proclamation of the Independent State of Croatia with German assistance, General Edmund Glaise von Horstenau was appointed German General in Zagreb, responsible directly to Field Marshal Wilhelm Keitel, Chief of the Armed Forces High Command. In mid-November Glaise's title was changed to Plenipotentiary German General in Croatia. His chief duty was to protect German military interests in Croatia, but he was also supposed to advise the Croatian government and army if asked to do so.[26] Glaise's counterpart for diplomatic and economic affairs between Germany and Croatia was the German Envoy in Zagreb, Siegfried Kasche.[27] The duties of the two officials were not strictly delineated, however, and in the complex wartime conditions they often duplicated each other's work or worked at cross-purposes, the more so as Glaise soon became an avowed opponent, and Kasche continued to the end a strong supporter of the Ustasha regime.

For more than a year and a half, Glaise had no troops, although he seems to have been responsible for the safety of the main Zagreb-Belgrade railroad line and therefore probably had under his full or partial command the railroad protection units stationed in Croatia. The German fighting forces stationed in Croatia were under the command of the Commanding German General (Bader) in Serbia and acted under his overall orders in 1942 in carrying out medium-scale military operations in Croatian territory (in eastern Bosnia in January, on the Kozara Mountain in northwestern Bosnia in June and July, and on the Fruška Gora in Srijem in August).

Germany had no desire to commit more troops to the territory of the Croatian puppet state, but it had little choice in the matter. As the war progressed and Partisan operations in Croatia expanded, the German involvement became ever larger; moreover the Croatian government was increasingly unhappy at having German troops in their territory under the operational command of the Serbia-based General Bader. Accordingly, in November 1942 a new command post, the Commanding General of German Troops in Croatia, was established, located at Slavonski Brod. General Rudolf Lüters was put in charge of the new command,

[26] Microcopy No. T-501, Roll 264, Frame 522. General Glaise, a former Austro-Hungarian general staff officer, was considered to be an excellent intelligence officer; he was an erudite man and a well-known military historian. He sided with the Nazis many years before the *Anschluss* and was in some pre-*Anschluss* Austrian cabinets as a representative of pro-Nazi elements. After the *Anschluss* he joined the Wehrmacht. Although he did not speak Serbo-Croatian, he had a wide acquaintance among the former Austro-Hungarian officers in Croatia who after the establishment of the Croatian puppet state assumed the leadership of the Croatian armed forces. He was outspokenly anti-Italian. See also RG 226, OSS–File No. XL13599.

[27] Envoy Kasche was an SA higher group leader and Nazi party official in Mecklenburg. It is said that he barely escaped the big purge of 1934. He had no diplomatic experience, and no special knowledge of Croatian or Yugoslav problems (nor of the Serbo-Croatian language), and was considered a very poor choice for the post of envoy.

which covered all Croatian areas between the Sava River and the German-Italian Demarcation Line, these areas being declared an operational zone. At the same time General Glaise was made responsible for operations in the Croatian territory lying between the Sava and Drava rivers.

Parallel with the establishment of a military occupation government in Serbia and of an important degree of military influence in the Independent State of Croatia through the Office of the Plenipotentiary German General in Croatia, the Germans either seized outright or put under their control all the important industrial, mining, trading, banking, and transportation facilities in Yugoslav territory, and obtained a lien on strategic mineral products in the Italian-controlled (bauxite) and Bulgarian-controlled (chrome ore) areas, and on agricultural surpluses and oil in Hungarian-controlled areas.[28] In contrast to the many changes that occurred in the German military and administrative structures in Yugoslav territory during the four years of their occupation, there was relative smoothness and efficiency in the utilization of economic resources within the limits allowed by guerrilla activity. Systematically, the Germans drew a growing share of Yugoslav manpower into the service or employ of the German military establishment or economy. They imposed large occupation costs on Serbia, which ran much beyond the cost of the occupation regime itself and to a large extent represented a tribute, and by special agreements with Croatia compelled it to undertake until 1943 the cost not only of maintaining German troops in Croatia but also of paying for various construction needs of the German forces, especially for the Luftwaffe. After January 1943 the Croatian government bore the larger share of the costs incurred by the German forces in Croatia.

Among the chief economic contributions of the Yugoslav territory to the German war machine were strategic nonferrous ores and metals: bauxite from the Italian-occupied parts of the country, copper, lead, zinc, and antimony from occupied Serbia, and chrome and in the later part of the war molybdenum from the Bulgarian-annexed parts. Other basic contributions were in food and agricultural raw materials (hemp, industrial alcohol) from the Banat and from Hungarian-annexed Bačka and Baranja, and timber and iron ore from Croatia. All important industrial enterprises were put directly or indirectly in the service of the German war economy, and all transportation facilities fell under German control: the Danube River for shipments of oil from Romania and ores and raw materials from Yugoslavia to Germany, and the railroads

[28] For various agreements that Germany made at this time with Italy, Bulgaria, and Hungary with regard to the exploitation of mineral resources see *DGFP*, Series D, Vol. XII, pp. 623, 630–32, 935.

for troop transport and for the sending of both military supplies and civilian supplies to and from Germany. The importance of Yugoslavia to the German war machine increased as the war went on and Germany's empire shrank under military reverses.

ITALIAN SYSTEMS OF CONTROL

The Italians used several different systems of control in Yugoslavia. In the part of Slovenia and in the Croatian lands that they annexed they introduced both a military and a civilian branch of government; in Montenegro the military commander from mid-July 1941 on was at the same time in charge of both the military and the civilian branches; in parts of Kosovo and western Macedonia that they annexed to Albania, there was also both a military and a civilian branch in operation. In the Independent State of Croatia, in parts first occupied, then cleared, and then reoccupied (within a period of months), the military commander was in charge of both military and civilian branches of government. The Italians' use of Chetniks as auxiliaries and to some extent their favoring of the Serbian element in these areas, while at the same time pursuing an outspoken anti-Croatian policy, led to numerous protests by the Croatian authorities as well as to German displeasure regarding the Italian policy.

The broad outlines of the relationship between Italy and the Croatian puppet state were set forth in a series of treaties signed in Rome on May 18, 1941. These were the Treaty on Frontiers, the Agreement on Military Matters Pertaining to the Coastal Area, and a twenty-five-year Treaty on Guarantee [of independence and territorial integrity] and Collaboration[29]—all of them humiliating to Croatia, and a severe setback to the Ustasha regime, which had a very narrow popular base from the beginning, and from which it never recuperated. (Moreover, it was agreed that King Victor Emmanuel would name a prince of the House of Savoy as Croatian king; he named his nephew Aimone, Duke of Spoleto, to this dubious honor, but since the latter's safety could not be ensured he never in fact set foot on Croatian soil.)

Under the terms of the Rome treaties, a strip of Croatian territory lying along the Adriatic coast (including most islands) was to be ceded to Italy; the rest of the territory, lying between the annexed zone and the Demarcation Line, was to be divided into two parts, of which the coastal zone was to be demilitarized. The Italians later called the annexed zone Zone I, the demilitarized zone Zone II, and the remainder of the territory to the Demarcation Line Zone III. Italy then withdrew the bulk of its forces from both Zone II and Zone III—though as we shall

---

[29] For the texts of these treaties see Independent State of Croatia, Ministry of Foreign Affairs, *Medjunarodni ugovori 1941*, pp. 49–59.

see, only temporarily—and those that remained there were formally considered until September 7, 1941, as allied troops stationed in Croatian territory by mutual agreement.[30]

The Italian Second Army, which had been the main Italian force in the invasion of Yugoslavia, remained in the country as the army of occupation[31] of a large territory bounded on the northwest by the old Italo-Yugoslav border and on the southeast by Montenegro and by the Adriatic Sea and the Italian-German Demarcation Line (some of this territory being formally annexed by Italy). This was a large army, numbering some 200,000 men, and it was never withdrawn during the roughly two and a half years of Italian control. On May 9, 1942, it was renamed Superior Command for Slovenia-Dalmatia, shortened to Supersloda. It was successively under the commands of General Vittorio Ambrosio (until January 1942), General Mario Roatta (1942), and General Mario Robotti, (earlier the commander of the Italian troops in Slovenia).

Within four or five months of the signing of the Rome treaties, Italian troops were back in Zones II and III in full force. Italy made the decision to reoccupy unilaterally, but it discussed the details with the Croatian government, and on September 7 General Ambrosio as Commander of the Second Army took over as supreme commander of both military and civilian affairs in these zones. (His proclamation of September 7 declared that he did so on the basis of an agreement with the Croatian government.)[32] A Croatian Administrative Delegate was designated to assist him in matters of administration, but practically all Croatian army units and all Ustasha Militia units were expelled to the German zone. The official reason given for reoccupation was the necessity of reestablishing law and order following the outbreak of the uprising toward the end of July and of safeguarding this area against possible British landings on the coast of Dalmatia. The much more important reasons, however, seem to have been the desire of having a stronger base for eventual further expansion into the rich Danube Basin if the opportunity should present itself and of keeping the Croats and, especially, the Germans away from the coastal areas. The Ustasha regime was unsuccessful in its appeal to Germany for help against the Italian reoccupation, Germany at this point having no wish to antagonize Italy. But early in 1942, after a difficult autumn, the Italians decided that they had overextended themselves militarily, and could not afford another year of operations over this vast area against the Partisans. On June 19 they reached a new agreement

---

[30] Italy, Stato Maggiore del R. Esercito, *Bollettini della guerra*, p. 541.

[31] Except, formally, for the period between the Rome treaties and September 7, 1941, the day when the two zones were formally and shortly thereafter also materially reoccupied.

[32] For the texts of the minutes of the conference on reoccupation between the Italian and Croatian representatives of August 26, 1941, and of General Ambrosio's proclamation see *Zbornik DNOR*, Tome XIII, Vol. 1, pp. 345-53, 374-76.

with the Ustasha government,[33] and during the summer they withdrew probably as much as a half of their forces from Zones II and III.

At the time of the invasion in April 1941 the Italian Ninth and Eleventh armies held Albania. After the Axis victory, the Ninth Army was given control of Montenegro, and of the parts of Kosovo[34] and western Macedonia that were incorporated into Albania for the Italian account. The Italians planned to make Montenegro an "independent" state closely allied with Italy, but the general uprising that occurred in Montenegro on July 13, 1941, forced them to abolish the post of civilian administrator which had been established and to put the military commander, General Alessandro Pirzio Biroli, in full control. A few months later (on October 3) the regime was redesignated the Governatorato of Montenegro, with Pirzio Biroli as Governor in full charge of both military and civilian affairs.[35] The troops under his command, the XIVth Army Corps of the Ninth Army, were redesignated on December 1, 1941, the Command of the Troops of Montenegro. No further changes were made during the period of Italian occupation.

The Italian military commitment in Yugoslav territory thus amounted to a very large force—ten divisions in the Supersloda, two or three more in the Command of the Troops of Montenegro.[36] In addition to these army forces, the Italians also had in Yugoslavia police and Blackshirt units, as well as air force units, and a special naval command—the *Maridalmazia*—was assigned to safeguard the eastern Adriatic coast.

Like the Germans, the Italians had in Zagreb an envoy—first Raffaele Casertano, and then Luigi Petrucci—and a representative of the Italian army as the counterpart of General Glaise, first General Antonio Oxilia (until August 1942), and later General Gian Carlo Re. For some time also the Italian Fascist Party had its special representative in Zagreb (Fascist Militia General Eugenio Coselschi).

The condominium in Croatia was the most important example of Italo-German collaboration in controlling and despoiling an occupied area, yet the relationship was characterized not by cooperation, but by constant rivalry and the systematic undermining of each other's position—in the end always at the expense of the Croatian people and the Italians, while German authority and military commitment steadily grew. Although the worsening of the Italian position was due mostly to Partisan activity, it is not surprising that, in view of the growing German

[33] For the German translation of this agreement, the various directives of the Croatian government on its implementation, and the "norms" of its application on the Italian side see Microcopy No. T-501, Roll 264, Frames 642–93.

[34] For the Italian and later German system of occupation of the Kosovo and Metohia regions see Hadri, "The Occupation System in Kosovo and Metohia, 1941–1944."

[35] *Zbornik DNOR*, Tome XIII, Vol. 1, pp. 412–13.

[36] For the deployment of the ten divisions of the Italian Second Army as of October 1, 1941, see *ibid.*, pp. 403–11.

military power in Croatia, the Italians looked upon General Glaise, the German Plenipotentiary General in Croatia and well-known Italophobe, as their archenemy.[37] On the other hand, according to a great many of Glaise's documents, almost all high Italian officers and officials on the Croatian scene were outspokenly anti-German, especially Roatta, Oxilia, Casertano, and Guiseppe Bastianini, who was the administrator of the annexed parts of Dalmatia. General Roatta, in particular, who followed a line of halfhearted cooperation with the Germans and was openly pro-Chetnik, was repeatedly accused by the Germans of sabotaging their attempts at pacification, which for the Wehrmacht was the principal problem and the chief objective of all German forces in the territory of the Croatian puppet state.

The Italo-Croatian relationship between May 1941 and September 1943 was thus more complex and quite different from what was intended by the provisions of the Rome treaties. The Italian quasi-protectorate over the puppet state was in fact conditional upon German consent and was qualified by a series of liens of an economic, military, and political nature which the Germans imposed upon Croatia before and after the Rome treaties and expanded as time passed.[38] These liens were kept secret from the Italians as much as possible, but their effects could not be covered, and it was soon apparent that, despite the Rome treaties, Italy's standing in Croatia was far lower than Germany's.

All in all, Italy got the short end of the economic spoils in Yugoslavia. All the production of the principal strategic resource in their territory, bauxite, was earmarked for the duration of the war for Germany. Italy made the most of the large timber reserves, but the area had low agricultural production, lacking grains especially, and food imports were necessary. To make matters worse, Partisan operations in large parts of Italian-controlled areas made it very difficult for the Italians to exploit the resources in these areas. Repeatedly, the Partisans attacked the railroad line from Karlovac to Rijeka, which was used for the transport of Romanian oil that came up the Danube to the port of Vukovar and then continued westward by rail, and the equally important line that ran through Lika and northern Dalmatia to Split.

Like Germany, Italy imposed on Croatia payment of maintenance costs for their troops. Legally, these costs were advances which were supposed to be repaid after the war, but in the second half of 1942, after Croatia ran into severe financial difficulties, Italy repaid a certain amount of these advances into Croatia's regular clearing account.

[37] Zanussi, I, 177, 215, 245.
[38] Compare e.g. the provisions of the Clodius Protocol of May 16, 1941, on German economic preferences in Croatia; arrangements about the so-called legionnaire divisions; and the agreement giving the status of state within the state to the German minority in Croatia.

THE INDEPENDENT STATE OF CROATIA

The Axis attack on Yugoslavia meant the culmination of the hopes of the exiled Ustashas, most of whom had spent the decade of the 1930's in Italy (some of them also in Hungary and Germany), where they received training in terrorist activities. Their role in the invasion was minor, consisting of some propaganda broadcasting from abroad and fifth-column activity in Croatia and Dalmatia during the brief days of fighting, but they reaped a fine reward: a few hours before German tanks entered Zagreb on April 10, and with the assistance of German agents, the Ustashas proclaimed the Independent State of Croatia. A few days later, Dr. Ante Pavelić, who had been agreed upon by Italy and Germany as the man to head the new puppet state, accompanied by two or three hundred uniformed Ustashas from the Ustasha camps in Italy, entered Zagreb in the dead of night. These Croats, along with a group of other Ustashas from Germany and Hungary and the small following at home, became the rulers of the new Independent State of Croatia—which was, of course, as a puppet state not independent at all.[39]

The Ustashas insisted that all of Bosnia and Herzegovina was part of the Croatian "historical and ethnic" territory, and they had been successful in getting the eastern frontier of their state placed along the line of the Drina River and the pre-1918 border between Herzegovina and Montenegro. Thus the state included close to two million Serbs, who accounted for approximately 30 percent of the total population. In order to substantiate their claim to Bosnia and Herzegovina, the Ustashas proclaimed the Moslems of that province to be the purest of all Croats.[40] In this way nearly 60 percent of the population of the province was considered as Croatian (about 23 percent Catholic Croats and close to 37 percent Moslem Croats).

[39] The exact number of sworn Ustashas at the beginning of April 1941 is not known; estimates range from about 900 to several thousand. There were also several tens of thousands of people who sympathized with the group. The Ustasha movement stood for extreme Croatianism, extreme anti-Serbianism, extreme anti-Yugoslavism, and anti-democratism. Its anti-Serbianism was a continuation of an ideological strain that developed in Croatia in the early 1890's under the leadership of Dr. Josip Frank, a Zagreb lawyer of German Jewish ancestry who was head of an offshoot of the Party of Rights, which had been established some thirty years earlier by Dr. Ante Starčević. Frank upheld this anti-Serbian policy to the end of his political career around 1910. His followers were known as *Frankovci*, and during the interwar period most of the Croats who displayed extreme anti-Serbianism and anti-Yugoslavism were dubbed by that name. After April 1941 the term Ustasha supplanted the term Frankovci, though not all of the real Frankovci were supporters of the Ustasha policies. For details on Frank see Šidak et al., pp. 18, 143–48, and *passim*.

[40] This was a gross exaggeration. The overwhelming majority of Moslems considered themselves neither Croat nor Serb but simply Moslem. And although a certain number of Moslems openly sided with the Ustashas, the majority was either directly opposed to them or neutral. Some of them sided with the Chetniks, some with the Partisans, and others were trying to achieve a special autonomous position for somewhat truncated Bosnia and Herzegovina directly under the Third Reich. See two articles by Rasim Hurem: "The Attempt of Some Moslem Bourgeois Politicians to Separate Bosnia and Herzegovina from the Independent State of Croatia" and "Conceptions of Some Moslem Bourgeois Politicians About the Situation of Bosnia and Herzegovina During the Period from the Middle of 1943 to the End of 1944."

Along with Jews and Gypsies, the Serbs were put outside the law by the Ustasha state. They were excluded from service in the armed forces (except for a few Serbs who were formerly Austro-Hungarian army officers, and except for their possible service as work battalions), from practically all government employment, from political life (a few persons excepted), from work in mass media and professions; their businesses were taken over by the government or by Croatian-owned firms; the use of Cyrillic script was forbidden.[41] The formula that was to be applied to the Serbian population was simple: about one-third would be expelled to Serbia, one-third would be converted to Roman Catholicism, and one-third would be exterminated. A program with these objectives was quickly launched—gaining momentum after Pavelić's first visit to Hitler early in June 1941. The final results bore out the formula. More than 120,000 Serbs were officially expelled and transported to Serbia, most of them within the first six months of the Ustasha regime, and a great many fled on their own; perhaps close to a quarter of a million were converted to the Roman Catholic faith with the assistance of at least a portion of the Croatian Catholic clergy; and several hundred thousand were massacred or met death in concentration camps.[42] (The same ruthlessness characterized the Ustasha treatment of Jews and of Croats who opposed the regime.) Appalling as the figures are, they would undoubtedly have been higher if the Ustashas had been allowed to proceed with their program without interference. Only the resistance of the Partisans and, to a much lesser extent, of the Chetniks, saved the Serbs in the territory of the Independent State of Croatia from total disaster. Thousands of Serbs, especially the young, who faced the alternative of going under the Ustasha knife or into the hills, went into the hills where most of them joined the Partisans. Until sometime in 1943, in fact, the majority of the Partisans in the territory of the Ustasha state were Serbs from that territory, although other Serbs from the Ustasha state were at the same time joining the Chetniks.

In the first months of the Ustasha regime neither Italy nor Germany showed much inclination to allow the regime to develop any sizable armed forces, and they systematically collected all but a token of the arms left by the old Yugoslav army in Croatian territory. The troops that the Ustashas could call upon during the first few weeks of their existence, in addition to a few detachments of their own militia, were those of the former paramilitary organization of the Croatian Peasant

[41] For the decrees and ordinances on the basis of which these policies were carried out see Independent State of Croatia, Ministry of Justice and Religion, *Zbornik zakona i naredaba Nezavisne Države Hrvatske—1941*, pp. 2, 10–11, 14–15, 19–20, 42–43, and *passim*.

[42] According to German data, the Ustashas had deported to Serbia as of about September 20, 1941, a total of 118,110 persons. *DGFP*, Series D, Vol. XIII, p. 570. There is a voluminous literature on conversions in wartime Croatia to Roman Catholicism and the extermination of the Serbian people, but since all figures are only estimates, no satisfactory references can be given. These problems will not be discussed further in this volume.

Party, the Civic Guards. The Guards helped them to establish their authority in some parts of the country, but they were soon disarmed by the government and replaced by newly organized army units (the *Domobrans*) and by units of the Ustasha party army or Ustasha Militia. There were also, during the first few months, a number of "wild" armed units which were organized by eager Ustashas in many localities on their own initiative. They played an especially prominent and ignominious part in the persecution and massacres of the Serbian population, and by government order were disbanded before the summer was over.

Although the Germans had hoped to use some of the Croatian manpower on the Russian front, only one Croatian volunteer regiment ever reached Russia. Three regular divisions composed of Croatian manpower and German officers and specialists (the so-called legionnaire divisions) were trained and outfitted in Austria for use in the Soviet Union, but the increasing activity of the Partisans in the territory of the Croatian puppet state forced the Germans to employ these divisions in Croatia instead, and they were also compelled to commit several divisions of their own in Croatia and to help the Croatian government to develop and arm its own forces for use at home. Thus as the war advanced and the southeastern European theater of war took on increasing importance, the Croatian army, along with more and more German troops, were vital to the security of German interests.

A statement submitted by Dr. Pavelić to the German Envoy in Zagreb on September 1, 1943, at a time when the Croatian quisling forces were numerically at their peak, gives the most authoritative information on the composition of these forces. The statement lists in the category of troops under German command the following: 62,020 troops within the German armed forces; 9,000 new recruits for these forces; 36,300 Croatian troops supplied by Germans and under German command; and 62,760 troops supplied by Croats but under German command—a total of 170,080 men. In the second category, troops under Croatian command, were 92,246 officers, noncommissioned officers, and men. The two categories combined came to a grand total of 262,326 men. Of this total, 28,500 men or 11 percent were the Ustasha Militia and Pavelić's Personal Guard. The largest single group of the approximately 92,000 men under Croatian command was the gendarmerie with around 18,000 men.[43]

At no time in the entire war did the Croatian armed forces function as anything more than essentially an instrument of the Wehrmacht. Whenever the German forces were engaged in operations in Croatian territory—that is from January 1942 on—the participating Croatian forces were under their command. Moreover, the German military commander had supreme executive powers in the operational areas, being

---

[43] Microcopy No. T-77, Roll 883, Frames 5,631,890–92.

formally in charge also of the Croatian administration, though he was assisted in this respect by the Croatian Administrative Delegate.

Despite its rather large size the Croatian army, the Domobrans, was not a good fighting force. The majority of its units were dispirited and most of its officers had no sympathy with the Axis cause. The Ustasha Militia, on the other hand, which was a party army, composed of fully indoctrinated volunteers and devoted to Pavelić, was excellent as a combat force; it was at the same time, however, extremely unruly and undisciplined and therefore almost constantly at odds with the regular Croatian army and with the German commanders in Croatia.

In sum, the Croatian puppet government was allowed very little freedom by the Germans and the Italians except in the matter of dealing with the Serbian population and with those Croats who were opposed to the Ustasha regime and thus also to the Axis occupation. And in these matters the regime followed a policy from which the overwhelming majority of the Croatian people shrank in horror.

THE SERBIAN PUPPET GOVERNMENT

The Serbian puppet government, unlike the Croatian, was composed of persons who had been closely associated with the prewar Yugoslav governments and in the period immediately prior to the invasion, as firm believers in German military superiority, had strongly advocated Yugoslavia's joining the Tripartite Pact. They were strongly anti-Communist and were confident that the Germans would win the war. Ironically, however, although they were made use of by the Germans, they were never trusted, especially by Hitler, because they were Serbs.

The first administrative body established by the Germans in occupied Serbia (May 30, 1941) was an Administration of Commissioners, headed by Milan Aćimović, a former chief of the Belgrade police and for a short time early in 1939 Minister of the Interior in the pro-Axis cabinet of Prime Minister Stojadinović.[44] This body was capable of handling routine administrative matters and of maintaining law and order under conditions of peaceful occupation, but it lacked the police and gendarmerie forces necessary to cope with the uprising that broke out in Serbia in July and continued with gathering momentum throughout the summer and autumn. Since the Military Commander in Serbia was himself short of police and military forces and was having trouble in getting reinforcements, he, in consultation with other German authorities, decided to appoint a strong-arm man to head a new Serbian puppet government and to allow him to build somewhat larger forces so that the Serbs themselves could be given the task of subduing the uprising.

The man chosen for this role was the former Minister of the Army

[44] Microcopy No. T-501, Roll 264, Frames 422–23; Kostić, pp. 20–21.

and Navy and Chief of General Staff Milan Nedić, who in November 1940 had been relieved of his cabinet post for urging that Yugoslavia join the Axis, and whom the Germans had not taken as prisoner of war to Germany in April 1941 although he was in command of the Third Group of Armies defending Macedonia against the Germans and Kosovo and Montenegro against the Italian forces invading from Albania. On August 29 Nedić organized what he called the Government of National Salvation.[45] He made certain oral agreements on the extent of his powers with the Military Commander in Serbia, General Danckelmann,[46] but after Danckelmann was dismissed in September these agreements were easily bypassed by his successors, and Nedić's powers were gradually reduced. Again and again, Nedić ran into difficulties with the German occupation authorities; several times he threatened to resign, and he made numerous changes in his cabinet, but although his authority toward the end of 1943 virtually ceased to exist, he continued in office until the end of German rule in Serbia in October 1944.

Obviously Nedić was in an awkward position: he had no real authority to make decisions, and he was quite aware of the fact that, although he was a tool of the Germans, he was not trusted by them and could expect little help from them. After January 1942 he also had to swallow the embarrassment of having most of his country occupied by Bulgarians, who were from beginning to end exceedingly unpopular; he had to deal more or less constantly with dissident elements in his cabinet; and he was challenged from the other direction by Chetniks, who successfully infiltrated nearly all levels of his armed forces and administration, and by the Partisans. Nor was he secure in his popular following. As an outright quisling and believer in German victory until sometime in 1943, he was looked upon with suspicion, sometimes loathing, by many Serbs.[47] In the early part of his regime, he apparently had the support of a sizable number of his countrymen who believed that he had saved many Serbian lives by cautioning the population at large against acts of violence, sabotage, and so on, warning them not to heed the words of the BBC and Radio Moscow which did not have the interests of the Serbian people at heart; but this support steadily declined as the war advanced and it appeared more and more certain that the Germans would lose.

Acting on his original understandings with the Military Commander in Serbia, Nedić established the Serbian State Guard. This soon absorbed the old gendarmerie and was commanded by former Yugoslav officers. It was allowed a maximum complement of about 17,000 men, and this was never exceeded. The Guard had three components: the Rural Guard

[45] Microcopy No. T-501, Roll 264, Frame 424.
[46] *Ibid.*, Roll 246, Frames 190–91, 333, Roll 256, Frames 1032–34.
[47] See e.g. the appraisal of the Chief of Staff of the Commander in Chief in Southeast Europe, General Hermann Foertsch, of August 1943 in Microcopy No. T-311, Roll 196, Frames 159–60.

in rural areas performing essentially the former duties of the gendarmerie, the police forces in the cities, and the Frontier Guard. Very quickly,
the Guard became infiltrated by Chetniks and throughout its existence
it was a poor and unreliable armed force. Arms and ammunition for the
State Guard were supplied by the Germans from war booty captured in
various parts of Europe; precautions had to be taken against pilfering
by the Chetniks who were known to be infiltrating the ranks.

Besides the State Guard, Nedić also had under his jurisdiction for a
time the Serbian Volunteer Detachments organized by the Serbian fascist
leader Dimitrije Ljotić, but commanded by former Yugoslav officers.
These were first organized with German backing in September 1941, and
by January 1942 they had reached a strength of about 3,700 men.[48] They
were a party force, consisting mainly of young pro-fascist volunteers.
Toward the end of 1942 these detachments were reorganized into the
Serbian Volunteer Corps, its strength limited to 3,600 men (it was somewhat enlarged after August 1943), and taken over by the German Commanding General in Serbia under his direct command.[49] The Volunteer
Corps fought well not only against the Partisans but also against the
Chetniks—it was, in fact, the only armed group of Serbs on the German
side that the Germans trusted and thought worthy of praise.[50]

Another special force organized by the Germans in occupied Serbia
was the Russian Protective Corps, recruited from among the Russian
exiles living in Serbia and elsewhere in southeastern Europe. The originally authorized strength of this corps was about 3,000 men, but according to corps' sources, at the beginning of September 1944 the corps
had 11,197 men.[51] It was commanded by former tsarist officers who
acted under the supervision of German liaison officers. Although the
corps was formally a part of the German armed forces,[52] it was mainly
used for guard duty in mines and industrial enterprises working for the
Germans and on railroads and roads, and only occasionally was put into
combat, in which it performed poorly.

Nedić and the Germans also had at their disposal, beginning as early
as August 1941, the Chetnik units of Kosta Milovanović Pećanac, and
to these were added the following autumn and on into 1942 a large portion of the Chetnik units that had been under the command of Pećanac's
rival, Colonel Draža Mihailović. The origin and early development of
these two kinds of Chetniks will be explained in the next chapter. As
part of Nedić's forces, their value was not great. The size of the Pećanac
units was limited, as of April 1942, to 8,745 men, and they could be used

[48] Microcopy No. T-501, Roll 247, Frames 756–58.
[49] Ibid., Roll 249, Frames 61, 142, 524.
[50] For mentions of bravery in German dispatches see e.g. ibid., Frames 60–63; Roll 253, Frames
936–37; Roll 256, Frames 596, 757.
[51] Vertepov, ed., p. 405.
[52] Ibid., Roll 249, Frame 142.

only in Serbia. The combined strength of both types of Chetnik units amounted on May 15, 1942, to 13,400 men, organized into 78 separate detachments.[53] That was probably the highest strength these detachments ever reached. The Germans did not trust Pećanac's Chetniks, and even less did they trust the Chetniks formerly under Mihailović. The Germans looked upon the legalization of the latter only as a temporary convenience for Mihailović until the appropriate moment arrived for these and other Mihailović Chetniks to turn their arms against the Germans. Consequently, during the summer of 1942 the Germans made the decision to disarm both groups of Chetniks, to transfer those that were considered reliable to the Ljotić volunteer detachments and to guide the remainder to productive work in the Serbian economy. By the end of the year detachments numbering over 12,000 men had been dissolved entirely, and other detachments had been severely reduced.

In all, the several segments of the Nedić military forces in the first year of his premiership amounted to a respectable size: about 21,000 men under arms in regular forces (Serbian State Guard and the Ljotić volunteer detachments) and over 13,000 men in auxiliary forces (Pećanac's Chetniks and Mihailović's legalized Chetniks). But after the reorganization and removal of the Volunteer Corps from Nedić's command and the disarming of his auxiliary troops, he had only the Serbian State Guard, the use of which was closely controlled by the Higher SS and Police Leader in Serbia. It was never a strong fighting force, and it deteriorated as the war advanced and it became more and more infiltrated by the Chetniks. Thus in comparison with the forces of the Croatian Ustasha state, the Serbian quisling forces were very limited.

The partitioning of Yugoslavia among the Axis powers and their satellites tore asunder the political, administrative, and economic fabric of the country developed during the preceding two decades. Each of the powers that obtained part of Yugoslav territory, as well as the puppet state of Croatia, followed their specific interests in administering these areas and utilizing their natural and manpower resources. Because of its overwhelming power, Germany was able to put a lien on the production of all strategic materials in the entire Yugoslav territory for the duration of the war. However, two groups, the Partisans and the Chetniks, which in time grew into large military and political organizations and enjoyed in specific periods strong support from the Great Allies, challenged the order established by Hitler in Yugoslav territory. Although both these groups desired and fought for the restoration of the Yugoslav state, their postwar aims were totally different, and during the war they followed totally different military and political strategies. And

---

[53] A report of the Commanding General in Serbia, *ibid.*, Roll 352, Frame 809.

since both of them wanted full, not partial, control of the postwar state, their opposition to each other was complete. It was thus that under the conditions of partition and foreign occupation and struggle against foreign enemies a civil war was fought in the country between the representatives of the old Serbian establishment and the Communist-led revolutionary forces.

PART TWO

The Army of the Homeland

CHAPTER FIVE

Early Stages of the Wartime Chetnik Movement

◄•••►

THE TRADITIONAL CHETNIKS UNTIL 1941

Rebellious activity akin to guerrilla warfare but on a small scale has a long tradition in the South Slav lands, especially in Serbia, Macedonia, Montenegro, and Bosnia and Herzegovina, which were for many centuries under Ottoman rule. It was one of the ways in which the people, or at least certain individuals, and groups of people, could show their opposition to the overwhelmingly powerful foreign rule. Although, until the beginning of the nineteenth century, such rebellious activity had the effect more often than not of worsening rather than lessening the oppression, it acted as a stimulus to the national psyche, as can be seen from the glorification of rebel leaders and groups in South Slav epic folk poetry. It helped to keep alive the people's hope for eventual liberation from the foreign yoke. Of course, armed action of individuals and small groups sometimes turned into or bordered on banditry. But if banditry was turned against the foreign oppressor it was considered heroic.

The First Serbian Revolution of 1804, which grew from a revolt against the terror and abuse of Turkish local chieftains and usurpers of power into a revolt against overall Turkish rule, actually began with operations of the existing guerrilla or "bandits'" companies (*hajdučke čete*),[1] and then under the leadership of Djordje Petrović (Karageorge, the founder of the Karadjordjević dynasty) took on the character of a general people's uprising.[2] The liberated territory under a rudimentary sort of government lasted until 1813, and was finally broken as much by internal troubles as by the Turks—by the tendency of many leaders of the revolution to enrich themselves and even to impose corvée on the

---

[1] The term Chetnik derives from the word *četa* (pl. *čete*), a company of soldiers or a group of men engaged in guerrilla warfare, and simply means a guerrilla fighter. The commander of a Chetnik company or area of activity is called *vojvoda*, and according to unwritten Chetnik law he has absolute power over his men and his *rayon*.

[2] Tudjman, *Rat protiv rata*, pp. 83–94, esp. pp. 86–87.

population, which of course sapped the revolutionary zeal; by the change from guerrilla tactics in battles to frontal operations with large units; and, as well, by developments in the international situation which made it possible for the Turks to strengthen their forces in Serbia. In the Second Serbian Revolution under Miloš Obrenović (founder of the rival Obrenović dynasty), which erupted in the spring of 1815, guerrilla warfare was again used to great advantage. The fighting stopped in the autumn, but by shrewd political maneuvering Miloš had by 1817 won the partial independence for Serbia. The same year he ordered the killing of his competitor Karageorge (when he returned from exile) and prevailed on the national assembly to proclaim him a hereditary prince. With a special ukase of the Sultan which was made public in 1830 Serbia was proclaimed an autonomous principality under Ottoman sovereignty and Russian protection. In 1833 the territory of the principality was markedly enlarged. Although the principality paid tribute to the Sultan and some Turkish garrisons were kept in Serbia until 1868, Serbia was after 1830 for all practical purposes independent, but it was only at the Berlin Congress in 1878 that it was given complete and formal independence.[3] Interest in guerrilla warfare in Serbia continued throughout these years, however, as indicated partly by the fact of there being two books on the subject, one an adaptation from the Polish by Matija Ban, published in Belgrade in 1848, and another by Ljubomir Ivanović which appeared in 1868.[4]

Early in the twentieth century some of the latent interest in guerrilla warfare came to the fore. Between 1904 and 1912 small groups of men, organized, outfitted, and financed in Serbia, turned up in Macedonia bent on securing the liberation of Macedonia from Ottoman rule so that it could be joined with Serbia. At first a private venture, the direction of these activities was soon taken over by the Serbian government, intensified or relaxed depending on the foreign political situation. These Chetnik units were, for the most part, under the command of officers or noncommissioned officers on active duty with the Serbian army. The members themselves were recruited, on a voluntary basis, from the army ranks, though after 1908 a certain number of these men came from among the Serbs outside Serbia, primarily from Bosnia and Herzegovina. Since the Bulgarians and the Greeks had even earlier dispatched their own guerrilla groups to Macedonia with the same purpose as the Serbs later on, and in areas claimed by the Serbs the Bulgarian guerrillas were quite successful, Serbian guerrilla groups in Macedonia had to

---

[3] Ćorović, pp. 416–28, 431–36, 443–61, 529.

[4] *Pravilo o četničkoj vojni* (Rules of Guerrilla Warfare) and *Četovanje ili četničko ratovanje* (Guerrilla or Guerrilla Warfare), respectively. Both publications were commissioned by Serbian authorities.

spend much of their time fighting their rivals.[5] The opinions of the rank and file of the Macedonian population as to their wishes in the matter were of course not considered; undoubtedly their sympathies were divided, ranging from the desire for unification with one of the three claimant states to the desire for full independence. But in Serbia, with the exception of the social-democratic press,[6] these actions met with approval, and from the point of view of the Serbian national interest as generally interpreted until the end of the interwar period, paid handsome dividends.

In the First Balkan War of 1912–13 against the Turks, Serbs, Bulgarians, and Greeks alike used their guerrilla detachments to great advantage. The Serbs used them in several ways: as vanguards for the advancing armies in order to soften up the enemy and make the advance easier, behind enemy lines for attack on communication facilities, for the spreading of panic and confusion, as field gendarmerie, and as a means for establishing rudimentary administration in newly liberated areas. The Serbian Chetnik units and the so-called mountain staffs that coordinated their activities were subordinate to army commands in the field, and their operations were closely coordinated with the needs of the various armies. Chetnik units were used again in the Second Balkan War against Bulgaria which broke out between the former allies over the division of the territorial spoils from the First Balkan War. When the Balkan wars were over, the Serbian government established "cruising" Chetnik detachments for the pacification of the liberated area—a pacification which sometimes involved terrorist actions against civilians.[7] Such activity reached a peak after the Albanian uprising in western Macedonia, which had been aided somewhat by Bulgarian guerrilla formations.

The value of Chetnik units having been proved in the Balkan wars, the Serbian army naturally put such detachments to use in the First World War, after much the same fashion. They again acquitted themselves well in battle but suffered great loss of life. With the Serbian army, the Chetnik detachments withdrew before the Austro-Hungarian forces by way of Albania to Corfu in 1915 and later were transferred to the Salonika front. Meanwhile, in the Bulgarian-occupied parts of southern Serbia, where the Bulgarian forces had instituted a harsh occupation regime, new Chetnik companies were being organized and put into action. Hearing about these activities and fearing that a large-scale upris-

---

[5] Šehić, *Četništvo u Bosni i Hercegovini (1918–1941)*, pp. 19–37, 39, 53, and *passim*. This study, my chief source for this section, contains a background of the traditional Chetnik movement prior to 1918 as well as its development from 1918 to 1941, not only in Bosnia and Herzegovina but in Yugoslavia as a whole.

[6] *Ibid.*, p. 52.

[7] *Ibid.*, pp. 37–39.

ing would lead to massive reprisals by the Bulgarians, the Serbian army sent to these areas one of the Chetnik *vojvodas,* Kosta Milovanović Pećanac, with strict instructions to prevent the outbreak of guerrilla warfare on a large scale until such time as the Serbian Supreme Command deemed advisable. But the Bulgarians aroused the Serbs by ordering them to be drafted, and hundreds of men began joining the Chetnik detachments. Early in February 1917 a general uprising, known as the Toplica Uprising, broke out, essentially under the leadership of *vojvoda* Kosta Vojinović, and to some extent also of Kosta Pećanac, who finally joined after seeing that his counsels against the rebellion were not being heeded. The uprising met with great success at first. A sizable area, including several towns, was freed; but by March 25 the Bulgarians, aided by reinforcements that were rushed to the scene, had put down all resistance. The defeat was followed by bloody reprisals against the civilian population. The following year, in connection with the breakthrough on the Salonika front, the Serbian army again used Chetnik detachments to great advantage. But shortly before the armistice the Chetnik detachments were ordered dissolved, with part of the men being absorbed by the regular army units and part of them released to their homes. It should be noted also that during the First World War there was some action by Montenegrin Chetniks against the Austro-Hungarian forces of occupation.[8]

Thus at the beginning of the new Yugoslav state, the Chetnik veterans, thanks to their record from 1904 to 1912 in Macedonia and to their actions in the Balkan Wars of 1912–13 and during the First World War, were one of the leading Serbian patriotic groups.

In 1921 the Chetnik Association for Freedom and Honor of the Fatherland was organized in Belgrade by Chetnik veterans. Its stated aims were to cultivate Chetnik history, to spread Chetnik patriotic ideas, and to care for the widows and orphans of fallen Chetniks and for disabled Chetnik veterans; obviously, however, it was meant also to be a political pressure group,[9] and from the beginning the questions of leadership in the organization and its political orientation were troublesome. The chief influence in the organization was the Democratic Party, but this was challenged by the Radical Party, the most important political party from 1903 to 1918 in Serbia and during the 1920's in the new Yugoslav state, by the very direct method of establishing opposing organizations:

[8] *Ibid.,* pp. 40–50. Pećanac's role in the Toplica Uprising was controversial, but he used it skillfully, and by building it up into a legend he managed to attain the leading position in the Chetnik Association. For the activity of the Chetniks between 1904 and 1918 see also *Vojna enciklopedija,* 2d ed. (1971), II, 259–61.

[9] The Chetnik Association had several kinds of members: regular (i.e. veterans), founding, supporting, honorary, and from 1922 also new members. In order to attract youth, membership was open to men aged sixteen and up. The mass membership was obviously related to the intentions of the association to become a mass movement. Šehić, pp. 55–57.

the pro-Radical, Great Serbian element of the Chetnik membership broke off from the parent association and established in 1924 two new organizations, the Association of Serbian Chetniks for King and Fatherland and the Association of Serbian Chetniks "Petar Mrkonjić."[10] In July 1925 the two organizations merged into the Association of Serbian Chetniks "Petar Mrkonjić" for King and Fatherland. Its actual leader until 1928 was Puniša Račić. Račić was elected to parliament as a Radical Party representative in September 1927, and it was he who, on June 20, 1928, shot and killed two Croatian deputies during a debate in parliament. The "Petar Mrkonjić" Association, plagued by dissension among its leaders, ceased to function sometime in 1928, and in 1929, after the introduction of royal dictatorship, it was dissolved. The former dissidents soon rejoined the original organization,[11] now the only Chetnik group in existence.

Kosta Pećanac became president of the Chetnik Association in 1932. He was interested in enlarging the organization, but his policy of admitting many new members who had no part in the Chetnik past and cared nothing for Chetnik ideals, joining only for political and economic reasons, aroused the opposition of the old-line Chetnik veterans. Some of them, including Ilija Trifunović-Birčanin—who had been president of the association from 1929 to 1932 and was head of another Serbian patriotic organization called the National Defense Association—withdrew and set up a rival organization called the Association of Old Chetniks, but it was no serious challenge. Between the assassination of King Alexander in Marseilles in October 1934 and 1938 the Pećanac-led association expanded on a large scale: in 1938, according to its annual report for that year, it had more than one thousand sections throughout the country with something like five hundred thousand members. After 1935, open activity of the organization was formally prohibited in the banovina (region) of Sava, and apparently also in those of Primorje and Drava, because of the opposition among the Croats and Slovenes against the Chetnik organization, but it appears that its sections in these areas continued to function also in the following years, although on a reduced scale and with some difficulty.[12]

At its height, under Pećanac, the Chetnik organization was composed essentially of people from the Serbian petty bourgeoisie and peasantry.

[10] *Ibid.*, pp. 55–56, 80, 109–10. The leading Chetniks were split not only between those who were nearer to the Democratic and Radical parties but also between those who were formerly friends of the two opposing officers' societies called the Black Hand and the White Hand. Both splits involved power, political principles, and deep emotions. The "Petar Mrkonjić" Association took its name from the nom de guerre of Prince Peter Karadjordjević, who participated as a guerrilla fighter in the uprising against the Turks in northwestern Bosnia in 1876. After the assassination of King Alexander, the last scion of the Obrenović dynasty, in 1903, he became king of Serbia, and in 1918 he was proclaimed king of the new Kingdom of Serbs, Croats, and Slovenes.
[11] *Ibid.*, p. 91.
[12] *Ibid.*, pp. 69, 92, 175–78.

At no time did it have any great number of intellectuals, and partly on this account it was never able to develop a politically attractive program. Even in the early 1920's it borrowed many of its ideas from the program of the Organization of Yugoslav Nationalists (ORJUNA), an organization that relied on force to spread the ideas of integral Yugoslavism. It also closely collaborated with the Serbian National Youth (SRNAO), a creation of the Radical Party. The Chetnik organization presented itself as the protector of the sacred heritage of the Serbian nation in the new Yugoslav state against both foreign and domestic enemies. Its framework was Yugoslav in the sense given to that concept by the Serbian ruling groups, in that it believed that Serbs, Croats, and Slovenes (it did not, of course, recognize the existence of a Macedonian or a Montenegrin nation) were three parts of one and the same nation, who should be united in a centralist, not federalist, form of government; but its orientation was exclusively Serbian nationalist, though much milder in tone than that of the splinter organizations between 1924 and 1929. Also, because it readily served the interests of the Serbian ruling groups, it became known for its anti-democratic, anti-liberal, anti-Communist point of view. But since the leadership of the organization was much of the time corrupt, and at least a portion of its membership was in no way dedicated to the proclaimed ideals and aims of the organization, its influence was never proportionate to its numerical strength.[13]

During the interwar period, a limited amount of instruction in the problems and tactics of guerrilla warfare was given in the military academies and army schools for reserve officers. A confidential manual, *Uput za četničko ratovanje* (Handbook on Guerrilla Warfare), published by the Ministry of the Army and Navy in 1929, distinguishes between two concepts of guerrilla warfare: (1) operations of guerrilla companies in which the special guerrilla units that have been created by regular forces operate either as the vanguard of large units or on their flanks or in the rear of the enemy, in all cases in tactical cooperation with large units, or in the rear of the enemy independently; and (2) the guerrilla or the small war (or what the Germans call *Kleinkrieg*), when the entire army of the country or a large part of it with or without cooperation with regular units switches to guerrilla or irregular war. In the first case the strength of the guerrilla units varies depending on specific tasks; in the second case the formational organization is fixed. In both cases the basic principle of operation is attack and surprise. Successful operation of guerrilla forces presupposes a friendly population and thus its support.[14]

13 *Ibid.*, pp. 105–63.
14 For a brief résumé of the organization of guerrilla units and principles of guerrilla warfare as contained in the handbook of 1929 see *ibid.*, pp. 190–92, or *Vojna enciklopedija* II, 320–21. In 1925 the Yugoslav military authorities issued a confidential handbook on guerrilla operations by Yugoslav Chetnik units in Hungarian territory in the event of war with Hungary. Šehić, pp. 192–95.

In 1938 the Yugoslav General Staff drew up a special report on the subject of guerrilla warfare under modern conditions and the possible use of members of the Chetnik Association in the event of war. The report represented a new attitude toward guerrilla warfare, revising many of the views in the 1929 manual, and without minimizing the Chetnik record in Macedonia and Serbia between 1904 and 1918, it came to the conclusion that operations similar to those carried on from 1912 to 1918 would be impossible in modern war.[15] The tasks formerly performed by the Chetniks in the enemy's rear would have to be entrusted to airborne troops, for example, and the maintenance of order in the country would be ensured by gendarmerie and/or reserve troops. Both this document and the Yugoslav war plans elaborated between 1938 and 1941 indicate that the Yugoslav army leadership did not contemplate any extended use of guerrilla warfare in the event of an invasion. Even less, apparently, did it intend to entrust any important functions to the Chetnik Association.

Nevertheless, as shown in Chapter 3, the Yugoslav government established in April 1940 the Chetnik Command (*Četnička komanda*) which in time organized six full-strength battalions and one partial battalion recruited on a volunteer basis from the regular army. The six complete battalions were assigned one each to the command of an army (there were seven armies in all) and located in Novi Sad, Sarajevo, Skopje, Karlovac, Niš, and Mostar. The Chetnik Command was first located in Novi Sad and then in Kraljevo. A few days after the beginning of the war in April 1941 it withdrew to Sarajevo where, together with the Chetnik battalion in Sarajevo, it surrendered to the Germans on April 18.[16] There is no record that any of the other Chetnik battalions was used for the purpose for which it was established or that any of them, or even portions of them, survived in an organized way or acted after the collapse of the Yugoslav army.

Furthermore, it seems that a short time before the invasion the army did turn to Kosta Pećanac, giving him authority, as well as arms and money, to organize guerrilla units. Of this more will be said presently.

Two things are important to remember in connection with the history of the Chetnik movement in the next four years of war and occupation: first, that the Yugoslav army leadership in the years prior to the invasion of April 1941 had no commitments to guerrilla warfare on a large scale and had made no serious preparations for such activity, and second, that it had no serious plans to utilize the membership of the Chetnik organizations in guerrilla operations. Since throughout the interwar period there were great differences of opinion and persistent squabbles among the leaders of various Chetnik organizations and within the

---

[15] Šehić, pp. 196–97.
[16] *Ibid.*, pp. 209–10.

rank and file as well, it was natural that following the invasion and occupation the interwar Chetniks should be divided. It was hardly to be expected that under the stresses of occupation and civil war, leaders and membership of the Chetnik organizations would unite in a set of common policies toward the armies of occupation, the quisling regimes, and the several resistance groups that were formed in the country. As will be shown, Pećanac soon emerged as an open collaborator with the Germans, Trifunović-Birčanin and the Bosnian Chetnik leader Dobroslav Jevdjević joined the Mihailović movement and became important commanders and his chief liaison officers with the Italian army of occupation, and some of the Chetnik rank and file joined or supported the Partisans.

THE BEGINNINGS OF THE WARTIME CHETNIK MOVEMENT

The nucleus of what later became the Chetnik resistance force was a small group of officers, noncommissioned officers, and men of the Yugoslav royal army, almost exclusively Serbs, who refused to surrender at their post near the town of Doboj in northern Bosnia at the time of the collapse of the Yugoslav army in mid-April 1941. Under the leadership of General Staff Colonel Dragoljub-Draža Mihailović, who at the time of collapse was Deputy Chief of Staff of the Yugoslav Second Army, these men retreated into the hills. Their aim was to move to the mountainous interior of Serbia where they hoped to find other parts of the Yugoslav army whom they would join and with whom they would continue the fight against the enemy. During the following weeks this group moved first southeast and then east toward Serbia. On its way, it encountered and was joined by several small straggling parties of soldiers, but it neither met nor heard of any units of the Yugoslav army offering resistance in the mountains. In the first few days of their retreat, the men were attacked by some German detachments and then later, after crossing into Serbia, by some gendarmes.

On April 28 there were about eighty men in the group, but during the next few days a number of officers and men, fearing hardship and uncertainty, left Mihailović. He himself sent a part of his men to the area of Rudnik Mountain, with orders to meet again about ten days later. Thus, on May 13 when Mihailović and his group reached the shepherds' huts at Ravna Gora, a grazing area on the western slopes of Suvobor Mountain at an elevation of perhaps fifteen hundred to two thousand feet, approximately halfway between the towns of Valjevo and Čačak in western Serbia, Mihailović had with him only seven officers and twenty-four noncommissioned officers and privates. One officer, a Croat, left after a few days and later joined Ljotić.[17] Between the time the Mihailović group realized that no remnants of the Yugoslav army

17 Mešković, "From Bosnia to Ravna Gora," p. 29.

were fighting in the interior mountains and the first days at Ravna Gora, they were faced with the decision of whether to surrender belatedly to the occupation authorities, and probably face stiff punishment, or to become themselves the nucleus of a resistance movement. Mihailović and his men chose the second alternative, and thus began the life of a very controversial resistance movement in Yugoslavia.[18] At Ravna Gora, these soldiers established their headquarters and center of action, hence the name Ravna Gora Movement (*Ravnogorski pokret*), that was and still is often used by the Chetniks when referring to their movement. A former Chetnik commander has given the following reasons for Mihailović's decision to center his organization at Ravna Gora:

Homogeneity of population and its clear national and democratic attitude; uneven and sheltered character of the terrain in relation to communications over which large forces of the occupation troops moved; relative proximity to the more important urban centers, especially to the capital, and more or less central position in regard to the country as a whole; excellent familiarity with the terrain in which Mihailović as a young lieutenant participated during the First World War in the victorious offensive of Suvobor Mountain.[19]

[18] There is a voluminous literature on the Chetnik movement during the Second World War and its leader General Draža Mihailović. From among the writings of former Chetniks themselves and their foreign sympathizers, I list the following as being probably the most important. The two volumes of articles and reminiscences edited by Radoje L. Knežević, *Knjiga o Draži*, were written by Chetnik veterans or ardent Chetnik sympathizers and show all the shortcomings and biases of such works, but they are nevertheless an important source of information especially on the early stages of the movement. Shortcomings and biases are also evident in a series of articles by Radoje Knežević, having the general title "The Yugoslav Government and Draža Mihailović," which was published in six issues of the London journal *Poruka* between November 1952 and November 1954, and in the two publications by Radoje's brother, Lt. Colonel Živan L. Knežević: *Why the Allies Abandoned the Yugoslav Army of General Mihailovich* and *General Mihailovich and U.S.S.R.* (both 1945). In somewhat the same category are four books by Topalović: *Pokreti narodnog otpora u Jugoslaviji 1941–1945* (1958), *Kako su komunisti dograbili vlast u Jugoslaviji* (1964), *Borba za budućnost Jugoslavije* (1967), and *Srbija pod Dražom* (1968), and Fotić's *The War We Lost*. Other useful works are Martin, *Ally Betrayed*; Seitz, *Mihailović: Hoax or Hero?*; Lazitch, *La tragédie du Général Mihailovitch*; Sergije M. Živanović, *Djeneral Mihailović i njegovo delo*; Vučetić, *Gradjanski rat u Crnoj Gori 1941–1945*; and Vukčević, *Na strašnom sudu*. The entire issue of *Glasnik SIKD 'Njegoš'* (a journal published in Chicago by Chetnik exiles) for June 1966 is devoted to the subject of Mihailović.

For views on the Chetniks held by Serbs who during the war were followers of the Ljotić movement or of General Nedić, written in exile, see Karapandžić, *Gradjanski rat u Srbiji 1941–1945*, and Krakov, *General Milan Nedić*. For a Croatian extremist's view of Mihailović see Omrčanin, *Isina o Draži Mihailoviću*.

For the official Yugoslav Communist interpretation of the Chetnik movement and its activities during the Second World War see (under Yugoslavia), Union of the Journalists' Associations, *The Trial of Dragoljub-Draža Mihailović*; *Dokumenti o izdajstvu Draže Mihailovića*, Vol. I; and *Sudjenje članovima političkog i vojnog rukovodstva organizacije Draže Mihailovića*. See also Mi. Mić. [Miloš Minić], "The Chetniks During the Second World War."

In a category by itself is the publication Allied Force, Mediterranean Headquarters, *The Chetniks: A Survey of Četnik Activity in Yugoslavia, April 1941–July 1944*. This publication is based on reports of British liaison officers with Mihailović's and Tito's forces, various reports submitted to the British by a number of Chetnik and Partisan officers, interrogations of various men who had knowledge about wartime Yugoslav affairs, the Yugoslav quisling press, and the copies of Mihailović's messages to the government-in-exile that were sent through the British communication channels.

For the beginnings of armed resistance in Serbia in 1941 and the attempts at Partisan-Chetnik cooperation and their later collision as described by a Yugoslav historian see two works by Marjanović, "Contributions to the History of the Conflict Between the National Liberation Movement and the Chetniks of Draža Mihailović in Serbia in 1941" and *Ustanak i narodnooslobodilački pokret u Srbiji 1941*.

References to other published materials, the German and Italian microfilmed wartime documents, and documents from collections in various archives will be given as we go along.

[19] Vučković, "The Uprising in Western Serbia," p. 129.

Most of Mihailović's followers and most of his domestic and foreign supporters, as well as many other people who are not well informed, claim that this was the first guerrilla force against the Axis powers in Europe, antedating in particular the emergence of the Yugoslav-oriented, Communist-led Partisans.[20] This claim is true only if one considers that simply going into the hills marks the beginning of a guerrilla movement. If one means by a guerrilla movement a political and military organization of relatively large numbers of men and armed operations that are intended to be carried on with determination and more or less continuously, it is certainly not true, for Mihailović, with perhaps only fifty to sixty men (including those he sent to the area of Rudnik Mountain), was hardly prepared to start guerrilla operations or to set off a general uprising in Serbia, let alone in other parts of the country, within six or eight weeks after reaching Ravna Gora. Writing about Mihailović's decision to go to the hills, Vučković stated: "On the following day (April 15) the Supreme Command issued the order about the cessation of hostilities. Mihailović refused to follow the order. On the contrary, he decided to depart for Serbia, hoping to meet some unbroken front or organized resistance and join it with his men."[21] The same statement was made by Mihailović to Colonel Robert H. McDowell, the leader of the last American military mission that was with Mihailović in 1944, from late August until November 1.[22]

A considerable number of other professional and reserve officers in Serbia also refused to surrender or managed to escape the German roundup in mid-April. Some of them joined Kosta Pećanac and a much larger number when they heard of Draža Mihailović and his group went to Ravna Gora and joined him. Since these men were mostly of junior rank, they did not question Mihailović's leadership. Many men who subsequently became important Chetnik commanders or important members at Mihailović's headquarters—among them Radoslav Djurić, Boško Todorović, Duško Todorović, Sima Uzelac, Aleksandar Mišić, Neško Nedić, Miloš Glišić, Zvonimir Vučković, Dragoslav Pavlović, Vučko Ignjatović, Velimir Piletić, Siniša Ocokoljić-Pazarac, Ljubomir Jovanović-Patak, Dragutin Keserović, Nikola Kalabić, Predrag Raković, Ivan Fregl, Rudolf Perhinek—came to Mihailović in this way.[23] Several who became important commanders later on were former civilians with reserve officer standing, such as Nikola Kalabić and Vojislav Lukačević. Yugoslav army officers who were from Montenegro were not kept long as prisoners of war by the Germans and Italians, but were released to

---

[20] Radoje Knežević, "The Beginnings of the Resistance Movement," p. 13, where it is reported that Mihailović himself claimed April 15, the day he decided not to surrender to the Germans, as the beginning of his guerrilla resistance; Knežević dates it from April 23, when Mihailović's group wrecked a bridge—that is, from their first sabotage act.
[21] "The Uprising in Western Serbia," p. 128.
[22] Interview with Colonel McDowell at Stanford University on March 19, 1968.
[23] Mešković, "At Ravna Gora," p. 55. Fregl and Perhinek were Slovenes.

their homes (since the Italians, who occupied Montenegro, had special plans with regard to that territory). A much larger proportion of Montenegrin officers joined the Partisans than was the case in Serbia, but many more joined the Chetniks and in time many of them became leading commanders of Chetnik forces, such as Bajo Stanišić, Djordjije Lašić, and Pavle Djurišić. Two Montenegrins who returned from exile with the first British-Yugoslav military mission, Major Zaharije Ostojić and Major Mirko Lalatović, assumed leading staff positions under Mihailović.

The chief activity of the Mihailović group from mid-May to August 1941 consisted in surveying the potential manpower available to their organization, registering those who were willing to join immediately and preparing mobilization lists of men of military age who could be called when the time came, collecting and setting up caches of arms and ammunition, communications equipment, and other supplies, and planning a strategy of resistance. Although the initial group that came with Mihailović from Bosnia and those officers who joined them in Serbia expected to engage in armed resistance against the armies of occupation, this did not mean that they planned resistance immediately: some delay, from their point of view, was not only logical and prudent but also under the existing conditions unavoidable. After all, they were only a few score in number, they were just starting to set up their organization, they did not know what the general mood of the people was, and they lacked arms, ammunition, and other necessary supplies. In fact, the fundamental component of their strategy from the outset was to organize and build up their strength, but to postpone actual armed struggle against the armies of occupation until the time when, under the onslaught of the Western Allies who they expected would land in Yugoslavia, these armies began withdrawing from Yugoslavia.

Soon after arriving at Ravna Gora Mihailović and his men organized a command post and designated themselves the Chetnik Detachments of the Yugoslav Army (*Četnički odredi jugoslovenske vojske*).²⁴ The name Chetnik was of course derivative, but the guerrilla organization was in no sense based on the prewar Chetnik Association or the Association of Old Chetniks nor did it grow out of the Chetnik Command of the Yugoslav Army that was established in April 1940. Nevertheless, Mihailović built his organization to some extent on the long and esteemed tradition of the Serbian fighting guerrillas.

In addition to the military headquarters at Ravna Gora Mihailović

---

²⁴ This name was subsequently changed to Military-Chetnik Detachments (*Vojno-četnički odredi*); after Mihailović established contact with the government-in-exile and was named Minister of the Army, Navy, and Air Force in January 1942 the name was again changed, to Yugoslav Army in the Homeland (*Jugoslovenska vojska u otadžbini*), and this was the official designation the Chetniks carried to the end of the war. See Mi. Mić., pp. 581–82. The last change in name denoted a formal change of the Mihailović organization from a guerrilla formation into a national army, the successor to the former Yugoslav Royal Army.

organized as early as August 1941 a Central National Committee, composed of a group of persons of some standing in Serbian political and cultural life. (Some of these same persons also served on a Belgrade Committee supporting Mihailović.) The three most important members of the Central National Committee were Dragiša Vasić, the former vice-president of the Serbian Cultural Club and member of the miniscule Republican Party; Dr. Stevan Moljević, a Bosnian Serb and lawyer; and Dr. Mladen Žujović, Vasić's law partner and a fellow member of the Republican Party. For a long time these men formed the Executive Council, and Vasić was specifically designated by Mihailović as the ranking member of a committee of three (including also Lt. Colonel Dragoslav Pavlović and Major Jezdimir Dangić) to succeed him in the leadership of the movement if anything should happen to him.[25]

The Central National Committee, especially the Executive Council, acted as advisers to Mihailović on domestic and international political matters and also maintained liaison with civilian followers in Serbia and other areas in which the Chetniks were strong. Mihailović needed the committee not only for its evident support but also for the political and administrative experience of its members, the kind of experience in which he and his officers were so lacking.[26]

PEĆANAC CHETNIKS UNDER OCCUPATION

In the dark days after the collapse of the country, many Serbs looked to the interwar Chetnik Association and to Kosta Pećanac, the man who had been its president since 1932, for action against the forces of occupation—never doubting Pećanac's patriotism, though recognizing him to be a controversial and reactionary figure. Shortly before the invasion Pećanac had been requested by the Yugoslav Ministry of the Army and Navy to organize guerrilla operations in the southern parts of Serbia, Macedonia, and the Kosovo region, presumably for the purpose of keeping the pro-Bulgarian and pro-Albanian population of these regions in check.[27] He was supplied with a certain amount of arms and money, and he succeeded in organizing and arming perhaps several hundred men, concentrated in the Toplica River valley in southern Serbia. This force was still intact after the Germans occupied Serbia, and its ranks were strengthened by Serbian refugees from Macedonia and Kosovo. Some clashes apparently took place between these detachments and Albanian bands in the early summer months of 1941, during the period

[25] Lazitch, "From the History of Ravna Gora," p. 171. According to Lazitch, Vasić wrote a history of the Ravna Gora movement, but the manuscript has never been found.
[26] For more data on the Central National Committee see The Trial of Draža Mihailović, pp. 316-19.
[27] Mešković, "At Ravna Gora," p. 65. Mešković says that Pećanac was authorized to cross the frontiers of the country if necessary. The most thorough study of the Pećanac organization and its activity from April to October 1941 is Petrović, "The Chetnik Organization of Kosta Pećanac in Occupied Serbia Until the Beginning of October 1941."

when Mihailović, still unknown to most of the Serbian population, was organizing his forces from Ravna Gora. In these early days of the occupation and for quite some time thereafter the term Chetnik was identified only with Pećanac's detachments, who were far better known than the *Dražinovci* or Draža's men.[28]

Pećanac was the absolute lord over his detachments. His commanders or *vojvodas* were all of his personal choosing—mainly former officers (including, briefly, one general), peasants, Orthodox priests, teachers, and merchants—men with no political talent or experience. The organizational structure was of the simplest sort.[29] But though the Pećanac detachments enjoyed a certain reputation and attracted more recruits during the first three months of occupation, they seem to have done no fighting except against the Albanian bands. With the appearance of the Communist-led Partisans Pećanac apparently decided to abandon any idea of becoming a resistance force, and by late August he had reached agreements with both the Serbian quisling government and the German occupation authorities to use his detachments against the Partisans.[30] In other words, within five months of the invasion, the Pećanac Chetnik organization had become an outright instrument of the occupation regime.

This role of course demanded a stronger organization, as well as supplies, arms, funds for salaries, and so on. There had to be trained officers, and for the purposes of liaison and coordination of activities a German officer was assigned to Pećanac's headquarters. Pećanac presented his requests in a lengthy aide-mémoire of October 7, 1941, addressed to General Nedić,[31] and in time he seems to have got most of what he asked for. As of January 17, 1942, according to German data, 72 Chetnik officers and 7,963 men were being maintained (fed, clothed, armed, and paid) by the Gendarmerie Command of the Serbian state.[32] This was somewhat short of the top authorized strength of 8,745 men, and it included perhaps two to three thousand Mihailović Chetniks who had legalized themselves since November 1941.

On August 18, 1941, at the time when Pećanac was about to conclude

[28] Petrović writes, p. 178: "Only after Kosta Pećanac became compromised at the end of August owing to his open declaration of support for quisling Nedić did the Draža Mihailović movement start to compete successfully with Pećanac's Chetnik organization."

[29] For the organization and some of the activities of the Pećanac Chetniks from early July to the end of September 1941 see a series of their documents captured by the Germans in Microcopy No. T-314, Roll 1457, Frames 577–98. For an interesting description of the organization and the conditions in the Pećanac detachments see also Drainac, *Crni dani*. Rade Drainac was a Serbian poet who spent some time with the Pećanac Chetniks in 1941–42. He died during the war and his book was published posthumously.

[30] Marjanović, *Ustanak 1941*, pp. 73–80, 126–27, 174–76, and *passim*; Petrović, "The Chetnik Organization of Kosta Pećanac," pp. 186–90.

[31] Microcopy No. T-501, Roll 246, Frames 501–9. The letter contains a shrewd, almost prophetic observation (Frame 504): "I do not understand the followers of Colonel Mihailović and their organization because they have united with the Communists, which is going to cost them their life. Mihailović thinks that he can outsmart the Communists, but he is utterly mistaken."

[32] *Ibid.*, Roll 247, Frame 757.

his arrangements with the Germans, an emissary of Mihailović brought a letter to Pećanac in which Mihailović suggested an agreement between the two whereby Pećanac would be in charge of the Chetnik organization south of the Western Morava River while Mihailović would be in charge in all other areas. Pećanac was not interested, but he suggested that he might offer Mihailović the post of his chief of staff and that Mihailović's detachments should disband and the men join his detachments.[33] On August 27 Pećanac issued an open challenge in the form of a "Proclamation to the Dear People," in which he described himself as the defender and protector of the Serbian people and called "on detachments that have been formed without his approval" (an obvious allusion to Mihailović's detachments) to unite under his command; all those in the forests were to return at once to their homes, under pain of death. He also warned that all those who were engaging in acts of sabotage against public buildings and communications as well as everything that belonged to the occupation authorities would be put to death.[34] It has been suggested by one writer that the representatives of Pećanac and Mihailović reached an agreement in September on the division of territory to be controlled by each and the nature of their activities against the Partisans,[35] but I have not found any confirmation of this assertion either in the wartime documents or in the more recent Yugoslav writings on the Pećanac Chetniks.

Pećanac was a willing tool of the Germans, who sought to ingratiate himself by suggesting on one occasion, for example, that sterner measures should be employed against the Partisans and by expressing views that even the Germans considered excessive,[36] but his career as a Chetnik leader for the Axis was soon ended. The Germans quickly discovered that his force of over eight thousand men was inefficient and unreliable and of little military help to them, and by March of 1943 they disbanded it completely as they did the Mihailović legalized Chetniks. Nothing is known of Pećanac's activities in the succeeding months, but for some time he was interned, apparently by the Serbian quisling authorities, and in June 1944 he was executed by the Chetniks of Draža Mihailović.[37]

More for showing the complexity of conditions in Serbia in the summer of 1941 and as an illustration of competition for the leadership of

[33] Mešković, "At Ravna Gora," pp. 65–66.
[34] *Ibid.*, pp. 66–68; Petrović, "The Chetnik Organization of Kosta Pećanac," pp. 188–89.
[35] Marjanović, *Ustanak 1941*, pp. 191–92.
[36] Microcopy No. T-501, Roll 247, Frames 1019–22. At the same conference, on March 18, 1942, Pećanac told the Germans that his commanders had made contact with Italian forces on the Albanian border and had received some arms from them—a statement that was confirmed by the Italian liaison officer who served with the German occupation forces in Serbia in early December 1941. The subject of discussion between Pećanac's representatives and the Italians was possible Pećanac aid against the Communists in the Italian-occupied parts of Sandjak. See Microcopy No. T-821, Roll 21, Frame 287.
[37] Mešković, "At Ravna Gora," pp. 67–68; RG 226, OSS–File No. L40002.

nationalist resistance forces than because of its intrinsic importance, it is necessary to mention here the case of a Yugoslav brigadier general named Ljubo Novaković (a Montenegrin by birth), who fled from a military hospital in Valjevo, Serbia, in the latter part of May 1941 and in June appeared at Mihailović's headquarters at Ravna Gora. Novaković got a cool reception from Mihailović and his men, who suspected him, because of his higher military rank, of having ambitions to supplant Mihailović as the guerrilla leader. Novaković soon left to join Pećanac, who put him in command of his detachments in Šumadija, an area not far from Mihailović's headquarters.[38] Seeing that Pećanac had started to collaborate with the Germans and that Mihailović was biding his time, Novaković issued on September 18 an order stating his objectives and calling on his commanders and their detachments to assemble on September 22 for action.[39] But practically no one showed up, and Novaković was relieved by Pećanac of his command.[40] He then left Serbia for eastern Bosnia, where he reportedly worked against the Partisans in that area. Toward the end of January 1942 he was captured by the Partisans and taken to Foča, where they had their headquarters.[41] He was kept under Partisan surveillance there for some time, possibly for eventual use to counteract Mihailović's influence among the Chetniks in eastern Bosnia. It happened that in March a British military mission (of which more will be said in Chapter 8), arrived at Partisan headquarters on its way to Mihailović. In mid-April when the mission left Foča (without telling the Partisans of their intentions) Novaković went along.[42] He eventually turned up in Montenegro, and it seems that toward the end of 1943 he began reassembling the disorganized remnants of the Chetniks there, but was caught by the Partisans, sentenced as a people's enemy, and shot.[43]

DRAŽA MIHAILOVIĆ

Colonel (later General) Dragoljub-Draža Mihailović was the man in whom during most of the war years rested the hopes and faith of a majority of Serbs within Yugoslavia and in exile. During these years Mihailović was not by any standards a brilliant or even a fairly good military leader, but there is much in his background that helps to explain why he became the commander of the pro–government-in-exile armed forces.

---

[38] Mešković, "At Ravna Gora," pp. 68–70; Marjanović, *Ustanak 1941*, p. 77.

[39] Microcopy No. T-314, Roll 1457, Frames 605–13. For a report of the Intelligence Officer of the Plenipotentiary Commanding General in Serbia of September 22 discussing the resistance groups in Serbia, including the one of Novaković, see *ibid.*, Frames 662–65.

[40] On Novaković's failure see the report of the Orašac County office to the Ministry of Interior of Sept. 23, 1941. *Ibid.*, Frames 575–76.

[41] *Zbornik DNOR*, Tome II, Vol. 2, p. 275.

[42] *Ibid.*; also Tome II, Vol. 3, pp. 390–91.

[43] *Ibid.*, Tome II, Vol. 2, p. 275.

Like many thousands of other Serbs who were officers or government employees in interwar Yugoslavia, Mihailović belonged to the second generation of urbanized peasants. He was born on April 27, 1893, in the small town of Ivanjica about fifty kilometers south of Čačak in southwestern Serbia, where his father was a county clerk.[44] Two of his uncles were army officers. He grew up at a time when Serbia, though still bound by the patriarchal traditions common to all the Balkan countries, was undergoing extraordinary political, economic, and military growth, and when the Serbian youth were imbued with a tremendous national pride and faith in the mission of their nation.

After the required six years of gymnasium Mihailović entered the Serbian Military Academy in September 1910. He participated in the Balkan Wars of 1912–13 as a cadet and in July 1913 was commissioned as a lieutenant at the top of his class. He served in the First World War and made the exodus with the Serbian forces over Albania in 1915, and later, on the Salonika front, earned a number of decorations.

Because of an incident at the beginning of the war, he had failed to obtain one of the regular promotions, but he advanced in the normal way during the interwar period. From 1921 to 1923 he attended the Graduate School of the Military Academy, and after additional preparation was shifted in 1926 to the General Staff branch of service. Between 1927 and February 1935 he was first Deputy to, then Chief of Staff of, the Commander of the Royal Guards. In June 1935, after a short stint in the Organizational Section of the General Staff, he was assigned to the post of military attaché at Sofia (duly promoted to the rank of colonel in September 1935), but he left that post the following April when the Bulgarian government, because of his contacts with some Bulgarian officers who were out of favor, requested his transfer. He was reassigned in the same capacity to Prague, where he remained until May 1937. During his two years of foreign duty he seems to have established good contacts not only with officers of the countries in which he was stationed but also with the Soviet military attachés whom he met, and he also acquired additional experience in intelligence work.

Between May 1937 and April 1941 Mihailović held several different positions in the Yugoslav military establishment, moving from Chief of Staff of the Drava Divisional Region in Ljubljana, to Commander of the 39th Infantry Regiment in Celje, Slovenia, then to the post of the Chief of the Fortifications Section in the Ministry of the Army and Navy, followed by a teaching assignment at the Military Academy, finally becoming Chief of the General Department of the Office of the

---

[44] Most of the data on Mihailović's life up to 1941 is taken from his personal file found by the Germans in the archives of the Yugoslav Ministry of the Army and Navy. See Microcopy No. T-314, Roll 1457, Frames 1203–7. See also the articles on Mihailović by Purković and Milosavljević in *Knjiga o Draži*, Vol. I, and Stojanović, "How Draža Mihailović Was Punished."

Inspector of the Army. His professional interest all along was infantry tactics, but toward the end of the 1930's he became interested in guerrilla warfare. Early in 1939, when in service at Celje, he drew up and submitted to his superiors a plan for reorganizing the Yugoslav armed forces on the principle of national origin—that is, Serbian, Croatian, and Slovene—apparently on the theory that divided rather than mixed units would improve the army's cohesion and defensive capabilities. The plan was sharply resented by his superiors and on November 1, 1939, he was punished with thirty days of strict arrest which was posted throughout the entire army. He was punished again with thirty days' arrest in November 1940 for attending, in uniform, without permission, a quasi-social quasi-political gathering arranged for the officials of the Association of Reserve Noncommissioned Officers by the British military attaché in Belgrade. After this second incident he apparently barely escaped being transferred out of the elite General Staff branch of service or being put on the retired list. Despite these incidents, however, in his personal army file he is described as "a persevering worker and excellent officer."[45]

Some months before the invasion Mihailović was made Deputy Chief of Staff of the Sixth Army Region in Mostar, a post described by one of his later commanders, Major Vučković, as "completely insignificant."[46] His wartime post of Deputy Chief of Staff of the Second Army, with which he was serving in northern Bosnia at the time of collapse, was equally insignificant. He was on friendly terms with Bora Mirković and he took part in the preparation of the revolt of March 27, 1941,[47] but since he was not in Belgrade at the time, one should interpret this probably as meaning that he, along with many other officers, was informed of the coup in advance by the leaders in Belgrade.

Until April 1941 Mihailović was thus no more outstanding than many another Yugoslav General Staff officer—somewhat above average, schooled in traditional military thinking, though displaying some independence of mind. He probably had only a slight knowledge of international affairs (of foreign languages he spoke French and Bulgarian), and of course he had no experience in political organization and management. Most assuredly, he had very little of the military and political acumen and flexibility required in a man who by chance became the leader of a resistance movement in a country already deeply divided by old national and religious differences, and now torn apart also by occupation and political and social revolution. What he did have was a deep devotion to the dynasty and to the Serbian-dominated political order in Yugoslavia, and during the war years, though he always spoke of

[45] See Microcopy No. T-314, Roll 1457, Frame 1206.
[46] "The Uprising in Western Serbia," p. 128.
[47] *The Trial of Draža Mihailović*, p. 333.

himself as simply an officer, he demonstrated that devotion with a stubborn determination and single-mindedness of purpose.

THE START OF ARMED RESISTANCE

Radoje Knežević in the first installment of the series of articles by him in *Poruka* ("The Yugoslav Government and Draža Mihailović") says that Mihailović's Chetniks had their first armed clash with the Germans as early as May 28, 1941, in the village of Ljuljaci, which lies on the highway between Kragujevac and Gornji Milanovac, and that they were therefore the first guerrillas in Europe in the Second World War.[48] No such incident is mentioned in German reports from Serbia; if one did indeed occur, it must have involved only a small armed group belonging to local authorities. It was certainly not a planned guerrilla attack on the Germans which was followed by other planned attacks, and it cannot be regarded as the start of armed resistance in Yugoslavia. Chetnik sources, furthermore, make it quite clear that Mihailović did not want an early military confrontation with the Germans, since from a military point of view such a confrontation was considered to be futile. There is one documented case of an isolated, obviously unplanned clash between a German unit and a group of Yugoslav soldiers who were hiding out in a village in northeastern Serbia during the early days of occupation. One German officer was killed, and in reprisal the Germans executed one hundred Serbs. This was done on the basis of an order by the Commander of the German Second Army, Colonel General Maximilian von Weichs, of April 28.[49] This was the first time that this formula was applied in occupied Serbia; it was to be applied later again and again on the basis of other orders. But the clash itself did not mark the start of a guerrilla war.

Some clashes also occurred in eastern Herzegovina prior to the outbreak of organized resistance. These began sporadically, between June 3 and 23, and grew to mass proportions before being quelled around July 7. Briefly, what happened was this. On May 20, two days after the signing in Rome of the treaties between Italy and the Independent State of Croatia, the Italians turned over the administration of eastern Herzegovina to the Croatians, though without immediately withdrawing their own garrisons. The Croatian authorities at once began appointing commune mayors and county prefects, setting up local units of the Ustasha, and bringing in several hundred gendarmes, Domobrans, and Ustasha militia men to maintain order. Since the Croatian (Catholic) popula-

[48] *Poruka*, No. 8, p. 5.

[49] For the description of this incident and the text of the order on repressing such attacks in the future, together with the announcement that 100 people had been shot in reprisal, see *Trials of War Criminals Before the Nuernberg Military Tribunals under Control Council Law No. 10*, XI, 799–801.

tion in eastern Herzegovina (in the counties of Bileća, Gacko, and Nevesinje) was only a very small minority, around 1.1 percent of the total, nearly all the appointed local officials and organized Ustashas were Moslems, who made up about 23.7 percent of the population of the area.[50] The new authorities at once began to consolidate their rule by mounting a hate campaign against the Serbian population which made up about three-fourths of the total. On June 1, in several towns and villages there occurred shootings of Serbs, and many shops owned by Serb merchants and artisans were seized on various pretexts. Two days later there were several instances of armed retaliation by villagers; those villages were then burned by Ustasha units, and there were mass shootings, and thus the scale of violence mounted. On June 24, two days after the German attack on the Soviet Union, the rebellion assumed mass proportions in which some three thousand men, including some Montenegrins, participated. The rebels overpowered several gendarmerie posts and seized or blockaded a couple of towns. Finally, under pressure of six to eight battalions of Croatian quisling troops equipped with several artillery pieces (and after being promised that they would not be punished), the bulk of the rebels gave up. The more determined ones fled to mountain hiding places, but by July 7 the Croatian quisling forces were again in full control of all towns and communications in the area.[51]

There is no doubt that the uprising in eastern Herzegovina was a spontaneous, unorganized outburst, and as such it was doomed to rapid failure. It must be stressed that neither the Mihailović Chetniks nor the leadership of the Communist Party of Yugoslavia, despite the reports of Croatian military authorities and later of various Yugoslav writers that the rebelling groups carried red flags, had anything at all to do with the abortive uprising. Rather, it occurred as a culmination of many resentments and conditions—the Ustasha terror, the mingled hate and fear of the new regime, the long local tradition of rebelliousness against the Turkish rule, the deplorable poverty of the region, and to some extent news of the invasion of Russia.

Of a completely different nature was the uprising that began in western Serbia early in July—and marked the start of armed resistance in Yugoslavia. This uprising was directly and fundamentally related to

[50] These are figures of the census of March 31, 1971, and have to be taken only as indicating the probable order of magnitudes existing in 1941. Yugoslavia, Federal Statistical Office, *Nacionalni sastav stanovništva po opštinama*, Statistical Bulletin No. 727, pp. 12–18. Present-day communes are approximately of the same size as counties in 1941.

[51] For General Glaise's reports on the uprising in Herzegovina, based on data furnished to him by Croatian military authorities, dated June 28, 30, July 1, 2, 3, 4, 10, and 12 see Microcopy No. T-501, Role 264, Frames 1185–1212. General Glaise, the German Plenipotentiary General in Croatia, thought that the Italians might have purposely refrained from interfering with the uprising. For Yugoslav interpretations of the uprising see the articles by Bajić; Kovačević and Skoko; and Piljević.

the German attack on the Soviet Union on June 22. In response to the appeals from Stalin and the Comintern to the European Communist parties to begin sabotage and attacks on the Germans in order to draw off some of the pressure on the Russian front, the Yugoslav Communist Party at a meeting of its leaders on July 4 in Belgrade decided to do the following things: to shift from sabotage and diversions to a general uprising, to move earlier organized shock groups to the countryside, to organize Partisan detachments and begin action, and to call upon the Yugoslav people to rise against the enemy. For the first time since April the Germans were vulnerable, having withdrawn practically all their forces from Yugoslavia for operations against the Soviet Union; and the psychological situation was favorable, since Russia was now a part of the anti-Hitler alliance. The Yugoslav Communists by and large were ready, with a countrywide underground organization with military committees that had been preparing themselves since April, and with a strong and undisputed leader, Josip Broz Tito, who could now assume the role of commander in chief.

The first fighting broke out on July 7 in the village of Bela Crkva near the town of Krupanj in western Serbia when the quisling gendarmerie tried to disperse a public meeting; in the fighting two gendarmes were killed. From there the fighting spread, and within a few weeks the uprising had acquired mass proportions in Serbia.[52] On July 13 fighting broke out in Montenegro, on July 22 in Slovenia, on July 27 in Croatia and in Bosnia and Herzegovina. In Macedonia, where the regional CPY leadership refused to follow the orders of the Central Committee, the uprising was delayed and started only on October 11, after the regional leadership had been changed. During the month of August the uprising in Serbia grew greatly in intensity and became a serious problem to both the German occupation authorities and the Serbian quisling regime.

From the German point of view it was very important to establish whether the uprising in Serbia was supported by the nationalist circles and by armed groups organized by nationalists, because they thought that only with nationalist backing could it acquire a mass character. Reports of August 1, 8, and 12 from Felix Benzler, representative of the German Ministry of Foreign Affairs with the Military Commander in Serbia, to his Ministry (and from there to Hitler's headquarters)[53] indicating that the strength of the Communist uprising might draw in nationalist forces as well, were followed by a request of August 14 from

---

[52] For the beginnings of the Partisan uprising in Serbia from the pen of individuals who had leading positions in the field see Čolaković, *Zapisi iz oslobodilačkog rata*, Vol. I, and Dudić, *Dnevnik 1941*. Rodoljub Čolaković, was a member of the Chief Headquarters of Serbia until the end of September 1941 when he was transferred to Bosnia; Dragojlo Dudić, a peasant and long-time CPY member, held both military and political positions until he was killed on November 29, 1941.

[53] For the gist of the telegrams of August 1 and 8 and the full text of the one of August 12 see *DGFP*, Series D, Vol. XIII, p. 308.

the Headquarters to the Military Commander in Serbia for further information. In his answer of the same day the Military Commander stated: "The spread to Serbian nationalist circles of Communist terrorist and sabotage activities, which as far as now can be established are conducted according to a uniform plan, which continue and are also directed against the Wehrmacht, cannot be proved at this time."[54]

On August 27 Benzler had more bad news for Berlin: "Since my telegram of August 12," he reported, "the situation has become more acute. The communist movement is spreading and is operating with nationalist slogans which begin to meet with a response. The misery of the Serbian refugees expelled from Croatia and Hungary and their stories keep adding to the fuel. Contacts with Communists and other rebels in Macedonia, Croatia, Montenegro, etc., are growing closer."[55] Two days later Benzler notified Berlin that German military and police forces in Serbia were insufficient to control the situation, and since reinforcements had been denied, the decision had been made to reorganize the Serbian government and to allow it to increase its armed effectives to have "the Serbs themselves crush this Communist activity so as to prevent the union of Communist and nationalist elements which is developing."[56]

By September, evidently after seeing the considerable success of the uprising and observing its wide, and growing, support among the people, the Chetniks realized that if they did not join in the fight against the Germans they would be forfeiting the leadership of the Serbian people completely to the Communists. Benzler reported this new development on September 12: "Under the influence of nationalistically camouflaged communist slogans, individual Chetnik groups are now also taking positions against the German occupation troops, although so far there has been no fighting involving them."[57] Later in the month some Chetnik detachments actually began fighting the Germans either in conjunction with the Partisans or on their own.

On September 16, obviously after receiving additional information, the Command Staff of the Military Commander in Serbia summarized in a report the development of the uprising thus far, and among other things said: "stimulated by partly successful fighting on the part of the Communists, the nationalist Serbs have also organized detachments against the Germans: [there is] cooperation of Communist and nationalist bands; and active fighting of both groups (partly together) against the German forces."[58]

In addition to Benzler's reports, we have another contemporary source

[54] Microcopy No. T-501, Roll 246, Frames 83–85.
[55] *Ibid.*, Frame 334.
[56] *DGFP*, Series D, Vol. XIII, p. 400.
[57] *Ibid.*, p. 411.
[58] *Ibid.*, p. 479.

of information about the early stages of the rebellion that comes from the Chetniks. This is a report prepared in the second half of September for the Yugoslav government-in-exile by Dr. Miloš Sekulić, a physician and prominent member of the Serbian Agrarian Party, after he reached Istanbul from occupied Serbia with regular traveling documents. Having had recent contacts with both General Nedić and Colonel Mihailović, as well as with Communist functionaries, he could be trusted to make an up-to-date report on conditions in Serbia, including the "tasks of the Yugoslav army" (Mihailović's forces), and Chetnik and Communist action. According to Sekulić, the actions of the army and of the Chetniks together represented "combined people's action," whereas the Chetnik leader Kosta Pećanac, who was collaborating with the enemy, had the backing of only a few. The Yugoslav army thought that it should fight until the victory over the Germans was achieved; it knew that it could not be of much influence on the developments on the main fronts, but it was convinced that the Allies would win, and that its duty was to resist whenever it was attacked and whenever it could, and that was what it was doing. The report continues:

[the army's] main task will be in the time of the interregnum, namely, at the time of collapse of the German army. At that time the army will have three objectives . . . First, to maintain law and order in the country so as to prevent robberies and banditry.

Second, to disarm the Germans, and if possible to kill them, in order that their graves might remind the Germans of the fate of those who attack much weaker enemies. . . .

Third, to punish all those who have helped the enemy . . .

In agreement with these objectives three kinds of companies are being organized in the country and they are headed by officers.[59]

Sekulić states that the Chetnik action "has a defensive character, and it only exceptionally engages in so-called sabotage. It is still in the phase of organization and it enters into action only when it gets in touch with the enemy." Of the Communist action he takes quite a different view:

Communist action is of an offensive nature. Their detachments are spread throughout the country . . .

These detachments are bound together by the central leadership and its orders.

. . . All those inclined toward the Communists and their friends, that is, not only the organized Communists but all those who are inclined to fighting and offensive action and demand an immediate attack on the Germans, enter into this action. One could say that often only the leader of the detachment is a Communist, while its members have not the slightest idea about Communism.

These detachments are headed by intellectuals, workers, peasants, and even reserve and active officers. The morale of these detachments is excellent and

[59] Archives of the Institute of Military History, Belgrade, Government-in-Exile Documents, Reg. No. 12/2, p. 53, Box 20.

the disposition is for immediate action and sabotage. . . . Evidently, they do not think about the situation in the period of the interregnum; they act immediately and directly in order to help the Soviet forces and to speed up the end of the war.[60]

But there is still more evidence to show that it was the Communists, not the Chetniks, who started the first guerrilla uprising against the Germans in Yugoslavia. One proof is contained in the protocol of the meeting held between Mihailović and the representatives of the Plenipotentiary Commanding General in Serbia in the village of Divci on November 11. At this meeting—of which more will be said below—one of Mihailović's close aides, Colonel Branislav J. Pantić, made this statement: "The Communists were the first to start the fight, whereas Mihailović stood completely aside and was preparing to strike in the direction of Bosnia and Sandjak. He wanted to take revenge on the Ustashas who had tortured to death hundreds of thousands of Serbs."[61]

Additional proof from the Chetnik side is to be found in a pamphlet prepared by Branko Lazitch (pseudonym of Branislav Stranjaković), one of the leaders of the Chetnik youth movement in Serbia, who was assigned by the Mihailović headquarters early in 1944 to do research and write on various outstanding political problems in Yugoslavia. Here is what this pamphlet says:

Second, they prove this [the anti-Serbian attitude of the Yugoslav Communists] by the fact that they started an uprising [*digli ustanak*] in Serbia and in Montenegro at a time when the Serbian population in Bosnia and Herzegovina and Lika and Banija was being exerminated. Instead of advising the Serbian people in other regions to defend their brothers from the Ustashas, the Communists turned them against the occupier; instead of seeing to it that by their intervention the number of Serbian victims in Croatia was reduced, the Communists pushed into misfortune the Serbs outside Croatia as well; and not only was the number of victims not reduced in Croatia, but the enemy was provoked elsewhere and this resulted in new victims. *Was it only a coincidence or a deliberate plan that at the same time when Pavelić carried out massacres of Serbs in Croatia, Josip Broz pushed the Serbs into uprising in Serbia and Montenegro?*

Third, the Communists proved their anti-Serbian character not only by the fact that they pushed the Serbs outside Croatia into death, but also by the fact that they started their action against the Serbs also in Croatia. During the most horrible massacres of Serbs in Croatia [in the summer of 1941], the Communist Party started the uprising in Serbia and Montenegro . . .[62]

---

[60] *Ibid.*, p. 55. Soon after the receipt of the Sekulić report, Prime Minister Simović received a new report by way of Lisbon, brought there by Gradimir Bajloni, a student, and member of a prominent Belgrade family. It confirmed the substance of Sekulić's report and by Chetnik sources described the situation as of October 1 as follows: "Serbia—Communist detachments throughout the country conduct open armed activity and sabotage against the Germans, under the slogan of a struggle for liberation. . . . They are active and in a fighting mood. They are especially active in western Bosnia, which they practically control. . . . Montenegro—There the uprising started in June [*sic*] and was led by the Communists. At the outset successful, the uprising led to a severe occupation regime in Montenegro and a large number of victims." Kljaković, in *Politika*, Nov. 4, 1970.

[61] Microcopy No. T-314, Roll 1457, Frame 1322.

[62] Lazitch, *Osnovne istine o radu i ciljevima Tita i komunista*, p. 56. The italicized question (in

Major Vučković, one of the important Chetnik commanders, in his article entitled "The Uprising in Western Serbia," also credits the Communists with having begun the resistance. One of the fundamental tasks of the Chetnik movement, he explains, was "at an opportune moment, when the prospects for the success of the action should be favorable, to inaugurate an uprising," but he goes on to say: "Thus the movement of Draža Mihailović, by the force of circumstances rather than by its own initiative, was induced to enter into action in September 1941 and to carry it on at great sacrifice."[63] The "opportune moment" of course meant when the Allies landed in the Balkans, and since there were no landings in the summer of 1941, the "force of circumstances" that brought Mihailović into action had to be the successful Partisan uprising. Not the least authoritative source is Mihailović himself, who at his trial conceded that it was the Partisans who started the uprising in Serbia.[64]

Another favorite thesis of Chetniks in exile is that the uprising in Serbia resulted from the intervention of Moscow with the British to start armed action behind German lines to relieve German pressure on the hard-pressed Russians. The best and most authoritative formulation of this thesis was given by Radoje Knežević:

The uprising in western Serbia, which Mihailović did not want in the first place —because as a professional soldier he knew that the "liberated territory" could not be held—erupted in August and September 1941, not under the pressure of the Communist Party, as the Communists maintain, and many believe. That uprising started because the Allies asked this from Mihailović, in order to reduce even slightly the German pressure on the Russian front. Mihailović never wanted to push the people into unnecessary military adventures, because to him it was not without meaning whether Yugoslavia was to be peopled by Yugoslavs or Chinese. But he agreed to this uprising, and led it masterfully, as an action necessary from the general Allied plan, and without regard to sacrifice.[65]

This thesis, accepted also by Major Vučković, is no more tenable than other Chetnik attempts to build up the history of the Chetnik role in the war. Neither Knežević nor Vučković goes as far as to say exactly when the British asked Mihailović to start an uprising in Serbia, but since we know that the first radio message from Mihailović's group was received at Malta on September 14, and that the first British agent,

---

the original) is intended to suggest a Communist-Ustasha conspiracy against the Serbian nation, a Chetnik thesis repeated many times throughout the war. After the war, Lazitch changed his mind: in his book *Titov pokret i režim u Jugoslaviji 1941–1946* (pp. 17–20) he claims that it was the Chetniks who were the first to start an uprising in Yugoslavia, referring, like Knežević, to the supposed incident near Ljuljaci on May 28, 1941.

[63] "The Uprising in Western Serbia," pp. 131, 134. Another Chetnik commander, Pavle Mešković, who was with Mihailović at Ravna Gora supports this: "Čiča [Mihailović] to the last moment avoided purposeless fighting against the Germans and was forced to accept the fight." "At Ravna Gora," p. 64.

[64] *The Trial of Draža Mihailović*, pp. 117–18.

[65] "On the Occasion of the Tenth Anniversary of the Death [of Draža Mihailović]," p. 339.

Captain Hudson, did not arrive at Mihailović's headquarters until the twenty-fifth of October, the British could not very well have called for an uprising in August or early September. The truth of the matter can be ascertained from several sources. The British-Soviet exchanges on conditions in Yugoslavia started soon after they established contact with Mihailović and heard from Hudson that there were two guerrilla groups in Serbia, one under Mihailović and another under the Communists, which were working at cross-purposes and indeed were engaged in armed struggle with each other. On November 13 the Yugoslav government-in-exile requested its envoy in Kuibyshev to ask the Soviet government to "send urgent instructions to the Communists to collaborate with Mihailović and to work under him in a united effort against the aggressor."[66] On November 24 the British Military Mission in Moscow submitted a memorandum to the Soviet Ministry of War in which it asked the Soviets "to intervene promptly with the rebels in Yugoslavia." This memorandum also stated:

At the particular request of the Soviet government the British government has encouraged the uprising in Yugoslavia, and therefore it is in the interest of the Soviet government to help bring about unity of the insurgents in Yugoslavia . . . the British government regards Colonel Mihailović as the only possible leader and that therefore all parties should obey his orders or should at least work with him.[67]

Knežević and Vučković would have us believe that these exchanges between the British and the Soviets, in which the Yugoslav government-in-exile also participated, bore a direct relation to the start of the uprising in Serbia. But the date of their occurrence, long after the uprising was under way, makes that impossible. The Soviets were simply hoping to get the British to do what they could to intensify the uprising, now that they had established contact with Mihailović, and the British and the Yugoslavs were hoping to get the Soviets to use pressure to bring the Partisans under Mihailović's command. The British, strongly pro-legitimist, agreed with the desires of Prime Minister Simović that there should be a united resistance under Mihailović: Mihailović was, after all, a professional officer, and a Serb, and could be expected to carry on a fight in the great tradition of the Serbian army during the Balkan Wars and the First World War; the Yugoslav Communists were military amateurs, and the British intelligence information from Yugoslavia up to the time of the German invasion had not been of a sort to make them feel optimistic now about the leadership capacities, homegrown initiative, and extent of following of the Yugoslav Communist Party.[68]

[66] Fotić, *The War We Lost*, p. 169.
[67] Quoted in *ibid.*, p. 170.
[68] Auty, MS pp. 7–9, 14, 17.

A general uprising that had started as a result of the initiative and leadership of the Communists rather than by people entitled to legitimacy, and had not started at a signal from the British, clearly did not fit the British formula. During August and September, before dependable information could be obtained and partly on the urging of Simović and at least one message from Yugoslavia by way of Lisbon, the BBC played down the uprising.[69] By mid-October, after it was evident that two different groups were involved, the British were firmly on the Chetnik side. They wanted the two groups to be unified, but on the basis of the Partisans submitting to Mihailović's overall command.

The Chetniks of Draža Mihailović were in fact drawn into the uprising only because they could not stand by and permit the leadership of the aroused Serbian population to fall completely into the hands of the Communists; they did not want the administration in liberated parts of the country to become exclusively Communist controlled, and they were afraid of Communist terror in liberated areas and wanted to prevent it.[70] But Mihailović never became fully committed to the uprising nor, as we shall see, did he stay with it for very long.

In the early stages of the resistance, when everyone faced a common enemy and common problems, some contacts and some cooperation arose naturally between Partisan and Chetnik detachments and leaders here and there in Serbia. (From the Partisan point of view, this was perfectly in accord with the Communist line of a Popular or National Front.) Tito himself has stated that the Partisan Chief Headquarters in Belgrade heard about Draža Mihailović and a group of officers hiding somewhere in the mountains around Ravna Gora, and that he himself had already in July ordered the staff of the Partisan Valjevo Detachment to contact Mihailović and try to persuade him to fight along with the Partisans.[71] Some contacts between the representatives of the two groups took place in Belgrade in July, and during the month of August there were several contacts between representatives of the two groups and apparently some understanding about not attacking each other and some other matters was arrived at.[72] But when Tito, who had just reached the free territory from Belgrade, met Mihailović at Struganik, a village near the town of Valjevo in western Serbia, on September 19 the two leaders both realized that the differences between their tactics and between the aims of their movements were too great for them to

---

[69] A former secretary of the American Legation in Belgrade, Karl Rankin, who left that city in mid-July arrived in Lisbon with a message to the effect that the BBC should stop broadcasting reports of armed actions in Serbia. *Ibid.*, pp. 11–13.

[70] This was how Mihailović explained his actions to the German representatives at the Divci meeting. Microcopy No. T-314, Roll 1457, Frames 1317–21.

[71] Tito, *Borba za oslobodjenje Jugoslavije 1941–1945*, pp. 207–8.

[72] Marjanović, "Contributions," pp. 183–92; *The Trial of Draža Mihailović*, pp. 110–11. See also Dedijer, *Josip Broz Tito*, pp. 301–3. For an early (August 30) statement on combined action of the Partisans and the Chetniks see *Zbornik DNOR*, Tome II, Vol. 1, pp. 44–45.

come to any real compromise.[73] Some tenuous agreements on minor matters were made, but even these lasted only a matter of weeks. By the end of October, all hopes of continuing cooperation had drained away in bickerings and outright violations of the agreements. During these weeks, too, it became clear that, whereas the Partisan leadership had no doubts about carrying on the struggle against the Germans and the Serbian quisling regime, the Chetniks were wavering and looking for a way of giving up the struggle and of directing all their power against the Partisans. It was a process of polarization which in Serbia took several weeks and produced some shifts in loyalties. Thus, for example, the Chetnik detachments of the Reverend Vlada Zečević and Lieutenant Ratko Martinović, which had been cooperating closely with the Partisans, switched completely to the Partisan side.[74] After more than a month of disagreements and minor collisions between the Chetniks and the Partisans, a series of developments which will be elaborated below culminated on November 1 in a Chetnik attack on the Partisans in and around the town of Užice where the Partisans had their headquarters. The Chetnik attempt to overwhelm the Partisans failed, and from that point on the Partisans and Chetniks became gradually more hostile, until they were locked in a determined struggle throughout most of Yugoslavia. This struggle grew to be the most important military and political problem of the war for Yugoslavia, and it was one that had extremely complex international implications.

One final question may be raised here with regard to the Chetniks in western Serbia in the fall of 1941—the question of their numerical strength. No satisfactory answer is possible. Contemporary Partisan sources indicate that in the last week of October the Chetniks had about three thousand men.[75] The problem is in knowing whom to count: only the men in established and operative detachments, or those plus the men who were registered and supposedly ready on call? Also, how many of those Chetniks actually fought? According to a statement of a captured Chetnik commander (Zdravko Drašković), the estimated strength of the Mihailović Chetniks as of October 8 was at least 10,000 men.[76] A German map showing the location of various rebel forces in Serbia as of October 29 indicates for Mihailović 10,000, under a question mark; a report of the Intelligence Officer of the Plenipotentiary Commanding

---

[73] Another meeting between Tito and Mihailović (to be discussed later) was held at the village of Brajići near Ravna Gora on October 27. For the Communist interpretation of these meetings see the two works by Jovan Marjanović pertaining to the conflict between the Chetniks and the Partisans in Serbia in 1941 and the National Liberation War in Serbia in 1941. For Chetnik views on these meetings see e.g. Sergije M. Živanović, III, 8–50. See also the interpretation of a pro-Ljotić writer, Karapandžić, pp. 94–96, 115–18.

[74] Zečević, formerly of the Democratic Party, apparently joined the CPY as early as 1942. Later he held high positions in the Partisan interim government and in the Yugoslav federal and Serbian republican governments. He died in October 1970.

[75] As referred to in Marjanović, *Ustanak 1941*, p. 184.

[76] Microcopy No. T-314, Roll 1457, Frames 351–52.

General in Serbia of November 1, indicates the strength of the Chetniks at between 5,000 and 10,000, but then adds: "The largest proportion of the rebel Chetniks had not yet entered into an open fight against the German forces."[77]

THE CHETNIKS ACHIEVE LEGITIMACY

In the first weeks as an incipient resistance force Mihailović's Chetniks made no effort to get in touch with the government-in-exile, apparently because they blamed the Simović government and the Supreme Command for the humiliating surrender that had occurred.[78] By July or August, however, Mihailović or his friends had made some contact through occasional business travelers from Serbia with Yugoslav representatives in Istanbul; these sources apparently relayed the news that the uprising that was taking place was not being led by former officers of the Yugoslav army, but rather by the Communist Party of Yugoslavia. These reports were duly passed on to the British authorities and to the Yugoslav government-in-exile in London. Reports about the uprising also appeared in the quisling press in Belgrade and in newspapers in various countries in Europe, and on August 8 were broadcast by Radio Moscow. The official British reaction to the happenings in Yugoslavia was expressed by Hugh Dalton, the cabinet member responsible for SOE affairs, in August 1941 as follows:

The Yugoslavs [i.e. the exiled royal Yugoslav government], the War Office and we are all agreed that the guerrilla and sabotage bands now active in Yugoslavia should show sufficient active resistance to cause constant embarrassment to the occupying forces, and prevent any reduction in their numbers. But they should keep their organization underground and avoid any attempt at large scale risings or ambitious military operations, which could only result at present in severe repression and the loss of our key men. They should now do all they can to prepare a widespread underground organization ready to strike hard later on, when we give the signal.[79]

The clear opposition of the government-in-exile to a premature uprising, especially to one not led by royal officers, was conveyed to the Yugoslav people in a speech by Prime Minister Simović over the BBC on August 12, which he concluded thus: "The royal government knows that a handful of unscrupulous men inflict great sufferings upon the people by their premature action. Innocent victims whom the Germans now shoot will be avenged both against the Germans and against those

---

[77] For the map see *ibid.*, Frame 1099 and for the November 1 report *ibid.*, Frames 1133–37. In the same map the Germans estimate the Partisan strength at about 12,700 men. Of course, Partisan estimates are considerably larger.

[78] Marjanović, "Contributions," pp. 196–97; Marjanović, *Ustanak 1941*, pp. 194–95.

[79] Ehrman, p. 77. The British continued to follow this policy at least until the end of 1942, the time when their strategy in the Mediterranean evolved to the point that a general uprising in Yugoslavia would fit well with their plans.

who are responsible for these victims. The hour of liberation is near, and the legitimate government from London will give the signal when the new struggle for liberty should begin."[80] This counsel that the insurgents should wait for the signal from London was to occur like a refrain in government messages to Yugoslavia, and as will be shown later, it agreed fully with Mihailović's views.

On September 13, on orders from British and Yugoslav military and intelligence authorities in the Middle East, a group of officers left Cairo by air for Malta on the first leg of a mission to find out what was going on in Yugoslavia. Their assignment was to establish contact with the insurgents and report on what was happening. The party consisted of Captain Duane T. (Bill) Hudson of the SOE, two Yugoslav air force majors, Mirko Lalatović and Zaharije Ostojić (both Montenegrins), and reserve air force sergeant Veljko Dragićević, as radio operator. Captain Hudson, known in Yugoslavia also under his nom de guerre "Marko," had been a mining engineer at the British-owned Zajača antimony mine in western Serbia but during the months preceding the invasion of Yugoslavia was working for the Belgrade unit of the SOE. He was fluent in Serbo-Croatian. Hudson and the two Yugoslav officers were briefed separately by their respective superiors in Cairo and took separate codes to Yugoslavia. The party was transported from Malta by submarine and landed on the Montenegrin coast on September 22.[81] They very soon encountered a detachment of Montenegrin Partisans who escorted them to the Partisan headquarters for Montenegro, where they also met Milovan Djilas, a delegate from Supreme Partisan Headquarters. From here Hudson filed some reports to his superiors favorable to the Partisans and their organization in the large area of Montenegro that they controlled. Later Hudson and Ostojić (Lalatović and Dragićević made the trip separately and at a slower pace), accompanied by a Partisan commander, Major Arso Jovanović, went to the Partisan headquarters at Užice in western Serbia where they met Tito.[82]

Meanwhile, on September 14, British radio monitoring services at Malta had picked up a message from Mihailović's headquarters identifying themselves and on September 24 had forwarded it, as requested, to the Yugoslav government-in-exile in London;[83] in reply, the British

[80] Kljaković, in *Politika*, Oct. 30, 1970.
[81] *Zbornik DNOR*, Tome II, Vol. 2, p. 209; Deakin, *The Embattled Mountain*, pp. 126, 129, 131, 138; Sweet-Escott, p. 96. The code name of the Hudson mission and its radio link with the British in Cairo was "Bullseye." The same link also carried the messages between Mihailović and the government-in-exile, but all messages that Mihailović sent to his government through British channels had the code name "Villa Resta." *The Četniks*, p. 83.
[82] Deakin gives a full account of Hudson's trip from the coast to Užice in *The Embattled Mountain*, pp. 131–34. See also Leković, "The Sojourn of the British Military Mission in the Liberated Territory of Montenegro and Southeastern Bosnia," pp. 301–2.
[83] For the way in which this contact was established and the authenticity of the radio sources in Yugoslavia verified see Radoje L. Knežević, "The Yugoslav Government and Draža Mihailović," *Poruka*, No. 8, pp. 5–14, esp. pp. 6–7.

promised to send Mihailović aid. On October 9 Hudson had received radio instructions from Cairo to move on without delay to Mihailović in Serbia because he needed safe codes,[84] so after a brief stay at Užice, Hudson and Ostojić continued on for Ravna Gora. They arrived there on or around October 25, and were later joined by Lalatović.[85] By that time Mihailović was already in contact with London and had learned that the British had decided to recognize him as the only legitimate commander of resistance forces in Yugoslavia and would send him aid. This was a turning point in the life of Mihailović's organization. From then on, the Chetniks were an arm of the Yugoslav government-in-exile. The British military mission that was sent to their headquarters imparted a great deal of prestige to the Chetniks; it was a visible expression of their officially having become a part of the Grand Alliance engaged in the struggle against the Axis. This kind of recognition and support was very important for Mihailović, especially now that he was faced not only by the German army of occupation and the Serbian quisling forces but also by the Communist-led resistance, the Partisans.

The recognition of Mihailović by the government-in-exile and the British as the chief of armed resistance in the country had several other consequences favorable to the Chetniks. First, Mihailović's speedy promotions between December 1941 and June 1942 to the highest military rank, his appointment as Minister of the Army, Navy, and Air Force in the government-in-exile in January 1942, and as Chief of Staff of the Supreme Command, which was transferred from Egypt back to the country, in June 1942, made it possible for him to bring under a measure of control the Chetnik and pro-Chetnik resistance groups that arose during the second half of 1941 without any participation of Serbian Chetniks and as a rule in close conjunction with the Partisans in Montenegro, Bosnia and Herzegovina, northern Dalmatia, southwestern Croatia (Lika, Kordun, Banija), and to some extent even in Slovenia. Additional prestige came from the Yugoslav and British propaganda which made him into a hero in the anti-Axis world. Second, Mihailović had the monopoly of contacts with the Western Allies and had normal contacts through the government-in-exile with the Soviet Union, whereas the Western Allies totally ignored the Partisans, even though they were the only force that was actively carrying on the struggle against the Axis powers and the domestic quislings.[86] Third, the Chetniks were the ex-

[84] *The Embattled Mountain*, pp. 130–31.

[85] *Zbornik DNOR*, Tome II, Vol. 2, p. 209. Major Ostojić later became the chief of the operational, organizational, and intelligence departments of the Mihailović forces, and Major Lalatović became a member of the Chetnik Supreme Command. Sergeant Dragićević stayed in Užice a few more days and since during these days the Chetniks launched their attack on Užice, he decided to stay with the Partisans. He became Tito's chief radio operator, promoted to the rank of major; he was killed in the German airborne attack on Partisan headquarters at Drvar on May 25, 1944.

[86] Until October 1942 the BBC did not even mention the Partisans in its broadcasts; when it began doing so, Mihailović was incensed at what he apparently regarded as a "threat to his claim to be the resistance leader." Deakin, *The Embattled Mountain*, p. 182.

clusive recipients for almost two years of what little material and financial help the British and the government-in-exile were able to provide. All these factors combined to strengthen the Chetniks' internal political position among the Serbs and in Montenegro, while at the same time inhibiting the Partisans' political position.

GROWING CONFLICT BETWEEN CHETNIKS AND PARTISANS

As we have seen, the success of the Partisan uprising in Serbia and the popular support that it received forced the hand of Mihailović's Chetniks, and in September some Chetnik detachments joined the Partisans in attacks on the Germans or fought the Germans alone. On September 24, for example, Major Dragutin Keserović, a former Pećanac commander who had switched to Mihailović, attacked the Germans in the area of Kruševac, killing twenty-three German soldiers.[87] In October Partisan units and Chetnik units under the command of Captain Radoslav Račić, Lieutenant Ratko Martinović, and the Reverend Vlada Zečević fought the Germans successfully in various parts of western Serbia.[88] But Mihailović himself was not committed to the uprising, and he soon shifted from a position of a reluctant late-joining partner in the Partisan-initiated resistance to an active opponent of the Partisans. The three principal reasons for this change in position were: the Draconian measures that the Germans were using in an effort to put down the uprising in Serbia, Mihailović's new status as the official leader of all resistance forces in Yugoslavia, enjoying the backing of the government-in-exile as well as of the British, and finally the realization that the Partisans represented the most serious challenge to the Chetnik position in Yugoslavia, both at that time and in the future.

Since the start of armed resistance in Serbia, the German occupation regime had become more severe day by day. Official announcements of and statistics on mass executions beginning on July 15 leave no doubt of this, nor does the documentation on the burning of houses, arrests, the taking of large numbers of hostages, and so on.[89] In the early months of the uprising the German occupation and quisling authorities ascribed the armed actions and sabotage acts exclusively to the Communists (and Jews), at the same time emphasizing that the rank and file of the Serbian population was behaving loyally toward the German and Serbian authorities.[90] German propaganda quite obviously wanted to drive a wedge between the more or less passive majority of the population and

---

[87] Microcopy No. T-314, Roll 1457, Frame 329.

[88] *Zbornik DNOR*, Tome II, Vol. 1, pp. 75–76, 89, 98.

[89] For these announcements and statistics issued by organs of the German occupation authorities or of the quisling regime see the texts in *ibid.*, Tome I, Vol. 2, pp. 297–376.

[90] German propaganda always referred to Communists and Jews together so as to capitalize on any possible anti-Semitic feeling existing among the population at large or to foment such a feeling.

the steadily growing minority who were more and more openly carrying on or supporting resistance.

Despite the demands of the Eastern front, the Germans soon found out that they must strengthen their forces in Serbia if they were to put down the uprising there. In mid-September they brought in a reinforced regiment (the 125th) from Greece and the 342nd Infantry Division from France, and in mid-November they transferred the 113th Infantry Division from the Russian front. On September 16 the policy of extreme brutality in suppressing the armed uprising in Serbia was officially set forth in two documents: Hitler's Directive No. 31a to Field Marshal List ordering him to put down the resistance movement in the southeast, and the Führer's order on the suppression of "Communist Armed Resistance Movements in the Occupied Areas," issued by the German Armed Forces High Command (OKW) under the signature of Field Marshal Keitel. The Führer's order specified that for each German soldier killed one hundred and for each German soldier wounded fifty hostages were to be executed.[91] The gruesome implementation of the order can be clearly seen from the German shooting of perhaps upward of five thousand people in the towns of Kraljevo and Kragujevac in mid-October 1941 as reprisal against attacks on German forces in which probably not more than a score of German soldiers were killed and a somewhat larger number were wounded.[92]

Mihailović thought that this kind of reprisal proved that guerrilla operations of any size would soon become impossible and that even very limited guerrilla activities and sabotage acts would cost an untold number of lives. He had been convinced from the start that the uprising was premature, because the overwhelming power of the Germans made it impossible to gain any lasting military results in terms of holding liberated territory and because the cost in lives would be too high in comparison with any temporary advantages that might be gained. Mihailović and others of his generation remembered vividly the grievous population losses of the First World War, when Serbia as a result of military operations and typhus epidemics lost about 20 percent of its population, and there were present horrors in the reports of great losses among the Serbian population in the Independent State of Croatia at the hands of the Ustashas. Thus Mihailović was only voicing the sentiments of a large proportion of the Serbian people when he urged the saving of

---

[91] For the text of Directive No. 31a see *Hitlers Weisungen*, pp. 128–29; for the text of the OKW order see International Military Tribunal, *Trial of the Major War Criminals*, XXV, 530–33. This order was formally intended to apply to all areas under German occupation but was strictly applied only in Serbia.

[92] German sources indicate the shooting of 1,736 male inhabitants and 19 women in the town of Kraljevo (*Zbornik DNOR*, Tome I, Vol. 1, pp. 554–56) and 2,300 inhabitants in the town of Kragujevac (*Trial of the Major War Criminals*, XXXIX, 366). Some estimates of the number executed on that occasion at Kragujevac alone go as high as 7,000, but the foremost authority on German terror in Serbia puts this figure for Kragujevac at about 3,000. Glišić, pp. 66–67.

Serbian lives. The same views were expressed by the Nedić government, by the Pećanac Chetniks, and by the government-in-exile. Obviously, to continue the resistance against the occupying forces would mean a steadily rising toll in Serbian lives, and there is no question that this certainty was a very important factor influencing Mihailović's behavior.[93]

The worsening military conditions for the rebels in Serbia in consequence of the large-scale German operations against the forces in free territory (the so-called First Enemy Offensive)[94] also increased the tension between the Partisans and the Chetniks; armed incidents between the two began to occur with increasing frequency, and there were numerous cases of the disarming of groups of Partisans by the Chetniks and vice versa. To iron out some of the difficulties and also to respond to the Chetniks' demand to present the Partisan point of view in detail, Tito on October 20 addressed to Mihailović a letter containing twelve points.[95] A meeting was arranged, and on October 27 the two leaders met at the village of Brajići near Ravna Gora.

The differences that emerged at this meeting were even more pronounced than those at the meeting at Struganik. At the meeting in Brajići it seems that at first four propositions, two from each side, were discussed: from the Partisan side that the combined struggle continue against the occupying forces without respect to consequences and that Colonel Mihailović join the Partisan Supreme Headquarters as chief of staff; and from the Chetnik side that the Partisan detachments be put under Mihailović's command and limit themselves to the type of action advocated and carried out by the Chetniks.[96] With each side trying to impose its views on the tactics of uprising and seeking to gain full control over the forces of the other group, agreement on these points was out of the question. Of the twelve points specified by Tito, the Chetniks apparently were unwilling to accept the four most important ones (1, 2, 6, and 7) dealing, respectively, with combined military operations against the Germans and the quisling forces and the establishment of a common operational headquarters; the combined maintenance of troops through a common operational staff; the organization of a temporary system of local government in the form of national liberation

---

[93] The saving of Serbian lives both from German punitive expeditions and from Communist terror was the primary concern expressed by Mihailović to the German representatives at the meeting at Divci. Microcopy No. T-314, Roll 1457, Frames 1317–18. See also Marjanović, "Contributions," pp. 186, 193–94.

[94] Most Yugoslav writers divide the military operations of the Axis forces against the Partisans into seven separate large undertakings or offensives, the first one being the German and Serbian quisling operations against the Partisans (and Chetniks) in western Serbia from about September 20 to the first days of December 1941.

[95] *Zbornik DNOR*, Tome I, Vol. 1, pp. 203–7. The Partisans published the text of their proposals in their newspaper *Borba* in Užice on November 11, 1941.

[96] Sergije M. Živanović, III, 44. The Yugoslav historiography does not mention the fact that Tito offered Mihailović the position of chief of staff at his headquarters, but it was confirmed by Tito himself in an interview with Raymond Tournoux, political director of *Paris Match*, published in the issue of November 16, 1968.

committees that would help maintain the armed forces, including the establishment of a central national liberation committee for the whole liberated territory and the use for the maintenance of law and order of the new people's guards rather than the old gendarmerie and police organs; and finally, the Partisan proposition to rely exclusively on volunteer forces, refraining from forced mobilization of manpower. Captain Hudson had arrived just a day or two earlier, and Tito and his comrades wanted him to participate in the meeting, but according to Hudson, Mihailović was opposed to this and either immediately before or after the meeting said to Hudson: "This attack which I am going to launch on the partisans, and my relations with them, is entirely a Yugoslav affair and I am the legitimate representative of my government."[97]

The meeting at Brajići did result in agreements on a series of less important points, namely, that both groups mobilize their manpower as they had before, that the forces stay approximately in their present positions and avoid conflicts in the future; that the booty be divided; that transport of troops and materials within the liberated area be free for both groups; that mixed courts be established for the trial of bandits and people's enemies; that the necessary aid be given to people and refugees; that twelve hundred rifles from the Užice rifle factory and a certain portion of money from the cache discovered in the safes of the National Bank branch at Užice be turned over to the Chetniks.[98] But it is clear that the Chetniks did not go to the meeting at Brajići or enter into these partial agreements in good faith. In Belgrade the following day, two of Mihailović's aides, Colonel Pantić and Captain Nenad Mitrović, told a German intelligence officer, Captain Josef Matl, whom they had contacted, that they had been empowered by Colonel Mihailović to establish contact with Prime Minister Nedić and the appropriate Wehrmacht command posts and tell them that he was willing "to put himself and his men at their disposal for fighting Communism." This decision must have been made prior to the meeting at Brajići or at least only moments after it. Pantić further declared that "Draža Mihailović personally gives his guarantee for the definitive clearing of Communist bands in Serbian territory both east and west of the Morava River and for the establishment of peace and order." For that purpose Mihailović needed "about 5,000 rifles, 350 light machine guns, and 20 heavy machine guns." From later developments it would appear that the two Chetniks also asked for some ammunition. They also made it clear that they expected that no German punitive expeditions would be undertaken during these operations.[99] The chief reason why Mihai-

[97] As quoted by Hudson in St. Antony's College, Oxford University, *Proceedings of a Conference on Britain and European Resistance 1939–45*, Yugoslav discussion section, p. 12.
[98] Marjanović, "Contributions," p. 208. Only a few hundred rifles and a small amount of money were actually delivered to the Chetniks.
[99] Memorandum of Captain Matl to the chief of his unit dated Oct. 28, 1941, Microcopy No. T-314, Roll 1457, Frames 1086–87.

lović turned to the Germans was that he had already decided to attack the Partisans but since the British were not sending him any arms and ammunition (the first British delivery of arms by air took place on November 9), he saw himself forced to seek these supplies from the Germans. The Germans on October 29 informed Pantić and Mitrović that they wanted to see Mihailović himself and would give him safe conduct.[100] This invitation apparently triggered Mihailović's order of October 31 for Chetnik troops to attack the Partisans in the areas of Užice and Požega, with the immediate objectives of capturing the airfield at Požega over which he expected to obtain supplies from the British, and convincing the Germans of the genuineness of his offer. The attack was started on November 1, and on November 3 Mihailović informed the German Plenipotentiary Commanding General in Serbia that he would be willing to meet with him but for the fact that the operations against the Communists in which his troops were engaged, which "apparently have turned into a general conflict," for the moment required him to remain at his headquarters.[101]

The meeting was not postponed for very long. It took place on November 11 in the village of Divci near Valjevo. Mihailović was accompanied by Colonel Pantić and Captain Mitrović and also by Major Aleksandar Mišić. The chief German spokesman was Lt. Colonel Rudolf Kogard, Intelligence Officer of the Plenipotentiary Commanding General in Serbia. Kogard's lengthy opening statement did not hide the fact that the Germans were there not to discuss Mihailović's offer of cooperation against the Partisans but rather to look over a man they considered dangerous, to explain to him the futility of fighting the Germans, and to demonstrate to him that the only way in which he could serve the cause of his people was to surrender immediately and unconditionally. Mihailović was extremely disappointed to find that his overtures were not being accepted, that he was there only to be lectured to, and he was especially chagrined at not being able to get any ammunition—pleading repeatedly that he must have some that very night. Nothing that he and his colleagues said seemed to convince the Germans that they were serious about their offer: pleas of such cooperation being in both the German and the Serbian interest, promises that they would not break faith, that under no conditions would they consider fighting the Germans, and that they would be willing to accept German liaison officers to check on their activities—all these made no impression at all on the Germans, and Kogard made it clear that if Mihailović did not surrender, the Germans would continue to fight the Chetniks. Mihailović steadfastly refused to surrender, and the Germans had no intention of accommodating his wishes, and so the meeting ended. Mihailović's

---

[100] *Ibid.*, Frames 1110–12.
[101] For Mihailović's letter in German translation see *ibid.*, Frame 1338.

final words were: "With arms and ideologically I am engaged in the fight against the Communists to the end."[102]

Two additional points should be made about this meeting at Divci. The first has to do with Mihailović's desire for secrecy. Mihailović stated that General Nedić by openly siding with the occupation power had made a mistake and that Pećanac by doing the same thing had lost his standing with and influence among the Serbian people, and that he did not intend to make the same mistake. He therefore asked for the strictest secrecy from the Germans not only about the meeting but also about any aid that the Germans might extend to him. In other words, as early as November 1941 Mihailović was willing to collaborate with the enemy provided it be kept secret, apparently not appreciating the fact that if open collaboration were looked upon with disfavor by the people, secret collaboration, if ever found out, would surely be viewed in the same way. The second point concerns Mihailović's silence about the identity of Partisan leaders. For whatever reasons—either because the Partisans had managed to keep Mihailović from knowing their true identity or because, though knowing, he chose not to talk—Mihailović gave the Germans no useful information about the Partisan leaders. On the contrary, he told them that they were all foreigners and mentioned specifically only a Jew named Lindermaier, a Bulgarian named Jenković, a Hungarian named Borota, two Moslems whose names he did not know, and an Ustasha, Major Boganić—all names that I have never seen mentioned anywhere else.[103]

Although no agreement was reached at Divci, the Chetniks continued their policy inaugurated at the beginning of November of fighting the Partisans but not fighting the Germans. One of the Chetnik actions that acerbated the relations between the Chetniks and the Partisans was that two days after the Divci meeting, a Chetnik commander of questionable allegiance to Mihailović and probably without the latter's knowledge, delivered to the Germans 365 Partisans whom the Chetniks had taken prisoner in the previous days; all but about thirty of these prisoners were subsequently executed or taken to concentration camps.[104]

Obviously unaware of the meeting held at Divci, Captain Hudson in the meantime was doing all he could to make peace between the two

---

[102] See the end of the protocol of the meeting, *ibid.*, Frame 1322. The German evaluation of Mihailović following this meeting was not unflattering—they found him to be a strong Serbian nationalist, a man of great physical stamina, and completely in control of his emotions even in face of bad news. *Ibid.*, Frames 1332–35.

[103] *Ibid.*, Frames 1318–20. For the meeting at Divci see also *The Trial of Draža Mihailović*, pp. 66–67, 127; *Wisshaupt*, pp. 63–64. Colonel Pantić was arrested by the Germans soon after the meeting in Divci and in March 1942 was taken to Germany as a prisoner of war. After the war he settled in Australia. His account of the meeting in Divci in Karapandžić, pp. 129–52, is radically at variance with contemporary German documents.

[104] The report of the delivery of these prisoners to the Germans first appeared in *Borba*, Nov. 20, 1941; reprinted in Communist Party of Yugoslavia, *Istorijski arhiv Komunističke Partije Jugoslavije* Tome I, Vol. 1, pp. 310–12. See also *The Trial of Draža Mihailović*, pp. 23, 129–30, Marjanović, *Ustanak 1941*, p. 367.

resistance groups, and in a message to his superiors of November 13 he suggested that pressure be put upon Mihailović:

I suggest that you tell Mihailović that full British help will not be forthcoming unless an attempt is made to incorporate all anti-fascist elements under his command. This attempt is to be made by me personally going to discuss terms of such incorporation with the Partisans at Užice, and reporting to you via our Mark III W/T set there, and his [Mihailović's] W/T set here. Such an attempt should be preceded by a strong appeal for unity by a Moscow broadcast to the Partisans.[105]

The Partisans, having successfully repelled the Chetnik attack in the area of Užice and Požega on November 1, mounted a counterattack. After some two weeks of continuous fighting, they surrounded the Chetnik headquarters at Ravna Gora. Captain Hudson commented some years after the event that the Partisans "came up and nearly took Ravna Gora while I was there."[106] Apparently, they would have had no difficulty in taking Ravna Gora, but according to Dedijer they were deterred by hearing Radio Moscow news broadcasts in Serbo-Croatian about fighting against the Germans in Serbia in which Mihailović was referred to as the leader of all resistance forces in Serbia. Although amazed by the broadcasts, Tito realized that the fight against the Chetniks and possible killing of Mihailović might cause the Russians some trouble with the British; he therefore ordered that the operation be stopped and that parliamentarians be dispatched to the Chetniks for further negotiations.[107] Between November 18 and 20 a mixed commission met in Čačak. At this meeting the representatives of the two resistance groups again agreed to stop fighting each other and undertake combined operations against the Germans, and to establish a new mixed commission for the settlement of problems and a mixed court for punishing those members of the two groups who acted against the agreement.[108] Such a commission did in fact meet several times, the last time being at Pranjani near Ravna Gora on November 27–28, but apparently without achieving any positive results. In the meantime, the Germans had started their final push for the liquidation of the Partisan free territory centering at Užice. On the twenty-eighth Tito made a telephone appeal to Mihailović for combined action against the Germans, but got nowhere: Mihailović told him that he could not accept frontal attacks and furthermore had to return his detachments to their home areas.[109]

[105] Deakin, *The Embattled Mountain*, p. 139.
[106] Hudson, p. 13; see also *The Četniks*, p. 10. For a statement of the Partisan Supreme Headquarters on the Chetnik-Partisan engagements of these days issued on Nov. 4, 1941, and published in *Borba* Nov. 7 and 8, 1941, see *Zbornik DNOR*, Tome I, Vol. 1, pp. 242–47.
[107] Dedijer, *Josip Broz Tito*, p. 308.
[108] Marjanović, "Contributions," pp. 219–20; Marjanović, *Ustanak 1941*, pp. 369–71.
[109] Marjanović, "Contributions," pp. 220–21. This was the last direct contact between the two leaders. See also Djelević, pp. 187–88.

The second basic reason that contributed to the break and ensuing collision between the Chetniks and the Partisans in western Serbia was the fact that Mihailović had established contact with the British and the government-in-exile and that this greatly increased his confidence and prestige. Although this deduction can be made from the general developments of the period, the following message of Hudson confirms it: "British promise of support had the effect of worsening Četnik-Partisan relations. When I first arrived at Ravna Gora and Užice, at the end of October, 1941, before Četnik-Partisan hostilities, Mihailović already knew by telegram that he would get British support. He felt rightly that no one outside the country knew about Partisans or that he alone was not responsible for the revolt."[110] On November 15, only a few days after Mihailović's meeting with the German Lt. Colonel Kogard at Divci, Prime Minister Simović, in a broadcast over the BBC, referred to Mihailović as the "commander of all Yugoslav armed forces that are fighting in the country" and urged all fighting men to rally under his supreme command.[111] This gave Mihailović the authority that he had been assuming for some time, and from then until the end of November, in all his dealings with the Partisans and in regard to all Partisan proposals for combined operations against the enemy and a combined operational staff, he was insistent that the Partisans get under his command because he was the only legitimate representative of the government.[112] The exile government, thereby backing up Mihailović's arguments, advised him to cease all attacks against the Germans, and to fight back only in self-defense, because they gave the Germans an excuse for bloody reprisals against the civilian population. Furthermore, on November 16 Hudson received the following message, obviously for transmittal to Mihailović: "His Majesty's government now consider fight should be Yugoslavs for Yugoslavia, and not revolt led by Communists for Russia, if it is to prosper. H.M.G. therefore asking Soviet government to urge Communist elements to rally Mihailović, collaborating with him against Germans, putting themselves unreservedly at disposal of Mihailović as national leader. Simović will also instruct Mihailović to refrain from retaliatory action."[113]

The British decision to recognize and support the Chetniks exclusively was to have a profound effect on the course of the resistance for many months. By their own choice they cut off the Partisans, canceled any possibility of influencing them or using them as a source of information, and in a real sense strengthened their mistrust. On the other hand, Mihailović was very displeased with Hudson in his role of me-

[110] Radio message quoted in *The Četniks*, p. 11.
[111] Kljaković, in *Politika*, Nov. 6, 1970.
[112] Marjanović, "Contributions," pp. 219–20.
[113] Deakin, *The Embattled Mountain*, p. 140; see also *The Trial of Draža Mihailović*, p. 131.

diator between him and the Partisans, thinking that he was trying to put pressure upon him directly and through his superiors (see Hudson's message of November 13). Hudson was dependent on Mihailović's radio transmitter for sending messages, but he had his own code, and on November 21 he was still skeptical of Mihailović as an ally, as he indicated in a message to his superiors: "My attitude to Mihailović has been that he has all qualifications except strength. At present the Partisans are stronger and he must first liquidate them with British arms before turning seriously against the Germans."[114] Mihailović was already making things difficult for Hudson, and about two weeks later, after conditions in western Serbia had radically changed, he withdrew all permission to Hudson to use his transmitter, thus cutting him off entirely from his superiors and the outside world.[115]

But the most important reason for the Chetnik decision to fight the Partisans was their utter opposition to the nature and the objectives of the Partisan movement. The Partisans were a Communist-led revolutionary force operating through the medium of a Popular Front and, with nationalist slogans, bent on maintaining full independence during the war, and pursuing a combined strategy of armed resistance against the occupying armies and the quisling regimes and a revolution against the old political and socioeconomic order. As such, they were a clear challenge to the Chetniks, who were an arm of the government-in-exile and defenders of the old order, and to their obvious aim of controlling the country after the war. The country had ruthlessly suppressed Communists in the interwar years, and there were many ardent anti-Communists not only among professional officers, bourgeois politicians, businessmen, and peasants but also among intellectuals, and none of

---

[114] Deakin, *The Embattled Mountain*, p. 141.

[115] The facts in connection with Hudson's radio sets and his radio communications have been difficult to unravel. The problem started when Deakin in his article "Great Britain and Yugoslavia, 1941–1945" (p. 48) asserted that Mihailović had succeeded in "preventing him [Hudson] from using his radio transmitter." Hudson explained at the Oxford conference in December 1962 that he took two transmitters into Yugoslavia, a small one which could only reach Malta, and soon burned out, and a heavy outmoded set, weighing fifty-five pounds, which could be operated only on electricity and had to be moved by pack animal. But Hudson left other points cloudy. My attempts to obtain further information from him by mail in the late winter of 1970 brought no result. However, Hudson's message of November 13 to his superiors (see p. 151 above) indicates clearly that he was not able to take his only working transmitter with him when he left Užice for Mihailović's headquarters late in October, because it arrived at Užice with Lalatović and Dragičević after he and Ostojić left for Ravna Gora and was kept there by the Partisans. Hudson's radio operator had stayed at Užice, and therefore Hudson, being unable to operate a transmitter himself, had to use and did use not only Mihailović's transmitter but also his operator. Hudson, disappointed at not getting any deliveries of arms after the single drop of November 9, probably suspected Hudson of sabotaging his efforts and of being pro-Partisan. Hudson attended some of the meetings of the mixed Chetnik-Partisan commission and went from there to Užice to further his efforts at mediation, arriving just in time to be evacuated with Tito and part of his staff on November 29 when the Germans attacked. While fleeing with Tito from Užice Hudson stumbled by chance on his large radio set, took it, and with great effort transported it to the area of Ravna Gora where he returned on the night of December 7–8 to join Mihailović. He found Mihailović and a few of his officers, but Mihailović refused to see him or to permit the use of his transmitter or of his radio operator, and Hudson's set, according to Bailey, was by this time "unserviceable." See Deakin, *The Embattled Mountain*, p. 146; Tito, "War Memoirs," pp. 48–54, 62; and Bailey's report of April 1944 after he returned from Yugoslavia, F.O. 371/44282, R21295/11/92, Appendix 3, p. 2.

them who had joined the Chetniks could be expected to favor long- or even short-range cooperation with the Communist-led Partisans. In ideology and wartime strategies and tactics as well as in postwar objectives, the positions of the two resistance groups could not be reconciled. The Chetniks, backed by the government-in-exile, naturally took the position that the Partisans must accept Mihailović as supreme commander and submit to his authority; the Partisans naturally refused, knowing that to submit would mean the end of their existence. But they were willing to come to some agreement with the Chetniks, following the reasoning that joining with them under the banner of a Popular Front would give them the chance to swallow up or emasculate the whole Chetnik movement. With the Communist Party in control of a Popular Front, their most dangerous domestic enemy, which had important connections with the Western Allies, would have been rendered impotent. The Chetniks of course had no intention of letting this happen, and since they were confident of an Allied victory, they could accept occupation and even quisling regimes in Yugoslavia as a temporary fact of life. The real danger lay in allowing the Communist-led Partisans to become so strong that, with Soviet Russia behind them, they might stand to become the controlling element at the end of the war and in postwar Yugoslav politics. The prize, in other words, was nothing less than the control of the future state: on the one hand, essentially a continuation of the pre-1941 political and socioeconomic order refashioned to strengthen the Great Serbian interests and Serbian hegemony, or on the other hand a totally new political and socioeconomic system built on the Communist model. For the Chetniks the choice was clear: they had to destroy the Partisans either alone or in aid to the Axis and quisling forces. The Partisans thus became the enemy against whom all means were permissible, including making pacts and arrangements with the occupying powers and the puppet regimes. The attack on Užice was the first attempt in this direction and from then on the elimination of the Partisans was the chief objective of Chetnik policy.

The reasoning on the Partisan side was similar: the Chetniks became the prime enemy because it was assumed that the Allies would win the war, and that with the departure of the occupying armies and quisling regimes from Yugoslav territory, the Chetniks as an arm of the government-in-exile who from the beginning had the support of the Western Allies would do everything they could to claim exclusive political control of the postwar state. Since the Chetniks were the defenders not only of Serbian hegemony but also of the old socioeconomic order, from the Partisan point of view they were the central and most important force of counterrevolution in Yugoslavia. To achieve their goal the Partisans had to defeat the Chetniks. For tactical reasons, they presented their struggle as being first and foremost a struggle against the occupying powers and the collaborators, open and secret—that is, against the quisling regimes and the Chetniks—and throughout the war they denied any Communist objectives, though they made no secret of the leading role of the Communist Party in the newly developed National Liberation Front and the National Liberation War. Although all Communist parties while in opposition have by definition the objective of seizing power and carrying out socialist revolution, and although some CPY officials stated as much during the early stages of the uprising, it was not until recently that it was candidly admitted in Yugoslavia that the CPY and the Partisans were engaged in both a war against the occupying powers and a civil war against the forces of the old regime at home. For domestic and international political reasons this was not generally admitted during the war.[116]

The Chetnik decision in November 1941 not to fight the Germans in western Serbia (and later not to fight either of the Axis Powers in areas outside Serbia) until the proper time arrived was not easily put into effect. Mihailović well understood at the meeting at Divci that if he did not surrender unconditionally the Germans would continue to fight him, and this they did, and without delay, on the assumption that the Chetniks were pro-Western, whatever they said, and would sooner or later turn their arms against the Germans.[117] On December 6–7, after concluding Operation Užice against the Partisans, the Germans undertook Operation Mihailović and overran Mihailović's headquarters at Ravna Gora. Mihailović barely escaped capture (see Chapter 7). Thus by early December 1941 the Germans had regained control of all the territory that the Partisans and the Chetniks had liberated in western Serbia; they had chased most of the Partisan remnants out of Serbia into Sandjak and had put the Chetnik forces into disarray—most of their detachments being disbanded, with some in the underground and others in the process of being legalized as part of General Nedić's quisling army.

THE SERBIAN NATIONALIST RESISTANCE OUTSIDE SERBIA

Forces that in time became known as the Chetnik movement of Draža Mihailović did not start in the early months of occupation as a unified movement. Mihailović had organized and was leading the Chetniks in Serbia, but the groups outside Serbia which later became identified as part of his movement in fact began either as part of the uprising led by

[116] Vojmir Kljaković, "About the Elements of Socialist Revolution in the Liberation War of the Peoples of Yugoslavia," paper read at a symposium held at Ljubljana in January 1972 on the theme "The Liberation Struggle of the Peoples of Yugoslavia as a General People's War and Socialist Revolution." MS in my files.

[117] See e.g. the report of Gerhard Feine, Counselor in the Office of the Plenipotentiary of the German Ministry of Foreign Affairs in Belgrade, of Dec. 3, 1941, in *DGFP*, Series D. Vol. XIII. p. 946.

the Communist Party of Yugoslavia, or started spontaneously on their own in defense of their lives and families. This was the case in Montenegro, in Bosnia and Herzegovina, in northern Dalmatia, and in southwestern Croatia (Lika, Kordun, Banija). During the first several months of the uprising in all these areas the fighting groups consisted both of Communists and their various National Front adherents and of Serbian nationalist elements, and the leadership of the armed detachments was mixed also.

Unlike the Partisans, who from the beginning of the uprising were directed by the Central Committee of the Communist Party and the Chief Headquarters—renamed Supreme Headquarters following the CPY leadership meeting at the village of Stolice in western Serbia on September 26, 1941, and with the help of the provincial or Chief Headquarters—the Serbian nationalist groups outside Serbia had no central military or political leadership. During the first three or four months of the uprising most of them, with the exception of detachments in eastern Bosnia, had little or no contact with Mihailović's group at Ravna Gora. Disregarding Communist coordinating activity, these Serbian nationalist groups worked independently, with no coordination among themselves even on a county let alone regional or provincial basis, their motivations being for the most part the simple ones of defending themselves and their families.

In some areas, such as the territory of the Croatian puppet state under Italian occupation, differences between the Communists and the Serbian nationalists arose almost as soon as the uprising started over the question of whether to fight both the Ustashas and the Italians as the Partisans wanted or only the Ustashas as the Serbian nationalist groups wanted, and the process of polarization between the two components of the resistance forces set in immediately. The leaders of the Serbian nationalist elements who were taking up arms in Bosnia and Herzegovina, Dalmatia, and parts of Croatia were former politicians or professional men—teachers, Orthodox priests, merchants—with long-standing affiliations with such Serbian patriotic organizations as the Chetnik Association,[118] National Defense, and the Yugoslav gymnastic organization Sokol. They were self-appointed leaders, many of them styling themselves *vojvodas* or chieftains, following the old Serbian tradition, and claiming absolute control over their detachments.

When news of these groups reached Mihailović he lost no time in sending his emissaries to take over command and bring them under his

[118] But according to Šehić, pp. 214–20, in Bosnia and Herzegovina, few of the active wartime Chetniks were leading members of the Chetnik Association before the war. Of 245 members of the governing boards of local Chetnik committees, only 57 joined Chetnik detachments; many were killed by the Ustashas in the course of 1941, still others joined the Partisans, remained inactive, and so on.

control. The first to be sent, toward the end of August, were Major Boško Todorović, who was made his chief delegate for Bosnia and Herzegovina, and Major Jezdimir Dangić, who was sent to eastern Bosnia. In the beginning their activities were directed primarily against the Ustashas and the Moslem population.[119] For some time in Bosnia, as in Serbia, there was tenuous cooperation between the Partisans and these delegates of Mihailović with the units they now had under their command. In eastern Bosnia a formal agreement was concluded on October 1 between the Partisan representatives and Mihailović's representatives. This provided for the establishment of a Combined Partisan-Chetnik Operations Staff for Eastern Bosnia and a joint administration of liberated territories, for the issuing of a joint proclamation to the people calling for the struggle against the enemy, and for the cessation of all fighting against the Moslem and Croatian population.[120] Since both sides—the Chetniks even more than the Partisans—had entered into this agreement with ulterior motives, it could hardly have proved workable, and after the Chetniks heard the news of Mihailović's rift with the Partisans in Serbia, the break between the two resistance groups in Bosnia was only a matter of time.

Mihailović also dispatched officers to establish contacts and set up regional commands in Montenegro, in other parts of Bosnia and Herzegovina, in Dalmatia, and in southwestern Croatia (Lika)—at first only on paper in many instances but gradually by and large in fact. But it was one thing to speed up the process of polarization between the two resistance groups and to start fighting the Partisans and to declare that all Serbian nationalist resistance groups were parts of the Yugoslav Army in the Homeland, and quite another to draw these disparate units into an efficient fighting force under a single military-political command. The circumstances under which the various groups had arisen and continued to operate differed greatly, and the character of each depended in great part on the strength and personal proclivities of the individual leaders, most of whom were quite jealous of their independence.

Nearly all the men that Mihailović sent out to take over commands in areas outside Serbia were young officers of the royal army who had refused to surrender in April or for some reason had not been sent to prisoner-of-war camps or were released from there after a short time (e.g. officers of Montenegrin birth). In some areas these officers were quickly accepted—in Montenegro, for example, because Mihailović sent or appointed there Montenegrins (who of course considered themselves really the best of Serbs)—but in other areas these officers, nearly all of them

[119] Marjanović, "Contributions," p. 202.
[120] Čolaković, *Zapisi iz oslobodilačkog rata*, II, 17–37; Yugoslavia, Vojnoistorijski institut, *Hronologija oslobodilačke borbe naroda Jugoslavije 1941–1945*, p. 122.

Serbs from Serbia, had only limited success in imposing themselves as commanders. Still, all the resistance leaders of a Serbian nationalist inclination outside Serbia accepted Mihailović in theory as their supreme commander.

Toward the end of February 1942, Partisans in Herzegovina captured Mihailović's delegate Major Todorović, who had shifted there from eastern Bosnia, and finding him in possession of compromising documents having to do with collaboration with the Italians, executed him after a quick trial. Mihailović replaced him with *vojvoda* Ilija Trifunović-Birčanin, giving him command of all Chetnik forces in southeastern Bosnia, Herzegovina, Dalmatia, western Bosnia, and southwestern Croatia.[121] Birčanin was recognized by all the pro-Chetnik commanders in his assigned area, but he was only partly successful in his attempts to replace some of the commanders with Mihailović's appointees. The local Chetnik leader in northern Dalmatia and western Bosnia, for example, Momčilo Djujić (an Orthodox priest and self-appointed *vojvoda*), refused to give up the post of the commander of the Dinara Division, though he remained loyal to Mihailović and made his intended successor first his deputy and later inspector of his troops.[122] In the German-occupied parts of Bosnia, several Chetnik leaders strongly opposed Mihailović's attempts to replace them or make them subordinate to his appointees. They insisted that they had carried the struggle against the enemy for a long time and could do their own commanding without any help from Serbs from Serbia.[123] But even they recognized Mihailović's supreme authority, though continuing to act independently. The self-appointed *vojvoda* Dobroslav Jevdjević, a member of the prewar Chetnik Association and former member of the Yugoslav parliament (Yugoslav National Party), who cooperated closely with Birčanin, remained a power among the Chetniks until the end of the war. In Lika, Mihailović's appointees, Lt. Colonel Ilija Mihić and Major Slavko N. Bjelajac, had somewhat better luck and for the most part succeeded in imposing their command over the local Chetnik groups.[124] In Slovenia, the originally appointed commander of pro-Chetnik groups, Colonel Jakob Avšič, soon shifted to the Partisans and his chief of staff, Major Karlo Novak, took over the Chetnik command, but the Chetniks in Slovenia never played an important role.

[121] Radmilo Grdjić, p. 264. Birčanin had been in Montenegro much of the time between April and October 1941 and had then gone to Split in the Italian-annexed part of Dalmatia.

[122] Stanisavljević, p. 101.

[123] For more on this see the minutes of a conference of Chetnik chieftains of the German-occupied parts of Bosnia held on Dec. 1, 1942, in the village of Kulaši (county of Prnjavor) in *Dokumenti o izdajstvu Draže Mihailovića*, I, 217–24, esp. 221–22. Two of the Bosnian leaders who were especially critical of the commanders sent to them by Mihailović were Stevan Botić and Mirko Djukanović. But even before the meeting in Kulaši, Mihailović was instructing his commanders that Botić must be "unconditionally stopped." *Ibid.*, pp. 474–75.

[124] Stanisavljević, pp. 112–14.

An extremely interesting development occurred in eastern Bosnia in the first half of 1942. In the autumn of 1941 the Partisans had in that area six detachments with an estimated seventy-three hundred men,[125] but except for a small number of CPY members (mostly workers and intellectuals), the overwhelming bulk of these forces were Bosnian Serb peasants who went to the hills to save their lives and to defend their families and villages against the Ustasha terror and were in no way committed to, or perhaps even interested in, Partisan political objectives. A good many of the Party members, who were mostly in positions of leadership, were Croats and Moslems. From the beginning the Party members sought to inculcate into their detachments the Party's beliefs in unity among all South Slav peoples, attempting to convince them that what was being done to the Serbs in eastern Bosnia and elsewhere in the Independent State of Croatia was the work of the foreign enemies and their domestic helpers and should not be blamed on the Croatian people or the Moslems in general, and that it was unity, rather than fratricidal war, that was needed in order to survive and regain liberty. The already mentioned Combined Operations Staff for Eastern Bosnia was dissolved on November 16 with the withdrawal of the Partisan representatives. The Chetniks then established their Interim Administration of Eastern Bosnia, but they were not yet ready to tackle the Partisans—in fact, a few Partisan and Chetnik detachments, by mutual agreement among their commanders, continued to cooperate. The Partisan position in eastern Serbia was further aggravated by lack of indoctrination and discipline in the detachments and a generally declining morale, due in part to the extreme severity of the winter.[126]

The new situation was thoroughly discussed at the conference of the Provincial Committee of the CPY for Bosnia and Herzegovina at the village of Ivančići near Sarajevo on January 7–8.[127] Since Tito and his chief aids with the First Proletarian Brigade had just arrived in the area, they also attended.[128] Being in fact the first meeting of the Partisan leadership after the disastrous developments in western Serbia, the discussion covered many problems. As far as the conditions in eastern and northeastern Bosnia were concerned the conference criticised the following mistakes: "vacillating attitude toward the Chetniks, lack of order

---

[125] Danilović, "The Crisis in the Uprising in Eastern Bosnia in the Spring of 1942," p. 386. For a detailed chronological account of these events in Bosnia by one of the leading Partisan functionaries see Čolaković, *Zapisi*, Vols. II and III, which cover the period from the end of September 1941 to November 1942. For the developments during the period August 1941 to April 1942 see also Vujasinović, pp. 13–370.

[126] Čolaković, *Zapisi*, II, 187–201; Danilović, "The Crisis," pp. 410–21.

[127] See Danilović, "The Conference in Ivančići," pp. 467–79; Vukmanović Tempo, pp. 651–61.

[128] The First Proletarian Brigade, made up of Serbian and Montenegrin Partisan detachments, was established by Tito on December 21, 1941, at Rudo, southeastern Bosnia, and was the first regular unit of what in time became the National Liberation Army of Yugoslavia. Partisan detachments continued to be established practically until the end of the war and operated as territorial troops.

in liberated territories, poor organization of Party work and the taking over of military duties by Party leaders, lack of vigilance, lack of care in developing younger cadres, and delay in forming mobile units." Certain decisions were made: to fight the Chetniks, to strengthen the Partisan detachments, and to accord a special status to those Chetniks who were willing to fight the Germans and the Ustashas under Partisan command but could not accept the Partisan program or its insignia (the red star). This was the beginning of the "volunteer army detachments."[129] A few days later the Partisan leadership issued a proclamation to the peoples of Bosnia and Herzegovina accusing the Chetnik leaders, and especially the Chetnik officers, of sabotaging the national liberation struggle and causing fratricidal war and calling upon all Serbs, Croats, and Moslems to take up "a common struggle against the Germans, Ustashas, and Chetniks."[130]

A week or so later the situation in eastern Bosnia took a new and critical turn when the Germans along with Croatian quisling troops launched a major operation (the Yugoslav-termed Second Enemy Offensive) to pacify the area.[131] When news of the operation reached Major Dangić and Major Todorović, they began spreading the word among the Chetnik commanders that the offensive was aimed only at the Communists and that the Chetniks need not become involved. Some Chetnik units promptly withdrew from the front lines they held, others let the Germans through, and some sent their men home. These actions undercut the Partisan defense and they lost a great deal of free territory and suffered a good many casualties in consequence. Obviously, any last shreds of cooperation between them and the Chetniks were now gone. Not even Tito's brief presence in the area with most of his Supreme Headquarters and the newly formed First Proletarian Brigade, though it temporarily bolstered the Partisans' position, could reverse the bad situation.

In the meantime, as will be described more fully in Chapter 7, Major Dangić, still under allegiance to Mihailović, was establishing contact with Nedić and the Germans and starting to negotiate with the latter the terms of his collaboration against the Partisans in eastern Bosnia. The agreement reached by Dangić with General Bader, the Commanding General in Serbia, on February 1, 1942, was never consummated because of the opposition of the Armed Forces Commander in Southeast Europe, General Walter Kuntze, and also of the authorities of the Independent State of Croatia who were supported by Kasche, the German Envoy in Zagreb, but there is no question that the Chetniks in eastern

[129] *Hronologija 1941–1945*, pp. 191–92.
[130] *Ibid.*, p. 189.
[131] Danilović, "The Crisis," pp. 389–98; see also the work by Djonlagić and Leković.

Bosnia, like Mihailović's forces in western Serbia some weeks earlier, had ceased to fight the Axis and were becoming active opponents of the Partisans. To complicate the situation still more, other Chetnik officers, for example Captain Radoslav Račić and Captain Milorad Momčilović, who had brought their detachments from western Serbia to avoid destruction at the hands of the Germans, threw them into the fight against the Partisans in eastern Bosnia. The Chetniks bombarded the Partisans with propaganda, some of it anti-Communist, some anti-Croat and anti-Moslem, and they continued a general anti-Croat and anti-Moslem program that extended beyond mere propaganda against them as the adherents of the Independent State of Croatia whose organs persecuted the Serbs to the carrying out of terrorist acts against the Croatian and Moslem villages in areas under their control.

The Chetniks' most effective anti-Partisan technique in this time before all-out conflict was that of subverting Partisan detachments from within. Between February 20 and the end of June 1942 the Chetniks carried out successful putsches in all but one of the six Partisan detachments in eastern Bosnia (as well as in many detachments in other areas) and in practically all detachments of the "volunteer army" and killed a great many Partisan commanders and political commissars. At the end of this process, sometime in June or July, the effective Partisan forces in eastern Bosnia were down to about six hundred men and fully isolated from other Partisan forces.[132]

Toward the end of January, under pressure of the Second Enemy Offensive, Tito and the First Proletarian Brigade had moved southward toward Foča, which in the meantime was cleared of the Chetniks by the Montenegrin Partisans, and from January 25 to May 10 Foča was the Partisan military and political headquarters. In Foča Tito established on March 1 the Second Proletarian Brigade consisting of the remaining Serbian detachments, and the two proletarian brigades and some of the volunteer detachments managed to retake some of the territory the Partisans had lost in eastern Bosnia (which they considered at that time important as a base for early re-entry into Serbia). They held it only briefly, however, for on April 15 the Germans, Croatian quisling troops, and Italians, with some help from the Chetniks, launched another large-scale offensive (the Third Enemy Offensive) in southeastern Bosnia, eastern Herzegovina, and Montenegro. By June 15 the Partisans had lost practically all their free territory in these areas.[133] With many units lost because of Chetnik subversion, the Partisans only just managed to pull out with their main forces at the end of June in the famous "long march" toward western Bosnia.

[132] Danilović, "The Crisis," pp. 398–410.
[133] Morača, *Prelomna godina narodnooslobodilačkog rata*, pp. 89–120.

The ascendence of the Chetnik forces in eastern Bosnia during the first half of 1942 was paralleled in all areas outside Serbia, and it was related to the two main developments already spoken of: first, the weakening or ebbing of the Partisan movement owing to the loss of the free area in western Serbia and serious reverses in eastern Bosnia, western Bosnia, Herzegovina, and Montenegro; and second, Chetnik accommodations with the Germans and Italians for a combined struggle against the Partisans. Mihailović's own position had, as we have seen, been tremendously strengthened during this period. Now, as the official representative of the government-in-exile, he could maintain direct control at least over some, though not all, Chetnik detachments, and since he seemed assured of the full and lasting support of the Western Allies, he was doubly secure in his position of power, being not only the chief wartime representative of the interwar Serbian political and social elite but also the hero of the Serbs outside Serbia, who had suffered greatly at the hands of the Ustashas (or of the Bulgarians or the Hungarians) and looked toward Serbia for leadership and protection. At this time, the Chetniks, with Mihailović as their leader, were in a very favorable position to emerge as the controlling group in the postwar period, whereas the Partisans seemed to be almost hopelessly out of the running. Even that early, however, the Chetnik position bore the two weaknesses that were ultimately to prove their downfall: (1) they were a purely Great Serbia oriented group and thus could not count on any real support among the other nations in Yugoslavia except in Montenegro, and (2) they had become collaborators with the enemy throughout the country, with all the perilous and unforeseeable consequences that such a policy entailed.

THE GOVERNMENT-IN-EXILE AND ARMED RESISTANCE

As explained earlier, the first reaction of the government-in-exile to reports about an uprising in Yugoslavia was a negative one. It was considered to be premature, it was started without any consultation with the government-in-exile or the British, and, above all, it was not, so reports indicated, being led by any groups that could be considered legitimate, but rather by the Communist Party of Yugoslavia. In his speech over the BBC on August 12, General Simović castigated the action and even threatened reprisals against the leaders after the war. The official line was set: the time for an uprising was not yet ripe, and the government-in-exile, obviously in conjunction with the British, would give the signal when the time did come. But when, as the uprising continued to gather momentum, the Chetniks, somewhat halfheartedly, took up arms, partly in cooperation with Partisans and partly in actions of their own, the government-in-exile changed its attitude toward the uprising, saw the advantages that it could derive from it, and began backing the Chetniks as a resistance force. Contact having been established between Mihailović and the two governments, the ball began to roll, and in a series of messages over the BBC, Simović, and after his dismissal his successor and King Peter, assured Mihailović of British aid and proceeded to advise him on what to do. On October 28, 1941, for example, Simović gave this advice:

> His Majesty the King and His Majesty's government are undertaking all necessary measures in order to give you all necessary aid as soon as possible. The problem [of aid] is satisfactorily solved. Preparations [are] under way. Therefore wait and advise everybody to be patient and to abstain from too hasty action, in order to avoid losses and to be able to hold out during the winter. Do not expose yourself now and wait for orders for action from here.
>
> Maintain steady contact with our people in Bosnia and Montenegro. Undertake measures for maneuvering in order to transfer troops from threatened places into areas outside of enemy's reach, for the case of need for wintering and for the forthcoming action.
>
> Until you receive the signal for combined action do not provoke the enemy except in greatest need.[134]

On November 15 Simović not only declared that Mihailović was the head of all resistance forces in Yugoslavia and that all fighters should get under his command, but also gave directives to Mihailović on what course to follow:

> There where the people are not in immediate danger be patient. We request that the acts of sabotage and of individual attacks, which only give an excuse to the enemy for the most brutal and criminal attacks against the peaceful civilian population, should immediately cease, in order to reduce the number of unnecessary victims and unnecessary loss of blood of our people.
>
> We feel very deeply about the sacrifices that are being made in the present struggle. We have advised you more than once that the moment for decisive struggle has not yet come.[135]

The government gave Mihailović every assistance in the form of rapid promotions and appointments to the highest military offices—Minister of the Army, Navy, and Air Force, and Chief of Staff of the Supreme Command[136]—and when it appealed for cooperation between the two resistance groups, it was always in terms of the Partisans accepting the command of Mihailović. This was consistent from October 1941 as long as Mihailović held his position in the government-in-exile, that is, until May 1944. As an example, one could quote a statement of King Peter

---

[134] Radoje L. Knežević, "The Yugoslav Government and Draža Mihailović," *Poruka*, No. 10, p. 11.

[135] *Ibid.*

[136] The promotion of Mihailović to brigadier general on December 7, 1941, came actually as a reward for his report of November 22 about the agreement between the Partisans and the Chetniks, which misled the government-in-exile and the British into thinking that the Partisans had accepted Mihailović's supreme command. Kljaković, in *Politika*, Nov. 7, 1970.

on March 27, 1942, over the BBC: "Now you have to recover after enemy attacks and you have to get together and to organize under the supreme leadership of General Mihailović. Beware of too early actions which could cause great sacrifices completely out of proportion with possible results. In the struggle against the enemy, everyone—Serbs, Croats, and Slovenes—will join when the right time comes and when the signal is given."[137]

The policy principles supposedly held by the government-in-exile under the Jovanović cabinets from January 1942 to June 1943 in regard to armed resistance in the country were reported by Radoje Knežević, the Minister of the Royal Court from March 27, 1941, to June 1943, and one of the staunchest supporters of Mihailović abroad, in a postwar article. These were, he wrote:

(1) First of all to bring about unification of the two rival resistance groups under the leadership of General Mihailović; and so far as this proved impossible to strive that their mutual fighting be terminated and a certain amount of cooperation in their actions against the enemy be achieved. (2) To transfer the maximum of resistance forces from Serbia and Montenegro into the territory of Pavelić state, so that with the action against the Ustashas a reduction and eventually a complete cessation of the annihilation of the Serbs can be brought about. (3) To unite all resistance elements throughout the whole country in order to make possible large-scale operations against the enemy wherever and whenever the interests of Allied strategy require them. This constant threat of organized forces would, in any event, be tying up in Yugoslavia a large number of enemy divisions. (4) A general uprising for the liberation of the country to be started at the moment of the Allied landings in the Balkans, or when the coalition of the free peoples organizes the storming of the "Fortress Europe." (5) With propaganda over the radio and by action in the country, to forestall the plans of perfidious enemies, who with the feeding of antagonisms among the various parts of the population, were undermining the very foundations of the Yugoslav state for the future.[138]

The important thing was, of course, not the actual or purported views of the government-in-exile on the armed resistance in the country, but rather what policies the government's representative in the country, General Mihailović, pursued. Just what these policies were will emerge in the pages that follow. They were never clear cut, but were full of twists and turns, varying from area to area and from one stage of the war to another; often, they seemed to be contradictory. Certainly no generalized characterization of them is possible. It can be said, however, that from the autumn of 1941, three features were at the bottom of all Chetnik thinking and action: first, they wanted to rebuild Yugoslavia around a Great Serbia including all areas in which Serbs formed a large or even only a substantial part of the population, with the Karadjor-

[137] "The Yugoslav Government and Draža Mihailović," *Poruka*, No. 10, p. 12.
[138] *Ibid.*, p. 10.

djević dynasty at its helm and the Chetniks in complete control of the state machinery; second, so far as possible, they would avoid fighting the much superior Axis forces until the final stages of the war and then only in conjunction with the Allies who they expected would land on the Adriatic coast and who in fact would be the main factor in throwing the enemy out of the country; and third, the Partisans were their foremost short-run and long-run enemy, and therefore they would collaborate with anyone, particularly the Axis occupation forces, who fought the Partisans. All other specific features of Chetnik behavior were only variations on or elaborations of these three basic features of their policy.

CHAPTER SIX

Chetnik Objectives and Organization

---◆◆◆◆◆▶----

THE MAIN OBJECTIVE: GREAT SERBIA

The main concern of Mihailović and the Chetniks, and of the government-in-exile as long as it was dominated by the Great Serbia forces, was to build up a superior power and maintain it throughout the war so that when the occupying armies were thrown out and the quisling governments collapsed, the Chetniks would be the strongest claimant to control of the postwar Yugoslav government. Starting from the assumption that the Axis was bound to lose the war, regardless of anything the Chetniks might or might not do, the Chetniks decided that their primary objective would best be served by not wasting their manpower in fighting the greatly superior Axis armies but instead concentrating on perfecting their organization and on fighting the internal competitors for postwar leadership of Yugoslavia, primarily the Communist-led Partisans, and turning against the Axis only in the final stages of the conflict, when the Allied forces would be there to help. A certain pretense of fighting the Axis was necessary, to maintain their reputation as a "heroic resistance group" so that they could remain in good standing with the Western Allies, but there was to be as little actual fighting as possible. In fact, there was a great deal of collaboration between the Chetniks on the one hand and the Axis powers and the quisling forces on the other in order better to fight the Partisans, their common enemy.

Until the Chetnik congress at the village of Ba in western Serbia in January 1944, of which more will be said in Chapter 11, the Chetnik objectives and program were expressed in a variety of documents, some quite unofficial, issued at various times and written by various persons or groups of persons, with some of the objectives outlined in more and others in less detailed form. The first of these documents, and the one that contains the most complete statement of Chetnik territorial aspirations for a Great Serbia—or as it was sometimes euphemistically called, a Serbian unit within a Great Yugoslavia—was a memorandum prepared by Dr. Stevan Moljević in June 1941, two months before he became a member of the Chetnik National Committee and of its Executive Council and, indeed, before he had even met Colonel Mihailović. Many of Moljević's ideas as expressed in this memorandum on "Homogeneous Serbia" are evident in most of the other Chetnik programmatic statements whether they came there from Moljević's memorandum, or Moljević's participation in the formulation of these statements, or were the result of similar thinking.[1]

Moljević's territorial plan for a "homogeneous Serbia" was based on the notion that the Serbs, because they had so long struggled against the Turks and had been the only people to resist the entry of the Germans into the Balkans, were entitled to the position of the leading nation in the Balkans. To assume that position with authority, however, they must first become the undisputed leaders of Yugoslavia. This they were to do, Moljević said,

by creating a homogeneous Serbia which has to include the entire ethnic area populated by Serbs and to secure for itself the necessary strategic and communication lines and hubs, as well as economic regions, which will give it the possibility of an assured free economic, political, and cultural life and development for all times.

Even if in some cases these strategic and communication lines and hubs, vital to the security, life, and existence of Serbia, do not at the present time have a Serbian majority, they have to serve Serbia and the Serbian people in order to avoid in the future the great sufferings which the Serbs' neighbors inflict upon them whenever they have an opportunity to do so.

Transfers and exchanges of population, especially of Croats from the Serbian and of Serbs from the Croatian areas, is the only way to arrive at their separation and to create better relations between them, and thereby remove the possibility of a repetition of the terrible crimes that occurred even in the First World War, but especially during this war, in the entire area in which the Serbs and Croats live intermixed, and where the Croats and Moslems have undertaken in a calculated way the extermination of the Serbs.

The territory of Great Serbia as proposed by Moljević (see Map 4) included not only the bulk of the old Yugoslav territory but also some areas that belonged to Yugoslavia's neighbors.[2] First of all, it was to include in addition to Serbia in its pre-1912 frontiers all the areas that were acquired by Serbia in the Balkan Wars of 1912–13, that is, Yugo-

---

[1] A copy of Moljević's memorandum, dated June 30, 1941, was made available to me by courtesy of Colonel Vojmir Kljaković of the Institute of Military History in Belgrade. The document is registered in the Archives of the Institute under Chetnik Documents, No. 4/1, Box 144. Moljević was born in Rudo, in southeastern Bosnia, in 1888. He was an attorney-at-law in Banja Luka, northwestern Bosnia, and chairman of the local section of the Serbian Cultural Club, but left his domicile on April 10, 1941, the day of the proclamation of the Independent State of Croatia. When he wrote the memorandum he was living in Montenegro.

[2] I have found two other maps of Chetnik origin on "Future Yugoslavia" in the Archives of the Institute of Military History, Belgrade: Chetnik Documents, Reg. No. 36/2 and Reg. No. 38/2, Box 7. Both of them have a corridor linking Yugoslavia and Czechoslovakia and thus separating Austria and Hungary. There are several minor differences between these two maps and between them and the one reproduced here, but in each one Croatia is reduced drastically in comparison with its present-day frontiers. According to the first of these maps, even the southern part of Istria is claimed for Great Serbia.

Map 4. A 1941 Chetnik conception of future Yugoslavia. (Based on a Chetnik leaflet entitled "Our Way" in the archives of the Institute of Military History in Belgrade.)

slav Macedonia and a part of Sandjak; then Montenegro and the part of Sandjak that went to Montenegro in 1912–13; all of Bosnia and Herzegovina; all of Dalmatia, with the city of Dubrovnik obtaining a special status, and the area of Dalmatia from the estuary of the Neretva River to the neighborhood of the town of Šibenik and some western Herzegovinian and Bosnian counties with Croatian majorities forming an autonomous area within Serbia. Of the territory of Croatia-Slavonia, Great Serbia was to take most of the area of Lika; practically all of Kordun and Banija; then the territory eastward to the town of Pakrac; then a corridor of land some fifteen to twenty-five kilometers wide extending from Pakrac north to the Hungarian border (including the counties of Daruvar, Grubišno Polje, Slatina, and parts of Nova Gradiška and Požega); parts of Slavonia including the towns of Osijek and Vinkovci; all of Srijem; and all of Baranja, Bačka, and the Banat that belonged to Yugoslavia during the interwar period. From Yugoslavia's neighbors

—which were currently aligned with the Axis powers against Yugoslavia —Great Serbia would claim the following areas: the northern part of Albania, the Kyustendil and Vidin districts from Bulgaria, the Reşita and Timisoara districts from Romania, and the districts of Szeged, Baja, and Pecs from Hungary. Slovenia would become a Great Slovenia, enlarged to more than twice its former size by adding Istria, the Slovene Littoral, a part of Italian territory, a very large part of Austrian-held Carinthia, and a chunk of Hungarian territory. Altogether, Great Serbia was to have some 65 to 70 percent of the total amount of territory and population. Croatia, reduced to less than half its territory and population (i.e. in terms of its post-1945 limits as the Socialist Republic of Croatia), would be effectively hemmed in between Great Serbia and Great Slovenia. Moljević believed that the Serbian statesmen had made a serious mistake in not carefully defining the frontiers of new Serbia in the newly established Yugoslav state in 1918, and he was insisting on the idea that the Serbs at the end of the Second World War should avoid that mistake and should seize all areas that they claimed and present the other nations of Yugoslavia with a fait accompli, and from that position talk about a federally organized Yugoslavia. His plan envisaged large-scale evictions of non-Serb population from various areas as well as large population exchanges, but he did not suggest any figures.

Moljević had definite ideas about the socioeconomic organization of the new Great Serbia. He conceived it as a nation in which work was "the basic goal and sense of life of every man" with just rewards; but the state was to be the chief investor and employer. Private capital was to be permitted to operate but only under state control. All citizens were to be guaranteed a chance to work, and provided with medical care and old age benefits. Freedoms of person, personal initiative, and private property, as well as of thought, religion, and the press, were to be guaranteed but could not be abused at the expense of others; the primary function of the press would be to serve the cause of the people and the state and to further public morality. The church was to be recognized and supported only if it were completely independent toward the outside world and had its head in the country itself; there could be no political parties formed on religious foundations. All this was to combine in a "people's renaissance," in which all segments of the Serbian population, divided into the various professions and inspired by the example of the intelligentsia and youth, would live and work in harmony.

Very similar to the territorial proposals of Dr. Moljević were those formulated by the Belgrade Chetnik Committee in the summer of 1941 and in September 1941 taken out of the country and later delivered to

the government-in-exile in London by Dr. Miloš Sekulić.[3] A map reportedly worked out on the basis of this document goes beyond Moljević, however, in setting forth the details of the large-scale population
shifts that would be necessary to make the Serbian unit purely Serbian
in terms of population. Specifically: from the projected Great Serbia
not less than 2,675,000 people would have to be expelled, including
1,000,000 Croats and 500,000 Germans; 1,310,000 would then be brought
into the newly defined Serbia, 300,000 of them Serbs from Croatia.
Some 200,000 Croats would be permitted to remain in the new Great
Serbia.[4] No figures are suggested for shifts of Moslems—Moslems are,
in fact, only briefly mentioned: "In the Serbian unit the Moslems present a grave problem and if possible it should be solved in this phase"
(meaning, apparently, in the final stages of the war and the early postwar period).[5]

We can assume that Mihailović endorsed all or most of the above
proposals having to do with the territory of a Great Serbia. He alludes
to them in a proclamation issued to the Serbian people the following
December,[6] and in a set of detailed instructions given on December 20
to his newly appointed commanders in Montenegro, Major Lašić and
Captain Djurišić, he makes specific references to them as part of the
Chetnik program. The objectives are, the directive says:

(1) The struggle for the liberty of our whole nation under the scepter of His
Majesty King Peter II; (2) the creation of a Great Yugoslavia and within it of
a Great Serbia which is to be ethnically pure and is to include Serbia [meaning
also Macedonia], Montenegro, Bosnia and Herzegovina, Srijem, the Banat,
and Bačka; (3) the struggle for the inclusion into Yugoslavia of all still un-
liberated Slovene territories under the Italians and Germans (Trieste, Gorizia,
Istria, and Carinthia) as well as [of areas now under] Bulgaria, and northern
Albania with Scutari; (4) the cleansing of the state territory of all national
minorities and a-national elements; (5) the creation of contiguous frontiers
between Serbia and Montenegro, as well as between Serbia and Slovenia by
cleansing [removing?] the Moslem population from Sandjak and the Moslem
and Croat populations from Bosnia and Herzegovina.[7]

The instructions also note that with "the Communist Partisans there
can be no cooperation because they are fighting against the dynasty and
for social revolution, which can never be our objective, because we are
only and exclusively soldiers and fighters for the King, Fatherland, and
the freedom of the people."

[3] For the text of the document see Marjanović, "Contributions," pp. 179–80. The program is
divided into four parts, dealing with the work during the war, work in the transition period,
preparations for normal conditions, and the question of the internal social and political organization.
[4] These figures in much greater detail are indicated in the map showing "Future Yugoslavia"
worked out on the basis of the memorandum of the Belgrade Committee. See Archives of the Institute of Military History, Belgrade, Chetnik Documents, Reg. No. 36/2, Box 7.
[5] Marjanović, "Contributions," p. 180.
[6] Zbornik DNOR, Tome I, Vol. 2, pp. 377–79.
[7] Dokumenti o izdajstvu Draže Mihailovića, I, 12.

The specific conditions of Bosnia and Herzegovina, northern Dalmatia, and southwestern Croatia (Lika) are the subject of a programmatic statement prepared by the Chetnik Dinara Division in March 1942 and accepted a month later by the commanders of these areas at a conference at Strmica, a village near Knin in northern Dalmatia. This statement closely follows Mihailović's instructions of the preceding December to Lašić and Djurišić in advocating the creation of a Great Serbia populated exclusively by Serbs, with a territorial corridor linking Herzegovina, northern Dalmatia, Bosnia, and Lika to Slovenia; it mentions the spreading of the national idea and the mobilization of all national (i.e. Serbian) elements for the cleansing of Herzegovina, Dalmatia, Bosnia, and Lika of other nationalities. But it contains a few additional ideas in the way of wartime strategy: collaboration with the Italians on a live-and-let-live principle, determined struggle against Ustasha formations and the Domobrans, as well as against the Partisans; decent treatment of the Moslems—for the time being, to keep them from joining the Partisans, though later they can be eliminated; and the formation of separate Croatian Chetnik units for pro-Yugoslav, anti-Partisan Croats.[8]

Late the following autumn another important and somewhat expanded version of the Chetniks' basic program emerged from a Conference of Young Chetnik Intellectuals of Montenegro and adjacent areas which was held at Šahovići, a village near the town of Bijelo Polje in Sandjak, between November 30 and December 2. Mihailović himself was not present but he was represented by three of his commanders, Ostojić, Lašić, and Djurišić, and the conclusions of the meetings bore an official stamp. The basic objectives were unchanged: retention of the monarchy under the Karadjordjević dynasty; a unitary Yugoslavia with the Serbian, Croatian, and Slovene units enjoying wide self-government, but all units having territorial links; wielding of all power in the country—with the agreement of the Crown—by the Chetnik organization for a period long enough for the rebuilding and renaissance of the country; a population consisting only of Serbs, Croats, and Slovenes (meaning a denial of nationhood to both Macedonians and Montenegrins), and excluding all national minorities. To these were added agrarian reform following the principle that "land belongs to those who till it"; guaranteed private initiative but nationalized industry, wholesale trade, and banking; an economy organized on the principle of "state cooperativism"; strong legislation against corruption; a gendarmerie recruited from among the Chetniks and under the supervision of the Chetnik organization; and greatly increased propaganda activity to expound Chetnik ideology.[9]

[8] Stanisavljević, pp. 96–100.
[9] *Dokumenti o izdajstvu Draže Mihailovića*, I, 14–25, esp. pp. 23–25.

At about this same time the Chetnik leadership prepared a manual
detailing the Chetnik organization and objectives and setting forth precise directives on how to achieve these objectives.[10] Some of the text re-
peats principles contained in earlier Chetnik programmatic statements,
but the bulk is new, especially in its details on the tasks of various components of the Chetnik organization in various stages of the war, and
the ways in which the Chetniks proposed to achieve their fundamental
objective: "Liberation of the Kingdom of Yugoslavia and of the brothers now living outside its frontiers and creation of conditions for a
sound and progressive life of the Yugoslavs." The manual divides the
war into three phases. Phase one was the April War and the "shameful
capitulation"—by others, but not by those men under the leadership
of Colonel Draža Milhailović who, true to the glorious traditions of
the Serbian people, had refused to lay down their arms and, animated
by "heroic nationalism," had started to gather all that was best in the
nation for a fight against the enemy. Phase two (the current phase) was
the period from the capitulation to the point when conditions would
warrant a general uprising against the enemy. This waiting, a basic
component of Chetnik strategy, is necessary, since the Yugoslavs are
without arms and the country is occupied, while the enemy is extremely
strong, but they will be organizing themselves for the decisive fight,
using unscrupulously all other means of struggle, and waiting to syn-
chronize their operations with favorable developments on other fronts.
Finally, in phase three, they will launch a general attack on the enemy
and throw him out of the country; at the same time they will eliminate
what remains of all competitors for power and assume sole control over
the country, expelling most of the national minorities and apprehend-
ing all internal enemies who have committed crimes against Yugoslavia.
Only by complete organization and careful preparations in phase two
can the movement be successful in the final phase, the manual cautions.
The two most important tasks in phase two are therefore the following:
"(a) Organization of the national struggle through the Yugoslav Army
in the Homeland on purely military foundations, without any (party)
political influences and tendencies, and (b) preventive incapacitation
of the internal enemies of the national struggle of the Yugoslavs (in the
first place of the Communists)." An outline of the working methods of
the movement during the second phase gives further details: "Secret organization combined with authoritative conduct; national, Yugoslav,

---

[10] I have a microcopy of this manual in German translation, a copy of the original (containing
all general material and some specific adaptations for application in Vojvodina, an area with
mixed population the majority of which at that time was non-Serb) having been procured by
agents of the German Security Police and *Sicherheitsdienst*, translated, and subsequently returned
without the Chetniks being aware of what had happened. The German translation runs to 75
single-spaced typed pages. With an introductory letter of July 15, 1943, it was distributed to all
German command posts in Yugoslav territory. Internal evidence suggests that the manual was
prepared during the late months of 1942 with Moljević's help. For the translation, see Microcopy
No. 311, Roll 192, Frames 312–90, esp. Frames 317, 319, and 320 for the portions here quoted.

uniting propaganda with the objective of creating a general popular movement; according to need, activation and employment of special, disciplined armed formations, preferably to be maintained by the purchasing of supplies for cash; sabotage executed only under orders of empowered authorities; use of unscrupulous tactics with the occupying powers and enemies; fighting the internal enemy at each and every opportunity; aid to units with money centrally accumulated and with strict accounting controls." This is followed by a detailed list, by groups, of tasks to be accomplished during phase three from the moment of the general attack against the enemy to the delivery of the country to the legal authorities appointed by the king and people, followed by demobilization. For the future, the manual foresees: "(*a*) a common state of Serbs, Croats, and Slovenes, and possibly later Bulgarians, with the form of state being of secondary importance; (*b*) radical social reform; (*c*) introduction of multi-annual state economic plans; (*d*) educational and moral renaissance; and (*e*) national churches if not one national church."

Although this manual pays some lip service to the idea of Yugoslavism (see Frames 376–78) and makes several statements about the need for expanding and gaining more support among all South Slav peoples, the idea of becoming a true, all-Yugoslav movement was not what the Chetniks desired, since it was inconsistent with the idea of a Great Serbia within a Great Yugoslavia. The Chetnik forces were, of course, almost exclusively Serbs except for a large proportion of Montenegrins who thought of themselves as Serbs. Obviously, the objectives of the movement as set forth in the manual and elsewhere could not be attractive to the non-Serb peoples of Yugoslavia; but on the other hand, the non-Serb peoples could not be disregarded. The Chetniks never succeeded in viewing the national question in Yugoslavia in realistic terms. Not even at Ba did they really approach a solution from the standpoint of Yugoslavia as a whole; the point of departure was always Great Serbia, always within the borders of Yugoslavia but disregarding the legitimate interests of the other nations of Yugoslavia, except the Slovenes, with whom the Serbs were not intermixed and with whom they had no contiguous borders and no differences of interests. The Chetnik solution was simply to claim both the Macedonians and the Montenegrins as Serbs and to claim as Serbian lands most of the territories in which Serbs lived even in relatively small numbers mixed with other South Slav nations, primarily Croats. This had been traditional Great Serbia thinking for many years. The new wartime feature—undoubtedly a reaction to the massacres of the Serbs in the Independent State of Croatia—was the plan to clear or "cleanse" these lands of non-Serb population.

The Chetnik manual of late 1942 discussed the question of Croatia at some length, with the idea of securing the cooperation at least of a sizable proportion of Croats with the Chetnik movement. Mihailović had a small group of followers among the Croats in central Dalmatia, especially from the area of Split and Šibenik, most of them either former members of the strongly pro-Yugoslav organizations of the early 1920's such as ORJUNA or younger people out of such families, but the group was too small to have any political or military significance.[11] A few Croats in the Croatian Littoral (Primorje) were also pro-Mihailović. In Slovenia there was a small pro-Mihailović group headed by Major Karlo Novak, and Mihailović also had a not very satisfactory working arrangement with the main anti-Communist armed and political forces of the province, consisting primarily of the followers of the Slovene People's Party. A few Sandjak and Bosnian Moslems also supported him.

A rather curious argument is presented in the manual, to the effect that the Serbs and Croats were equally the victims of unscrupulous politicians of all sorts during the interwar period. The manual even asserts—with no suggestion of proof—that in all Serbia, and especially in Belgrade, there were more Croats than Serbs in government service and that "the Serbs were not in the least in a favored position, rather it was the Croats." Furthermore, it was not the Croatian people who were the enemy of the Serbs but only the Frankovci (that is, the wartime Ustashas), and therefore the Chetniks should look upon the Croatians as they did upon the Serbian people and should call upon all Croats of "correct behavior" to cooperate with them and form Croatian military units under the Chetnik banner. They should also invite the Croatian army to shift to the Chetnik side. But any Ustashas who offered armed resistance should be dealt with summarily and executed on the spot. This broad program of establishing new relations with the Croats would have to be carried out gradually and intelligently, but firmly. Discussions of population exchanges should not be anticipated but should wait until the frontiers of the various national units had been decided. Nor should the question of religion be brought up yet.[12] All these important matters relating to the national question were, in other words, to be settled after the Chetniks had achieved their goal of phase three—the complete control of the country—and had determined the limits of the Serbian unit.

Since the war, the Chetnik policy on the all-important national question has been analyzed with a good deal of objectivity by Dr. Živko Topalović, who as president of the Yugoslav National Democratic Union established at the Ba congress was one of the leading figures in the po-

---

[11] See Radmilo Grdjić, pp. 262–68, and Stanisavljević, pp. 81, 113.
[12] Microcopy No. T-311, Roll 192, Frames 368, 371–72.

litical wing of the Chetnik movement from January 1944 until the collapse. He especially stresses the close connection between religious affiliation and national belonging, and makes the differences between the Chetnik ideology and the Partisan ideology, particularly in multinational and multireligious areas under Italian occupation (parts of Sandjak and Bosnia and Herzegovina), very clear:

> Anti-Croatianism, anti-Moslemism, and anti-Yugoslavism, this is the ideology of the Serbian Chetniks....
>
> Experience has shown, however, that in addition to mutual extermination the religious-chauvinistic ideology had one basic consequence—it pushed the Serbs, the Croats, and the Moslems into dependence upon and submission to the foreign conqueror. It was only in this fashion that one could save his own people and struggle against the members of the other denominations. The Communists, however, took another way, the way of union of all South Slavs and the way of religious tolerance. They succeeded in finding understanding for this policy among the younger generations of Serbs, Croats, and Moslems, especially in the multinational and multireligious areas.[13]

Although this characterization is supposed to fit primarily the religiously and nationally mixed areas, it also fits the Chetnik movement at large.

The simple truth was that the Chetnik movement had no postwar solution of the national question to offer the non-Serb nations of Yugoslavia because Mihailović, like Nikola Pašić and King Alexander, and practically all other Serbian politicians and high-ranking officers of the interwar period, did not understand that a strong and workable Yugoslavia had to be something quite different from an expanded Serbia, and that it required a totally different political and psychological attitude on the part of the leaders and the population at large in every one of the five South Slav nations, but especially in Serbia and Croatia. Obviously, Mihailović and his advisers only vaguely comprehended the enormousness of the changes that were taking place in the country as a result of the surrender and occupation and of the Communist-led resistance and revolution. Their main thought was to bring back what had been lost, to restore the monarchy and the Serbian-controlled state apparatus. During the interwar period Serbians had dominated all state coercive power, including the entire army and the police, and through long years of practice of political patronage also the government bureaucracy—all forces working for Serbian hegemonism. This had now

---

[13] Topalović, *Pokreti narodnog otpora*, pp. 52–53; also pp. 16–17, 103. See also Chapter 7, n. 172. Some Mihailović followers in exile took sharp issue with these interpretations in their reviews of Topalović's book. See e.g. Radoje L. Knežević in *Poruka*, No. 50–51, pp. 17–18, and Vukčević in *Glasnik SIKD 'Njegoš'*, December 1958, pp. 113–25, esp. pp. 120–22. Topalović's views are essentially sound, but as his critics realize, if one accepts the thesis that the Great Serbia doctrine and other narrow policies made the Chetnik movement unacceptable to the majority of the people of Yugoslavia, one cannot very well argue also—as they wish to do—that Mihailović and his movement failed because they were victims of an unholy alliance involving Great Britain, the Soviet Union, and their Yugoslav helpers Tito and Šubašić.

been reduced to a small, loosely organized, and poorly led Chetnik army, made up almost solely of Serbs and Montenegrins, pursuing a narrow nationalist policy and engaged in a military venture that was directed almost exclusively against fellow Yugoslavs rather than against the foreign powers who had brought on the country's disaster. If Mihailović appreciated the true nature of the situation, he gave no sign. And of course he had reason to feel confident as long as he had the unquestioned backing of the government-in-exile and the Western allies.

He also had the support of the Serbian Orthodox Church, which as a national church long identified with the national destiny and aspirations of the Serbian people was naturally inclined to identify itself with the movement that had the backing of the king and the Serbian-dominated government-in-exile. Most of the clergy had been outspokenly anti-Communist before the war, and continued to be so. Dr. Djura Djurović, secretary general of the Chetnik Central National Committee from June to September 1944, testified at his trial in the summer of 1945 that "three-quarters of the Orthodox clergy supported the Draža Mihailović movement."[14] That seems a fair estimate. Of course, most of this support was secret, but a certain proportion of Orthodox priests openly expressed their adherence to the Chetnik movement. There were, naturally, a great many limitations on the activity of the church in occupied Serbia and even more in some other areas. The Germans were extremely suspicious of the church and did not hesitate to intern any churchman, however high, who seemed uncooperative with the quisling and occupation authorities. Patriarch Gavrilo, strongly anti-German, was at first interned in a monastery in the Banat and later taken to the Dachau concentration camp (and finally released shortly before the end of the war); also first interned at home and then taken to Dachau was the Bishop of Žiča, Nikolaj Velimirović, the best-known Serbian churchman of the interwar period (also released shortly before the end of the war).

The Serbian Orthodox Church headed by the Patriarch included not only the church in Serbia but also the church in Macedonia, in Montenegro, in parts annexed by Hungary, and in the territories that in April 1941 were made part of the Independent State of Croatia (it had also a few bishoprics abroad). Because these areas were subjected to different regimes of occupation in April 1941, the conditions under which the church existed during the war years differed greatly from area to area. In Montenegro, where the church was not persecuted, Metropolitan Joanikije followed the lead of the Chetnik commanders in collabo-

[14] *Sudjenje članovima rukovodstva organizacije Draže Mihailovića*, pp. 81–82.

rating with the Italians, and after them with the Germans, as well as in resolutely opposing the Communist-led Partisans.[15]

In Macedonia, all the top members of the church hierarchy as well as a great number of Orthodox priests were expelled by the Bulgarians, who annexed most of the area in April 1941, because these bishops and priests were considered as foremost carriers of Serbdom and Serbian Orthodoxy in Macedonia. Undoubtedly one of the many reasons for the strong church support of the Chetniks was the latter's stand on Macedonia as an integral part of Serbia and Macedonians as Serbs and thus for full control by the Serbian Orthodox Church over Macedonia— whereas the Communists acknowledged that the Macedonians were a separate nation entitled to a state of their own within the Yugoslav federal union.[16]

Most difficult was the situation of the church in the puppet state of Croatia, where the church and the Serbian Orthodox population were systematically and ruthlessly persecuted. Three Orthodox bishops and many scores of priests were killed; many churches and monasteries were destroyed; and the killing of the Serbian population, forced conversion to Roman Catholicism, and expellings to Serbia were practiced on a mass basis. In June 1942 the Orthodox Church in Croatia was separated from the body of the Serbian Orthodox Church by decree and constituted as an independent Croatian Orthodox Church. The head of the puppet state, Pavelić, named Germogen (the former Archbishop of Ekaterinoslav in Russia, who had lived in Yugoslavia for many years as a guest of the Serbian Orthodox Church) as Metropolitan of Zagreb and head of the new church.[17] Persecution of the Orthodox population continued even after the separation, however.

Both in Montenegro and in the puppet state of Croatia, just as in Serbia, the great majority of Orthodox priests sided with the Chetniks, and in the puppet state some of them—for example, the Reverend Momčilo Djujić and the Reverend Savo Božić—became well-known Chetnik commanders. On the other hand, in all areas a small number of Orthodox priests joined the Partisans. It should be noted, too, that the Partisans generally underplayed the traditional anti-church tenets of Communist ideology, even to the point of allowing regular chaplains with some of their fighting units. Estimates on the number of Orthodox

---

[15] *Dokumenti o izdajstvu Draže Mihailovića*, I, 186–92.

[16] The fear of the church hierarchy about the future of the Orthodox Church in Macedonia, or more precisely its control by the Serbian Church, was clearly evident in some private statements to American officials made in April 1945 by Acting Patriarch Josif, who first as Bishop of Bitola during the 1920's and then as Metropolitan of Skopje between 1932 and 1941 when he was chased out by the Bulgarians had helped to develop the church organization and its educational institutions. See RG 226, OSS–File No. XL9761, pp. 5–7.

[17] See Kašić, "The Serbian Church in the So-called Independent State of Croatia."

priests who lost their lives during the war as a result of persecution or other unnatural causes vary widely; most authoritative is the total figure of 515 used by Kašić.[18]

THE MILITARY ORGANIZATION

Since Mihailović's main goal was the restoration of the monarchy and the establishment of a Great Serbia, it followed that he conceived his Chetnik resistance in military rather than political terms and had no particular interest himself in making his forces anything more than the army of the exile government. Mihailović, as we have seen, first designated his small group of officers and men at Ravna Gora the Chetnik Command of the Yugoslav Army. This designation was changed to Chetnik Detachments of the Yugoslav Army, and from January 1942 on—that is, after Mihailović was made Minister of the Army, Navy, and Air Force in the government-in-exile—it bore the official designation Yugoslav Army in the Homeland.

The first Chetnik armed detachments in Serbia, usually named after the mountain or river of the area or the particular county, were mustered for the most part by young professional officers sent out by Mihailović, though some arose spontaneously on their own before Mihailović's emissaries arrived and were then recognized by Mihailović and made part of his military organization. These armed detachments, generally numbering fifty to two hundred men, occasionally more than that, were under the command of men who were responsible to Mihailović and operated under his general instructions but nevertheless had a wide latitude of independent action. This freedom was to some extent a matter of necessity, owing to difficulties, especially at the outset, of communicating with headquarters, but it was also a way of allowing the local commanders to take into consideration the local conditions. This was the state of the Chetnik forces in September 1941 when they began sporadic fighting in the uprising that had been going on since July under the leadership of Communist-led armed units. For the greater part of the following year, the Chetniks continued in this loose fashion. More detachments, as we have seen, were brought under the Chetnik banner in Bosnia and Herzegovina and Montenegro, and Mihailović made efforts, not always successful, to replace local commanders with his own men, but the overall command still lacked organizational strength. The troops were united in fighting "For the King and the Fatherland" and for the freedom of the Serbs and of Yugoslavia, as

---

[18] Kašić, "The Serbian Church Under German Occupation," p. 231. In Kašić's study of the Serbian Church in the Independent State of Croatia (p. 191) the figure of 219 is given for the number of Orthodox priests killed in the Croatian puppet state during the war. Paris, pp. 285–89, gives a list of 171 Orthodox priests, including three bishops, killed by the Ustashas in the early part of the war. See also Smiljanić et al., p. 13.

the Chetnik manual emphasized, but they were just soldiers, over-whelmingly of peasant origin, steeped in Serbian tradition, and totally ignorant in terms of political ideas and interrelationships. Even so, the Chetnik leaders made no attempts at systematic political education or indoctrination of the members of their forces or of the population at large in the areas in which they operated.

Practically from the start of their organization the Chetniks began establishing three kinds of companies.[19] Sometime in the spring of 1942, realizing that local commanders were often ignoring the instructions, Mihailović issued the important Directive No. 5 which specified in detail the principles of Chetnik military organization. The three categories of companies were: Category 3, mobile, operative troops, consisting of manpower between the ages of twenty and thirty; category 2, companies with manpower of ages thirty-one to forty, these to concentrate on sabotage activity against communications (roads, bridges, railroads); and category 1, local and supporting troops, consisting of manpower of ages forty-one to fifty, whose duty was to maintain law and order and protect their own villages. Two to four companies would form a battalion and two to five battalions a brigade. Each county was to have a commandant who would be in charge of companies 1 and 2 in the county. Directive No. 5 also specified certain other duties of the county commandants, such as organization of intelligence and propaganda services in their areas, boring into enemy units, and so on.[20]

Late in 1942 this basic organization was amended, presumably to meet the needs of the rapidly developing war against the Partisans, in the direction of greater mobility and versatility. Under the new plan, which went into effect on January 1, 1943, the basic unit was the *trojka* or three-man unit, consisting of a leader, a deputy, and a third member for liaison tasks between the other two and between the trojka and the superior authorities—a revival, in fact, of the traditional Serbian guerrilla unit long considered to be convenient and efficient. Fifteen to thirty trojkas were to form a company, three companies a battalion, and three battalions a brigade. There were also corps, consisting of three to five brigades (some of these were started even before the plan

[19] The Sekulić report of September 1941 mentions these three kinds of companies, and they are referred to by Marjanović in his "Contributions," pp. 169–70. In parts of Bosnia and Lika and in northern Dalmatia, however, as early as the winter of 1941–42, some of the large Chetnik units were called regiments and divisions, e.g. Regiment "King Peter II" and Dinara Division.

[20] A copy of the text of Directive No. 5 is to be found in the Archives of the Institute of Military History, Belgrade, Chetnik Documents, Reg. No. 10/3, Box 1; reports on its application can be found in a directive letter of Major Ostojić to the Chetnik commanders of July 30, 1942, Reg. No. 14/2, Box 1, and a report of Major Miodrag P. Pološević to Mihailović of Nov. 5, 1942, Reg. No. 34/2, Box 1.

On the basis of intercepted radio messages between Mihailović's headquarters and his various commanders in the field, the German radio monitoring service in Belgrade was able to reconstruct in great detail the entire Chetnik military organization and to identify practically all the commanders, and on September 11, 1942, it submitted a detailed report entitled "The Organization of the Draža Mihailović Movement." See Microcopy No. T-312, Roll 470, Frames 8,060,380–435.

officially went into effect).[21] Elite brigades, consisting of the best and youngest manpower, were designated as "flying brigades."

According to the Chetnik manual already referred to, during the second phase the Chetnik command staffs were supposed to operate within certain specified territories, with all levels—corps, brigade, battalion, and company—carrying out specific tasks. These tasks are described in detail for the second and third phases, using Vojvodina as an example of a typical organization. As before, the commandant of each county was in charge of companies 1 and 2, as well as of labor companies. With the beginning of phase three, the overall command of each area, heretofore lodged in the corps or brigade commander, would split into two parts: the operational troops (based on companies of category 3) under the operational commanders, and the territorial troops (based on categories 1 and 2) under county commandants. As new areas were gradually liberated by the operational troops, the territorial troops would take over the role of military government and carry out the tasks assigned to them as listed in the manual.[22]

Much later—in the spring of 1944 when the Chetniks in Serbia were under great pressure from two Partisan divisions which penetrated deep into Serbian territory from the southwest and fought there for some time—several shock corps and groups of shock corps, consisting of the best flying brigades pulled from regular corps, were formed, but that was the only change that occurred in the basic army structure established in January 1943.

How large was the Chetnik army, and where did it get its manpower? The second part of the question is the easier to answer. The first Chetnik units in Serbia were of course volunteer forces, consisting of men who desired to follow Mihailović in a resistance against the armies that had invaded and occupied their country. But as the months wore on and the Partisans became the prime enemy as well as a rival resistance force that was attracting many volunteers, the Chetniks found it necessary to resort to a system of drafting men wherever needed—that is, in areas under their control where, as the official Yugoslav Army in the Homeland which had the backing of the king and the government-in-exile, they could assert their authority. Not all these forces were on active duty at all times; most were only registered on mobilization rolls and on call, presumably ready to respond in time of need.

Besides the illegal Chetniks, there were from late 1941 on the legalized Chetnik troops which served as auxiliaries of the Italian army or of the quisling armies in Serbia and the Independent State of Croatia.

[21] See Vučković, "Guerrilla Formation of the Yugoslav Army in the Homeland"; also Ratković, pp. 99–106.
[22] Microcopy No. T-311, Roll 192, Frames 323–45.

Soon after the Italian collapse most of the Chetnik units throughout the country began to serve as German auxiliaries against the Partisans on the basis of formal written or informal oral agreements, and were given arms, ammunition, and other supplies to carry on this fight. But all of these units were always counted by the Chetniks as parts of the Yugoslav Army in the Homeland.

Because of this diversity of forces, and also because of the Chetnik habit of exaggerating figures for propaganda purposes, it is very hard to determine just how large the Chetnik forces actually were. In his December 1941 proclamation to the Serbian people, Mihailović said that the Chetniks had "in the country a strong military organization with more than 300,000 people."[23] Later on there was frequent mention of the army of "200,000 to 250,000" Chetniks. Evidently, some figures included not only troops on active duty but also men who were registered and on call and probably men of certain age classes who were registered on mobilization rolls and were assumed to be present in areas under Chetnik control. For example, a telegram of Mihailović to the government-in-exile dated March 20, 1943, speaks of having organized at least 1,000 men per county in 180 out of the 338 counties in the country, or a total of 180,000 men; in most of the remaining counties, particularly those in Vojvodina, northern Croatia, and northern Slovenia, he was working secretly.[24] But according to Major Vučković, one of Mihailović's top commanders, "what was true in the wartime reports were the figures of soldiers from specific territories who in the case of a sufficient supply of arms could be made available."[25] At the end of 1943, Vučković says, the strength of the various corps in western Serbia was between 2,500 and 3,000 men, but much less than that in eastern Serbia and the flat areas of the country. Another source—a Nedić official who was forced to serve with the Chetniks for some time during the autumn of 1943 and who later returned to the Nedić fold—tells us that the 67th Corps under the command of Major Velimir J. Piletić (the principal Mihailović commander in northeastern Serbia) was made up of five brigades numbering in all about 600 active Chetniks, with a staff of about 60.[26]

About Chetniks in Montenegro and the Independent State of Croatia we can be more certain. At the beginning of 1943 there were some 40,000–50,000 Chetniks in Montenegro and the Italian zone of the Independent State of Croatia; in the German zone at the end of 1942 about 10,000 Bosnian Chetniks had live-and-let-live agreements with the Cro-

[23] *Zbornik DNOR*, Tome I, Vol. 2, p. 377.
[24] Živan L. Knežević, *Why the Allies Abandoned*, Part 1, pp. 6–7.
[25] Vučković, "Guerrilla Formation," p. 72.
[26] Deposition to German interrogators of Dec. 31, 1943. Microcopy No. T-311, Roll 189, Frames 232, 237.

atian quisling authorities, but the number of "rebel" Chetniks actively working against the Croatian government was undoubtedly much less than that.[27] For the country as a whole at the end of 1943 the Germans estimated Chetnik actual strength as follows: Slovenia, 500; northern Dalmatia and Lika, 2,000; western Bosnia, 1,500; eastern Bosnia, 3,000; Herzegovina, 3,000; Montenegro, 5,000; southwestern Serbia, 2,500; northwestern Serbia, 3,000; middle Serbia, 3,000; Kapaonik Mountain area, 1,500; southeastern Serbia, 3,000–4,000; and northeastern Serbia, about 2,000. This adds up to a total force of 30,000–31,000 men.[28] Of course, as will be shown later, there was a large increase in Chetnik forces in the course of 1944 both in Serbia and the puppet state of Croatia.

It is fair to assume that if the Allies had executed a large-scale landing on the Dalmatian coast, as the Chetniks had hoped they would do, the Chetniks would have been able to carry through their plan to increase their strength by general mobilization in areas under their control, and those detachments that were collaborating with the German and the Croatian forces would have turned their arms against them. According to the 1942 manual, they also planned to organize the employees in railroad and river shipping lines and in the telephone and telegraph services in occupied areas, who were expected to stage mass civil disobedience at the beginning of phase three for the purpose of impeding enemy countermeasures against the general uprising.[29] It is not likely, however, that either the old or the newly recruited troops would have become overnight a very efficient armed force, and it would certainly not have been an all-Yugoslav one, since the Chetniks never had had more than a token following outside the Serbian and Montenegrin nations. Furthermore, even if the Allies had landed on the Dalmatian coast, immense political and military complications would have arisen for the Chetniks—the Partisans also would have cooperated with the Allies, and the Croatian Domobrans, too, who were eagerly awaiting that moment, would have shifted en bloc to the Allied side and insisted that they be recognized as a separate army.

With the exception of the flying brigades and later of shock corps, the Chetnik army remained throughout the war a loose agglomeration of forces, a sort of territorial militia, nominally under the command of Mihailović—in some cases various units being under his direct command—but in fact many units often acting quite independently. Lack of mobility was a characteristic of most Chetnik units, and combat morale was usually not at a high level, especially in the case of freshly

---

[27] Microcopy No. T-501, Roll 264, Frames 568–69, 583. For details, see Chapter 7, p. 229.
[28] Microcopy No. T-311, Roll 189, Frame 262.
[29] *Ibid.*, Roll 192, Frames 355–57.

drafted units and when fighting away from home areas. Chetnik units also lacked a strong political ideology capable of sustaining them in critical periods. There was a lack of strict discipline, from the top levels on down, and individual commanders were frequently jealous of one another's position and standing with the Supreme Command, so that there were squabbles and petty rivalries. Mihailović and his Supreme Command often seemed unable to enforce their orders or to induce various commanders to work together effectively.[30] Without strong guidance and strict lines of command, local commanders often tended to resort to expediency and to regard their particular areas as something like fiefs. As one former officer in exile who strongly supported Mihailović and his Chetniks has put it: "Very rare were the cases where various regional commanders cooperated sincerely and helped each other. It seems that these commanders agreed only in one respect: all of them sent to General Mihailović very optimistic reports about the conditions in their areas and magnified their personal merits."[31] There were also cases where various commanders struggled against one another, and according to Mihailović's own testimony the Inspector of all Chetnik forces, Colonel Jevrem Simić, was killed by the Chetniks when he was passing through the Raković territory.[32]

This extreme decentralization of the Chetnik forces did have an advantage in that it made for easier maintenance, though to the extent that this led to great resentment among the people on whom the burden of maintenance fell, even that advantage was not unmitigated.[33] In the early stages of the movement at Ravna Gora, the Chetniks could count on their supporters for voluntary contributions of money and supplies, but as time went on a system of more or less compulsory contributions

[30] The lack of discipline was such that in the very important telegram No. 487 of November 7, 1943, ordering the mobilization of all disposable armed forces in all Serbian provinces and immediate and most energetic attacks against the Communists, Mihailović saw fit to say: "All commanders who do not execute this order will be punished for treason." Archives of the Institute of Military History, Belgrade, Chetnik Documents, Reg. No. 19/1, Box 3.

[31] Putnik, pp. 39–40. Ostojić's directive letter of July 30, 1942, implored the Chetnik commanders "to avoid conflicts and arguments and to live and work in peace." See also two reports of Major Palošević, an officer who joined Mihailović while he was on the move from Bosnia to Ravna Gora in April and May 1941, in which he complains about the behavior both of his superiors and of his subordinate commanders: Archives of the Institute of Military History, Belgrade, a letter of Palošević of Nov. 5, 1942, Chetnik Documents, Reg. No. 34/2, Box 1, and a letter of April 29, 1943, Reg. No. 3/2, Box 2, both letters being addressed to General Mihailović personally; also a letter of Lt. Colonel Ljuba Jovanović-Patak, a Chetnik commander in eastern Serbia (no date available), to General Mihailović, Reg. No. 49/2, Box 129.

[32] *The Trial of Draža Mihailović*, p. 377; see also pp. 162, 190, 250, 335–36, and *passim* for similar admissions by Mihailović that his commanders frequently disobeyed his orders and instructions. In regard to Raković, willfulness of various Chetnik commanders in Serbia, and Mihailović's inability to control them see also Topalović, *Srbija pod Dražom*, pp. 18–20.

[33] *Dokumenti o izdajstvu Draže Mihailovića*, I, 592–96. Because of their behavior and probably also their often extravagant mode of living, the Chetnik commanders in Serbia came to be referred to by many of the population as *rasovi*, derived from the Arabic word *ras* and especially used to denote local chieftains in Ethiopia. The term became popular in Yugoslavia during the Italian invasion of Ethiopia, but during the war in Serbia, as well as in the Independent State of Croatia where it was applied to Ustasha commanders, it took on a mocking, derogatory connotation.

was found necessary to support the growing number of units.[34] The villages were expected to provide in one way or another for the units stationed in their areas, supplying food and animals and money, sometimes in the form of loans to be repaid as soon as possible.[35] More will be said about the problems of supplying and arming the Chetniks in later chapters—the problem of securing arms and ammunition for fighting the Partisans became, indeed, one of Mihailović's chief worries, and it has been often presented as the principal reason for Chetnik collaboration with Axis and quisling forces. The "legalized" Chetnik units were, of course, supplied and armed and paid, to one degree or another, by the armies to which they were attached as auxiliaries, and it became possible for the illegal Chetniks of Mihailović to draw off some of the matériel by surreptitious means. To a very small extent, until the end of 1943, the British provided supplies and money. There is no evidence, however, that the Chetniks ever systematically engaged in the Partisan technique—common to Communist-led guerrilla forces everywhere—of obtaining arms and supplies by capturing them from the enemy in military engagements.

General Mihailović, as the appointed Minister of the Army, Navy, and Air Force of the exiled government and Chief of Staff of the Supreme Command, had the authority of an official army leader and as a trained general staff officer thought along traditional military lines; he had studied guerrilla warfare, however, and could have been expected to apply his knowledge. One observer, Lt. Colonel Albert B. Seitz, who for several months in 1943 was the ranking American officer attached to the British military mission with Mihailović, has placed him "next to Lawrence [of Arabia] in excellence" of knowledge and skill in guerrilla warfare. According to Seitz, Mihailović's "principles of success" were roughly as follows:

1—Always lead and provide inspiration. 2—Know your terrain as the palm of your hand. 3—Train your people, fighters and peasants, to report all movements and actions of the enemy. 4—Weed out your traitors and talkers. 5—Strike only when you can gain advantage. 6—Keep your fighters hard, fit and fed. 7—Use as few fighters as possible, drawing reserves from peasantry trained to fight your way, for specific action. 8—Never give the enemy a chance to attack you. Hit him hard and disengage and disappear while he is still in shock. Be like the drops from a bucket of water thrown on the ground. 9—Requisition your needs from the enemy in battle or from those who can spare it. Help the poor. This will keep the people on your side. 10—Hold to your cause with

[34] Microcopy No. 312, Roll 470, Frames 8,060,420–21.

[35] In his "Directive on Mobilization" issued on January 7, 1942, Mihailović ordered that those called upon to serve were to take along food for three days. Thereafter, assembled units were to send one or two men to the villages for food. *Dokumenti o izdajstvu Draže Mihailovića*, I, 9–10, 32–34.

God, and the people will hold to that cause because it means freedom, and without freedom a man is better dead.[36]

These are sound principles as far as they go, and they may well have been what Mihailović held as the ideal. Almost nothing exists, however, in the way of written material about actual guerrilla operations from the Chetniks themselves.[37] We know that guerrilla warfare manuals did exist and that some training in guerrilla warfare was carried out. We also know that both the Italians and after September 1943 the Germans often stated that they could not afford to give up the Chetniks as allies because they had proved themselves as excellent fighters against the Partisans. (Of course in these cases the Chetniks acted as Italian or German auxiliaries, were supplied by them and, to a large extent, were under their tactical command.) Despite all this, the fact remains that the Chetniks did not prove themselves, when acting independently, to be a superior fighting force either as guerrillas or in operations by large units.[38] During much of the war they had a very broad base of support in both Serbia and Montenegro, but they lacked proper military and political leadership, an overwhelming commitment among all the commanders and units for their cause as a whole, and a strong ideology, and therefore the movement was never able to draw itself together into a cohesive force.

POLITICAL ORGANIZATION AND PROPAGANDA

The Chetnik Central National Committee that was formed at Ravna Gora in August 1941 was intended to be an advisory body. It included some former politicians—mostly from the fourth-ranking Serbian party the Serbian Agrarians and the miniscule Republican Party—and some leading members of patriotic and cultural organizations such as the Serbian Cultural Club. The Executive Council of the Committee which for the first two years or so consisted of Dragiša Vasić, Dr. Stevan Moljević, and Dr. Mladen Žujović handled a multitude of tasks, however, such as administrative matters, some liaison work with important supporters of the Mihailović movement, and propaganda—tasks for which Mihailović's military commanders were not suited. Practically all the men on the Committee and all three members of its Executive Council were men of a narrow, that is, Great Serbian, outlook rather than of a

[36] Seitz, p. 39.

[37] A collection of Chetnik wartime documents is presently in the process of publication by the Institute of Military History in Belgrade.

[38] According to Vučković, "Guerrilla Formation," p. 73, Mihailović's headquarters published toward the end of 1941 a handbook, *Uput za četničko ratovanje* (Handbook on Guerrilla Warfare), which was for some time used as a training manual. Unfortunately I was unable to consult this publication and could not compare it with the instructional manual under the same title published by the Yugoslav Ministry of the Army and Navy in Belgrade in 1929. See also Djelević, p. 184.

broader or Yugoslav political outlook, and they had little or no political experience.

Although both Mihailović and his political advisers repeatedly assert-ed that the Chetnik organization centering around the Yugoslav Army in the Homeland was only a military organization dedicated to the lib-eration of the country, the freeing of those Yugoslavs still under foreign rule, and the restoration of the monarchy and the legitimate govern-ment, and not at all a political organization, the Chetnik organization as an instrument of the government-in-exile and as an exponent of Great Serbian objectives was eminently also a political organization. This is clearly indicated by the following facts: the Chetniks endeav-ored, even during the war, to annihilate all competitors for power in postwar Yugoslavia, in particular the Communist Party of Yugoslavia which from the beginning appeared the most serious and dangerous competitor; the Chetniks defined and fought for the realization of the Great Serbian territorial objectives within Yugoslavia; claiming that they were not engaged in political activity, they insisted also that no other political groups should engage in such activity while the war was still on; and finally, they were preparing to introduce a Chetnik dicta-torship after the war for a period long enough to carry out most of their program. It does not matter that the political decisions were made not by civilian politicians but rather by Mihailović and his military com-manders.[39]

Essentially, these attitudes never changed, despite the democratic-sounding principles contained in the resolution that came out of the Ba congress—which was in any event too late in the day to count for much either as propaganda or as proof of a change of direction. None of the Chetniks really had a change of heart, though some, including Mihailović himself and a few of his civilian advisers, realized eventually that they must widen their political base by cooperating with the repre-sentatives of various Serbian political parties in order to counteract the existing impression that the Chetniks were striving toward a system of military dictatorship and, also, to survive against the Partisans. A re-port prepared in May 1945 by the Serbian anti-Communist politicians, intellectuals, and economists describes the atmosphere in the Chetnik camp during the war as follows:

... colonel Draza Mihailovic, later promoted to general rank, was surrounded by people of whom some had failed in the political and public life, who did not see the whole importance of the movement and the complicatedness of a fight to be led at the same time against the occupator, the "ustashas," the Quislings in Serbia and Montenegro and finally against the communist party

[39] For the nature of the Chetnik political organization and decision making see the revealing statements by Djurović at his trial in August 1945. *Sudjenje članovima rukovodstva organizacije Draže Mihailovića*, pp. 69–83, 481–500.

which fought for its special aims. Devoid of any political spirit, anxious to keep the positions they kept with the war minister Draza Mihailovic, lacking broadness of view on the whole Yugoslav problem, which arose again in its full seriousness after the debacle of Yugoslavia, these counsellors of Mihailovic surrounded themselves with a Chinese wall against all the politicians who would have been able to help them in the interest of the nation. With their narrow-minded notions and ill advice, they gave Mihailovic—who was only an army officer without political horizon—they were of disastrous influence on the brought decisions and the attitude of the movement against the occupator, the allies, the communists and the own people. Besides, some of Mihailovic's local commanders, as a result of the bad communications, became independent and violent in such a degree that they began to be an evil to the people. Their willful, often bloody acts were condemned by the people, and although they used terror, unquestionable misgivings could be heard.[40]

In the spring of 1942 a Serbian National Committee was established in Split by *vojvoda* Trifunović-Birčanin, and in July of the same year a Committee of Montenegrin Nationalists was established. Neither of these was formally subordinate to the Central National Committee because these organizations for tactical reasons maintained that they were not aligned with Mihailović, but they were intended to function, and did function, as regional political bodies supporting Mihailović and the Chetnik movement.

As long as Mihailović held official positions in the government-in-exile he personally was the head of the domestic branch of the legitimate Yugoslav government and he exercised the prerogatives of the government in the name of the king. In all areas that were effectively under Chetnik control, including those which by acquiescence of the occupying forces were left to the Chetniks to administer (e.g. in much of Montenegro and certain parts of the territory of the Independent State of Croatia under Italian occupation), the Chetniks maintained the old Yugoslav system of local administration, simply putting it under their own men. This was one of the expressions of Chetnik conservatism and one of the fundamental differences between them and the Partisans, who thoroughly wrecked the old administrative system and established a completely new one.

Perceiving the political importance of youth for the Chetnik movement, the Chetniks established in November 1942 the Yugoslav Ravna Gora Youth (*Jugoslovenska ravnogorska omladina* or JURAO). This organization, based on the pre-1941 youth sections of the Serbian Cultural Club, the Democratic Party (almost purely Serbian), and the Ser-

[40] RG 226, OSS–File No. XL13541, p. 6. This report, obviously in a crude English translation, was submitted secretly to the U.S. military attaché in Belgrade and relayed by him to Washington in July 1945. The criticism of this group about Mihailović's wartime entourage seems to have been primarily directed against Vasić and Moljević. For Vasić's background and some of his characteristics, see the pamphlet entitled *Dragiša Vasić* by his colleague Mladen J. Žujović. For Vasić's reported views about Moljević and to some extent about Mihailović, as well as about himself, see Topalović, *Srbija pod Dražom*, pp. 16–20.

bian Agrarian Party, was under the overall control of the Supreme Command and was organized on a regional basis by means of staffs (e.g. Staffs 708 and 801 for Montenegro and Staffs 501, 601, and 701 for Serbia). The most important branch was apparently Staff 501, whose area included the city of Belgrade and all of western and central Serbia, where Mihailović's command was located after June 1943; most of the information we have about JURAO concerns this area.[41] A directive issued by Staff 501 on February 15, 1943, describes something of how the organization functioned in urban areas.[42] The objective, as outlined therein, was to assemble and organize all Serbian "nationally [politically?] uncompromised" young men, to indoctrinate them in the Chetnik spirit, and to prepare them for the fulfillment of all tasks "which the interests of the Serbian people and our superiors require." The basic organizational unit was the same as in the revised army, the trojka, and there were special sections, following the trojka principle, for high school youth, university students (although the University of Belgrade was closed), people in the Nedić government-sponsored Youth Labor Service, and young people in industry and handicrafts. Disciplinary rules were the same as those of the Yugoslav Army in the Homeland, and the Ravna Gora Youth members were subject to call by the corps or brigade commander of the area. Limited as it was in its Serbian outlook, and limited also, at least to some extent, by the Chetnik bias against women, the Chetnik youth movement was no rival to the United Alliance of Antifascist Youth of Yugoslavia and especially to its core and controlling force, the United Communist Youth of Yugoslavia—though it undoubtedly contained many dedicated and well-disciplined young men.

One of the fundamental differences between the Chetnik and Partisan movements was in their attitude toward women. The participation of women in Partisan fighting ranks and mass organizations of the Partisan movement was of such importance that all Partisan officials agreed that without the women the Partisans could never have won. Whereas the Partisan fighting ranks numbered between 15 and 20 percent women, I have never found any references to women among Chetnik fighters. Indeed, there were no women at all in Chetnik fighting units; women were used only for nursing and occasionally for intelligence work.[43] Since the status of peasant women in the parts of the country where the Chetniks were the strongest (Serbia, Montenegro, Bosnia and Herzegovina) was very low, a skillful policy of mobilizing women would un-

[41] One of the rare statements on the Ravna Gora youth movement is an article by two of its former leaders, Milorad M. Drachkovitch and Branko Lazitch, containing their recollections of its organization, functioning, and underlying ideology, "Staff 501 of the Ravna Gora Youth." On p. 97 they say that "the Yugoslav name [of the youth organization] did not correspond to its Serbian content." See also Borković, p. 308.
[42] Microcopy No. T-311, Roll 189, Frames 433–41, esp. Frame 434.
[43] Sergije M. Živanović, I, 118–21.

doubtedly have been beneficial to the Chetniks militarily, politically, and psychologically. But the Chetniks do not seem even to have considered this possibility, and they made women who had joined the Partisan ranks or who supported them a favored butt of their propaganda (which undoubtedly was also directed at conservative-minded men). One Chetnik leaflet, for example, asserted that the Partisans killed all Serbs who married in churches, and that in Montenegro 4,000 illegitimate children were fathered by the Partisans and many girls who had been dishonored by them had drowned themselves.[44] Mihailović himself used the word prostitutes in speaking of the women Partisans: he told Prime Minister Purić in a telegram of December 12–13, 1943, that there were many women in the Communist ranks, who as a rule were either prostitutes before they joined or became such during their stay in the Communist forces.[45] And General Nedić, Prime Minister of the Serbian puppet government, who came from the same social background as Mihailović, is reported to have said that women who left their homes and joined the Partisans and those who engaged in propaganda for them were "immoral women, women without homes, women without reason, public prostitutes."[46]

Propaganda was recognized by the Chetnik Supreme Command and the Central National Committee to be of tremendous importance, both at home and abroad, and the main Chetnik headquarters contained an active propaganda department. Vasić was head of this branch in 1942 and part of 1943, and Dr. Moljević apparently continued his work. From August 1943 to September 1944 Dr. Djurović was also very active in propaganda work, especially with respect to radio propaganda directed to Great Britain and the United States. In March 1942 Mihailović commented in a letter to one of his Montenegrin commanders, Colonel Bajo Stanišić, "At the present time propaganda is of the same great value as armed action."[47] One of the main thrusts of Chetnik propaganda throughout the war was, naturally, to gain active support among the people for the Chetnik movement. Major Ostojić, of the Supreme Command, in a directive letter of July 30, 1942, urged all Chetnik commanders to "develop the strongest possible oral and written propaganda. The people must be persuaded that the Chetniks are their only friends and that it is from them that they can expect freedom and a happy life.... Work day and night and maintain the spirit of the people; the hour of freedom is near. Allied aid for the Chetniks is

[44] *Sudenja članovima rukovodstva organizacije Draže Mihailovića*, p. 245, testimony of Lt. Colonel Keserović, one of the defendants.

[45] Jovan Djonović, "The Connections with General Mihailović from the Middle East," p. 20.

[46] Martinović-Bajica, p. 321. One entire chapter of this book is devoted to a scornful account of women in the Partisan ranks.

[47] *Dokumenti o izdajstvu Draže Mihailovića*, I, 27.

assured, and the whole world is admiring them."[48] The other basic feature of Chetnik propaganda after the collision between the Chetniks and Partisans in western Serbia in the autumn of 1941 was anti-Communism.

The extreme complexity of conditions under which the Chetniks operated of course made their propaganda task complex also. A directive issued by Mihailović in September 1942 listed the specific intents of Chetnik propaganda in this way:

a) struggle against the Communists who, in order not to disturb the relations of the government-in-exile with the Soviet Union, were to be attacked as Trotskyists;
b) elaboration of mass atrocities committed by the Communists, the Ustashas, and the German troops of occupation;
c) publicizing the mass shootings of hostages by the German occupation troops;
d) helping the recruiting for the Yugoslav Army in the Homeland; and
e) strengthening confidence in the final victory of the Allies.[49]

Another directive, entitled "People's Committees of Ravna Gora and Our Propaganda," issued in the summer of 1944, outlined the setting up of committees throughout the country so that "our propaganda may envelop the whole country and the entire population." The system was to have an orderly sequence: village committees, followed by commune committees, county committees, district committees, and finally provincial committees headed by the various area commanders; propaganda in Serbia itself was to be directed from the Supreme Command. In any given area, corps or groups of corps were to be responsible for propaganda work both through their own special sections and through the village, commune, and county committees, though these last three kinds of committees were to be directed by the county Chetnik commandants.[50]

One section of the manual of late 1942 was devoted to the organization of propaganda and intelligence services—distinct but closely cooperating branches—and it outlined in detail the principles of organization, the kinds of personnel to be employed in each task, and specific approaches to be followed in certain aspects of propaganda, as for example among the Croats and in defense of the monarchy.[51] The principal target of Chetnik propaganda was the Communists, which Mihailović repeatedly emphasized. In the already quoted telegram to his commanders of November 7, 1943, for example, he said: "Address your-

[48] Archives of the Institute of Military History, Belgrade, Chetnik Documents, Reg. No. 14/2, Box 1.
[49] Microcopy No. T-312, Roll 470, Frames 8,060,434–35.
[50] Archives of the Institute of Military History, Belgrade, Chetnik Documents, Reg. No. 43/2, Box 7.
[51] Microcopy No. T-311, Roll 192, Frames 345–55. The manual even suggests how certain probable ticklish questions, e.g. the role of the Yugoslav Army in the Homeland in the political field after the end of the war, should be answered.

self with proclamations to the people and explain the whole danger from the Communists. Call into our ranks all Moslems and all Croats of correct behavior. Counteract the Communists' lies about their numbers and their strength. . . . Issue leaflets and show the people the danger from the Communists and the necessity of fighting them until they are destroyed."[52]

One part of Chetnik political activity during the war referred to their contacts with the anti-Communist resistance and political groups in the other countries in southeastern Europe—Albania, Bulgaria, Greece, Hungary, and Romania—in an effort to devise common policies against the Communist-led forces in those countries as well as in Yugoslavia.[53] But whereas the Communist groups were bound together by a common revolutionary and internationalist ideology, by their allegiance to Stalin and the Soviet Union, and to the Comintern until its dissolution in May 1943, the nationalist forces were all more or less chauvinist and expansionist at one another's expense; their only common bond was their anti-Communism. Of course, once the Chetniks began to experience great difficulties with the British, and especially after the Partisans had been recognized as an Allied armed force and the Chetniks had been jettisoned by the Western Allies, all Chetnik schemes for cooperation with similar groups in the neighboring countries lost practically any significance. But all of these anti-Communist forces continued to hope for salvation from a British-American landing in the Balkans and an arresting of the threatening Soviet tide. These, however, proved to be forlorn hopes.

CHETNIK MODES OF THINKING AND BEHAVIOR

Certain facts and certain Chetnik ideas and attitudes were of fundamental importance for Chetnik behavior throughout the war; pointing them out here will help in understanding the policies and activities of the Chetniks as discussed in succeeding chapters.

1. The Chetnik resistance movement was started by and was led by professional officers, and they overrated their own military expertise. This was evident on many occasions when Mihailović and other Chetnik officers referred to their own military training and lack of the same in the commanders of the Partisan forces. The government-in-exile used the same argument when it pressed for the submission of the Par-

---

[52] Archives of the Institute of Military History, Belgrade, Chetnik Documents, Reg. No. 19/1, Box 3.

[53] *The Trial of Draža Mihailović*, pp. 420–23, 470–80, 497–99. For some indications of Chetnik contacts with the Bulgarians which were carried out by Lt. Colonel Jovanović-Patak, Chetnik commander in eastern Serbia, see the Archives of the Institute of Military History, Belgrade, Chetnik Documents, Reg. No. 49/2, Box 129; and Microcopy No. T-312, Roll 470, Frame 8,060,326. For some of the contacts maintained by Jovan Djonović from abroad with the anti-Communist forces in Albania see his article, "My Connections with Draža Mihailović from the Middle East."

tisans to Mihailović's command. Professional soldiers are prone to scoff at the ability of civilians to conduct military operations. But modern guerrilla warfare, especially of the sort employed in the national liberation wars led by the Communists in economically underdeveloped countries, has taken on certain political, socioeconomic, and psychological aspects which clearly distinguish it from guerrilla operations of the traditional sort. The Chetnik forces under the leadership of traditionally trained professional officers proved totally incapable not only of carrying on a successful guerrilla war but also of fighting the Communist-led guerrillas and the army that grew out of these guerrilla detachments. Among the Partisans, too, of course, there were a good many former Yugoslav officers, whose knowledge was fully utilized; but the leading Partisan front-line commanders were civilians who had fought with the Loyalist army in the Spanish Civil War and had real battle experience.

2. For the first two and a half years of their existence as a wartime movement, the Chetniks saw no necessity for and in fact did not have a political organization embracing the rank and file of the population supporting them. They thought it sufficient to have a very small Central National Committee (established in August 1941 and somewhat enlarged early in 1943), and since this was merely an appendage of the Supreme Command. Mihailović's military organization was also his political apparatus. It was not until January 1944 that the Ba congress established the Yugoslav National Democratic Union, and at the same time further enlarged the Central National Committee, and even then neither of these bodies had any real power. Even the Ravna Gora People's Committees which began to be established late in 1943 and after the Ba congress served as local organs of the Union were in fact established by county military commandants.[54] Moreover, Dragiša Vasić, who well into 1943 was the leading member of the Executive Council of the Central National Committee and Mihailović's chief political adviser, seems to have been quite unsuited for such a role, because of his personality as well as his lack of political experience. But even after Vasić's eclipse and the ascent of Moljević to the role of principal political adviser, the quality of the political advice given to Mihailović does not seem to have improved.

3. The Chetnik leaders and their followers were extremely conservative and traditional-minded. Not only in much of their military thinking but also in their garb and their long hair and beards, and, often, in the willful behavior of many commanders, they harked back to the experiences of the Serbian Chetnik detachments in Macedonia in pre-

---

[54] Djurović's statement at his trial; *Sudjenje članovima rukovodstva organizacije Draže Mihailovića*, p. 489.

1912 days, even though Serbian traditions of this sort had no meaning whatsoever for anyone in Yugoslavia except Serbs and Montenegrins. In addition, Mihailović and the other leading Chetnik commanders, as well as the civilian Vasić, were extremely suspicious and even antagonistic toward the professional politicians, and took a substantial number of them into their fold only after the Ba congress. Finally, like many other organizations led by professional soldiers, the Chetniks were outspokenly anti-intellectual, and their ranks included practically no writers and artists.[55]

4. The Chetniks overrated their capability of using to advantage, in a Machiavellian, unscrupulous manner, some of their enemies, the principal method of which was the collaboration with the armies of occupation and the quisling forces against their main domestic enemy, the Communist-led Partisans. This sort of policy can of course be practiced equally well or better by the opposing forces—as it was in Yugoslavia, primarily by the Axis powers. Moreover, it has many inherent dangers, such as the difficulty of extricating oneself from the policy once it has been set in motion, the negative reaction to it by both one's own rank and file and the general public, its exploitation as propaganda ammunition by one's opponents, and so on.

5. The Chetniks underrated the Communist Party of Yugoslavia, whose leaders organized and assumed both the political and the military conduct of the Partisan forces. In the beginning, of course, Mihailović had good reason to doubt the effectiveness of the Communist leadership, which during most of the interwar period had been rather inept. Not being in a position to know how much Tito had accomplished since taking over as head of the party, Mihailović could hardly have expected the Communists to be successful either politically or militarily under the much more difficult conditions that followed the partition and occupation of the country. The general uprising ordered by the Communists while the Germans were at the zenith of their power and the various mistakes and grievous losses of the Partisans until the middle of 1942 seemed to confirm Chetnik views. But the Chetniks paid little attention to the gradually accumulating evidence that the Partisans were learning quickly from their mistakes. Had they looked at the evidence, they would have seen that by the end of 1942 the Partisans had developed into accomplished military and political organizers, whose forces, led by capable and bold commanders, were showing high fighting morale, and that they had developed a true, mobile army and a

---

[55] I have been told on good authority that there was much talk in the Chetnik camp during the first half of 1944 that several Serbian writers, including Ivo Andrić the later Nobel Prize winner who during the war lived in Belgrade, were ready to join the Chetniks in the mountains. This never happened, and it may simply have been propaganda to counteract the news that many writers, artists, and intellectuals, including several poets, painters, and sculptors of great distinction, had for some time been with the Partisans.

large number of territorial guerrilla detachments, both supported by a well-organized and rapidly growing Communist Party and its front organizations, as well as by a rudimentary structure of revolutionary government.

6. One of the most revealing Chetnik statements about the Partisans as their military adversaries is found in section X of Directive No. 1 of January 2, 1943, pertaining to Chetnik plans to attack and destroy the Partisans in Bosnia. It is a statement that requires no comment. In this section entitled "The Tactics of the Enemy," the Supreme Command— that is, Mihailović—has this to say about what he calls the "Partisan-bandit bands":

The units are very poorly led and commanded owing to the lack of trained commanding cadres;

Actions of various groups are not coordinated either as to tasks or to time, and amount essentially to speedy and sudden attacks particularly during the night;

In defense, and sometime even in offense, they avoid decisive battles, and in cases when they meet a superior enemy, they avoid battle and they try to get away from every difficult situation;

Killing of our officers [for purposes of wrecking our system of organization and command] and the operation of trojkas [for spreading panic in our ranks] are the main features of their actions;

. . .

Partisan units are composed of a motley of rascals, such as the Ustashas, the most blood-thirsty enemies of the Serbian people, Jews, Croats, Dalmatians, Bulgarians, Turks [Moslems], Hungarians, and all other nations of the world . . . Because of this mixture, the fighting value of the Partisan units is very low, a fact partly due to their poor armament;

The Partisans are masters of propaganda, which they mostly base on their fight against the occupier, as if the occupier did not arm them for the struggle against the Serbian people. In misleading the masses their chief argument is bluff, which they use very successfully, both in counteracting our propaganda and in spreading their own.[56]

7. Despite the term "Yugoslav" in the official name of his army and occasional references to the Yugoslav state and idea in Chetnik propaganda, neither Mihailović himself nor the leading political and military men in his movement were committed to the Yugoslav idea and the Yugoslav state in the true sense of the word. Their Yugoslavism was a shell filled with Great Serbian content and intended to serve only Serbian interests. Because of that Mihailović and the Chetniks could not count on any real support from the non-Serb population of the country, only on their opposition. But since the idea of Yugoslavism originated as a defensive and unifying ideology intended to serve all South Slav

[56] Archives of the Institute of Military History, Belgrade, Chetnik Documents, Reg. No. 13/3, Box 1.

peoples, and since the South Slavs, and indeed Slavs in general, were threatened with obliteration during the Second World War, it was natural that some political group, despite the almost total discrediting of the idea of Yugoslavism during the interwar period, would try to recast this idea in a new fashion and use it as a unifying and defensive ideological tool during the war. This was done by the Communist Party of Yugoslavia. Indeed, in the subtle political hands of Josip Broz Tito, a new idea of Yugoslavism flourished. Combining elements of both the narrower nationalism of individual South Slav nations and overall Yugoslav nationalism, this new idea became a powerful ideological force not only against foreign invaders but against domestic opponents like the Ustashas, who wanted to break up Yugoslavia for good, and the Chetniks, who sought to reconstitute it in a manner that would serve essentially the interest of a single South Slav nation.

8. The Chetnik leaders, and Mihailović in particular, were confident that the Western Allies because of their opposition to the possible spread of Communism would never allow the Russians to acquire a decisive influence in the Balkans. The Chetniks made the erroneous assumption that they were indispensable to the Western Allies and therefore must be supported by them. In his telegram of November 7, 1943, to his commanders, Mihailović put this idea in a nutshell: "England can never relinquish the Balkans to the Russian influence, because in that case it loses the Mediterranean—this is clear to everybody."[57] From the standpoint of long-term political considerations based on traditional power relations in Europe, Chetnik thinking seemed to have a great deal of sense. But unfortunately for the Chetniks, the crucial decisions were ultimately determined not on the basis of long-term political considerations but rather by Prime Minister Churchill and his military advisers on the basis of short-term military needs in which the fighting strength and dependability of Tito's Partisans were more important than their Communist tendencies (which, anyway, seemed to have been watered down). Moreover, Russian influence in Europe in general, and in southeastern Europe in particular, had never been as great as it was at the end of the Second World War. Once again it was demonstrated how risky it is for political groups in small nations, or even small nations as a whole, to assume that they are indispensable, especially under the conditions of coalition wars dominated by a few Great Powers. History has repeatedly shown that in such wars, and even in great diplomatic crises, small nations and especially political groups in such nations are always expendable.

[57] *Ibid.*, Reg. No. 19/1, Box 3.

CHAPTER SEVEN

The Chetniks and the Foreign Enemy

THE POLICY OF AMBIVALENCE IN SERBIA

Once the Chetniks realized what the objectives of the Communist-led Partisans were, they knew that the Partisans were their main enemy. Unless they defeated the Partisans, their goal of restoring the monarchy and the Serbian hegemony in postwar Yugoslavia would be impossible of realizing. Obviously, the fight was going to require arms and supplies, and since the Chetniks had so far, in early November 1941, received only one small delivery of arms from the British, they came to the conclusion that they would have to start looking elsewhere for support. They also knew that to fight the Partisans effectively they must avoid antagonizing the armies of occupation and the quisling forces and running the risk of being caught between them and the Partisans. "Use of the enemy"—as the Chetniks liked to call their form of collaboration—to the degree needed, seemed the only answer, and this was the course the Chetniks decided to pursue. Thus, over a period of time, and in different parts of the country, the Chetniks reached arrangements on collaboration first with the Nedić forces in Serbia, then with the Italians in Montenegro and in the Italian-controlled parts of the Independent State of Croatia, then with some of the Pavelić forces in the German-controlled parts of Bosnia, and after the Italian collapse also with the Germans directly. In all these arrangements, the collaboration was for both sides a matter of short-term convenience for the sake of a common goal—the defeat of the Partisans —rather than an arrangement based on mutual long-term interests, although the destruction of the Partisans was obviously also in the long-term interest of all collaborating forces. The Axis powers and the quisling regimes, who had no illusions about the Chetniks' basic pro-Western attitude, understood that the Chetniks would very likely at an opportune moment in the future turn their arms against them; and the Chetniks understood equally well that after the Partisans had been destroyed, the Axis, no longer in need of their help, could turn and destroy them too.

The Chetniks also tried at the same time to preserve their good relations with the Western Allies by fighting the quisling forces and the Germans occasionally to maintain an appearance of active resistance—and they steadfastly denied accusations first by the Partisans and later also by the Russians and the British that they were collaborating with the enemy.

Almost from the first days of the Mihailović Chetnik movement—out of several different motives on the two sides—there were contacts between Mihailović's representatives and the collaborationist Aćimović administration in Serbia.[1] One of Mihailović's close political confidants, Aleksandar Aksentijević, testified, for example, at his own trial in August 1945 that in June 1941 a radio transmitter was acquired in Novi Sad for Mihailović and Aćimović knew about it.[2] The acting commander of the Serbian gendarmerie under Aćimović and for some time under Nedić, Colonel Jovan N. Trišić, extended various kinds of assistance to Mihailović.[3] Aćimović himself, both as head of the commissioner government and later as Minister of the Interior in the Nedić government, had full knowledge of Mihailović's organization in Belgrade and took no action against it, and he in fact rendered many real services to Mihailović in the course of the war. Aćimović had been one of the most determined antagonists of the Communists prior to April 1941, and it is therefore possible that so far as action against the Communists was concerned he was fully in the service of the Germans, but also wanted to help Mihailović, who had come to be considered by a majority of Serbs as a Serbian patriot; perhaps, too, he was not ruling out any possibilities and wanted to hedge on Mihailović.

Whatever the reasoning, contacts between the Serbian quisling government and Mihailović's representatives were expanded after General Milan Nedić took over the government on August 29, 1941. As early as September 3, General Nedić met Mihailović's representatives, Lt. Colonel Dragoslav Pavlović and Major Aleksandar Mišić, and asked them to forward the following proposals to Mihailović: (1) that Mihailović was to move his armed detachments to Bosnia and Herzegovina to help the Serbian population defend themselves against Ustasha terror; (2) that if Mihailović submitted the necessary requests for funds, Nedić would endeavor to supply them; and (3) that Nedić would back Mihailović's venture in Bosnia by giving him as many arms and other supplies as he could secure from the Germans. Mihailović did not answer Nedić's proposals, and sometime later Nedić drafted a second proposal to the effect that Mihailović should withdraw his troops from areas in which Nedić's troops were active against the Partisans if he did not want to act

[1] Marjanović, "Contributions," pp. 167–69.
[2] *Sudjenje članovima rukovodstva organizacije Draže Mihailovića,* pp. 502–3.
[3] Trišić, pp. 37, 61–62; *The Trial of Draža Mihailović,* pp. 115, 149.

directly against them. This second message was intercepted by the Partisans[4] and apparently never reached Mihailović. Obviously, Nedić had hoped to neutralize Mihailović by getting him to break off all cooperation between his Chetniks and the Partisans, after which Nedić could concentrate his military and police power against the Partisans and ultimately bring about a state of peace and order in Serbia. Only then would there be an end to the ruthless German reprisals against the insurgents and the innocent civilians.

With the expansion of the uprising in Serbia after mid-September as a consequence of more and more volunteers going to the Partisans and more and more Chetnik units joining the fight, followed by the arrival of German reinforcements in Serbia, the German reprisals increased in number and in harshness. Thousands of hostages were taken and shot and thousands of dwellings were burned. There is no question that these reprisals were one of the major reasons for Mihailović's increasing reluctance to go on with a resistance that he had from the outset regarded as premature. But it was his fear of the Communists—who had started and put themselves at the head of the uprising—that led him to try to arrange for secret collaboration with the Germans at Divci and altered his relationship with the Nedić administration.

Having reached the decision to abandon even limited cooperation with the Partisans and to adopt a policy of open enmity, Mihailović was in a position to encourage some of his troops to cooperate with Nedić's forces. This he seems to have done around the middle of November, because during the latter part of November, that is, during the second phase of the large-scale German offensive against the Partisans in western Serbia, seven of Mihailović's commanders—Predrag Raković, Miloš Glišić, Vučko Ignjatović, Manojlo Korać, Nikola Mladenović, Radovan Stojanović, and Nikola Kalabić—together with their detachments amounting, according to Communist sources, to about two thousand men, legalized themselves by declaring their willingness to accept the command of Nedić and collaborated with his forces in operations against the Partisans.[5]

We have already seen how Mihailović, by refusing at Divci to give in to the German demand for unconditional surrender, had antagonized the Germans to the point where they were determined to put him out of the way. First the Partisans had to be disposed of in western Serbia through Operation Užice; this done, the Germans launched Operation

[4] Krakov, I, 149–54. This version of the first contacts between Nedić and Mihailović's representatives comes from Nedić's principal apologist, a relative of his and one of the leading newspapermen in occupied Serbia until his arrest by the Germans sometime late in 1943 or early 1944. See also Marjanović, *Ustanak 1941*, pp. 192–93.

[5] Krakov, I, 281; Višnjić, "The Offensive of Occupation and Quisling Forces in Western Serbia in 1941," p. 26. Krakov maintains that by this action these Chetnik detachments saved themselves from destruction at German hands.

Mihailović with the objective of capturing Mihailović and the Chetnik headquarters at Ravna Gora and dispersing the Chetnik detachments. Operation Mihailović was carried out on December 6 and 7.[6] On December 6 Mihailović was at the home of Major Aleksandar Mišić at the village of Struganik with a group of his people. They were apparently betrayed and surrounded, but Mihailović succeeded in escaping. Two of his coworkers, Majors Mišić and Ivan Fregl, were caught and later shot. Mihailović first hid in the area of Ravna Gora, then fled toward the east, and later headed in a southwesterly direction toward the Italian-occupied territory of Sandjak.[7] The German command posts in Serbia disagreed as to how successful Operation Mihailović had been: the 342nd Infantry Division report summing up the operation thought that the Chetnik group around Mihailović had not been liquidated but that the breaking up of its command post had been a serious blow; Bader, the Commanding General in Serbia, more sanguine, thought that the "Mihailović group" had been broken up, but he put a bounty of 200,000 dinars on Mihailović in hopes of catching him.[8]

Mihailović remained in hiding for several months, but by March the Nedić government knew of his whereabouts and a meeting took place between him and Aćimović, with German knowledge and permission. On March 26 General Bader was informed that Mihailović had renewed his offer to the Serbian government "to put himself at its disposal for the struggle against the Communists." Since Mihailović was now Minister of the Army, Navy, and Air Force in the Yugoslav government-in-exile, his new offer, though essentially the same as the one made at Divci in November, was quite different in its implications. Nevertheless, Bader refused the offer and ordered this decision to be conveyed to Nedić, indicating that Nedić was free to make the refusal public.[9]

In the spring of 1942 the center of Chetnik organization and Chetnik activity shifted to Montenegro and Bosnia and Herzegovina. By June, when Mihailović arrived in Montenegro to establish his headquarters,

[6] Microcopy No. T-501, Roll 256, Frame 1149. On December 5 Aćimović, now Minister of the Interior in the Nedić government, and Colonel Kosta Mušicki of the Serbian Volunteer Detachments were in contact with Mihailović, perhaps (though there is no proof) because they knew something about the impending German operation and wished to warn Mihailović. This contact did not escape the Germans and it put Nedić in a bad position, but he managed to convince them that he had had no knowledge of it and had in fact expressly forbidden Aćimović to have anything to do with what he called the "Mihailović Question." Aćimović kept his post in the government for another year and continued to maintain contacts with the Mihailović organization throughout the war. See *The Trial of Draža Mihailović*, pp. 393–94. Colonel Mušicki was jailed but later freed at Nedić's intervention and still later put in command of the Serbian Volunteer Corps. After the Germans were driven out of Serbia in October 1944 and the Chetniks had fled to Bosnia, Aćimović became Mihailović's chief contact man with Envoy Hermann Neubacher in Vienna.

[7] For the order to carry out Operation Mihailović see Microcopy No. T-501, Roll 250, Frames 442–43; for the report on its execution by the German 342nd Infantry Division, see *ibid.*, Roll 246, Frames 732–73. There were no German casualties in the operation; one Chetnik officer and 11 men were killed, and 7 officers (apparently including Mišić and Fregl), 475 men, and 2 women were taken prisoner. In addition, the Germans captured a sizable amount of booty. *Ibid.*, Frame 741.

[8] *Ibid.*, Frames 736, 750. For a copy of a bounty poster see *ibid.*, Roll 256, Frame 1155.

[9] *Ibid.*, Roll 247, Frame 920; Roll 257, Frame 1232.

Chetnik commanders there had already concluded several collaboration agreements with the Italians. Mihailović brought no Chetnik troops with him, but he was soon followed by Majors Ostojić and Lalatović, several other officers, and the British liaison officer Captain Hudson, who traveled by truck disguised as Nedić troops,[10] and later in the year several members of the Chetnik political staff, including Dragiša Vasić and Stevan Moljević, also reached Montenegro.

This left in Serbia about twenty legalized detachments serving under Nedić's authority, but not much else in the way of organized troops. Legalizing the detachments had in fact been about the only way in which Mihailović had been able to save his forces, and so far as it meant that they were being fed and maintained as units but presumably were ready at any time to turn against the Axis, this fitted in with Mihailović's strategy. In the meantime, they were helping the Germans to preserve law and order in Serbia, thus reducing the loss of Serbian lives; and finally, that move was to put him in a better position to fight the Partisans in Serbia both in a military and in a political sense. Many of the illegal Chetnik detachments had been disbanded after Operation Mihailović and sent home. Some Chetnik officers were still in Serbia, however, with orders to set up an underground Chetnik organization according to principles provided by the Supreme Command, and there were also a few detachments with greatly reduced manpower in the hills. There were, too, many Chetnik leaders operating under cover.[11]

The legalized Mihailović Chetnik detachments became a part of Nedić's auxiliary troops comparable in status to the Chetnik detachments of Kosta Pećanac which had joined the Nedić government forces in August. By an order of General Bader dated April 10, 1942, all the detachments of volunteers and all Pećanac and legalized Mihailović Chetnik detachments were put under the command of the German garrisoning divisions in various areas. They were assigned special numbers (D-1 to D-19 to the volunteer units, C-20 to C-38 to "independent Chetniks," i.e. legalized Mihailović Chetniks, and C-39 to C-101 to Pećanac Chetnik detachments), and their activity was to be tightly controlled: they were assigned special territories from which they would not be permitted to move without German orders; all operations of these units, still under Nedić's command, were to be reported in advance

---

[10] *The Trial of Draža Mihailović,* pp. 138–39. Upon arrival in Montenegro, Hudson wrote Mihailović a letter on June 11, offering his services to further the Chetnik cause. *Ibid.,* p. 122.

[11] Compare e.g. a report of the Commander of the Bulgarian Occupation Corps General Nikoloff to the German Commanding General in Serbia of September 1942 in which he says that "in the area of the corps exist well-camouflaged organizations (staffs) of the National movement of Draža Mihailović, but so far there has not been any formation of fighting detachments in the mountains. Members of this movement hide behind the official positions and authorities. They are found among the leaders of the government Chetniks, among the officers of the Serbian State Guard, among the priests, teachers, and government employees." This is followed by a list of 194 such persons who should be arrested and 18 persons whose guns should be confiscated. Microcopy No. T-501, Roll 257, Frames 1174–81.

to the German area or district command in whose area they were located; when engaged in operations, all these detachments had to have German liaison officers; all the ammunition requirements of these units which heretofore were routed to the German authorities through the Serbian government were henceforth to be submitted directly to the German area or district commands of the areas in which the detachments were located.[12] In November 1942 the volunteer units were reorganized into the Serbian Volunteer Corps and put under the direct command of the Commanding General in Serbia,[13] but by the end of the year both kinds of legalized Chetniks, having little value as fighting units and being at the same time very unreliable, were almost completely disarmed. Altogether, over 12,000 legalized Pećanac and Mihailović Chetniks were dissolved and many of their officers were arrested and sent to Germany to prisoner-of-war camps.[14] The last two detachments (a Pećanac detachment commanded by Mašan Djurović and a Mihailović detachment commanded by Lt. Colonel Matić) were dissolved in mid-March 1943. By then, the choice was clearer: knowing what had happened to many of their comrades in the course of dissolution of their detachments, a great many men in the last two units escaped and fled to the hills to cast their fate with the illegal Mihailović detachments.[15]

During the summer and autumn of 1942 the illegal Chetniks, gradually regaining strength, engaged in occasional minor attacks on the units of the Serbian State Guard and especially those of the Serbian Volunteer Corps and carried out occasional acts of sabotage against communication lines. In some cases the actions were initiated by impatient local commanders, and some of the action, especially sabotage against rail lines, was undertaken because of pressure from the British, who were anxious to impede the flow of supplies to German troops in Greece and Africa.

On August 9, 1942, for example, Mihailović ordered his contact man in Belgrade, "506," to recruit dependable employees of the Serbian railroads to sabotage locomotives and railroad cars. On August 26 he instructed Major Djurić in southern Serbia to order an agent named Ratko to organize trojkas for sabotage work on the railroad line from Vranje (85 kilometers south of Niš) to Belgrade and to provide the necessary equipment. The German radio monitoring service in Belgrade which picked up this message noted in transmitting it to headquarters:

---

[12] *Ibid.*, Roll 247, Frames 1118–19; Roll 257, Frame 1135. D stands for *Dobrovoljci* (Volunteers), C for Chetniks. See also a report on these units of Nov. 18, 1942, in *ibid.*, Roll 352, Frames 571–74.

[13] *Ibid.*, Roll 249, Frame 142.

[14] *Ibid.*, Frame 61.

[15] *Ibid.*, Frames 5–6, 56–58, 98. About half of the 6,000 legalized Pećanac and Mihailović Chetniks ordered dissolved up to December 1, 1942, had also gone into the hills with their rifles. But of the 900 men in the Djurović and Matić detachments only 110 surrendered with their arms, and another 111 rifles were surrendered. *Ibid.*, Roll 352, Frame 809; Roll 249, Frame 98.

"With this order General Mihailović took for the first time a definite position against the occupying powers," and added that the order was obviously British-inspired and had for its purpose the stopping of railroad traffic through Serbia which was of great importance for German operations in Africa. On that same occasion the Germans also intercepted an order of Mihailović to some of his principal commanders in Serbia (Lt. Colonel Pavlović, Major Djurić, Major Ocokoljić, and Captain Saša Mihajlović) to organize a service for collecting intelligence data about German military railroad traffic through Serbia and for sabotaging the railroads. Mihailović requested that daily reports about this matter be prepared and sent to him. On September 8 Mihailović ordered his commanders in Serbia and many other areas of the country to collect and submit to him regularly intelligence data on the military units and activity of the occupying forces, quisling forces, and Communists.[16] That same summer, as harvesting began, two of Mihailović's commanders in Serbia, Keserović and Ocokoljić, issued a general directive urging the peasants to hide their grain, fodder, and livestock, and on August 27 Mihailović ordered his commanders in Serbia to buy quantities of grain from the peasants, who were to store it themselves and receive payments at a later date. According to German sources, in many cases Nedić officials were helping the Mihailović Chetniks in these grain purchases. Such activities of course helped to keep some food supplies out of the hands of the Directorate for Food Supplies (DIRIS) and/or the occupation authorities.[17]

These Chetnik orders and activities, which to the Germans probably indicated an early start of Chetnik operations, were followed by several German decisions. In an exchange of opinions between the Military Commander in Serbia and the Chief of the Armed Forces High Command early in September, it was agreed that Mihailović should be caught and that a special company of soldiers was to be brought to Serbia for that purpose (of course Mihailović was at that time in Italian-occupied Montenegro). On September 9 General Bader issued a special order on the reconnoitering and combatting of the Chetniks. During these days the Germans also brought to Serbia from the Banat the SS Division "Prinz Eugen," composed of the *Volksdeutsche* from that area, which during the following three months committed many acts of terror against the sympathizers of both the Chetniks and the Partisans.[18]

On November 21 General Bader reported to the Armed Forces Commander in Southeast Europe that Mihailović had called for "general disobedience" in Serbia but that there had been little response so far

[16] Microcopy No. T-312, Roll 470, Frames 8,060,425–26, 8,060,429–30.
[17] *Ibid.*, Frame 8,060,432.
[18] Microcopy No. T-501, Roll 352, Frames 6, 45–47, 72–75; Glišić, 128–31.

because people feared German reprisals. Nonetheless, to forestall any intensification of rebel activities—by Partisans as well as by Chetniks—he was issuing a proclamation warning people not to follow the orders of Mihailović and the Communists and stating that all offenses would be decisively suppressed. Every act of sabotage on railroads, bridges, telegraph and telephone communications, and industrial enterprises would be answered by the occupation authorities by shooting up to one hundred hostages.[19] This new policy would be in addition to the policy still in effect of shooting hostages for attacks on German and quisling government personnel. During the month of December, German daily and special reports indicated that German troops had engaged in fighting Chetnik groups on several occasions.[20] The severity of the German reprisals for attacks on personnel is indicated by an announcement of the occupation authorities on December 26 that for the killing of four and the wounding of two German citizens, all employees of the Organization Todt, by the Chetniks on December 14 in the county of Žagubica in eastern Serbia, 250 followers of Mihailović had been shot as hostages. On Christmas Day the Germans announced the execution the preceding day of forty Communists and ten other persons for the wounding of two German officers by a Communist in the town of Mladenovac.[21]

A former officer of the Division "Brandenburg" (a German commando division mostly used against the insurgents) has told how, as a company commander, he made an agreement with the Mihailović Chetniks in northeastern Serbia for combined actions against the Partisans, but this obviously was an isolated occurrence.[22] The report of the Commanding General in Serbia for the month of February 1943 mentions Chetniks along with Communists as the object of smaller operations by the Germans. The same report says that the prompt shooting of hostages had prevented new sabotage acts called for both by Tito and by Mihailović, but that the Communists in a surprise attack had killed a regimental commander and a group of men who accompanied him.[23] The Commanding General in Serbia also issued an order to the troops under his command, dated March 24, 1943,

[19] Microcopy No. T-501, Roll 352, Frames 587, 592–94.

[20] See esp. the report of Dec. 16, *ibid.*, Frames 736–37. In 1965 the Yugoslavs published compilations of monthly reports of the Serbian quisling authorities on Partisan attacks for the period July 1941–November 1942 and the weekly reports and various bulletins of the Department of Internal Security of the Ministry of the Interior for the period December 1942 to the summer of 1944 (see *Zbornik DNOR*, Tome I, Vol. 21, *passim*). Much of their documentary value has been destroyed, however, because the editors deleted all texts that did not refer to "actions of Partisan units, local Partisans, and the activities of the Communist Party and Communist Youth organization," and that means the activities of the Chetniks. *Zbornik DNOR*, Tome I, Vol. 21, p. 1.

[21] Microcopy No. T-501, Roll 352, Frames 668–69. Many of the German documents referring to these reprisal measures are found in the *Trials of War Criminals Before the Nuernberg Military Tribunals Under Control Council Law No. 10*, Vol. XI, pp. 912–1031 (the "Hostage Case").

[22] Kriegsheim, pp. 238–64, 312. This is a novelized history of the Division "Brandenburg," with a chronology of its operations at the end. From the text it is impossible to see how long this collaboration lasted.

[23] Microcopy No. T-501, Roll 249, Frame 43.

dealing specifically with ways of fighting the rebels in Serbia (apparently both Chetniks and Partisans), pointing out that "despite the operations of the German troops and despite the shooting of many hostages, *one cannot say that the country had been pacified* . . . and that the developments in Herzegovina and Montenegro [meaning the steadily mounting strength of the Partisans] as well as the possibility of Allied landings in Dalmatia, could lead to a significant worsening of the situation in Serbia." In addition to the maintenance of security in the country, the main task of the troops was still to secure communication lines, particularly the Belgrade-Niš-Salonika, Belgrade-Niš-Sofia, and Lapovo-Kraljevo-Skopje lines and the Danube waterway, as well as the economic enterprises working for Germany. "The basic principle to observe in fighting the enemy," the order says, "is that the enemy bands have to be searched out in their hiding places and destroyed." The order concludes with a special code name for the arrest of all those Serbs who in the case of a general uprising would assume leading roles; all German and Bulgarian army units, police units, and area and district commands had special lists of names falling in that category and these lists were to be kept up to date.[24]

With the coming of spring, the situation had begun to change. The situation report of the Commanding General in Serbia for the first half of April describes it as a period in which various groups of Serbs have been settling accounts among themselves, whereas because of the continued policy of prompt reprisals—during this time 170 Communists and 165 Mihailović followers had been shot as hostages—the reserved attitude of the population, and the spring sowing, the activity of the rebel bands has been reduced. When Communist units are forced to fight, the report notes, they fight furiously and not without skill. As for the Chetniks:

> The Mihailović movement is in a great crisis. London threatens to revise its relations with Mihailović if he continues to fight the Croats and the Communists instead of the Axis powers. Not only on the part of his order-giving Allies, but also on the part of a large proportion of his followers there is no longer any understanding of the political fratricide war. Therein undoubtedly lies also the main reason for the obvious military failure in Herzegovina and Montenegro. Under the existing conditions, only two alternatives remain to Mihailović: either to give in to the double pressure or to retreat from the political scene in the Balkans. In this connection certain political possibilities may arise.
>
> The Mihailović movement in Serbia is completely passive in its attitude to the occupation power, but it continues to engage in military espionage, political propaganda, and its settlement of accounts with the Communists.[25]

[24] *Ibid.*, Frames 128–30.
[25] *Ibid.*, Frame 300.

The last two legalized Chetnik detachments having been dissolved in March, there were now in Serbia only illegal detachments—two, perhaps three score, according to a report on public safety prepared by the Nedić Ministry of the Interior in April. Most of these detachments, though not all, were active, and most of their efforts, fairly vigorous and systematic, were being directed against the Partisans.[26] Thus, even though the Chetniks were now altogether an illegal force, they were, by fighting the Partisans, actually helping the Germans to keep Serbia relatively pacified and thus the more easily exploited. The above report of the Serbian Ministry of the Interior makes this point clear:

> Endangered by the activity of the nationalist illegal formations [Chetniks], the Communist bands are forced to withdraw from the forested and mountainous areas into the plains, where it is much easier for the Serbian State Guards to pursue and annihilate them.
>
> . . .
>
> It is observed that among practically all illegal detachments [Chetniks] there exists unity of action in regard to the annihilation of Communists which is proceeding on a much larger scale and more methodically than during the month of March. These detachments have so increased in power that in some districts they conduct independent and successful action against the Communists. In some districts (Kragujevac and Požarevac) these actions have been so sharpened that the illegal detachments liquidate even persons who were with the Partisans for only a single day.
>
> In propaganda meetings the illegal detachments, now even more than earlier, advise the population to be loyal to the occupying authorities and obedient toward our authorities.[27]

Meanwhile, after suffering repeated defeats at the hands of the Partisans in Herzegovina, southeastern Bosnia, and Montenegro between March 7 and May 10 and after the Germans disarmed some of his elite troops in Montenegro (to be described in full later in the chapter), Mihailović made his way back to Serbia. After his return to Serbia, the British military mission at his headquarters and sub-missions at some of the regional headquarters in Serbia began applying pressure on the Chetniks to step up their activity against the German and Serbian quisling troops. A few limited operations were carried out, but not nearly enough to satisfy the British—and in contrast to the Partisans, who, with increasing strength, were intensifying their attacks. German reports give detailed information on sabotage and other attacks of the guerrillas in Serbia from March to October 1943 on a biweekly basis classified into sabotage of railroads, roads, telegraph and telephone lines, attacks on buildings, attacks on Germans and Bulgarians, on

---

[26] For these illegal Chetnik detachments, their commanders, and districts of their activity see the report of April 1943 in *Zbornik DNOR*, Tome I, Vol. 21, pp. 430–40.

[27] *Ibid.*, p. 440.

quisling troops, killings and abductions, plunder of food, and sabotage of crops.[28] These reports do not indicate who was responsible for these acts—Chetniks or Partisans—but from data referring to the period July–September communicated by the First Bulgarian Occupation Corps on October 13 to the Military Commander in Southeast Europe, General Felber, it is clear that in areas under Bulgarian occupation, at least—which can be taken as indicative of all Serbia—it was the Partisans who were chiefly responsible:[29]

	July	August	September
1. Attacks (not specified as to nature):			
by Chetniks	62	78	138
by Partisans	178	205	253
desertions from the Serbian State Guard	20	54	68
2. Killings of Germans and Bulgarians:			
by Chetniks	1	7	14
by Partisans	9	13	19
3. Killings of Serbs (in the service of occupation forces):			
by Chetniks	6	25	30
by Partisans	60	70	88

In the meantime, the Chetniks' loose collaboration with the Nedić regime became more and more a systematic effort to infiltrate the Nedić forces and administration, an undertaking in which the Chetniks were very successful.

THE MAJOR DANGIĆ INCIDENT

An interesting minor incident in German-Nedić-Chetnik relations at the turn of 1941–42 was one involving Major Jezdimir Dangić, a former gendarmerie officer, a Serb from Bosnia, who was sent to eastern Bosnia in August 1941, not long after joining Mihailović, to head the pro-Chetnik formations in that area. In accordance with Chetnik policy at that time, Dangić and his troops cooperated, but tenuously, with the Partisans and continued to do so to some extent after the break came between the Chetniks and the Partisans in Serbia. But according to a report of the *Abwehr* (German Military Intelligence) unit in Belgrade of September 29, 1941, based on reports of one of their dependable confidence men who was in contact with Dangić, Dangić practically from his arrival in Bosnia maintained contact with and was supported by the Nedić administration in Serbia; the report says that he has "had good relations with the Germans and does everything in order to avoid collision between his troops and the Germans."[30] Dangić's original

---

[28] For details see Microcopy No. T-501, Roll 267, Frames 221–31.
[29] *Ibid.*, Roll 253, Frames 519–20.
[30] Microcopy No. T-314, Roll 1457, Frames 702–4, 711–12; Microcopy No. T-501, Roll 256, Frame 1138, and Roll 257, Frame 1223. See also Miletić, pp. 135–39.

objective was to protect the Serbian population against the Ustashas. After the break between the Partisans and Chetniks in Serbia, however, he became the chief factor in the polarization between the two groups in eastern Bosnia. Under the existing circumstances, the Germans were interested in strengthening the anti-Partisan front in eastern Bosnia, and any aid that Dangić forces, reportedly numbering about ten thousand men, could give them would of course be welcomed by Bader, the Commanding General in Serbia, who for purposes of fighting the insurgents had jurisdiction over Croatia as well. In January 1942 Dangić's cooperation was considered even more valuable because Tito and the First Proletarian Brigade had arrived in eastern Bosnia. In fact, when the Germans and Croatian quisling troops launched their operation on January 17, 1942, for the pacification of eastern Bosnia—the operation known in Partisan terminology as the Second Enemy Offensive—Dangić's orders to the Chetniks were not to resist the enemy forces; the operation succeeded within a few days in overrunning some Partisan positions and resulted generally in pushing the Partisans southward toward the Italian-occupied zone.[31] But obviously to enlist the Chetniks' aid and to intensify the split between the Partisans and the Chetniks in eastern Bosnia, Dangić—though he was still maintaining contact with Mihailović—was invited toward the end of January to Belgrade to confer with General Bader and General Nedić; an agreement was concluded between Bader and Dangić, but was not signed.[32] These negotiations had not been cleared in advance with the Armed Forces Commander in Southeast Europe General Kuntze, and he was only informed on February 5, after the agreement had been concluded.[33] Neither had the authorities of the Croatian puppet state been consulted

[31] For General Bader's directive of Jan. 3, 1942, on operations against the rebels in Croatia, in fact in eastern Bosnia, see Microcopy No. T-501, Roll 247, Frames 677–90. For a Yugoslav account of this offensive see Djonlagić and Leković, *Njemačka ofanziva na istočnu Bosnu—januar–februar 1942*. See also Microcopy No. T-501, Roll 257, Frame 1283, and Microcopy No. T-314, Roll 1457, Frame 1091. Recent Yugoslav sources indicate that the strength of troops directly under Dangić's command early in 1942 was about 4,500 men. Miletić, p. 138.

[32] See Microcopy No. T-501, Roll 256, Frames 1098, 1105–11, 1130, for minutes and official German reports of the conferences between the German officials in Belgrade, Nedić, and Dangić, held between January 30 and February 2, 1942; the text of the abortive agreement, dated February 1, 1942, is in Frame 1123. By this agreement, Dangić and his detachments in the area bordered by the Drina, Sava, and Bosna rivers, and in the south by the German-Italian Demarcation Line, were to put themselves at once under German command (specifically under General Johann Fortner, commander of the 718th Infantry Division who had also the executive power in the area), with the promise to remain on the German side even in the event of general uprising. Dangić's assigned seat of command was Zvornik. He was to help pacify northeastern Bosnia, by observing the principle that each Serb, Croat, and Moslem of the area should live in peace; murder was punishable by death. All Croatian authorities in this area were to be maintained, and where they were not in existence were to be established. Dangić was to assist the Germans in certain special ways: by spreading news about the agreement among the people in order to calm the population; by fighting the Communists, if necessary, even outside the agreement area; by protecting the railroads in the agreement area; and by protecting industrial and mining enterprises in the area according to the instructions of the commander of the 718th Division. Ammunition for Dangić's troops was to be provided by the Commanding General in Serbia. Prisoners already held by Dangić were to be freed.

[33] Microcopy No. T-501, Roll 257, Frame 1278.

in advance, although that state was a German ally and the agreement referred to a very sensitive part of its territory. But when invited to Belgrade in this connection, the Croatian representatives and the German Envoy in Zagreb, Kasche, as well as the representative of the German Foreign Ministry with the Commanding General in Serbia, Benzler, all opposed the agreement. This opposition led to General Bader's change of heart and decision not to sign the agreement. Kuntze himself was suspicious that Dangić, being a Serb, was just buying time, using eastern Bosnia as a training ground for his troops and helping to prepare this area for incorporation into Serbia at a later date, and on February 12 he vetoed the conclusion of the agreement. Despite the fact that the agreement was never signed and despite Kuntze's veto, the parties concerned seem to have gone ahead with some collaboration for a few weeks, though apparently with the clear understanding that Dangić would act only in Bosnia; but early in April Dangić made the mistake of going to Serbia, where he met Nedić's representatives and various Chetnik leaders.[34] Shortly after these meetings, by order of the Armed Forces Commander in Southeast Europe, Dangić was arrested and sent to a prisoner-of-war camp in occupied Poland.[35] The Germans were also glad to have Dangić out of the way because they suspected that he and some other Chetnik officers in southeastern Bosnia and Herzegovina were trying to make certain arrangements with the Italians in case they should move into eastern Bosnia beyond the Demarcation Line. The Croatian Ustashas were very annoyed and extremely worried by the whole Dangić affair and the various German, Italian, and Chetnik moves in eastern Bosnia, believing them to be a conspiracy against the Croatian state. Powerless as they were, they did manage to refurbish their Black Legion (about 1,500 men) and early in April sent it into the area between Sarajevo and the Drina River where it inflicted large losses on the Chetniks and engaged in massacres of segments of the Serbian population.

Although the agreement between Dangić and General Bader never became operative, it did help to clarify relations among the Germans, General Nedić, and various Chetnik leaders, and it established a pattern that for a time was followed by the Germans in maintaining contact

---

[34] *Ibid.*, Frame 1117 for the collaboration. On March 26, 1942, Mihailović noted in his diary (a copy of which is in the Archives of the Institute of Military History in Belgrade) the main points of a report of Major Djurić on his inspection trip to eastern Bosnia—all very disapproving of Dangić. Dangić was behaving in a willful manner; his command was not at all organized and his commanders were not disciplined; his accounts of money sent to him from Serbia were careless; and most important of all, he lacked both authority and popularity in his area, and he was further compromised by being in touch with the Germans through Captain Matl.

[35] *Ibid.*, Frames 1103, 1215. After the liberation of Poland Dangić was returned to Yugoslavia. In 1946 he was found guilty of war crimes by a court in Sarajevo, sentenced to death, and executed. Miletić, p. 135. For an appraisal of Dangić's activities from a pro-Nedić point of view see Krakov, II, 70–77, 106–7, 128–46.

with some Chetnik leaders. The Armed Forces Commander in Southeast Europe in a directive of April 15, 1942, for example, forbade Wehrmacht units to deal with former rebel groups or any unofficial armed units, because such dealing not only could be interpreted as a weakness on the part of the German armed forces but also gave a legal standing to such groups, limited the freedom of action of the Wehrmacht, and tended to create conflict within the German troops in executing their orders. Maintaining contacts with former rebel groups for purposes of surveillance, which he deemed necessary, was a matter reserved exclusively for the *Abwehr* and the police organs, which for this task should use confidential people and other undercover agents. The Commanding General in Serbia could charge the police organs with tasks exceeding surveillance only with the permission of the Armed Forces Commander in Southeast Europe.[36]

COLLABORATION WITH THE ITALIANS IN MONTENEGRO

In Montenegro, unlike other parts of Yugoslavia, the uprising of the summer of 1941 was of a general, popular character, in which both the Communists and their sympathizers and the nationalist Montenegrins or Whites *(bjelaši)*, who stood for close ties with Serbia, took an active part. Against them were aligned the Italians and the Montenegrin separatists or Greens *(zelenaši)* under the leadership of Sekula Drljević and the old Montenegrin General Krsto Popović.[37] The uprising broke out on July 13, 1941, but it was not well prepared and after a few weeks of success it met with serious reverses. The pro-Serbian nationalists admitted defeat and wanted to quit; the Partisans were determined to continue the fight. The result was a parting of ways. Sometime in the autumn the nationalists established contact with the Italians, offering their assistance against the Partisans. The trend toward collaboration was greatly strengthened after the Montenegrins heard about the split between Mihailović's Chetniks and the Partisans in Serbia. To ascertain what the situation was in Serbia and to get in direct touch with Mihailović, the nationalist groups in Montenegro toward the end of November dispatched Major Djurišić to Serbia. During that visit Mihailović gave Djurišić oral instructions and appointed him commander of all Chetnik

[36] Microcopy No. T-501, Roll 257, Frame 1213.

[37] Drljević was the principal Montenegrin separatist leader who helped the Italians to organize the proclamation of the "independent" state of Montenegro on July 12, 1941, a move that collapsed under the impact of the general uprising which began the following day. The Italians, believing that Drljević's life was in danger, in September sent him to an internment camp in Italy, but after a few months he managed to escape and made his way to the German-controlled part of the Independent State of Croatia. Sometime in 1944 Drljević launched a Montenegrin State Council in Croatia and worked on the establishment of a Montenegrin state with the help of Croatian and German authorities. Toward the end of the war he became active in connection with Djurišić's Montenegrin Chetniks (see Chapter 12). Pajović, "Political Action of Sekula Drljević," pp. 75–80.

detachments in Sandjak; he appointed Major Lašić commander of all Chetnik forces in Old Montenegro. In the instruction of December 20 (discussed in the preceding chapter) Mihailović outlined the Chetnik program in general and also indicated specific tasks regarding the organization and future activities of the Chetniks in Sandjak and Montenegro. In the second half of December Djurišić and Lašić began mobilizing men in Montenegro and organizing them into separate units in competition with Partisan detachments, and by the middle of January these units were in armed conflict with the Partisans.[38] The conflict between the two groups was spurred on by two developments on the Partisan side. One was the debacle the Partisans suffered in their attack upon the Italian garrison in the town of Pljevlja at the beginning of December, in which they sustained several hundred dead and wounded and which resulted in large-scale desertions from Partisan to Chetnik ranks. The other was the "left deviation" engaged in by Partisans in Montenegro and the Partisan use of mass terror against their actual and potential enemies, on the grounds—not always true—that they were collaborating with the enemy.

By mid-February individual Chetnik commanders and the commanders of various Italian divisions had begun to make their first formal agreements. The first, on February 17, was an agreement between a representative of Colonel Bajo Stanišić and the commander of the Italian Taro Division.[39] This was soon followed by an agreement between a representative of Captain Djurišić and the Military Governor and Commander of the Italian Troops in Montenegro, General Pirzio Biroli, on collaboration between the Djurišić Chetniks and the Italian forces in areas in which the Venezia Division was deployed, and on March 6 an agreement was concluded between Colonel Stanišić and General Pirzio Biroli.[40] All these agreements involved either joint action or independent Chetnik action against the Communist-led Partisans, with the Italians in both cases giving the necessary arms and supplies to the Chetnik formations. On March 9 a large number of Montenegrins who had been professional or reserve officers in the royal Yugoslav army held a conference at Cetinje at which they elected General Blažo Djukanović commander of all nationalist forces in Montenegro, a selection which General Mihailović fully accepted and which indeed he may have suggested.[41]

Between March and June of 1942 the Chetniks thus acquired a degree

[38] Jovanović, I, 441–85.

[39] *Dokumenti o izdajstvu Draže Mihailovića*, I, 65. Colonel Stanišić was a Yugoslav officer who took part in the July 13 uprising and was a member of the Montenegrin rebel headquarters. After the uprising suffered reverses he withdrew from action, but in February 1942 he came out strongly in favor of the Chetniks and remained so until his death in October 1943.

[40] *Ibid.*, 40; Jovanović, pp. 508, 511–12.

[41] Jovanović, p. 497.

of power in Montenegro, partly because of their agreements with the Italians and the arms and other supplies that they got from them, and partly because of the weakening of the Partisans, which was to a large extent due to the excesses of the Partisans along the lines of "left deviation." Since the principal objective of the Italians in reaching agreements with the Chetniks was to keep Italian troop losses at a minimum, the Chetniks were heavily relied on in the successful drive to push the Partisans out of Montenegro and eastern Herzegovina in the spring of 1942 (the Third Enemy Offensive in Partisan terminology).[42]

As the war advanced, Chetnik-Italian collaboration in Montenegro went beyond the first formal agreements between individual Chetnik commanders and commanders of various Italian divisions, which had applied to specific areas only. In order to expand the areas covered and to strengthen all Chetnik forces in Montenegro and keep them in fighting condition so that the Italians could hold their casualties at a minimum, a comprehensive agreement between General Djukanović and General Pirzio Biroli was worked out and signed on July 24, about two months after Mihailović reached Montenegro.[43] Since the agreement apparently remained in force during the year Mihailović was in Montenegro, one can fairly assume that he knew about it and was satisfied with its provisions. This can be inferred also from Mihailović's own statements (see below, p. 219).

The Pirzio Biroli–Djukanović agreement contained several detailed provisions: the Chetniks were to continue uncompromising struggle against the Communists and were to cooperate with the Italian occupation authorities in the restoration and maintenance of law and order in the country; three "flying detachments" (similar to the units of the *Milizia volontaria anti comunista* or MVAC's in the areas under the command of the Italian Second Army) under the command of Djurišić, Stanišić, and Popović, respectively, of 1,500 men each were officially recognized;[44] arrangements pertaining to pay, rations, arms, and aid to the families of Chetnik volunteers were to be made by mutual understanding; a Committee of Montenegrin Nationalists of seventeen members was to be established (it in fact sanctioned an already existing committee headed by General Djukanović). The agreement also stated that the Nationalist Movement and the committee that led it had no political objectives, except to crush Communism and to safeguard law and order and the well-being of the Montenegrin population. The con-

---

[42] *Oslobodilački rat*, I, 212–18.

[43] For the text of this agreement see *Zbornik DNOR*, Tome III, Vol. 4, pp. 527–30.

[44] These flying detachments were in fact already in existence and had been used by the Italians, as proved by the order of General Pirzio Biroli of June 10, 1942, for operations against the Partisans, although the map attached to that order shows that they were not used as one block of troops but rather were deployed between large Italian units. Microcopy No. T-821, Roll 60, Frames 3–6.

cluding provision of the agreement was particularly significant: "The Committee of Nationalists of Montenegro obliges itself to undertake everything that is in its power and authority to preserve order and discipline in the country and will counteract all possible actions that could be directed against the Italian authorities."[45]

The Chetniks in Montenegro became an important part of the Italian occupation regime, controlling the rural areas and in that way allowing the Italians to concentrate on maintaining their rule in towns and safeguarding communications between towns. The Montenegrin separatists had of course been collaborating with the Italians from the beginning of occupation, and during the first half of 1942 the separatists and the Chetniks came to some understanding about joint collaboration with the Italians; but because their objectives were diametrically different, relations between the two groups were always rather tenuous. In some crucial instances, as for example the Montenegrin Chetnik expedition to Herzegovina during the Battle of the Neretva River, there was no collaboration at all between them. Both groups were interested in getting as much as possible out of the Italians—organizing their forces to the limit allowed, having these troops armed, paid, and maintained by the Italians, and having food brought in by the Italians for the civilian population that supported them—all in order to wage a better fight against the Partisans. Here, as in Serbia with the legalized Chetniks, Mihailović wanted to have a ready-made army which at the opportune moment would turn against the enemy and unite with other Mihailović forces, and with the help of the Western Allies carry Mihailović to power. For nearly a year—from June 1942 to about April 1943—the Chetniks were eminently successful in their scheme in Montenegro: in addition to the 3,500 men whom they organized as Italian auxiliaries in Montenegro under terms of the Pirzio Biroli–Djukanović agreement, they had several times that number of men under arms who were not Italian auxiliaries but were likewise engaged in fighting the Partisans.[46] In fact the Chetniks controlled a very large part of the whole province.

On one occasion—during the Battle of the Neretva River, the final stages of Operation Weiss—the Italians made use of the Montenegrin Chetniks outside their own province, though they were also under concurrent orders from Mihailović to fight the Partisans.[47]

[45] For the text of this agreement see *Zbornik DNOR*, Tome III, Vol. 4, p. 530.

[46] An internal memorandum of the Italian Ministry of Foreign Affairs of January 2, 1943 (Microcopy No. T-821, Roll 247, Frames 736–40), estimates that in addition to the 3,500 men in the auxiliaries (actually according to the Pirzio Biroli–Djukanović agreement the Chetniks had only 3,000 men in these units) there were in Montenegro 31,500 armed Chetniks. The latter figure is totally unrealistic, except possibly as an estimate of the number who could be mobilized in areas under Chetnik control.

[47] *Dokumenti o izdajstvu Draže Mihailovića*, I, 424.

COLLABORATION WITH THE ITALIANS IN CROATIA

Chetnik collaboration with the Italians in the Italian-annexed parts of Dalmatia and the Italian-occupied parts of the Independent State of Croatia was similar to the collaboration that went on in Montenegro, except that conditions were more complex because Croatian quisling and German interests were directly involved, and disagreements between Communist-led groups and Serbian nationalist groups partaking in the July 1941 uprising in these areas appeared much sooner than in Montenegro.[48] The Partisans lumped the occupation forces and the Croatian quisling forces all together as the fascist enemy; the Serbian nationalists hated the Ustashas but balked at fighting the Italians, and had indeed tried as early as July and August to get the Italians to help them in countering the brutal anti-Serbian measures of the Ustashas.[49] These early contacts, in which a Serb politician from Lika, Stevo Radjenović, played an important part, are clearly set forth in a report of the commander of the Italian VIth Army Corps, General Renzo Dalmazzo, to the Italian Second Army of January 17, 1942, entitled "Contacts with the Leaders of the Chetnik Formations."[50] In addition to contacts with Radjenović, Dalmazzo took special note of the contacts with and the views and policies of two other Chetnik leaders who played a leading role in this area, *vojvodas* Ilija Trifunović-Birčanin and Dobroslav Jevdjević. Both these men were favorably disposed toward the Italians and, in the belief that the expansion of Italian occupation over the whole area of Bosnia and Herzegovina was the best wartime solution for the Serbian population of the province, sought an alliance with them against the Ustashas and the Partisans.[51]

General Dalmazzo's policy toward the Chetniks had two objectives: first, to avoid any fighting with them, and second, to induce most if not all of them to join the fight against the Partisans, which he thought would be an "enormous advantage" to the Italians. He proposed to strengthen only the detachments that were known to be friendly to the

---

[48] Practically all these Serbian nationalist groups identified themselves during the latter months of 1941 as Chetnik groups.

[49] On August 11, 1941, before the resistance became polarized, both Chetnik and Partisan representatives from Lika met with representatives of the Italian army in the western Bosnian village of Otrić. The Chetnik representatives issued a statement, which the Partisans also signed, in which they declared that the main reason for the uprising was the Ustasha persecution of the Serbian people; no fighting and no sabotage would be directed against the Italians, and "together [with the Italians] they would counteract all Communist actions in these areas." All the Chetnik and Partisan signatories were arrested shortly afterward by units of the Partisan command in western Bosnia. Pressure from the peasant population of the area quickly brought their release, but no Partisan group signed anything like this statement in the future. See Stanisavljević, pp. 68–71. See also Žurić, pp. 200–202.

[50] Microcopy No. T-821, Roll 53, Frames 697–702. This report seems to have been prompted by the conclusion six days earlier of a preliminary agreement with the Chetniks, since this agreement, to be discussed presently, was attached to the Dalmazzo report as an appendix.

[51] See the report of General Roatta, the new commander of the Italian Second Army, to the Chief of General Staff of the Army, dated Feb. 2, 1942, and the enclosed memorandum by Jevdjević, *ibid.*, Frames 1162–71.

Italians and to disarm detachments that were vacillating; also, in areas in which the Serbs were in a majority, he would remove Croats from local government and replace them with Serbs.[52] As will presently be shown, the policy of Italian-Chetnik collaboration was greatly advanced and systematized under the guidance of General Roatta, commander of the Italian Second Army during 1942, and was applied by all Italian commanders in the Italian-annexed or occupied territories of Croatia, Dalmatia, and Bosnia and Herzegovina, and in Slovenia with the forces supplied by the anti-Communist groups.

I have not found texts of any agreements between the Chetniks and the command of the Italian Second Army comparable to the Djukanović–Pirzio Biroli agreement for Montenegro, but texts of several less general agreements are available and there is much other evidence of close Chetnik-Italian collaboration in the area occupied by the Italian Second Army. The first agreement seems to have been the preliminary agreement concluded on January 11, 1942, between the representative of the Italian VIth Army Corps, Captain Angelo De Matteis, and the representative of the Chetniks from southeastern Bosnia, Mutimir Petković.[53] The agreement was to become effective after it had been signed by both the Italian command and the Chetnik command of the area as well as by Major Boško Todorović, Mihailović's chief delegate in Bosnia and Herzegovina. Later developments suggest that the agreement was signed by all concerned. The agreement contains seven specific provisions: (1) If the Italians should occupy eastern Bosnia, they and the Chetniks of the area would refrain from using arms against each other; (2) Chetnik detachments in eastern Bosnia would be allowed to keep their arms, since they would need them after the Italian withdrawal from the area; (3) in areas liberated by the Chetniks (meaning, presumably, from the Croatian quisling forces or from the Partisans) all Croatian military and police formations would be disarmed; (4) in all areas in which the Roman Catholics (Croats) were in a minority, Croatian local authority would be replaced by Serbian authority which would function alongside the Italian military administration; (5) in these areas the Serbian population would be guaranteed personal, national, and religious freedom, as well as property rights; (6) the Italians should help in obtaining the release of Serbs from these areas who were held in Croatian concentration camps, because this would greatly help to counteract Communist propaganda against the Chetniks; and (7) a trade agreement would be concluded between the Chetniks and the Italians.

Although the January 11 agreement was directed essentially against

[52] *Ibid.*, Frame 701.
[53] For the text of this agreement see *ibid.*, Frames 704–5. Petković was one of the officers whom Mihailović sent to Bosnia to work on the organization of the Bosnian Chetniks. *The Trial of Draža Mihailović*, p. 134.

the Croatian Ustashas, because the Chetniks and the Partisans had not yet completely split, there is no doubt that the Italians were very aware, as General Dalmazzo stated, of what assistance they could get from the Chetniks against the Partisans. And very soon—if not yet at that time— the chief interest of both the Chetniks and the Italians would be to help each other to fight the Partisans.

In order to develop a Policy Directive (*Linea di condotta*) on relations between his command and the Croats, Chetniks, and Partisans, General Roatta addressed between January 30 and February 9, 1942, a series of memoranda to General Vittorio Ambrosio, his predecessor as commander of the Second Army who was now the Chief of the General Staff of the Army.[54] Roatta was primarily interested in withdrawing a large portion of the Italian troops from Zones II and III and regrouping the remainder in a series of strong garrisons in order to reduce troop casualties; the problem was how to fill the vacuum that would be created without seriously prejudicing Italian interests. Since the chief danger lay in the Partisans, the obvious counterbalancing force, besides the Croatian quisling troops, was the Chetniks. In a reply of February 13 to Roatta's memoranda, General Ambrosio said that in regard to the Croats, maximum loyalty was to be shown, but Italian policy should show toward them "no uncertainty, or weakness, and a strong hand, if necessary." With the Chetniks, he said, the situation was fluid partly because the policy of their various chiefs was not clear. In view of the Italian policy toward the Croats, all negotiations with them should be avoided; but contacts with the Chetniks when situations and local convenience required were advisable. As for the Communists: "struggle to the bitter end."[55] In other words, whereas policies toward the Independent State of Croatia and the Communist-led Partisans were well defined, Roatta was more or less free to make his own policy in regard to the Chetniks.

The use he made of that freedom is shown in his report on the Chetniks of March 6, 1942, submitted to the General Staff of the Army. His policy had four points:

> To support the Chetniks sufficiently to make them fight against the Communists, but not so much as to allow them too much latitude in their action; to demand and assure that the Chetniks do not fight against Croatian forces and authorities; to allow them to operate against the Communists for their own account (so that they can "slaughter each other"); and finally to allow the Chetnik bands to operate in a parallel way with Italian and German forces, as do the nationalist bands [Chetniks and separatists] in Montenegro.[56]

[54] Microcopy No. T-821, Roll 53, Frames 1162–64, 1173–79.
[55] *Ibid.*, Frame 1161.
[56] *Ibid.*, Frame 1068. In a meeting of Italian, German, and Croatian generals on March 28, 1942, shortly before the launching of the so-called Third Enemy Offensive, the question of the Chetniks was again considered with great care. General Roatta stated on that occasion that all

In his postwar memoirs Roatta explained his policy more fully:

> The political label of the "Chetniks," their indirect relations with the "Allies," and their program for the future did not interest this commander, and these things he "ignored." He only established and exploited the existing fact, that in the territory under his command, the "Chetniks" acted in our favor. So much the worse for the Croats and the Germans in other regions who did not want to or did not know how to make out of the "Chetniks" their own allies.
>
> Thus, despite the protests of Berlin and Zagreb, and the efforts of the government in Rome (which often changed its opinion and finally adopted the German view), we continued on our part to collaborate with the "Chetniks." The formations in question were furnished arms, etc., and so regularized (as were the other voluntary formations) until they reached a total strength of about 30,000 men.[57]

The Ustasha government was of course opposed to the Italian policy, but it had no choice in the matter, and by the terms of the Italian-Croatian agreement concluded in Zagreb on June 19, 1942, concerning the withdrawal of about half of the Italian forces from Zones II and III, it assumed the burden of maintaining the Chetnik anti-Communist militia which had been established and maintained up to that time by the Italians—provided of course that the Chetniks recognized the sovereignty of the Croatian state.[58]

Thus during 1942 and 1943 an overwhelming proportion of the Chetnik forces in the Italian-occupied parts of the territory of the Croatian puppet state were organized as Italian auxiliary forces in the form of Voluntary Anti-Communist Militia (*Milizia volontaria anti comunista* or MVAC). According to General Giacomo Zanussi, who while still a colonel was Roatta's Deputy Chief of Staff, there were 19,000 to 20,000 Chetniks in the MVAC in the Italian-occupied parts of puppet Croatia, and they were furnished by the Italians with the following supplies: 30,000 rifles, 500 machine guns, 100 mortars, fifteen pieces of artillery, 250,000 hand grenades, 7,000,000 rounds of ammunition, 7,000–8,000 pairs of shoes. Some other supplies that were promised were apparently not delivered because Roatta was removed from his post.[59] Probably, too, the list does not include supplies that were delivered to the Chetniks during the three stages of Operation Weiss in the winter of 1943, which must have been considerable.

The strength and deployment of the MVAC units in the area of the

---

Communists were enemies and that no negotiations would be held with them. The Chetniks were a different matter: "The Chetniks are actually enemies of Croatia, but not enemies of the Axis, and therefore it is expedient for the time being to negotiate with them. . . . The fight against the Chetniks will necessarily be undertaken later, together." Microcopy No. T-501, Roll 257, Frame 1108.

[57] Roatta, p. 177. On January 3, 1943, shortly before he was shifted from his command, Roatta told Marshal Ugo Cavallero, Chief of the Italian Supreme Command, that the Chetniks were the only "little white ball" in the area of his command, so it was necessary to keep them on the Italian side. Cavallero, p. 429. See also Stanisavljević, pp. 95, 125, 129, 137.

[58] Microcopy No. T-501, Roll 264, Frames 649–61, esp. Frames 658–61.

[59] Zanussi, I, 248–49.

TABLE 4

MVAC Units in Italian Service, February 28, 1943

Unit	Orthodox	Catholics	Moslems	Total	Units	Divisions
Vth Army Corps	4,313[a]	—	—	4,313	20	Lombardia 2, Re 18
VIth Army Corps	8,385	511	780	9,676	22	Marche 6, Messina 2, Murge 14
XVIIIth Army Corps	7,816[b]	321	—	8,137	21	Sassari 17, Bergamo 4
Total (occupied zone)	20,514	832	780	22,126		
Slovenia (XIth A.C.)				5,145	40	Isonzo, Cacciatori delle Alpi, Frontier Guards
Dalmatia (XVIIIth A.C.)				882	13	
Kotor (VIth A.C.)				1,474	3	
Total (annexed zone)				7,501		
Grand total				29,627		

SOURCE: Microcopy No. T-821, Roll 31, Frames 218–23.

[a] All Chetnik MVAC units in the area of the Vth Army Corps were under the command of Lt. Colonel Ilija Mihić.

[b] Of these, 2,807 men were brought to northern Dalmatia from Herzegovina and were under the command of Major Petar Baćović. The name of the principal Chetnik commander in this area, *vojvoda* Momčilo Djujić, is not mentioned, however.

Supersloda as of the end of February 1943 are shown in Table 4, based on detailed Italian tabulations. As a matter of policy, these units, which varied in size from only a score or two of men per unit to units numbering a thousand, were spread over a vast area and were subject to the command of a great many Italian divisions. In the area of the VIth Army Corps (southern Dalmatia and most of Herzegovina) some MVAC units were composed solely of Catholics or of Moslems, and in the area of the XVIIIth Army Corps there was a small all-Catholic MVAC contingent.

A very important document pertaining to the Anti-Communist Militia is a memorandum of the General Staff of the Army of March 20, 1943, bearing the title, "The Conduct of the Chetniks." After discussing the strength of the Chetniks organized in the Anti-Communist Militia, their control by Draža Mihailović, and probable objectives of these forces, the memorandum raises the possibility of hostile reorientation of these troops against Italy in view of the changing military situation in the Balkans, especially the possibility of an Anglo-American landing in Yugoslav territory. Considering the remarkable contribution which these troops have made in the common struggle against subversion and the fact that the Chetnik conduct has been affected by profound changes in the military situation in the Balkans, it is necessary, the memorandum says, to adopt intensive measures to ensure their control. To that end the following measures seem to be of special interest:

to keep the Chetnik forces in small detachments strictly observing the territorial principle, avoiding especially the union of the Montenegrin and Herzegovinian units with the units of the Dinara area, Lika, and Slovenia, in order to make it impossible for these forces to acquire a unified and organic character, which in the course of time could constitute a center of support for the reconstruction of a unified Great Yugoslavia; avoid formation of new units; provide arms and ammunition only in absolutely necessary quantities.[60]

By March 1943, however, as this memorandum was being drafted, the situation in the Italian zone was changing rapidly, and various reflections of this memorandum were overtaken by developments of which more will be said later.

The commander of the Chetnik units organized as MVAC as well as other Chetnik formations in Dalmatia, Herzegovina, western Bosnia, and southwestern Croatia was *vojvoda* Trifunović-Birčanin, who came to Split from Montenegro in October 1941 and received his command from Mihailović in the spring of 1942.[61] Both Chetnik and Italian documents clearly show that his role as liaison officer between the Chetniks and the Italian Second Army was just as important as his command over the Chetnik formations in these areas. Under Birčanin there were several important Chetnik commanders. In northern Dalmatia there was the self-appointed *vojvoda* Momčilo Djujić; in Lika were Lt. Colonel Ilija Mihić and Major Slavko N. Bjelajac, both appointees of Mihailović; in Herzegovina and southeastern Bosnia were Lt. Colonel Petar Baćović, a Mihailović appointee, and the self-appointed *vojvoda* Dobroslav Jevdjević, who was closely associated with Birčanin in liaison work with the Italians. Birčanin, who had long been in poor health, died in February 1943, but his chief lieutenants (Jevdjević, Djujić, Baćović, Radovan Ivanišević) promised the Italians that they would carry on his policies of close collaboration with them and continued struggle against the Partisans.[62] A few weeks later Mihailović appointed Lt. Colonel Mladen Žujović (known also as Aćimović), a lawyer in civilian life and a member of the Chetnik Central National Committee, to succeed Birčanin, and he held that position until the collapse of Italy.[63]

---

[60] Microcopy No. T-821, Roll 247, Frames 746–48.

[61] Stanisavljević, pp. 80–83 and *passim*.

[62] See the message of General Umberto Spigo, commander of the XVIIIth Army Corps, to Supersloda of Feb. 5, 1943, Microcopy No. T-821, Roll 247, Frame 774. The Italians had maintained a personal hold over Birčanin, whose family was with him in Split, and also over Jevdjević, whose brother and fiancée were interned in Italy; see *ibid.*, Roll 252, Frame 303.

[63] *The Četniks*, pp. 68–74. According to the same source, at the time of the Italian collapse both Žujović and Bjelajac escaped to the Allies in Italy and later went to Cairo. Bjelajac went to the United States after the war and became an officer of the United States Army, apparently specializing in unconventional and psychological warfare. Since his retirement he has published a series of articles on guerrilla warfare and counterinsurgency, but not with reference to Yugoslavia.

The question may be raised whether General Mihailović knew of this collaboration of his commanders with the Italians. Many of the documents quoted above prove that he did, and Mihailović himself admitted the knowledge in a speech at Gornje Lipovo on February 28, 1943 (see Chapter 8). During his trial Mihailović confessed that he knew about the collaboration of his commanders with the Italians and that he saw it as soon as he arrived in Montenegro.[64] Not only Mihailović, but also the Yugoslav government-in-exile, as we shall see, heard of this collaboration in a number of ways during the course of 1942.

There is a plethora of other documents on Chetnik collaboration with the Italians. Among the most interesting are those regarding the meetings between Trifunović-Birčanin and General Roatta in September 1942, of which more will be said below. There are also an order of General Roatta of January 11, 1943, on "Winter Operations" (i.e. Italian participation in Operation Weiss 1), which among other things specifies the tasks of the collaborating Chetnik anti-Communist militia, and the text of an agreement presumably dating from early 1943 between Jevdjević and the Italians dealing with the problem of legalizing more Chetnik units in southeastern Bosnia and eastern Herzegovina, that is, increasing the effectives of the MVAC, including the provision of supplies, arms, and pay for them.[65] The voluminous correspondence among various Chetnik commanders in these areas also reveals this collaboration.[66]

Some especially interesting information is included in a report of General Glaise to the Commander in Chief in Southeast Europe of January 13, 1943, concerning a visit made by General Roatta to Zagreb shortly before he was transferred from the command of Supersloda. The report says:

In regard to the Chetnik problem which was raised by Pavelić, it came out that Roatta had under his flag 3,000 Chetniks around Plaški and Vrhovine [Lika], 8,000 around Knin [northern Dalmatia], of which 3,000 were from Herzegovina, and 8,000 in Herzegovina—that is, a total of 19,000 Chetniks. That these Chetniks do not make even a step without the concurrence of DM [Draža Mihailović] is known to us from absolutely unimpeachable documents; 7,000 of these Chetniks were armed, supplied, and paid by the Italians. And only a few weeks ago Roatta swore to the Croats that he had only 1,500 Chetniks in his service, and that he would no longer supply them with even a single rifle! Furthermore Roatta told Pavelić that probably the time might come when for the pacification of Herzegovina also the 20,000 Chetniks who are located in Montenegro and are in the service of the Italians should be called upon. It was also planned to enlarge this contingent with a further 10,000 men. Considering

[64] *The Trial of Draža Mihailović*, pp. 146, 194.
[65] *Dokumenti o izdajstvu Draže Mihailovića*, 1, 351–57.
[66] See esp. the correspondence during the crucial period of the last stages of Operation Weiss, *ibid.*, 1, 394–487.

all this, Roatta surely does not think of disarming his Chetniks. It is also interesting to note that Count Ciano a few weeks ago told the Croatian Envoy in Rome, Perić, that the Croats should turn to the German Wehrmacht and through it exert some pressure on the Italian Comando Supremo in regard to the Chetnik problem.[67]

In fact, Roatta and Pavelić agreed at that meeting that a contingent of Montenegrin troops would be sent immediately to the central parts of western Bosnia for operations against the Partisans. This plan was soon given up but, as will be shown later, during the Battle of the Neretva River in February and March 1943 the bulk of Montenegrin Chetniks who served as Italian auxiliaries was sent to Herzegovina to help fight the Partisans.[68]

In collaborating with the Italians in the Italian-occupied parts of the Independent State of Croatia the Chetniks had both immediate and long-range objectives. The fundamental consideration was the fight against the Partisans, but they also were engaged in actions against the Croatian quisling forces and authorities both as representatives of a state idea unacceptable to the Serbs and as the enemies of the Serbian population in these areas. This collaboration therefore became one of the chief stumbling blocks in the relations between Italy and the Ustasha state. The critical Croatian reaction to this collaboration can be seen from a multitude of Croatian complaints, both written and oral, on important but also frequently trivial things to the Italian Second Army, to the Italian representatives in Zagreb, and occasionally to the highest Italian political and military authorities in Rome.[69] In their replies to the Croats, the Italians tended to speak lightly of this collaboration and to stress its temporary character: it would last only until the Partisans had been liquidated, with Chetnik aid, and then the Chetniks would be dealt with.[70]

COLLABORATION WITH THE ITALIANS IN SLOVENIA

In the beginning of their rule in part of Slovenia, the Italians, hoping to gain the acceptance of the rank and file of the Slovene people, showed themselves a more civilized occupying power than their allies the Germans. Most of the leading members of the now outlawed Slovene

---

[67] Microcopy No. T-501, Roll 264, Frames 568–69.

[68] *Dokumenti o izdajstvu Draže Mihailovića*, 1, 326–50, 373–76, and *passim*.

[69] See esp. the protest submitted by the Croatian envoy in Rome, Stijepo Perić, on Dec. 29, 1942, to Marshal Cavallero, Chief of the Italian Supreme Command, in Microcopy No. T-821, Roll 247, Frames 783–89.

[70] See e.g. General Roatta's report of April 13, 1942, on his visit to Zagreb, on which occasion the Croatian puppet government showed great concern and protested against Italian collaboration with the Chetniks and Roatta's efforts to mollify the Croatian leaders, in *ibid.*, Roll 65, Frames 299–301. The Italians were forced in time to make some concessions to the Croats in this respect, the more so as behind the Croatian protests there was also considerable German pressure. See e.g. Leković, "Mihailović's Plans for the Destruction of the 'Partisan State' in Western Bosnia in the Second Half of 1942."

People's Party—the Catholic-oriented party which had controlled the political destiny of Slovenia throughout the interwar period—who were still in the country justified full collaboration with the Italians as a way of saving the zone from the large-scale deportation and denationalization practices that the Germans were following in the parts of Slovenia under their control. These included Dr. Marko Natlačen, the last Ban of Banovina Drava (Slovenia), Dr. Lambert Ehrlich, a theology professor at the University of Ljubljana and head of one of the extreme right wings of Catholic Action's youth organizations, and Dr. Gregorij Rožman, Bishop of Ljubljana, as well as other political and business leaders and even a former Yugoslav army general, Leon Rupnik, who in June 1942 was appointed mayor of Ljubljana by the Italians. (The head of the party, Dr. Miha Krek, and some other members were with the government-in-exile in London.) During the invasion and the ensuing collapse and disintegration of the Yugoslav army and state apparatus Natlačen had organized the Slovene Legion for the purpose of helping maintain law and order. This group was put at the disposal of the Italians on their entry into Ljubljana and continued to exist as a collaborating group under the Italian rule.[71] But there were other elements in Slovenia that were interested in building up a force to oppose the occupation regimes. One of these groups consisted of a portion of the former officers, and some noncommissioned officers, of the Yugoslav army who were not taken as prisoners of war or who returned to their native Slovenia from prisoner-of-war camps in Germany and Italy. The Communist Party of Slovenia, a branch of the Communist Party of Yugoslavia, was the most active, however, and it was instrumental in helping to organize at the end of April 1941 the Anti-Imperialist Front, composed of Communists, the left wing of Christian Socialists, a portion of the Yugoslav gymnastic organization Sokol, and a large number of liberal intellectuals and artists. This coalition—renamed the Liberation Front (*Osvobodilna fronta*) after the Germans invaded the Soviet Union— was open to all groups and individuals (including a few of the former Yugoslav army officers) who were in favor of immediate and determined resistance against the occupying powers and all groups and individuals who collaborated with them. The Communist Party of Slovenia was undoubtedly the most thoroughly organized and disciplined section of the Front, and through one of its leading members, Boris Kidrič, who became secretary of the Front's executive committee, the party for all practical purposes exercised a controlling influence in the Front.[72] The uprising in Slovenia under the leadership of the Liberation Front started on July 22.

[71] Škerl, pp. 19–21.
[72] *Ibid.*, pp. 28–31, 52–53.

News about the Mihailović resistance group in Serbia reached Slovenia during the latter part of the summer of 1941 and apparently elicited keen interest among some of the former Yugoslav officers. In October two of these officers, Colonel Jakob Avšič and Major Karlo Novak, with the approval of the Liberation Front, went to Serbia to see Mihailović, and were appointed by him commander and chief of staff, respectively, of the proposed Slovene Chetnik forces. A month later, when Mihailović abandoned his tenuous cooperation with the Partisans in Serbia in favor of outright armed hostility, Avšič opted for the Liberation Front (he eventually became one of the Partisan generals in Slovenia).[73] Novak opted for the Chetniks and became commander of the Slovene Chetniks, but most of the other officers and noncommissioned officers of the royal army who were in the Italian-annexed parts of Slovenia were arrested the following March and taken to Italian prisoner-of-war camps as a precautionary measure.[74]

The main anti-Communist forces in Slovenia were not the Chetniks, however, but the armed formations established by the adherents of the former Slovene People's Party—Natlačen's Slovene Legion and another group called the Village Guards. These two organizations and a few other armed units were able to maintain contact with Slovene People's Party representatives in the government-in-exile, and by way of BBC broadcasts their members received periodic messages of advice and encouragement. On February 1, 1942, for example, the Reverend Alojzij Kuhar, one of the Slovene leaders in London, broadcast a message saying that the fate of the Slovenes would be determined by the West, that in the relations with the enemy it was necessary to be wise and cautious, and that the leaders should see to it that the people did not follow political adventurers who by their actions caused the burning of Slovene homes and the killing of Slovene people.[75] On April 26 of the same year, Dr. Krek, Vice-Premier in the exile cabinet, told the Slovene people that the Yugoslav government-in-exile was the only government of Yugoslavia recognized by the Allies, and that no fighting group in Yugoslavia other than the one led by General Mihailović was recognized by the Allies; all men of military age, he said, were subject to call by Mihailović and all those who failed to heed his call would be considered traitors and deserters and would be dealt with by military courts. In short, the only path open for Slovenia was to be a part of free Yugoslavia, and all Slovenes must join in that platform. He called upon all youth organizations, members of Sokol, and regular and reserve officers to follow the

[73] For the letter from Partisan headquarters in Serbia to the Partisans in Slovenia informing them of the change in Mihailović's policy see *Zbornik DNOR*, Tome VI, Vol. 1, pp. 146–49.
[74] Novak, pp. 317–18, 320; Mikuž, I, 280–81. There was also a small political group led by Dr. Črtomir Nagode that stood behind Novak.
[75] Saje, pp. 251–52, 266–67.

orders of General Mihailović.[76] It was only a few weeks later that the Slovene bourgeois political parties under the leadership of the Slovene People's Party organized the Slovene Alliance (*Slovenska zaveza*), as the political organization of the anti-Communist forces which at the same time stood politically and organizationally behind the existing anti-Communist armed formations.[77] In a political sense, the Chetniks under Major Novak were also a part of the Slovene Alliance, but they had no influence whatsoever in it.[78]

There were thus in Slovenia—which, unlike most of Yugoslavia, is nationally and religiously almost completely homogeneous—three distinct categories of armed formations: first, the Slovene Legion, the Sokol Legion, the Village Guards, and for some time also a minuscule group of the so-called White Chetniks, acting more or less independently but controlled by the Slovene Alliance;[79] second, the pro-Mihailović Chetniks under Major Novak; and third, the armed formations of the Liberation Front, that is, Partisans under the leadership of the Communist Party of Slovenia. Those people, including some former officers, who might have been expected to take sides but instead tried to remain neutral, in distinction to people who belonged to the Liberation Front and were dubbed OF's, were derisively referred to as OR's (*oprezne riti,* literally cautious arses).

The Italians in Slovenia, as in other areas of Yugoslavia under their control, were eager to use the anti-Communist forces as auxiliary troops. This accorded well with the desires of the Slovene bourgeois political parties and organizations, especially the adherents of the Slovene People's Party, which were to strengthen their armed groups and obtain Italian recognition and assistance in order to carry on their fight against the Partisans—who for them, as for the Chetniks, were a much more dangerous enemy than the occupying powers. These desires of the Slovene anti-Communist forces were first clearly formulated in a memorandum that Dr. Ehrlich presented on April 1, 1942, to the commander of the Italian troops in the Italian-annexed part of Slovenia.[80]

In September 1942, according to a report of General Roatta, there

[76] *Ibid.*, pp. 256–57. For another programmatic statement by Dr. Krek of Oct. 18, 1942, see Mikuž, p. 260.

[77] Mikuž, pp. 257–61.

[78] Novak, pp. 320–23. In Liberation Front terminology the forces under the control of the Slovene Alliance were known as the White Guards (*bela garda*) and the forces under Major Novak were the Blue Guards (*plava garda*).

[79] An important component of the Slovene Legion seems to have been young men who after 1932 were organized and indoctrinated by youth organizations of Catholic Action, the one at the University of Ljubljana organized by Dr. Ehrlich and popularly known as Guards (*stražari*) and the other organized at the high school level by a Catholic layman, Ernest Tomec, popularly known as Fighters (*borci*). The names were derived from the journals published by the two groups: *Straža v viharju* (Guards in the Storm) and *Mi mladi borci* (We Young Fighters), respectively. See Mikuž, pp. 263–71; Saje, pp. 135–219.

[80] For what seems to be a paraphrase of this memorandum see *Proces proti vojnim zločincem in izdajalcem Rupniku, Rösenerju, Rožmanu, Kreku, Vizjaku in Hacinu,* pp. 151–54; see also Saje, pp. 273–314, and Mikuž, pp. 278–84.

were in Slovenia about one thousand Slovenes in units that were organized as *Milizia volontaria anti comunista*. Subsequently, owing to pressure exerted by General Roatta and General Robotti, the commander of the XIth Army Corps deployed in the Slovene area under Italian rule, on various Slovene leaders and especially on the influential Bishop of Ljubljana, Dr. Rožman, these forces were greatly increased. In a memorandum to General Robotti of September 12, 1942, Bishop Rožman proposed that the Village Guards be enlarged under Italian auspices and put under the command of certain Slovene officers presently in Italian prisoner-of-war camps (who were to be released according to lists to be supplied by the Bishop), and that a special secret anti-Communist police force of Slovenes be established for the city of Ljubljana. Robotti approved all these proposals and they were at once put into effect.[81] The officers were released; Lt. Colonel Ernest Peterlin became the chief of the Slovene units in Italian service, and their number rapidly increased, reaching by the end of February 1943 the strength of 5,145 officers and men (see Table 4 above).

Although the existence of these forces, which owed allegiance not only to the Italians but also to the government-in-exile, including General Mihailović as their theoretical commander-in-chief, made the Chetnik forces that Novak had been trying to organize redundant, Novak did not withdraw. Acting on Mihailović's orders, Novak early in 1943 set up a special staff, consisting mostly of officers released by the Italians and including two representatives of the Slovene Alliance. Colonel Ivan Prezelj became his deputy and liaison officer with the Slovene Alliance, and there were officers in charge of propaganda, intelligence work, staff affairs, and supplies, as well as command officers. But there were no troops. Following directives from General Mihailović, Novak tried to induce the Slovene Alliance to shift to his command at least 2,500 members of the Village Guards who were in the MVAC—supposedly to be ready for light operations against the Italians. But the Slovene Alliance, not liking to have part of its troops going into illegality and at the same time professing that its forces owed allegiance to General Mihailović, refused to authorize their release. As Novak explained it, these Slovene forces owed primary allegiance to the Slovene Alliance and only secondary allegiance to Mihailović. Novak was allowed to form one small "illegal" detachment, however, which in the next several months increased through shifts of other units and new recruits to some three or four hundred men. This was the largest Mihailović Chetnik army ever

---

[81] Microcopy No. T-821, Roll 252, Frames 313–17. Robotti stated that a significant number of these units were commanded by Roman Catholic priests. On the whole problem of the MVAC units in Slovenia see also Saje, pp. 487–646. Apparently Robotti was for some time opposed to the arming of Slovene anti-Communist forces, but relented because of the growing strength of the Partisans.

to exist in Slovenia. Thereafter, the Slovene Alliance and its military leaders under Lt. Colonel Peterlin effectively sabotaged Novak's efforts to increase their size, although the troops were supplied with arms and ammunition by the Italians.[82] In September 1943 this small force came to a decisive end. Between September 8 and 10, during the days of the Italian collapse, the Partisans surrounded the main Chetnik unit, the Central Chetnik Detachment, numbering around two hundred men, in the village of Grčarice, some fifty kilometers southeast of Ljubljana, and killed or captured practically the entire complement (according to Novak about ten men escaped).[83] Major Novak was not at Grčarice, and a few weeks later, after writing a strong protest to the Slovene Alliance and breaking relations with it, he left for Italy where he stayed during the remainder of the war.

As of August 15, 1943, the MVAC units in the Italian-occupied part of Slovenia numbered 6,049 men, while the Partisan forces in the same area (four brigades, three detachments, and one independent battalion) had a total of 2,958 men. As the Italian collapse neared, the chief preoccupations of the Slovene anti-Communist forces were how to participate in the disarming of the Italian troops, how to reach the Adriatic coast, and how, in view of their collaborationist record, to arrange their acceptance by the Western Allies who, they confidently hoped, would be landing there.[84] The anti-Communist forces in Slovenia were now known as the Slovene People's Army and were an integral part of the Yugoslav Army in the Homeland and thus formally, though not actually, under Mihailović's command. Unlike the Partisans, the anti-Communist troops had little luck in trying to disarm some of the Italian forces.

The Slovene Alliance forces, thrown into disagreement over strategy when the Allies failed to land, gave the Partisans the chance to take advantage of their indecision to inflict another decisive defeat. Around September 9 several units, totaling around 1,600 men, of the Alliance forces assembled in the area of the castle of Turjak, about twenty-five kilometers southeast of Ljubljana. Strong Partisan forces laid siege to the castle. The anti-Communist forces that were outside the castle succeeded in extricating themselves, though with huge losses, but the forces inside the solidly built castle walls remained where they were, undecided whether to attempt a breakout or not and hopeful that help might arrive. After ten days of siege, during which they suffered only a few casualties, the force of 695, including 26 Catholic priests and seminarians, surrendered to the Partisans. Subsequently, many of those captured

---

[82] Novak, pp. 323–30. According to an oral statement of one of Novak's former officers, the system of supply was "indirect" and Novak himself had no contacts with the Italians.
[83] For the story of the Partisan attack see *ibid.*, pp. 330–31; Grum and Pleško, pp. 68–76; Petelin, "The Defeat at Grčarice and Turjak," pp. 9–12; and Saje, pp. 757–95.
[84] Petelin, *Izmedju Triglava i Trsta*, pp. 52–53; Grum and Pleško, pp. 33–44.

at Grčarice and Turjak were put before the military tribunals, and a large number of leaders were sentenced to death; most of the rank and file were put into labor battalions and some were even absorbed into Partisan ranks.[85]

After the Germans took control of most of the Slovene territory following the Italian collapse, the Slovene anti-Communist forces that earlier collaborated with the Italians started to collaborate with the Germans. These forces, now called the Slovene Domobrans, were in time built up to a strength of over ten thousand men; amply provided with arms and supplies, they were put under the command of General Rupnik and used by the Germans in their operations against the Partisans until the final days of the war.

COLLABORATION WITH THE CROATIAN USTASHA STATE

Like nearly all the later Chetniks outside Serbia, the Serbian nationalist groups in parts of eastern, central, and northwestern Bosnia that lay east of the German-Italian Demarcation Line cooperated with the Partisans in the uprising of July 1941 and during the ensuing four or five months—that is, until the split occurred between the Chetniks and the Partisans in Serbia and polarization began to take place in the rest of the country.

After the split the Chetnik forces in these areas and the population that supported them were caught between the Croatian and German forces on the one hand and the Partisans on the other. Major Dangić's efforts to arrive at a modus vivendi with the Germans in eastern Bosnia at the beginning of 1942 failed, and local leaders had to seek a new solution to their problems. The Chetnik groups were in fundamental disagreement with Croatian authorities on practically all problems, but they did face a common enemy in the Partisans, and this was the overriding reason for the collaboration that ensued between the Croatian authorities and many Chetnik detachments. In order to achieve that collaboration, however, the two parties had to reach an agreement—at least temporarily and not without reservations—on a great number of other issues: in other words, each had to pay a price for collaboration. (Since the Croatian quisling forces in these areas as operational zones

---

[85] Petelin, *Izmedju Triglava i Trsta*, pp. 60–72; Petelin, "The Defeat at Grčarice and Turjak," pp. 12–24; Grum and Pleško, pp. 8–110, 128–49. Throughout, the struggle between the followers of the Liberation Front and the anti-Communist forces controlled by the Slovene Alliance was extremely bloody. For the various "crimes against the fatherland" perpetrated by the latter group as interpreted by a Communist writer see Saje, *passim*. The Partisans themselves had an efficient and ruthless Security and Intelligence Service (*Varnostno-obveščevalna služba* or VOS) which sentenced to death and executed a number of important anti-Communist leaders, including both Ehrlich (May 26, 1942) and Natlačen (Oct. 13, 1942). In 1944 the political organizations behind the anti-Communist forces, undoubtedly with the assistance of the Catholic Church, published a "Black Book"—*Črne bukve o delu komunistične Osvobodilne fronte proti slovenskemu narodu*—giving their version of the background and bloody activities of the Liberation Front and its subsidiary organizations. Besides Dr. Metod Mikuž, two other Roman Catholic priests who were members of the Front are among those indicted for war crimes. See also Arnez, pp. 78–118.

had been under German command from January 1942, and all of Bosnia between the Sava River and the Demarcation Line became in October 1942 an operational zone under supreme German authority, these agreements represented also an indirect type of Chetnik collaboration with the Germans.)

The first formal agreement between the Croatian state authorities and the Bosnian Chetniks was concluded on May 28, 1942, simultaneously and in one document with the Ozren Mountain and Trebava Mountain detachments in the village of Lipac, covering that portion of eastern Bosnia adjacent to the Bosna River and the Sarajevo-Brod railroad.[86] During the next three weeks three additional agreements were signed for areas of central and northwestern Bosnia, and then on January 16, 1943, an additional one for an area in eastern Bosnia.[87] The most comprehensive agreement in regard to the area covered, forces involved, and the nature of provisions was the first agreement signed on May 28. By this agreement the commanders of the Ozren Mountain and Trebava Mountain detachments recognized the sovereignty of the Independent State of Croatia and expressed loyalty as its citizens to the state and its head; both Chetnik detachments were as of that day to discontinue any hostilities against the military and civilian authorities of the Croatian state; the Croatian authorities were to establish in these Chetnik areas regular administration, and the Chetnik detachments promised to help them in the normalization of general conditions. As long as the extraordinary conditions lasted the Chetnik chieftains were to exercise administrative authority in their areas under the supervision of the Independent State of Croatia. The main provision (Art. 5) of the agreement was as follows:

As long as there is danger from armed Partisan bands, the Chetnik formations will cooperate voluntarily with the Croatian military forces in fighting and destroying the Partisans and in these operations they will be under the overall command of Croatian armed forces. In these operations Chetnik commanders will be in command of their own detachments.

The Chetnik formations can engage in operations against the Partisans on

[86] For the text of the agreement of May 28, 1942, see Microcopy No. T-314, Roll 566, Frames 734–36. The agreement was amended on July 9, 1942, by a statement that its provisions applied also to the relations of the two Chetnik detachments with German and Italian forces in Croatian territory. *Ibid.*, Frame 739. Although the Croatian authorities did not list them, it appears that two similar agreements were signed earlier—one with Uroš Drenović, the commander of the Chetnik Detachment "Kočić" at Varcar Vakuf (Mrkonjić Grad) on April 27 and another one with Lazo Tešanović, the commander of the Chetnik Battalion "Mrkonjić" on May 23, 1942. For the text of the agreement with Tešanović see *ibid.*, Frames 359–61. For a discussion of Chetnik collaboration with the authorities of the Independent State of Croatia in Bosnia see also Kačavenda, pp. 37–67, and Hurem, "The Collaboration Agreements Between the Authorities of the Independent State of Croatia and Some Chetnik Detachments in Eastern Bosnia in 1942," pp. 294–325.

[87] These were two agreements with Radoslav Radić, commander of the Chetnik Detachment "Borja," the first one signed in Banja Luka on June 9 affecting the western region controlled by these Chetniks and the second one signed on June 14 in Prnjavor for their eastern region (Microcopy No. T-314, Roll 566, Frames 740–43); one agreement with Borivoje Kerović, commander of the Majevica Mountain Detachment, in eastern Bosnia, signed in the village of Lopare on June 15 (*ibid.*, Frames 746–47); and the one signed on January 16, 1943, in the village of Kovanje in eastern Bosnia with the Chetnik commander Radivoje Kosorić (*ibid.*, Frames 712–13).

their own, but this they have to report, on time, to the Croatian military commanders.[88]

The necessary ammunition requirements would be supplied to the Chetnik forces by the Croatian military authorities. Chetniks who were wounded in operations against the Partisans would be cared for in Croatian military hospitals and the widows and orphans of Chetnik soldiers fallen in the struggle against the Partisans would be given government financial assistance comparable to that given to the widows and orphans of Croatian soldiers. If possible, the Croatian authorities would arrange the release and return to their homes of men who had been taken to concentration camps, but only upon the specific recommendation of Chetnik leaders (not, presumably, including Partisans or Partisan sympathizers). Until they returned, their families, if in need, would be given financial assistance. All refugees were to be permitted to return to their homes and if in need would be given state assistance comparable to that given other citizens of the Independent State of Croatia. The Serbs were to be allowed to engage in trade like other citizens.

As a sort of recapitulation of the agreements with the Bosnian Chetniks, the Chief Headquarters of the Poglavnik (that is, the head of the Independent State of Croatia) sent on June 30, 1942, under the signature of Marshal Kvaternik, a statement to the Ministry of Social Welfare (*Ministarstvo udružbe*) summarizing the provisions of these agreements under twenty points, which generally correspond to the points enumerated above. Copies of the statement were to be sent to the welfare committees of the county courts which were in charge of deciding upon welfare payments made to families of Croatian soldiers entitled to them and which also made the decisions regarding the payments to the Chetnik families entitled to them under these agreements.[89]

The Germans were in favor of these agreements for several reasons. First, they were directed against the Partisans who from the summer of 1941 were the chief German problem in Yugoslavia, including the portions of Bosnia under German control; second, the involvement of the Chetniks against the Partisans tended to reduce somewhat the number of German troops assigned to these areas; and finally, these agreements tended to contribute to the pacification of Bosnian areas, the northeast and northwest in particular, in which Germany had major economic interests (iron ore, timber, heavy chemicals, steel, and important railroad lines).[90] On July 15, 1942, General Glaise even proposed to a

[88] *Ibid.*, Frame 736.

[89] A copy of this report was made available to me by courtesy of the State Archives of the SR Croatia in Zagreb. Another résumé of these agreements is available in Microcopy No. T-314, Roll 566, Frames 709–10.

[90] A report of General Lüters, the Commanding General of German Troops in Croatia, dated Nov. 18, 1942 (Microcopy No. T-314, Roll 566, Frames 357–58), points out both military and economic positive effects of these agreements between the Croatian authorities and the Chetniks.

Croatian general, Ivan Brozović, at Banja Luka, that a central office be established in Zagreb for the implementation and supervision of these agreements.[91] Nothing came of this proposal at that time because such an office would certainly have been an embarrassment to the Ustasha regime; but as will presently be shown, a central office was later put in charge of these agreements. There is no doubt, however, that the agreements covered the majority of Chetnik forces in Bosnia east of the Demarcation Line, because Glaise's report of November 16, 1942, to the Armed Forces Commander in Southeast Europe indicates that about ten thousand Bosnian Chetniks had live-and-let-live agreements with the Croatian government.[92] A map prepared by the General Staff of the Croatian Armed Forces and dated January 17, 1943, classified the Chetniks in the territory of the Independent State of Croatia into three groups: Italian Chetniks concentrated in the area of Otočac in Lika, the area of Knin in northern Dalmatia, and in eastern Herzegovina; collaborating Chetniks centering in central and parts of eastern Bosnia near the Bosna River; and rebel Chetniks holding smaller pockets in northeastern Bosnia and the area east of Sarajevo.[93]

In the meantime, on December 22, 1942, the Chief Headquarters of the Poglavnik informed the Croatian liaison officer with the German 718th Infantry Division of a directive issued on October 9, 1942, by the Directorate for Public Order and Security of the Ministry of the Interior relating to the negotiations and conclusion of any agreements between the Croatian military and civilian authorities and Chetnik detachments. This directive stated that no one could engage in either formal or informal discussions with the Chetniks without the approval of Department X of the Directorate. The principles to be followed in these discussions and agreements were as follows: (1) Chetniks who were strong opponents of Croatia were to be excluded from negotiations; (2) no negotiations were to be held with Chetnik leaders who were not born in or had not acquired citizenship in the territory of the Independent State of Croatia; (3) the military and civilian authorities of Croatia must be recognized; (4) hostile Chetnik elements must be disarmed; (5) when it proved necessary to allow Chetnik detachments to keep their arms in order to help maintain law and order, Croatian authorities must participate in that work and Chetnik units must inform the authorities about the number of their men and arms; and (6) in Italian-occupied zones, agreements between the Croatian authorities and the Chetniks could not be contrary to the Italian-Croatian agreement of June 19, 1942.[94]

[91] Microcopy No. T-501, Roll 267, Frames 457–58.

[92] *Ibid.*, Roll 264, Frame 583.

[93] A copy of the map was made available to me by courtesy of Colonel Vojmir Kljaković of the Institute of Military History in Belgrade.

[94] Microcopy No. T-314, Roll 566, Frames 706–8. The same directive also stated that collective retribution against the Chetniks could not be undertaken no matter how grievous their actions

Department X of the Directorate for Public Order and Security seems to have been an oblique realization of the idea proposed by Glaise the preceding July, hiding its function behind a nondescript designation. Obviously after getting news of the Directive of October 9, 1942, General Glaise informed the Chief Headquarters of the Poglavnik on January 20, 1943, that all agreements with Orthodox [Chetnik] fighting detachments in the "operational zone"—meaning the whole area between the Sava River and the Demarcation Line—must be reported to and agreed upon by the Commanding General of German Troops in Croatia.[95]

Despite these agreements, however, not only the noncollaborating but also some of the collaborating Chetnik detachments in Bosnia engaged occasionally in some sabotage and other activities unacceptable either to the Germans or to the Croatian authorities—in other words, did not give up completely the idea of rebellion. Consequently, following the completion of Operation Weiss against the Partisans, of which more will be said below, General Lüters issued orders on March 28, 1943, for the partial and gradual disarmament of recalcitrant Chetnik detachments. To force compliance, the Germans had some of their troops in readiness and had planned, for example, in the area of Ozren Mountain, a special Operation Teufel. In the execution of this order the 369th Infantry Division (Croatian legionnaires) concluded on May 1, 1943, agreements with the Ozren Mountain Chetnik Detachment and the Zenica Chetnik Detachment, whereby they promised not to interfere with the German and Croatian forces, to refrain from sabotage acts, and to surrender within five days a portion of their arms. At the same time the Germans guaranteed the Chetniks that "no illegal acts against the Serbian population" would be undertaken (presumably by the Croatian formations). The Germans knew, as Lüters's order clearly indicated, that neither political nor military preconditions existed for a significant degree of disarmament of the Chetnik detachments, and the records show that they were satisfied with the return of a few hundred rifles and a few machine guns.[96]

These agreements between the Chetnik detachments and the authorities of the Independent State of Croatia were significant for both sides. For the Independent State of Croatia, they were an admission of political and military impotence and of the failure of its policy against the Serbian population—although without the Partisans to contend with (and until well into 1943 the majority of the Partisans in the territory

---

might be; that efforts should be made to induce Chetnik fighters to return home from the forests so that they could engage in useful work or go to Germany for work; and that Serbs charged with committing murder and other crimes must be tried by regular courts and not punished at the discretion of individual officials.

[95] *Ibid.*, Frame 701.

[96] For the text of Lüters's order of March 28 see *ibid.*, Frames 320–22, and for the agreements of May 1 regarding the partial disarmament of the two detachments see *ibid.*, Frames 685–700.

of the Croatian puppet state were recruited from the Serbian population), the Croatians could, of course, have dealt more rigorously with the Chetniks. For the Chetniks, the agreements and various concessions which they granted to the Serbian population testify to their strength— but their strength could have been much greater had there been more unity and better organization. Though many of the Chetnik leaders abused their position, they were tolerated by the people as long as they could provide some protection against the Ustashas, and up to the end of the war they kept the support of a portion of the Serbian population of the Independent State of Croatia.

Chetnik collaboration with the Italians in particular, but also with Nedić and the Croatian quisling forces and through them with the Germans, was, as we shall see, well known to the British by the end of 1942. As long as the Mediterranean theater of war was not an area of major Allied operations, what went on in Yugoslavia did not matter much, and the Chetniks' collaboration with the Axis was allowed to pass. But when the Allies launched their North African offensive on November 8, 1942, opening up the prospect of an invasion of Italy or of the Balkans, or both, the activities of the Chetniks and the Partisans became a matter of direct concern to Western Allied strategy. Mihailović and his Chetniks, the Allies discovered, were incapable of and/or unwilling to play the role assigned to them without simultaneous Allied landings on the Adriatic coast or in Greece, and from the end of December 1942 on, the British government, both indirectly through the Yugoslav government-in-exile and directly through its own missions with Mihailović, made strenuous and sustained efforts to persuade Mihailović to stop collaborating with the enemy and fighting the Partisans, and to start fighting the Axis forces, but in vain.

THE BATTLE OF THE NERETVA RIVER AND ITS AFTERMATH

The high point of Chetnik collaboration with the Axis powers was reached during the Battle of the Neretva River in the winter of 1943, which was the final phase of Operation Weiss or, in Yugoslav terminology, the Fourth Enemy Offensive. The Battle of the Neretva River had a long and complicated background on the Chetnik and Axis side, and for the Chetniks, a fateful aftermath.

During the first six months of 1942, as a result of the Second and Third Enemy Offensives, the Partisans had suffered great losses in eastern Bosnia, Herzegovina, Sandjak, and Montenegro, and owing to these losses as well as to the successful Chetnik subversion of many Partisan detachments and to some serious mistakes of the Communist leaders, especially the so-called "left deviation," Partisan activity in these areas had been brought almost to a standstill and their position had become untenable. At the same time, the Chetniks in these areas had been building up their strength partly by subverting Partisan units and partly by collaborating with the Italians, and in certain areas to some extent with the Croatian quisling forces, and thus indirectly with the Germans. In consequence of these developments, the Partisans were obliged at the end of June 1942 to move toward western Bosnia where other Partisan units had certain areas under their control. Four Proletarian brigades with the bulk of the Partisan political and military leadership started to move toward western Bosnia late in June, and the one brigade and one detachment that stayed in Herzegovina also subsequently moved westward because of Chetnik pressure. The Partisan decision to move westward proved to be very sound for a number of reasons, most important of which was the fact that the Italians were withdrawing a large part of their occupation troops from Zones II and III on the basis of the Zagreb agreement concluded on June 19 and the Croatian puppet state had neither time nor strength to provide sufficient protection. On their way north the Partisans liberated several towns, among them Prozor, Gornji Vakuf, Duvno, and Livno, and after joining with Partisan detachments from central Dalmatia and western Bosnia they also liberated some Dalmatian localities, and later the Bosnian towns of Mrkonjić Grad and Jajce.[97] At the beginning of November western Bosnian and Croatian brigades captured the Croatian quisling stronghold of Bihać on the Una River, thereby establishing direct connection between the Bosnian liberated areas and those of southwestern Croatia (Lika, Kordun, Banija).[98] Although in the meantime they had lost Prozor to the Italians, Livno to the Croatian quisling forces, and Jajce to the Germans, the Partisans nevertheless controlled by the end of 1942 an area extending from the western approaches to the Neretva River in the south close to Karlovac in the north, an area some two hundred fifty kilometers long and forty to seventy kilometers wide. The crisis in Partisan fortunes seemed to be over: they now had nine divisions and many independent detachments, their military organization had been tightened, they had in these areas a rudimentary system of governmental administration in the form of national liberation committees, and politically they were asserting themselves by convening an assembly in the newly liberated Bihać, which constituted itself as the Anti-Fascist Council of National Liberation of Yugoslavia (AVNOJ). It was evident that they were now in a position to intensify their activities both against the Axis and the Croatian quisling forces and against the Chetniks.

All this alarmed the Chetniks. They were particularly unhappy be-

[97] *Oslobodilački rat*, I, 269–92; see also Leković, *Ofanziva proleterskih brigada u leto 1942*.
[98] *Oslobodilački rat*, I, 286–92.

cause Partisan control of western Bosnia interfered with their hopes of establishing the corridor between Herzegovina and Lika and then Slovenia which was part of their essential strategy based on the assumption that the Allies would land on the Dalmatian coast. Since September they had been trying to persuade the Italians to undertake a "large operation" against the Partisans in their domain—knowing that unaided they were incapable of defeating them. *Vojvoda* Trifunović-Birčanin met with General Roatta on September 10 and 21 to urge him to undertake "as soon as possible" a large operation to chase the Partisans from the Prozor-Livno area and offering 7,500 Chetniks as aid on condition they were furnished the necessary arms and supplies.[99] He was successful in obtaining some arms and promises of action. Early in October the Italians launched an operation called Alfa against the Partisans northwest of the middle course of the Neretva River in which about three thousand Herzegovinian and southeastern Bosnian Chetniks under the leadership of Lt. Colonel Baćović and *vojvoda* Jevdjević participated. In this operation the town of Prozor and some smaller towns in the same area were taken. But the Chetnik forces, acting on their own, burned villages and carried out mass killings of the civilian Moslem and Croatian population. Their behavior quite naturally aroused the anger of the Croatian quisling government, and the Italians had to order the Chetniks to withdraw. Some Chetniks were discharged altogether, others were sent later to northern Dalmatia to aid the forces of *vojvoda* Djujić. In another minor undertaking, Operation Beta, launched later in October, the Italians took several localities in the area of Livno and Croatian quisling forces took Livno.[100]

But the Chetnik leadership had larger hopes. The Chetnik Supreme Command, now in Montenegro, decided that it would undertake a "March on Bosnia" of its own, an operation that would have Italian logistic support and would also use the Chetnik units serving as Italian auxiliaries but would be under sole Chetnik command. The idea was to use Chetnik formations in Lika, northern Bosnia, northern Dalmatia, and Herzegovina, with help from the Montenegrin Chetniks, to encircle and destroy the Partisan troops in their free territory. This would give the Chetniks partial control of the Adriatic hinterland, making

---

[99] In the meeting on September 10 (Microcopy No. T-821, Roll 252, Frames 309–12) Birčanin told Roatta that he was not under the command of Draža Mihailović but that he had seen him on July 21 at Avtovac and had his approval of his cooperation with the Italians. For the meetings of September 21–22, in which Birčanin was accompanied by Jevdjević and at times by Radmilo Grdjić, another leading Chetnik from Herzegovina, see *ibid.*, Roll 31, Frames 346–53. In a letter of late September or early October Mihailović, replying to a letter from Birčanin of September 20, congratulated him on his conduct and "high comprehension of the national line" in these talks. Archives of the Institute of Military History, Belgrade, Chetnik Documents, Reg. No. 22/3-1, Box 1. See also *The Trial of Draža Mihailović*, pp. 327, 446, and Leković, "Mihailović's Plans," pp. 85–91.

[100] Leković, "Mihailović's Plans," pp. 91–97. At approximately the same time the Germans and Croatian quisling troops operating out of Banja Luka and Travnik retook Jajce and Mrkonjić Grad.

it possible for them to assist and join the Allies when and if they landed troops on the coast. Mihailović put his chief of operations, Major Zaharije Ostojić, in charge of the proposed operation and in mid-December sent him to set up a Forward Headquarters in Kalinovik, southeastern Bosnia. On January 2 Mihailović issued Directive No. 1 (to become operative at a date to be indicated later), outlining in detail his plans for the destruction of the Partisan forces.[101] Mihailović had also drafted late in December an amazingly ambitious top-secret plan of operations to be used when the Allies landed on the coast. According to this plan, Colonel Stanišić from Montenegro was to come up the coast and take Split. There he would enter under the command of *vojvoda* Trifunović-Birčanin, and their combined forces would join those from northern Dalmatia, western Bosnia, and Lika and move northward. Lt. Colonel Baćović was to take Sarajevo, then move toward northeastern Bosnia where he would join with Major Račić's forces coming from Serbia. This force would then move through Slavonia and Baranja to the Hungarian town of Pecs. Meanwhile, the combined troops of Birčanin and those from northern Bosnia and Lika would move between the Bosna and Una rivers northward through Slavonia toward Hungary, with the larger segment going toward Zagreb to destroy Pavelić's forces and then further north in the direction of Varaždin. The Slovene forces cooperating with the Chetniks were to help in operations in Croatia, but their chief objectives were to push into Carinthia and toward Gorica. That Mihailović was serious about this plan is indicated in part by the fact that he communicated at least some of it to the government-in-exile.[102]

The Italians were themselves greatly worried about the growing size and strength of the Partisan domain. Since the middle of November the Germans had been urging them to take part in combined large-scale winter operations against the Partisans and to disarm the Chetniks in their service. But neither the commander of Supersloda, General Roatta, nor his superiors in Rome thought that such large operations would be successful.[103] Moreover, with the Italian armies in great peril in North Africa and Russia, they had no desire to undertake new large commitments in Yugoslavia.

The Germans, too, were facing critical days. With the American and British landings in North Africa (Algiers and Morocco) and the steady advance of the British forces from Egypt, the defeat of the German forces in North Africa had become only a matter of time. On the Russian front the disaster at Stalingrad was in the making. The Balkans, along with

---

[101] Archives of the Institute of Military History, Belgrade, Chetnik Documents, Reg. No. 2/3, Box 1; Reg. No. 13/3, Box 1.
[102] *Ibid.*, Reg. No. 9/3-1, Box 1; Živan L. Knežević, *Why the Allies Abandoned*, Part 1, p. 16.
[103] Roatta, p. 182.

the Italian islands and mainland and the south of France, had to be regarded as potential areas of landings by the Western Allies. The poorly defended and strategically vulnerable Balkan area could prove to be of extraordinary military significance for the Germans. And one of the key areas in the Balkans was the territory of the Croatian puppet state, in the center of which was the large Partisan free area and in several other areas large contingents of Chetniks.

In the opinion of the German generals in the field (Löhr, Bader, Glaise) the consolidation of the Croatian state was to be achieved not by military means alone but by a combination of military and political means, the latter being primarily a policy of tolerance and equity toward the Serbian population of the state. Hitler disagreed: he thought that consolidation could be brought about in a purely military manner by destroying or disarming both the Partisan and the Chetnik forces in the state, a move which would at the same time make it impossible for either of the resistance forces to help the Allies if they should land on the eastern Adriatic shores. Naturally, it was Hitler's reasoning that prevailed.[104]

The German idea was to exert the utmost pressure upon their ally the Italians to cooperate with them in destroying the Partisans and, at the same time, to renounce the services of the Chetniks and to disarm them in the territory of the Independent State of Croatia and later also in Montenegro. Hitler discussed the problem of the Chetniks and the action against the rebels in the Croatian territory on the occasion of Dr. Pavelić's visit to his headquarters on September 23, 1942.[105] On November 11 General Löhr, the Armed Forces Commander in Southeast Europe (from December 28 Commander in Chief in Southeast Europe), who had been present at the Hitler-Pavelić meeting, issued an order on the disarming of the rebels, but at that time the Germans were short of troops in Croatia, and the German Plenipotentiary General in Croatia was of the opinion that nothing successful could be undertaken without additional German forces.[106] Work on the plan continued, however: Löhr discussed the idea with General Roatta during November and the issue was also raised by Hitler with the Chief of the Italian Supreme Command, Marshal Ugo Cavallero, and Foreign Minister Ciano when they visited him on December 19. [107] Details of the forthcoming opera-

[104] Kljaković, "Enemy Preparations for the Fourth Offensive," pp. 66–68.
[105] *Ibid.*
[106] Microcopy No. T-501, Roll 264, Frames 582–85. Glaise wrote Löhr on November 16 that the Partisans and the Chetniks had at least 35,000 to 40,000 armed men in the area between the Drava River and the German-Italian Demarcation Line, that immediately south of the Demarcation Line, in what Glaise called the "Partisan State," Tito had 30,000 to 35,000 relatively well armed and organized men, and that still further to the south there were over 20,000 Chetniks serving as Italian auxiliaries. The already mentioned report of General Lüters of November 18, 1942 (n. 90), also raised the problem of disarming the rebels but noted, as did Glaise, that at that time it was impossible to carry it out.
[107] *KTB/OKW/WFSt*, Vol. II (1942), Part 2, pp. 1157–58; Cavallero, p. 421.

tions, known under the code name "Weiss," were discussed by General Löhr and Italian high commanders in Rome in the first days of January and then again by General Roatta and General Lüters on January 9 in Zagreb. Finally, but with the greatest reluctance, the Italians agreed to the plan. As originally conceived, the plan consisted of three phases— Weiss 1 and Weiss 2 for the destruction of the Partisan forces and their "state," and Weiss 3 for the disarming of the Chetniks in the territory of the Independent State of Croatia[108]—but as will be shown below, many changes took place in the course of its implementation.

For the execution of Operation Weiss the Germans employed from the beginning the 717th and 718th divisions, parts of the 714th Division, the 7th SS Division "Prinz Eugen," the 187th Infantry Reserve Division, several Croatian quisling brigades, as well as about ninety German and Croatian aircraft, and from February 27 on, the 369th Infantry Division (Croatian legionnaires). The Italians used the Lombardia, Re, and Sassari divisions from the beginning, as well as about 6,000 Chetnik auxiliaries from Lika and northern Dalmatia.[109] Later, they used also parts of the Bergamo, Marche, and Murge divisions. In the final phase, the Battle of the Neretva River, the total number of Chetnik auxiliaries and other Chetnik formations closely working together with the Italians was between 12,000 and 15,000 men.

Operation Weiss 1 started on January 20 with the Prinz Eugen Division advancing south of Karlovac and the 717th Division and parts of the 714th, with some Croatian formations, advancing south and west of Banja Luka, and corresponding though much less decisive moves on the part of the Italian divisions and their Chetnik auxiliaries. The German forces operating from northern Bosnia and the Italian forces operating from northern and central Dalmatia were supposed to link approximately in the middle of the "Partisan State." This was to be followed by a tightening of the ring around the Partisan forces to the west and their annihilation. Not all went as planned. In brief outline, what happened was this: Partisan forces in the western part of their region gave stiff resistance in battles in the vicinity of and on the Una River. But the attackers soon discovered that the main Partisan forces, consisting of the 1st and 2nd Proletarian divisions, the 3rd and 7th Shock divisions, and the newly formed 9th Division (made up of the 3rd, 4th, and 5th Dalmatian brigades), were in the southern part of the Partisan-held region, outside the area of operations of Weiss 1. As soon as Tito perceived the Axis objective he ordered these troops in an offensive toward the southeast in order to avoid the encirclement, to clear the

---

[108] For the Italian and German orders to launch Operation Weiss see *Zbornik DNOR*, Tome IV, Vol. 9, pp. 509–48. See also *KTB/OKW/WFSt*, Vol. III (1943), Part 1, pp. 89, 102–3.
[109] Microcopy No. T-78, Roll 332, Frames 6,290,085–89; *Oslobodilački rat*, I, 362–63, 481–83.

escape corridor to the south, and also to save about four thousand sick and wounded Partisan soldiers.[110] Throughout Weiss 1 the Italians dragged their feet, and confronted with the determined resistance of the Partisan forces the Axis troops were slowed down. Partisan operations toward the Neretva River, which for some time endangered also the safety of the bauxite mines in the Mostar area, forced the Axis to change and keep changing its plans and its operations. At a meeting of General Robotti with General Löhr in Belgrade on February 8 Weiss 3 was scrapped because of Italian objections that it was unnecessary and politically dangerous.[111] Weiss 1 ended by February 15, without accomplishing its objectives, and on February 25 Weiss 2 and a special operation, Mostar, for the securing of the bauxite mines, were begun. The general objective, in addition to the securing of the bauxite mines, was to prevent the Partisans from crossing the Neretva River and heading southeast and to destroy them in the canyons of the Rama and Neretva rivers.

But the Germans were not giving up the idea of involving the Italians more fully in the fight against the Partisans and in disarming the Chetniks. During the last week of February, Hitler sent Foreign Minister von Ribbentrop and General Walter Warlimont, the Deputy Chief of the Operations Staff of the Wehrmacht, to Rome to try to bring the Italians around to the German point of view. The two men carried a letter from Hitler to Mussolini in which Hitler stressed the absolute necessity of disarming the Chetniks because of their potential danger in the event of an Allied landing on the Dalmatian coast.[112] The outcome of the Rome conference, in which the Germans used strong pressure, was an Italian acquiescence for a more active participation in operations Weiss 2 and Mostar, and a definite promise by the Italians to disarm the Chetniks in the Independent State of Croatia as soon as the Partisans had been defeated, and even a promise to disarm the Montenegrin Chetniks at a date to be specified later.[113] But as soon as the German representatives left Rome, the Italians had a change of heart. In meetings on

---

[110] For a brief outline of the Partisan plans and operations in the course of Operation Weiss, see "The Fourth Enemy Offensive," *Enciklopedija Jugoslavije*, II, 587–94. For a more complete discussion of these problems see *Oslobodilački rat*, I, 345–413; Kladarin, *Slom Četvrte i Pete okupatorsko-kvislinške ofanzive*; and Trgo, *Četvrta i Peta neprijateljska ofanziva*. For a detailed description and analysis of these operations, especially of the Battle of the Neretva River, written by participants, see the three-volume *Neretva*. For a running, nontechnical description of the course of the Fourth Enemy Offensive and the developments from the middle of March to the end of April see Dedijer, *Dnevnik*, II, 59–247.

[111] Microcopy No. T-821, Roll 125, Frame 815; *KTB/OKW/WFSt*, Vol. III, Part 1, pp. 102–6.

[112] Microcopy No. T-821, Roll 125, Frames 531–35; *Hitler e Mussolini, lettere e documenti*, pp. 132–36. This letter as here published seems to include parts of other letters, and the microfilm copy of it in the National Archives in Washington is only partly usable because several of the pages are overexposed and unreadable. Just prior to the Rome conference (and again on March 5) the Germans sent the Italians transcrips of intercepted radio messages between Mihailović and his commanders, in support of their contention that Mihailović's Chetniks ought to be disarmed. *KTB/OKW/WFSt*, Vol. III, Part 1, pp. 169, 192–93.

[113] *KTB/OKW/WFSt*, Vol. III, Part 1, pp. 162, 168–74, 191–92, 195–96, esp. p. 192.

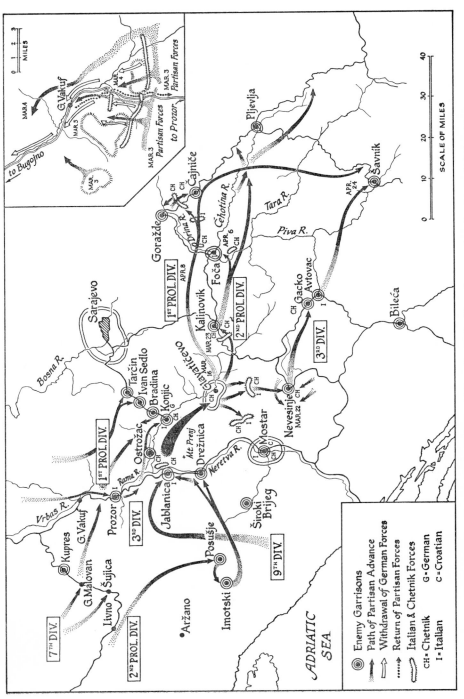

Map 5: Battle of the Neretva River and its aftermath. (Based on a series of maps in Fabijan Trgo, *Četvrta i Peta neprijateljska ofanziva* [The Fourth and Fifth Enemy Offensives], Belgrade, 1968.)

March 3 and 4 in Rome of the highest Italian officials and of General Robotti, the former commander of Italian troops in Slovenia who had replaced Roatta as commander of Supersloda, and the Military Governor of Montenegro General Pirzio Biroli, the situation was considered anew. As a result of these discussions the decision was made to delay the disarmament of the Chetniks in the Independent State of Croatia as long as possible and to prolong its execution; the disarmament of the Chetniks in Montenegro was considered impossible and contrary to Italian interests and was simply taken off the agenda. In both instances the justification was that the Italians could not afford to lose the Chetniks as allies against the Partisans.[114]

The main Partisan objective at this time was to reach the Neretva River (see Map 5) in its middle course and to cross it and then to invest the Chetnik- and Italian-controlled eastern Herzegovina, southeastern Bosnia, Sandjak, and Montenegro, and to move to the Kosovo area and Serbia in order to build up their units and to intensify the national liberation struggle in these areas. First of all, they had to reach, take, and hold the town of Konjic on the Neretva River, from which a road led into eastern Herzegovina. In between the Partisan forces and Konjic lay the stronghold of Prozor, now held by parts of the Italian Murge Division. With the 1st and 2nd Partisan divisions widening and holding the walls of the corridor, the 3rd Division was to take Prozor. The first onslaught on February 16 was repulsed, but the following day the Partisans took the town and killed or captured over a thousand Italian soldiers; they also captured huge stores of arms and ammunition, including some tanks and lorries, which they immediately put to use.[115] Konjic proved to be another matter. This town was jointly held by Italians and Chetniks, and in the course of the battle for its control it was reinforced by some German and Croatian and additional Chetnik troops.[116] Neither a weak attack of two battalions of the 1st Division on February 19 nor repeated attacks of the 3rd Division between February 22 and 26 succeeded in dislodging them, although the Partisans did manage to block the advance of the troops from Konjic downstream toward Jablanica.[117] On the western side of the corridor (about 30 to 40 kilometers as the river flows), the Partisans took the railroad station of Drežnica from the Italians and held it against Italian and Montenegrin Chetnik troops advancing from Mostar. Although not less than five road or railroad bridges existed between Konjic and Drežnica, none of them

[114] Microcopy No. T-821, Roll 125, Frames 816–20; Roll 252, Frames 319–23. See also Warlimont, pp. 331–32.

[115] Trgo, *Četvrta i Peta neprijateljska ofanziva*, pp. 32–33; Raičević, pp. 169–80. For an Italian analysis of the loss of Prozor see *Zbornik DNOR*, Tome IV, Vol. 11, pp. 368–74.

[116] See the report of Major Vojislav Lukačević, the Chetnik commander in the Konjic area, to Major Ostojić, of Feb. 23, 1943, in *The Trial of Draža Mihailović*, pp. 76–77, 203–4.

[117] *Oslobodilački rat*, I, 383–86, 411; *Neretva*, I, 75–79, 196–202.

gave access to a road leading toward eastern Herzegovina, only to rough trails on the northeastern lower slopes of the formidable Mount Prenj.

The Chetniks were dismayed by the Italian loss of Prozor, but with the Partisans being pushed from three sides into an ever shrinking pocket in the canyons of the Rama and Neretva rivers, the Chetniks saw a fine opportunity to help bring about their destruction and thus achieve the objective outlined in their Directive No. 1 early in January (though under completely different circumstances and in another area). On February 17 and 18 Mihailović sent two messages to the Montenegrin Chetnik commander Stanišić, who was en route to Mostar and operations on the Neretva, in which he appraised the Partisan situation and outlined his strategy: he had ordered Baćović, with his troops in northern Dalmatia and western Bosnia, to hit the Partisans in the rear and to push toward the Neretva River; he had instructed Ostojić to take offensive action with the disposable forces in the middle course of the river; and he had ordered Jevdjević to provide political support for these operations—presumably by working on the Italians, whose position, in Mihailović's words, had become softer because the Partisans had captured 2,000 of their men in the Jablanica-Prozor area. The concluding words of the messages were similar: "Now is the unique moment to square our accounts with the Communists once and for all."[118] Thus at the end of February some 12,000 to 15,000 Chetnik troops were at or near the Neretva River banks from Mostar to Konjic and in the southeast around the towns of Kalinovik and Nevesinje, with Baćović's troops moving from the north and Djurišić's from the south toward the middle course of the Neretva.[119] For some time a part of the Stanišić troops with the Italian Group Scotti were shifted about twenty to thirty kilometers west of Mostar where they met with Baćović's forces and operated against

---

[118] *Dokumenti o izdajstvu Draže Mihailovića*, I, 111–12. This quotation is from the message of February 18; the concluding statement in the message of February 17 expresses the same idea, but adds ". . . if we act wisely. Otherwise we run the risk of being beaten piecemeal." How the Chetniks went about implementing this plan can be seen from the instruction of February 18 issued by Major Ostojić (see Archives of the Institute of Military History, Belgrade, Chetnik Documents, Reg. No. 18/1, Box 2), and from the instruction of Major Borivoje Radulović, the Delegate of the Chetnik Supreme Command in Herzegovina, of March 6, *Dokumenti o izdajstvu Draže Mihailovića*, I, 119–21. For day-to-day orders and instructions of Ostojić and Radulović and messages of various commanders during the period from about February 20 to March 18 see *ibid.*, pp. 109–26, 433–72. One of Ostojić's recurring orders to his commanders was to kill all Communists in various Herzegovinian towns, and one order said to kill all captured Partisans after brief interrogation. *Ibid.*, pp. 433, 436, 447, 452.

[119] The exact number is not known. A calculation, apparently by Major Ostojić, put the number of Chetnik troops in the area of Konjic and in Herzegovina as of February 25 at 11,667, exclusive of the troops of Baćović and Djurišić which were on the way (Archives of the Institute of Military History, Belgrade, Chetnik Documents, Reg. No. 53, Box 3). At his trial Mihailović said that there was a maximum of 12,000 to 15,000 troops at Neretva (see *The Trial of Draža Mihailović*, p. 172). The chief Chetnik writer on the battle, Major Borivoje Radulović ("The Battle on the Neretva River," p. 81), says about 20,000. In the 1968 symposium dealing with the battles of the Neretva and Sutjeska rivers, some writers claimed that as many as 26,000 Chetnik troops participated in the Neretva River operation; others were inclined to put the figure at about 20,000 (*Neretva-Sutjeska 1943*, pp. 157–58, 583–84). All depends on the dates and areas to which one refers. It should be mentioned that among these troops for a brief time were also two detachments of Moslems, whose political leader was Dr. Ismet Popovac, a pro-Chetnik lawyer (*Dokumenti o izdajstvu Draže Mihailovića*, I, p. 436). Popovac later was killed by an assassin.

portions of the Partisan 9th Dalmatian Division which was moving with some of the sick and wounded toward the Jablanica area.[120]

It would appear that the Chetniks, though certain that the Partisans would be annihilated in the canyons of the Neretva and Rama rivers, were worried lest the Germans should decide to push on into eastern Herzegovina, which they considered their domain. For this reason, Jevdjević concluded an agreement with the Germans on February 23 providing that the Germans would not cross the Neretva and also that contact between German and Chetnik troops should be avoided.[121]

Apparently to make sure that the crucial operation on the Neretva would be carried out successfully and also to be present at the scene of the kill, Mihailović himself moved from Montenegro to Kalinovik where he joined Ostojić, who had up to this point been in command of the operations in Herzegovina. On March 9 Mihailović wrote to Colonel Stanišić:

I manage the whole operation through Branko [i.e. Ostojić, Mihailović's Chief of Operations]. No action is ordered without my approval. Branko is keeping me informed of even the smallest details. All his proposals are reviewed, studied, approved or corrected. In this we follow these principles: we work for ourselves alone and for no one else; we are concerned only with the interests of the Serbs and of future Yugoslavia; for the achievement of our objectives we use one enemy against another, precisely as do all our enemies without exception, and achieve our objectives with the least sacrifice, but are prepared even for the greatest sacrifices if this is necessary in the general interest, and to safeguard the people from all unnecessary exposure to danger in their homes.[122]

The position of the Partisans certainly appeared hopeless. Not only did the corridor to the Neretva have to be kept secure toward both Konjic and Drežnica, but time must somehow be gained to assemble and transport to Jablanica and across the Neretva the four thousand or so troops who were wounded or suffering from typhus, who were immediately menaced by the German forces advancing from the north.[123] Apparently both as a precautionary measure against possible Chetnik attacks from the left bank of the Neretva and as a ruse to mislead the

---

[120] *Neretva*, I, 290–99.

[121] *Dokumenti o izdajstvu Draže Mihailovića*, I, 458–59, 471. Of course it was not the agreement with Jevdjević but their overall plan, the nature of their relations with the Italians, and the fact that they had achieved the basic objective of Operation Mostar—namely, the occupation of the bauxite mines area west of the town of Mostar—that kept the Germans from crossing the Neretva and moving southeastward at that time.

[122] *Ibid.*, pp. 116–17. But at his trial Mihailović stated that "there the operations were led by Ostojić, because I had no time to occupy myself with these matters, since I had really come to visit my troops and get acquainted with the real state of affairs." In regard to collaboration with the Germans carried on by Lukačević at Konjic with Ostojić's knowledge, he said, "but they only told me what they wanted to, because all the main links were held by Ostojić, who jealously kept them from me, thus trying to increase his influence." *The Trial of Draža Mihailović*, pp. 171, 174.

[123] *Neretva*, I, 335–55, esp. 350. This figure does not include patients in the small divisional and brigade hospitals. Of the 4,000, about 1,500 were moved on horseback, and about 800 were stretcher cases. The others walked.

enemy about the direction of an intended breakthrough out of the encirclement in the canyons of the Rama and Neretva rivers, Tito on
February 28 ordered the blowing up of all five bridges across the Neretva
from Ostrožac below Konjic to Karaula, about thirty kilometers downstream. During the first three days of March the Company of Pioneers,
attached to the Supreme Headquarters and commanded by Vladimir
Smirnov, a White Russian civil engineer who before the war had worked
on construction projects for the Yugoslav State Railways, blew up the
road bridge at Ostrožac and a railroad and a road bridge at the other
end of the corridor near Karaula (standing about a hundred meters
apart), leaving untouched the road bridge at the confluence of the Rama
and the Neretva and the railroad bridge at Jablanica, about seven kilometers downstream. When he reported to Tito about only partially
fulfilling the task, he was ordered to blow up the two remaining bridges
as well, and did so within a few hours.[124]

In the meantime, Tito had ordered the 1st and 2nd Proletarian divisions to assemble in the area of Prozor where the 7th Shock Division
was in action against the German and Croatian quisling forces, and on
March 3 he ordered the three divisions to open a counteroffensive against
the 717th and parts of 718th German divisions and two Croatian brigades. This undoubtedly heightened the impression that the Partisans
might be trying to break out westward and strengthened the ruse of
the blowing up of the bridges over the Neretva. In three days of fighting
the Partisans succeeded in pushing the enemy back beyond Gornji
Vakuf (about 25 to 30 kilometers).[125] This action gained them the time
they needed to transport the sick and wounded to Jablanica, and in fact
temporarily relieved the entire Partisan force from crushing German
pressure. After providing for a strong rear guard (the 1st Proletarian
Division), all Partisan troops were directed toward Jablanica and across
the Neretva River.

After the Partisans established a bridgehead at the site of the wreck
of the railroad bridge at Jablanica on the night of March 6–7, Smirnov,
following earlier orders, began to build a makeshift bridge. Using the
collapsed construction for support, a narrow wooden bridge, only a
few feet above the water, was built within a day, and while the bridge-

[124] Tomac, *Četvrta neprijateljska ofanziva*, p. 106; *Oslobodilački rat*, I, 389; *Neretva*, I, 359–72.
The wisdom and true reasons for the destruction of all five bridges over the Neretva, which
thereby made it immensely more difficult to cross the river, have been questioned in recent years
by some of the Yugoslav officers who at that time held high positions in Partisan forces. One of
these officers has said that it perhaps was more beneficial to the enemy than to the Partisans.
The official interpretation is that the action was a ruse, that it succeeded in misleading the enemy
about the direction of an intended Partisan breakout of the encirclement, and that its success
confirmed its wisdom. See the articles by Velimir Terzić and Jovo Vukotić in *Neretva*, I, p. 56 and
pp. 156–57, respectively, and the corrections of the text executed by the editorial board of this
symposium in the Errata.
[125] *Oslobodilački rat*, I, 388–94; Tomac, *Četvrta neprijateljska ofanziva*, pp. 107–13; *Neretva*,
I, 98–117, 157–62, 248–51; Trgo, *Četvrta i Peta neprijateljska ofanziva*, pp. 40–44.

head was steadily extended, Partisan troops, the sick and wounded, and refugees began crossing on March 8 and kept on crossing, much of the time under Axis air attacks. By March 15 the crossing was completed, including the troops that secured the crossing, though the heavy equipment and vehicles could not be taken and had to be blown up or sunk. When the German forces reached Jablanica on March 17 they found the town empty of Partisans.[126] Operations Weiss 2 and Mostar were over, only that part of them relating to the takeover of the bauxite mines having been completed successfully. Although the Partisans avoided the destruction of their main forces and saved the sick and wounded, the Germans exacted a tremendous toll during Operation Weiss. According to a report of General Lüters of March 31 to General Vilko Begić, State Secretary in the Ministry of Armed Forces of Croatia, the German and Croatian forces together killed (counted or estimated) 11,915 Partisans; 616 more were executed upon capture, and another 2,506 were captured, of whom 775 were sent to concentration camps.[127]

While engaged throughout Operation Weiss with its main forces in a combination of withdrawal and offensive actions, the Partisan Supreme Headquarters availed itself of two other tactical elements and a special gambit in an attempt to gain time to withdraw across the Neretva. First, it ordered the 1st Croatian Corps in Lika and the 1st Bosnian Corps in northwestern Bosnia to fight with all their power against the Axis forces participating in Operation Weiss—which they did in such a manner that, in spite of certain reverses, they did materially slow the enemy's advance.[128] Second, Partisan forces in Lika and western Bosnia which the Germans thought they had destroyed in Weiss 1 were by early March beginning to reestablish new pockets of liberated territory and to interfere with the communications and German and Croatian garrisons left there.[129]

The special gambit was to engage in negotiations with the Germans on the vital issue of mutual application of the rules of international law of war, primarily in regard to the treatment of prisoners, exchange of some prisoners, and a series of other questions. The nature of these "other questions" has still not been completely cleared up. It is a subject that Yugoslav writers avoid, and outside Yugoslavia it has not been satisfactorily covered. A brief discussion here is appropriate in that it bears some relation to the question of collaboration with the Germans not only by the Chetniks but also by the Partisans.

[126] *Neretva*, I, 117–25, 162–66, 372–84; and II, 268–71; *Oslobodilački rat*, I, 394–402.

[127] *Zbornik DNOR*, Tome IV, Vol. 11, p. 599. These estimates of Partisan dead undoubtedly included some civilians who were moving with the Partisan troops as refugees or were inhabitants of villages which the Germans considered to be hostile.

[128] Kladarin, pp. 153–62; Trgo, *Četvrta i Peta neprijateljska ofanziva*, pp. 24–26, 44; *Oslobodilački rat*, I, 362, 378, 380, 386–87, 389–90.

[129] Microcopy No. T-78, Roll 332, Frames 6,289,918, 6,290,028, and 6,290,062.

Before Operation Weiss began, the Partisans and the Germans had carried on lengthy negotiations and on September 5 and November 17, 1942, had exchanged some prisoners.[130] On November 17 the Partisan representatives delivered a letter directed to General Glaise, the German Plenipotentiary General in Croatia, in which they apparently explained that the Army of National Liberation of Yugoslavia was an independent armed force with military discipline and not an agglomeration of bands, and proposed mutual application of the rules of international law of war, especially in regard to prisoners and wounded, a regular exchange of prisoners, and a sort of armistice between the two sides.[131] Not only Glaise but also Kasche, the German Envoy in Zagreb, and the representatives of the German economic agencies there favored this contact and exchange of prisoners as a way of deriving some useful intelligence, and they also wanted a modus vivendi with the Partisans because in the areas they had liberated there were some important mining facilities. Generally, they hoped for a pacification of the Croatian areas south of the Sava River and a cessation of sabotage on the vital Zagreb-Belgrade rail line. But Hitler and von Ribbentrop were much opposed to any modus vivendi, fearing that any formal arrangement with the Partisans would give them the status of a regular belligerent. Their opinion of course prevailed, and the Partisan proposals remained unanswered.

Sometime in late February or early March the Partisans captured German Major Strecker and about 25 soldiers; they already had about 100 Croatian army personnel and 15 Italian officers and some 600 non-commissioned officers and privates as prisoners of war. Since the Partisans were now in extreme peril and desperately needed additional time to effect their crossing of the Neretva, they decided to use Major Strecker to initiate new negotiations with the Germans. These negotiations took place at Gornji Vakuf on March 11. The importance that the Partisans attached to them is indicated by the rank of their delegates: Koča Popović, the commander of the 1st Proletarian Division; Milovan Djilas (posing as Miloš Marković), a member of the Supreme Headquarters of the Yugoslav Army of National Liberation and of the Politbureau of the CPY; and Dr. Vladimir Velebit (posing as Dr. Vladimir Petrović), a Zagreb lawyer, one of Tito's confidants. The Germans were represented by Lt. General Benignus Dippold, commander of the 717th Infantry Division, a younger officer on his staff, and, curiously, a representative of the Hitler Youth. In their written statement the Partisan delegates indicated the number of various groups of people they had

[130] Odić, pp. 29–36, 67–77.

[131] Unfortunately I have not been able to locate a copy of this letter, but I base my knowledge of it on the text of the statement by the Partisan representatives of March 11, which repeated much of the November 17 letter.

to offer and which persons in particular they wanted to get in exchange, and said that the exchange of prisoners should be settled as soon as possible. Point 2 of the statement, though somewhat unclear, seems to say that if the German Command would accept the Partisan proposal, especially in regard to wounded and captured, the Yugoslavs would guarantee that their units would do the same. Point 3 stated the opinion of the Headquarters of the Army of Liberation as being the following:

a) That in the present situation there is no reason why the German Wehrmacht should commit acts of war against the Army of Liberation of Yugoslavia especially in consideration of the situation, the adversaries and the interests of both sides—accordingly, it would be in the interests of both sides if hostilities ceased. In connection with this, the German Headquarters and this delegation should determine their proposals concerning a possible zone, and lay down the aims of the economical and other interests.

b) The Army of Liberation of Yugoslavia considers the Chetniks as the main enemies.

Point 4 proposed that during the negotiations all acts of war between the two sides should cease (i.e. an armistice), and Point 5 stated than any possible definitive agreement would have to be signed by their higher headquarters.

During the negotiations the Partisan delegates made it clear that their proposals did not constitute an offer of capitulation, that the Army of Liberation "would also take up combat against the English, if the latter were to land"—something the Chetniks would not do because they were only waiting for this to happen—and that they had slanted their propaganda toward Moscow only because they did not want to have any relations with London.[132]

A few days after this meeting, on March 17, Envoy Kasche addressed a report to the Foreign Ministry in which he repeated the Partisan offer and urged the continuation of discussions, and asked for instructions. In the meantime Djilas and Velebit had been brought to Zagreb where they continued negotiations with General Glaise and Kasche's representatives, apparently on the entire agenda of the March 11 meeting. Kasche had two additional exchanges with Berlin, in one of which he supported the negotiations and some arrangement with the Partisans on the grounds that complete victory over them could not be reached by military and police measures alone and therefore political means should also be used. In the end the instructions from Berlin were in the negative and the discussions with the Partisans on the "other questions" came to nothing. By the end of March, however, a new group of

[132] German originals of the documents pertaining to the conference at Gornji Vakuf registered under No. NOKW-1088 are found in Microcopy No. T-1119, Roll 16, Frames 68–74; official English translations are found in *ibid.*, Frames 75–81. The citation is from Frames 78–79. In his *Conversations with Stalin*, pp. 9–10, Djilas only briefly mentions these March 1943 negotiations.

prisoners was exchanged, and later on a program of almost regular exchange was inaugurated.[133]

Since no evidence on the "other questions" has been forthcoming from Yugoslavia, one cannot be certain precisely what motivated Tito in these negotiations. Were they only an excuse to gain time to execute the crossing of the Neretva, or did the Partisans seriously seek some modus vivendi of longer duration with the Germans? Had they arrived at a modus vivendi, would this not have knocked out the Partisans' chief propaganda line against the Chetniks—namely, that they were collaborating with the enemy? Finally, why has the subject been taboo in Yugoslavia for so many years? The last question is the easiest to answer: obviously, if the systematically nurtured legend that the Partisans never had any dealings with the Axis forces beyond the periodic exchanges of prisoners is to be maintained, there can be no public mention of incidents from which it appears that the Partisans, like the Chetniks, were prepared in certain periods of time to make arrangements with the enemy if by so doing they could stiffen their fight against their main domestic enemy, the Chetniks.

On the other hand, the record of German-Partisan relations from 1941 to 1945 taken as a whole proves that the Partisans could never have reached with the Germans an arrangement going much beyond the exchange of prisoners. It ought therefore to be evident that the attempt of March 11, 1943 (if not the one of November 17, 1942), to reach some agreement, was made under extreme circumstances when the Partisan main forces, their leadership, and some 4,000 sick and wounded, were facing almost certain and complete destruction, and that it cannot be put in the same category as the systematic and enduring Chetnik collaboration described in this study, although that collaboration was not based on ideological affinity and was not without reservations either.[134]

Throughout the Battle of the Neretva River the Chetniks collaborated very closely with the Italians and were dependent on them for all sup-

[133] The November 1942 and March 1943 prisoner exchanges were negotiated by the Partisan Supreme Headquarters. Dr. Vladimir Velebit and Marijan Stilinović negotiated the November exchange, and in March 1943 Velebit, Djilas, and Popović were involved. Sometime late in 1943 new exchanges were negotiated and from then on until the end of the war steady exchanges took place. The negotiations were now carried on by the Partisan Chief Headquarters of Croatia—for some time by Stilinović, then briefly by Dr. Josip Brnčić, and from March 1944 on by Boris Bakrač. Between March 1944 and May 1945 Bakrač had about forty meetings with German representatives (of which 25 were in Zagreb under safe conduct) and secured the exchange of some 600 to 800 Partisans. From the beginning of these exchanges a German mining engineer, Hans Ott, who was one of the persons exchanged in November 1942, played a leading role on the German side. Information supplied by Dr. Vladimir Bakarić, Zagreb, in a letter of June 6, 1966. When Bakarić held the post of Political Commissar of the Partisan Chief Headquarters of Croatia, Stilinović reported to him on his negotiations with the Germans. It should be noted also that in July 1944 the Slovene Partisans in the Slovene Littoral made offers of an armistice to the Germans. Microcopy No. T-311, Roll 195, Frames 717–22, 736. It seems that later an agreement was made, but it was never consummated.

[134] Hagen, pp. 258–68, simply reports on the Partisan-German negotiations, but Jukić, pp. 148–53, and Roberts, pp. 106–12, put the Partisan overtures to collaborate and Chetnik collaboration in the same category.

plies and transportation. Although according to German-Italian arrangements the Italians were supposed to keep the Chetnik troops from making contact with German and Croatian quisling troops, in the course of operations in the area of Konjic they not only established contact but found themselves fighting together, and the Germans supplied some ammunition to the Chetniks. For the Germans, such collaboration was not exactly comfortable. This is clearly indicated in a statement concerning the end of the last phase of Operation Weiss that was issued by General Löhr to his troops on March 14. All remaining rebel forces, of all colors, must be destroyed, he said, but as for the operation just concluded: "It is especially necessary to state that temporary shoulder-to-shoulder fighting with the Chetniks in certain areas against the Partisans was a necessary evil which had to be accepted, because the fight against both groups at the same time would not have permitted the destruction of either."[135] For the Chetniks, their failure to hold the left bank of the Neretva and prevent the Partisans from breaking through into the interior of eastern Herzegovina and further southeast was undoubtedly an unexpected and terrible loss. For the Axis forces the Partisans' escape from the trap was yet another failure to administer a death blow to the Partisans. And for the Partisans, it was their finest victory up to that time.

The Partisan determination to exploit their breakthrough at the Neretva River bend to the utmost had two tactical aims: to keep the Chetnik and Italian forces under such unrelenting pressure that they would have no chance to regroup and mount a successful counterattack, and to put as much distance as possible between their forces and any Germans who were in pursuit. But in fact as soon as the crossing of the Neretva River seemed to be assured, a new and very ambitious plan began to develop in the Partisan headquarters: the destruction of the main Chetnik forces. Having at the Neretva River experienced a great danger from the Chetniks when they operated as auxiliaries of and in parallel actions with the Axis powers, Tito made the destruction of the Chetniks the first priority and issued a series of orders to that effect. On March 9 he notified the 7th Shock Division that in the direction of their new advance the chief enemy would be the Chetniks, both local and those brought from Montenegro, and all captured leaders and commanders should be treated without mercy—that is, after a brief interrogation they were to be shot on the spot—while the rank and file if misled or innocent were to be coaxed into the Partisan ranks or held as prisoners. The order urged the troops to do their utmost: "In your fight against the enemy you must display the greatest possible offensive

---

[135] Microcopy No. T-314, Roll 554, Frame 637. See also *KTB/OKW/WFSt*, Vol. III, Part 1, p. 212.

spirit, recklessness, impudence, and push, in order to annihilate his men and destroy his units. In order to achieve this, you must in every encounter with the enemy engage in speedy maneuvering, attacking especially his flanks and rear."[136] The Central Committee of the CPY on March 29 instructed the Provincial CPY Committee for Bosnia and Herzegovina to send an eastern Bosnian brigade to Sandjak to help the divisions presently under Tito's direct command, for "Our most important task now is to destroy the Chetniks of Draža Mihailović and to break up his administrative apparatus, because they represent the greatest danger for the further course of the national liberation struggle."[137] And on March 30 in a letter to the staff of the First Bosnian Corps Tito identified the Chetniks as being temporarily the principal enemy, and directed that the main action be concentrated against them.[138]

Moving between the eastern slopes of Mount Prenj and the Neretva, the Partisan divisions first captured Glavatičevo, a Chetnik stronghold. The 1st and 2nd Proletarian divisions then moved directly east. Between March 20 and 22 they engaged in a fierce battle with the Chetniks around the town of Kalinovik, captured it, and continued toward the Drina River. Despite the failure to cross the Drina on the first try and some reverses after crossing, the Partisan forces beat the Chetniks and the Italians on that front during the first half of April and in the next two weeks moved southward into Montenegro.[139] The 3rd Shock Division followed by the 7th Shock Division,[140] partly before reaching Glavatičevo and partly immediately after it, took a southwesterly route. After some temporary reverses they seized the towns of Nevesinje, Gacko, and Avtovac, and early in April moved across the Piva River into Montenegro. On about April 24 they came into the area of Šavnik, somewhat south of the area into which Partisan forces from the north were advancing.[141] Thus by late April the Chetniks from Sandjak and Mon-

---

[136] *Zbornik DNOR*, Tome II, Vol. 8, pp. 275–76.

[137] *Ibid.*, p. 359.

[138] *Ibid.*, p. 361. This message obviously alludes to the talks between Tito's representatives and the commander of the German 717th Infantry Division in this remark: "Taking advantage of the contact for the exchange of prisoners, we have succeeded in neutralizing [isolating?] the Germans from the Chetniks and the Italians."

[139] *Oslobodilački rat*, I, 400–404, 407–10, 413–19.

[140] The 9th Shock Division, after serving as rearguard during the crossing of the Neretva River and crossing itself on March 14–15, was given the task (aided by one brigade of the 7th Shock Division and some Italian prisoners of war) of transporting the Partisan sick and wounded around Mount Prenj from Krstac to Glavatičevo. It completed this arduous task, but at such great loss in casualties as a result of enemy air and artillery attacks, as well as miseries of cold, hunger, typhus, and exhaustion, that when reassigned, its fighting power was seen to be greatly diminished. A number of groups of men began deserting to return to their home areas in Dalmatia; toward the end of April, therefore, the Partisan Supreme Headquarters disbanded the division and its unimpaired units were shifted to other divisions. *Neretva*, I, 276–85, 305–17. The division was reconstituted on September 8, 1943, in Split.

[141] *Oslobodilački rat*, I, 404–6, 419–20. Around March 23, *vojvoda* Jevdjević through the Italians, as well as the Italians themselves, asked the 7th SS Division "Prinz Eugen," which had taken over the area of bauxite mines in western Herzegovina, for assistance in the defense of Nevesinje, but the Germans refused to oblige. They said that the troops were tired and were in need of rest and that they had been reserved for other tasks. *Zbornik DNOR*, Tome IV, Vol. 11, pp. 507–8,

tenegro who took part in the Battle of the Neretva River or in ensuing battles in eastern Herzegovina and southeastern Bosnia had been pushed deep into their home territories with the Partisans close on their heels.

The climax of the operation as it developed from February on was, of course, the Partisans' successful crossing of the Neretva River between March 7 and 15—by means of which action they were able to shake off the crushing pressure of German and Croatian quisling forces, leaving them only the Chetniks and the Italians to contend with, and in a much better situation militarily (that is, with more room for maneuvering and with more suitable terrain). This action was decisive so far as the Chetniks' basic strategy was concerned: because of it, the Chetnik position was totally altered. On February 24 the Chetniks had announced that Partisan forces in western Bosnia had been completely broken up and chased out of that territory and that they were in the process of disintegration; the statement concluded with the words: "Our situation is very favorable."[142] A month later, on March 25, Mihailović was ordering Major Djurišić, then fighting in eastern Herzegovina, to resist with all power the Partisan advance toward Sandjak and Montenegro, and on March 28 he advised Ostojić, his chief of operations, that the Drina-Piva rivers line—some eighty to ninety kilometers southwest of the Neretva River bend—was the best line for the defense of Sandjak and Montenegro.[143] But the Chetnik troops with portions of the Italian Taurinense Division which held the Drina line were defeated by the Partisans during the first half of April, and when they turned southward toward the heart of Montenegro they were about ten to fifteen kilometers east of the Piva River. By this time, the Chetniks had lost a large proportion of their troops and could expect little if any logistic or artillery support from the Italians, who had themselves suffered heavy losses and were beginning to change their policy toward the Chetniks. To stem the Partisan advance into Montenegro and Sandjak after the break of the Drina-Piva defense line Mihailović ordered the mobilization and shift of two Chetnik corps from Serbia, with the help of which, and with the remaining forces in Sandjak and Montenegro, he planned to give decisive battle to the Partisans on the front between Nikšić on the Zeta River and Bijelo Polje on the Lim River. The two corps from Serbia (under Keserović and Raković) arrived in the area of Bijelo Polje around May 7, but the advances made in the meantime by the

---

510, 530–31. Whether the negotiations under way between the Germans and the Partisans had anything to do with this German reply is not known.

On the operations of the Italian units during the second half of March and early April in eastern Herzegovina and for the repeated criticism of the Italian command posts of their Chetnik auxiliaries see the messages of the Italian VIth Army Corps to various units and to Supersloda in *Zbornik DNOR*, Tome IV, Vol. 11, pp. 323–603.

[142] Archives of the Institute of Military History, Belgrade, Chetnik Documents, Reg. No. 20/1, Box 2.

[143] *Ibid.*, Reg. No. 34/1 and 37/1, Box 2.

Partisans and the reports Mihailović got from the Italians that the Germans were soon to enter Montenegro and intended to capture him, prevented Mihailović from even attempting to fight against the Partisans as planned but rather made him decide to return with his two Serbian corps to Serbia.[144]

The Chetniks' failure at the Neretva River and during the following weeks was due to a combination of mistakes and inadequacies: poor planning, poor leadership by Mihailović and his commanders, a lack of cooperation among the commanders, too much confidence in themselves and too low an estimate of the Partisans, and the reluctance of commanders and men to fight the seasoned, superbly led, and—at the Neretva River—desperate Partisan troops.[145] The overconfidence was so great among some of the Chetnik officers, it has been reported, that they began to squabble about which of them would get the credit for the coming victory.[146] The looseness and disunity of Mihailović's agglomeration of territorial detachments, willing to defend only their own immediate areas and unwilling to fight resolutely away from home, were never more in evidence.

General Löhr, the Commander in Chief in Southeast Europe, in his Situation Report for March 1943, which includes also a rather detailed report on the final phase of Operation Weiss, had this to say: "The battles thus far fought show that Mihailović as a military leader has failed. By not recognizing the existing possibilities because of his lack of knowledge of the area, and the terrain, and the demands of time, he has been chiefly responsible for the failure so far."[147] Bader, the Commanding General in Serbia, made much the same sort of observation in his Situation Report for the second half of March; referring to the Chetnik-Partisan fighting on the Neretva River and in eastern Herzegovina, he commented: "The forces of Draža Mihailović have not passed their first serious test. Many reasons contributed to this: inability, cowardice, and lack of discipline on the part of the commanders, lack of

---

[144] Pajović, "The Chetnik Movement and the National Liberation Movement in Montenegro," pp. 397–99. According to the testimony of Major Lukačević at his trial the two Serbian corps numbered altogether 2,000 men. *Sudjenje članovima rukovodstva organizacije Draže Mihailovića*, p. 142. On May 18 Mihailović issued a special order praising the soldiers of Raković's corps for promptly coming to the assistance of their brothers in Sandjak and Montenegro; it also contained another tirade against the Communists. Archives of the Institute of Military History, Belgrade, Chetnik Documents, Reg. No. 12/2, Box 2. From a popularly written book on the Chetnik movement during the Second World War by one of Djurišić's admirers, it appears that at a meeting between Djurišić and Mihailović near Kolašin, just before Mihailović began the trek toward Serbia with the two Serbian corps, there had for the first time been strong words between the two men, and their parting was anything but friendly. Minić, pp. 197–98.

[145] Ostojić tried without success to enforce discipline and obedience by threatening courts martial and summary executions. *Dokumenti o izdajstvu Draže Mihailovića*, I, 114–15, 123.

[146] Vučetić, pp. 102–3.

[147] Microcopy No. T-78, Roll 332, Frames 6,290,062–63. At least two of his own commanders were very critical of Mihailović's conduct of operations at this time. Colonel Bailey, in a report of November 1944 dealing with Chetnik matters, stated: "Both Lt. Col. Ostojic and Major Lukacevic ... maintained that Mihailovic's foolhardy, though brave, tactical handling of his forces contributed largely to the failure of operations." F.O. 371/44282, R20526/11/92. See also *Sudjenje članovima rukovodstva organizacije Draže Mihailovića*, p. 141.

stern leadership of soldiers, and by no means of least importance the overrating of the fighting power of their own troops on the part of the highest command posts."[148]

Tito in a contemporary report on the Partisan-Chetnik fighting in the course of March and April said that although the Chetniks were fully convinced that with the Axis forces and the Ustashas they would finally liquidate the Partisans, they had succeeded in exposing their true character to the people, and "instead of marching on western Bosnia, they had met complete military and political defeat and had been reduced to small bandit detachments without any support among the masses."[149]

The chief Chetnik chronicler of the Battle of the Neretva, Major Radulović, recognizes the success of the Partisans, but his account, written from memory, not only is biased from the personal and the Chetnik point of view but also contains many inaccuracies and inconsistencies. Naturally he says nothing about Chetnik collaboration with the Italians and the Germans, nor anything about the poor Chetnik leadership and the unwillingness of the troops to fight. Had the Chetniks been defeated by the German forces, this could be easily explained by the superiority in men and matériel, and pride could be preserved. The defeat at the hands of the Partisans, whom they so hated and underrated, was humiliating.[150]

Although Operation Weiss 3 for the disarming of the Chetniks as well as Italian promises of the end of February to do the same had long since been scrapped, the defeats that the Partisans had inflicted upon the Chetniks by and following the breakthrough into eastern Herzegovina had in fact temporarily removed the Chetniks as a problem in the Croatian puppet state. But the Partisans were still a force to reckon with, not only in eastern Herzegovina but also in Sandjak and Montenegro; and so too were a portion of the Chetniks in Montenegro. While the Partisans and the Chetniks were locked in battle during the early spring, the Germans prepared their Operation Schwarz, the aim of which was the disarming of all Chetniks and the destruction of all Partisans in Montenegro and Sandjak. The operation, known as the Fifth Enemy Offensive in Partisan terminology, was on such a scale as to demand additional forces. One of the German elite divisions, the 1st Mountain Division, was brought from the Russian front to join the Prinz Eugen Division, the 369th Infantry Division, the 118th and large parts of the 104th Light Infantry divisions (the former 700-series in-

[148] Microcopy No. T-315, Roll 64, Frame 556.
[149] See Tito's report on the military developments of this period published in *Bilten Vrhovnog štaba NOV i POJ*, January–April 1943, reprinted in *Zbornik DNOR*, Tome II, Vol 1, pp. 223–27, esp. p. 224.
[150] Borivoje Radulović, pp. 82–89.

fantry divisions now outfitted for mountain warfare), a regiment of the Brandenburg Division, several Croatian independent brigades, and the 61st Bulgarian Infantry Regiment, which had been brought from Serbia. In the immediate area of operations, but intended essentially to seal off the possible escape routes, the Italians had three divisions, the Taurinense, the Ferrara, and the Venezia. On the perimeter of the area there were four more Italian divisions and one German division. In all, the Axis forces amounted to about 117,000 men and an appropriate number of German and Italian aircraft. On the Partisan side in this operation there were about 19,000 men (the 1st and 2nd Proletarian divisions and the 3rd and 7th Shock divisions, the last two burdened with about 3,500 sick and wounded).[151]

The purpose of Operation Schwarz as officially stated was to remove the eventual danger from the Partisan and Chetnik troops to the bauxite mines in Herzegovina and the lead and chromium ore mines in the southern parts of Serbia, Kosovo, and Macedonia; but it is obvious that the basic reason, as in Operation Weiss, was the threat of an Allied invasion of the Balkans and the need to remove the two resistance groups as forces which could aid the Allies in such a landing.[152] The main strategic objective was to surround the Partisan and Chetnik forces in Montenegro and Sandjak and to push them through concentric attacks to the high plateau and mountains (Durmitor and Sinjajevina mountains) between the Tara and Piva rivers, an area known for its scarcity of food and lack of communications, where nature itself would prove a most cruel enemy.

Before the start of Operation Schwarz, however, another incident worth relating took place. On May 10 Lt. Colonel F. W. Heinz, commander of the 4th Regiment of the Brandenburg Division, which was attached to the 1st Mountain Division in Montenegro, held a conference with Chetnik commander Pavle Djurišić in Kolašin. Heinz was interested in inducing Djurišić to collaborate with the Germans against the Partisans. Djurišić was quite willing to do this and was even ready to go on after the Partisans had been destroyed to fight with a part of his men on the Russian front. He told Heinz that Mihailović had been away from Kolašin since the end of 1942, and he repudiated Mihailović's current policy, calling him "an unsteady visionary wandering through the land," whose head had been turned by propaganda and who was "overrated." The "serious enemy" was only Tito. The day after the conference Heinz submitted to General Lüters, who was in charge of Operation Schwarz, and to the 1st Mountain Division a proposal sug-

---

[151] *Oslobodilački rat*, I, 430–32, 439; *Sutjeska*, I, 314–16; Microcopy No. T-78, Roll 332, Frames 6,290,240–43.
[152] See General Lüters's order regarding Operation Schwarz of May 5, 1943, Microcopy No. T-501, Roll 250, Frame 274. See also Bojić, pp. 125–34.

gesting a way to make use of the Italian legalized Chetniks in Montenegro until Tito was destroyed. This was "to legalize Djurišić's forces
and with his help disarm the illegal Chetniks. After the destruction of
Tito legalize only weak Djurišić detachments."[153] Heinz seems to have
got into some trouble with his superiors for making this contact with
Djurišić (though his account of the incident many years later tends to
exaggerate its importance and does not, in fact, agree with his own
report of May 11, 1943).[154] The reaction of his superiors to his proposals
was at any rate evident in the events as they occurred: early on May 14,
an advance group (*Vorausabteilung*) of the 1st Mountain Division consisting of five companies having great firepower and mobility entered
Kolašin and captured and disarmed Major Djurišić and about 1,500
to 2,000 of his troops. Djurišić offered no resistance and there were no
casualties. The Italians protested the incident but they were overruled
and Djurišić and his troops were taken to prisoner-of-war camps.[155] On
May 12 General Lüters had informed the 4th Regiment of the Brandenburg Division as follows: "The chief goal of the Brandenburg Regiment
remains capture of the person and staff of Draža Mihailović and securing of files. At the same time, the destruction of Tito and his staff is also
desired."[156] Since Mihailović had just started to withdraw with the two
Serbian corps toward Serbia, except for the disarming of some additional
Chetnik units, Tito and the Partisans thus became the sole target of the
Axis forces.

But as in the Konjic area during the Battle of the Neretva River, so in
the course of Operation Schwarz there was for a brief period some unexpected and unplanned German-Chetnik collaboration against the
Partisans. Some days after the disarming of the Djurišić Chetniks, the
98th Regiment of the 1st Mountain Division discovered a force of two
to three thousand Partisans holding a mountainous area west of Kolašin,
and also in the area a large group of Chetniks. Friendly contact was
established with the Chetniks, German noncommissioned officers were
attached to the Chetnik units as tactical commanders, and in a combined action the Partisans were dislodged from their positions.[157] When
the higher German command posts heard about this collaboration, they
informed the 1st Mountain Division that the previous order to disarm
all Chetniks that were encountered still stood. The Chetniks who had
collaborated with the 98th Regiment—1,546 men— were therefore disarmed by May 26, but ten officers and 800 men were used by the Germans
as guides for pack animals and carriers of supplies for German troops.[158]

[153] Microcopy No. T-315, Roll 64, Frames 653–54.
[154] See his story in Roberts, pp. 123–25; see also Kriegsheim, p. 313.
[155] Microcopy No. T-78, Roll 332, Frames 6,289,989–90.
[156] Microcopy No. T-315, Roll 64, Frame 650.
[157] *Ibid.*, Frames 1194–96.
[158] *Ibid.*, Frames 1180, 1227.

Furthermore, General Roncaglia, the Italian commander in the Kolašin area, who had vigorously protested the disarming of Djurišić, himself ordered on the basis of higher orders the disarming of those Chetnik units that were connected with General Mihailović, with the Lašić Chetniks, for example, specifically exempted.[159] According to Yugoslav estimates, the total number of Chetniks disarmed by the Germans and Italians in these weeks in Montenegro, southeastern Bosnia, and Herzegovina was about 7,000.[160]

When launched on May 17, Operation Schwarz caught the Partisans by surprise. In fact by that time the wider encirclement by the Axis forces was almost complete and went on almost as planned. The four Partisan divisions (the 1st, 2nd, 3rd, and 7th with the entire Partisan leadership and the Partisan central hospital with about 2,200 sick and wounded) were soon encircled with an almost completely closed ring.[161] Fighting desperately, and with great losses, the 1st, 2nd, and 7th divisions (the latter also moving about 600 wounded and sick) succeeded between June 5 and 8 in getting out of the first ring at Tjentište on the Sutjeska River before it shut fast, and then between June 9 and 15 broke the second German barrier near Kalinovik and escaped into eastern Bosnia. The 3rd Shock Division which served as a rear guard and which now was responsible for the central hospital swerved first toward the southeast, and finding its way blocked, turned north by the route previously taken by the other divisions. But it was too late: the ring was closed tight. The 3rd Division's attempt on June 13 to break through the ring at Tjentište proved futile, and the division was almost completely destroyed. Altogether, losses in the Partisans' four divisions amounted to about 35 percent of their effectives, and about 1,300 of the sick and wounded were also lost.[162] But the Partisan leadership and the three divisions that broke out and, in conjunction with the Partisan divisions from northern Bosnia, mounted an offensive undertaking into eastern Bosnia, were immensely strengthened in a moral and political sense, since in terms of Partisan warfare victory meant surviving and not being incapacitated for further action. Commenting on the outcome of the Fifth Enemy Offensive, Tito wrote in the summer of 1943: "Draža Mihailović was finished precisely in areas in which he used to be the strongest, as, for example, in Montenegro, Sandjak, and Herzegovina.

---

[159] *Ibid.*, Frames 1201, 1226, 1231.

[160] Vujošević, p. 146.

[161] It was during these fateful days, on the night of May 27, that the first British exploratory military mission under the leadership of Captains William F. D. Deakin and William F. Stuart reached the Partisan headquarters. This mission, of which more will be said in the following chapter, added tremendously to the prestige of the Partisans and had far-reaching consequences. Captain Stuart was killed on June 9 in an attack by German aircraft in which also Tito was slightly wounded.

[162] *Oslobodilački rat*, 432–66; Trgo, *Četvrta i Peta neprijateljska ofanziva*, pp. 55–83. On the whole epic of Partisan operations in the Fifth Enemy Offensive there is also the five-volume work written by the participants, *Sutjeska*, Belgrade, 1959–61.

Since then he no longer represents anything in a military sense and politically he has exposed himself in his true character."[163]

The Partisan success at the Sutjeska River was perhaps an even more spectacular military feat than their victory at the Neretva.[164] This was the last great German-Italian operation against the Partisans. Thereafter the Germans were to use smaller groupings of troops but occasionally more imaginative operations against the Partisans—none of them, however, any more successful than the earlier ones.

The Chetnik position was now extremely weakened and serious: first had come the series of defeats at Partisan hands from March 7 to about May 10, then the disarming and removal of Djurišić and his forces from Montenegro and the disarming of other Chetnik units in Montenegro and Bosnia and Herzegovina, and finally the departure of Mihailović for Serbia. The Chetniks' strength and influence outside Serbia were almost completely broken. Moreover, the Italians, who had for so long supported and used the Chetniks, began disarming Chetnik units in Montenegro and Herzegovina—partly because of German pressure and partly because they realized that the remaining Chetnik units in their area would be of little help against the Partisans.[165] The period of Chetnik-Italian collaboration and of great assistance in arms, supplies, and finance from the latter to the former was rapidly coming to an end.

After June 1943 the strength of the Italians themselves in the Balkans, though they still had large forces in the field, began to decline rapidly.[166] One of the indications of this decline in the Yugoslav territory was the gradual entry of German forces into certain areas of the Italian occupation zone prior to the Italian collapse. The German takeover on March 16, 1943, of the bauxite mines area near Mostar (as per agreement of March 10), had been understood by the Italians to be only a temporary

[163] From a statement of Tito on the Fifth Enemy Offensive in *Bilten Vrhovnog štaba NOV i POJ*, June–July–August 1943, reprinted in *Zbornik DNOR*, Tome II, Vol. 1, pp. 277–82, esp. p. 279.

[164] Proof that Operation Schwarz finally evolved almost exclusively into an operation against the Partisans, though it was conceived as an operation against both the Partisans and the Chetniks, is best indicated by German estimates of losses inflicted upon the two groups: the Report on the Enemy Position in the Southeast No. 53 of June 20, 1943, issued by the General Staff of the German Army, estimated that the Partisans had 12,000 killed and 1,500 captured, and the Chetniks only about 3,000 captured and disarmed. Microcopy No. T-78, Roll 332, Frames 6,290,244–46. The shooting of Partisan prisoners, a practice consistently followed by the Germans, probably reached its peak during Operation Schwarz. Of the 498 prisoners taken during this operation by the 1st Mountain Division, 411 were shot. *Ibid.*, Frame 6,289,997.

[165] One of the contributing factors to this Italian change of policy toward the Chetniks were the radio messages among the Chetnik commanders of late 1942 and early 1943 which were intercepted by the Italians. In these messages the Chetniks expressed themselves deprecatingly and arrogantly about the Italians, talked about disarming them and seizing their arms at an opportune moment, and so on. For the gist of some of these messages see Microcopy No. T-821, Roll 31, Frames 370–79.

[166] According to a report of the Italian Supreme Command, the Italians had in the Balkans as of August 1, 1943, a total of thirty-two divisions and six brigades with approximately 672,000 men. Of these, 213,000 were in Greece and Crete, 55,000 in the Aegean Islands, 108,000 in Albania (of which probably 25,000–30,000 were in the Yugoslav areas of western Macedonia and Kosovo), 71,000 in Montenegro and the Bay of Kotor area, and 225,000 in areas under the command of Supersloda. Thus in Yugoslavia alone, counting also the forces in Albanian-held Yugoslav areas, the Italians had about 321,000 men. Microcopy No. T-821, Roll 252, Frames 64–85.

arrangement, but on May 28 another agreement between the two armies permitted the Germans to occupy the whole area of Mostar, definitely replacing the Italians.[167] This was followed early in June by a German takeover of some areas of Sandjak, and on September 3 by a takeover of certain areas with bauxite mines in the neighborhood of Split in Dalmatia.[168] On June 1 General Sandro Piazzoni, commander of the Italian VIth Army Corps, ordered the disarming of all units of the Chetnik MVAC in his area of command.[169] But the Chetniks, knowing that the Italians were on their way out, simply disregarded the order, and as General Piazzoni told the commander of the Prinz Eugen Division (General von Oberkamp) on August 12, of about 8,000 Chetniks in Herzegovina only 120 surrendered their arms.[170] The Italians even that late treated the Chetniks in different areas differently: for example, on August 11 General Robotti and the Italian envoy in Croatia Luigi Petrucci were still talking about the possibility of supplying no more arms to the Chetniks and gradually disarming them.[171] But the Chetniks could not hope to stand alone in areas where they had depended heavily on Italian arms, supplies, and finance, and as will be shown in Chapter 9, soon after the Italian collapse they began to make collaboration arrangements with the Germans.

CHETNIK TERROR

No study of the Chetniks and their policies during the Second World War would be complete without a discussion of the Chetnik use of mass terror against their various enemies. The Chetniks were by no means the only offenders in Yugoslavia: the use of terror on a large scale and in innumerable forms was practiced by all parties engaged in war in Yugoslavia and was a ubiquitous phenomenon in all parts of the country. I bring up the Chetniks as perpetrators here because some of the most outrageous incidents of Chetnik terror took place in the time period covered in this chapter, that is between October 1942 and February 1943, and also because it was practiced on the largest scale in areas under Italian control and thus, one might say, under the Italian security umbrella.

In Yugoslavia, as in all the Balkan countries, there was a certain traditional inclination to the use of terror as a political tool. Living for centuries under foreign rule, frustrated in their repeated attempts to gain freedom, their rewards as a rule being only increased oppression, the peoples of the South Slav nations grew accustomed to the use of terror as a means of dealing with an enemy. By 1941, several more recent

---

[167] Microcopy No. T-314, Roll 554, Frames 633–34, 668–71.
[168] Microcopy No. T-821, Roll 247, Frame 839; Microcopy No. T-314, Roll 554, Frames 1387–88.
[169] Microcopy No. T-314, Roll 566, Frame 750.
[170] *Ibid.*, Frame 316.
[171] Microcopy No. T-821, Roll 31, Frames 266–72.

grievances had been added to the long-standing antagonism between the Christians (especially Orthodox) and the Moslems who, rightly or not, were reminders of the hated Turkish rule; there were mutual grievances between the Croats and the Serbs especially, and after the invasion, the Serbs had fresh grievances in the treasonable activities of some Croats and the subsequent persecution of Serbs in the Independent State of Croatia by the Ustashas.

Chetnik mass terror was thus directed principally against three groups of people. First, there were the Croats in areas where Serbs and Croats were living mixed and where the Ustashas were using mass terror against the Serbs (in other words, counterterror). These people had strong religious differences as well as national and ideological differences, and the terror and counterterror were indeed only an aspect of the newest phase in the thousand-year-old feud between the Serbian Orthodox and Catholic churches. The second group, the Moslem population in Bosnia and Herzegovina and Sandjak, was one of the primary victims of Chetnik terror. Here, the centuries-old religious and political Christian-Moslem antagonism had been aggravated during the First World War when many Bosnian Moslems joined the Austro-Hungarian *Schutzkorps*, which engaged in anti-Serb activities, and again after April 1941 when a great many Moslems joined the Ustashas and participated in atrocities against the Serbs. The Moslems were thus a traditional enemy, and it was only after mid-1943, when the potential political value of the Moslem population of Bosnia and Herzegovina and Sandjak took on importance for the Chetniks, that they suspended their acts of terror against the Moslems. The third group against whom the Chetniks used mass terror was, of course, their principal enemy the Partisans. Against them, whatever their nationality or religion, from the late fall of 1941 the Chetniks used terrorist methods at every opportunity.[172] At the same time, the Partisans did not hesitate to use terrorist methods against the Chetniks, labeling them collaborators with the enemy, and in the period of "left deviation" from about December 1941 to May 1942, especially in Montenegro and Herzegovina, used terror even against people who, though not collaborators, were because of their class standing looked upon as potential enemies in a later period of revolutionary development. Thus a terrible pattern of terror and counterterror emerged.

A brief summary of Chetnik terrorist activities in various forms and

---

[172] Topalović's views in *Pokreti narodnog otpora* on the psychological background of the Serbian population in areas outside Serbia help to explain Chetnik terrorist practices. After saying that in areas outside Serbia the Chetnik movement arose as a defense against the Ustashas and that in terms of ideology it knew only of Serbianism, he continues (p. 52): "The Chetnik movement identified the national and state belonging with religion. A Serb—that is, a member of the Orthodox Church—considers every Catholic a Croat and every Moslem a Turk. In a Serbian state these, as enemies, were to be annihilated or expelled.

"According to this primitive political ideology the Partisans were not Serbs either, but identical with the Turks and Ustashas, and even worse than that—they were godless. Since in the Partisan ranks the Orthodox were together with Catholics and Moslems, this meant for the Chetnik leaders treason against Serbdom and cooperation with the enemies of one's religion and one's people."

in various parts of the country during the Second World War may be found in the explanation of the verdict of the Military Tribunal that tried General Mihailović and his codefendants in the summer of 1946.[173] One of the earliest incidents was the series of massacres of Moslems in southeastern Bosnia which took place in December 1941 and January 1942, especially in the area of the town of Foča, in which probably over two thousand people perished. Eastern and southeastern Bosnia were, in fact, severely hit both by Ustasha terror against the Serbs and by Chetnik terror against the Moslem and Croatian population. Additional Chetnik terrorist outbursts against the Moslems in the area of Foča took place in August 1942. The worst of the Chetnik terror against the Moslems occurred in Sandjak and southeastern Bosnia in January and February 1943. According to a statement originating with the Chetnik Supreme Command dated February 24, 1943, these were punitive countermeasures prompted by the "aggressive actions of the Moslems who had attacked Serbian villages and killed some Serbian people."[174] Chetnik units which had been mobilized in December 1942 in Montenegro and readied for the planned, but delayed, "March on Bosnia" were ordered early in January and again early in February to undertake what were known as "cleansing actions" against the Moslems, first in the county of Bijelo Polje in Sandjak and in February in the county of Čajniče and part of the county of Foča in southeastern Bosnia, and in part of the county of Pljevlja in Sandjak. Chetnik losses were nominal; Moslem losses were estimated at about 10,000 persons. More details are revealed in the reports that Major Djurišić, the officer in charge of these operations, submitted to the Chief of Staff of the Supreme Command (Mihailović). According to Djurišić's report of January 10, thirty-three Moslem villages had been burned down, and 400 Moslem fighters (members of the Moslem self-protection militia supported by the Italians) and about 1,000 women and children had been killed, as against 14 Chetnik dead and 26 wounded.[175] The cleansing action carried out in early February took an even more staggering toll: according to Djurišić's report of February 13, in this action the Chetniks killed about 1,200 Moslem fighters and about 8,000 old people, women, and children; Chetnik losses in the action were 22 killed and 32 wounded. In addition, the Chetniks destroyed all property except livestock, grain, and hay, which they seized. It may be observed that Moslem casualties would certainly have been even greater had not a great number of Moslems already fled the area, mostly to Sarajevo; and all who could escape to safety of course did so as soon as the February action

[173] *The Trial of Draža Mihailović*, pp. 519–23, esp. pp. 520–21.
[174] For a copy of the statement see Archives of the Institute of Military History, Belgrade, Chetnik Documents, Reg. No. 20/1, Box 2.
[175] *The Trial of Draža Mihailović*, p. 261.

started.[176] Although "cleansing actions" in Sandjak and southeastern Bosnia were represented by the Chetniks as countermeasures against Moslem aggressive activities, all circumstances indicate that the operations were a partial implementation of the Chetnik plans mentioned specifically in Mihailović's directive of December 20, 1941, to Djurišić and Lašić about the cleansing of Sandjak of Moslem and of Bosnia of Moslem and Croatian populations.

One of the worst Chetnik outbursts against the Croatian population in Dalmatia took place in the first days of October 1942 at the village of Gata south of Split, in reprisal against the people of this village and other villages nearby for destroying some roads in the area; the reprisals were, in fact, taken by the Chetniks for Italian account. In all, about one hundred people were killed, and many homes were burned.[177]

Mention has already been made of the behavior of Chetnik formations under Lt. Colonel Baćović and *vojvoda* Jevdjević who were participating in the Italian Operation Alfa in the area of Prozor that same October. The Chetniks burned many villages and massacred over five hundred Croats and Moslems until being ordered out of the area at the insistance of the Croatian quisling regime.[178]

In terms of the number of victims and the cruelty of dispatching them, the Croatian Ustashas were, of course, far more guilty of crimes against humanity than were the Chetniks, though the Chetnik massacres of Moslem people in Sandjak and southeastern Bosnia were in essence of the same kind. It should also be pointed out that the Ustasha atrocities were undertaken first, and that at least to some extent the Chetnik terrorist activities against the Croatian and Moslem populations were in the nature of a reaction.

In Serbia, aside from some terrorist acts against Nedić's and Ljotić's men, and in Montenegro against the separatists, Chetnik terror was directed exclusively against the Partisans and their families and sympathizers, and it was based solely on ideological grounds. The goal, as Chetnik documents prove again and again in general and specific orders, was nothing less than the complete destruction of the Partisans. Total figures of Partisan dead will never be known. Indiscriminate terror being impossible because Partisans and their sympathizers lived together with other Serbian and Montenegrin people, lists of individuals marked for liquidation were compiled, and occasionally specific individuals were singled out by the Chetnik officers, as for example by Colonel Jevrem Simić, the Inspector of all Chetnik forces.[179] To carry out these acts of

---

[176] *Ibid.*, p. 202. For this whole episode see also Pajović, "The Massacre of Moslems," pp. 510–17.
[177] Gizdić, pp. 573–83.
[178] Leković, "Mihailović's Plans," p. 91.
[179] See e.g. the lists prepared in the area commanded by Lt. Colonel Dragutin Keserović in southern Serbia in *Sudjenje članovima rukovodstva organizacije Draže Mihailovića*, pp. 223–30,

terror special units, known as "black trojkas," were trained.[180] The standard method employed in these liquidations, especially in rural areas, was slaughter by knife—the Chetniks, like the Ustashas, being followers of the "cult of the knife." (The Partisans and other adversaries gave them the sobriquet *koljači*, the slaughterers.)

For a few months in the summer of 1942 even the BBC was used as a means of implementing one of the Chetnik terror schemes. This was the period of the "Z" lists. These lists, broadcast over the BBC in the news program in the Serbo-Croatian language, which was fully under the control of the Yugoslav government-in-exile, were lists of Nedić and Ljotić supporters (the names were supplied by Mihailović) who were marked for liquidation or at least were to be scared into compliance with Chetnik wishes.[181] No Partisans were included in the lists, since they were outside the "Chetnik" law and apparently the Chetnik leadership did not bother to publicize their liquidations.[182] The broadcasting of the "Z" lists was quickly stopped when the British authorities discovered their sinister purpose, but the Chetniks continued the selective terror practice, singling out their targets one by one. In this way a number of prominent Serbs were assassinated: Vojko Čvrkić, a former member of parliament (who had supposedly organized an assassination attempt against Mihailović) in the summer of 1942; Colonel Miloš Masalović, *chef de cabinet* of General Nedić, in March 1944; Deputy Minister of the Interior Ceka Djordjević in May 1944; and Kosta Pećanac in June 1944.[183]

It will be apparent that the German and Italian occupation authorities would have been able to put a halt to mass terror practiced by the Ustashas and the Chetniks and would not have tolerated it had they not considered it to be to their advantage. Obviously, as long as the various groups in Yugoslavia were busy killing one another, they were not going to form a united front against the occupying powers, and so their terror and counterterror made the task of the Axis in Yugoslavia all the easier. Besides, both Axis powers practiced terror on a large scale themselves in all Yugoslav territories under their control in order to enforce their rule or to retaliate against the rebellious activities of the population against the occupying powers.

The Chetnik manual of December 1942, previously referred to, makes

and a copy of Simić's order of July 10, 1943, to the commander of the Smederevo Corps in the Archives of the Institute of Military History, Belgrade, Chetnik Documents, Reg. No. 36/2, Box 2.

[180] See *The Trial of Draža Mihailović*, pp. 351–56.

[181] Chetnik enemies insisted that the letter "Z" stood for the word *zaklati* (to slaughter), whereas the Chetniks said that it stood for the word *zastrašiti* (to frighten).

[182] For a list of 75 names on the "Z" list broadcast over the BBC and another list of 25 names which were communicated by Mihailović to the government-in-exile but were not broadcast see Radoje L. Knežević, "The Letter Z," pp. 257–62.

[183] *The Trial of Draža Mihailović*, pp. 231, 352. For a report of the execution of Pećanac on June 6, 1944, see RG 226, OSS–File No. L40002.

it clear that the Chetniks were prepared to use terror during the concluding stages of the war and for some time after. One section entitled "The Problem of Revenge" discusses revenge as the sacred duty of the Serbian people against those who had wronged them during the war and occupation. This of course assumed that the Chetniks were going to emerge as the controlling power at the end of the war. The manual opposed disorderly and unsystematic retributions by individuals and groups; it advocated collective retribution, that is, by the state on the basis of proper legislation and carried out according to sentences of special people's courts by special troops. Aside from the Communists, who were of course the Chetniks' chief enemy, the main targets of postwar retribution were to be the Croatian Ustashas and their followers and backers, and a portion of the Croatian intelligentsia (presumably the extreme nationalist and Catholic intelligentsia). The authors of the manual opined that the elimination of these segments of the Croatian population would be as much in the interest of the Croatian people as of the Serbian people and that it would strengthen the unity of the two nations. They also thought that the elimination of these groups would break down any remnants of pro-Austrian sentiment among the Croats and in that way help the Croats to rediscover their national soul. Although the manual does not say specifically how many Croats were to be liquidated, the order of magnitude is stated obliquely as follows: "One should not fear that the retribution executed in this manner would not be complete as far as the number of executed is concerned. If there are not more, then there are at least as many Frankovci and members of a certain intelligentsia, as there were Serbs who were killed." (Chetnik estimates of the Serbs killed by the Ustashas run to between 600,000 and 800,000.) For the punishing of Serbs who as government officials acted against other Serbs special administrative courts were to be established. Finally, the manual says that the legal and orderly administration of the retribution will strengthen rather than diminish the cultural and moral prestige of the Serbian nation, which is an important consideration because the Serbs desire to be the leading nation among the Balkan peoples whether they are combined into a common state or not.[184]

[184] Microcopy No. T-311, Roll 194, Frames 362–65, 370, 372. The quote is from Frame 372.

CHAPTER EIGHT

The Government-in-Exile and Relations with the British

King Peter, all the main leaders of the March 27 revolt, the civilian government ministers, and a number of high government officials flew from Yugoslavia to Greece on April 14 and 15, 1941, and after a stop in Athens to Jerusalem where the British gave them temporary shelter. On June 21, 1941, the king and most of the cabinet arrived in London, adding another member to the already large group of European governments-in-exile resident in the British capital. Several of the ministers, however, and also the Ban of Banovina Croatia, Dr. Ivan Šubašić, went on to the United States or Canada, where some of them were to remain for the better part of the war years. A number of politicians, diplomats, and other government officials were also stationed in Cape Town, South Africa, as a sort of reserve, and in Cairo the exile government established a Yugoslav Supreme Command, with General Bogoljub Ilić, Minister of the Army and Navy, filling also the post of Chief of Staff. The token Yugoslav forces that had succeeded in leaving the country were located in Egypt and in Palestine. The government also named a special representative in the Middle East, Jovan Djonović, and put him in charge "of propaganda and affairs related to contacts with the country."[1]

Governments-in-exile are seldom great successes, and that of the Yugoslavs was less successful than most. Its history falls into four distinct phases. The first lasted from the flight into exile until January 9, 1942, during which the government was headed by General Dušan Simović; it included all the ministers who escaped, and was supported for most of the time by all the officers who participated in the revolt of March 27 and/or went into exile. The second lasted from January 11, 1942, to August 10, 1943, when the cabinet was headed first by Professor Slobodan Jovanović and then briefly by Miloš Trifunović. During most of this phase the cabinet included all the leading party politicians who had

---

[1] Jovan Djonović, "From the Wailing Wall to the Land of the Pharaohs," p. 28.

been ministers in the Simović government; a newcomer, General Mihailović, who although in Yugoslavia was made Minister of the Army, Navy, and Air Force, was its most outstanding member. The third phase lasted from August 10, 1943, to June 1, 1944, under the premiership of Dr. Božidar Purić, a professional diplomat. Apart from Mihailović, who retained his post, all the posts in this cabinet were filled not by politicians but by government officials and technicians. During the fourth phase, which began on June 1, 1944, the cabinet, headed by Dr. Šubašić, was composed mostly of party politicians, but it did not include any exiled politicians representing the Serbian political parties, nor did it include General Mihailović. The chief objective of this cabinet was to come to an agreement with Marshal Tito on fusing the government-in-exile with the Partisan interim government. When this was achieved on March 7, 1945, the government-in-exile went out of existence.

In a substantive sense the history of the Yugoslav government-in-exile falls into two periods: the first, from the flight into exile until June 1944, was the period of Serbian domination and alliance with Mihailović and his Chetniks; the second, the period under Prime Minister Šubašić, was marked by the absence of Serbian party politicians, officers in exile, and General Mihailović, in fact or by influence, and by the working out of an agreement with Marshal Tito on the merging with his interim government. Two other features of the cabinets in exile may be noted here. The first is the national representation. Beginning with the Simović government-in-exile through the government of Prime Minister Trifunović, it became more or less the custom for each of the political parties in exile to be represented in the cabinet by two members. Since the Croats and Slovenes had one political party each, they were always in a minority position, even on occasions when the representatives of the Independent Democratic Party, which had among its members Serbs, Croats, and Slovenes, voted with them, because the Serbians had representatives of four political parties in exile and furthermore on three occasions had non-party persons as Prime Minister (Simović, Jovanović, Purić), and first Ilić and then Mihailović as Minister of the Army, Navy, and Air Force. This practice gave the Serbs from Serbia a tremendous advantage in the control of the government, although the spoils of power during the years of exile were small indeed. During the period from April 15, 1941, to August 10, 1943, three were four cabinets composed of politicians (including here also Simović, Jovanović, Ilić, and Mihailović). If we weigh the post of the Prime Minister with two points and all other members of the cabinet with one, even when they held more than one portfolio, and include the Minister of the Royal Court who, though not a cabinet member, exercised great power (not included when only in an acting position), there were in all sixty-two cabinet positions during these twenty-eight months, of which thirty-six were held by Serbs from Serbia, eleven by Serbs from outside Serbia, eight by Croats, and seven by Slovenes.[2] The post of Chief of Staff of the Supreme Command was also held by a Serb (first Ilić and then Mihailović), and the ambassadors in Washington, London, and Moscow were Serbs from Serbia. The second feature is the pronounced influence of the British government on all major decisions of the cabinet. The influence grew as the war went on, reaching its peak at the time of the Purić and Šubašić cabinets.

Although the March 27 revolt had inspired goodwill for the new Yugoslav government in the Western world, most of that goodwill evaporated as a consequence of the extremely poor showing of the government and the Army in the April War. The government already had to bear the burden of the undistinguished record set by the interwar governments, all of which had been characterized by failure to deal with the national problem, Serbian hegemonism, corruption in public life, poor economic policies especially with regard to the peasantry, and after 1929 royal dictatorship. In the early days of exile, most Serbian members of the cabinet were preoccupied with trying to fasten the blame for the collapse of the army on the Croatian Ustashas, or even on the Croats as a nation. If the Croats could be held responsible for the ignominious collapse of April 1941, and of course assuming that no radical changes would occur during the war, the representatives of the old Serbian ruling groups might look for a return to power in the liberated country under essentially the same conditions as before—namely, Serbian hegemonism. The Croatian representatives in the cabinet had to fight against these allegations and try to prove that only one small group of Croatian extremists, the Ustashas, had been guilty of fifth-column activity in April 1941 and that they alone, as tools of the Germans and Italians, and not the Croatian people, were responsible for the suppression and widespread terror against the Serb population that later followed. Until the advent of the Šubašić cabinet the Croatian ministers sought to make the reaffirmation of the Cvetković-Maček Agreement of August 26, 1939, the basis of the postwar organization of the Yugoslav state, because it was only under that agreement that they could preserve their party's postwar standing and the continuation of the autonomy that was granted to Croatia in August 1939. Neither the Serb nor the Croat politicians in exile, in other words, seemed to comprehend the great significance of the military and political collapse that had occurred in April 1941, let alone the changes in the body politic that were under way in Yugoslavia in the course of the war.

[2] Data on members of the Simović and Jovanović cabinets from Yugoslavia, *Službene novine*, No. 1, Aug. 19, 1941; No. 4, Jan. 16, 1942; and No. 11, Mar. 21, 1943; and of the Trifunović cabinet from the *American Srbobran*, June 29, 1943 (a Pittsburgh newspaper which was and still is the chief organ of the Serbian immigrants in the United States).

With running disagreements among the representatives of various national groups, but especially between the Serbs and Croats, the government was incapable of coming face to face with the national question, which was the most serious problem to be solved in postwar Yugoslavia. Constitutionally, the national question could be solved only by adopting a truly federalist form of organization in which all the South Slav nations (Serbs, Croats, Slovenes, Macedonians, and Montenegrins), as well as the province of Bosnia and Herzegovina, were organized as individual states united in a federal union, and in which the legitimate rights of all national minorities would be safeguarded. This sort of federal organization was abhorrent to the representatives of the Serbian ruling groups in exile as well as to the Chetnik leadership in the country, but rather early both groups came to accept the idea of a federal setup that would include only Serbian, Croatian, and Slovene units, but in which the Croatian and Slovene units would in fact be mere appendages to the Great Serbian unit—all of which would be decided upon only after the war was over, when, they hoped, all power would be concentrated in Chetnik hands. Moreover, the country was supposed to rid itself of all national minorities.

The many problems that the government brought with it into exile were overshadowed and greatly aggravated, however, by those that were created by events in the country after its collapse and occupation. These were the dismemberment of the country and the establishment of the Croatian puppet state, the Ustasha massacres and persecution of the Serbian population in that state, the Chetnik massacres of Croatian and especially Moslem populations, and above all the rise of armed resistance led by two groups, the revolutionary Communist-led Partisans and the pro-government Chetniks, and the civil war between these two groups.

The Ustasha atrocities against the Serbian population gave the Serbian forces in exile new reason for their anti-Croat attitude. When the Croat ministers in the cabinet did not join in repeated denunciations of Ustasha atrocities against the Serbs, the Serb ministers were quick to condemn their reluctance.[3] It did not matter that there was great doubt about the number of reported victims in that the information that was coming out of Yugoslavia was primarily from Serbian, and therefore probably biased, sources, nor that some of the information from Serbia was apparently reaching London with German knowledge and possibly

---

[3] On several occasions the Croatian ministers in the government-in-exile publicly condemned the Ustasha crimes. Vice-Premier Dr. Juraj Krnjević, speaking over the BBC on October 11, 1941, said: "In my first speech over the radio I castigated most decisively the crimes that are being perpetrated by the Ustashas on the innocent Serbs. I said on that occasion, and I am saying it again to the whole world: the Croatian people have nothing in common with these crimes and they castigate these crimes most decisively. Never in its whole history did the Croatian people use such means of policy. These crimes are the works of a handful of individuals educated in Nazi Germany and Fascist Italy, who have come into Croatia on the heels of the German army." See the *American Srbobran*, Oct. 23, 1941.

even German assistance. The best known and most damning example of this kind of information was contained in two memoranda of the Serbian Orthodox Church which church leaders submitted to the successive military commanders in Serbia, the first to General Schröder on July 9, 1941, and an enlarged one to General Danckelmann (often referred to also as the Danckelmann Memorandum) in August, asking them to request the Reich government to intercede on behalf of the Serbian population in the Independent State of Croatia. Copies of these memoranda were brought to London via Istanbul and Cairo in October 1941 by Dr. Miloš Sekulić. Moreover, as stated in Chapter 5, Sekulić wrote for the Yugoslav government-in-exile an extensive report on conditions in Yugoslavia between the April collapse and the end of August, including a discussion of the Chetniks and the Partisans and their respective activities.

The memoranda of the Serbian Orthodox Church were based on information supplied by deportees and refugees from the Croatian puppet state and the second memorandum included a detailed list by counties and even localities of the number of Serbs murdered in the territory of the puppet state and the amount of damage inflicted upon their churches and monasteries. The total number of Serbs killed in the Ustasha state up to early August 1941—that is, in the first four months of the Ustasha regime—was indicated as amounting to the staggering figure of over 180,000.

Numerous people in the country and among the exiles criticized the memoranda for their ingratiating attitude toward the Germans, who were themselves just beginning to use extremely brutal methods to put down the uprising in Serbia. But as I have been told by one of the drafters of the memoranda, this tone was intentional (*Nemcima je trebalo podići*); pleas rather than anger, it was hoped, would bring out magnanimity in the German authorities, and thus intervention in Zagreb.[4] Copies of the memoranda were also made available to the British government and to the Church of England and they were later published in the United States.[5] Since the memoranda implied that the Croatian people as a whole must share part of the responsibility for the Ustasha outrages, they brought an immediate reply from the Croatian ministers in the government-in-exile.

The reply or Commentary prepared on behalf of the Croatian ministers by Dr. Rudolf Bićanić denied collective responsibility of the

---

[4] I am not at liberty to divulge the name of my source. He told me, however, that the final texts of the memoranda were written by Pero Slijepčević, a Serb from Herzegovina, who during the 1930's was a professor on the Faculty of Philosophy at Skopje.

[5] The text of the first memorandum appeared in the *American Srbobran* on November 4, 1941. The full text of the second memorandum was published by the same newspaper in its issues of October 23, 27–30, and November 2, 4–6, 1942. For the effect of these memoranda on the relations among ministers in the cabinet and the sharpening of antagonisms between the Serbian and Croatian immigrants in the United States see Kosanović, pp. 13–32, and Čubrilović, pp. 62–76.

Croatian people for the Ustasha atrocities and put the blame on the Germans, Italians, and Ustashas. It also pointed out numerous inconsistencies in the memoranda, and charged that they had been taken out of Serbia with the knowledge and assistance of the Germans, who sought by this means to further their political and military objectives in Serbia and provoke dissension between the Serbs and Croats in the government-in-exile.[6] There can be no doubt that the memoranda did aggravate dissension in that they were used not only by the Serbs in and near the government as an illustration of the sacrifices by the Serbian people for the Allied cause and of Croatian inhuman behavior, but also by such immigrants' newspapers in the United States as the *American Srbobran* in its reckless anti-Croatian propaganda. This propaganda had the support of Konstantin Fotić, the Yugoslav envoy in Washington, and was most conspicuously carried on by Jovan Dučić, a leading Serbian poet and Yugoslav diplomat who soon after the conquest of Yugoslavia panicked and in July 1941 abruptly abandoned his post as Yugoslav envoy in Madrid and went to live with relatives in Gary, Indiana. In his new activity his well-known Serbian chauvinism was complemented by extreme anti-Croat and anti-Yugoslav views.[7]

But great differences existed not only between the Serbian and Croatian politicians in exile; they also appeared between the two groups of officers in exile (practically all of whom were Serbs)—the group of older officers headed by General Simović, who held the offices of Prime Minister, Minister of the Army and Navy, and the few command posts that the Yugoslavs maintained in exile, and the group of younger officers in London and Cairo who were associated with the former in the March 27 revolt. The younger officers, led by Major Živan L. Knežević, were dissatisfied because their participation in the revolt had not earned them higher ranks or an important voice in the affairs of the government. Živan's older brother Radoje was Minister of the Royal Court, a position which, because of the king's youth and inexperience, was very influential, and partly on this account these younger officers, referred to

---

[6] The text of this Commentary was made available to me by the late Dr. Bićanić himself. Dr. Bićanić, who from 1946 to his death in 1968 was a professor at the University of Zagreb, was in 1941 the vice-governor of the National Bank of Yugoslavia (in exile), but he was active in both political and economic spheres of the government-in-exile and as a skillful writer and an erudite man he was often asked by the Croatian ministers to ghostwrite for them. Soon after this Commentary Dr. Bićanić prepared another memorandum, which became known in government-in-exile circles as the "Bićanić Memorandum," in which were elaborated the causes of the Serbo-Croatian dispute, the principles of the Cvetković-Maček Agreement, and the postwar aims of the Croatian people. For its text with opposing editorial comments see the *American Srbobran*, April 23, 1942.

[7] For a biography of Dučić see Pavlović, *Jovan Dučić*, esp. pp. 293–306. Three series of articles by Dučić, published in the *American Srbobran* as coming from a "Competent Pen" in 1941 and 1942, were issued in 1942 by the Chicago-based Serbian National Defense Council of America as separate pamphlets in Serbo-Croatian, under the titles, *Dr. Vlatko Maček i Jugoslavija, Jugoslovenska ideologija,* and *Federalizam ili centralizam.* The Office of Strategic Services was fully aware of Dučić's activities and under the date of January 19, 1943, prepared a report on his political views and propaganda activities. See RG 226, OSS–File No. 27360.

occasionally as the League of Majors, were successful, as we shall see, in acquiring and together with Radoje Knežević holding for some time great influence in the government-in-exile.

Even at the outset, the Simović government which took over on March 27, 1941, was not in agreement on the basic issue of peace or war with Germany. The manner and swiftness of the country's collapse brought new disagreements to add to the old: there were now disagreements about who had brought on the collapse, about the status of the Cvetko-vić-Maček Agreement, about the assignments of various ministers in exile, who was to fill the post of envoy in London and in Washington, and so on. The reports of the massacres and persecution of the Serbs by the Ustashas in the Independent State of Croatia added a new and explosive point of disagreement, especially between the Serbian and Croatian ministers. Finally, the resistance in the country led by two opposing groups which soon started to fight each other and the international complications which arose from this situation created new and ever growing difficulties for the government.

Personal problems, too, along with matters of policy, began to complicate the situation in the government, centering on the actions of Prime Minister Simović. The Serbian ministers, especially Foreign Minister Ninčić, began accusing Simović of dictatorial tendencies. Simović in response turned more and more for support to the Croatian and Slovene ministers, thus further antagonizing the Serbian ministers, and when he tried to win them back by slighting the Croats, the latter also became his determined opponents. Recently opened documents of the British Foreign Office show that as early as the autumn of 1941 the British were disappointed with the performance of the Yugoslav government-in-exile. According to a student of these documents, the British considered the Simović government "to be weak, divided, difficult, ignorant, obstinate, proud and unaccommodating, and some of these adjectives were certainly thought to be applicable to General Simović himself."[8]

Besides being a target of the younger officers and the politicians, Simović drew the resentment of the Royal Court as well for trying to make cuts in the budgetary appropriations for the maintenance of Queen Dowager Marie and King Peter.[9] But it was the emergence of Colonel Mihailović as a new and rapidly rising star, a man in the field who was receiving the full political and propaganda support of the Western Allies, that precipitated Simović's downfall. Many of the younger and more ambitious putschist officers in exile, who moreover had good contacts with the court, and all Serbian politicians switched their

---

[8] Auty, MS p. 13. For an appraisal of the conditions in the government-in-exile in November 1941 by Mihailo Petrović, a Yugoslav newspaperman then in London, see Marić, p. 434.
[9] Kljaković, in *Politika*, Nov. 13, 1970.

allegiance to Mihailović. In December 1941 King Peter was induced by these enemies of Simović to say that the revolt of March 27 had been carried out by the "younger and middle ranks [of officers] of the Yugoslav army," thus indirectly denying any credit for it either to Simović or to Mirković. Even after Simović had lost his post, his enemies still carried on their attack. They accused him, anonymously, of poor leadership and meek surrender in April 1941, and alleged that General Ilić had shown abject panic in the final days of the war before the government fled the country. They also complained that Simović had not given full support to Mihailović and his gallant warriors who, they firmly believed, were waging a superhuman struggle against the Axis powers in the free mountains of Yugoslavia.[10]

Simović's fall came early in January 1942, clearly by arrangement between the cabinet ministers and the king: all the cabinet members present in London submitted a collective resignation, stating that General Simović was unable to provide the leadership demanded by the seriousness of the times. The king then sent Simović a letter in which he told him that from his conversations with the ministers and with Simović himself it was clear that no further cooperation between them was possible and that he had named Slobodan Jovanović as the new prime minister, in whose cabinet all political groups would be represented.[11]

Simović did what he could to defend his policies in two long memoranda addressed to the king. In these he tried to explain the problems that he was faced with—the complicated disagreements among the various political groups and individuals, the actions and motives of his opponents, and so on. To the contention of the politicians that they actually represented the people and were at the same time both the government and some sort of parliament, he retorted that the politicians did "not represent any expression of people's preference nor have anybody behind them" and therefore could not be considered any kind of parlia-

---

[10] Pavelić, *Kairska afera*, pp. 55–57, gives the text of a report of Major Knežević to Prime Minister Jovanović of February 12, 1942 (after Simović's dismissal), containing an extremely critical appraisal of Simović and his policies. An anonymous pamphlet (which Pavelić ascribes to Knežević) which began to circulate in London at the beginning of April 1942 was even more critical of Simović. For the text of this see *ibid.*, pp. 58–64. A. S. Pavelić, a Yugoslav diplomat, became Šubašić's secretary in December 1941 and apparently held that position until the merger of the government-in-exile with the National Committee of Liberation, the Partisan interim government, on March 7, 1945. In that post he had access to various documents of the government-in-exile after Šubašić became prime minister, some of which he published in the above study and in an article to be cited later.

[11] An insider's history of Simović's dismissal is presented by the chronicler of the changes in the government-in-exile, Kosta St. Pavlović, a career diplomat who held the position of *chef de cabinet* of the prime minister from January 1, 1942, until the end of the Purić government in May 1944. See his article "The Fall of the Simović Cabinet." For an interpretation of the reasons for Simović's dismissal by one of his main antagonists, Radoje L. Knežević, see his "Slobodan Jovanović in Politics," pp. 31–32. See also Pavelić, *Kairska afera, passim*; and Plenča, *Medjunarodni odnosi Jugoslavije*, pp. 90–97. Simović's interpretation of his dismissal is to be found in his memoirs. See Kljaković, in *Politika*, Nov. 12–22, 1970.

ment.[12] The memoranda only made Simović's position worse, and he entered into full political eclipse.[13]

Simović's downfall was followed within two weeks by the removal from their posts of all of his high-ranking supporters in the Yugoslav officer corps in Cairo. The putschist group of officers was now split in two, the older group of leaders (Simović, Mirković, Ilić) being out of power, and the League of Majors and friends being on the threshold of power. (Practically all Air Force officers abroad supported the generals.) In a larger sense, the Serbian group of politicians who were installed by the putschists and especially the younger officers who participated in the revolt no longer needed to maintain the personal symbol of the revolt as a rallying cause because there was now a much more interesting rallying point and symbol—Draža Mihailović. Mihailović was soon to be raised to the highest military rank, highest military offices, and highest political influence and thus to become the chief asset, aside from its legitimacy, of the government-in-exile and of the Serbian groups that controlled it.

THE JOVANOVIĆ CABINET

Simović's successor, Slobodan Jovanović, a former vice-premier, had before the war been president of the politically influential Serbian Cultural Club and as a well-known historian and professor of constitutional law at the University of Belgrade he had frequently been consulted by the Crown and the government on constitutional matters. He was undoubtedly the only intellectually brilliant man among the Yugoslav ministers abroad, but he had no experience in practical politics, and at the age of seventy-three he could hardly have been expected to adjust his views to new realities or, considering his personality, to become a vigorous chief executive.

Jovanović's cabinet, composed of the same members as that of Simović, immediately made two important innovations in the government-in-exile. First, on January 11, 1942, the day of its installation, it appointed

[12] Pavlović, "The Fall of the Simović Cabinet," pp. 73–80.

[13] In May 1943 when the Jovanović cabinet entered its final period of crisis, Simović addressed another long memorandum to the king expressing his political views and his concern about the Yugoslav armed forces in exile and offering his services to the Crown and the country; he was not taken up on his offer. A similar offer made in July to General Petar Živković, the acting Minister of the Army, Navy, and Air Force in the Trifunović cabinet, was also rebuffed. After the arrival of the Partisan military mission in London Simović established contact with it, and on February 20, 1944, he made a declaration over the BBC in support of the Partisans. Toward the end of 1944 and early in 1945 he was one of the candidates for the council of three regents who according to the Tito-Šubašić agreements of the previous months were to exercise royal prerogatives until the peoples of Yugoslavia decided in elections whether they did or did not want the reinstatement of the monarchy, but again his candidacy fell through, reportedly because a 1941 memorandum from him to his Minister of Foreign Affairs in which he advocated continued neutrality of Yugoslavia (see Chapter 2) was brought to the attention of Prime Minister Šubašić. Simović returned to Belgrade in May 1945 and lived there on a pension from the new government until his death in 1962. See Kljaković, in *Politika*, Nov. 24, 1970. For Simović's reaction to being dropped from proposed membership in the regency council see his letter to Prime Minister Šubašić dated Feb. 6, 1945, in *Glasnik SIKD 'Njegoš'*, December 1962, pp. 73–75.

Mihailović (with British blessings) to the cabinet post of Minister of the Army, Navy, and Air Force. Since Mihailović could not participate in cabinet meetings, Jovanović acted for him, and in Yugoslavia Mihailović exercised many powers that normally belonged to the Prime Minister. Second, it established the Military Office of the Prime Minister, with Major (later Lt. Colonel) Živan Knežević, as its chief.

The chief preoccupation of the Jovanović cabinet was to strengthen Mihailović's position both at home and abroad. On January 19 the cabinet advanced him to the rank of divisional general, and on June 17 to general of the army, and on June 10 it named him Chief of Staff of the Supreme Command.[14] These marks of political and military legitimacy were primarily intended to certify his authority at home and enhance his status in dealing with the Allied military commanders in the Middle Eastern theater of war.[15] The exile government further hoped that Mihailović's legitimacy would induce the Axis powers to recognize his forces as the regular Yugoslav army, a continuation of the old Royal Yugoslav Army, rather than as merely a force of francs-tireurs. The Axis never recognized his forces as legitimate, however, maintaining that the Royal Army had vanished with its unconditional surrender in April 1941. On an international plane, the government tried, first, to obtain aid in arms and other military matériel for Mihailović; it asked both the British and the United States governments to furnish a number of aircraft that could be manned by Yugoslav crews and used for delivering supplies to Mihailović as well as for maintaining contact with him. These requests were turned down because of shortages, both of aircraft and of arms. The Yugoslav government was equally unsuccessful in its attempts to induce the British government to order its highest military authorities to send to Mihailović "all requests for sabotage, political propaganda, military intelligence, and anything else that had to be done in Yugoslavia."[16]

Another step undertaken by the Jovanović government to strengthen both its own and General Mihailović's position was to arrange a visit of King Peter to the United States in June 1942. The king was cordially received by President Roosevelt and American officialdom in Washington, and he spent some time touring war industries in the United States. The Chetnik cause was probably then at its zenith of popularity, and both Peter and Fotić wanted to enhance even more the position of General Mihailović. Moreover, in the official meetings Fotić always emphasized the role of the Serbs, pointing out that the Independent State

---

[14] Purković, pp. 4–5. Apart from Mihailović, few officers in the Yugoslav Army in the Homeland were promoted by more than one or two grades in rank because of military regulations which imposed strict limitations on wartime promotions.

[15] Radoje L. Knežević, "The Yugoslav Government and Draža Mihailović," *Poruka*, No. 13, p. 9.

[16] *Ibid.*, pp. 10–11.

of Croatia had declared war on the United States, that the resistance consisted practically only of Serbs, and that massacres of Serbs were being carried out both by Axis powers and by the Croatian Ustashas.[17] The king received with a great display of approval the representatives of the pro-Mihailović Serbian organizations in the United States and praised the writing of the Serbian newspaper the *American Srbobran*, thereby helping to sharpen the bitterness and rivalry among the newspapers and organizations of various South Slav groups in the United States.[18]

King Peter had come with certain specific requests: he wanted the Americans to allow use of their services in establishing direct communications between his government and General Mihailović; he wanted a decision on supplies to be delivered to Mihailović by the United States; he wanted Yugoslav airmen to be trained in the United States. He was successful in getting a lend-lease agreement signed with the U.S. government, and about fifty Yugoslav airmen were brought to the United States for training. In the crucial matters, however, King Peter got nowhere: because Yugoslavia was within the British-controlled theater of operations, the United States refused for a long time to take any action to help Mihailović with supplies or to bypass the British in establishing separate communications with him. It was not until August 1943 that the U.S. government allowed its Navy channels to accept messages from Mihailović to Fotić on a one-way basis, and no action whatever was taken on supplies until October 1943, when the United States turned over to Yugoslavia four Liberator bombers to be attached as a unit to the U.S. Fifteenth Air Force in Italy for general assignments and possibly also (though this never happened) for carrying supplies to Mihailović's Chetniks.[19]

During Jovanović's term of office the League of Majors exercised great powers.[20] Besides Court Minister Radoje Knežević, who was its most influential friend, two of its members, Majors Svetislav Vohoska and Vlastimir Roždjalovski, the aides-de-camp, had a direct line to the king, and Živan Knežević was chief of the most sensitive and most important executive office directly under the prime minister. Further-

---

[17] Fotić, *The War We Lost*, pp. 175–80.

[18] Kosanović, pp. 10, 31.

[19] Fotić, *The War We Lost*, p. 228. According to Fotić some American food supplies intended for Mihailović's forces were held up in Egypt by the British and were never delivered. *Ibid.*, 213–16.

[20] The League of Majors, undoubtedly only an informal group, was evidently formed in the days preceding the revolt as a group of colleagues with similar ideas. In addition to Knežević, generally acknowledged to be the leading member, and Majors Roždjalovski and Vohoska, its other prominent members were Majors Nikola Kosić and Danilo Zobenica, and Lt. Colonel Stojan Zdravković. With the exception of Kosić, who became a prisoner of war and spent his war years in Germany, and Zdravković, who, it seems, was a prisoner of war in Italy, all the others were in exile. In the heat of the Cairo officers' affair General Ilić (Pavelić, *Kairska afera*, p. 21) accused Knežević of starting to form his clique soon after they fled the country and mentioned the following officers as belonging to the group: Lt. Colonels Lozić and Luka Baletić, Majors Milovan Gligorijević and Pavle Novaković, and Captain Kosta Lekić. Undoubtedly, part of the group operated in London and part in Cairo.

more, Radoje and Živan Knežević installed their brother Nikola, a foreign service official, as chief of the Code Department in the Ministry of Foreign Affairs, thus making it possible for them to keep an eye on all communications flowing to and from the government.[21] With such direct means of influence, and taking advantage of Jovanović's disinclination to become embroiled in the constant bickering over policy within his cabinet,[22] the League could make the most of its favored position.

Western diplomats accredited to the Yugoslav government-in-exile grasped the situation at once. Sir George Rendel, British ambassador to the Yugoslav government, though respecting Prime Minister Jovanović as an intellectual, knew that "he was never a man for a crisis," and he was fully aware of the power that rested in Court Minister Radoje Knežević, "who was by no means working in harmony with the government."[23] One of the British wartime intelligence handbooks dealing with Yugoslav personalities had this to say about the Knežević brothers: "They may certainly be regarded as the most powerful forces in the exiled Yugoslav Government and the most instrumental in carrying through its chauvinistic Great Serb and anti-Partisan policy."[24] And the American ambassador to the Yugoslav government Anthony Drexel Biddle, Jr., in a report to Secretary of State Hull on October 19, 1942, listed among "unfavorable factors" facing the government the tendency of some Serb extremists "to exploit . . . the division of opinion among the Cabinet members." Biddle added:

This element is composed of a group of army officers around King Peter. Assuming credit for a large part of the responsibility for the March 27 *coup d'état*, these officers have "muscled in" to the political arena and are attempting to take things into their own hands. This group consists of Major Knezevic, Chief of Prime Minister Jovanovic' War Cabinet and brother of Minister Knezevic, Master of the King's Household, and Major Rozdjalovski and Major Vohoska, both Aides-de-Camp to the King. The officers, moreover, throw their support behind the activities of the Serbian Extremists: the Agrarians under the direction of the Minister of Justice Gavrilovic, and the Radicals under the direction of the Minister of Foreign Affairs, Nincic.[25]

The British skepticism of the Yugoslav government-in-exile that had begun during Simović's tenure was, as it turned out, hardly modified by the change in prime ministers. Jovanović seemed no more able than Simović had been to bring a halt to the constant bickering of his min-

[21] *Ibid.*, pp. 10–11. For the views of a former Yugoslav diplomat on the Knežević brothers and generally on the conditions in the Yugoslav government-in-exile as of May 12, 1943, see RG 226, OSS–File No. 34849.

[22] *FRUS 1942*, III, 829–30.

[23] Rendel, pp. 219, 221.

[24] Allied Force Headquarters, Mediterranean Branch, *Handbook of Jugoslav Personalities.* Entries in this handbook are arranged in alphabetical order, without pagination.

[25] *FRUS 1942*, III, 829.

isters or to achieve progress in defining the war aims and postwar organization of his country. Besides, there were new problems with the officers in Cairo, the activities of the Knežević brothers, and the difficult personality of Foreign Minister Ninčić. The growing British impatience is brought out in a confidential report of the London office of the OSS to the headquarters in Washington of December 17, 1942:

> I may add that, of late, I have been hearing only harsh or sarcastic comments about the Yugoslav Government-in-Exile—and those who utter such comments include the British Ambassador to Yugoslavia, Mr. Rendell [sic], men from the Foreign Office, as well as men from the Ministry of Information. I think that I can say without any risk of overstatement that the relations between the Yugoslav and British Governments are strained and that the Yugoslav Government-in-Exile rates low in the estimation of the British Government (as early as last April Mr. Eden told me in the presence of an American witness that "the Yuogslav Government was making a bad impression in London"). When one adds to that the almost hostile relations between the Soviet and the Yugoslav Governments, one can't help concluding that the inter-allied position of the Yugoslav Government is rather grave. As usually happens in such cases, everybody realizes the situation except the Yugoslav Foreign Minister, Mr. Nincich.[26]

The same report contains information received from an unidentified British Major X (probably Major Peter Boughey of the London SOE headquarters, of whom more will be said presently) who stated: "We receive much information from Yugoslavia. We know that the people have for a long time asked the Yugoslav government to do something, to get together, to send political and military directives. We know that by now the people have written off the Yugoslav Government in London. This Government has become the laughing stock in Yugoslavia." Furthermore, Major X was incensed by the fact that the Yugoslav government had for some time been playing off the United States against the British, making untrue and unfair accusations against the British, and concluded by saying "They think we don't know what they are doing."

Prime Minister Jovanović was from the beginning openly Great Serbian in his views and policies and was therefore opposed by the Croatian and Slovene ministers, especially the Croats led by Dr. Juraj Krnjević, as well as by Ban Šubašić in the United States.[27] These ministers dis-

---

[26] RG 226, OSS–File No. 27302. In June 1942 when King Peter and Foreign Minister Ninčić were in Washington, they also saw, on the 24th, Prime Minister Churchill. In the discussion of the government's handling of the Cairo affair, of which more will be said later, Churchill showed his dissatisfaction and ended his remarks by saying to Ninčić (but obviously addressed to the Yugoslav government as a whole): "You are beginning to tire your friends." Pavelić, *Kairska afera*, p. 95.

[27] For some details on Dr. Krnjević's activities in the various exile cabinets from the Serbian point of view see the series of articles on the fall of successive cabinets by Pavlović, cited in the Bibliography, as well as the article by Radoje L. Knežević, "Slobodan Jovanović in Politics," pp. 38–40. For the Croatian interpretation see Martinović, pp. 66–79. Martinović's analysis convincingly shows that Krnjević was not concerned about Yugoslavia as a whole but only about Croatian interests and the interests of his party as he saw them.

agreed with the Prime Minister on the meaning of the Cvetković-Maček Agreement, on his views about the postwar aims and the future state of Yugoslavia, on the position of Šubašić, the anti-Croat activities of Envoy Fotić, the naming of an ambassador to Great Britain, and so on. Often they were joined in their opposition by the Serb politicians from areas outside Serbia, notably Sava Kosanović, Srdjan Budisavljević, and Branko Čubrilović, and though they were still outnumbered by the Great Serbian forces they constituted a vocal minority that added to the Prime Minister's difficulties. Foreign Minister Ninčić, besides being very intransigent toward the Croats and having doubts about the possibility of reestablishing Yugoslavia as a unified state, seemed unable to get along either with the British or with the Russians.[28] Then in addition to the Partisans and the Russians, the British also started to accuse General Mihailović and his Chetniks of collaborating with the enemy.

The quarrel between Fotić and Šubašić and some of the ministers who were in the United States was becoming particularly embarrassing. Šubašić and the ministers had been sent to the United States in the autumn of 1941 for the purpose of promoting the cause of Yugoslavia with the United States government and helping to mobilize support for Yugoslavia among South Slav immigrant groups there and in Canada. But as Fotić and the Legation began taking a more and more aggressively pro-Serb and pro-Chetnik and anti-Croat position, these ministers, especially Šubašić and Kosanović and others who were strong believers in a federal democratic Yugoslavia, found themselves spending most of their time defending the very idea of Yugoslavia as a state against Great Serbia propaganda emanating mostly from the Yugoslav Legation; and against veiled pro-Ustasha propaganda coming from some Croatian immigrant sources.[29] In an effort to promote the work of the ministers the Yugoslav government in January 1942 established a Yugoslav Information Center in New York, to which the information service from the Legation in Washington was transferred. Bogoljub Jevtić, Minister Without Portfolio and a Yugoslav-oriented Serbian politician, who was the highest ranking member of the group, was over-all head of the Center, but the various departments functioned more or less on their own. An Office of Economic Reconstruction for the study of postwar reconstruction problems was headed by Sava Kosanović, Minister Without Portfolio, who also directed work among the Serbian immigrants. The Slovene office was headed by Franc Snoj, Minister Without Port-

[28] It should be noted as a piece of historical irony that Ninčić's daughter Olga was a member of the Communist Party of Yugoslavia, married to one of the leading Bosnian Communists, Avdo Humo (a Moslem), and served as Tito's secretary throughout the war, even accompanying him to the meeting with Prime Minister Churchill in Naples in August 1944.

[29] See e.g. the text of a speech by Šubašić entitled "Yugoslavia and the World," delivered before an audience of Americans of Yugoslav origin in San Francisco on November 29, 1942, in *Yugoslavia*, Jan. 6, 1943, pp. 5–8, and various memoranda and letters by Kosanović, pp. 16–27 and *passim*.

folio, and an office of the Ban of Croatia, Dr. Šubašić, engaged especially in working with Croatian immigrants. The Press Department proper was headed by Bogdan Raditsa, who had been in charge of the press service at the Legation in Washington and, as a Croat, was much opposed to Fotić's views.[30]

The Information Center began as simply pro-Yugoslav, as opposed to the pro–Great Serbian, pro-Chetnik Legation in Washington. In time Kosanović and some members of the staff, including Raditsa and to some extent Šubašić, became more and more pro-Partisan, because they felt that the Partisans were going to establish a truly Yugoslav state and government.[31] These men were especially critical of Fotić, and in this they had the support of the Croatian ministers and a few others in the cabinet in London. But Fotić (who was elevated to ambassador in September 1942) had strong backing in the cabinet as well as a high personal and professional standing with the United States government, and in September 1943, after Prime Minister Purić took office, Fotić succeeded in getting the Information Center closed and having all the information services returned to Washington. From that time on, with the Embassy strongly pro-Mihailović, Kosanović, along with several professional assistants from the Center, turned their support more and more to Tito and the Partisans and joined forces in their propaganda with Louis Adamic, an American writer of Slovene birth who was a leading member of the United South Slavic Committee in New York and from late in 1942 a staunch and very effective Partisan supporter.[32]

Among the immigrant groups from Yugoslavia opinions about what was happening in the old country changed as the war went on. Most Americans of Serbian origin (much less numerous than Americans of Croatian and Slovene origin) were strongly behind the Chetniks. The Croats were overwhelmingly opposed to the policies of the Ustasha regime, but they were also opposed to the restoration of Serbian hegemonism in Yugoslavia, and the Croatian press consistently denounced the accusations of the *American Srbobran*, which got its inspiration

[30] According to a letter of Professor Raditsa, now at Fairleigh Dickinson University, of April 4, 1972.

[31] For the story of the relationship between Fotić and the Embassy on the one hand and the Šubašić-Kosanović group in the Information Center on the other and how the Chetnik-Partisan conflict reflected itself among Yugoslav exiled politicians and Yugoslav diplomats see Raditsa, pp. 118–22, 138–42. In the second half of 1942 a motion picture entitled *The Četniks* was produced in Hollywood by Twentieth Century–Fox. Dr. Miloš Sekulić was technical adviser. Because of its too open Chetnik bias, most of the functionaries of the Yugoslav Information Center refused to attend its premiere in New York on March 18, 1943. Raditsa's letter of April 4, 1972.

[32] Like all Americans of Serbian and Montenegrin origin and practically all Yugoslav-oriented Americans of Croatian and Slovene descent, Adamic was pro-Mihailović as long as nothing was known in the United States about the true activities of the Chetniks and the existence of the Partisans. His views began to change in the summer of 1942 when the first reports of Chetnik accommodations with the quisling and Axis forces started to appear in the Communist press in England and the United States. He described the process of awakening to the truth in an article entitled "Mikhailovitch: Balkan Mystery Man" in the *Saturday Evening Post*, Dec. 19, 1942. Both the article and Adamic's book *My Native Land*, which was published in late 1943, were for the Partisans propaganda coups of the first magnitude.

from Fotić and Dučić. When it appeared that the conflict among the Yugoslav immigrant groups might be hampering the American war effort, the Office of War Information arranged a meeting of representatives of various South Slav organizations and their press for the purpose of promoting tolerance and cooperation. At that meeting, held in Washington on September 18, 1942, all those present except the representatives of the *American Srbobran* signed a pledge to follow the leadership of the United States government in promoting unity among all Americans without regard to national or racial origin, to further the winning of the war, and to resist all attempts at creating discord among Americans of South Slav origin.[33] The *American Srbobran* continued as before, until on June 10, 1943, Elmer Davis, director of the OWI, found it necessary to admonish the publisher. The key passage in Davis's letter read:

For some time, several branches of the United States goverment, including the Office of War Information, the Department of Justice and the Department of State, have watched with concern the policies of the *American Srbobran*. Its violent attacks upon all peoples of Croatian extraction and their clergy, its strong anti-Catholic attacks, and its veiled efforts to defend the Quisling Neditch, who supported the Nazi regime in Serbia, often have the effect of aiding the Nazi campaigns of intolerance and race hate, and are damaging to the American war effort.[34]

Davis's appeal had no effect. The *American Srbobran* continued its editorial policy as before—becoming, if anything, even more openly intolerant of its enemies as Mihailović's fortunes waned. At the same time, however, Mihailović's support generally in the United States, not only among Croats and Slovenes but among Serbs as well, began to decline as the truth about Chetnik and Partisan activities became known—and much of the support turned to the Partisans.[35]

[33] In a long report to its readers, the *American Srbobran* on September 28, 1942, explained in detail why its three representatives, in spite of their full agreement with the letter and spirit of the resolution, could not sign it: it was evident that the Americans of Serbian descent were loyal to the United States, and they did not deem it necessary to take a new pledge of allegiance; some of their adversaries might accuse them of being separatists, but in their opinion this was an effort to reduce the recognition due the Serbs (in the old country) for their contribution to the Allied cause and at the same time an effort to give a share of that recognition to those who did not deserve it but had in fact declared war on the United States (meaning the Croats); several participants in the conference were representing nobody but themselves; one participant in the conference was spreading Communist views in his paper; and all participants in the conference who signed the resolution did so as individuals and not as representatives of various organizations.

[34] For the full text of the letter see the *American Srbobran*, June 18, 1943, and Kosanović, pp. 56–57. See also *FRUS 1943*, II, 1014–15.

[35] The change in attitude of the American press began on July 26, 1942, when the Communist *Sunday Worker* in New York published a dispatch from Turkey disseminated by the Soviet news agency Inter-Continent Press giving the gist of a resolution passed by a Partisan-sponsored meeting of delegates from Montenegro, Sandjak, and Boka Kotorska held on June 16, which accused Mihailović and his commanders in Montenegro of collaboration with the Italians against the Partisans. After this article, pro-Partisan and anti-Chetnik news began to appear in the liberal and pro-Communist press of the various Slav immigrant groups. Much of this news originated with Radio Free Yugoslavia broadcasting from Tiflis on the basis of reports from Partisan sources in Yugoslavia. The Chetnik spell over the American press was thus broken, and toward the end

In London, Prime Minister Jovanović resorted to a reorganization of the cabinet as a way of ridding it of some ministers, both there and in the United States, who were causing dissension. He did this by resigning, on January 1, 1943, and two days later forming a new cabinet which dropped Foreign Minister Ninčić and all the ministers then in the United States (Čubrilović, Jevtić, Kosanović, Marković, and Snoj).[36] Jovanović himself took the position of Acting Foreign Minister. A provision of the decree setting up Banovina Croatia kept him from dismissing Šubašić: according to Article 8 of the decree, the new Ban had to countersign the ukase on the dismissal of the old Ban, and since under the existing conditions in the government-in-exile a new Ban could not easily be found, the dismissal of the old one was impossible. Fotić also stayed, of course, but the Prime Minister wrote him a firm letter (January 14, 1943), instructing him to try to improve relations among the various national groups of Yugoslav immigrants in the United States and not to side with any of the feuding parties, and telling him and his subordinates that "in an appropriate way they should show themselves as an active element in the promotion of the idea of integrity of the Kingdom of Yugoslavia."[37]

These changes may have helped to clear the air somewhat, but they did little to soften the growing irritation of the British with the Yugoslav government's irresolution and bickering. The accumulating evidence of Chetnik collaboration with the Axis was becoming a sore point of division between the Yugoslav government-in-exile (and General Mihailović) and the British government and military. During the last six months of Jovanović's term relations cooled noticeably. This was the first phase of developments which ultimately led to a total break between Mihailović and his supporters in the government-in-exile and the British. Most importantly for future events, in the last weeks of the Jovanović cabinet the British established what proved to be the beginning of regular liaison with the Partisans and began to send them military aid.[38]

The anti-Simović forces in the government-in-exile and among the younger officers in London had first proved their strength by engineer-

---

of 1942 the *New York Times* and other big city newspapers began printing news about the Partisans, and their reports about Mihailović and his Chetniks became more realistic.

[36] Marić, p. 253.

[37] Radoje L. Knežević, "Slobodan Jovanović in Politics," pp. 36–37. Jovanović discussed this matter with Ambassador Biddle and showed him the directive he sent to Fotić. See *FRUS 1943*, II, 966–68, 971–72, 1020–21.

[38] From the time in mid-February 1943 when the British decided to seek contacts with the Partisans, first with the help of the Russians and, when they refused to cooperate, on their own, the Foreign Office through its spokesmen kept the U.S. government informed about the progress of their undertaking, so that the regular reports to the State Department from Ambassador Biddle (after December 1943 from Ambassador Lincoln MacVeagh), and to some extent from John G. Winant, Ambassador in the United Kingdom, present a secondary record of the changes in the British policy both toward the Chetniks and toward the Partisans. See e.g. various reports in *ibid.*, pp. 974–77, 984–85, 1015–16, 1018, 1023–25.

ing the removal of General Simović from the office of prime minister. Among the leaders in this undertaking were the Knežević brothers, whose long-term objective apparently was to make sure that they had a direct share in power with General Mihailović after the war was over and a Chetnik-dominated state had been organized. That meant, first of all, getting rid of the competition from older officers who had led the coup—that is, General Simović, General Ilić, who was still Chief of Staff of the Supreme Command, and General Mirković, Chief of the Air Force and the principal architect of the revolt.[39] These three generals had the support of most exiled officers of the rank of colonel, practically all the Air Force officers, and many officers of the lower rank; and General Mirković and Colonel Žarko Popović, the Chief of Military Intelligence, and some of the other officers also had excellent connections with the British Military Intelligence and the SOE, with whom they had cooperated closely before and during the March 27 revolt.[40]

The ax fell immediately after the first Jovanović cabinet took office in January 1942. General Mirković was dismissed as Commander of the Air Force by abolishing his command and General Ilić was relieved of his post as Chief of Staff of the Supreme Command. On January 15 Lt. Colonel Miodrag Lozić was named Acting Chief of Staff of the Supreme Command, although he was outranked by four generals, eight colonels, and one lieutenant colonel in exile. The two generals refused to acknowledge the orders, saying that they were unclear and of doubtful authenticity. They appealed to Queen Dowager Marie, accused Major Knežević of having deserted during the war (referring to his leaving his battalion in Palestine and moving to London without proper orders), and declared that their dismissal endangered the order, unity, and prestige of the Yugoslav armed forces in exile and the interests of the resistance in the country. The government took the position that the actions of the generals and some other officers represented open mutiny, but it responded by simply putting General Ilić on the retired list. When General Mirković, as the ranking Yugoslav officer in Egypt, took over Ilić's post as Chief of Staff of the Supreme Command, he, too, was or-

---

[39] The forces the Yugoslavs had in exile were small indeed. According to a report submitted by Prime Minister Jovanović to the cabinet on February 23, 1942, these forces consisted of an incomplete Royal Guards battalion with 505 officers, noncommissioned officers, and enlisted men (the latter mostly Slovenes from the Slovene Littoral who had been in the Italian army and after being captured by the British in Africa had volunteered to join the Yugoslav forces); one submarine, two torpedo boats, and a squadron of hydroplanes with a total of 105 officers, noncommissioned officers, and men; and 346 airplane-crew members and other air force personnel but without planes, the planes that were able to escape to Egypt having been turned over to the British. Counting also the various military missions, there was a total of 1,072 military personnel abroad, comprising 246 officers, 2 military clerks, 327 noncommissioned officers, 25 men from the military bands, and 472 corporals and privates. Radoje L. Knežević, "The Yugoslav Government and Draža Mihailović," *Poruka*, No. 8, p. 7. The plan of the government-in-exile to recruit volunteers from among Yugoslav immigrants in the United States and Canada never got under way.
[40] At his trial General Mihailović claimed that all the officers who came to him from Cairo were opposed to General Mirković and General Simović. *The Trial of Draža Mihailović*, pp. 333–34.

dered into retirement. Mirković stalled for several weeks, while his British friends tried to help smooth the difficulties, but finally on March 4, with British agreement, he gave up the command, and Lt. Colonel Miodrag Lozić, a member of the League of Majors, took over as Acting Chief of Staff of the Supreme Command. The officers who supported Mirković refused to recognize Lozić, however (there were even some threats of force on their part), and in consequence some 430 officers, noncommissioned officers, and enlisted men—almost half of the entire Yugoslav forces—were hurried off to a British detention camp. But when Lozić on the first day in his new post requested the British to remove Mirković and his friends from Cairo and also to deliver into Yugoslav custody Colonel Popović and two other officers for trial by courts martial for mutiny—which in time of war carried death penalty—the British ordered him and his staff to vacate their posts. The same day, March 5, despite protests on the part of the Yugoslav envoy in Cairo, the British, clearly annoyed by the whole mess, named one of their own officers, the Commander of the British Troops in Egypt, Lt. General R. G. W. H. Stone, as Acting Chief of Staff of the Yugoslav Supreme Command.[41]

Since mismanagement of the Cairo situation had brought the British openly into action, it was also necessary to achieve the resolution with their cooperation. For that task the Yugoslav government dispatched to Cairo Colonel Miodrag Rakić. The British tried first to bring about a rehabilitation and reinstatement of General Mirković. When this failed, they agreed to take him and his followers into the British forces with no loss of rank. The British were also willing to turn over the post of Acting Chief of Staff of the Supreme Command to Colonel Rakić on the condition that he should not relinquish it to Lt. Colonel Lozić. These proposals were put into effect on May 7. In June the government transferred the Supreme Command to Yugoslavia by appointing General Mihailović as Chief of Staff, and in Cairo a new Command of the Yugoslav Forces in the Middle East was established under Colonel Rakić. The following November 19, a protocol was signed by the representatives of the two governments which provided that General Mirković and some of his closest friends would be taken over into the British forces for service away from the Middle East and the Balkans and that another group of officers would be given an opportunity to join the British forces, but if they refused they would not be accepted

[41] The best and most complete study of this affair, known in Yugoslav writings as the Scandal of Cairo, is the previously cited book by Pavelić, *Kairska afera*. It contains a great number of basic documents and the testimonies of some of the participants. See also Fotić, *The War We Lost*, pp. 166–67, and Rendel, pp. 214–15.

Radoje L. Knežević does not mention the Scandal of Cairo in his series of articles in *Poruka* on the relations between the government-in-exile and General Mihailović, and in his long obituary of Slobodan Jovanović, in *Poruka*, No. 53–54 (January–March 1959), he mentions it but once (p. 33) and commends Jovanović for the manner in which he handled this and several other matters. For Yugoslav Communist views on the Scandal of Cairo see Plenča, *Medjunarodni odnosi Jugoslavije*, pp. 118–23, and Marić, pp. 191–96, 211–14.

back into the Yugoslav forces. Neither of these two groups would be allowed to return to Yugoslavia without the permission of the Yugoslav government. Other officers, noncommissioned officers, and men who supported General Mirković, and who on July 2, 1942, had been organized as the British 244th Temporary Battalion of the King's Own Royal Regiment, were to be given the choice of continuing in the British service or returning without penalty under the Yugoslav flag. A large number of these men returned to the Yugoslav flag and together with other Yugoslav soldiers made up the battalion of Yugoslav Royal Guards, which numbered in January 1943 some 850 men. This was in fact the bulk of the royal military forces in exile and later most of them decided to join Tito's National Liberation Army.[42]

The resolution of the whole matter represented a partial and temporary victory for the Jovanović cabinet and the League of Majors over the pro-Simović officers, but it was a costly victory in that it damaged the government's standing with the Western Allies and lost potential aid for Mihailović. In fact, it could be said that the so-called Scandal of Cairo was the forerunner of the much greater troubles that later befell the Great Serbian forces in exile and contributed substantially to the downfall of General Mihailović.[43]

BRITISH ACTIVITY REGARDING YUGOSLAVIA, 1941–1942

From the time when first reports about the armed uprising in Yugoslavia began reaching London in the summer of 1941, the Yugoslav government was in close touch with the British authorities. Since these early reports indicated that the resistance was under Communist leadership, Prime Minister Simović's government reacted in a negative fashion, castigating the instigators, and saying that the uprising was premature and that when the time came the government would give the signal. That time would be, of course, whenever for purposes of British strategy in the Mediterranean a general uprising in Yugoslavia was thought appropriate. Nonetheless, when it appeared that an uprising was indeed under way, the British, as the statement of Hugh Dalton quoted in Chapter 5 indicates, decided that a certain amount of sabotage and activity was a good thing, both as a way of keeping the enemy from withdrawing its forces from the country and as a way of develop-

---

[42] Pavelić, *Kairska afera*, pp. 91–113. It may be noted that after the signature of the November 19 protocol certain changes in British policy with respect to Yugoslav affairs began to take place. Thus, for example, the BBC began to mention the actions of the Partisans in its broadcasts, and broadcasts of news in Serbo-Croatian over the BBC which were fully under the control of the Yugoslav government were terminated a few months later.

[43] Rendel, p. 215, gives the impression that it was chiefly the Scandal of Cairo and its consequences that led the British to abandon the Serbian-controlled government-in-exile, and with it also General Mihailović and his Chetniks, and to embrace the Partisans. A much more important cause, however, was the evidence of Chetnik collaboration with the enemy, to which was added Mihailović's refusal to follow British instructions.

ing a resistance force that would be ready when the British gave the signal.

It was the success of the Partisans as the leaders of the uprising that first drew the attention of the Great Powers, and that success soon brought the Serbian nationalist forces, inclined toward the government-in-exile and the Allies, into the action, although this went against their better judgment. The appearance of the Serbian nationalists as a resistance force altered the stand of the British and the government-in-exile, for obviously they could not let them down under the existing circumstances. Thus, when the nationalist forces succeeded in establishing contact with the British at Malta and through them with the government-in-exile, the British realized that they could use the revolt in Yugoslavia as an instrument of psychological warfare against the Axis, since it proved that Hitler was not, after all, the complete master of occupied Europe that he boasted of being. The British resolve to stand behind the uprising in Yugoslavia was also conveyed in a message of the Chiefs of Staff to the Commander in Chief Middle East of October 15, 1941, which said: "From our point of view the revolt is premature, but the patriots have thrown their caps over the fence and must be supported by all means."[44]

As the uneasy and partial cooperation between the Chetniks and the Partisans during September and most of October began to wear thin, Mihailović's appeals for arms from the British grew more insistent, and thus also the pleading of the government-in-exile to the British. On October 13 King Peter submitted three aides-mémoire on the Yugoslav situation to Prime Minister Churchill. A week later Simović, in response to an urgent appeal from Mihailović, addressed a follow-up letter to Churchill asking specifically for "120 Light Machine Guns, 300 Bren Guns, 72 Trench Mortars, 8–10,000 Hand Grenades," as well as surgical supplies for about ten thousand wounded. He stated that the number of guerrillas in Yugoslavia was eighty to one hundred thousand.[45]

Churchill's reply to Simović of October 26 explained that the question of assistance to Yugoslavia had been examined and no aid could be sent from England, but that British military authorities in the Middle East had been instructed to send aid as soon as possible and to the greatest extent possible; he assured Simović that "authorities in the Middle East are already in touch with Serbian patriots."[46] On October 31 General Sir John G. Dill, Chief of the Imperial General Staff, notified Simović that the authorities in the Middle East would parachute some supplies to Yugoslavia within a very short time and that possibly some

---

[44] As quoted in Howard, *Grand Strategy*, IV, 386.
[45] Archives of the Institute of Military History, Belgrade, Government-in-Exile Documents, Reg. No. 32/6-2, Box 180a.
[46] *Ibid.*, Reg. No. 32/6-3, Box 180a.

would be sent by submarine; that same day Simović conveyed to Churchill, Eden, and Dill another message from Mihailović appealing for speedy help while the weather was still fine.[47]

In the meantime two things had taken place: first, the field liaison officer, Captain Hudson, had arrived at Mihailović's headquarters on October 25, and though handicapped by not having his own radio transmitter, had used Mihailović's transmitter to inform his superiors of some of his observations in the field; and second, fighting had broken out between the Chetniks and the Partisans. As we have already seen in Chapter 5, Hudson's original instructions had been to work with all the groups in Yugoslavia that were resisting the enemy. The British decision to throw their full support behind Mihailović—with whom they had established contact after Hudson's departure—put him in the unenviable position of trying to mediate between the Partisans and a stubborn Mihailović who refused to cooperate, and who insisted that he was the only legitimate representative of the government and was entitled to sole command under which all other groups should submit. Mihailović also seems to have resented the way in which Hudson, a mere British captain, was presuming to give him advice on Yugoslav affairs. After two weeks of frustrating attempts to mediate between the Chetniks and the Partisans, Hudson informed his superiors (on November 13) that he was going to the Partisan headquarters at Užice and would make further attempts at mediation there and report from there directly.

In London on November 13 Simović informed Eden of a message from Mihailović apprising him as follows: "The Communists have attacked us, and forced us to fight at the same time against Germans, Communists, Ustashas, and other factions." This message was, of course, a total distortion of the truth, since it was Mihailović who had attacked the Communist-led Partisans and not the other way round, and there were no Ustashas present in Serbia. Simović also reported Hudson's impressions to the effect that the Communists were also opposed to the Axis, that Montenegro was organized by the Partisans, that Chetnik leaders were openly saying that they preferred to collaborate with Nedić rather than with the Communists, and that many Communists would switch to the Chetniks if Mihailović received the aid that had been promised him. Simović said that he had approached the Soviet government to influence the Partisans to help Mihailović against the Germans and now asked the British government to support his efforts with the Soviet government. This the British agreed to do, by intervening with the Soviet authorities to influence the Partisans toward cooperation with Mihailović.[48]

[47] *Ibid.*, Reg. No. 32/6–5, 6–6, Box 180a.
[48] *Ibid.*, Reg. No. 32/6–8, 6–9, 6–10, Box 180a.

Within five days the British had misgivings, as we can see from a letter addressed to Simović by Sir Alexander Cadogan, the British Permanent Under Secretary for Foreign Affairs, on November 18. The letter begins judiciously by saying, "His Majesty's Government wish to do all in their power to heal the breach which has occurred between followers of Colonel Mihailović and the Communist elements," but it goes on to refer to a message from Mihailović from which it appears "that he intends to liquidate the Communists when the necessary arms are available." Sir Alexander seems to be implying here that Mihailović wanted arms to use not against the Germans but against the Partisans. The letter continues: "Retaliatory measures are clearly to be avoided if possible, and you may think it desirable to issue instructions to Colonel Mihailovic in this sense"; this is a reference to a message of Mihailović of November 12 by way of Malta in which he said that "he would be able to liquidate the Communists" as soon as he got the arms he requested.[49] The obvious inference from Sir Alexander's letter is that the British were fully aware of the incipient civil war between the Chetniks and the Partisans and knew that any arms sent to Mihailović without prior agreement having been reached between the two groups would surely be used by the Chetniks against the Partisans.[50] Certainly if the strife continued, the effectiveness of both groups against the Axis would be reduced, if not ended completely, and British relations with the Soviet Union would no doubt be complicated; and, as well, the already difficult political situation in Yugoslavia, both present and for the future, would be worsened. The British were therefore pleased to learn that "Colonel Mihailovic has sent a message which seems to show that he has composed his quarrel with the Partisans"—an erroneous report which both the Yugoslav government and the British government interpreted to mean that the Partisans had accepted Mihailović's command.[51] In the same letter Eden wrote Simović that they had con-

[49] *Ibid.*, Reg. No. 32/6–10, Box 180a; Kljaković, "Great Britain, the Soviet Union, and the Uprising in Yugoslavia in 1941," p. 88, quoting from the unregistered radiograms of Mihailović by way of Malta during the period September–December 1941 in the Archives of the Federal Secretariat of Internal Affairs. This article is the best documented and clearest presentation of the somewhat involved relations between the two Great Powers and Yugoslavia during the second half of 1941.

[50] Deakin, *The Embattled Mountain*, p. 139, says that Mihailović's accusations that the Partisans had provoked armed clashes with the Chetniks should have revealed to the British and Yugoslav governments that "any supplies of arms, under such conditions, to Mihailović would be used in civil strife. There is no evidence that this point of critical importance for the future was immediately appreciated, at least by the British." On the contrary: Mihailović's message of November 12 and the above quotation from Sir Alexander's letter prove that the British were indeed fully aware of this contingency. If the British authorities had paid more attention to Mihailović's message of November 12 and Hudson's messages of November 13 and 20, they might have been more cautious.

[51] Eden's letter to Simović of November 28 in Archives of the Institute of Military History, Belgrade, Government-in-Exile Documents, Reg. No. 32/6–11, Box 180a, was referring to a message of Mihailović of November 22, in which he said: "I have done all I could on my part and have succeeded in stopping fratricidal struggle caused by the Communists. In the fights up to now against the Communists and the Germans my detachments had used up almost all ammuni-

gratulated Mihailović on the new agreement, "But we are making it clear that the continuance of our help will be dependent on the maintenance of a united front under his leadership."[52] The same spirit of a united front under the "military and political leadership of Colonel Mihailović" which should "not only be maintained but also strengthened" was expressed by Simović in his letter to Eden of December 3.[53] It was sometime between December 7 and 10 that Hudson returned from the Partisans to the area of Ravna Gora, as described in Chapter 5, to find Mihailović refusing to talk with him or to let him use his radio transmitter and radio operator. With this Hudson was cut off from his superiors, and he separated from Mihailović. This ended the first phase in British relations with the two Yugoslav leaders—with Mihailović on the way of being built up by Yugoslav and British propaganda into an international hero, and Tito for the time being officially discounted.

For the next four or five months Mihailović and Hudson were not in contact. They hid and moved in various parts of Serbia separately, and Hudson's superiors heard nothing from him. Sometime in April 1942 Hudson established contact with Ostojić and through him with Mihailović. In a postscript to a report of April 26 to Mihailović, Ostojić wrote: "Marko [Hudson] is with me. I explained to him the principles of our work. He is now our great friend and has recognized his mistakes. At my suggestion, Radovan gave him a severe reprimand. He is now soft as cotton and does not get in our way."[54]

Alarmed at Hudson's silence, the SOE lost no time in dispatching other missions to find out what had gone wrong and to get information on the Chetnik resistance. The first mission, a two-man team using the code name "Henna," was landed by submarine on January 27, 1942, on the eastern shore of the island of Mljet.[55] Its objective was Split. A

---

tion. I am making the greatest efforts to unite all popular forces and to reorganize for a decisive fight against the Germans." See Radoje L. Knežević, "The Yugoslav Government and Draža Mihailović," *Poruka*, No. 8, p. 13. See also Kljaković, in *Politika*, Nov. 7, 1970. Partly because of this report, following the Chetnik-Partisan conferences of November 18 to 20, Mihailović was advanced to the rank of brigadier general.

[52] Government-in-Exile Documents, Reg. No. 32/6–11, Box 180a. Even after they lost contact with Hudson and Mihailović, the British continued to urge over the BBC a peaceful settlement of differences between the Chetniks and the Partisans, but the Chetnik Command on January 16, 1942, ordered that this British endeavor should be explained away in oral propaganda as a Chetnik gambit to entrap and liquidate the Communists. On the same day Mihailović issued an order to his commanders stating that "the Communist danger is one of the worst. These evildoers and killers of our people *should be annihilated* without mercy." Marjanović, "Contributions," p. 226.

[53] Archives of the Institute of Military History, Belgrade, Government-in-Exile Documents, Reg. No. 32/6–13, Box 180a.

[54] Quoted from a copy of this report in *ibid.*, Chetnik Documents, Reg. No. 7/2, Box 1. According to Colonel Kljaković, "Radovan" was Ronald Houghton Jones, an Australian officer who was captured in Greece by the Germans in the spring of 1941, jumped the train while going through Serbia as a prisoner of war, and later joined the Chetniks. He was in Herzegovina at the time of Mihailović's meeting with *vojvoda* Trifunović-Birčanin and others at Avtovac on July 22–23, 1942, and was captured by the Italians on July 25. Microcopy No. T-821, Roll 252, Frames 297–98.

[55] All information on code names of these missions is from Deakin, *The Embattled Mountain*, p. 155.

Yugoslav reserve lieutenant, Stanislav Rapotec, was in charge, and he was accompanied by a radio operator, Stjepan Šinko (both men were Slovenes). Rapotec arrived at Split in the first days of March and established contact with Trifunović-Birčanin, the Chetnik commander for southwestern Yugoslavia and chief liaison man between the Italian Second Army and the Chetniks. He failed to establish contact with Mihailović or to find out what had happened to Hudson. Later he moved inward, to Zagreb and Ljubljana, and then made his way out of the country and arrived in July in Istanbul.[56]

On February 4, a week after mission Henna had landed, a second mission, with the code name "Hydra," was landed on the Montenegrin coast by the same submarine. The mission consisted of Major Terence Atherton, a former British newspaperman who before the war had lived and worked for about a decade in Belgrade and was married to a Bosnian Moslem girl; a radio operator, Sergeant Patrick O'Donovan; and a Yugoslav officer, Captain Radoje Nedeljković. Atherton was carrying with him a large sum of money: one million Italian lire and about two thousand British gold sovereigns. As had happened with the Hudson party the previous September, Atherton and his group encountered a contingent of Partisans soon after landing, and were taken by them to their Montenegrin headquarters. Later under an escort, but apparently without the radio set which was supposed to be sent after them, they were taken to the Partisan Supreme Headquarters at Foča in southeastern Bosnia. There Atherton associated with the already mentioned General Ljubo Novaković (Chapter 5, p. 129), who was living there under Partisan surveillance. Around April 15, Atherton and his companions together with General Novaković secretly left Foča, presumably with the intention of reaching Chetnik headquarters. Atherton and O'Donovan on April 22 separated from Novaković and Nedeljković and apparently set out for Serbia in search of Mihailović and Hudson, escorted by Spasoje Dakić, a bandit who seems to have had some contacts with the Chetniks. They were never heard of again. The Chetniks tried to place the responsibility for Atherton's disappearance on the Partisans, but according to later investigations in the field by Hudson and Bailey, Atherton and O'Donovan were murdered and robbed by Dakić near the village of Tatarevina not far from Foča. Atherton never made contact with Mihailović or Hudson, and his superiors never received any radio messages from him.[57]

The third mission sent by the SOE, under the code name "Disclaim,"

---

[56] On Rapotec's trip and later report see Kljaković, "Dalmatia in Perception and Action of the Government-in-Exile and the Western Allies During 1941–1942," MS pp. 14–15. Šinko reportedly joined the forces of the Reverend Djujić, the Chetnik leader in northern Dalmatia.

[57] Deakin, *The Embattled Mountain*, pp. 155–56, 162–77, esp. p. 174. See also Leković, "The Sojourn of the British Military Mission in the Liberated Territory of Montenegro and Southeastern Bosnia," esp. pp. 324–28.

and consisting of one British officer, Major Cavan Eliot, a British radio operator, and two Yugoslav officers, was parachuted "blind" into the area of Romanija Mountain, east of Sarajevo, on February 5. All four men were caught soon after landing by Croatian quisling forces and handed over to the Germans.[58]

From Deakin's book it would appear that in the course of 1942 the SOE made several other attempts to slip men into Yugoslavia, by sea or air, but with a singular lack of success until Christmas night, when Colonel S. W. Bailey, an important SOE official, was parachuted near Mihailović's headquarters in Montenegro. (Deakin mentions, however, a British signal group led by Lieutenant P. H. A. Lofts which was successfully dropped in August near Mihailović's headquarters in Montenegro.)[59] Deakin may be correct in describing the SOE attempts as failures, but he overlooks other British intelligence services which sent in teams of their own, both Yugoslav military personnel and British operatives, during 1942. A former Yugoslav officer, Major Nedjeljko Plećaš, who himself was parachuted by the British into Yugoslavia in September 1942, has listed nine groups, none of which is mentioned by Deakin, as having been dropped into Yugoslavia between April and September 1942 (some successfully, some not).[60] It would be reasonable to assume that from these groups, and surely also from other sources at their disposal, the British received at least a certain amount of intelligence from the Yugoslav territory, including intelligence pertaining to Chetnik activity. Deakin's description of the situation, "the curtain was impenetrable, the picture dark," is a rather vivid exaggeration.[61] Indeed, the very makeup of mission "Typical" which on the night of May 27, 1943, was dropped in the neighborhood of Tito's headquarters in Montenegro indicated that at least two British services were operating in Yugoslavia, since Captain Deakin was representing the SOE and Captain William F. Stuart was representing the Military Intelligence. Both of them were under orders from General Headquarters Middle East but each had his own assistant and his own radio operator,[62] obviously so that they could make their reports independently to their own superiors. But it is true enough that for about half a year—that is, from November 28, 1941, when he went to Užice to sometime in early June 1942—the British had no contact with Hudson. Likewise from the last message to the government-in-exile on December 5 until January 6 there was no radio contact with Mihailović. Between June and August 1942 Hudson sent some messages over Mihailović's transmitter, and

[58] Deakin, *The Embattled Mountain*, pp. 155, 158.
[59] *Ibid.*, p. 150.
[60] Plećaš, pp. 40–44.
[61] Deakin, *The Embattled Mountain*, p. 177.
[62] *Ibid.*, pp. 215–17.

then starting in August he used the radio transmitter of Lieutenant Lofts.[63]

During the first six months of 1942 especially, when the two resistance movements in some parts of Yugoslavia were still in the process of polarization, the British were mainly interested in finding out what the Chetniks were doing and trying to help them with some arms and especially with propaganda. Naturally, the Partisans were somewhat uneasy about having occasional British groups passing through their territory, and uneasy too when they heard about other groups of British and Yugoslav officers parachuted into Chetnik territory or learned of the appearance of new Chetnik detachments under strongly pro-British leaders. They had no desire to make trouble for the British missions, partly because they were British but also because they did not want to be a cause of difficulties between the Russians and the British, but they were uncertain how far they should cooperate. After hearing of the arrival of the Atherton mission at the Partisan headquarters in Montenegro, for example, Tito asked the Comintern how to handle these British missions and was advised to receive British officers, to be careful (about what he told them?) and to find out what they really were after.[64] On the other hand, the British did not want to antagonize the U.S.S.R. by being openly against the National Liberation movement which they assumed enjoyed Soviet sympathies.

THE COLLABORATION ISSUE

In addition to information supplied by their own services in Yugoslavia, the British gleaned a certain amount of information from the British-controlled channels of communications linking the Yugoslav government-in-exile and Yugoslav sources abroad, which communicated to the government what information they received from the country. The chief Yugoslav lines of information to London in addition to Mihailović were the Yugoslav legations in the Vatican and in Switzerland, and diplomatic and intelligence channels in the Middle East, and later also the legation in Madrid (which had its informants in the Madrid legation of the puppet state of Croatia.)[65] It would appear that in the course of 1942 the British government and to a large extent the Yugoslav govern-

[63] *Ibid.*, p. 154. At the Oxford conference Hudson himself contradicted Deakin's statement that Hudson was not in touch with his superiors for almost a year after the end of 1941, by saying that from about July or August 1942 he was able to inform them about the Montenegrin Chetnik leaders. See Hudson, pp. 11–12. Moreover, according to Bailey's report of April 1944, the British had from July to September 1942 two Yugoslavs (Captains "Robertson" and Vemić) at Mihailović's headquarters serving as their independent agents who had "direct cypher communication with Cairo." F.O. 371/44282, R21295/11/92, Appendix 3, pp. 2–3.

[64] *Zbornik DNOR*, Tome II, Vol. 2, pp. 441–42, and Vol. 3, p. 42. Deakin (*The Embattled Mountain*, pp. 155–72), considers this problem together with the movements and disappearance of Atherton and his companion O'Donovan. See especially Tito's confidential letter to the Central Committee of the Communist Party of Croatia of April 8, 1942, *ibid.*, pp. 169–71.

[65] Kljaković, "Dalmatia in Perception and Action," MS pp. 7–20.

ment-in-exile as well acquired a pretty clear picture of what was going on in Yugoslav territory, including the fact that the Mihailović Chetniks were engaged in anti-Partisan collaboration with the Italians in the Italian-controlled areas, with the Nedić forces in Serbia, and with some of the forces of the Independent State of Croatia in German-controlled parts of Bosnia, and thus indirectly with the Germans, and that it was the Partisans who were really fighting the Axis and the quisling forces. But the British, even with this knowledge, still continued to send Mihailović some aid and to help the Chetnik cause by means of propaganda and exclusive recognition as a resistance group in Yugoslavia, and for some time they did not protest the Chetnik behavior to the government-in-exile. By the autumn of 1942, however, British strategy in the Mediterranean had reached the point where Mihailović had to demonstrate his goodwill and effectiveness. The emerging British view was that Mihailović must somehow be persuaded, through the government-in-exile and directly, to make an about-face: to cease collaborating with the Italians and the quisling regimes, to stop fighting the Partisans, and to start fighting the Axis forces on his own or preferably together with the Partisans.

To achieve such a shift was undoubtedly the purpose of Bailey's mission to Mihailović in December 1942. Also, on December 20 Sir Orme Sargent, Deputy Under Secretary in the Foreign Office, broached the subject to the Yugoslav Assistant Foreign Minister Vladimir Milanović, and informed him that the Communists were "the only ones now fighting in Yugoslavia, that Mihailović had stopped fighting in October 1941, which makes it difficult to fight Soviet propaganda against Mihailović."[66]

The issue was even more bluntly set forth by Major Peter Boughey to Major Živan Knežević, the chief of the Military Office of the Prime Minister, on December 29. Boughey was a member of the Masterson Service, the SOE unit that was responsible for contacts with and aid to Mihailović. When he visited Knežević to discuss the delivery of copies of the official gazette (*Službene novine*) to Yugoslavia and the request of King Peter to Prime Minister Churchill of December 9 for additional arms and food for Mihailović, he told Knežević frankly that as a member of the Masterson Service he had been assigned to give the opinion that served as basis for the answer to King Peter's request, which was to the effect that delivery of arms to Mihailović for fighting the Partisans was out of the question, because the Partisans were the only ones who were

[66] Milanović went to the Foreign Office to ask British help in doing something to answer the broadcasts of the Partisan radio station Free Yugoslavia from the Soviet Union. The Yugoslav government wanted a strong favorable statement on the Chetniks which they could circulate abroad and broadcast to Yugoslavia over radio station Karadjordje in Jerusalem. This station, which began broadcasting on November 27, 1942, was manned by Yugoslav citizens but was under tight British supervision. Its broadcasts had a purely Chetnik slant, and eventually it fell victim to the disagreements between the British and the Chetniks. Its activities were suspended by British order on March 27, 1943. See Petković, "The Chetnik Radio Station Karadjordje."

fighting the Axis.[67] Boughey also informed Knežević that the British "had reliable information from teams in Yugoslavia not stationed with General Mihailović" according to which (so Knežević noted) certain things were known:

General Mihailović openly cooperates with the Italians, and his detachments, fully armed, are transported in Italian lorries to western Bosnia, to fight against Partisans, and this in cooperation with Italian troops. He said that at that very moment a battle was being waged north of Mostar, in which one of Draža's detachments of 2,400 men from Montenegro was fighting with the Italians, against the Partisans.

Major Boughey said: "Draža Mihailović is a quisling, just like Nedić, for Nedić is cooperating with the Germans and Draža with the Italians."

Major Boughey was of the candid opinion that Mihailović's detachments were not fighting at all at that time, and that the British had to have Mihailović start fighting immediately, not after the British had landed in the Balkans; by then it would be too late, and it would make no difference to the British who joined them—Nedić, Antonescu (of Romania), or Mihailović. In fact, he suggested, Mihailović should perhaps be removed from his position and replaced by someone else. In any event, before the British decided whether to aid General Mihailović or not he should be given instructions by the government-in-exile regarding its views on Yugoslavia and its (future) organization, because Mihailović was fighting for "Great Serbia," and he ought to be given precise instructions on what his relations should be toward the Partisans and the occupying powers. Knežević's remarks at the conclusion of this conversation were a play on the theme that the Chetniks were indispensable to the British: "Do you British want a Bolshevik Yugoslavia and civil war, or do you want a democratic Yugoslavia and law and order? If you want the latter, you must support the Yugoslav government and General Mihailović."

Boughey was not merely talking tough. In the days since Colonel Bailey's arrival at Mihailović's headquarters, both Bailey and Hudson had been transmitting information freely by radio to their superiors and in a series of over two hundred telegrams had given ample confirmation of widespread collaboration of the Chetniks with the Italians, with Nedić, and to a certain extent with the Croatian quisling authorities, and indirectly with the Germans.[68] The telegrams greatly impressed

[67] Full texts of the notes made by Milanović and Major Knežević on their talks with Sargent and Boughey (including the parts quoted here) were published in the final installment of Radoje L. Knežević's article, "The Yugoslav Government and Draža Mihailović," *Poruka*, No. 24, pp. 11–13. Excerpts from both notes were first published in *The Trial of Draža Mihailović*, pp. 464–65, 467–68. For the text of King Peter's request, see Živan L. Knežević, *Why the Allies Abandoned*, Part 2, pp. 23–24. For the efforts of the government-in-exile to obtain supplies for Mihailović, see also Plenča, *Medjunarodni odnosi Jugoslavije*, pp. 128–30, 133–34.

[68] Until August 1943 communications between Mihailović and the government-in-exile in London were carried on exclusively through British military channels, but the way in which these

the British military and political authorities and resulted in an immediate reexamination of Great Britain's relations with Mihailović and,
eventually, in a shift in British policy and recognition of the Partisans.[69]
In this shift of policy a major contribution was made by the persistent
reports from the Partisan radio station Free Yugoslavia operating from
the Soviet Union and news from Yugoslavia coming through newspapers
and other channels in Sweden, Switzerland, and Turkey to the effect that
the Chetniks were collaborating and the Partisans fighting—as indeed
the British were able to confirm through their own intelligence sources.

After these discussions among the lesser British and Yugoslav officials
regarding Mihailović and his policies, Prime Minister Jovanović on December 31 took up the matter with British Ambassador Rendel, and the
following day got from him the assurance that the Foreign Office still
had full confidence both in the Yugoslav government and in Mihailović; he was also informed about Colonel Bailey's mission at Mihailović's
headquarters.[70] That same day Jovanović resigned. On January 3 he
organized his second cabinet, but since Mihailović was retained as Minister of the Army, Navy, and Air Force, British-Yugoslav relations remained strained, and they were soon put under new stress by an incident
that occurred on February 28, 1943, at the village of Gornje Lipovo in
Montenegro. There, at a private celebration, Mihailović, in a somewhat
inebriated state, made a speech in which he expressed many views objectionable to the British. Bailey reported details of the speech to Cairo
and London, and on March 29 Churchill, acting for the absent Foreign
Secretary Eden, sent Jovanović a sharp note.[71]

His Majesty's Government, Churchill told Jovanović, was "becoming
seriously disturbed at recent developments in Yugoslav affairs and increasingly apprehensive in regard to the future unless steps are taken to

communications were managed is still a matter of much discussion among Chetnik writers in the
Western world. Chetnik writers maintain that these communications were fully under British
control and that the British often delayed, garbled, mutilated, or failed to deliver messages in
both directions, and in that way were infringing on the sovereign rights of an Allied power. The
Yugoslavs considered this situation an outright affront. The problem of communications therefore
caused a great deal of trouble between the government-in-exile and Mihailović on the one hand
and the British on the other. Radoje L. Knežević, "The Yugoslav Government and Draža Mihailović," *Poruka*, No. 13, pp. 10–11, and No. 23, pp. 9–10.

Later in the war the government-in-exile and Mihailović were able to set up other communica-
tion channels free of British control, including from August 1943 to September 1944 a one-way
channel from Yugoslavia to Ambassador Fotić in Washington through the facilities of the United
States Navy. See Fotić, *The War We Lost*, p. 228. There were also channels through Istanbul and
Algiers. The connection through Istanbul was established in December 1943 and the one through
Algiers somewhat later. See Jovan Djonović, "The Connections with General Mihailović from the
Middle East." But by the time these channels were in full operation most of the fateful Allied de-
cisions which spelled the doom of Mihailović forces at home had already been made and rendered
fruitless the support efforts of his representatives abroad and many foreign backers.

[69] The messages from Bailey and Hudson later served as the principal raw material for the British intelligence handbook *The Četniks*, issued by the Allied Force, Mediterranean Headquarters, in
September 1944.

[70] Radoje L. Knežević, "The Yugoslav Government and Draža Mihailović," *Poruka*, No. 24,
p. 14.

[71] The text of this note, No. R2538/2G., was first published in 1945 by Živan L. Knežević in his
Why the Allies Abandoned, Part 2, pp. 2–3, which source I have utilized. The italics are in the
original.

effect a greater measure of unity, not only among the various elements of resistance within the country, and among the Serbs, Croats and Slovenes, but also among Yugoslav circles abroad." He realized the difficulties, he said, of reaching any permanent settlement under present circumstances, but he was disturbed by the fact that "division of thought and opinion is becoming ever more accentuated." In particular, he knew from reports of the Liaison Officer (Bailey) that a "virtual [state] of civil war" continued between the Chetniks and "other units of resistance," and that *"in this struggle General Mihailovic has associated himself directly, or indirectly with the Italian army of occupation."* He then referred specifically to Mihailović's speech of February 28, as "reported by Colonel Bailey who was present":

3. In the course of this speech General Mihailovic said that the Serbs were now completely friendless, *that the English, to suit their own strategic ends, were urging them to undertake operations without the slightest intention of helping them either now or in the future, and that the English were now fighting to the last Serb in Yugoslavia.* He continued that the English were trying to purchase Serbian blood at the cost of an insignificant supply of arms, but that he would never be a party to this "shameful commerce typical of English traditional perfidy." Far from being guests the Yugoslav King and Government were virtually prisoners of the English. They were forgotten and confined by His Majesty's Government who shamelessly violated Yugoslav sovereignty by negotiating direct with the Soviet Government on internal Yugoslav problems. The B.B.C. with revolting cynicism had dropped its support of the sacred Serbian cause. The Allies' lust for fraud was satisfied by the untimely, hypocritical and anti-Yugoslav activity of the Partisans—but let the Allies realize that nothing they could do or threaten, could turn the Serbs from their vowed and sacred duty of exterminating the Partisans. *As long as the Italians remained his sole adequate source of benefit and assistance generally,* nothing the Allies could do would make him change his attitude towards them. *His enemies were the Partisans, the Ustashi, the Moslems, and the Croats.* When he had dealt with them, he would turn to the Italians and Germans. In conclusion he said that he needed no further contact with the Western democracies whose sole aim was to win the war at the expense of others.

4. You are aware that it has always been the policy of His Majesty's Government to give General Mihailovic their full support in his struggle against the Axis and to send him all possible material assistance. For two years they have carried out this policy to the limit of their power and they are on this account all the more shocked to observe General Mihailovic's reaction. I appreciate that words spoken in heat may not express a considered judgment, and that General Mihailovic may feel himself temporarily aggrieved at the small amount of assistance which it has unfortunately for reasons beyond the control of His Majesty's Government been possible to send him recently. You will appreciate, however, that His Majesty's Government cannot ignore this outburst nor accept without explanation and without protest a policy so totally at variance with their own. They could never justify to the British public or to their own Allies their continued support of a movement, the leader of which does not scruple publicly to declare that their enemies are his allies—whether temporary or permanent is immaterial—and that his enemies are not the German and Italian

invaders of his country, but his fellow Yugoslavs and chief among them men who at this very moment are fighting and giving their lives to free his country from the foreigner's yoke.

Churchill added diplomatically that he did not believe that this policy had the sanction or in any way reflected the views of the Yugoslav government, but since Mihailović was the Yugoslav Minister of War, the Yugoslav government should be aware of his views and should "take the necessary steps to see that General Mihailovic is fully and properly informed of their own views on these matters and that he is instructed henceforward to adopt a line more in consonance with the attitude of the Yugoslav Government and of His Majesty's Government." The final sentence of Churchill's letter left no question about the British position: "You will, I am sure, appreciate that unless General Mihailovic is prepared to change his policy both towards the Italian enemy and towards his Yugoslav compatriots who are resisting the enemy, it may well prove necessary for His Majesty's Government to revise their present policy of favouring General Mihailovic to the exclusion of the other resistance movements in Yugoslavia." Of course, by this time the situation was quite different. Mihailović's forces had been beaten at the Neretva River and in eastern Herzegovina and he was neither militarily nor politically what he had been only a month earlier, and this was soon to be reflected by British relations with Mihailović and the Partisans.

Jovanović, without revealing the text of the note to his cabinet and after several meetings with Ambassador Rendel, tried to minimize the significance of the Bailey report.[72] Mihailović's speech, he explained to Churchill, was directed to only a small group of people and was not for the general public: "it must be taken to express no more than a temporary mood." At the same time he "deeply regretted the expressions used by General Mihailović against Great Britain," and in the most recent communications, he said, Mihailović rejected the accusations of collaboration with the Italians.[73] Following this exchange, both the Yugoslav government-in-exile and the British government for a time made a determined effort to patch up relations between the British and Mihailović. The British Foreign Office drafted a formal set of propositions on mutual conduct of affairs (dated May 7, 1943) for Mihailović's approval, and Mihailović accepted it, although some of its terms could not have pleased him. The chief points in these propositions were that Mihailović's primary object should be resistance to the Axis, that all

[72] Ante Smith Pavelić in his article "The British and Draža Mihailović" refers on p. 235 to a newspaper article of 1956 by Dr. Juraj Krnjević, Vice-Premier in the Jovanović cabinet, who said that he saw the full contents of Churchill's letter not less than thirteen years after it was written. Pavelić published in this article in Serbo-Croatian translation many of the Yugoslav-British exchanges pertaining to Mihailović and the Chetniks, including Churchill's letter.

[73] See Jovanović's letter to Churchill of April 6, 1943, in Živan L. Knežević, *Why the Allies Abandoned*, Part 2, p. 8.

collaboration with the Italians and General Nedić must definitely cease, that "every effort must therefore be made by all concerned to reach a peaceful settlement with the Partisans and in any case no operations against them should be carried out by General Mihailović except in self-defense," and that "the British Military Command is primarily concerned with the contribution which resistance movements in occupied countries can reasonably be expected to make in the prosecution of the war." Increased British aid would be forthcoming only if Mihailović accepted these propositions.[74] Also the agreement stipulated that General Mihailović was to follow the orders of General Henry Maitland Wilson, the British commander in the Middle East, who was responsible for delivery of all aid to and the maintaining of all contacts with the Chetniks, including liaison at Mihailović's headquarters.[75]

Mihailović was at that time in a very difficult position, his main forces from Herzegovina and Montenegro having been crushed by the Partisans after Operation Weiss, and much of what was left being even now stripped of their arms by the Germans and to some extent by the Italians. Settling his differences with the British and obtaining their larger military and political aid was now Mihailović's only hope of survival, and he accepted the propositions with little hesitation. He vehemently denied, however, that he had collaborated with the Italians and the Nedić forces and declared that he had fought the Partisans only in self-defense—thus squarely contradicting all the evidence supplied by British SOE officers and other intelligence sources.[76]

It is necessary at this point to return to a proposal made early in 1943 by Colonel Bailey to his superiors in Cairo after he had studied the situation in Yugoslavia at first hand. He suggested that the British should divide Yugoslavia for purposes of administering military aid to resistance groups into two separate zones, one in which the Chetniks would be recognized as exercising control and as solely entitled to British aid and the other in which only the Partisans would be recognized and aided. The problem, obviously, would be to determine the limits of the two zones, and following that to convince the Partisans that they should cooperate with the British proposal and with their plans. As time went on, other developments in the Mediterranean theater of war,

[74] *Ibid.*, pp. 10–14, the quotation being from p. 12. See also a Foreign Office report entitled "Relations Between General Mihailovic and His Majesty's Government," dated July 27, 1944, pp. 4–5. F.O. 371/44276, R12712/11/92.

[75] This was one of the complicating factors impeding aid to Mihailović. The Mediterranean Command in North Africa under General Eisenhower was in a much better position than the British Middle East Command to help Mihailović but lacked jurisdiction to do so (the line of demarcation ran through the middle of the Adriatic Sea). This jurisdictional situation obtained until January 1944, when General Wilson succeeded Eisenhower as Supreme Allied Commander in the Mediterranean. Wilson appointed a special officer in charge of assistance to Tito's Partisans and other British-supported resistance groups in the Balkans. See Churchill, *The Second World War*, V, 330–31, 422–24, 447–48.

[76] Mihailović accepted the British proposal with his telegram No. 1597 of June 1, 1943, to the government-in-exile. Živan L. Knežević, *Why the Allies Abandoned*, Part 2, pp. 13–14.

notably the forthcoming invasion of Italy, suggested even more convincingly to British intelligence and military authorities the idea of investigating the possibility of working with the Partisans in a drive against the Axis in Yugoslav territory.

Bailey made a specific proposal, based on Chetnik-supplied information that Partisan strength in western Bosnia amounted to only about four thousand hard-core Communists and some ten thousand "misled" troops which could easily be converted to Chetnik views. The Communists, he proposed, should be induced to move to the mountainous area west of Zagreb, while the Chetnik forces would move into the Bosnian areas cleared by the Partisans. With the Chetniks and Partisans thus separated, Mihailović would no longer have the excuse of having to fight the Partisans in self-defense instead of the Axis forces; and by dispatching Hudson to Tito, Bailey thought that the British might be able to secure direct control of further operations of the Partisans in Croatia. This proposal greatly underestimated Partisan strength and overestimated Chetnik strength. It was also quite naïvely, almost ridiculously, in error in assuming that Hudson would be able to convince the Partisans that they should move from western Bosnia to the area west of Zagreb.[77] Wittingly or unwittingly, Bailey was offering for serious consideration to his superiors the very objective that the Chetniks wanted to achieve with the planned "March on Bosnia," although the Chetniks actually wanted to destroy the Partisans, rather than push them away. But on January 20 Operation Weiss had been launched against Tito's forces in Banija, Kordun, Lika, and western Bosnia by German, Italian (along with Chetnik auxiliaries), and Croatian quisling troops, and the Mihailović Chetniks were preparing to enter the battle at the appropriate time with the bulk of their forces to give the Partisans what they thought would be the final coup. Bailey must have learned about this Axis operation fairly soon after it began, but the Chetniks apparently tried to keep him in the dark about the part that they were to play both as Italian auxiliaries and in coordinated parallel actions.

Bailey's proposal was discussed and rejected by British military and political authorities: the Foreign Office opposed it on several grounds and the War Office contended that Bailey was not accurately informed on the Partisans in Bosnia and Croatia and on the extent of pro-Partisan and anti-Chetnik feelings in most parts of the country.[78] But then the situation began to change rapidly and made those British discussions pointless. As explained in the preceding chapter, after the Partisans succeeded in crossing the Neretva River into eastern Herzegovina in

---

[77] Deakin, *The Embattled Mountain*, pp. 178–80.

[78] *Ibid.*, pp. 180–81. The position taken by the War Office is further proof that the British had other sources of intelligence in Yugoslavia besides the SOE.

the middle of March, they inflicted a series of defeats upon the Chetniks and pursued their remnants all the way into Sandjak and Montenegro. This setback and the disarming of Djurišić's Chetnik units and some others by German troops which entered Montenegro around May 12 forced Mihailović to withdraw in the direction of Serbia with some two thousand troops which he had hurriedly summoned from Serbia to help him stem the Partisan advance.[79]

The British Command in the Middle East, undoubtedly relying on reports from Bailey, informed London in the second half of May that its impression was that the Ibar River in Serbia "represented a real dividing line between the retreating Četniks and the advancing Partisans,"[80] and issued orders to General Mihailović which if followed would have divided Yugoslavia into two separate zones, one Chetnik and the other Partisan, but with territories totally different from those originally proposed by Bailey. This detailed "operational decision" of General Wilson was delivered in writing to General Mihailović by Bailey on May 28. Referring to the earlier agreements, Wilson ordered Mihailović to "cooperate totally" with the Allied forces. The British decision, the order noted, was based on these propositions: that the Chetniks do not represent "a fighting force of any importance west of Kopaonik Mountain [in south-central Serbia]," that Mihailović's units "in Montenegro, Herzegovina, and Bosnia are already annihilated or else in close cooperation with the Axis," and that "it is also difficult to say that his units exist in Croatia, Slovenia, and Slavonia." Furthermore, the order continued, "the Partisans represent a good and effective fighting force in all parts where only the quislings represent General Mihailović." After these preliminaries, the order gave the following specific instructions: (1) Mihailović was to stop all cooperation with the Axis forces; (2) he was to move immediately to the area of Kopaonik Mountain in Serbia (east of the Ibar River), using force if necessary; (3) henceforth the British would consider only the area east of the Ibar River as Mihailović's domain and would send him there ample aid by air. The Middle East Command also requested that the BBC should attack as traitors all quislings fighting together with the Italians, among whom were specifically named three Chetnik leaders—General Djukanović, Colonel Stanišić, and *vojvoda* Jevdjević. Bailey was instructed to present this order in a most categorical manner and to obtain a "quick and nonambiguous consent in a favorable sense."[81]

[79] *Ibid.*, p. 187. Cairo reported to London that Mihailović was withdrawing to Serbia with 1,000–2,000 men. The figure must have originated with Bailey, who at this time was withdrawing with Mihailović toward Serbia. As we have seen in Chapter 7, n. 144, the higher figure was later confirmed by Lukačević.

[80] *Ibid.*, p. 187.

[81] For the full text see Živan L. Knežević, *Why the Allies Abandoned*, Part 2, pp. 14–15. This is a retranslation from Serbo-Croatian into English. The message was also approved by British authorities in London.

Mihailović considered this order totally unacceptable, and without replying, he communicated both the order and his thoughts about it to the government-in-exile. Not only was the manner of the order—requesting an immediate written answer and compliance—an insult, but also its implications were infuriating to Mihailović. Although he claimed as Minister of the Army, Navy, and Air Force and Chief of Staff of the Supreme Command to exercise jurisdiction over the entire country, the British were ordering him to withdraw to a corner of the country and telling him that they would recognize his authority only in this part, while in most other parts of the country they wanted by implication to recognize the jurisdiction of the revolutionary movement of Tito. Mihailović interpreted the order as a request for capitulation to the British. Since he and his fighters did not recognize the capitulation to the Axis, they certainly would not capitulate to the British, he said, and furthermore, according to the Yugoslav Constitution and military regulations, only the government had the authority to reply to such an order. He was also deeply hurt that the British threatened to call his officers Djukanović, Stanišić, and Jevdjević traitors because of their alleged collaboration with the Italians; that was something that only the Yugoslav government had the right to do, and on the basis of information furnished by the Central National Committee, and for the British to do so represented intervention in Yugoslav internal affairs. I will not, he declared, "bear this sort of insult any longer."[82]

In issuing this order the British may very well have hoped to force Mihailović out. He might become angry enough to resign, or he might refuse to comply and in so doing leave himself open to charges of insubordination which the British would not hesitate to make use of at the proper time.[83] But Mihailović simply refused to acknowledge the order, and it was soon withdrawn by the British authorities, who stated that as soon as Mihailović accepted the earlier conditions stipulated by the British government—which he in the meantime did—new discussions should be inaugurated on operational possibilities.[84]

The whole affair did much to worsen Chetnik-British relations. The controversial order itself indicates what lay at the heart of Chetnik-British difficulties—that is, the British attempts to assume operational command over Mihailović and his Yugoslav Army in the Homeland and Mihailović's stubborn but quite understandable determination not to accept that command, since he was the chief of that army and the legiti-

[82] *Ibid.*, p. 15.
[83] Deakin in a conference of Yugoslav military and other historians (with many nonhistorians and foreign specialists participating) held at Sarajevo between June 27 and July 2, 1969, interpreted this order as the first step in the process of jettisoning Mihailović. See *Neretva-Sutjeska 1943*, pp. 404–5.
[84] See the Foreign Office report entitled "Relations Between General Mihailovic and His Majesty's Government," p. 5.

mate representative of a sovereign state and therefore in a better position than the British to know what was good for his troops and for his
people in the short and in the long run. The British position was not
helped by the fact that they were investing practically nothing in terms
of military supplies and were giving Mihailović no promises of substantial material aid for an all-out guerrilla war against the Axis or,
especially, of landings along the Dalmatian coast.

Colonel Bailey's original proposal for dividing Yugoslavia into two
resistance zones implied the establishing of direct relations between the
British and the Partisans. To avoid the danger of making Yugoslavia
another Spain, he had urged that support of Yugoslav guerrillas should
be an Anglo-Soviet undertaking. Though rejecting the idea of two zones,
British authorities decided on March 3, 1943, that along with further
support to Mihailović, "British officers were to be infiltrated into other
resistance groups, and, if information from these officers justified it, all
possible support was to be sent to such groups." This decision was the
formal basis for later action of British services in establishing contact
with the "Croat guerrillas," meaning the Partisans.[85] Exploratory contacts made in April and May showed that the Partisans were ready and
willing to carry out tasks which the Allies were not able to induce the
Chetniks to take. These preliminary contacts were followed by de facto
recognition of the Partisans as an Allied fighting force and the giving
of some aid. The next phase was that of "equal assistance" to both Partisans and Chetniks, but with a strong bias in favor of the Partisans.
After that came the formal recognition of the Partisans as an Allied
force at Tehran, followed in the next few months by the withdrawal
of formal recognition, as well as of military missions and all aid, from
the Chetniks, and the transfer of all military, political, and diplomatic
assistance to the Partisans. With this step, Mihailović acquired another
enemy, and the Partisans a powerful ally. Thus the military defeats in
March and April 1943 in eastern Herzegovina, southeastern Bosnia, and
Montenegro at the hands of the Partisans ushered in the losing phase
of the Chetnik movement. By September its position had become ap-
preciably worse, though Mihailović continued to claim authority over
the whole Yugoslav territory and his forces still fought the Partisans
in Serbia and elsewhere and undertook some attacks against the German and quisling forces.

By an agreement arrived at between Colonel Bailey and General Mihailović sometime in January or February 1943, nine British sub-missions were sent, beginning in April, to various regional Chetnik commands in Serbia. These missions were equipped with radio transmitters
to be used for reporting on the organization and strength of the Chet-

[85] Deakin, *The Embattled Mountain*, pp. 180, 185–86.

niks, but they were also, if necessary, supposed to engage in "independent sabotage operations, against lines of communications and valuable mining installations."[86] Things appeared to be going somewhat more smoothly—in September the mission at Mihailović's headquarters was upgraded by appointing Brigadier C. D. Armstrong as head although apparently without much hope that relations would improve greatly—and Mihailović even sounded a little more cooperative. On August 7 he said in a circular letter sent to his troops: ". . . during June and July I was obliged to take a hard stand in the defense of the interests of our people and Yugoslavia. My message to our allies the British was sharp, full of bitterness and reproach . . . I am pleased to tell you now that our relations with the British High Command are again those of allies, and for this much credit goes to you, because our forces have shown themselves steadfast and faithful to the King and Fatherland."[87]

This optimism was short-lived. The differences between the British and the Chetniks were too serious and too pervasive to be patched up. At many of the regional Chetnik headquarters also there was trouble between the Chetnik commanders and the British officers assigned to them; the reports sent by the British, according to Deakin, "Almost without exception . . . were unfavorable to the Chetniks as a fighting force and . . . these messages completed the critical impressions being formed both by S.O.E. and the British G.H.Q. Middle East of the Mihailović movement even in Serbia."[88] The Chetnik commanders were equally critical of the British liaison officers. Two illustrations have to suffice. On July 18, 1943, Lt. Colonel Keserović informed the Second Kruševac Brigade that a British captain would be visiting the brigade's area. He asked that he be well received and safely escorted, but that his movements be directed only to areas where he could see Chetnik power and organization. The message concluded: "It is necessary to keep in mind that these "allies" of ours wish to buy much but sell little. Do not give them any information. Tell them only of the power of our people and their strong devotion to General Draža Mihailović, and that there were no other armed forces in Serbia."[89] The second illustration is to be found in a letter from Major Puniša B. Vešović, Chetnik commander in the area of the Bor copper mines in northeastern Serbia, to Major Erik Greenwood, the chief British liaison officer attached to his unit. This is a long letter of protest (dated September 27, 1943) written following a verbal clash that occurred after a military mistake. The letter tells how Greenwood and his colleagues urged Vešović to attack a German column

[86] *Ibid.*, pp. 180, 183.
[87] Archives of the Institute of Military History, Belgrade, Chetnik Documents, Reg. No. 3/3, Box 2.
[88] Deakin, *The Embattled Mountain*, p. 183; see also *The Četniks*, pp. 16–17.
[89] Archives of the Institute of Military History, Belgrade, Chetnik Documents, Reg. No. 13/1, Box 129.

despite a four-to-one German superiority in numbers and even a greater superiority in arms. The actions of British officers on that occasion revealed the Chetnik positions to the Germans and apparently resulted in a number of wounded, including some British. Greenwood also tried to force Vešović to attack the Bor mines. When Vešović brought up the fear of reprisals against civilians, Greenwood answered, "Without regard to reprisals you must attack the Germans and execute our orders; you are wearing British uniforms." Vešović was very angry at these attempts of the British officers to assume operational command, and in this letter he sets forth all his complaints—which amounted to a general list of Chetnik complaints—against the British: little military assistance, often of the wrong kind; close checking and recording of parachuted supplies; frequently unfriendly behavior, almost that of a foe, toward the Chetniks; lack of appreciation for what the Serbian people had done for the British; British officers acting against what Vešović considered to be British government policy; support of the Communists; coddling of the Croats; anti-Chetnik broadcasts over the BBC; foolhardy approach of British officers to operations; lack of consideration for reprisals against the civilian population, and so on.[90] As in the relationship between Mihailović and the British officers at his headquarters, here, too, the fundamental issue was the open efforts of the British officers to impose themselves as operational commanders over the Chetniks. It must have seemed to the Chetniks that the British were trying to treat them as if the Yugoslav Army in the Homeland were a home force in a British colony. Had the British delivered a great amount of arms and other military supplies, had their government continued an anti-Partisan and completely pro-Chetnik course, had there, especially, been immediate hope of an Allied landing on the Dalmatian coast, the situation would have been somewhat different. But with only scant amounts of supplies delivered, steadily growing support for the Partisans after May 1943, constant criticism of Mihailović and attempts to remove him and replace him with some other leader who would do their bidding, it was not strange that neither Mihailović nor his local commanders wanted to surrender their authority and become British pawns.

The British had a problem deciding what to do about Mihailović. What they most wanted was for him to do an about-face and become an ally of the Partisans against the Axis. In the short run, that would have done the most harm to the Axis forces and in the long run it would have enabled the British to continue their support of the legitimate government and its Minister of War in the country, to have helped return that government to power after the war, and in the process also, it could be hoped, to have enabled the government to render innocuous the

[90] *Ibid.*, Reg. No. 19/1–2, Box 129.

Communist-led Partisans and thus avert the threat of postwar Russian influence in the country. Since Mihailović would not cooperate, the next best thing seemed to be to replace him with one of the other Chetnik leaders, one who would be more willing to go along with their plans. But this too proved impossible.[91] At last it was concluded that the only way to put a stop to his activities was to weaken him to the point of insignificance and/or to remove him with the help of King Peter, and continue cooperating with and aiding the Partisans.

The first important evidence of increased British pressure was the resignation of Slobodan Jovanović as prime minister of the government-in-exile on June 17, 1943. Since Jovanović was one of Mihailović's staunchest supporters and by far the most influential of the Yugoslav ministers in exile, his departure presaged the beginning of the end of the Chetnik domination of the exile government. Mihailović lasted almost another year as Minister of the Army, Navy, and Air Force, but both his and the government's position became more and more insecure. The British had much to lose: the Chetniks, provided they could be brought around to obeying their orders, were important to them as representatives of the Serbian nationalist forces with a strong following in Serbia, as strong supporters of the Karadjordjević dynasty which the British wanted to preserve, as a movement of strong pro-Western orientation, and in the long run as a strongly anti-Communist force. But the more immediate military considerations were also persuasive — and eventually the most compelling. As long as Mihailović was unwilling or unable to change his policies to respond to the needs of the Western Allied strategy in the Mediterranean, British-Chetnik relations were bound to deteriorate, and of this fact the British, the exile government, and Mihailović himself were well aware.[92]

BRITISH MATERIAL AND FINANCIAL AID TO THE CHETNIKS

There were several aspects to British aid to the Chetniks while it lasted, including, as we have seen, political and propaganda aid, as well as technical assistance in providing communication facilities between the Chetniks in Yugoslavia and the government-in-exile.

There is no doubt in this writer's mind that the British propaganda aid was of enormous value so far as the popularization of the Chetnik movement and of Mihailović himself was concerned, not only abroad but to some extent at home, and was indeed mostly responsible for the

[91] The British even considered at one time having Mihailović called to Cairo to report to King Peter and then detaining him there. But since it was assumed that he would not follow any such order, the plan was discarded. Biber, in *Vijesnik u srijedu (VUS)*, June 21, 1972, p. 34.

[92] Part of Bailey's messages to his superiors were acquired by chance by Mihailović's men. For Mihailović's messages to the government-in-exile of August 28 and 30, 1943, containing excerpts from Bailey's messages and some of Mihailović's comments see Jovan Djonović, "Mihailović's Telegrams About British Missions at His Headquarters and British Policy in the Country," *Glasnik SIKD 'Njegoš'*, June 1960, pp. 24–29.

creation of the Mihailović legend. From both the internal and the international points of view the chief British political aid to the Chetniks until the autumn of 1942 consisted in ignoring the Partisans. By acting as if the Partisans did not exist, the British offered a great advantage to the Chetniks at home, strengthening their legitimacy and casting them in the role of the accepted future rulers of the country. In addition, British support greatly enhanced the Chetnik position abroad, and for a long time the Chetniks were able to derive great propaganda advantages from this support.

Detailed data on British material and financial aid to the Chetniks are contained in a number of reports submitted by British authorities to the Yugoslav government-in-exile. The first supplies by air were dropped to Mihailović on November 9, 1941. These were followed in January 1942 by some deliveries of matériel by submarine, and four deliveries by air in April 1942. There were several deliveries of matériel between June and October 1942, and deliveries, again by air, in December 1942 and in February, March, and April 1943. Finally there is a report on deliveries between May and October 1943. The total amount of arms and ammunition delivered by the British to Mihailović, according to these reports, was: 43 mortars, 860 shells for mortars, 307 pistols, 1,203 automatic pistols, 1,866 rifles, 136 light machine guns, 217 submachine guns, 104 antitank guns, 8,728 hand grenades, 1,029,450 rounds of ammunition for various arms, and 5,220 pounds of explosives. There was in addition some clothing, footwear, radio equipment, medical supplies, and the like. Some of this material was damaged on delivery and some of it reportedly was dropped by mistake into enemy-controlled areas. The British services also delivered to Mihailović certain sums of money, amounting (after the ascertained losses) to 45,410 British pounds in gold, 5,000 U.S. dollars in gold and 99,420 dollars in bills, 75,980,000 Italian lire, 2,015 napoleons, 13,064,000 Nedić dinars, 11,540,-000 Bulgarian levas, and 1,014,000 Romanian leis.[93]

The British also delivered to the Chetniks a certain amount of money through various channels out of funds supplied by the Yugoslav government-in-exile. Aid to Mihailović from this source amounted to about 50,000 pounds sterling, 52,000 U.S. dollars, 2,500 napoleons, 10 to 15 million Romanian leis, and some millions of Nedić dinars.[94] The Yugoslav government-in-exile and its intelligence operatives in Cairo and Istanbul also discussed with the British the possibility of establishing a domestic fund in Belgrade which Mihailović could use for his needs. The amount considered was 100 million Nedić dinars. The funds were supposed to be contributed by industrialists and merchants in occupied

[93] D. [Dušan J. Djonović], "Aid Sent by Great Britain [to General Mihailović]."
[94] Dušan J. Djonović, "Aid in Money Sent by the Yugoslav Government to General Mihailović." *Glasnik SIKD 'Njegoš'*, December 1960.

Serbia who would in turn be credited abroad for their contributions. Nothing tangible ever came of these discussions.[95]

The Chetniks were disappointed and angered by the meagerness of the aid they were receiving, and both Mihailović and the government-in-exile repeatedly asked the British for more in the way of supplies. The British answer, as long as they were supporting Mihailović, invariably was that aircraft necessary for making deliveries were in short supply and that many other higher priorities had to be met. But even though British aid in military supplies was extremely limited and therefore of little consequence in a military sense, it was of great political and psychological significance for a time. As long as it was coming it was a proof that the Western Allies stood behind the Chetniks; when it ceased to come, it indicated that support was declining and would soon end entirely.

THE GOVERNMENT-IN-EXILE AFTER JUNE 1943

Early in 1943 the British government began suggesting to the government-in-exile that it move from London to Cairo, ostensibly in order to be nearer its country during the important pending operations concerning Yugoslavia.[96] It would not, I think, be incorrect to say that this suggestion came in part also as a culmination of the British government's growing irritation at the bickerings within the government-in-exile, the Scandal of Cairo, and the accumulating evidence of Chetnik collaboration with the enemy. Indeed, as we have seen, the British had been disappointed with the operations and behavior of the Yugoslav government since the autumn of 1941, and as time went on conditions only became worse.

The British government was dissatisfied among other things with King Peter—his entourage, his lack of interest in his studies, and the absence of a systematic program to prepare him for his duties as a monarch. In February 1943, acting on a British suggestion, King Peter accepted the appointment of a British officer, Major Archibald Dunlop Mackenzie, as aide-de-camp, replacing Major Vohoska. Mackenzie's job was a thankless one, but he remained at it until March 1944.[97]

On June 17, 1943, Jovanović resigned, having failed to achieve the cohesion within the cabinet that was needed for the making of important decisions, and facing increasing British pressure regarding changes

---

[95] *Ibid.*, *Glasnik SIKD 'Njegoš'*, December 1961.

[96] Pavlović, "The Fall of the Jovanović Cabinet," esp. p. 4. Pavlović, though he was *chef de cabinet* of the prime minister and therefore cognizant of the real issues, writes only about what he calls "internal political issues" of the government, avoiding important questions about the government's relations with the Great Allies and the civil war in the country, and the implications that these questions had for the future of Yugoslavia as a state.

[97] Biber, in *VUS*, July 5, 1972, p. 33. A very negative appraisal of King Peter is found in a report of June 30, 1944, submitted by Colonel Bailey, who accompanied the king on a tour of the central Mediterranean area. F.O. 371/44292, R11324/44/92.

in Mihailović's policies. Writing after Jovanović's death, Radoje Knežević made it clear that he thought the British had interfered: "The Jovanović cabinet was toppled by a foreign hand. . . . The overthrow of
the Jovanović government (and thereafter the so-to-say automatic fall
of the Trifunović government) was the indispensable precondition for
the realization of the plan of putting Yugoslavia after the war under
the tutelage of two Great Powers."[98] Quite clearly, Great Britain desired
Jovanović's removal, but the real reasons for his fall were the great increase in the power of the Partisans, the establishment of direct relations between the British and the Partisans, the weakening of the overall Chetnik position both at home and with the Great Allies, and his
refusal to alter his Great Serbia policy even though it was clearly un-
workable at home and unacceptable to the British.[99]

During his seventeen-and-a-half-month tenure as prime minister, Jovanović did nothing definite toward resolving the national question or
the problem of the federal reorganization of the state—although anything that the government-in-exile might have done in these respects
would, under the circumstances, have had only academic significance.
Nor did Jovanović, being himself strongly pro-Chetnik and surrounded
by even more ardently pro-Chetnik military and political advisers, do
anything toward resolving the conflict between the Chetniks and the
Partisans. Jovanović had also to contend with a long series of other problems in London: the proposed marriage of King Peter to the Greek
Princess Alexandra, to which he and all the Serbian party politicians
were opposed, fearing that it might produce unfavorable effects for the
king and dynasty at home;[100] the issue of a government declaration on
postwar reorganization of the country and policies of the government;[101]
the strong opposition of the Croatian ministers to practically every proposal that the Prime Minister made and their insistence that at least
one ambassadorial post, either in London or in Washington, be given
to a Croat, and that a special budget for Banovina Croatia to be used
at the discretion of Ban Šubašić be approved; Šubašić's refusal to communicate with the government and his insistence on maintaining direct
relations with the king; the controversial propaganda activities of Ambassador Fotić in Washington; British pressures to move the government to the Middle East; and the mounting difficulties with the British
over the policies of Mihailović and his Chetniks. Thus facing unsolvable
problems within his cabinet and after seeing that a basic and unfavor-

---

[98] Radoje L. Knežević, "Slobodan Jovanović in Politics," p. 33.
[99] For a discussion of the shift in British policy toward the two competing groups in Yugoslavia
during the first half of 1943 and the fall of the Jovanović cabinet see Kljaković, "The Change in
the Policy of Great Britain Toward Yugoslavia in the First Half of 1943," esp. pp. 44–56.
[100] King Peter's desire to marry Princess Alexandra was also opposed by his mother, Queen
Dowager Marie, and it led finally to a break in their relations.
[101] For the draft of the declaration see FRUS 1943, II, 1012–14. See also FRUS 1942, III, 827–
30, and Rendel, pp. 216–17. For the Serbo-Croatian text see Poruka, No. 53–54, pp. 37–38.

able change had taken place in the British policy toward the government-in-exile and the Chetniks by establishing direct contact with the Partisans and extending them aid, Jovanović had no choice but to resign.

Jovanović was succeeded in the office of prime minister on June 26, 1943 by Miloš Trifunović. Trifunović was a professional politician of mediocre abilities, a former minister, and an important representative of the Radical Party of Serbia, but he was seventy-two years old, strongly set in his Great Serbian ideas, and quite clearly not disposed to undertake any innovations in his relations with the Croatian ministers in the cabinet, or in the established policies toward the Chetniks and the Partisans, or in the exile government's relations with the British. His cabinet of fourteen members consisted mostly of the chiefs of the various political parties and groups in exile (and with Jovanović as the third vice-premier in addition to Krnjević and Krek); Mihailović continued as Minister of the Army, Navy, and Air Force. Only the Independent Democratic Party was not represented (because they refused to participate in a cabinet in which General Petar Živković was a Minister Without Portfolio and Acting Minister of the Army, Navy, and Air Force). But there was one very important change: Radoje Knežević, Minister of the Royal Court since March 1941, was replaced, on an acting basis, by a professional diplomat, Niko Mirošević-Sorgo. This ended Knežević's political power, and he was removed from the London scene by being appointed chargé d'affaires of the Yugoslav legation in Lisbon.

Trifunović proved no better at working out solutions to the welter of problems facing the government than his predecessor had been. The contradictions in and difficulties of the government-in-exile were so great that no political maneuver of the Prime Minister, as long as he upheld the Great Serbia policy, could bring about agreement, and without agreement, none of the problems could be solved.

At the outset, the new government tried to make an important ploy in strengthening the Chetnik cause from abroad. Acting Minister of the Army, Navy, and Air Force Živković submitted on July 14 a plan for establishing an army of about one hundred thousand men abroad. This army was to be raised by recruiting Yugoslav prisoners of war and political deportees in Italy and Slovenes from the Slovene Littoral and Croats from Istria who had been captured by the British in Africa while serving in the Italian army. It was to be outfitted and maintained by the Western Allies and landed on the Dalmatian coast to fight the Germans under Allied command, but its real purpose would be to support the Chetniks who would immediately rally around the landing force. The government submitted the plan to the Big Three along with a request for permission to start recruiting among the Italian prisoners of war.[102] The Big Three governments, and especially the Western Allies, having no plans whatever to land on the Dalmatian coast, ignored the proposal, and the Trifunović government suffered a bad setback.

After a month or so of constant disputes between the Serbian and Croatian ministers in the cabinet, some of the Serbian leaders, including Prime Minister Trifunović, came to the conclusion that the situation could not continue and that probably a cabinet under a non-party personality with government officials and technicians as ministers would have to take over. Reports of such talk must have reached the king and the British, for on August 3, Foreign Secretary Eden, who acted as the shepherd of the Yugoslav government, met with Trifunović and several other Serbian, Croatian, and Slovene ministers and renewed the suggestion that the Yugoslav government should move to Cairo to be nearer the scene of forthcoming operations which would follow upon the soon expected Italian collapse.[103] For the first time, all the ministers seemed to indicate agreement on the matter, but when the cabinet next convened the Croatian ministers brought up their former conditions for agreeing to a transfer of the government: appointment of a Croat as ambassador to Washington or to London, and a budget for Banovina Croatia. The Serbian ministers charged political blackmail, and the cabinet was again at an impasse.[104]

These events also must have become known to the British immediately, for on August 9 the British suggested to King Peter that the new government ought to limit itself to routine matters and allow the king sufficient time and freedom to find a more satisfactory solution for a number of pending important issues.[105]

It was following this intervention of the British that King Peter requested Trifunović's resignation. Trifunović complied, on August 10, indicating for the record that the principal reason for his resignation was the impossibility of getting cooperation from the Croatian representatives in the cabinet.[106] In view of the difficulties that all the wartime cabinets had experienced because of national, ideological, and personal

[102] Plenča, *Medjunarodni odnosi Jugoslavije*, pp. 200–201.

[103] Pavlović, "The Fall of the Trifunović Cabinet," pp. 65–66.

[104] Marić, pp. 323, 330–32.

[105] Plenča, *Medjunarodni odnosi Jugoslavije*, p. 202. The degree of British dissatisfaction with the Yugoslav politicians in exile is stated candidly in an internal memorandum of Sir Orme Sargent of the Foreign Office of March 25, 1943: "I sometimes think that it would be better if there were no Yugoslav Government at all and if the Yugoslav politicians in this country were to agree among themselves to give up all this play-acting of forming a government with Ministers occupying administrative posts when they have nothing to administer, and cannot even agree among themselves on current appointments, such as the Yugoslav Ambassador to H.M. Government, still less on future policy. . . .

"It seems to me that if we are to save the young King, so that he may play his part on the liberation of Yugoslavia, it is essential that he should cease to be identified with his miserable Government and with the discredited and out of date politicians who happen to be in this country . . . One thing seems clear, and that is that with the virtual breakdown of the Government and emergence of Mihailovitch as a pan-Serb leader, the King is the only remaining symbol of the unified Yugoslav ideal." F.O. 371/37630, R2580/2578/92.

[106] Marić, pp. 335–36; Pavlović, "The Fall of the Trifunović Cabinet," pp. 68–69.

disagreements among the ministers, a government composed of men who were not politicians seemed a workable solution—pleasing to the king, who could not get permission to marry from a cabinet headed by a politician, and pleasing to the British, who had had their fill of bickering. It had also been made clear that the new prime minister would be a Serb from Serbia (the names considered were Dr. Božidar Purić, former envoy in Paris, Ambassador Fotić, and Ilija Šumenković, the ambassador in Ankara), and that General Mihailović would continue in office.

King Peter settled on Dr. Purić, and within an hour of Trifunović's resignation Purić had taken the oath of office.[107] The swiftness of the change, in which the British role was implicit, and the departure from precedent in appointing a prime minister and a cabinet who were not leading party figures (or not leading political figures at all) amounted to a sort of coup d'état on the part of the king.[108] But the king could not have undertaken the change without the backing of at least some Serbian party politicians. Purić was acceptable to these party politicians because, quite as much as Jovanović or Trifunović, he represented the pro-Chetnik Great Serbian forces. The party politicians grumbled about the manner in which the change had been effected and the British role in it, but most of them consoled themselves with the thought that Purić's tenure would be of short duration, or, like Branko Čubrilović, who himself aspired to the office of prime minister, began at once to plot his downfall.[109]

Prime Minister Churchill had written Prime Minister Jovanović quite frankly back in March (in the letter quoted extensively above) that if Mihailović did not "change his policy both towards the Italian enemy and towards his Yugoslav compatriots who are resisting the enemy" it might "well prove necessary for His Majesty's Government to revise their present policy of favouring General Mihailovic to the exclusion of the other resistance movements in Yugoslavia." Throughout the spring and summer the British continued to press this point, and they became more insistent after Purić took office, because it had now become imperative to create a strong diversion against the Axis forces in Yugoslav territory in order to reduce pressure on the Allied forces fighting in Italy.[110] Mihailović still refused to cooperate with the Partisans, and the exile government supported everything that he did in the country, because the Serbian politicians were convinced that he was defending their cause—the cause of the Serbian people—and that he had the pres-

[107] Purić was the son-in-law of Nikola Pašić, the pre-1918 Serbian and later Yugoslav Prime Minister who was for many years head of the Serbian Radical Party.
[108] It seems that Purić himself boasted that Foreign Secretary Eden and King Peter put him in the post of prime minister. See Marić, pp. 340–41.
[109] *Ibid.*, pp. 330–42; Čubrilović, pp. 156–89, 198–202.
[110] See Pavlović, "The Fall of the Purić Cabinet," pp. 7–32, esp. pp. 12–22.

tige and power to restore their regime, perhaps even without the help of the British. Even Purić, although appointed with British blessings, resisted British pressure for removal of Mihailović with great vigor as long as he remained in office.

One move of the Purić cabinet was the dispersal from London of the group of majors headed by Živan Knežević. Knežević was sent to the embassy in Washington as military attaché, and the two former aides-de-camp of the king, Roždjalovski and Vohoska, were apparently sent to a British base for training in parachute jumping, ostensibly so that they could be dropped to the Chetniks in Yugoslavia (which, however, never happened). Purić also removed Miroševič-Sorgo from the position of acting Minister of the Royal Court and replaced him with his cousin, Vladislav Marković-Brale, thus establishing a close control over the king's entourage and the contacts he was able to maintain.[111]

The Purić cabinet, not having the continual squabbles between the Serbian and other ministers that had plagued the Jovanović and Trifunović cabinets, was also able to come to decisions on certain matters that had been pending. The government moved to Cairo in mid-September; Bogoljub Jevtić was named ambassador to London; King Peter was granted permission to marry Princess Alexandra, and did so on March 20, 1944. But as a cabinet of government officials and technicians it did not presume to act on matters of potentially major significance such as issuing a declaration on postwar plans of the government. In sum, the Purić government, quite as much as the two exile governments that had preceded it, was simply the foreign representative and protector of the interests of General Mihailović and his Chetniks, and thus of the interests of the traditional Serbian ruling groups.

But postponing a decision on the Chetniks *vs.* the Partisans was no longer possible. The increasing strength of the Partisans was all too evident, to the Yugoslav government and certainly to the Great Powers. It was certain, however, that the problem could not be solved in a political and military manner acceptable to a Chetnik-dominated government-in-exile. Since the beginning of 1943 changes in British policy toward the two competing forces had been taking place with unusual rapidity. Between April and September 1943 British policy toward the Partisans moved from one of establishing preliminary contacts to the granting of full equality with the Chetniks as far as military aid was concerned. After a period of continued worsening relations between the British and the Chetniks (decisions of the Tehran conference, testing of Mihailović by giving him orders they knew he would refuse to execute), the final step—reached by early March 1944—was the with-

---

[111] Marić, pp. 338–40, 350, 381; Čubrilović, p. 201.

drawal of all recognition and aid from the Chetniks and the concentration of military, propaganda, and political aid on the Partisans.

As the makers of Western Allied policy for Yugoslavia, the British almost from day to day increased their pressure on King Peter and the Purić government to get rid of Mihailović. Still they resisted, and it was not long before there was a complete breakdown in relations between the British authorities and the Great Serbian forces that controlled the government-in-exile. When, finally, the British decided to recall their military missions to the Chetniks, they were sufficiently aware of the embarrassment that this would cause the Purić government and Mihailović not to publicize the action (which was announced simultaneously on March 1, 1944, to Purić in Cairo and to a representative of Mihailović in Yugoslavia), but General Wilson made Mihailović personally responsible for the safety of the British missions and the British also delayed the departure of Major Lukačević and Lt. Colonel Baćović until they saw how the Chetniks managed the evacuation of their men.[112]

One of the examples of the extraordinary pressure exercised by the British on King Peter was a conference between Prime Minister Churchill and King Peter on April 13, 1944, which was attended also by the Ambassador to the Yugoslav government R. C. Skrine Stevenson. Churchill urged the king to dismiss the Purić government as soon as possible and in that way get rid of Mihailović because during the coming months Mihailović might act in a manner—by, for example, opposing the Russian forces if they should cross into Yugoslav territory—which would prove very embarrassing to the king. If the king followed this suggestion, Churchill promised to aid him so far as possible in matters of publicity. In this meeting and another one with Ambassador Stevenson the following day, the king seemed ready to take Churchill's advice.[113] But he soon had a change of heart, presumably after talking to Prime Minister Purić, for on April 17 he sent an urgent letter to President Roosevelt in which he declared that he could not dismiss his best prime minister and relieve General Mihailović of his position without perpetrating an act of treason on his nation. His people were united behind him and his government, he said, and he implored the President for understanding and help. It is not clear whether Roosevelt sent a reply to King Peter or not, but the draft of Roosevelt's contemplated reply gives no encouragement to the Yugoslav king, even expressing doubt about some of the information contained in his letter, and generally agrees with the wisdom of the British handling of Yugoslav affairs.[114]

[112] Biber, in *VUS*, June 28, 1972, pp. 33–34.
[113] F.O. 371/44309, R6007/658/92. One should not be surprised that King Peter changed his mind after these two meetings because he was well known for his lack of independent thinking. As Colonel Bailey wrote in one of his reports, the king often reflected the views of the person to whom he talked last.
[114] *FRUS 1944*, IV, 1359–61, 1366–68.

It was inconceivable that the British, once having broken relations with Mihailović and having ordered the withdrawal of their military missions from areas under his control, would for long tolerate a Yugoslav government-in-exile that persisted stubbornly in its pro-Chetnik, Great Serbia policies. The British wanted a government that would help them to bring about a modus vivendi between the Chetniks and the Partisans in the interests of creating a strong Yugoslav state, friendly to the British, and if at all possible, under the aegis of the Karadjordjević dynasty.

After a series of moves and pressures upon King Peter extending over several months, the British government got what it wanted: the dismissal of Purić and his cabinet, which included also the removal of General Mihailović as Minister of the Army, Navy, and Air Force. It was hardly to be expected that any Yugoslav government-in-exile headed by a Serb, whether politician or not, would undertake the task of removing Mihailović, although his removal was clearly required both by the internal situation in the country and by the international situation of the country as understood by the Allies and by their strategic needs. A suitable non-Serbian politician had to be found for the job. The Serbian politicians, aware of what was in the offing, tried to prevail on the king to choose a man of their own group—either Milan Grol, the chief of the Democratic Party, or former Prime Minister Jovanović— to replace Purić. But the British had made it clear to King Peter that Mihailović must go; Tito was insistent in his demand for it and had stated firmly that he would not enter into discussions with the government-in-exile until Mihailović had been removed from office. The British similarly made this the fundamental condition for their support of any new exile government. The king, with no choice in the matter, dismissed the Purić cabinet and on June 1, 1944, named Dr. Ivan Šubašić prime minister. Until July 7, when the ukase of the appointment of other ministers was issued, Šubašić was in charge of all cabinet posts.[115]

Šubašić was the British choice.[116] He had always displayed a truly Yugoslav orientation, and he had the reputation of believing in political compromise.[117] Yugoslav sources state that Churchill informed Tito as early as May 9, 1944, about the selection of Šubašić as the new head of the government-in-exile. The proposed appointment was acceptable to Tito provided that Mihailović was not named Minister of the Army, Navy, and Air Force and that the new government issued a declaration

[115] See Pavlović, "The Fall of the Purić Cabinet," pp. 25–26, 32; Čubrilović, p. 224.

[116] Biber, in *VUS*, Aug. 2 ,9, 23, 30, and Sept. 27, 1972.

[117] Šubašić had made his position clear not only in public statements and speeches in the United States such as the one already cited, but also in numerous messages to the government in London (copies of which the British undoubtedly had in their files). For a series of passages from these statements and messages as found in the files of the Yugoslav government-in-exile see Kljaković, "The Yugoslav Government-in-Exile and the Allies in Relation to the Problem of Croatia, 1941–1944," Part I, pp. 108–12, 116, 122, 136.

castigating all those who collaborated with the enemy.[118] Šubašić's appointment opened a new chapter in the history of the government-in-exile and its relationships with the Chetniks and the Partisans. Thereafter the Great Serbia forces and the Chetniks had no influence whatsoever upon the actions of the government. They tried, without success, through British and American friends of the Chetniks, to prevent the Šubašić government from entering into and carrying out various agreements with Marshal Tito which they considered to be injurious to themselves, to the dynasty, to General Mihailović, to the Serbian people, and to the Yugoslav state in general. Similarly, the Chetnik Central National Committee which met on July 20–23 issued a statement declaring its lack of confidence in the Šubašić government and retaining for itself freedom of action (see Chapter 11). Šubašić's policies were also opposed by the leading member of the Croatian Peasant Party in exile, Dr. Krnjević—although several other prominent members of the party in exile, notably Šutej and Bićanić went along with Šubašić—and by the leader of the Slovene People's Party in exile, Dr. Krek. But this opposition was ineffectual, for it was now firm British policy, assented to by the United States and the Soviet Union, to give full support to the Tito-Šubašić agreements.

By mid-1944 conditions in Yugoslavia and the thinking of the Big Three about Yugoslavia had so evolved that the new Šubašić government could have no reasonable objective except that of coming to an agreement with the Partisans. The consolidation of the government-in-exile and the Partisan interim government took place on March 7, 1945, and marked the end of the government-in-exile. At last the Western Allies could look for an intensification of the Yugoslav war effort against Germany, and for an end to the disagreements in and over Yugoslavia which had for so long been festering relations among the Big Three; and they could also seriously hope that it might still be possible, with Western aid, to prevent the formation of a one-party Communist dictatorship in Yugoslavia after the war.

[118] *Hronologija 1941–1945*, p. 748.

PART THREE

Decline and Disaster

CHAPTER NINE

From the Italian Collapse to the Battle for Serbia

The failure of the Axis–Croatian quisling–Chetnik forces to annihilate the Partisans in the course of Operation Weiss in the winter of 1943 marked the beginning of the decline of Chetnik fortunes in Yugoslavia. For the Chetniks, the failure was an especially painful one, since in the decisive phase of that operation, the Battle of the Neretva River, they were bested by their greatest and most detested enemy, the Partisans, when the Partisans broke the encirclement at the sector held by the Chetniks and then beat them repeatedly in a series of engagements and drove them into Sandjak and Montenegro. Tito, the British, and the Germans all recognized that the Partisan victories of March and April had been a crushing military defeat of the Chetniks. On the heels of that defeat had come another German operation, Schwarz, lasting from mid-May to mid-June, the objective of which was to disarm the Chetnik forces in Montenegro, to seize Mihailović and his staff, and to destroy the Partisan troops and Tito and his staff. Even before the offensive began, one of Mihailović's ablest commanders, Major Pavle Djurišić, was removed from the action when he and his troops were easily captured and disarmed in the area of Kolašin. Additional Chetnik troops in Montenegro and some in southeastern Bosnia suffered a similar fate, and the Italians, under German pressure and possibly out of their own motivation, also disarmed some of the Montenegrin Chetniks. Thus by the middle of May, Mihailović, realizing that it was unsafe to remain in Montenegro, had begun a retreat with about two thousand Chetniks in the direction of Serbia.

Mihailović was now in a most unenviable position, being a commander who, having risked collaboration with the occupying enemy, was now set to lose not only the support of his ally the British but also the prospect of remaining on the winning side in the war. When the British established contact with the Partisans first in Croatia in April and then in Montenegro in May and began to give them various kinds of assistance, Mihailović lost prestige among many who had until then supported his movement. The Chetnik plight was compounded in June when, under British pressure and because of the untenable position of his cabinet, Mihailović's staunch supporter, Slobodan Jovanović, was forced to resign as prime minister of the government-in-exile. The spring of 1943 was thus in a number of ways a turning point for the Chetniks. From that time on they steadily lost ground, while the Partisans grew steadily stronger.

The surrender of Italy on September 8 and the withdrawal or removal of the Italian forces from their zone of occupation did not mean only that the Chetniks lost a valuable source of supplies; it meant also the loss of control over a large part of rural areas in Montenegro, Herzegovina, northern Dalmatia, western Bosnia, and Lika, where for about a year and a half they exercised that control with Italian acquiescence. At the same time, the Partisans profited greatly by the Italian collapse—in that they acquired control of much new territory and captured from the Italians large amounts of arms and ammunition and other military stores, gained many thousands of new volunteers (including some Italians), improved their communications with the Allied forces in Italy, and not the least, experienced a great boost in morale, since the collapse of Italy presaged the collapse of Germany.

After the summer of 1943, Western Allied aid to the Chetniks started to diminish whereas aid to the Partisans, at first small, rose steadily. The successes of the Red Army against the Germans were a propaganda and political boon for the Partisans, and by the same token a further setback for the Chetniks. And at the end of November the second session of AVNOJ at Jajce declared AVNOJ to be the sole representative of Yugoslav sovereignty and established an interim government in the form of a National Committee of Liberation of Yugoslavia (*Nacionalni komitet oslobodjenja Jugoslavije* or NKOJ) preparatory to a later reorganization of the country on a federal principle—denying the right of the government-in-exile to act for the people of Yugoslavia and forbidding the king to return to the country after the war until elections had been held on the question of continuing the monarchy.[1] Thus the Partisans had made their challenge to the Chetniks clear also on the internal political and diplomatic planes.

Finally, at Tehran at the end of November, the Big Three recognized the Partisans as an Allied armed force and promised to give them all military aid possible. A few months later the British withdrew their official recognition of the Chetniks and recalled their military missions.

---

[1] For the decisions of the second session of AVNOJ see *Zbornik DNOR*, Tome II, Vol. 11, pp. 421-35.

In May 1944 they cut off Mihailović's last shred of official support by forcing the ouster of the pro-Mihailović Purić government and with it Mihailović as Minister of the Army, Navy, and Air Force; and in August Mihailović was removed as Chief of Staff of the Supreme Command by abolition of that command by the Šubašić government. Then on September 12 King Peter, acting on the advice of the British, in a speech over the BBC to the people in Yugoslavia urged "all Serbs, Croats, and Slovenes to unite and join the National Liberation Army under Marshal Tito." Though he did not mention the Chetniks or Mihailović by name, he said by way of a warning: "All those who lean for support on the enemy against the interests of their own people and their future, and who do not respond to this call, will not succeed in freeing themselves from the onus of treason, either before the people or before history."[2]

CHANGE IN THE GERMAN ATTITUDE TOWARD THE CHETNIKS

We have seen how, during the whole time from the autumn of 1941 to the collapse of Italy, the Germans were suspicious of Mihailović and his Chetniks despite their occasional local collaboration, some overtures by the Chetniks for a modus vivendi, and their steady fighting of the Partisans. What the Germans especially feared was that the Chetniks would turn the full measure of their arms against them if the Allies made a landing on the Adriatic coast or in Greece. To undercut that prospect, the Germans gradually disarmed the legalized Chetniks in Serbia and fought the illegal ones when necessary; they supported the collaboration agreements between the Croatian authorities and the Chetniks in Bosnia; they insisted that the Italians disarm the Chetniks in their service, and finally in May 1943 themselves disarmed a part of the Chetnik forces in Montenegro and southeastern Bosnia. When the Allied forces landed in Sicily, and shortly thereafter on the Italian mainland, rather than in the Balkans, the threat of the Chetniks as a potential opponent diminished greatly, and soon after the Italian collapse the Germans were generally ready to accept the Chetniks as collaborators. They would never trust them completely, but at least there was little risk involved in working with them against their common enemy the Partisans, especially if the collaboration was on their own terms and the Chetniks were given the minimum amount of aid. The Germans realized that the Chetniks could be particularly useful in helping to keep the Partisans out of Serbia, so important for railroad

---

[2] For the text of King Peter's speech see Radoje L. Knežević, ed., *Knjiga o Draži*, II, 118–19. Later on, in his memoirs, Peter wrote about this speech: "I felt that I was letting down my best friends and giving full recognition to a group basically opposed to the monarchy and all democratic principles. The seeds of dictatorship were planted. I was powerless to do anything about it." *A King's Heritage*, p. 162.

lines and for its supplies of nonferrous metals and food—and fundamentally important, of course, to the Chetniks themselves because it
was the principal domain of their military and political organizations
and popular support.

The few isolated, and unsustained, instances of direct Chetnik-German collaboration that occurred before the collapse of Italy (Chapter 7)
were the result of individual initiative of both German and Chetnik
commanders in the field. In May 1943 the Commanding General in
Serbia ruled that negotiations for some Chetnik-German accommodation which were asked for by Chetnik commander Nikola Kalabić could
not be entered into.[3] Kalabić was one of Mihailović's top commanders
in Serbia, and his attempt to negotiate with the Germans is indicative
of the changing situation among the Chetniks. Undoubtedly, the defeats
of the Chetniks in Herzegovina, southeastern Bosnia, and Montenegro
in the spring of 1943 and Mihailović's withdrawal toward Serbia influenced Kalabić's decision to seek an accommodation.

By the end of the summer of 1943, when the Chetniks were faced
with the prospect of a very hard fight against the Partisans in defense
of their main stronghold, the need for arms and ammunition for their
troops in Serbia became extremely urgent. The Germans were the only
possible source of supply, if not directly then indirectly through the
Nedić administration. On the German side, the necessity of having to
police a greatly expanded area of responsibility in southeastern Europe
and at the same time carry on the struggle against the Partisans compelled them to develop other forces or to combine and expand the
existing ones. The inauguration of this change in policy began with
Hitler's Directive No. 48 of July 26, issued in expectation of the Italian
surrender, and it was further implemented by additional orders from
Hitler, the Wehrmacht High Command, the Commander in Chief in
Southeast Europe, and the Military Commander in Southeast Europe.
The largest forces available to fill this need in Yugoslav territory were
those of the Croatian puppet state, which at that time numbered in
excess of a quarter of a million men. They were, however, ill-trained
and poorly led; their equipment was inadequate and would have to be
greatly improved with German aid; and furthermore many of the
troops, of all ranks, were Partisan sympathizers. Hitler's order of September 7 on the "Improvement in the Defense Power of the Croatian
Army" was supposed to take care of the deficiencies, but the undertaking
did not prove to be very successful.

For almost a year prior to the Italian surrender, many German
generals and diplomats in the Balkan sector had been convinced that

---

[3] Microcopy No. T-501, Roll 249, Frame 372.

a purely military approach to the struggle against the Partisans could not succeed. Generals Löhr, Bader, and Glaise, as well as the German Envoy in Croatia, Kasche, had urged that a combined military-political approach should be inaugurated. But it was not until the Italian collapse that Hitler's headquarters came to a realization that they must find additional allies to help them carry on their greatly increased responsibilities in the Balkans, and especially the struggle against the Partisans, who rebounded with new vigor after every setback. If the struggle against the Partisans was to be waged on both a military and a political plane, however, it would require a considerable degree of flexibility. Somehow, the Germans would have to reach an agreement with the Chetniks and increase their effectiveness against the Partisans, and they would have to induce the Serbian people to support the new policy, primarily by relaxing the long-held policy of mass reprisals. The man chosen to coordinate the new policy, Hermann Neubacher, was dispatched to Belgrade in October with special powers which were to extend over all of southeastern Europe.

Hitler's orders to Neubacher are contained in his directive of October 29, 1943, entitled "The Unified Conduct of the Struggle Against Communism in the Southeast." The chief provisions of the directive, in paraphrase, were the following:

1. The Communist danger in the Southeast requires a unified counteraction.
2. The political conduct of the counteraction is the task of Envoy Neubacher, the Special Plenipotentiary of the Foreign Ministry, who gets his directives from the Reich Foreign Minister. The Special Plenipotentiary conducts this action in closest cooperation with the Commander in Chief in Southeast Europe and the Military Commander in Southeast Europe.
3. The task of the Special Plenipotentiary is to organize politically the national anti-Communist forces in various countries of the Southeast and to direct their efforts in the struggle against the Communist bands. He alone is empowered to conduct, allow, or deny the negotiations with the leaders of the bands.
4. The economic policy in the Southeast, especially in regard to the supplying of the population, is to be so organized as to make a contribution to the united anti-Communist action. The Special Plenipotentiary is given full powers to establish the principles of economic policy in the Southeast and to carry them out.

· · ·

6. The civilian German agencies in the Southeast will be streamlined and their personnel reduced. The national administrations in various areas of the Southeast should be given a greater say in the conduct of the administration and economy, provided that this is politically unobjectionable ...

· · ·

8. The handling of the measures of atonement [reprisals] is to be agreed upon with the Special Plenipotentiary.[4]

[4] Microcopy No. T-120, Roll 753, Frames 365,533–36. See also Neubacher, pp. 164–70.

The directive contained several other points including those relating to the position and jurisdiction of the German military and diplomatic representatives in the Independent State of Croatia. In fact, as was often true in the German occupation regimes, Neubacher's activity did not extend to the limits of his powers as outlined in the directive. For one thing, Neubacher, despite the wording of the directive, had little to do either with the conclusion or with the implementation of the armistice agreements, once the policy of collaboration with the Chetniks had been worked out. And he had practically no influence on Germany's economic policies in Serbia, or in other areas of the southeast, except in Greece. The Economic Plenipotentiary in Serbia, Neuhausen, was too powerful and too successful in running the Serbian economy to Germany's great advantage to permit outside interference. Furthermore, Neuhausen's powers had just been expanded as a consequence of the streamlining of the occupation regime, which made him also Chief of the Military Administration. Neubacher did, however, have a considerable influence on the policy of mass reprisals in Serbia, and he was responsible for a drastic reduction in the harshness of this policy. The gruesome formula of shooting fifty hostages for each German killed, which had superseded the one hundred–to–one formula in February 1943, was now removed altogether. No fixed ratio was named as binding for the military commanders, and thenceforth the shooting of hostages was much less frequent and involved relatively few people. It is unlikely that this change in policy, although welcome indeed, made any great difference in the attitude of the population at large—the earlier savageries were still too vivid—and it was no doubt taken as a further indication of the Germans' waning fortunes.

Point 6 of the October 29 directive empowered Neubacher to enlarge the authority of the national governments in the southeast, including the Nedić regime in Serbia. But since Hitler consistently opposed the specific proposals that Neubacher submitted in that respect, Nedić remained as powerless as before. Neubacher did help, however, in bringing the Chetniks into a degree of collaboration with the Germans, and soon after his arrival in Belgrade a series of so-called armistice agreements were concluded between several of the leading Chetnik commanders and the German forces.

Despite the wording of the Neubacher directive (Point 3), the authority to conclude armistice agreements with the Chetniks and to decide questions of aid rested with the Commander in Chief in Southeast Europe (von Weichs), who in the case of Serbia delegated it to the Military Commander in Southeast Europe (who was also Military Commander in Serbia), and to the Commander of the Second Panzer Army for Yugoslav areas under his command.[5] The actual negotiations, based on principles announced by the Commander in Chief, and the signing of the agreements were handled by low-ranking officers, mostly majors and captains. Similarly, on the Chetnik side, it was never Mihailović who negotiated with the Germans but rather his various field commanders or deputies of these commanders. There seems no doubt that this was a planned effort on the part of the Chetnik high command: if Mihailović was not personally involved in the negotiations, they could always say (as they later in fact did) that he had never authorized the agreements and that they were concluded by individual commanders acting on their own and therefore could not be charged to him. Nevertheless, it seems certain that he knew of these agreements and approved of them. After all, as will presently be shown, they were concluded by some of Mihailović's principal field commanders and by the Inspector General of all Chetnik troops; they were part of broad Chetnik policy; and they affected large and strategically important territories and territory in the immediate vicinity of his headquarters. And most significantly, both in the directive of the Commander in Chief in Southeast Europe of November 21, 1943, and in the texts of the agreements themselves, there seems to have been a studied effort not to implicate General Mihailović in the collaboration, and even to exonerate him of any sins of collaboration.

CHETNIK-GERMAN COLLABORATION AGREEMENTS IN SERBIA

The formal basis of all these so-called armistice agreements (*Waffenruhe-Verträge*) between the representatives of the Military Commander in Southeast Europe and the leaders of the various Chetnik groups was the November 21 directive of Field Marshal Maximilian von Weichs, Commander in Chief in Southeast Europe, which listed the rules upon which these agreements had to rest:

1. As a consequence of negotiations started some time ago in close cooperation with the Special Plenipotentiary of the Ministry of Foreign Affairs [Neubacher] and the Commander in Chief in Southeast Europe with leaders of the Chetnik forces, an agreement was concluded, which stipulates local armistices and foresees common operations against the Communists, which will be concluded from case to case.

2. The conditions for this agreement were—and the same will apply for any possible additional agreements—that the Chetnik forces:

   a) Stop all fighting and sabotage operations against the German forces, their allies, and the domestic forces which cooperate with them, as well as against the Moslems [Moslem militia battalions],

   b) In the case of combined operations against the Communists the Chetniks put themselves under German command,

[5] Microcopy No. T-313, Roll 488, Frame 245.

c) Give up all liaison with the powers which find themselves at war with Germany, and deliver the liaison officers now present with them,

d) Take part in joint propaganda against Communism.

3. All [German] officers are to be informed about the following:

a) The now existing prohibition of cooperation with Chetnik forces and single groups corresponded to the definite decision of the Supreme Chetnik leader Draža Mihailović to pursue the struggle against Germany and its allies, a determination which he has *not* as yet given up.

b) The declaration of *individual* Chetnik leaders to pursue the struggle against Communism together with the German armed forces, resulted from the appraisal of the general situation in the Southeast, which considers the Communist guerrilla and its proved ideological and material support by the U.S.S.R. as the basic danger, and thus led to a reappraisal of the Chetnik offers [for cooperation?].

c) The lately loyal behavior of *individual* Chetnik units *cannot* be generalized, because even today there are still some attacks and sabotage acts by Chetnik bands.

d) The troops are forbidden from now on to conduct any negotiations with Chetnik troops. Unauthorized actions in this respect can lead to disturbances in the negotiations initiated by the highest political and military posts and result in injury to the policies in the entire Southeast.

e) Local Chetnik leaders who offer to participate in the common struggle must be referred to the next higher *Abwehr* or SD [*Sicherheitsdienst*] post.

f) The propaganda campaign against the Chetniks is to cease, its resumption to depend on the developments in the newly created situation.[6]

This document is interesting in several ways. It shows that the highest German political and military authorities in Serbia seriously desired to make a success of collaboration with the Chetniks and for this reason prohibited the local commanders from making arrangements on their own, and even from engaging in negotiations.[7] The emphasis on *individual* Chetnik units as cooperating in the struggle against Communism and the reference to Mihailović's continuing struggle against Germany removed Mihailović himself from any participation in the agreement and from any responsibility for Chetnik-German collaboration. This would appear to have been intentional, so that if Chetnik-German collaboration tended to undermine the Chetnik's standing with the population at large, the Chetnik leader would at least not bear the responsibility. Since both sides urgently needed each other, mutual concessions had to be made in the interest of achieving the basic aim, that of strengthening the front against the impending Partisan penetration into Serbia from the west and southwest; but the studied effort to exonerate Mihailović from guilt for the actions of his commanders would, they hoped, have the effect of preserving his standing with the people

---

[6] Microcopy No. T-77, Roll 883, Frames 5,631,870–71.

[7] The Chetniks took the same precautions, authorizing only certain persons to negotiate with the Germans and prohibiting all others from such activities. See *Dokumenti o idajstvu Draže Mihailovića*, I, 687.

and with the Western Allies if they should find out about the agreements. The Chetnik leadership wanted to have their cake and eat it, and von Weichs's directive would seem to indicate that they succeeded. Thus while in Serbia the Chetniks continued to pursue a policy of ambivalence, their relationship to the Germans was direct, rather than indirect through the Nedić regime, and fairly intensive, and at least for some months was based on formal agreements.

Between mid-November and the end of December 1943 four short-term agreements were concluded between the Chetniks and the Germans. The first, concluded on November 13 and signed six days later (it is alluded to in the von Weichs directive), was between the Military Commander in Southeast Europe and Major Vojislav Lukačević, chief of the Chetnik Staff No. 148.[8] The second, of November 26, was between the Military Commander in Southeast Europe on the one hand and Major Nikola Kalabić and Colonel Jevrem Simić acting for the Chetniks. The third, of December 14, was between the Germans and Captain Mihailo Čačić, commander of the Chetnik Ravanica Brigade. In all three the signatory for the Germans was Cavalry Captain Prince von Wrede, the Ic (Intelligence Officer) to the Military Commander in Southeast Europe; the Chetnik commanders, except Čačić, were represented by one of their staff members (e.g. Major Lukačević by Captain Milorad Mitić, and Kalabić and Simić by Lt. Colonel Janko Mijatović). A fourth agreement was concluded between Lt. Colonel Ljuba Jovanović-Patak, commander of the Chetnik forces in eastern Serbia, and German Major Müller acting for the district command (*Kreiskommandantur*) Zaječar on December 23–25. Each of these agreements consisted of ten to twelve points, which were to be in effect for a period of five to ten weeks. They all specified, or implied, that if they were loyally executed they would be renewed: thus on January 17, 1944, a new agreement between the Germans and Colonel Simić was concluded, covering a few more counties than the earlier Kalabić-Simić agreement of November 26, and specified to be in effect until March 31, 1944.[9]

One German report refers to an agreement that had been concluded,

---

[8] On November 3, 1943, the Chetnik commander holding the area south of Užice found his troops threatened by the Partisans and turned to the commander of the 24th Bulgarian Division for assistance with ammunition. The request was passed on to the Germans, who answered that as long as the Chetniks fought the Partisans, the Germans would not attack them from the rear and that they would furnish them the necessary medical supplies but no ammunition because they thought the Chetniks had enough. The Germans also stated that the Chetniks could fight against the Partisans in front of the German lines, but any further arrangements would have to wait. Microcopy No. T-501, Roll 253, Frame 740. The implication is clear that some talks were going on between the Germans and the Chetniks but that no definite arrangements had as yet been made.

[9] For the excerpts of the Lukačević agreement see Microcopy No. T-77, Roll 883, Frames 5,632,502–4; for those of the Kalabić-Simić agreement Frames 5,632,500–1. Full texts of the Lukačević, Kalabić-Simić, Čačić, Jovanović, and Simić agreements, all under No. NOKW-1082, are found in U.S. National Archives, *World War II Crimes Records—Record Group 238.* The full text of the Simić agreement of Jan. 17, 1944, is given also in Microcopy No. T-77, Roll 883, Frames 5,632,508–10.

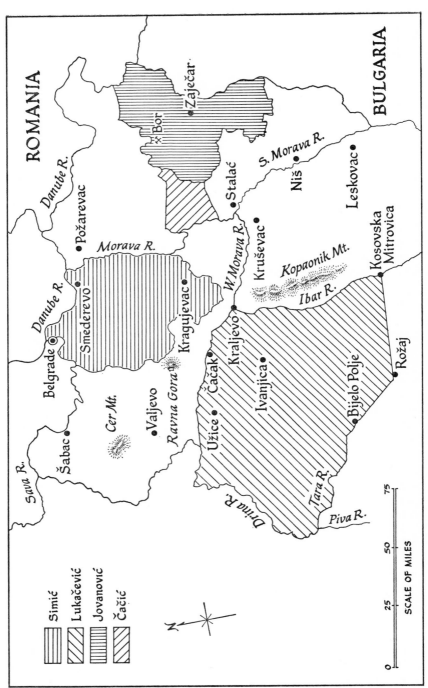

ROMANIA

BULGARIA

Danube R.

Danube R.

Sava R.

Šabac

Belgrade

Požarevac

Smederevo

Morava R.

Cer Mt.

Valjevo

Ravna Gora

Kragujevac

Bor

Zaječar

Stalać

S. Morava R.

Niš

Leskovac

W. Morava R.

Kruševac

Kopaonik Mt.

Ibar R.

Kosovska
Mitrovica

Kraljevo

Čačak

Užice

Ivanjica

Bijelo Polje

Rožaj

Drina R.

Tara R.

Piva R.

Simić

Lukačević

Jovanović

Čačić

N

SCALE OF MILES

0   25   50   75

Map 6. Areas in Serbia covered by Chetnik-German armistice agreements

or was about to be concluded, with the Chetnik commander Popović in the area of Leskovac in southern Serbia, to be in effect until February 21, 1944.[10] I was unable to find the text of this agreement, nor could I confirm by means of documentary evidence Neubacher's assertion that an armistice agreement was concluded also with Lt. Colonel Dragutin Keserović, another leading Chetnik commander, although, as will be shown later, he did collaborate intensively with the Germans during the summer of 1944.[11]

With the exception of Captain Čačić, the Chetnik commanders who concluded the above agreements were among the half-dozen highest standing of Mihailović's field commanders in Serbia. Both Lukačević and Kalabić, though of low military rank, were supreme commanders in their areas. Simić was the Inspector of all Chetnik forces, and Jovanović was Mihailović's top commander in eastern Serbia.[12] The military importance of both Lukačević and Kalabić (and Simić) and of the agreements signed with them is best indicated by the large area under their command, to which therefore the provisions of the agreements applied. The area covered by the four agreements that were in existence around January 20, 1944, is indicated in Map 6. The territory of the Lukačević agreement of November 19, 1943, was delimited by the following points: Bajina Bašta, the Drina River, the Tara River, Bijelo Polje, Rožaj, Kosovska Mitrovica, the Ibar River, Kraljevo, Čačak, Užice, Bajina Bašta. The Simić agreement of January 17 included the following counties: Posavina, Vračar, Grocka, Podunavlje, Jasenica, Kosmaj, Mladenovac, Oplenac, Orašac, Kačer, Kragujevac, Gruža, Lepenica, Veliki Orašac, and Kolubara, and a five-kilometer-wide strip of land to the west of the railroad line between Obrenovac and Gornji Milanovac. The Čačić agreement covered a smaller area, consisting of the counties of Paraćin and Ćuprija and the southern part of the county of Despotovac, but through it ran a section of the vital railroad connecting Belgrade and Salonika and within the area were four coal mines valuable to the German war effort. The Jovanović agreement included the counties of Negotin, Salaš, Zaječar, Boljevac, Andrejevac, Knjaževac, and the southern portion of the country of Jabukovac—an area containing the great copper mine at Bor as well as several other mining enterprises of lesser importance.

A number of things can be said about these agreements, and said more pertinently by direct reference. For this reason I reproduce, as an example, the complete text of one of these agreements, the Simić

[10] Microcopy No. T-501, Roll 256, Frame 10.
[11] See Neubacher, p. 166.
[12] Simić had been Mihailović's classmate, but Mihailović, though granting him a high position in his military organization, did not think well of him and did not trust him because of his habit of lying. See *The Trial of Draža Mihailović*, p. 358.

agreement of January 17, 1944. Two considerations make this full analysis warranted: first, the importance of the Chetnik-German agreements, despite their short duration, as showing Chetnik policies not only toward the Germans but also toward the Partisans and the Western Allies; and second, the persistent denials on the part of General Mihailović that he knew of such agreements and the denials by Chetnik and pro-Chetnik writers since the war either that the agreements existed at all or that, if they did, they were part of overall Chetnik policy. The argument of these writers is that the agreements were made solely for the purpose of getting ammunition from the Germans and were entered into only by a few local commanders acting on their own, and were in fact no different from similar accommodations that the Partisans made with the Germans in the course of the war.

The Simić agreement was one of the last to be concluded and was the most comprehensive, and it can be fairly assumed to have been worded with care. Its text was as follows:

The following armistice agreement is concluded between the Military Commander in Southeast Europe [Felber] as the supreme organ of the occupying powers in Serbia and as the representative of the German Reich with the Serbian government on the one hand and the Inspector of the Chetnik forces of Draža Mihailović, Colonel Jevrem Simić, on the other:

1. The purpose of the agreement is the joint struggle against the Communist Partisans, for which all the units under the command of Colonel Simić of the DM Chetniks will be embodied in the fight by the German and Bulgarian troops as well as the troops of the Serbian government against the Communists.

2. The agreement includes the following counties: Posavina, Vračar, Grocka, Podunavlje, Jasenica, Kosmaj, Mladenovac, Oplenac, Orašac, Kačer, Kragujevac, Gruža, Lepenica, Veliki Orašac, Kolubara, and besides in the westerly direction the territory extending for 5 kilometers west of the railroad line Obrenovac–Gornji Milanovac.

3. In the area covered by the armistice, arrests of and actions against the followers of the DM movement will not be undertaken for the duration of the agreement, unless such measures become necessary by the committing of punishable acts on the part of individual followers of DM.

4. Colonel Simić confirms that in the agreement area, with units under his command, no members of armed forces of countries which are at war with Germany are present either as liaison officers or in any other capacity.

Colonel Simić assumes for the agreement area the obligation to forbid [functioning of] all channels which could furnish information to the enemy on the German and the Bulgarian armies and on the German military movements.

5. oFr the duration of the agreement the DM Chetniks will abstain from any enemy activity against the German, Bulgarian, and Serbian troops and police units, as well as against their military and civilian organs. The recruiting of troops for the Serbian government forces is not to be interfered with, not even by propaganda. Likewise, the Chetniks are to stop all reprisals and threats against the families of Serbs who as soldiers, officials, employees, workers, or in any other capacity are in the service of the Serbian government or of the armies of occupation.

6. Should any DM Chetnik units, with which no armistice agreement has been concluded, appear in the agreement area, Colonel Simić will either put these units under his command, or see to it that they leave the area. Colonel Simić is responsible for the actions of the members of such units which might run against the provisions of this agreement. Subordinates of Colonel Simić who refuse to recognize this agreement are to be removed from the agreement area.

7. The DM Chetniks devote themselves in the agreement area exclusively to the fighting of the Communist Partisans and thereby support the struggle of the forces of law and order in Serbia.

8. Should DM Chetniks receive information that members of the German, Bulgarian, or Serbian units or other posts, or individual persons, engage in Communist activity or maintain contact with the Communists, the Chetniks will not interfere on their own initiative in dispensing justice, but will deliver the incriminating evidence, and in the case of danger, also the persons involved, to the German authorities.

9. The DM Chetniks must report as rapidly as possible to the nearest organ of the forces of order the appearance, the origin, the marching direction, and so on, of any Communist units [entering] in the agreement area, as well as their strength and armament.

The DM Chetnik units must take up the fight against these units immediately, if their forces suffice. For this purpose, and according to need, they will be given ammunition and medical supplies.

In the case that the DM Chetnik units are not sufficient, the forces of law and order will give them aid in troops, and in the case of need also in heavy arms. The wounded DM Chetniks will be cared for in the German military hospitals.

10. For the fight against the Communists the DM Chetniks put unconditionally at the disposal of the forces of order their scouting and their intelligence services.

For the purpose of mutual exchange of information a liaison group will be detailed to the staff of Colonel Simić. Furthermore, the posts of the occupying armies and of the [Serbian] government in the agreement area will be instructed to cooperate in the sense of this agreement with the DM Chetniks and to transmit the messages.

11. By mutual agreement the DM Chetniks take the obligation to protect the transport routes and transport equipment against attacks, plunder, and sabotage, including such acts committed by Anglo-Americans by way of land operations.

In particular, the DM Chetniks take the obligation within the agreement area to cooperate, by active military operations, in the securing of the following communication lines:

a) The road Ripanj [near Belgrade]-Topola-Kragujevac-Kraljevo.
b) The railroad Obrenovac-Lajkovac-Gornji Milanovac, including the branch line Lazarevac-Arandjelovac-Mladenovac.
c) The railroad Belgrade-Mala Krsna-Velika Plana, with the branch line to Požarevac.
d) The railroad Belgrade-Mladenovac-Lapovo.

The stopping and inspecting of trains of all kinds [by the DM Chetniks], even when they are in stations, is considered an unwarranted interference with the railroad traffic, and is forbidden.

12. The conclusion of this agreement is to be kept secret. It enters into effect immediately upon its signature and is valid until March 31, 1944.[13]

For the most part, each successive agreement was more detailed and specific than previous ones, and the Simić agreement just quoted is extremely exact. Also, specific conditions in various areas played a certain role in formulating the provisions of these agreements. Some of the early agreements stipulated that the agreement areas were entrusted to the Chetnik commanders for independent struggle against the Partisans, stating that only in the case of larger undertakings the German and Chetnik forces would operate together and under German command. Some of the agreements say explicitly that the agreements on the German side are binding also for the Bulgarian troops, Nedić troops, the Serbian Volunteer Corps, the Russian Protective Corps, and the Moslem Legion in Sandjak; others refer simply to German and "other forces of law and order." Since the Germans had trouble keeping the Serbian labor working in the mines, both the Čačić and the Jovanović agreements have specific provisions obliging the two commanders to return to the mines the workers who deserted, even if they had joined their ranks, and generally to safeguard these mines against sabotage.

As Map 6 indicates, the agreement area (except for a corridor in the middle, of which more will be said later) extended from the suburbs of Belgrade to the southern borders of Sandjak, and included also the economically strategic area of eastern Serbia.[14] It should be mentioned, however, that Chetnik-German collaboration at this time was not limited to agreement areas but was actively pursued in some other areas as well. For example, a report of the Area Command No. 599 (Belgrade) for the period November 15–December 15, 1943, says: "Peace and order were not disturbed in the area of the Belgrade Area Command and the Požarevac District Command. In the Požarevac district the Chetnik detachments are determined to step up the fight against the Communists, although they have not concluded an agreement with the occupation power. The conclusion of the agreements between the occupation power and the Chetniks for combined struggle against the Communists was almost generally acclaimed, perhaps with the unspoken thought that this will help to avoid the reprisals in these hard times."[15] The Chetniks in the Požarevac area were under the command of another important officer, Lt. Colonel Simeon Ocokoljić (known also as Siniša Pazarac), and his collaboration with the Germans is reported also by the Nedić authorities. A similar situation existed in the district of Šabac

---

[13] Microcopy No. T-77, Roll 883, Frames 5,632,508–10.

[14] On the maps that accompanied biweekly Situation Reports of the Military Commander in Southeast Europe to the Wehrmacht Operations Staff, indicating the areas controlled by specific guerilla groups in Serbia, the areas covered by the agreements are indicated as controlled by the "Contractual Chetniks" (*Vertrags-Chetniks*). See e.g. Microcopy No. T-501, Roll 267, Frame 232.

[15] *Dokumenti o izdajstvu Draže Mihailovića*, I, 593.

in northwestern Serbia, where Chetniks stepped up their action against known and suspected Communists and were not interfered with by the German and Serbian quisling authorities.[16]

The curious aspect of the agreement areas as shown in Map 6 is the corridor, wider in the west and narrower in the east, that separated the Simić area from the Lukačević area. The land not covered by any agreement lay north of the Kraljevo-Čačak-Požega line and included the counties of Ljubić, Takovo (except for some parts west of the railroad line from the north to Gornji Milanovac), and most of the county of Požega. In the western part of this area, on one of the slopes of Mount Suvobor, was Ravna Gora, where General Mihailović had his headquarters, and also the village of Pranjani (where in April 1944 the Chetniks made a makeshift airstrip); there, too, was the village of Ba, where the Chetnik congress was convened during the last week of January 1944. Within this corridor also were the railroad and good roads between western and eastern Serbia. Thus Mihailović sat in his headquarters (moving frequently within this general area), not bound by any provisions of the agreements with the Germans. The situation was hardly circumstantial, but if it was, as I assume, a concession that the Germans granted, it was not a costly one.

The text of von Weichs's November 21 directive, with its italics and its careful noting of Mihailović's continued resistance, seems to support the conclusion. The Chetniks and the Germans had good reason to collaborate, but there were constraints on both sides: for the Germans, Hitler's orders that agreements must be with individual commanders, and thus by definition for smaller areas, and that when aid was extended in arms and supplies, the operations must be well defined and under overall German command; for the Chetniks, Mihailović's insistence that his position both with the people and with the Western Allies must not be compromised by open collaboration with the Germans.[17] In fact, a German agreement with Mihailović personally would have taken on something of a general Serbian or Yugoslav character and thus in view of Hitler's specifications was impossible in principle. Mihailović's professed determination to continue fighting the Germans at the same time

---

[16] See *ibid.*, pp. 558, 561, 596–99.

[17] On November 20, 1943, the Germans intercepted a radio message from Mihailović to *vojvoda* Djujić, his commander in northern Dalmatia, instructing him to cooperate with the German forces. He himself, he says, "cannot go along because of public opinion." Microcopy No. T-311, Roll 196, Frame 223. This refusal to have any personal dealing with the enemy was a policy that Mihailović departed from only on four or five occasions—the Divci conference in mid-November 1941, two conferences with Envoy Neubacher's representative, Rudolf Stärker, in the autumn of 1944 (the first one in western Serbia, at which Mihailović accompanied Colonel Robert H. McDowell, the chief of the American military mission at his headquarters, and the second one in northeastern Bosnia), and a final conference with Stärker at Vučjak Mountain early in April 1945. One Chetnik commander known to have advised Mihailović to use such restraint was Lt. Colonel Petar Baćović, in regard to Chetnik dealings with the Italians. See *The Trial of Draža Mihailović*, p. 448. It is interesting that Neubacher in his book, pp. 166–68, also tries to exonerate Mihailović from the onus of collaboration.

that his commanders were concluding armistice agreements with them proves nothing. Certainly he took no disciplinary actions against those commanders. And for the Germans, the delineation of the agreement areas to exclude Ravna Gora was in some ways a convenience, although even before these agreements the Germans were well informed about Mihailović's whereabouts.[18] After the agreements had been concluded Mihailović had a smaller area to move in and from Ravna Gora he was in no position to threaten the Germans.[19]

Another point can be made: one of the stipulations of all Chetnik-German agreements was that the commanders of the agreement areas could not have at their headquarters or with any of their units any liaison or other officers representing powers at war with Germany (meaning, obviously, British, American, and Russian officers). Mihailović continued to have British and American liaison officers until May 1944, and then again American officers from August 1944 to the second half of September when he was forced out of Serbia (and in northeastern Bosnia until November 1, 1944).

The signing of these agreements was in a number of ways helpful to the Chetniks. They were now safe from the Germans in times when they were engaged in fighting the Partisans, and they were assured of a measure of ammunition (though much less than they had hoped for) to use in pursuing that struggle, as well as the necessary medical supplies and care of their wounded in German military hospitals. They acquired a large measure of freedom to work on the improvement of their military, political, and intelligence organization, and virtual freedom of forced recruiting of manpower even in the plains areas.[20] To some extent also the agreements made it easier for them to obtain supplies and money contributions from the people, some of whom at least were induced by this show of strength to swing from Nedić or from a neutralist position to the Chetniks, and they increased the Chetniks' ability to infiltrate the Nedić governmental and military apparatus. At the same time, of course, this outright collaboration sent many other people to the Partisans' side, and it was the fear of this that made the Chetniks so much interested in keeping the agreements secret. Sporadic outbursts by some Chetnik units against the Germans even after the agreements were signed may perhaps have been an attempt to counteract unfavor-

---

[18] Colonel Klamroth of the German General Staff after an inspection trip to the Balkans in August 1943 reported: "The surveillance of Draža Mihailović is good. The German service posts quickly get to know his continually changing location." Microcopy No. T-78, Roll 332, Frame 6,289,881.

[19] The shepherds' huts of Ravna Gora, located on one of the slopes of Mount Suvobor (865 m.), are easily accessible from all sides. If the Germans had wanted to drive Mihailović from his base after he returned to Serbia in June 1943, or take him prisoner, they probably could have done so with little effort.

[20] See the report of the Military Commander in Southeast Europe to the Commander in Chief in Southeast Europe of Dec. 23, 1943, Microcopy No. T-501, Roll 253, Frames 1,020–21.

able public reaction, and the canceling of the Simić agreement in mid-February 1944 may also be attributed to this. Indeed, a British liaison officer, Major H. B. Dugmore, who was with the Partisans in eastern Serbia from the beginning of November 1943 to mid-June 1944, reported to his superiors that during this time the number of Partisans in Serbia rose from about 1,700 to over 13,000.[21]

After the agreements, Chetnik activity against the Partisans increased throughout Serbia. Ample proof of this can be found in the periodic reports of the German commands and of the county and district prefects of the Nedić administration.[22] In mid-December 1943 Mihailović issued an appeal to all able-bodied Serbs to enlist in his forces for a determined struggle against the Partisans, and in parts of Sandjak the SS commander of the Moslem Legion, Karl von Krempler, posted announcements stating that the Lukačević Chetniks were being allowed to mobilize "the national forces" from among the Serbian population of the area.[23] Major Lukačević showed such zeal in fighting the Partisans in parts of Sandjak that on December 22 Colonel Remold, commander of the Remold Group, commended him in a special order, and he was also permitted to keep some of the arms he captured.[24]

In order to assure better overall cooperation between the German and collaborating Chetnik forces and particularly to provide for more efficient aid in arms and ammunition in various operations, special liaison officers were assigned to the Chetnik units that had formal agreements or collaborated informally with the Germans. These liaison officers were also giving advice on tactical problems in various operations. Among the Germans performing such functions one of the best known was Lieutenant Heusz; until December 22, 1943, he was liaison officer with Major Lukačević and later he was liaison officer with Lt. Colonel Djurišić.[25] Another was Major Weyel, who maintained liaison with Captain Neško Nedić, chief of staff to the Chetnik Commander of Serbia General Miroslav J. Trifunović; Weyel was also in direct command of a Chetnik force that was attached to his group of units.[26] Even Keserović admitted at his trial that Weyel came to southern Serbia in the summer of 1944 as the representative of the German command in Serbia and coordinated the operations of the Račić, Kalabić, and Kesero-

---

[21] According to the communication of a reliable British source.

[22] *Dokumenti o izdajstvu Draže Mihailovića*, I, 513, 591, 596–98, 605, and *passim*.

[23] Report of the *Abwehr* troop 381 of Dec. 20, 1943, in Microcopy No. T-313, Roll 488, Frame 249. For Colonel von Krempler's announcement see *ibid.*, Frame 350.

[24] *Ibid.*, Frames 230–32. This order of the day angered the Second Panzer Army Command, and the Vth SS-Mountain Army Corps, under which the Remold Group operated, was given orders to instruct its lower commands that such actions—meaning official praise of the Chetniks—were undesirable and should not be repeated without prior permission of divisional commands.

[25] *Ibid.*, Frames 171, 225.

[26] See e.g. the Daily Reports of the Military Commander in Southeast Europe to the Commander in Chief in Southeast Europe for May 1944, Microcopy No. T-501, Roll 256, Frames 669–99, and *KTB/OKW/WFSt*, Vol. IV, Part I (1944), p. 710.

vić Chetnik units with those of the German, Serbian quisling and Bulgarian units against the Partisans.[27]

No reference to the Chetnik-German agreements was ever made in the published exchanges between Mihailović and the Yugoslav government-in-exile. It is not surprising that no information about these agreements reached the government-in-exile through communication channels under British control; but there are no traces of such communications through any other channels. Conceivably, the government-in-exile could have learned of them from Major Lukačević in person after he left Yugoslavia with Colonel Bailey in February 1944 and called upon Yugoslav and British officials in both Cairo and London. But if he ever communicated anything to Prime Minister Purić or to any other government-in-exile official, the facts have, to my knowledge, not been made public. One must therefore concede that it is possible, even probable, that even the most ardently pro-Chetnik members of the government-in-exile, including Purić, had no knowledge whatsoever of the existence of these agreements as long as they were in office, and were therefore honest in their denials as pertaining to that time. They knew only as much as Mihailović communicated to them: namely, that there was no collaboration between the Chetniks and the enemy.[28] Of course, the British government, from December 1942 on, communicated to the government-in-exile a certain amount of their information on Chetnik collaboration.

But the important question is, did the British know about the existence of these agreements? Since no British intelligence reports from Yugoslavia have been made public except the excerpts that are contained in various autobiographical works such as those of Churchill, Eden, Maclean, and Deakin, we had until recently no official proof of whether or not the British got wind of these agreements, and if they did, when and how.[29] But circumstantial evidence in the materials thus far published and the recently opened Foreign Office documents dealing with Yugoslav affairs and a series of British-initiated moves indicates that the British at least strongly suspected that agreements were being concluded, and they may well have had definite information about them within days of their signing.[30] Two points especially bear out this sur-

[27] *Sudjenje članovima rukovodstva organizacije Draže Mihailovića*, p. 215.

[28] I did not consider it necessary to contact and inquire specifically of former Prime Minister Purić whether he knew anything about the existence of the Chetnik-German agreements at the turn of 1943–44; I am sure that he would say that he did not, since his official and private position was always one of supporting General Mihailović, who insisted that there were no such agreements.

[29] The previously quoted British pamphlet *The Četniks* (September 1944), which contains an abbreviated version of the Kalabić-Simić agreement with the Germans, states explicitly (p. 19) that it had been reported by a British intelligence officer in June 1944. This may, of course, have been a case of shifting of dates and other details to protect the agents involved.

[30] It seems definite from declassified reports of the SOE liaison officers with Mihailović that they did not have documentary proof of Chetnik collaboration with the Germans. But the British could have obtained that proof from their other agents in Yugoslavia or Berlin, or from other

mise. First, the Lukačević agreement with the Germans was signed on November 19, and the Kalabić and Simić agreement on November 27; on November 29 the British military authorities in the Middle East asked their group of liaison officers in northeastern Serbia, headed by Lt. Colonel Jasper Rootham (and probably liaison officers in other areas as well), whether they "could estimate the reactions of the local commanders if Mihailovich were to be replaced, and secondly, whether any of them had to our knowledge received orders from Mihailovich to collaborate with the Axis." Rootham later wrote that even though he knew that the British were dissatisfied with Mihailović and that many of Mihailović's supporters disagreed with his policies, he had never given a thought to Mihailović's collaboration with the Axis or his removal and therefore the message came as a "tremendous shock."[31]

The second point is that on December 16, General Wilson, through Brigadier Armstrong, issued written orders to General Mihailović for the Chetniks to blow up a railroad bridge over the Morava River south of the railroad hub of Stalać on the main Belgrade-Athens line and also a railroad bridge over the Ibar River between Kraljevo and Kosovska Mitrovica on the secondary line connecting Belgrade and Skopje (and thence Athens) and to carry out these actions by December 29.[32] Lt. Colonel Rootham also got an order from the Middle East on December 9 to sabotage the main railroad line near his area of activity.[33] There was to my knowledge no German-Chetnik agreement covering the area on the Morava River south of Stalać, but the western bank of the Ibar lay within the area covered by the Lukačević agreement. The Lukačević agreement did not specify, as did the Simić agreement of January 17, 1944, in point 11, that the Chetniks were obliged to protect the railroads against sabotage precisely of the type General Wilson ordered Mihailović to undertake, but it was perhaps considered self-evident and the Chetniks apparently stood ready to honor it. At first, Mihailović replied to Brigadier Armstrong that they could not blow up either of the bridges, because they had no equipment, because there was danger of German reprisals, because they lacked the military supplies to protect

---

sources. In fact, after this study was in page proof, the author saw, through the courtesy of Professor Phyllis Auty, a series of reports submitted to a symposium she and Professor Richard Clogg organized on July 6–8, 1973, at Cumberland Lodge, Windsor Great Park, England, under the title *British Policy Towards Resistance in Yugoslavia and Greece in the Second World War* (soon to be published by Macmillan), in which it was stated that the British had broken German codes and that from intercepted radio messages they knew what was going on between the Germans and the Chetniks. The source of this information was considered so important that in order to protect the secret the intercepts were circulated only to a highly select group of people. Nor did the British react directly to information in these intercepts in order not to arouse German suspicion. See also below, p. 366.

[31] Rootham, p. 171.

[32] For the partial text of Wilson's order specifying the targets to be sabotaged see Mihailović's correspondence with the government-in-exile in Jovan Djonović, "The Connections with General Mihailović from the Middle East," p. 19. Mihailović's reactions to this order communicated to the government-in-exile are found in *ibid.*, pp. 19–22.

[33] Rootham, p. 175.

surrounding civilian population against such reprisals, and so on. Eventually, Mihailović signified that he would issue an order for the blowing up of the bridges, and he seems to have done so, but the command was never executed.[34]

A third indication that the British knew about these agreements and that they were very disgusted by them was the order issued to Rootham, dated December 13, that he had the discretionary power to lead his party to the nearest Partisan units, which, according to the information supplied by the same wire, were seventy-five to one hundred forty-five miles away. Rootham and his companions did not, however, shift to the Partisans, but rather set out toward Ravna Gora, where the chief British military mission was winding up its affairs and from where, some five months later, they were evacuated to Italy.[35]

It should be made clear that not all the Chetniks, however strongly anti-Partisan, were willing to follow the collaboration agreements. The Simić agreement (Point 6) clearly foresaw such unwillingness by stipulating that it was the obligation of the agreement area commanders to remove uncooperative Chetniks by expelling them from the area. And Lieutenant Heusz, while still liaison officer with Lukačević, reported on December 1, 1943, that there was some grumbling among Lukačević's men because of the agreement he had made with the Germans.[36] The Chetniks themselves were fully aware of the unfavorable effect that these agreements would probably have on their standing with the population at large. But the collaboration could not be hidden, and the result was an inevitable erosion of the morale in the ranks of the Chetniks. In other words, the policy of ambivalence tilting toward closer collaboration with the Germans contained obvious dangers for the Chetniks.

Under the circumstances, the armistice agreements failed to satisfy either side. Some Chetnik units still engaged in sporadic attacks and acts of sabotage against the quisling forces and even Germans; certain provisions they simply ignored, and in general they used the agreements as a convenient cover to strengthen their organization and to extend their infiltration of the Nedić administration. They even boasted that the agreements were an expression of German weakness.[37] This attitude was particularly in evidence at the Ba congress held in late January 1944 (to be discussed fully in Chapter 11), which could not have been held

---

[34] Many years later, on July 23, 1961, Brigadier Armstrong, in a speech given in the hall of the Serbian Church in London at the invitation of the Serbian emigrants' group "Oslobodjenje," said that he and Mihailović did send some officers to the Morava River to blow up the bridge but the commander of the local Chetnik corps, Radomir Cvetić, would not allow the action to be carried out because his area was endangered by the Partisans. Speech quoted by Vukčević, "From Tehran to the Establishment of the Šubašić Government," pp. 45–46. Cvetić may have been acting on his own, but it is not inconceivable that he was following other orders of Mihailović, as a way of protecting the Chetniks with the Germans and at least Mihailović also with the British.

[35] Rootham, pp. 176–77.

[36] Microcopy No. T-313, Roll 488, Frame 524.

[37] Microcopy No. T-501, Roll 256, Frame 39; Microcopy No. T-311, Roll 286, Frames 185–87.

except by tacit German approval and ironically became the occasion of an outpouring of anti-German sentiment. The Germans reacted by issuing orders that some of the Chetnik leaders, including Čačić, who failed to observe the agreements were again to be regarded as enemies who should be captured and whose detachments should be destroyed.[38] In a conference between the Commander in Chief in Southeast Europe von Weichs and Envoy Neubacher on February 1, it was established that most of the Chetnik leaders were not living up to the terms of the agreements and that therefore not only should the agreements not be renewed but also the Chetniks should again be militarily pressed.[39] In more general terms, General Felber in a circular letter of February 2 and a letter to General August Meyszner of February 11 stated frankly that the armistice agreements had not achieved their objective of assuring Chetnik collaboration against the Partisans. He directed the German troops as well as the Serbian quisling troops to proceed decisively against the Chetniks whenever they acted against the Germans or quisling forces and authorities. Attempts of the Chetnik leaders to conclude new agreements were to be repulsed, on the grounds of the numerous breaches of the earlier agreements.[40] And when Colonel Simić canceled his agreement on February 11 but with the proviso that he might withdraw the cancellation later, the Germans accepted it as definite. The reason given by the Chetniks for the cancellation of this contract was that the Germans were not enforcing the agreement on the Serbian Volunteer Corps: specifically, there had been some difficulties over a train carrying Volunteer Corps wounded and in the ensuing fight twenty-five Chetniks had been killed and twenty-two taken prisoner, with no losses on the Volunteer Corps side.[41] The Area Command 599 (Belgrade) in its report for the period January 15–February 15 stated also, and quite significantly, that one of the reasons for the cancellation of the Simić agreement was that the Chetniks were condemned by the population because of the collaboration with the occupying power.[42] The final outcome of this disagreement was an order of the Commander in Chief in Southeast Europe of February 23, 1944:

It is again stressed, that on the basis of experience thus far, any further conclusion of agreements with the subordinate leaders of DM [Draža Mihailović] is forbidden. Only the agreement with Lukačević in southwestern Serbia remains in force. The Commander in Chief in Southeast Europe retains the right to terminate this agreement also if the Chetnik leaders in that area should not fulfill their obligations. The requests for ammunition coming from the

[38] See the order of the Military Commander in Southeast Europe of Feb. 2, 1944, Microcopy No. T-311, Roll 286, Frame 24.
[39] Microcopy No. T-501, Roll 256, Frame 3.
[40] *Ibid.*, Frames 26, 54.
[41] *Ibid.*, Frames 7, 55.
[42] *Dokumenti o izdajstvu Draže Mihailovića*, I, 594.

Chetniks must be carefully scrutinized before being submitted to the Commander in Chief. In case of doubt it should be always assumed that the requests are too large in comparison with the objective of replenishing the ammunition supplies of the DM movement.[43]

The last two sentences are ambiguous, to say the least, but they would seem to indicate that some agreements were still functioning. Moreover, as later developments showed, even without the formal agreements Chetnik requests for ammunition were accepted and honored after due investigation of their reasonableness and proposed use.

It was not only the infringement of the provisions of these agreements on the part of the Chetniks that worked against their continuation in a formal manner. Both Nedić and Ljotić were against the agreements, which tended to push them aside as German puppets in favor of the Chetniks. And General Meyszner was apparently against them from the beginning. In February he opened a veritable campaign against them, trying to persuade the military commanders to declare that Germany was "in a state of war" against the Chetniks. He strongly opposed further arming of Djurišić and Lukačević, not simply because they were (untrustworthy) Chetniks and Serbs, but on the grounds that they had broken their agreements with the Germans, and that the Moslem population in Albania, Kosovo, and Sandjak had expressed concern over the strengthening of the Chetniks by the Germans; the Croats, too, he said, were very concerned about the strengthening of the Chetniks.[44] At the same time (February 22) General Asen Nikoloff, the commander of the Bulgarian First Occupation Corps, also indicated his opposition to all agreements with the Chetniks.[45]

Meanwhile, the primary reason for Chetnik-German collaboration— the Partisan danger to Serbia—grew in importance. Partisan military preparation on the western approaches to Serbia, along with the steady advance of Soviet armies from the east, clearly suggested that the Partisans' chief area of operations in the second half of 1944 would be Serbia. For the Chetniks, therefore, collaboration with the Germans, or at least arms and ammunition from them, was essential. In May, the withdrawal of the head of the British mission, Brigadier Armstrong, and all other British liaison officers, dashed all hope of more arms and supplies from the British. Mihailović was still confident that the Western Allies would in the end come to his rescue, but he realized that he could not expect any help from them for the approaching struggle against the Partisans. The problem, therefore, was to hold out, to hang on to some territory, and to prevent the Partisans from overwhelming the Chetniks

[43] Microcopy No. T-501, Roll 256, Frame 97.
[44] Ibid., Frames 18, 128, 144, and Microcopy No. T-311, Roll 286, Frame 185.
[45] Microcopy No. T-501, Roll 256, Frame 16.

in Serbia. In order to do these things, continuing collaboration with the Germans was unavoidable.

INFORMAL COLLABORATION IN SERBIA

Despite certain objections, as we have seen, the Germans after the cancellation of most armistice agreements with the Chetniks were eager to preserve the agreement with Lukačević, who controlled the vital areas of Sandjak and southwestern Serbia and could be very useful in helping to prevent Partisan penetration into Serbia. From the minutes of a conference between Generals Felber and Meyszner of February 24, 1944, it would appear that the Lukačević agreement was still in force as of that date,[46] but soon thereafter the Germans lost contact with Lukačević. The agenda for a conference between Felber and Envoy Neubacher of March 4 includes the question, "Where is Lukačević hiding now?"[47] In fact, Lukačević was already out of the country—on his way via Italy and Cairo to London, where he was to be the representative of Mihailović at King Peter's wedding.[48] By March 4 the Germans had arrested and were about to bring to Belgrade Lukačević's chief of staff, Major Rudolf Perhinek, because of the attacks his Chetniks had been making on German troops.[49]

It thus appears that by early March 1944 the only formal operative arrangement between the Germans and the Chetniks was the one with Lt. Colonel Djurišić, who was in command of the Montenegrin Volunteer Corps, a unit established by the Germans and Nedić the previous autumn for the purpose of combatting the Partisans in Montenegro, but who also owed allegiance to Mihailović.

With the cancellation of the Chetnik-German armistice agreements by the end of February 1944, the Chetniks again became formally an enemy of the occupying forces. The report of the Military Commander in Southeast Europe for the period January 22–February 20 notes that "Except for single infringements there were up to now no [Chetnik] attacks and sabotage acts of significance."[50] Repeated pronouncements and continuing actions of both Germans and Chetniks in Serbia show, however, that both sides were ambivalent about the collaboration or lack of it: the only thing that bound them together and forced them to

---

[46] *Ibid.*, Frame 128.

[47] *Ibid.*, Frame 218.

[48] In London Lukačević was received by King George VI and high British officials including Foreign Secretary Eden. But his efforts to drum up support for Mihailović were ignored. He returned to Yugoslavia at the end of May just at the time when the chief of the British military mission, Brigadier Armstrong, was leaving Mihailović's headquarters. See the article by T. Z., "Vojislav Lukačević," pp. 97–100.

[49] Microcopy No. T-501, Roll 256, Frame 218. Perhinek, a Slovene, was the only non-Serb holding a high position among the Chetniks in Serbia.

[50] *Ibid.*, Frame 106.

cooperate was the growing danger from the Partisans. Between March 1944 and the end of the following August, this ambivalence was evident: a certain cooperation prevailed, without formal agreements, but the Germans reserved the right to use force whenever the Chetniks transgressed against them, or against the Bulgarians or the Serbian quisling forces or authorities. In practice, such force was not often applied during the course of 1944, but the few instances of it are worth noting. The largest and best known was Operation Treibjagd which began in mid-February against the Chetnik detachments of Kalabić in central and south-central Serbia. It was a joint German, Bulgarian, and Serbian quisling action, under the command of Colonel Diesener, otherwise commander of the Railroad Security Section Staff No. 5. The operation was concluded by March 5 with 81 Chetniks dead, many wounded, and 913, including many officers, taken prisoner.[51] Smaller actions were frequent. The German Daily Report of March 31 mentions an action against the Belgrade DM organization in which three corps commanders, two brigade commanders, and some other Chetnik officers were arrested.[52] The Daily Report for April 25 notes that an operation against the Chetniks near Ljig was called off, having achieved no success.[53] The same report also cites Partisan and Chetnik losses at the hands of the Germans from March 16 to April 15: for the Chetniks, 182 dead, 127 taken prisoner; for the Communists, 1,586 dead, 94 taken prisoner, 40 hostages shot, 200 arrested in Belgrade. But Chetnik commanders were apparently still trying to conclude new agreements, for in a conference between the Commander in Chief in Southeast Europe and the deputy of Envoy Neubacher on March 28, the Commander in Chief stated that the "general policy line toward Mihailović should be that one should continue to play with him, but no promises should be made. His offers should be declared as being of no interest to us."[54]

The most serious Partisan threat at this time was the penetration of two of their divisions, the 2nd and the 5th, numbering about five thousand men, into southwestern Serbia from Sandjak and Bosnia. The objective of these divisions was to cross the Ibar River and Mount Kopaonik in order to join forces with the strongest and most active Partisan units in Serbia, which were operating in the areas of Mount Jastrebac and the Toplica and Jablanica valleys in southern Serbia, and thus intensify Partisan activities in Serbia and prepare the ground for the entry of other Partisan forces from Bosnia and Sandjak.[55] The danger prompted immediate and intensive collaboration among the Germans,

[51] *Ibid.*, Frames 57, 224.
[52] *Ibid.*, Frame 380.
[53] *Ibid.*, Frame 590.
[54] *Ibid.*, Frame 360.
[55] *Oslobodilački rat*, II, 227–35.

the Bulgarians, the Serbian quisling forces, and the Chetniks. General Felber, referring to the new situation in Serbia in his report of April 22, took note of the cooperation: "DM himself is reported to have asked in a speech for loyal cooperation with the occupying forces in order to remove the Communist danger in Serbia. A visible sign of this new development is the fact that in southern Serbia, the Germans, the Serbian Volunteer Corps, and the Chetniks fight shoulder to shoulder." But in the same report Felber also stated: "The DM movement is split. While a part is actively fighting with the Germans against the Communists—without thereby giving up any of their reservations against all the occupiers—smaller DM bands in central and eastern Serbia continue their mischief as before."[56] Many other reports from this period refer to Chetnik-German collaboration against the Partisans. For example, in the Daily Report of the Military Commander in Southeast Europe of April 8, dealing with Operation Kammerjäger, which had been launched against the Partisan divisions that had broken into Serbia, it is stated that Chetnik detachments of Captain Raković, a leading Chetnik commander, have been badly beaten by the Partisans.[57] Ten days later (April 18) the Chief of Staff of the Serbian Volunteer Corps, Lt. Colonel Radoslav Tatalović, reported to General Felber that "cooperation with the Group Cvetić [an important Chetnik commander from south-central Serbia] is very good."[58] And in an order of General Felber of April 28, on the final phases of operations against the 2nd and 5th Partisan divisions near Požega in southwestern Serbia, Chetnik units are mentioned as taking part in operations with the German and Bulgarian forces.[59] Even more interesting is the information in the Daily Report of General Felber of May 1, in which it is said that about one thousand Chetniks are included in a German unit led by Major Weyel, who at that time was closely working with Chetnik Captain Neško Nedić on the coordination of German-Chetnik operations against the Partisans. The same report also states that on the line Požega-Kosjerići-Ražana-Povlen in the same area there are about five thousand Chetniks to various units of which German liaison officers have already been posted. The report continues: "DM, who has taken the overall command over these Chetnik forces, will establish radio contact with the German command."[60] (I cannot, however, offer any confirmation of this

---

[56] Microcopy No. T-501, Roll 256, Frames 549, 552.

[57] *Ibid.*, Frame 450.

[58] *Ibid.*, Frame 502.

[59] *Ibid.*, Frame 622. That the British liaison officers with the Chetniks were aware of this Chetnik-German collaboration in southwestern Serbia is clearly shown in *The Četniks*, pp. 22–23. See also *The Trial of Draža Mihailović*, p. 188, where Mihailović agrees that at the time there was some "parallel action, but not collaboration," with the Germans.

[60] Microcopy No. T-501, Roll 256, Frames 669–70. At his trial Mihailović admitted that through Major Lalatović he was directing the operations of the Chetnik forces against the two Partisan divisions that penetrated into Serbia. *The Trial of Draža Mihailović*, p. 224.

suggestion that Mihailović maintained direct radio contact with German command posts, and considering his pattern of behavior throughout the war, it is hardly likely that he did.)

In a conference held in Čačak on April 26 between SD Chief Biermann and Captain Predrag Raković, the commander of the Chetnik Second Corps and one of the principal Chetnik liaison links with Nedić and the Germans, Raković observed that his power to transact business with the Germans by order and in the name of General Mihailović had been withdrawn by the general and that he was therefore not participating in the conference as a representative of Mihailović.[61] The obvious inference is that Mihailović was quite aware of the agreements and contacts and was giving the authorization for them, and also, that despite these powers having been withdrawn, Raković was maintaining contact and transacting business with the Germans.

As during the period of the armistice agreements, now in the period of informal collaboration, both parties apparently were still trying to keep things secret. In the field, of course, secrecy was hardly possible, but elsewhere there was ample reason to preserve silence. In May, when the Belgrade German-language newspaper *Donau-Zeitung* published an item saying that the Chetniks were fighting under German command, some political difficulties arose for the Chetniks.[62] But Chetnik-German collaboration continued. General Felber told Commander in Chief in Southeast Europe von Weichs on May 13 that the Chetniks (meaning certain Chetnik leaders) had assured him that they were giving up all action against the Germans and that they wanted to participate in the fight against the Communists until the final victory. These Chetniks were led, he said, by Captain Neško Nedić and Major Weyel of the German army. He also poined out that it was extremely difficult to find the proper way of handling Mihailović and the Chetniks, but he gave the order that whenever they fought on the German side against the Communists, they would be handled "accordingly" (presumably, that is, in a friendly manner), and that whenever they turned arms against the Germans, they would be sharply met with arms.[63] Three days later (May 16) General Felber followed this up with a directive outlining in detail the proper conduct of the German authorities and troops toward the Chetniks, who had been and still remained an enemy; the Chetniks' enemy No. 1 was the Partisans, but the occupation power was their enemy No. 2. Chetnik cooperation with the Germans was for the purpose of replenishing ammunition supply, and the Chetniks in general did not fight the Partisans with determination, in order to shed as little blood as possible; therefore all the Chetnik measures which un-

[61] Microcopy No. T-311, Roll 286, Frame 314.
[62] Microcopy No. T-501, Roll 256, Frame 647.
[63] *Ibid.*, Frames 723–24.

favorably affected the interests of the Germans or of the Nedić government, attacks on the same, recruiting for Chetnik detachments, interference with the local administration and with the delivery of agricultural and livestock products must be considered as "enemy behavior"
and dealt with accordingly, and all Chetnik actions to strengthen their
staffs and central organs must be prevented with all means. On the other
hand, all Chetnik groups actively fighting the Partisans were not to be
hindered or fought, but rather helped with ammunition. For that purpose a limited delivery of ammunition, for actual and local engagements
and under strict German supervision, was necessary as well as the supplying of medical materials and care of the wounded. All aid in ammunition must be approved by the Military Commander in Southeast
Europe.[64]

Even after the 2nd and 5th Partisan divisions, hard pressed by combined attack of the Germans, Bulgarians, Serbian quislings, and Chetniks, had been forced to withdraw to Sandjak early in May, the Chetniks continued to collaborate with the Germans against the domestic
Partisan units in Serbia. The same motives continued to sustain the
collaboration: a need for arms and supplies on the part of the Chetniks,
and a mutual Chetnik-German need for help against the Partisan threat.
On June 30, for example, the Chetnik leader in eastern Serbia, Lt.
Colonel Ocokoljić, whose forces had on an earlier occasion attacked a
German arms depot to seize arms, was pleading for new arms and ammunition. Ocokoljić bolstered his plea with the argument that the Partisans from southeastern Serbia planned to push into northeastern Serbia and move toward the Danube River where they would meet Soviet
airborne troops for combined operations against the Germans. Ocokoljić also told the Germans that the principal propaganda theme of the
Tito forces in Serbia was the aid that they were getting from the Anglo-
Americans by air and that the government of King Peter was engaged
in negotiations with Tito (the Tito-Šubašić agreement of June 16 had
in fact already been signed), and he cautioned them that the Chetniks
must insist on the secrecy of their negotiations for arms, since otherwise
"they would lose all credit with the population."[65]

In July the Germans, again with the help of the Bulgarians, the Serbian quislings, and elite Chetnik units, launched a drive against the

---

[64] *Ibid.*, Frames 754–55. References to the lack of determination on the part of some Chetnik
units in Serbia in fighting the Partisans are found also in Chetnik documents. See e.g. orders of
General Trifunović of July 19, 1944, in *Dokumenti o izdajstvu Draže Mihailovića*, I, 86–87.

[65] Microcopy No. T-311, Roll 286, Frames 556–67. In addition to helping the Partisans in Serbia
with airborne supplies, the Western Allies, beginning in April 1944, staged a series of bombing
raids on railroad installations in Belgrade and several other Serbian towns and on some towns in
which, according to Partisan information, there were strong German forces (though inevitably
there were in all cases many civilian casualties as well). These raids, in conjunction with the approaching Soviet forces and the preparations of the Partisans in Bosnia and Sandjak for an assault
on Serbia, presaged the speedy end of the German occupation regime in Serbia and probably acted
in a political sense also against the Chetnik position there.

Partisan forces in southern Serbia (Operation Trumpf, see Chapter 11). While this operation was in progress German and Chetnik representatives held discussions on further combined action against the Partisans, with the Chetniks always especially concerned about securing more arms and ammunition for their units.[66]

Perhaps the most interesting conference, however, was the one held on August 11 at Topola between a German group led by Cavalry Captain Prince von Wrede, representing the Military Commander in Southeast Europe, and a Chetnik delegation consisting of three important commanders: Major Dragoslav Račić, Captain Neško Nedić, and Captain Nikola Kalabić. The purpose of the conference was to work out the terms for a meeting between General Mihailović and Envoy Neubacher and to set forth the conditions of the two parties for increased collaboration. Prince von Wrede in a report of August 12 formulated the position of the two sides as follows:

(1) DM wishes to speak with the Plenipotentiary of the Führer for the Southeast Neubacher; (2) he demands an alliance of all Serbian nationalist forces; (3) he demands mobilization and arming of all able-bodied nationalist Serbs for a struggle against the Communists, arming and leadership to be in the hands of the Wehrmacht; (4) DM requests that he himself remain in illegality; (5) the members of the Chetnik movement should not be put in German uniforms; (6) the meeting place should under no circumstances be Belgrade or a large town.
Against this our own wishes are: (1) DM has to agree that only an oral and not a written agreement be made; and (2) the Chetniks promise to stop all measures directed against the German military administration and to protect it.[67]

Obviously connected with the proposals made by Mihailović's delegates at the Topola conference is a message from German headquarters in Belgrade stating that Mihailović is pressing the Germans for a decision by August 20; the message also makes the point that Mihailović has been in touch with Prime Minister Nedić and has agreed with him on the way in which German aid is to come and be used. The message says that considering the weakness of the German troops in Serbia and superior armament of the Partisans who had already started systematic infiltration of Serbia as well as the uncertainty of the future behavior of the Bulgarian forces, the Germans cannot afford to dispense with Chetnik assistance.[68]

The Mihailović-Neubacher meeting was never held, but Neubacher became an even stronger advocate of a reasonable measure of arming the

[66] For example, the conference held between Captain Neško Nedić, the chief Chetnik liaison officer with the Germans and the German representatives on July 14. Microcopy No. T-311, Roll 195, Frames 725–26. During this time General Trifunović, the Chetnik commander for Serbia, also maintained contact with Envoy Neubacher and informed him that Mihailović was in a position in which he had to collaborate with the Germans. See Microcopy No. T-501, Roll 256, Frame 458.
[67] Microcopy No. T-311, Roll 286, Frames 508–11.
[68] Microcopy No. T-77, Roll 883, Frame 5,631,180.

Chetniks for the coming struggle against the Partisans—though only as far as technically feasible and as long as it was in German interest, which meant that the Chetniks had no chance of building up an arms supply to continue the struggle against the Partisans after the Germans had been forced to withdraw.

At approximately the same time, Mihailović made another contact with the Germans through a German agent named Jefto. The conditions and requests were essentially the same as those that had been presented by his representatives at Topola, with an additional offer that the Chetniks would not turn their arms against the Germans even in the event of a Western Allied landing on the Dalmatian coast but would continue to fight the Partisans and try to prevent the linking up of Partisan and Allied troops after the landings.[69]

One of the most telling proofs that active collaboration continued between the Chetniks and the Germans even after the last formal agreements had lapsed is found in the briefs prepared by the staff of the Commander in Chief in Southeast Europe Field Marshal von Weichs for his conference with Hitler on August 22, 1944. In a general introductory statement on the prevailing military and political situation in Serbia and elsewhere in Yugoslavia von Weichs noted that the recent behavior of the Mihailović Chetniks had been marked by the following characteristics: (*a*) active fighting against the Communist enemy in Serbia, Croatia, and Montenegro, which, owing to the numerical and armament superiority of the Communist bands, was in each case connected with risks for the DM forces; (*b*) failure to execute general and specific sabotage orders of the Allies; (*c*) local collaboration, sometimes very active, between the DM Chetniks and the German security troops, the *Abwehr*, and the German organizations established for the economic exploitation of the land; (*d*) an absolute readiness to obey the tactical directives given by the German liaison officers; and (*e*) repeated attempts, in exchange for proved loyalty, to obtain arms and ammunition for the fight against the Communist enemy.[70] In contrast to this general behavior, there had been some transgressions on the part of the Chetniks, especially in the form of attacks upon food and ammunition transports; but, the report pointed out, these attacks were of no great significance and the Chetniks always made an effort not to hurt German personnel.

The same document goes on to state that, although General Nedić had had some reservations about General Mihailović, he had now become Mihailović's advocate and spoke for him to the Germans, so that there was at last a united anti-Communist Serbian front, with General Mihailović commanding the support of over 90 percent of all Serbs. Von

[69] *Ibid.*, Frame 5,631,178.
[70] Microcopy No. T-311, Roll 195, Frame 960.

Weichs knew that such extravagant ammunition requests as those of General Nedić for 3 million rounds were totally unrealistic, and he proposed that at the outset only 250,000 rounds be delivered. The Chetniks were talking of raising an army of 50,000 men; von Weichs considered an army of this size impossible for technical reasons and proposed instead to establish three regiments of about 6,000 men in all, to be formed out of the seasoned troops of Chetnik commanders Keserović and Račić, and to give them the requested arms (about 5,000 Italian rifles, 40 Italian heavy machine guns, 30 light mortars).[71]

By the time von Weichs had to leave Belgrade to submit his report to Hitler, Nedić and Mihailović had had their meeting on August 20. According to information received by von Weichs, the position of the two generals in the new setup was politically conditioned: "Out of regard for the Serbian population and because of considerations for the future, DM will stay, as up to this time, in the background. He will, however, lead the struggle against Communism, while the political ties to the occupying power will continue to remain in the domain of Prime Minister Nedić." Von Weichs was aware that there was a certain risk involved in arming the Chetniks in Serbia, but he was nonetheless convinced that in view of the conditions prevailing there and the probable events that lay immediately ahead and also on the basis of past experience, the DM movement was at the moment "the *most positive* element in the struggle against Communism, which for the time being the Germans can under no circumstances give up." This was so because in the event that Bulgarian troops were withdrawn, the Germans in Serbia would lack sufficient forces and would thus be open to the advance of Tito's troops, and even if Bulgarian troops were to remain, the German troops in Serbia were insufficient to replace the Chetnik formations; and finally, the Chetniks in many cases directly or indirectly made the economic exploitation of Serbia secure, and under the existing conditions that was of fundamental significance for the German military industry.[72]

Another document prepared for this report to Hitler dealt with the losses of the Serbian nationalist forces in fighting against the Communists between March 15 and August 15, 1944. They were detailed as follows:

	Killed	Wounded	Missing
Serbian Volunteer Corps	140	312	69
Serbian State Guards	157	107	26
Serbian Frontier Guards	3	13	2
Loyal Chetniks	1,749	2,089	120

71 *Ibid.*, Frames 960–62. On the whole problem of Nedić's and Mihailović's efforts to obtain arms and ammunition from the Germans and their apportionment see also *The Trial of Draža Mihailović*, pp. 242–44.

72 Microcopy No. T-311, Roll 195, Frames 963–64.

Losses of the loyal Chetniks by months were as follows: March 16–April 15, 228; April 16–May 15, 231; May 16–June 15, 290; June 16–July 15, 594; and July 16–August 15, 406. The Germans could not precisely establish the losses of Chetnik units that had fought the Partisans independently, but they estimated them to be at least as high as those of the loyal Chetniks.[73] Since the Chetniks could not have been fighting without ammunition, which they had to be getting from the Germans, these figures imply that there was close collaboration between the Germans and a large portion of the Chetniks in Serbia even after March 1944, that is, after all armistice agreements had presumably been voided.

Von Weichs's brief in support of collaboration with and extension of aid to the Chetniks perhaps overstates the case for the Chetniks, but von Weichs of course had military reasons for trying to convince Hitler that the aid of the Chetniks must be enlisted on the German side even more than before. At that stage in the war, and pressed on all sides, the Germans had little material help to spare, and Hitler was more than ever reluctant to give anything but the smallest amount to the Chetniks. His reply to von Weichs, given first orally and confirmed by telegram, was explicit: "Solely individual Chetnik formations which have proved themselves thus far can be used in locally limited and tactically small undertakings and under German command and control."[74] This order tied the hands of the German commanders in Serbia, and dashed Mihailović's hopes for sizable German assistance for the struggle against the Partisans. Hitler's anti-Serbian bias, to which now several other factors were added (the loss of Romania and the approaching loss of Bulgaria, fear of a coup in Hungary, and even fear of an anti-German shift in the Croatian Ustasha state), precluded the extension of any large amount of aid to the Chetniks.[75]

A new plea for substantial aid in arms and ammunition to the Chetniks was submitted to the German Ministry of Foreign Affairs by Envoy Neubacher on August 28, after Hitler had only partially accepted von Weichs's proposal. Neubacher argued that lack of German aid was causing dissatisfaction in the Chetnik ranks and that because of this— and also because of other reasons including the dumping of Mihailović by the Western Allies, and his subsequent loss of his one remaining position as Chief of Staff of the Supreme Command, the approach of Russian forces from the east, and the beginning of strong attacks by the Partisans on Serbia—the Chetniks were threatened with disintegration. In view of the limited forces that the Germans had in Serbia, such disintegration was against German military interests, and Neubacher sug-

[73] *Ibid.*, Frame 968.
[74] Microcopy No. T-77, Roll 781, Frame 5,507,576.
[75] See in this regard *KTB/OKW/WFSt*, Vol. IV, Part 1 (1944), pp. 708–11.

gested that, since the German arms supply was low, arms should be taken from caches of Yugoslav arms which had been in Hungarian hands since the time of invasion in 1941.[76] This was a well-reasoned argument, but it, too, was unsuccessful. Under the circumstances, with arms in short supply, Hitler was more than ever unwilling to extend substantial aid to two Serbian generals whom he had never trusted, and he still feared the possibility of an Allied landing in the Balkans, with the Chetniks turning German arms against the Germans. He also feared that the extension of aid to Great Serbia forces might help the Serbs to regain the position of the leading political and military factor in the Balkans, a contingency he wanted to prevent and against which even a strengthening of Communists might be preferable.[77]

One of the fateful mistakes of the Chetniks up to the middle of 1943 was to underrate the political acumen and the military leadership and resilience of the Partisans. Even after General Mihailović returned to Serbia in June 1943, and in the course of the following year, this under-estimation prevailed. This tone of overoptimism marks also Mihailović's circular letter of May 1944 containing instructions for the corps commanders, especially those in Belgrade, as well as a letter from Mihailović to Jevdjević written in June 1944.[78] Among many things, Mihailović speaks in this letter to Jevdjević about Partisan weakness and Chetnik strengths:

> During the past two or three months the Communists have sustained heavy losses and many successive defeats. The Communists are today much weakened in all areas. We hope that soon they will become even weaker and will be completely liquidated. The most important thing is that the people nowadays rise more and more against them because they have perceived all their crimes and plans.
> On the contrary, we are today considerably stronger than we were a year ago and our organization advances and spreads more and more. Our armed forces number in fact in the whole land over 100,000 men, while the number of recruits who could be armed reaches over half a million. We do not feel it necessary to announce such things publicly, nor do we need to exaggerate these figures as the Communists do. The Communists claim that they have over 200,000 soldiers, while in fact they have no more than a few tens of thousands.

Mihailović's reports to the government-in-exile were similarly optimistic, and his optimism did not flag after he lost his post in the government-in-exile; his reports to his representatives abroad in the sum-

---

[76] Microcopy No. T-77, Roll 883, Frames 5,631,201–6.

[77] According to General Jodl's notes quoted by General Warlimont, on August 22, 1944, when Field Marshal von Weichs came to Hitler's headquarters to ask for permission to arrange a common struggle with General Nedić and Mihailović against the Partisans in Serbia, Hitler told him that "Germany must combat to the utmost all Great Serbia projects. A Serbian army must not be created. Even a certain Communist danger is more acceptable." Warlimont, p. 499.

[78] Microcopy No. T-311, Roll 286, Frames 451–56, esp. Frame 452, and Frames 471–75 for the letter to Jevdjević.

mer of 1944—on July 12 and 27, for example—are generally hopeful about the Chetnik situation.[79] But the next three months were to show how ill-founded that optimism was.

However strong Mihailović's following may have been among the Serbian people and however successful his organization may have been in infiltrating the governmental and military apparatus of the Nedić regime, outside Serbia, and especially among the Western Allies, his support was rapidly deteriorating. The British, who were responsible for policy making for the Western Allies in Yugoslavia and the Balkans, had abandoned him, and the United States was unwilling to undertake anything substantial in his behalf, or in the Balkans in general, because this was against policy principles developed at the highest levels of the American government and army. Moreover, Mihailović had been stripped of his two government positions, and therefore had no legitimate standing, and the government-in-exile was becoming an instrument of the Partisans. As time went on, more and more of his followers in Serbia, realizing that Mihailović's cause was hopeless, turned away. The disintegration within Chetnik ranks which was noted by Neubacher in August 1944 had in fact been evident for some time. The previous May, Major Radoslav Djurić, the Chetnik commander of southeastern Serbia, defected to the Partisans with a number of his officers and men,[80] and in August the Ibar Chetnik brigade shifted to the Partisans.[81]

This, then, was the state of affairs in the Chetnik camp in Serbia in late August 1944. To the east, the Soviet forces were approaching the Yugoslav borders; the Partisans had already started attacks against both the Germans and the Chetniks in Serbia from the west and southwest, and the Bulgarians were preparing their exit from the alliance with the Germans and the withdrawal of their forces from Serbia and Macedonia. On August 25 Bulgaria declared its neutrality and sent its representatives to Cairo to seek contact with the Western Allies. On September 5 the Soviet Union declared war on Bulgaria. Three days later Bulgaria declared war on Germany, and the day following that it capitulated to Soviet forces.

[79] See Mihailović's reports as published by Jovan Djonović in "The Connections with Draža Mihailović from the Middle East and North Africa," pp. 56–57, 61–65.

[80] *The Četniks*, pp. 24–27. Some pro-Mihailović Serbs who have written postwar accounts of wartime conditions in Serbia maintain that Djurić was from the beginning inclined toward the Partisans and stayed with the Chetniks as a Communist Trojan horse. Similar charges were also made by a pro-Nedić Serb writer in exile against the chief political adviser of Lt. Colonel Keserović, Professor Mihailo Knežević. See e.g. Karapandžić, pp. 264–67. Djurić's actions in the critical days of October and November 1941 in western Serbia and his later efforts to minimize the struggle between the Chetniks and the Partisans in Serbia indicate that he was quite different from most other Chetnik commanders. After his defection, he became deputy chief of staff of the Partisan Chief Headquarters for Serbia. Mihailo Knežević was killed by the Chetnik commander Captain Raković, or on his orders. See *Sudjenje članovima rukovodstva organizacije Draže Mihailovića*, p. 530.

[81] Microcopy No. T-77, Roll 883, Frame 5,631,204. In June 1972 I heard in Belgrade from a historian specializing in Serbian history during the Second World War that a group of about sixty Communists was present in this brigade before it made the shift to the Partisans.

COLLABORATION OUTSIDE SERBIA TO OCTOBER 1944

As explained earlier, the revised German policy of mobilizing all anti-Communist groups in southeastern Europe for the struggle against the Communist-led forces following the Italian collapse in September 1943 was first set forth in Hitler's directive to Special Envoy Neubacher of October 29 and was expanded in the directive of the Commander in Chief of Southeast Europe of November 21. We have seen that the power to conclude armistice (in fact collaboration) agreements with the Chetniks was delegated to the Military Commander in Southeast Europe for occupied Serbia and to the Second Panzer Army for areas under its command, which included most of the other Yugoslav territory as well as Albania. Although Montenegro was in the domain of the Second Panzer Army, the Military Commander in Southeast Europe, for reasons to be explained later, was involved in the implementation of the new policy in that area. Furthermore, certain changes in German policy toward the Chetniks in the territory of the Independent State of Croatia had taken place by decision of the Second Panzer Army, most probably after clearance with higher authorities, even before the new German policy acquired its final formulation.

Let us first discuss the less important Montenegrin case. Although the Chetniks had been greatly weakened by the defeats at Partisan hands during the spring of 1943 and by the disarming of a large portion of their troops in Montenegro and some in southeastern Bosnia, they still had sizable forces in Montenegro. In the course of the summer they were reorganized by General Blažo Djukanović, who, assisted by Colonel Bajo Stanišić and Major Djordjije Lašić, remained in command. It seems that General Mihailović had issued orders that these troops resist with arms the entry of German troops into Montenegro after the Italian collapse in order to save that area as a possible bridgehead for the expected Allied landings. However, Stanišić while calling upon the Partisans to get under his command for fighting the Germans, on September 12 also wrote to Jevrem Šaulić, mayor of the town of Nikšić and his confidant, that he had issued orders to his troops not to attack the German forces passing through his territory. Furthermore, he advised Šaulić that if he considered it necessary, he should contact the German commander in Nikšić, inform him about Stanišić's order, and ask him not to interfere with the Chetniks while they were doing the work they had begun (meaning, that is, fighting the Partisans).[82]

But whatever plans Djukanović and Stanišić had for adjusting to the German presence in Montenegro could not be implemented because in mid-October they were surrounded by the Partisans in the monastery of

---

[82] *The Četniks*, pp. 63–64.

Ostrog and killed.[83] In the meantime, the Germans had entered Montenegro and had established a military government in the form of Area Command No. 1040 (*Feldkommandantur* No. 1040) under General Wilhelm Keiper, at the same time continuing, though without allowing it much real power, the Montenegrin Administrative Council composed of representatives of both "Whites" and "Greens" (i.e. the pro-Serbian and pro-Chetnik group and the Montenegrin separatists). Since the Area Command had few German troops at its disposal, it reorganized and increased the former provincial gendarmerie and soon also entered into agreements with what was left of the domestic "national forces"—that is, the Chetniks—who were under the command of Major Jovo Djukanović. As early as December 1943 the Germans used these forces against the Partisans, and in April 1944 they used them again on a larger scale, but in both cases with little success.[84]

The changing situation of the German military government in Montenegro can be inferred from the way in which Area Command No. 1040 was subordinated to higher command posts. When it was established on September 26, 1943, it was put under the German General in Albania, who at the same time was the German Commanding General in Montenegro. Later it was shifted to the jurisdiction of the Vth SS-Mountain Corps, then to the Second Panzer Army. Finally, in April or May 1944, it was raised in rank to an Independent Area Command and put directly under the command of the Military Commander in Southeast Europe (Felber), who was also Military Commander in Serbia, with the seat in Belgrade.[85] This last change was the result of a scheme of Envoy Neubacher to establish a federation consisting of Serbia, Sandjak, and Montenegro, to which in time also a part of eastern Bosnia was to be attached—the purpose of which was to strengthen the Nedić regime and in that way the whole anti-Communist force in Yugoslav territory. Because of Hitler's opposition, this plan was never accepted, but certain military arrangements between General Felber and General Nedić with regard to Montenegro were made. In these arrangements Major Pavle Djurišić, who as we have seen in Chapter 7 was captured and disarmed on May 14, 1943, and taken into captivity, played an important role.

Djurišić was taken to a prisoner-of-war camp in Galicia (the area of the town of Stryi, during the interwar period part of Poland, now in the Ukraine). He escaped from captivity, reportedly in August 1943, and after some time reached Serbia. He was caught by the Serbian quisling authorities and was immediately taken over by the Germans and in-

---

[83] See Puniša Perović, "The End of the Two Greatest Montenegrin Traitors," and Pajović, "The Liquidation of the Chetnik Leadership in Ostrog in October 1943."

[84] See the "Concluding Report on the Military Government in Montenegro," prepared in April 1945, in Microcopy No. T-501, Roll 258, Frames 679–84; and Vujović, pp. 491–94.

[85] Microcopy No. T-501, Roll 258, Frame 675.

carcerated. But since it was known that Djurišić enjoyed a good reputation among the Chetniks and pro-Chetnik population in Montenegro,
and the other two senior Montenegrin Chetnik leaders had been killed,
Neubacher, Nedić, and Felber thought that Djurišić could be used to
advantage in Montenegro in fighting the Partisans and in promoting
closer ties between Serbia and Montenegro. Djurišić was therefore set
free and named by General Nedić as assistant to the commander of the
Serbian Volunteer Corps.

When the Independent Area Command No. 1040 was put directly
under Felber's command, the Germans, Nedić, and Ljotić assisted Djurišić in establishing the Montenegrin Volunteer Corps, some of whose
units were first used in Sandjak, and later in all of Montenegro. For
some time in the spring of 1944 a battalion of the Serbian Volunteer
Corps was sent to Sandjak to assist Djurišić, and a former Nedić minister and close associate of Ljotić, Mihailo Olćan, was sent with this
battalion to Sandjak to serve as liaison between Djurišić and Nedić (for
some time Ratko Parežanin served as liaison officer).[86] The Montenegrin
Corps was made up in part of some of Djurišić's former troops who had
been released by the Germans from captivity, but the majority were
Chetniks who remained at large in Montenegro under the name of
"national forces." Major Djukanović, formerly at the head of these
forces, was also absorbed by Djurišić's organization and was given the
command of the Lovćen Corps.[87] Altogether, including troops that were
part of the Montenegrin Volunteer Corps proper and other Chetnik
troops that joined, Djurišić developed a fighting force in Montenegro
and Sandjak of perhaps some seven to eight thousand men.

The Germans assigned Djurišić a watchful eye in the person of liaison
officer Lieutenant Heusz, formerly the liaison officer with Major Lukačević. On May 30, 1944, Heusz was sent a detailed briefing on his duties
with Djurišić, including the instructions that he was responsible "for
control and assuring of the execution of the directives issued by the
German command posts" and "liaison between the staffs and units of
the Montenegrin Volunteer Corps on the one hand and the German
command posts on the other, especially in the course of operations
against the bands [the Partisans]." He was cautioned to be tactful and
to establish a feeling of confidence between the German command posts
and the Montenegrin Volunteer Corps, and he was of course to keep
the Military Commander in Southeast Europe informed on the condi-

---

[86] Parežanin, pp. 485–87; Karapandžić, pp. 311–17. Both these sources give an interpretation of
Djurišić's role in Montenegro at that time from the point of view of General Nedić and Ljotić. The
Chetnik version of his action is given in his biography in *Glasnik SIKD 'Njegoš'*, June 1960, pp.
85–93, which presents him as one of the leading Chetnik and Serbian heroes of the Second World
War. See also Neubacher, p. 145.
[87] Vujović, p. 505.

tions in the corps, its fighting qualities, personnel and supply problems, and so on.[88]

In terms of the organizational setup, formal allegiance, channels of command, and logistics, Djurišić and his forces were a part of the German-organized and German-maintained quisling forces closely related to the Serbian Volunteer Corps. Despite all this, however, Djurišić, and therefore also his troops, continued to owe their first allegiance to Draža Mihailović and his Chetnik organization.

The Montenegrin Chetniks justified their collaboration with the Germans, both prior to and following Djurišić's return, with the same arguments they had used to justify their earlier collaboration with the Italians—that is, the necessity of fighting the Communists and putting an end to the civil war that was bringing death and destruction to many of their supporters in Montenegro. They had another compelling reason however—the necessity of bringing in food supplies to the province from areas under German control and by means of German transport. In some parts of the province food was so scarce that near-starvation conditions existed. The collaboration of the Chetniks and the Germans did little to alleviate the situation, however, and the population blamed both for the shortages.[89] They were also losing favor day by day among the people because of several other developments outside their control: the mass overflights of Allied aircraft over Montenegro and the occasional air attacks on the town of Podgorica (in one of these attacks the Chetnik leader Lašić was killed), the entry of the Partisan and Soviet forces into Serbia and the withdrawal of Mihailović and his Chetniks from that territory, and finally the realization, more and more accepted, that the Germans and therefore all their allies would soon be going down to defeat.

In July the Germans decided to reorganize the National Administrative Council, which had lost all popular support, and when Djurišić refused to allow any of his representatives to sit on it, dissolved it altogether.[90] The collaboration between Djurišić's forces and the Germans continued that summer and on into the autumn, marred by occasional difficulties, but early in December (as we shall see in Chapter 12) both the Germans and the Djurišić forces were obliged to withdraw from Montenegro, going part of the way together, the Germans in the direction of Austria and Djurišić and his forces to northeastern Bosnia to join Mihailović.

---

[88] Microcopy No. T-501, Roll 256, Frame 862.

[89] The Italians during their period of occupation imported into Montenegro (according to reports the Germans considered reliable) between 1,200 and 1,500 metric tons of food monthly, principally cereals. The German food shipments from Serbia never exceeded 250 to 300 tons monthly. Lack of means of transportation was given as the main excuse. See the "Concluding Report . . . ," *ibid.*, Roll 258, Frame 679.

[90] *Ibid.*, Frames 679–82; see also *ibid.*, Roll 256, Frames 550–51.

All the Chetnik detachments in the Italian-controlled parts of the
Independent State of Croatia had at some time or another collaborated
with the Italians against the Partisans. After the Italian surrender and
the failure of the Allies to land in Dalmatia, these Chetniks were more
or less forced into collaboration with the Germans in order not to be
caught between them and the Partisans. Some Chetnik units in fact
embarked on this course at once, rendering services to German divisions
while they were still in the process of taking over the areas formerly
under Italian control.[91]

The high German command posts apparently still believed that the
Chetnik detachments in these areas had to be made innocuous by re-
moving their leaders from the scene: an operative of the *Abwehr* in
Dubrovnik, for example, was ordered around September 20 to arrest all
Chetnik leaders who were present in that city, and the 114th Infantry
Division in northern Dalmatia was ordered on September 23 to arrest
the commander of the largest existing Chetnik formation, Momčilo
Djujić.[92] But the German field commanders had different ideas. They
needed the Chetniks as allies against the Partisans, who had been greatly
strengthened by the capture of many arms and supplies from the Italians
and by the influx of many thousands of new volunteers. And they still
regarded the Chetniks as potentially dangerous in the event of the still
feared Allied landings on the coast. For both reasons they were unwilling to jeopardize any possible arrangements with the Chetniks by
arresting any of their leaders. They therefore ignored the orders at first
and then, it seems, prevailed upon the higher commands to alter the
policy, with the result that on September 29 the Second Panzer Army
issued a comprehensive order regarding policies to be followed toward
the Chetniks in the territory fo the Independent State of Croatia. A day
later this order was communicated by the XVth Army Corps (the former
command post known as the Commanding General of German Troops
in Croatia, which had been redesignated in August) to the subordinate
divisions and independent groups in the following message:

(1) In cases of extreme local necessity, the commanders of divisions and leaders of independent groups may find themselves in the situation of having to
conclude, exceptionally, and with regard to time and place limited, arrangements with the Chetnik bands for joint action against the Communists.

(2) Such arrangements must be reported immediately to the Intelligence Officer of the XVth Army Corps.

(3) Political negotiations are forbidden on principle. If such negotiations
seem to be appropriate, this should be reported.[93]

Since in the areas of Croatia that had always been under German control collaboration agreements had customarily been concluded by the

[91] Microcopy No. T-314, Roll 566, Frame 342.
[92] Microcopy No. T-501, Roll 267, Frame 1034; Microcopy No. T-314, Roll 566, Frame 790.
[93] Microcopy No. T-314, Roll 566, Frame 681.

Croatian authorities (though after January 1943 cleared with the Germans), the new order of the Second Panzer Army actually applied to all the Chetnik detachments that were in the Croatian puppet state. It seems that the first arrangement that was made on the basis of the new order was the one between the 373rd Infantry Division (Croatian legionnaires) and the Chetnik leader Mane Rokvić, who was in control of an area including parts of western Bosnia and parts of Lika.[94]

A report of the XVth Army Corps to the Second Panzer Army of November 19 gives interesting details on the specifics of the German-Chetnik collaboration. Chetnik troops were being used at that time for the safeguarding of railroads and of important industrial enterprises, and for scouting against and action in the rear of Partisan troops, but no written agreements were made. Besides their usefulness as guard troops, the Chetniks were also helpful to the Germans in intelligence work concerning the Partisans and as guides, and in acquiring livestock from the people, partly by making possible the holding of livestock market days. The report also points out that if the Germans were to break off this collaboration, the Orthodox population (the Serbs) standing behind the Chetniks would be at the mercy of the Ustashas, and under that pressure the Chetnik formations would either have to become robber bands or join the Partisans, both alternatives being against German interests.[95]

In practice, the collaboration took the form of assigning specific areas of action to various Chetnik groups, always within the command area of one or another German division or independent group, with special German officers charged with maintaining liaison with their Chetnik counterparts for purposes of coordination. The Chetniks were given arms and ammunition, as well as food and other supplies, sufficient to cover all or the largest part of their needs, the doling out of supplies being a way of forcing the Chetnik detachments to carry out the assigned tasks; when the Chetniks failed to follow German orders, supplies could be cut off.[96] But the details of the arrangements were always handled informally, partly to avoid offense to the Croatian government, and apparently no written orders were ever issued.[97]

The collaboration in Croatia grew more intense during the winter of

---

[94] *Ibid.*, Frame 678.

[95] *Ibid.*, Frames 342–43.

[96] See *ibid.*, Frames 85–86. Many documents show how the supplies were distributed. See e.g. an intelligence report of February 1944 that Djujić Chetniks obtained provisioning for approximately two-thirds of their formations from the Germans while the remainder was maintained from their own resources, in Microcopy No. T-311, Roll 286, Frame 232; a report on the supplying of the Herzegovinian Chetniks with arms, ammunition, and food of May 27, 1944, in Microcopy No. T-77, Roll 883, Frame 5,631,760; a report on the supplying of Djujić Chetniks with arms and ammunition of Sept. 27, 1944, in Microcopy No. T-501, Roll 257, Frames 1074–75.

[97] It may be noted that in his memoirs Colonel General Lothar Rendulic, the commander of the Second Panzer Army, devotes seventy-eight pages to the period he spent on assignment in Yugoslavia, but he sheds absolutely no light on the relations between the units under his command and the Chetniks in the territory of the Independent State of Croatia. *Gekämpft, Gesiegt, Geschlagen,* pp. 151–229.

1943–44, though it was under continual strain in the case of the Croatian quisling forces and the Chetniks. The figures cited in General Glaise's report of February 26, 1944 (based on official Croatian data), reveal the extent of the collaboration: as of February 11 there were in the territory of the Independent State of Croatia thirty-five specifically named Chetnik groups, some of them small (200–400 men), others, for example Djujić's group, as large as 2,500 men. Of these, nineteen groups, with a total of 17,500 men, collaborated with the Germans and Croatian authorities; sixteen others, with 5,800 men, were counted as rebellious Chetniks. With the exception of Uroš Drenović's detachment in north-western Bosnia, which had about 400 men whom the Croatian authorities considered completely loyal, all the Chetnik collaborating groups were considered by the Croatian authorities to be especially friendly toward the German forces in order to obtain more arms and ammunition from them but at the same time unfriendly toward the Croats and their state.[98] A somewhat later report of Croatian authorities, dated April 14, 1944, lists eighty-seven Chetnik leaders known to be in the territory of their state around that time and indicates which of them were born in Serbia or Montenegro.[99]

It will be seen that, just as the Chetnik-German collaboration in Serbia had to some extent to contend with the sensitivities of General Nedić and Ljotić, so in the puppet state of Croatia, but to a much greater degree, the Germans had to contend with the persistent opposition of the Ustasha government. And in Croatia the situation was further complicated by the fact that, though it was actually occupied territory the Germans considered it formally an independent state and were therefore obliged to observe the formalities. Difficulties between the Germans and the Ustashas with respect to the Chetniks began almost immediately after the Italian collapse. We see this from a complaint of the Croatian government lodged in a conference with German officials in Zagreb and reported by Envoy Kasche on October 19, 1943, regarding the use of the Chetniks and the pro-German Italians as guards in various Dalmatian towns while at the same time the Germans were not allowing Croatian troops to move into these areas.[100] As time went on and the Germans relied more and more on the Chetniks, the issue of German-Chetnik collaboration became by far the most troublesome one between German command posts in Croatia and Croatian military and civilian authorities. The Croats were particularly annoyed by the fact that practically all Chetnik commanders in their territory—although most of them denied it—swore allegiance to General Mihailović, that is,

---

[98] Microcopy No. T-311, Roll 286, Frames 224–28. For a detailed description of these units and names of their principal officers see *ibid.*, Frames 230–39.

[99] *Ibid.*, Frames 336–42. Another report (*ibid.*, Frame 343) claims that as of that same date there were in Croatian territory about 35,000 Chetniks—a figure that seems to me too high.

[100] Microcopy No. T-77, Roll 883, Frame 5,631,876; Microcopy No. T-501, Roll 264, Frame 795.

to the leader of a greatly detested military and political group in another country, and that there were indeed a considerable number of officers from Serbia and Montenegro holding important positions in the Chetnik formations in the Ustasha state. This ran counter to the Ustasha policy of keeping its Serbian population isolated from the Serbs in Serbia and forcing it to owe allegiance exclusively to the Croatian state. The presence of Serbia-born officers with Chetnik units in Croatia threatened even the pretense of sovereignty of the Croatian state, and on this and other grounds the Croatian authorities protested repeatedly to the Germans—against their cooperating with the Chetniks, against fraternizing between German and Chetnik troops, and so on. Some such protests were lodged by Pavelić directly to Hitler. But the Germans needed the Chetniks: they were short of troops of their own, and most of the Croatian Domobrans and even the legionnaire divisions were of very limited use against the Partisans as their members deserted to them en masse. At least some of the Chetnik units were considered excellent fighters against the Partisans, and few of them (except the new draftees), because of the atrocities they had committed against the Partisans and their sympathizers, were likely to desert to them.[101] Indeed, they were counted on as probably proving loyal even in the event of Allied landings in Dalmatia. German documents originating in Croatia often included the statement, familiar to us from similar documents regarding German-Chetnik collaboration in Serbia, that they cannot afford to dispense with the Chetniks as allies.[102] On the other hand, the Germans had no desire to aggravate the Ustasha authorities too far, for they also needed the Croatian quisling troops, and they were aware, as the German military attaché in Zagreb reported to the Operations Staff of the Wehrmacht, that with an appropriate use of nationalist slogans and as long as the chief danger lay in the Partisans and the Soviets, the Germans could still get a great deal out of the country.[103] They were therefore prepared to grant the Croats some concessions, of a minor sort not contrary to German interests.

Perhaps the most important attempt to assuage the Croatian sensitivities was the "Directive on the Employment and Subordination of the Croatian Combat Groups" issued by the Second Panzer Army on May 11, 1944.[104] The directive began with the proposition that "in the course of further pacification of the Croatian territory the Germans cannot

[101] See e.g. the report of the German liaison group with the Djujić forces of Sept. 27, 1944, in Microcopy No. T-501, Roll 257, Frames 1072–75.

[102] See the directive of May 11, 1944, discussed below, and the report of the commander of the 369th Infantry Division (Croatian legionnaires) to the Commander in Chief in Southeast Europe, of Aug. 7, 1944, in Microcopy No. T-311, Roll 195, Frame 672.

[103] Telegram of the Attaché of Aug. 30, 1944, in Microcopy No. T-77, Roll 883, Frame 5,631,327. The attaché thought, however, that this would not be the case if the Western Allies made landings on the Dalmatian coast, because the Croatian masses considered these troops to be the only possible salvation of their personal and national existence.

[104] For the text of this directive see Microcopy No. T-311, Roll 286, Frames 423–25.

dispense with the cooperation of the Orthodox population which is fighting against Communism. This necessity is recognized by the Commander in Chief in Southeast Europe." The specific order was promulgated on the basis of a decision by Hitler and was formulated in nine separate points. Under point 1 it was stated that because of the continual misunderstandings between the Croatian and German commands regarding the Chetnik formations (composed of Orthodox people of Croatian citizenship and declared loyalty to the Croatian state), these formations were to be renamed "Croatian Combat Group ———" indicating whatever Chetnik leader was in charge. These groups were then to be divided into smaller units and subordinated to various German (and also Croatian) units, and their supervision and command was to be assured by appropriate German liaison personnel. Under point 3 it was ordered that the Croatian Combat Groups which were subordinated to German units and supervised by German personnel, and which thereby lost some of their independence, were to be supplied with arms, ammunition, rations, and medical supplies depending on the extent of combat tasks assigned. Point 4 stated that the Chetnik formations were entitled to German protection so far as they fulfilled the conditions of cooperation. The final objective of this measure was to attach at some time in the future all "combat groups" to the regular Croatian military units. Point 7 declared that all support was to be withdrawn from Chetnik troops that refused to be subordinated to German units in the sense of this directive, but as long as these groups conducted an active struggle against the Communist bands they would not, for the time being, be interfered with by force of arms. If such groups should, however, show any hostility toward German or Croatian troops they would immediately be disarmed. All collaboration with Chetnik groups from Serbia proper was forbidden, and their return to Serbia was urged. All Chetnik leaders from Serbia present in Croatia were in the case of their apprehension to be turned over to the Croatian government. In view of the varied conditions in different areas, the manner of execution of this directive was to be left to the discretion of the various German commands (apparently of divisional and regimental rank).

This attempt to soothe Ustasha indignation failed. Although a sizable number of Croatian Combat Groups were organized under the supervision of various German divisions, neither the Croatian political and military authorities nor the Chetnik formations ever genuinely accepted the designation Croatian Combat Groups. Many Croatian units, obviously with approval from Zagreb, sabotaged as far as they could the collaboration with the Chetniks.[105] And the Croatian authorities con-

---

[105] See e.g. a report of Aug. 11, 1944, on the behavior of the 2nd Croatian Light Infantry Brigade which was attached to the 373rd Infantry Division (Croatian legionnaires), in *ibid.*, Roll 195, Frame 674.

tinued to complain to the Germans about their collaboration with the Chetniks, bombarding them with information on the presence of Serbia-born officers in important command posts with the Chetnik units in Croatian territory, on fraternization between German soldiers and Chetniks, Chetnik unreliability and pro-Western attitude, and so on.[106] But the XVth Army Corps brushed all this aside, ordering lower echelon commands "to disregard Ustasha protests,"[107] and collaboration with the Chetniks continued as before.

The Germans still had many reservations about the collaboration. The reservations were well formulated in a memorandum on a conference of several interested officers with the Intelligence Officer of the Second Panzer Army on July 29, 1944.[108] According to this memorandum, German army units were not actively to support the crossing of the Chetniks from Serbia into Croatian territory or to give ammunition to these Chetniks, but on the other hand were to prevent the Ustasha battalions from closing the frontier toward Serbia or engaging in fighting the Chetniks who crossed over. What the Security Forces (*Sicherheitsdienst*) did with regard to the Chetniks did not concern the army, the memorandum noted, but neither was it the responsibility of the German army forces to hinder the movement of Chetniks from Serbia into Croatia, especially since the Intelligence Officer of the Military Commander in Southeast Europe (Prince von Wrede), who knew of Chetnik intentions of crossing over and "who at all times keeps the Chetniks on the string," had done nothing against it. It was necessary, however, to see to it that the Chetniks did not threaten the interests of the Croatian state. The memorandum further noted that the army forces issued no written directives. In the case of Croatian complaints it was always to be pointed out that the Chetniks were behaving correctly, that with the limited troops that the Germans had at their disposal they were not in a position to prevent the Chetniks from coming from Serbia and that the Germans must avoid the danger of having Chetniks fight against them and the Croatian forces. It was true, the memorandum pointed out, that clear directives existed from the higher commands that Serbs were not to be helped in any way, but this should not cause much hesitation and all arrangements (with the Chetniks) should be defended on military grounds referring to Germany's own (limited) forces, and the support of the Croats should be sought.

[106] Among the wealth of material on this point see e.g. Microcopy No. T-77, Roll 781, Frames 5,507,627–36, and Roll 883, Frames 5,631,326–27; Microcopy No. T-311, Roll 286, Frames 336–43; Microcopy No. T-313, Roll 488, Frames 267–68; Microcopy No. T-501, Roll 264, Frames 464–67.

[107] Microcopy No. T-314, Roll 566, Frames 67, 73. In fact, at the beginning of 1944, when some Ustasha officers interfered with the Chetniks who were working for enterprises in Bosnia which were important for the Germans and were otherwise proving obnoxious to German local units, the XVth Army Corps, the Second Panzer Army, and even the Commander in Chief in Southeast Europe, decided to use force against Ustasha units if these provocations did not stop. See *ibid.*, Frames 233–49. Later developments show that conditions did not move to this critical stage.

[108] Microcopy No. T-501, Roll 257, Frame 1042.

But such considerations on the part of the Germans apparently did not satisfy the Croats. General Glaise reported on August 24, 1944, about a visit to Pavelić in which Pavelić especially requested that the German troops should maintain a greater distance from the Chetniks in order to improve the attitude of the Croats toward the Germans.[109] The following month Pavelić brought up the Chetnik question with Hitler when he visited him at his headquarters (Wolfsschanze) near Rastenburg in East Prussia, and received the promise that "the collaboration of the German Wehrmacht with the Chetniks would be given up systematically and gradually, and that no aid of any kind would be given to them."[110] But that was obviously not what the Germans meant, and even though after September there was occasional fighting between the Germans and some of the Chetnik groups from areas other than Serbia, the Germans nevertheless continued to give aid to all Chetniks when they were engaged in fighting the Partisans.

Had the decision on collaborating with the Chetniks depended on the German military alone, it would most probably have started much earlier than it did and also probably would have been more intensive. It was not until the end of 1943 that the higher authorities realized that "the Italians had handled the matter more wisely by arming the Chetniks and shifting to them a part of the struggle against Tito's forces."[111] Even then, the German field commanders were constrained by Hitler's mistrust, hate, and fear of Serbs, so that when collaboration became militarily and politically necessary after the Italian collapse and the reversing of the tide against the Germans, it could be staged only within narrow limits prescribed by Hitler. In all areas in which Chetnik collaboration with the Germans and the quisling forces was carried on, and that means in all areas in which the Chetniks were operating, this collaboration played into the hands of the Partisans and tended to undermine the strength of the Chetniks, especially after it became clear to everyone that the Germans would lose the war and after the Chetniks were jettisoned by the Western Allies and the latter's military, political, and diplomatic aid was concentrated in support of the Partisans.

[109] *Ibid.*, Roll 264, Frame 756.
[110] Microcopy No. T-311, Roll 196, Frame 332.
[111] *KTB/OKW/WFSt*, Vol. III (1943), Part 2, p. 1537.

CHAPTER TEN

Relations with the Allies

———◆•◆•◆———

THE BRITISH BREAK WITH THE CHETNIKS

In the summer of 1943 the British inaugurated a policy of "equal assistance" to and equal treatment of the Chetniks and the Partisans. One of the formal signs of this policy was the appointment of brigadiers as heads of the military missions both at Mihailović's headquarters (C. D. Armstrong) and at Tito's (Fitzroy Maclean); Colonel Bailey, until then head of the British mission to the Chetniks, was made political officer and second in command. The chief reason for upgrading the British mission to the Chetniks, aside from the policy of equal treatment with the Partisans, was the desire to push the Chetniks more forcefully into action against the Germans, on their own and, if possible, in combination with the Partisans. To a small extent British pressure was successful. In late September and October, partly in expectation of Allied landings on the Dalmatian coast and partly to dispel the prevailing notion that they were not active against the Germans, the Chetniks engaged in new mobilization of men in eastern Bosnia and undertook a series of successful operations which were interpreted by the German forces in the area as presaging a possible general uprising on the part of the Chetniks. Most important was the operation in which the Chetniks took Višegrad on the Serbia-Bosnia border and in which some British and two American officers from the British mission to Mihailović also participated.[1] The Chetniks also engaged in some small operations against the quisling and German forces in Serbia. But these operations petered out a few weeks later, and the British, feeling that they did not represent any basic change in Chetnik policy, renewed their pressure on Mihailović. Mihailović ignored the pressure, and in December the British stopped delivery of all supplies to the Chetniks, and

---

[1] See e.g. the reports of the 369th Infantry Division (Croatian legionnaires) of Sept. 29 and Oct. 10 and 11, 1943, in Microcopy No. T-314, Roll 554, Frames 931, 1065, 1362, and Seitz, pp. 26–30.

simultaneously expanded their military and political assistance to the Partisans.

For some time the Chetniks had shown signs of resenting British policy. They were particularly vexed at not having been informed in advance of the negotiations for the Italian surrender, and they blamed the British for not having directed the Italian troops in Yugoslavia to surrender with their stores to the Chetniks. The British had not so informed the Partisans either, nor their liaison officers with the Chetniks and the Partisans. They all heard the news of the surrender over the Allied radio stations. In the conditions of the armistice signed on September 3 it was provided that the Italian forces were to surrender unconditionally (this provision was later eliminated) and that they were immediately to withdraw to Italy "from all participation in the current war from whatever areas in which they may be now engaged." After the surrender on September 8, General Wilson broadcast a message to Yugoslavia in which he stated that the Italian forces were now under his orders and not those of the Germans, and that he had ordered them to stop all hostilities against Yugoslav forces. He told the Yugoslav forces—he did not specifically mention either the Partisans or the Chetniks—not to hinder Italian troops from leaving for Italy and not to fall for any German trickery which might involve them in new fighting with the Italians. He also said, "to those who had been openly fighting against the Axis"—and this could of course be interpreted as meaning only the Partisans—"do everything in your power to obtain without fighting Italian arms and equipment, which will enable you to continue your glorious struggle against the enemy with even greater success. Wait for our signal for general uprising."[2]

One Italian division, the Venezia, located in Berane (now Ivangrad), Montenegro, did actually surrender to Colonel Bailey and Chetnik Major Lukačević, but Lukačević's troops failed to bring the division securely under their control. Partisan troops, accompanied by British liaison officers, that turned up in Berane shortly thereafter succeeded where the Chetniks had not—using both persuasion and threat—and the division joined the Partisans.[3] Other Partisan units also succeeded in disarming five or six other Italian divisions and persuaded a sizable number of Italian soldiers to form special units and join them.

The Chetniks also had complaints about the increasingly pro-Partisan

[2] For the documents on the armistice see Great Britain, *Documents Relating to the Conditions of an Armistice with Italy (September–November 1943)*; for the leaflet containing General Wilson's proclamation see Microcopy No. T-313, Roll 151, Frame 7,404,932. Marshal Pietro Badoglio, Italian prime minister at that time, said in his memoirs: "By means of the Allied intelligence services we tried to send instructions to the troops in the Balkans and in Greece to join the Partisans, and we ordered forces in the occupied areas of Italy to form guerrilla bands." *Italy in the Second World War*, p. 101.

[3] Jovan Djonović, "Mihailović's Telegrams About British Missions," *Glasnik SIKD 'Njegoš'*, June 1960, pp. 30–32; Seitz, pp. 102–3.

slant of the BBC broadcasts. This slant first appeared in the summer of 1943. At times, as when the Chetnik Višegrad operation was credited to the Partisans, it was ridiculous.[4] Mihailović made a point of informing the government-in-exile on October 20 that "the people" (presumably in Serbia) were "very disappointed" in the BBC, and that few listened to it because they considered it an Ustasha-Communist radio.[5]

Mihailović's complaints about Colonel Bailey have already been gone into in some detail (Chapter 8). As the months passed and Mihailović continued to hold off fighting the Germans and kept on fighting the Partisans, Bailey made an attempt to begin subverting some of the Chetnik officers, hoping to get Mihailović replaced and taking thereby a positive step toward bringing the Chetniks and the Partisans into some form of combined action against the Germans. Mihailović accused Bailey of having tried to bribe one of his important commanders, Major Keserović, with money and of having promised postwar support to other Chetnik officers. Keserović did in fact accept money from Bailey, but he did not fall in with Bailey's plan; instead, he entered the money in his records as state revenue and informed both Bailey and Mihailović that he had done so. Mihailović also accused the British mission of trying to set one group of his officers against another, just as they had done in Cairo, he said, among both Yugoslav and Greek officers, and he was pleased to report that all their attempts in this regard had failed.[6]

At certain times, the Chetniks came into possession of copies of some of Bailey's candid reports to his superiors, parts of which Mihailović relayed during the summer and autumn of 1943 to the government-in-exile along with his own angry comments. Some of these messages not only were very unflattering to the Chetniks but also explicitly showed that the British were intent on trying to make use of Mihailović and the Chetniks, both in their wartime strategy and in postwar plans. On August 23 Mihailović commented: "I am spending the last reserves of money. The British are trying to break me by not giving me the means for life and work"; on August 30: "With the help of money the British are blackmailing us"; on October 23: "You should know that the Brit-

---

[4] According to a reliable British source, Hudson said in his last report before leaving Yugoslavia, filed from Berane in mid-March 1944, that Mihailović had been very bitter about the Višegrad operation broadcast; it was as hard to listen to Chetnik complaints about the BBC crediting their actions to the Partisans, Hudson said, as it had been to listen to Tito in 1941, when Partisan actions in Serbia were credited by the BBC to the Chetniks.

[5] Jovan Djonović, "Mihailović's Telegrams About British Missions," *Glasnik SIKD 'Njegoš'*, June 1960, pp. 33–35. British propaganda policy and thereby also the BBC broadcasts were directed by the PWE (Political Warfare Executive), an organization consisting of a policy-making interministerial committee (at first the Foreign Secretary and the Ministers of Information and Economic Warfare, later only the first two) and an executive staff with R. H. Bruce Lockhart as director general. He says, the "fluctuating situation in the Balkans was a perpetual source of trouble to our propaganda on account of the conflicting policies or rather series of improvisations devised, not by the Foreign Office, but by the Prime Minister and the Chiefs of Staff." *Comes the Reckoning*, p. 290. For PWE weekly directives for BBC Yugoslav Service, see F.O. 371/44289, R14503/25/92.

[6] Jovan Djonović, "Mihailović's Telegrams About British Missions," *Glasnik SIKD 'Njegoš'*, June 1960, pp. 27–28. See also note 24, p. 367.

ish are leaving us without financial means. They are also using this means as pressure against us so that we might carry out their requests without regard to our interests and the sacrifices of the people. They request even such actions as would result in tens of thousands of people shot as reprisal. And in spite of this they do not give us any military supplies or any money. They blackmail us for every airplane load [of supplies] as if they were the worst merchants. We believe that if it were not for the Germans, the British would be the worst people." In a message of early October (No. 104) sent to General Petar Živković, who held the position of deputy to the Supreme Commander of the Yugoslav Army (that is, to King Peter), Mihailović reported that the Chetniks had acquired a message from Bailey to his superiors in Cairo in which Bailey said: "Request the moving of Partisan troops, along with British liaison officers, to areas west and south of Mihailović's forces [in Serbia?]." Mihailović's comment on this was: "Our greatest enemy is Colonel Bailey. All difficulties which we have emanate from him. He is our worst enemy."[7] One gets the impression from several of Mihailović's messages that Colonel Bailey was Mihailović's whipping boy for his problems with the British.[8]

Mihailović was of course pleased by one of Bailey's reports to his superiors of August 1943 in which he said that there was in fact no one to work with but Mihailović, and that "a well-managed Mihailović" was the "ideal instrument to use his forces for our purposes"; Mihailović, the report said, had moral authority over the civilian population, and this authority could not be reduced "as long as his military authority over his local commanders remains steadfast. The only way that would be certain to be successful [in breaking his authority] would be public dismissal by the king. I think that this will not, repeat, will not occur soon."[9]

The Germans seem to have been well informed on the presence of Allied liaison officers both with the Chetniks and the Partisans. One German document states that British liaison officers with the Chetniks moved rather freely through various parts of Serbia, provided sometimes with papers issued by the Nedić authorities in which their nationality was given as "Slovene refugee."[10] Another German document

---

[7] For the text of some excerpts of Bailey's messages communicated by Mihailović with his comments to the government-in-exile and as published by Djonović see *ibid.*, pp. 25–30; and *ibid.*, December 1960, pp. 54–55.

[8] Nevertheless, after Bailey left, both Mihailović and Moljević sent him on May 28, 1944, very friendly letters of thanks for his labors. See F.O. 371/44273, R10605/11/92.

[9] *Ibid.*, pp. 25–27.

[10] Microcopy No. T-501, Roll 256, Frame 903. This document refers primarily to Christie Lawrence, who was not in fact a liaison officer but a British commando who after being captured in Greece in June 1941 escaped from a German transport and in Serbian territory established contact with various Chetnik groups, including those of Kosta Pećanac. He moved around a good deal until he was arrested in June 1942 by one of the Pećanac Chetnik leaders (Mašan Djurović) and delivered by him to the Germans. See Lawrence, pp. 257–58.

lists the names and locations, as of February 1, 1944, of about three hundred liaison, intelligence, and other officers and men of foreign powers in Yugoslavia, Albania, and western Romania.[11] But the Chetniks were apparently able to keep their dealings separate, so there were no chance encounters between the British and American liaison officers and the German liaison and other officers, and for the most part the Allied officers never got close to German troops. Only on three occasions is there known to have been an error. First was the case of Major N. B. Selby, a British army demolitions expert who was operating in the area controlled by Major Keserović. According to Deakin, Selby was disgusted with what he saw at the headquarters he was assigned to and radioed his superiors on August 23, 1943, that he was moving to the nearest Partisan units. En route, he was somehow betrayed and caught by Serbian quisling troops, who handed him over to the Gestapo. He was taken to Belgrade and subsequently was killed trying to escape from prison there.[12] Two other cases were those of a Captain Nash and a Captain Vercoe.[13] Nash, a Polish officer of Polish-Serbian parentage, was an agent of the British in northeastern Serbia and had the special task of helping to free Polish slave workers in the Bor copper mines and taking them to the Chetniks. He was killed in action on December 12, 1943, and on that same occasion a British Lieutenant Hargreaves was captured by the Germans. Vercoe was dropped by parachute in eastern Serbia but was badly injured in landing. For more than six months he was sheltered and cared for by Chetniks and peasants, until being captured by the Germans in March 1944 and taken to a prisoner-of-war camp. He was later repatriated.

The assigning of Brigadier Armstrong to Mihailović's headquarters in September 1943 was supposed to improve relations between the Chetniks and the British; it was hoped that a man of his rank could induce Mihailović to agree to cooperate with the Partisans, or if not that, at least to come to some accommodation with them and turn his troops on the Germans instead of the Partisans. Armstrong could do none of this—and in view of all that had passed between the British and Mihailović, his failure probably surprised no one. The British would gladly have given up the unmanageable Mihailović, but they could not easily abandon the Chetniks. Their large following in Serbia, as well

[11] Microcopy No. T-311, Roll 189, Frames 449–66.

[12] For the German document mentioning the capture of Selby see *ibid.*, Frame 458. The first British report of Selby's capture seems to be a letter of Captain Charles Robertson of August 24, 1943, to a Captain Boon, which says that Selby and Sergeant Boxer were captured by Serbian State Guards in the village of Kulino near Mali Jastrebac. Archives of the Institute of Military History, Belgrade, Chetnik Documents, Reg. No. 16/1–1, Box 129. On the death of Selby see especially the statement by Selby's friend Deakin, who conducted his own investigation after the war, in St. Antony's College, Oxford University, *Proceedings of a Conference on Britain and European Resistance 1939–45*, Yugoslav discussion section, p. 8.

[13] Microcopy No. T-311, Roll 189, Frame 464; Rootham, pp. 119–20, 179, 182, 205–6.

as tactical considerations having to do with the Partisans, made them hard to write off, and this Mihailović realized. He continued to play along with the British, but he made it clear that he resented being used. On October 20 in a message to the government-in-exile (No. 138) he complained of the British attitude: "They give us little but desire much. It is especially evident that they wish to exercise strong influence both now and later." The Chetniks, he said, had received the British officers courteously and with an open mind, on the assumption that complete honesty would contribute most to the common aim, the defeat of the enemy. "However," he went on, "these officers have proved to be insincere and their presence here is harmful. They are obsessed with their political role and have failed to inform their superiors about the importance and seriousness of our action. Undoubtedly, they have contributed to the success of the pro-Communist propaganda and thereby have caused much damage to our interests." On another occasion, referring to one of Bailey's messages that the Chetniks had acquired, he said that the British were wrong if they thought that he was their "ideal instrument." "I am," he said, "standing steadfast in the defense of the rights of the Crown which they are trying to destroy in the interest of their dirty schemes."[14] This comment is interesting because the British policy from the middle of 1943 was precisely to save the Crown by sacrificing Mihailović.

Something of the nature of the work of the British mission is brought out in a letter from Brigadier Armstrong to Mihailović of November 15, 1943, summarizing a conference that he and Colonel Bailey had had with Mihailović on November 13. On that occasion, Armstrong admonished Mihailović for his lack of activity against the enemy and told him that his inaction was very difficult for the Western world to comprehend. Mihailović, he said, seemed to be completely occupied with the internal struggle against the Croats, Moslems, and Partisans, particularly in Bosnia and Herzegovina and to a lesser extent in the Sandjak, all of which was a drain on the possible Yugoslav contribution to the war effort of the United Nations; Mihailović had never given him any plans for action against the Germans in Serbia, and the Chetniks' apparent inactivity against the enemy could have regrettable consequences for the Serbian people and for the postwar appraisal by the Serbian people of what Mihailović did during the war. He fully understood Mihailović's desire to save Serbian lives and he was in sympathy with the Chetnik cause and wished to help as much as possible, but he saw no advantage in the Chetnik policy of delaying action and refusing po-

---

[14] For these comments see Jovan Djonović, "Mihailović's Telegrams About British Missions," *Glasnik SIKD 'Njegoš'*, June 1960, pp. 28, 33–34, and *ibid.*, December 1960, pp. 54–55.

litical cooperation (i.e., apparently, with the Partisans) and activity against the Germans.[15]

Mihailović forwarded this message to his government (by non-British radio channels), along with his comment that Armstrong had gone beyond his powers as head of a friendly military mission and "had entered into the realm of politics in a manner which cannot be forgiven in such a high Allied officer." Mihailović also informed the government that he had notified Armstrong that his letter had been turned over to the Central National Committee for study. He quoted his letter to Armstrong, in which he told him that the interests of the Serbian people were directly involved in the unwarranted threats that Armsrong had expressed in regard to the future of the Serbs and that in the meantime the British mission ought to learn more about the great sacrifices in blood and property that had been made by the Chetniks and the Serbian people while fighting alone, without foreign aid, for which they had asked in vain for many months. Mihailović concluded his message to the government-in-exile thus: "I consider Armstrong to be one of our great enemies and think that we will not be able to achieve anything with him, because he is favorably inclined toward the Communists."[16]

In the late autumn of 1943 the British received new information showing that "Mihailovic was still determined to play his own game and was not fulfilling the conditions laid down" in earlier agreements. After reviewing its policy once again at the end of November the British government made up its mind about Mihailović:

(*a*) Mihailovic was not only of *no military value* to the Allies but had become *a standing obstacle* to any sort of *Yugoslav unity* either then or in the near future;

(*b*) he was so *obsessed with the Communist menace* that he appeared openly to admit that the protection of Nedic and the Germans was preferable to submission to the Partisans;

(*c*) there was no definite evidence that he was himself collaborating with the Germans, but his subordinates were: either, then, he was impotent to control his subordinates or he was guilty of approving their arrangements;

(*d*) *his followers did not all share his extremist views*;

(*e*) the Partisans would in no circumstances collaborate with him, but there was nothing to show that they would refuse to deal with other leaders.[17]

Within days of this policy statement, the Big Three meeting at Tehran formally recognized the Partisans as an Allied armed force to which

---

[15] *Ibid.*, June 1961, pp. 36–37.

[16] *Ibid.*, pp. 37–38. *Ibid.*, December 1960, pp. 54–55, contains this acid comment about Armstrong, sent by Mihailović to the government-in-exile on October 23, 1943: "He is a common sergeant, like Bailey, who is strictly carrying out British policy according to instruction of his command in Cairo. He is trying to exert strong pressure on me, but I know them well and keep in mind the interests of the people and the existing situation."

[17] Great Britain, Foreign Office, "Relations Between General Mihailovic and His Majesty's Government," of July 27, 1944, p. 6. F.O. 371/44276, R12712/11/92.

all possible aid would be granted. The published Military Decisions did not mention the Chetniks. After the Tehran Conference was concluded, Prime Minister Churchill had a conversation with King Peter and Prime Minister Purić in Cairo in which he told them that the strength and significance of the Partisans was such that it might be necessary to dismiss Mihailović from his cabinet post and that the king's only hope for the future might lie in reaching an agreement with Tito, with British mediation, before the Partisans became even stronger. The Russians had already, he said, agreed to support his scheme.[18]

The British authorities in Cairo must have known, or at least strongly suspected, that the Chetniks had concluded a series of armistice agreements with the Germans for the purpose of combined action against the Partisans in Serbia. In Cairo shortly after leaving Tehran Eden in discussions with General Wilson, British Ambassador to Yugoslavia Ralph Stevenson, and Brigadier Maclean "heard of reports that Mihailović was uncooperative and was told of evidence that some, at least, of his subordinates were working with the Germans and their puppets." Writing in his memoirs, Eden recalls: "I was unhappy about this and it was decided by the Prime Minister, Wilson and myself that Mihailović should be asked to carry out an operation so that we might further test his intentions. General Wilson therefore sent a message to Mihailović on December 8th asking him to attack two specific bridges on the Belgrade to Salonika railway."[19] Recently opened Foreign Office documents make the intentions of the test very clear. In the already quoted Foreign Office document, "Relations Between General Mihailovic and His Majesty's Government," it is stated (p. 6): "At the beginning of December a new complication arose by the decision of the Special Operations Committee at Cairo that, *as most of the evidence* regarding *Mihailovic's collaboration with the enemy could not be published,* the case against him should be strengthened by calling upon him to carry out by a given date some specific operation known to be within his powers —*in the certain knowledge that he would fail to do so.*" Such a request had been made before Churchill saw King Peter in Cairo: on December 16 Mihailović was delivered written orders by Brigadier Armstrong to blow up an important railroad bridge south of the railroad hub of Stalać on the main Belgrade-Salonika line, and also simultaneously a bridge on the secondary line going from Kraljevo over Kosovska Mitrovica to Skopje then Salonika, and to execute this order by the twenty-ninth of December.[20]

---

[18] Churchill, *The Second World War*, V, 467–68.

[19] Eden, p. 500.

[20] For the text of Wilson's order and Mihailović's preliminary comments on the order relayed to the government-in-exile see Jovan Djonović, "The Connections with General Mihailović from the Middle East," pp. 19–20.

A few days after Armstrong delivered Wilson's order to Mihailović, Armstrong and Mihailović met again. Mihailović told Armstrong that the bridges would be destroyed, if not by December 29 then during the first half of January, because such an undertaking required considerable preparations. But he raised two other questions: first, the need for the coordination of Allied operations in the Balkans with those of the Chetniks, requiring the necessary information in advance, and second, the problem of ending the civil war in Yugoslavia, so that all forces could be directed against the occupying powers. He put all the blame for the civil war on the Partisans, using this as a reason for not trusting them, and said that it would be necessary for British officers to serve as mediators.[21] This certainly appeared to be a reversal of Mihailović's former position, which he had as recently as November 12 defined to the government-in-exile as follows: "Our policy abroad should neither recognize nor even mention the Communists, that is, the so-called People's Liberation Army. Unity of the Yugoslav Army in the Homeland and popular nationally oriented elements with the Communists is impossible, repeat impossible. Therefore, abroad such unity should be neither defended nor recommended."[22] The Tehran Conference and the second session of AVNOJ could only have strengthened Mihailović's attitude. That he now—perhaps for tactical reasons—seemed to be considering the possibility of cooperating may well have been the result of the bad news of Churchill's remarks to King Peter and Prime Minister Purić in Cairo, of which he must have learned. How sincere Mihailović was in this feeler for an agreement with the Partisans is best indicated by the fact that it was precisely at that time that some of his leading commanders in Serbia were concluding agreements with the Germans for combined action against the Partisans in Serbia; in areas outside Serbia, most of his commanders were already collaborating with the Germans. At any rate, as General Mihailović stated at this trial, Brigadier Armstrong informed him on January 3, 1944, that the British government was not willing to mediate.[23] It could hardly have done anything else, since the British had apparently made the decision to drop Mihailović. On January 2, in a note to Foreign Secretary Eden, Churchill summed it up neatly: "Mihailovic is a millstone tied around the neck of the little King, and he has no chance till he gets rid of him."[24]

Mihailović never executed General Wilson's orders regarding the bridges, but the situation had so deteriorated that even if he had done

---

[21] For Mihailović's report to the government-in-exile about this conference see *ibid.*, pp. 21–22.
[22] Jovan Djonović, "Mihailović's Telegrams About British Missions," *Glasnik SIKD 'Njegoš'*, December 1960, p. 57.
[23] *The Trial of Draža Mihailović*, p. 212.
[24] *The Second World War*, V, 470. For some correspondence of March and April 1944 between Bailey and Armstrong about the possibility of a "palace revolution" against Mihailović and Foreign Office commentaries, see F.O. 371/44269, R4937/11/92.

so it would not have helped him; as the Foreign Office paper put it, the British "attitude towards him depended upon much larger considerations" and the opinion of the Special Operations Committee was "that we could not regard last-minute repentance as being sufficient to outweigh his record of two years' inactivity."[25]

The same paper reveals (p. 6) that on January 13, 1944, evidence was received from British officers both with the Partisans and with the Chetniks, establishing the following facts:

(i) over a long period certain Chetnik commanders in Yugoslavia had been openly collaborating with the Axis forces—German, Italian, Croat, and Bulgar, according to locality;

(ii) there was no evidence of direct personal collaboration between Mihailovic and the enemy, but there was no doubt that he was aware of the acts of his subordinates and had in certain cases specifically condoned them;

(iii) *Mihailovic had personally directed operations against the Partisan forces in the Neretva Valley in March 1943*, as partner in the joint German-Italian-Croat offensive.

In his memoirs Churchill says that early in December 1943 the British "withdrew official support from Mihailovic and recalled the British missions operating in his territory."[26] The severing of relations with Mihailović was a good deal more complicated than these words would indicate. It seems to be true that some members of the British mission, Hudson for one, got orders to withdraw toward the coast or toward Partisan territory as early as mid-December; and Bailey left Chetnik headquarters in western Serbia on January 5. (Bailey was evacuated in mid-February and Hudson in mid-March.) And British liaison groups in northeastern Serbia also were given discretionary power on December 13 to move, if they so desired, after December 15 to the nearest Partisan units.[27] The government-in-exile and Mihailović were notified about the withdrawal of all members of British missions on March 1, but the last members, including Brigadier Armstrong as well as some American and British airmen who had bailed out over Chetnik territory and some Chetnik politicians, were not evacuated until the last three days in May. In the intervening months, the British who were still at Chetnik headquarters were scarcely on speaking terms with any of the Yugoslavs. According to Topalović, all personal communication between Armstrong and Mihailović ceased after January. For four months Armstrong's aide, Major H. S. K. Greenlees, appeared at Mihailović's office every morning at eleven o'clock to communicate the desire of his chief to be received by Mihailović, but each time the answer was the same:

[25] Foreign Office, "Relations Between General Mihailovic and His Majesty's Government," p. 6.
[26] *The Second World War*, V, 467.
[27] Rootham, p. 176.

"The General is occupied." Thus they communicated by polite letters and did not meet even when Armstrong departed.[28]

Armstrongs' quite understandable frustration is evident from one of his reports of April 1944. "From the operational point of view," he said, "Mihailović's orders for inactivity are known and followed almost without exception. . . . The main pre-occupation ever since the end of October has been propaganda. This has never wavered from the line that Serbia is hitched, for better or worse, to the Anglo-American star and that no compromise is possible with the occupying powers. Equally strong is the propaganda against the Partisans who have, in the minds of the people, taken the place of the Germans as Enemy No. 1." Although the British mission had no evidence of collaboration, he said, it appeared from the behavior of the Chetnik commanders that "a sort of non-aggression pact existed which conduced to the comfort of all concerned." He concluded that the Chetnik organization because of "military ill-preparedness and moral defeatism" could now do little more than accelerate by a few days the already inevitable withdrawal of the Germans and that it "will continue to fight the Partisans with such weapons as it has, either until it is finally beaten or until there is a Partisan representation in the Yugoslav Government."[29] Armstrong seems to have been totally unaware that the Chetniks and the Germans were even then collaborating on a large scale against the two Partisan divisions that had penetrated into Serbia, and one must interpret his scanty intelligence about the Chetniks as being due, in part at least, to the fact that since the British liaison officers were preparing to leave the country, the Chetniks for obvious reasons were using extreme caution to keep them from acquiring any knowledge about their activities outside headquarters.[30]

In London, the efforts of the Churchill government to oust the Yugoslav cabinet headed by Dr. Purić were finally successful, and with the ouster of the Purić government they also eliminated General Mihailović from the position of Minister of the Army, Navy, and Air Force, though he continued briefly in his post as Chief of Staff of the Supreme Com-

[28] Topalović, "The Departure from the Country," pp. 56–58. In a brief article laudatory of Mihailović (in which there are several factual errors), Armstrong makes no mention of their extremely strained relations during the last part of his stay at Chetnik headquarters. *Naša reč* (London), No. 172–73 (June–July, 1966), pp. 16–17.

[29] *The Četniks*, pp. 21–22.

[30] Bailey was back in London by early March and had a series of talks not only with his superiors and intelligence authorities but also with Eden and Churchill. In April 1944 he submitted his "Report on Mission to General Mihailovic & Conditions in Yugoslavia," consisting of 37 sections or appendixes. Declassified, less sensitive portions of the report (F.O. 371/44282, R21295/11/92) suggest that the entire report was several hundred pages long. Since in January 1970 I was still in the dark about some matters regarding relations between the British military mission and General Mihailović, I addressed a series of questions to Colonel Bailey but never received any answers, although we exchanged several letters. Through the recently released Foreign Office documents and other sources, however, I was able to clear up all the controversial points.

mand. On May 24 Churchill told the House of Commons: "The reason why we have ceased to supply Mihailovitch with arms and support is a simple one. He has not been fighting the enemy, and, moreover, some of his subordinates have made accommodations with the enemy." In this speech Churchill repeatedly emphasized that the main idea that shaped the policy of the British government was "beating the enemy as soon as possible and to gather all forces for that purpose in priority to any other purpose."[31] The length of time it took for the British to come to a decision on this matter suggests that they were prepared to continue their support of the Chetniks, whom they considered to be the only important political and military force in Serbia proper, if they saw any fundamental change in Chetnik policy such as a complete switch from intermittent collaborating with the Germans to fighting them with resolution and some real moves toward cooperating with the Partisans. Any such reversal in the Chetnik policy was, of course, highly unlikely. But as long as the British mission remained at Mihailović's headquarters, even if their relations were almost hostile, a pretense of some British-Chetnik cooperation could be maintained. Similarly, the Chetniks no doubt knew that the departure of the British mission would be the unmistakable sign that the British had severed relations with the Chetniks, and that such a move would inevitably have unfavorable consequences for Mihailović and the Chetniks in military, political, and psychological respects, and would serve as a boon for the Partisans.

Armstrong's final leavetaking was marred by some petty incidents which, though interpreted quite differently by Chetnik and British sources, are indicative of the impasse which their relations had reached. What happened was that two Chetnik commanders, Major Vojislav Lukačević and Lt. Colonel Petar Baćović, who were returning to Yugoslavia from Cairo, were thoroughly searched by the British at Bari, and apparently most of the money, valuable gifts, and letters that they were carrying were impounded, apparently for purposes of investigation to see whether they were connected with a robbery in the Yugoslav headquarters in Cairo. They arrived back in Serbia just as Brigadier Armstrong was about to leave, and insisted that he should be held as a sort of hostage until their impounded articles had been brought from Bari.[32] Cooler heads prevailed, but the incident was an unpleasant conclusion to the always difficult Chetnik-British relations.

Around May 18, simultaneously with the demise of the Purić government (including Mihailović), a Partisan military mission under Major

[31] Great Britain, *Parliamentary Debates*, Session 1943–44, Vol. 400, pp. 775–76.

[32] Topalović, "The Departure from the Country," pp. 56–65, gives an unflattering picture of British behavior. But Field Marshal Wilson, *Eight Years Overseas, 1939–1947*, pp. 213–14, gives an equally unflattering picture of the Chetniks.

General Vladimir Velebit arrived in London. Its purpose was to facilitate Partisan-British cooperation on the British side, but it also served to maintain contact between the Partisan authorities and the new Yugoslav government of Dr. Šubašić, which on June 1 took over the conduct of Yugoslav affairs abroad.

There is a rather interesting item from the days following Mihailović's removal as Minister of the Army, Navy, and Air Force. On July 10, 1944, the German services intercepted a letter addressed to Jevdjević, without date but apparently written early in June, which they ascribed to Mihailović. In this letter Mihailović told Jevdjević, after referring to the return of Lukačević and Baćović from Cairo, that "British officials in high posts and widely visible have let us know that we should liquidate the Communists as soon as possible. As soon as we have carried out the liquidation of the Communists there will be a change in the situation —that is, the Allies will immediately change their attitude, their propaganda, and what is the most important, their politics."[33] According to this letter, both Lukačević and Baćović were convinced that the existing policy toward the Partisans was only a matter of temporary tactics, and that the Allies would change their policy as soon as the Chetniks had defeated the Partisans. Since Mihailović still had many friends among the British officials, it is entirely possible that such a message was sent to him, but it is obvious that it could not have been sent by any official who at that time had an important say in formulating British policy toward Yugoslavia.[34] Certainly, if the Chetniks had been able to defeat the Partisans in the second half of 1944, their position would have been greatly improved and the Allies would have faced new decisions, but both because of the Partisans' own strength and the strength of the approaching Soviet army, such a victory was out of the question.

In spite of the royal decree abolishing the Supreme Command in Yugoslavia, signed on August 24, and King Peter's speech broadcast on September 12 calling upon all Serbs, Croats, and Slovenes to switch under the command of Marshal Tito, Mihailović did not give up. Most of his Chetniks still remained loyal to him, and in accordance with the resolution of the Central National Committee of the preceding July 23, in which the committee reserved for itself the right to undertake measures for the protection of the nation and state, Mihailović and the Chetnik leadership continued to uphold the idea that the Supreme Command of the Yugoslav Army in the Homeland was still in effect and that Mihailović was its legitimate head. The Chetnik army continued to exist, but after its defeats in Serbia and withdrawal to Bosnia it was a steadily

[33] Microcopy No. T-311, Roll 286, Frame 473.
[34] At his trial Mihailović stated that the message came from Tom Masterson, of the Cairo office of SOE, who was known for his pro-Chetnik attitudes. *The Trial of Draža Mihailović*, p. 305.

dwindling force. And the support of the civilian population, too, was fast eroding.

The memoirs of both Churchill and Eden show that the British were in many ways reluctant to drop Mihailović, knowing that in so doing they would be alienating the whole Chetnik movement in Yugoslavia and Mihailović's friends not only among the Yugoslav politicians in exile but also among the officials and people in Great Britain and the United States, and they did their best to induce Tito to give assurances that King Peter would be treated fairly.[35] An essential political objective of this sacrifice of Mihailović and support of Tito was to save the monarchy and thereby also some democratic institutions and perhaps, as well, some British influence in postwar Yugoslavia. But Tito gave no guarantee beyond professing the democratic character and intentions of the Partisan movement and asserting that the decisions on the monarchy would be made by general and free elections after the war. It was only after such assurances, however, that the king, against the advice of the overwhelming majority of the exiled politicians, gave in to Churchill's pressure and completely abandoned Mihailović and the Chetniks.

HOPES OF SALVATION FROM THE UNITED STATES

In the spring of 1943, when relations between the Chetniks, backed by the government-in-exile, and the British military mission and government first began to turn really sour and as news of Chetnik-Axis collaboration appeared with increasing frequency in the press of Great Britain and the United States, the government-in-exile and Ambassador Fotić in Washington once again tried to involve the United States more fully on the side of the Chetniks. On May 5, Fotić, just back from London, took up the matter with Roosevelt. Fotić was mainly interested in persuading Roosevelt, who was known to lean toward the Serbs and the Chetniks, that there was no truth in the stories of Axis-Chetnik collaboration which, though mostly originating from Soviet news services on the basis of information from Partisan sources, were now being repeated by the press in both England and the United States, and also in convincing him that the fundamental objective of the Partisans was to prepare the ground for a Communist takeover of Yugoslavia after the war.

Fotić urged Roosevelt to send impartial army observers, men not previously involved in Yugoslav matters, to Mihailović's headquarters in order to make a fair evaluation. On May 12 Fotić learned from Undersecretary of State Sumner Welles that Roosevelt had decided to send "two American officers to Mihailović and two others to Tito."[36] This

---

[35] See e.g. Churchill, *The Second World War*, V, 466–78; Eden, pp. 500–502, 546–47.
[36] Fotić, *The War We Lost*, pp. 205–7. See also *FRUS 1943*, pp. 1006–7. There is no record of Welles's communication in *FRUS 1943*, and it may have been made in an informal fashion. But other documents in this publication, even of a somewhat later date, do not hint at any decision of

was rather more than Fotić had desired in the way of ascertaining true conditions in Yugoslavia, but he was in no position to object.

Early in August, before any Americans had arrived at Chetnik headquarters, a German agent who was working for the *Abwehrstelle* in Belgrade and had direct contacts at Mihailović's headquarters reported that "according to allegedly true information, General Mihailović will try, because of the rivalry between the British and the Americans, to derive some advantage for future Yugoslavia."[37] This was, indeed, the apparent Chetnik objective. On August 18 the first American officer, Captain Walter R. Mansfield, arrived at Mihailović's headquarters.[38]

Captain Mansfield has written several articles on the Chetniks. His first article (1946), a simple "narrative of a marine's adventures as an OSS officer," shows no trace of understanding of the background of the Chetniks or their wartime policies, and gives no hint of their collaboration with either the Italians or the Germans.[39] Another article, entitled "Mihailović and Tito," was prepared in 1946 at the time of Mihailović's trial, but it was not published until 1956. This article contends that Mihailović always fought the Germans and never collaborated. "The American mission," Mansfield says, "had never seen Mihailović in the course of 1943 and 1944 collaborating with the Germans." He concedes that a few Chetnik commanders did make arrangements with the Germans, but only in order to maintain their units and obtain arms until the time came to turn against the Germans, and in order to fight off Partisan efforts to annihilate the Chetniks who refused to accept Communism.[40]

Lt. Colonel Albert B. Seitz and Lieutenant George Musulin were parachuted into Serbia together with Brigadier Armstrong toward the end of September 1943. Like Captain Mansfield, they were attached to the British mission, and Seitz reports that he was told by Armstrong immediately after their arrival that the whole thing "was a British show" and that he would be permitted to communicate with Mihailović only in the presence of British officers, in Serbian only, not in French, with Col-

---

this sort by Roosevelt at that time. It probably was made only after the British established contact with the Partisan headquarters through mission Typical (Deakin-Stuart) and was communicated to Fotić later than he indicates.

[37] Microcopy No. T-311, Roll 196, Frame 150.

[38] The formal status of the American officers with the Chetniks underwent several changes during the course of time. From August 1943 to May 1944 the American officers were attached to the British military mission and under its command; from late July to late August 1944 some American officers were with the Chetniks solely to facilitate the evacuation of Allied (mostly American) fliers who bailed out over Chetnik-controlled territory; and from late August to November 1, 1944, there was an independent American intelligence mission with Mihailović.

[39] "Marine with the Chetniks," *Marine Corps Gazette*, January and February 1946.

[40] "Mihailović and Tito," pp. 349, 355–56. In an earlier speech published also in *Knjiga o Draži*, Vol. II, Mansfield apparently accepts (p. 362) the Chetnik contention that British and American statesmen had betrayed Mihailović at Tehran and Yalta. After this book was in page proof, I obtained Mansfield's report "Mihailovic and His Forces" dated April 24, 1944 (F.O. 371/44271, R7885/11/92), which is limited in perception though relatively realistic, but also contains some strong Mihailović apologia. See also below, p. 468.

onel Bailey acting as interpreter.[41] Seitz protested to his superiors, but Armstrong was upheld on all points except that of editing Seitz's dispatches (but he was entitled to read them). Of this period at Mihailović's headquarters, Seitz says:

> We, the Americans, were thus relegated to a supernumerary news gathering capacity, and to sending in items gathered by the "Štab" (headquarters) from various "Korpus" (corps) Commanders by radio and courier. This intelligence could not be checked and, I felt certain, would have to be almost totally discounted.
>
> I felt that the war had to be an Allied show, and that America had a definite task to perform in the Balkans. It might be only supplies, but supplies are the sinews of war.[42]

Frustrated by this situation at headquarters, both Seitz and Mansfield were eager to get into the country so that they could gather information firsthand and check the accuracy of what the Chetniks were telling them. The Chetniks welcomed the idea, seeing that it was an opportunity to make a good impression on the American officers and in that way, no doubt, build up a counterbalance for the Chetnik cause to offset the negative attitudes of the British mission and the British command posts in the Mediterranean. Early in November, Seitz and Mansfield, without waiting for authorization from their superiors in Cairo but with the approval of Brigadier Armstrong, set out on a tour of inspection. They were accompanied by Hudson and Captain Borislav J. Todorović, an English-speaking Chetnik liaison officer, and were guided by the groups of Chetniks representing the commanders of areas through which they passed or by the commanders personally. They were shown what they asked to see, they asked questions of persons they met, and they inspected and reviewed Chetnik armed troops and unarmed reserves. On one occasion they observed actual fighting between a Chetnik brigade and Communists.[43] Everywhere, they were treated with utmost courtesy and were dined and wined daily by their Serbian hosts.[44] Seitz and Mansfield interpreted their relative freedom of movement throughout the trip as proof that the Chetniks controlled the areas through which they passed. The truth was, of course, that in two areas at least, those under the commands of Captain Kalabić and Major Lukačević (see Map 6, p. 325), a state of German-Chetnik collaboration existed and the Chetniks were

[41] Seitz, p. 13. Seitz has good things to say about both Bailey and Hudson, but he describes Armstrong as "an admirable little man in many ways, but rather slow thinking," who seemed unable to understand either the Americans or the Serbs (p. 40).

[42] *Ibid.*, p. 14.

[43] *Ibid.*, p. 52. One of the pro-Ljotić and anti-Chetnik Serbs in exile, B. M. Karapandžić, maintains (*Gradjanski rat*, pp. 260–61) that in order to impress the Anglo-American inspection commission (Hudson, Seitz, Mansfield) Chetnik commanders Račić, Kalabić, Marković, Smiljanić, Keserović, and others engaged in military operations not against the Germans but against troops of Nedić and Ljotić where prior to that time peace reigned, and in so doing killed several Ljotić commanders and more than a hundred Serbian Volunteer Corps members.

[44] Seitz, pp. 48–49.

being supplied with ammunition by the Germans. Receiving Allied officers in their midst was a violation of the terms of the agreements with the Germans, and a few months later these formal agreements were canceled or expired; but there is no doubt that at the time of the visit of the Allied officers, both Kalabić and Lukačević (for whom Seitz had much praise) were collaborating.[45] It is curious therefore that Seitz should say: "The fable of collaboration could not be taken seriously; I had been with too many Chetnik leaders at the time the certainly ill-informed or lying Tiflis radio had accused them of collaboration." Seitz outdoes even the Chetniks in some of his claims—as when he says that the Chetniks by their revolt under Mihailović rendered "incalculable benefit to Russia" in forcing Germany to postpone its attack on Russia from April to June 1941, and that the Chetniks held down thirty enemy divisions during the winter of 1941–42. There is not a grain of truth in either one of these statements.[46]

After several months in Yugoslavia, Seitz and Mansfield, along with Hudson, received orders to end their mission. Since the Chetniks had not even a makeshift airstrip at that time, evacuation had to be by sea, or by airlift from Partisan territory. They chose the sea route, and with Captain Todorović as guide, set out for the Adriatic coast; but Seitz and Hudson, accompanied by two British officers who joined them en route, broke away and went instead to Partisan-controlled territory in Montenegro.[47] Colonel Bailey and some other British officers, as well as Major Lukačević, also went to the coast, and they, along with Mansfield and Todorović and another Chetnik commander, Lt. Colonel Baćović, were evacuated in mid-February 1944 by a British naval craft from an area south of Dubrovnik. Seitz and Hudson reached Berane and were safely evacuated from there by air around March 18.[48]

Seitz's wartime operational reports have not been declassified and were not available to me. The views expressed in his book, which most probably reflected the tenor of his wartime reports, differ markedly from those that were being conveyed to the British and American commands by other, primarily British, and much more experienced and knowledgeable observers.[49] From the developments that followed, it

[45] As shown earlier, in February and March the Germans conducted a special operation, Treibjagd, against Kalabić, and some operations against Čačić, in order to destroy their forces, but some months later these Chetnik commanders were again collaborating informally with the Germans.

[46] See Seitz, pp. 128, 138–39.

[47] For Todorović's experiences as liaison officer with Seitz, Mansfield, and Hudson on their inspection trip as well as his account of the ordeal of the trek to the coast and evacuation there see his article "Notes of a Liaison Officer," pp. 372–412. Especially interesting, however, is that portion of Todorović's narrative where he relates how all Chetnik officers who came out with Bailey were arrested after their arrival in Cairo and detained several days in a military prison (pp. 408–12).

[48] For Bailey's report on his evacuation from Yugoslavia, see F.O. 371/44282, R21295/11/92, Appendix 5. For Seitz's observations on his stay in Partisan territory, see his book, pp. 94–96.

[49] According to a reliable British source, Hudson submitted a full report following his inspection trip with Seitz and Mansfield. This report, dated March 17, 1944, from Berane, presented a balanced picture of the development of the Chetnik movement from the summer of 1941 and included

appears that Mansfield's and Seitz's reports favorably impressed **Briga-dier** General William J. Donovan, director of the OSS, and other American officials. Donovan wanted not only to leave Lieutenant Musulin with Mihailović but also to enlarge the American mission, and he got the full support of the State Department for his plan. A letter from Secretary Cordell Hull to Donovan of May 18 replying to Donovan's letter of April 7 describes the functions of the proposed mission as "military intelligence, special operations, arranging supply lines, technical air force intelligence, and morale operations against the enemy."[50] The British thought that it would be a mistake to leave an American mission with the Chetniks since it might be interpreted as showing disagreement between the two Allies. Churchill intervened to squash the plan, and Musulin was withdrawn at the same time as Brigadier Armstrong.[51] But this did not mean the end of American efforts to have an intelligence mission, at least, with Mihailović, the more so as pressure continued to be exercised on American authorities by Mihailović's supporters in the United States to have such a mission.

It appears also that the reports of Mansfield and Seitz somewhat hardened the position of those persons in the United States government, including Secretary of State Hull, who were of the opinion that the United States should proceed slowly in enlarging the relations with the Partisans. In a letter to President Roosevelt dated May 17, 1944, Hull suggested that the President should not personally reply to an earlier letter of Marshal Tito because of the conflict existing between the Partisans and the government of King Peter which the United States recognized. Hull particularly objected to the proposal to send a Partisan military mission to the United States comparable to the one that had just arrived in London. He believed that such a mission not only would make it more difficult to settle various issues between the government-in-exile and the Partisans but would tend to aggravate disputes among the various South Slav groups in the United States.[52] Hull's objection was accepted and no Partisan mission was ever sent to Washington.

The United States had several good reasons for wanting to be involved in Yugoslav affairs in a limited way. First of all, the American military and intelligence authorities wanted to maintain a link with the Chet-

detailed observations about the inspection trip. The report suggested that the idea that Mihailović and his Chetniks were really combatants was supported by the frequent clashes with the Serbian Volunteer Corps, by the occasional disarming of Nedić forces, and by the killing of the remnants of the Partisans in Serbia, while the Germans remained generally indifferent to this fighting among various Serbian groups.

[50] *FRUS 1944*, IV, 1369–70.

[51] *Ibid.*, pp. 1349–50; Martin, p. 229; Roberts, pp. 255–56.

[52] For Tito's letter of March 15, 1944, to Roosevelt see *FRUS 1944*, IV, 1356–57; for an excerpt from Hull's note to Roosevelt of May 17, the draft of an answer to Tito to be signed by the future chief of American military mission to the Partisans, and a letter from Hull to General Donovan of May 18, see *ibid.*, pp. 1368–70.

niks in order to rescue American airmen who were forced to bail out over Chetnik-controlled areas on their way back to Italian airfields from raids on targets in southeastern Europe. These authorities, as well as the government in Washington, wanted to know whether or not, and if so to what extent, the Partisans were using American-supplied arms and other military equipment against the Chetniks; and the American intelligence services wanted to obtain firsthand intelligence from the Chetnik areas as well as intelligence from other countries in southeastern Europe through channels maintained by the Chetniks.

Beginning in July 1944, American policy in Yugoslavia had conformed to the policy outlined in a directive formulated by the Political Advisory Staff of the Supreme Allied Commander, Mediterranean Theater, applying to all forces under the Balkan Air Force, and sent by the U.S. Mission in Algiers for State Department approval in Washington. The portion of the draft referring to Yugoslavia read as follows:

> The general policy is that all possible military support should be accorded to those elements willing and able to resist the enemy. The final goal is to further the cause of national unity throughout the country in preparation for post-war settlements. No action should be initiated which would commit us to a recognition of any claims to the revision of pre-war frontiers. Such questions must be held in abeyance for settlement at the peace conference. This means in Yugoslavia that we should provide the fullest aid to Tito's Partisans. We should encourage the union of all the fighting units in Yugoslavia with the National Army of Liberation in a single front in accord with the provisions of the Tito-Subasich agreement. No support will be furnished the Mihailovich forces. Support will not be furnished the Partisans where it is obvious that they will use it not against the Germans, Bulgarians, Ustashi and other definitely accepted Quislings, but merely against the Chetniks. Support may be given, however, in cases where Partisan forces are fighting Chetniks who are definitely collaborating with the Germans, Bulgarians or Quisling Serbian units and in cases where the Partisans find active opposition in attacks on mines, lines of communication or other objectives of a military value. We would use as our guiding principle, except for the two exceptions already noted, the idea that we must not become involved in or a party to purely internal conflicts or domestic issues in Yugoslavia.[53]

The U.S. Mission in Algiers thought that such a policy implied virtual exclusion of Mihailović from Allied aid, and since the idea persisted that Mihailović might still be doing some fighting against the Germans, there was, it believed, an implied contradiction to the policy that aid should be given to all elements that were willing and able to fight the enemy. This objection was later upheld by the State Department[54] and the directive may have been slightly changed. The Partisans, on the other hand, in fact had full freedom in the use of arms against the Chet-

[53] *Ibid.*, p. 1383.
[54] *Ibid.*, pp. 1384, 1386–88, 1407–8.

niks, because the Chetniks in general were collaborating with the Germans and the quisling troops against the Partisans.

As for the rescue of American fliers from Chetnik-held territories, American intelligence services and the Fifteenth Air Force repeatedly requested British permission to establish contact with the Chetniks and to send American officers to arrange the evacuation of the fliers who were in hiding with them. Contact was finally made around July 20, and on August 2 Lieutenant George Musulin was parachuted near Ravna Gora. He was followed on the night of August 9 by First Lieutenant (later Captain) Nick Lalich, who assisted Musulin and later became head of the air crew rescue unit operating in Chetnik territory under the code name "Halyard." On the nights of August 9 and 10 from a crude airstrip at the village of Pranjani, which had been built by the Chetniks and peasants the previous April, sixteen transport planes evacuated the Allied fliers. During the next three months three additional flights for the same purpose were made to northwestern Serbia and north-central Bosnia. The last flight, which included Lalich, was made on December 27 from an airstrip at Boljanići near Doboj. In all, 417 fliers were rescued, including 343 Americans.[55]

The mission to Mihailović led by Colonel Robert H. McDowell was of a totally different sort from those so far described. The following account of McDowell's mission is based on an interview with him at Stanford University, March 19, 1968, talks with a member of the Chetnik Committee of Experts who participated with the other members of the committee in an interview of Colonel McDowell in Serbia, various radio messages of the Chetnik Supreme Command to lower commands on statements supposedly made by McDowell as intercepted by German monitoring services, and the statement that he submitted in 1946 to the Commission of Inquiry of the Committee for a Fair Trial for Draja Mihailovich, the last named being, so far as I know, his only published statement. From this statement as well as from our interview, it was evident that his sympathies lay with the Chetniks and that he was greatly disturbed by the drastic shift in attitude among the policy-making British authorities away from the Chetniks and in favor of the Partisans which took place during the second half of 1943 and finally led to the jettisoning of the Chetniks. He had full opportunity to watch the change in British policy toward the two competing groups in Yugoslavia since he was a member of the JICAME (Joint Intelligence Collection Agency Middle East) in Cairo, and was dissatisfied with it, as were

[55] Report of 1st Lt. Lalich of Jan. 10, 1945, on Halyard Mission, RG 226, OSS–File No. XL5727. Since Lalich was charged exclusively with the evacuation of Allied fliers and not with intelligence work, he did not file any intelligence reports. In this report, nevertheless, he put down what he had "heard and seen" in Chetnik territory, but nothing is really worth dwelling upon. See also Vučković, "The Rescue of American Fliers."

some of the British SOE officers in Cairo who strongly supported Mihailović. McDowell first asked for an assignment in Yugoslavia in March 1944, but was turned down; a second request in June was also turned down. The reason for refusal was opposition by the British, who apparently feared that the presence of an American mission with the Chetniks might bring increased friction among the Big Three with regard to the Yugoslav question, and might also further complicate the Yugoslav internal situation by seeming to encourage the Chetniks, who by that time had been officially jettisoned by the Western Allies. However, Brigadier General Donovan, Chief of the OSS, pushed the dispatching of such a mission, and on August 26, 1944, after six unsuccessful tries, Colonel McDowell and four others—Captain John Milodragovich, Lieutenant Ellsworth Kramer, Master Sergeant (later Lieutenant) Michael Rayacich, and a radio operator—were parachuted into Chetnik territory not far from Mihailović's headquarters. Nick Lalich, the head of the air crew rescue unit, was also attached to McDowell. Kramer was soon detailed to the headquarters of Lt. Colonel Keserović.

Colonel McDowell told me that his task in Yugoslavia was to gather general intelligence—mainly, of course, from the Chetnik camp—and to establish contacts (with the help of already existing Chetnik channels) with the representatives of the pro-Western political forces in Hungary, Romania, and Bulgaria. Since the position of the Chetniks in Serbia and elsewhere in Yugoslavia worsened drastically soon after McDowell joined Mihailović, it appears that most of his time was taken up with the problems of the Chetniks.

A former member of the Chetnik Committee of Experts told me in July 1967 in Belgrade that the entire committee met with Colonel McDowell shortly after he arrived in Serbia in order to ascertain whom he really represented and what his real assignment was. They were especially interested in finding out whether he was a special emissary of President Roosevelt, of Secretary of War Stimson, or of Chief of Staff Marshall, or just another representative of the OSS—in other words, just how much influence he might actually have. Colonel McDowell's answers at this meeting (which he could not recall when I asked him about it) were evasive, and the Committee of Experts rightly deduced that he was an OSS operative, that is, just another intelligence officer. Since earlier Chetnik experiences with both British and American intelligence officers had been disappointing, to say the least, McDowell's real importance and influence were greatly discounted. Nevertheless, at that juncture in the Chetnik situation, Colonel McDowell appeared to be a real asset in a psychological and propaganda sense, and there was at least an outside chance of his being able to persuade American military and political authorities to show some real support for the Chetniks. That Mihailović appraised the McDowell mission in this sense can be seen from two documents: a circular telegram, No. 677, "only for corps commanders and higher officers," sent shortly after McDowell arrived, and a letter of Mihailović to Fotić dated November 18, 1944— that is, shortly after McDowell left Yugoslavia. In the circular telegram Mihailović said: "The Chief of the American military mission, Colonel McDowell, who arrived at my headquarters on August 26, had wide political powers. With him I have elaborated a detailed, allied, political and military plan. Now it is necessary for every commander to do only whatever I order him to do. Any initiative beyond my orders can spoil everything. Therefore I order that no action can be undertaken without my orders, save against the Communists."[56] In his letter to Fotić, Mihailović wrote that McDowell left "as our great friend." McDowell, he said, had accompanied him through much of western Serbia and northeastern Bosnia and had "had the opportunity to see our military forces as well as the close ties between the army and the people"; he had visited various political meetings, and in Bosnia he was "delighted with our work on developing close ties with the Moslems and Catholics." Mihailović went on to say that he trusted "that [McDowell's] report, together with the reports of Seitz and Mansfield, would be one more confirmation of the real conditions in the country in our favor." Mihailović also said that McDowell had visited military hospitals with him and had talked with Chetniks whose wounds were mostly inflicted by the Partisans and that he told him that there would be a great scandal if the American people heard that nationalist soldiers were killed by American arms delivered by American aircraft (to the Partisans). Mihailović suggested to Fotić "to guard McDowell's name so that he might not be blocked in his work." Mihailović also added this suggestion: "I think that we should try to seek the greatest possible reliance on America for support because America has great economic interests in the Balkans, and it would be in our economic interest also to tie ourselves to America."[57]

The Chetniks badly needed support from America, and naturally they tried not only to cultivate the American mission but also to make the greatest political and propaganda capital out of the rescue of the downed airmen. Their hopes were stimulated by a good deal of wishful thinking, but unquestionably McDowell himself had a share in raising Mihailović's hopes. Neither his report after he came out of Yugoslavia, dated November 22, 1944, nor his statement to the Commission of In-

[56] Archives of the Institute of Military History, Belgrade, Chetnik Documents, Reg. No. 33/3, Box 129. Mihailović's statement about McDowell's powers and about having elaborated with him "a detailed, allied, political and military plan" are obviously expressions of wishful thinking rather than fact, and were probably intended to raise the morale of his commanders. Later his telegram was read to the troops.

[57] For the text of this letter see *Knjiga o Draži*, II, 171–74.

quiry of the Committee for a Fair Trial for Draja Mihailovich[58] says anything about what statements he made to Mihailović or to various political meetings while in Yugoslavia. There are some hints in the messages of the Chetnik Supreme Command, however. One, to the Area Staff for Dalmatia, dated October 17, 1944, says, in a paraphrased form, that "the Chief of the American mission to the Supreme Command, Colonel McDowell, has declared explicitly in political meetings that a British-American invasion of the Balkans is imminent and that the Balkans will never be given up to the Russians and thus to bolshevization." And a message of October 22 to all lower commands says: "Colonel Mc-Dowell, chief of the American mission at the Supreme Command, stated that Churchill is afraid that after the war England would be the only country in Europe which would have to represent the monarchic idea, and therefore it would support any monarchistic party, including the Mihailović movement."[59] An official statement of the (Chetnik) Command for Serbia cites McDowell even more specifically as having made these points: (*a*) that the Allies had ceased to supply the Partisans because they had not used the supplies to fight the occupying armies; (*b*) that the landing of only American troops in Yugoslavia was to take place shortly and this was to assure the people that they could express their democratic principles without any pressure; and (*c*) that in France and Italy the Allies had disarmed all Partisan detachments and allowed the existence of only the regular army. This statement and some others were issued in the form of leaflets and distributed in large numbers throughout Serbia.[60] Not surprisingly, McDowell's mission and his statements came up at Mihailović's trial. Mihailović testified that McDowell made a number of comments soon after his arrival, such as: "Your present situation is difficult, but the future is yours"; "Germany has lost the war; your fight against the Germans does not interest us. You have to keep your position among the people—I have come to help you"; and "When the Russians appear on the frontier, and see our arrival, the Red Army will not enter Yugoslavia." On another occasion McDowell told Mihailović that he had to hold some terrain.[61]

It need hardly be said that none of the quoted statements attributed to Colonel McDowell represented official policy. When McDowell spoke to Mihailović about the landing of American troops in Yugoslavia—ob-

---

[58] For the text of McDowell's statement to this committee see Committee for a Fair Trial for Draja Mihailovich, *Report of Commission of Inquiry*, pp. 12–16.

[59] Microcopy No. T-311, Roll 189, Frames 1096, 1073. These messages of the Supreme Command to the subordinate commands are paraphrases that were included in the daily reports of the German monitoring service (Kommandeur der Nachrichtenaufklärung 4, which apparently until October 18, 1944, was covered by designation Dienststelle Feldpostnummer 31208). The messages were probably in code, but it is well known that the Germans broke all Chetnik and Partisan codes in no time.

[60] For texts of these statements and texts of leaflets see Kostić, pp. 169–72, or Karapandžić, pp. 368–70.

[61] *The Trial of Draža Mihailović*, pp. 269, 307–8.

viously a vital matter for the Chetniks—he could not have been speaking either on the basis of his original briefing before he undertook the mission or on the basis of new instructions from his superiors during his stay with Mihailović, because a decision for an invasion of Yugoslavia by the Anglo-American forces, much less for the American forces alone, had never been made nor could have been made in view of established U.S. policy. Throughout the war, the United States considered the Balkans outside its direct political and military interest and therefore opposed any operations, either American or British, in Yugoslavia beyond aid to the fighting guerrillas in supplies and air support and occasional commando actions. There were varied military reasons for this caution in terms of overall American strategy: military operations in the Balkans would have overextended the lines of communication and thus greatly increased the problems of supplying the troops in that area; also, expanded operations in the Balkans might have delayed the massive assault on Europe in Operation Overlord and might have created an awkward situation with the Russians.[62] McDowell therefore must have been speaking on his own, apparently not realizing how his statements would be interpreted—or perhaps merely trying, somewhat thoughtlessly, to boost the Chetniks' morale. Possibly, it is true, these statements were simply invented by the Chetnik Supreme Command and attributed to McDowell, again for the purpose of boosting morale, but this is scarcely probable because statements from Chetnik sources differ little from those attributed to McDowell by anti-Chetnik Serbian (pro-Nedić and pro-Ljotić), Partisan, and German sources.[63]

The Partisans were unhappy at having Colonel McDowell attached to Mihailović's headquarters, and Tito made vigorous protests to Brigadier Maclean. He could not understand, he said, the presence of this American officer with the Chetniks in view of the generally proven collaboration of Mihailović with the Germans, and after "even King Peter had publicly denounced him."[64]

According to a telegram of September 7, 1944, from the U.S. Political

---

[62] For more on American policy against involvement in any extensive Balkan operations see e.g. Stimson's memorandum to the conference at Quebec in August 1943 in Stimson and Bundy, pp. 436–38, and especially conferences of Roosevelt and the Joint Chiefs of Staff aboard the SS *Iowa* held between November 15 and 19, 1943, preparatory to the meetings at Cairo and Tehran, in Matloff, pp. 343–44, 505. See also Wedemeyer, pp. 228–34.

[63] Not that the Chetnik authorities were above fabricating news about McDowell. For example, the Area Staff East Bosnia informed the Area Staff Herzegovina on November 26, 1944, that Colonel McDowell had returned from Washington to the Chetnik Supreme Command on the preceding day. See Microcopy No. T-311, Roll 189, Frame 1253. The motive of such an obvious untruthful statement is baffling; it could only have been made in desperation. An earlier case of news fabrication for purposes of boosting the morale of the Chetnik forces was the circular announcement of the Chetnik Supreme Command to all lower commands of October 10, 1944, to the effect that a Yugoslav army of about 100,000 men was being formed abroad (Italy) which would include also many Yugoslav officers and men from Switzerland (former Yugoslav prisoners of war in Italy who after the Italian collapse succeeded in moving to Switzerland). *Ibid.*, Frame 999.

[64] See the message of the U.S. Political Adviser on the staff of the Supreme Allied Commander, Mediterranean Theater, to the Secretary of State, of Oct. 31, 1944; *FRUS 1944*, IV, 1415–16.

Adviser on the staff of the Supreme Allied Commander, Mediterranean Theater, Colonel McDowell while attached to Mihailović's headquarters had a meeting with a German intelligence operative (Rudolf Stärker) who represented Special Envoy Hermann Neubacher, Plenipotentiary of German Ministry of Foreign Affairs in the Balkans. Stärker proposed an arrangement

with British and Americans whereby all German troops would withdraw in Balkans approximately up to Danube-Sava line without any interference on part of Allies in return for German promise to employ these troops against Russians. OSS representative replied that conversations on basis of trickery or Allied disunity were out of question but that he would be glad to confer with German representative on an early end of German resistance in Balkans and disposition of German troops and would transmit any serious proposals that Germans might wish to make.[65]

Since any local surrender of German commanders could be discussed, according to Allied agreements, only in terms of unconditional surrender, nothing came of these conversations.

McDowell's stay with the Chetniks was terminated because Churchill, with whom it had not been cleared and who, it will be remembered, had intervened with Roosevelt the preceding April, strenuously objected. Churchill did not learn that McDowell was in Yugoslavia until early September. He immediately reminded Roosevelt of his promise not to send a mission. Roosevelt acknowledged the mistake, and directed General Donovan to recall McDowell.[66] McDowell told me, however, that he delayed his departure, claiming lack of facilities from which to be airlifted, and stayed with the Chetniks until November 1. Upon returning to Italy he was received by appropriate American and British officers to brief them on his mission, but that done and his report (of November 22) submitted, all British doors in Italy were closed to him and he was sent back to Washington. There he got a mixed reception. Some persons, he told me, wanted to give him a medal for a job well done, while others were talking about hauling him before a court martial for disobeying orders (meaning, presumably, for postponing his departure from Yugoslavia).

Colonel McDowell told me in our interview (and I was able to confirm this through other sources) that in his report of November 22, 1944, he made the following recommendations: (1) The Allies should order all parties in Yugoslavia to stop fighting one another and committing acts of violence, under penalty of losing aid from the Allies. (2) Allied

---

[65] *Ibid.*, I, 549–50. It should be mentioned, however, that this contact, initiated by the Germans, took place at a time when the Allied air forces from Italy and Partisan ground forces were carrying out a special operation (under the code name "Ratweek") against Yugoslav communications for the purpose of impeding the German withdrawal from Greece and the movement of German troops and supplies within Yugoslavia. More details on this will be given in Chapter 11.

[66] F.O. 371/44262, R 13335/8/92; Roberts, pp. 256–57.

teams should be sent to all the larger towns in Yugoslavia to establish basic government services by cooperating with whatever group was in control of the town. (3) A new government should be established for Yugoslavia, to be composed of one third Chetniks, one third Partisans, and one third persons selected by the Allies from the ranks of the Yugoslavs. The government was to prepare free elections and carry them out under Allied supervision. (4) This government should accept the surrender of both the Chetnik and Partisan forces and form from them a unified Yugoslav army to be put under Allied command against the Germans.

McDowell thought that the execution of his recommendations would require only small Allied contingents, which was much better than having the prospect of continuing civil war which the Allies might be called upon to stop and for which purpose much larger forces would be required. He expected that at first there would be some grumbling in Yugoslavia against such an Allied policy, but he thought that it would soon be accepted by 85 percent of the Yugoslav population.

One can imagine the reaction to these recommendations among the British authorities and among the American authorities who supported British policy in Yugoslavia. Not only were recommendations of this sort in the realm of high politics preempted essentially by Prime Minister Churchill, but also they were heavily in favor of the Chetniks, who had been let down by the Allies after many months of consideration, who had been badly beaten by the Partisans and with the help of the Russians forced to leave Serbia, and whose following among the people of Yugoslavia was limited almost exclusively to Serbs and Montenegrins and a few Slovenes. Furthermore, these recommendations disregarded British policy, which was designed to bring about a basic change in Yugoslavia by arranging a merging of the government-in-exile and the Tito provisional government, as well as the British arrangements with the Russians on the sharing of influence in Yugoslavia on a fifty-fifty basis just concluded in October in Moscow, and acquiesced to by the United States. In other words, the recommendations could hardly have been taken seriously. For the Chetniks, McDowell's failure to help was another in a series of disappointments in a rapidly deteriorating situation.

McDowell's statement to the Commission of Inquiry of the Committee for a Fair Trial for Draja Mihailovich is essentially concerned with two questions: that of alleged collaboration between Mihailović and the Axis, and that of the relative contribution of the Chetniks and the Partisans to the common struggle against the Axis. On the first question, McDowell's statement says: "The undersigned has seen and heard of absolutely no evidence serving to connect General Mihailovich personally, or officers under his direct command, with any form of collabora-

tion with the Germans. This evidence includes not only personal observation but the totality of documents seen and conversations held with
U.S., Allied, and even enemy, personnel. This includes very highly
placed and responsible British officials."[67] McDowell of course acknowl-
edges that certain Chetnik leaders who were not under Mihailović's
direct command made truces and arrangements with the Germans, but
he accuses the Communist leaders of having done the same thing. In
short, McDowell completely exonerates Mihailović from any complicity
in and responsibility for Chetnik collaboration.

McDowell regards the relative contribution of the Chetniks and the
Partisans against the Axis as a moot point. He thinks that all Partisan
claims have been unrealistic or exaggerated. Mihailović, he says, was
especially active against the Axis powers during 1941–42 and significantly helped Allied operations in North Africa by harassing German
communication lines; in 1944–45, he explains, existing circumstances
prevented both the Partisans and the Chetniks from lending any substantial aid. In view of the evidence presented in this study there is no
need to argue with McDowell's views.

The American officers were not the only ones responsible for raising
false hopes among the Chetniks, however. There were also optimistic
messages from Lt. Colonel Živan Knežević, the Yugoslav military attaché in Washington from the summer of 1943 to July 1944, which were
relayed to Mihailović by Mladen Žujović, his representative in Cairo
after September 1943 (over the Chetnik radio channel in Istanbul). In
a message of June 8, 1944, for example, Knežević told Mihailović of the
German airborne attack on Tito's headquarters at Drvar and said that
the Partisans had been beaten in all areas and that only remnants were
present in three places in Yugoslavia. He concluded the message thus:
"Tito has never been weaker. One should not be surprised if the Russians drop Tito and acknowledge you because Tito did not succeed in
bolshevizing the Balkans." In a message of June 19 relayed to Mihailović by Žujović on June 21, he said: "British sources are confirming
news about actions in the Balkans. It is thought that they will begin in
two weeks. One mentions the coast between Split and the Neretva estuary." And in a message of July 1, Knežević said in part: "General Marshall is in London negotiating about the invasion of Yugoslavia. After
the fall of Ancona the [Italian] front will be stabilized and then they

---

[67] *Report of Commission of Inquiry*, p. 13. The last sentence in this quotation is particularly
interesting in that it implies support of some British officials for McDowell's contention that Mihailović and the Chetnik commanders under his immediate command did not collaborate with the
Germans. When I called McDowell's attention in our interview to the British intelligence publication *The Četniks*, he told me that he had been informed by a British general that the material in
that publication was "doctored"—a charge that was later categorically denied to me by a person
in London who was personally involved in helping to put together that publication. Indeed, practically every statement about Chetnik collaboration made in that publication can be confirmed by
captured German and Italian documents.

will hit our country.... The Russian mission declares that Tito is not serious, lacks officers, the soldiers lack discipline and are not close to the people. They consider Draža a strong and serious force."[68] Most of these messages were pure fantasy, but coming from the top Yugoslav official intelligence officer in Washington, who also had many British contacts as a result of his service as chief of the Military Office in the Jovanović government, they were taken very seriously by Mihailović and seem to have had considerable influence on his thinking and decisions. Knežević's reasons for sending Mihailović such promising reports are hard to fathom, since he surely knew that King Peter had been told by the responsible British authorities even before April that there would be no Allied landings in the Balkans.[69]

Žujović himself was also occasionally an unreliable source of information, as in the following message sent to Mihailović on November 6, 1944:

(a) In connection with the decisions of the Moscow conference, the maintenance of the Serbian units is absolutely necessary. General Mihailović must be in a position to count on the support of the Serbian people and on the fighting powers of his army.

(b) Militarily speaking, it is advisable that all Chetnik units should be concentrated in one or two areas which are considered safe within and without.

(c) General Mihailović is strongly advised to deny the rumors that he plans to flee to Italy.

(d) The persons who are supporting the Mihailović movement in Great Britain and the United States give assurance that the change in the course of Allied policy with regard to the Yugoslav question is imminent, provided only that the Chetnik army can hold out in the meantime.[70]

But one should remember that Mihailović's reports to the government-in-exile until May 1944, and after that, for some months at least, to his representatives abroad, especially Djonović and Fotić, invariably painted a rosy picture.[71] Not until after the Chetnik withdrawal from Serbia in September and October 1944 did Mihailović's reports begin to sound gloomy—as if at last he realized the seriousness of his predicament. By then, he had the burden of several tens of thousands of disorganized and dispirited soldiers and refugees on his hands, and he was

---

[68] These dispatches were published with other messages to and from Mihailović by Jovan Djonović in "The Connections with Draža Mihailović from the Middle East and North Africa"; see esp. p. 53.

[69] See King Peter's letter to President Roosevelt of April 17, 1944, in which it is also said, "We have been told that there will not be any landing in the Balkans. If such a fatal decision was taken I implore you to change it." *FRUS 1944*, IV, 1359–61, esp. 1360.

[70] Microcopy No. T-311, Roll 189, Frame 1234. The message was sent by Žujović on October 28 from Cairo but was intercepted by the German monitoring service when broadcast by the Chetnik secret radio station in Istanbul on November 6. This station, managed by Dušan Petković, operated from December 10, 1943, to May 10, 1945. See Petković's article, "How the Contact with General Mihailović from Istanbul Was Established."

[71] See Jovan Djonović, "The Connections with Draža Mihailović from the Middle East and North Africa," pp. 51–65.

truly being driven toward a tragic end by forces that he could not influence, much less overcome.[72] Ironically, during the last four or five months of the war, one very influential correspondent of Mihailović from inside Serbia turned out to be none other than the Yugoslav Communist secret police, operating as a Chetnik source, who fed Mihailović bogus information along with accurate information for the purpose of raising false hopes, which were of course reflected in Mihailović's reports to Ljotić stationed in the Ljubljana Gap and to representatives abroad.[73] (For Mihailović, as we shall see in Chapter 12, the consequences were disastrous.)

In Great Britain and the United States, the lack of complete information on what was going on in Yugoslavia worked to the Chetniks' advantage so far as the general public, and even many government officials and military personnel, was concerned. Long after the Chetnik cause had lost favor with top officials in the British and American governments, a large part of the public was still on the Chetniks' side and tended to discount Partisan, Russian, and even British accounts of Chetnik collaboration as being Communist-inspired propaganda. At the same time, stories about the saving of American fliers by the Chetniks appealed to American sentiment. Most of these stories were somewhat exaggerated, as later evidence proved. Of the roughly fifteen hundred Allied fliers who were evacuated from Yugoslavia (with a few from Albania), less than a third were saved by the Chetniks; the others came from territory controlled by the Partisans and were assembled and evacuated with their aid. As with the members of the American military missions, the Chetniks did their best to solicit the help of rescued fliers in presenting their case to the American commands and public; they considered them, as one of the Chetniks now in this country has stated, "as ambassadors of truth."[74] This was only reasonable, of course, and the Partisans were following much the same policy, though rather more subtly.

Konstantin Fotić had lost his post as ambassador when the Šubašić cabinet took over, but he remained in Washington as representative of Mihailović and the Chetniks and did what he could to promote their cause. In a letter addressed to President Roosevelt on October 14, 1944, he asked for the protection of the Serbian people until their duly and freely elected representatives were in a position to make vital decisions for them. Roosevelt's reply, of November 3, was not encouraging. It

---

[72] See Jovan Djonović, "The Reports of General Mihailović from the End of 1943 and 1944."
[73] *Ibid.*, pp. 70–71; Kostić, pp. 238–39.
[74] For the friendly treatment of Allied, especially American, fliers by the Chetniks and the Chetnik aid in carrying out their successful evacuation see Vukčević, "The Americans at Ravna Gora." There were some cases of fliers being robbed by the peasants, but the Chetnik authorities proceeded sternly against the offenders. See e.g. Archives of the Institute of Military History, Belgrade, Chetnik Documents, Reg. No 33/2, Box 129.

reiterated the American policy of not interfering in the internal affairs of Yugoslavia and expressed the hope that after the war had been won a spirit of mutual consideration and understanding would prevail in the organization of new national life in Yugoslavia—which was simply another way of expressing the Big Three policy of trying to arrange a merger of the government-in-exile and the Partisan provisional government and of totally disregarding the Chetnik movement. Two additional letters from Fotić to Roosevelt were answered in the same vein.[75]

The Chetniks' expectations of aid from the United States in the form of a landing of American forces on the Adriatic coast foundered on one fundamental fact—namely, the firm opposition of the top American political and military authorities to any expansion of the Western Allied military role in the eastern Mediterranean and the Balkans. Whatever assurances Mansfield, Seitz, and McDowell may have given to the contrary, strong American support to the Chetniks was never forthcoming. The assurances may have been based on the assumption that the very presence of the American officers at Mihailović's headquarters implied a willingness to assist them on a large scale: they could scarcely have been given otherwise, because American and British policy was totally the other way—against landings in Yugoslavia. In fact, while Mansfield and Seitz were still in Yugoslavia the British had stopped delivering any aid to the Chetniks.

The Chetniks obviously did not grasp the extent of the British influence on Allied policy in Yugoslavia and the Balkans. The Americans and Soviets seemed to agree with that policy by giving support, but the Chetniks apparently failed to realize that the Americans were flatly opposed to large-scale operations in the Balkans, and that without their support the British could not engage in such operations even if they wanted to do so.[76] As long as the British did not make unreasonable demands for ground troops, their conduct of Balkan policy was accepted; and as we have seen, the two allies agreed completely on the expansion of aid to the Partisans and on the severing of aid to the Chetniks. The Chetniks, however, made no discriminations in putting the blame on both the British and the Americans: in Djonović's words, "Our great Allies simply betrayed us and helped the Communists to acquire power in Yugoslavia."[77]

---

[75] Fotić, *The War We Lost*, pp. 288–92.

[76] In the immediate postwar period there was considerable talk of there having been a basic policy disagreement on Mediterranean strategy, with the British favoring large-scale operations against the Germans through the Balkans and the Americans opposed. Leighton in "OVERLORD Revisited: An Interpretation of American Strategy in the European War, 1942–1944" (esp. pp. 922, 928, 932, 937); and Howard in *The Mediterranean Strategy in the Second World War, passim,* both show convincingly that there was no specific British plan to invade the Balkans, though there was talk of it, especially by Churchill, and that the Americans finally accepted the necessity of the Mediterranean front, centering in Italy as subsidiary front against the Germans.

[77] Jovan Djonović, "The Reports of General Mihailović from the End of 1943 and 1944," p. 63.

HOPES OF AN ALLIANCE WITH SOVIET FORCES

Diplomatic relations between Yugoslavia and the Soviet Union, which were severed by the Soviets in May 1941, were resumed with the government-in-exile after the U.S.S.R. was itself invaded that June. The relations were correct, but trouble was brewing between the pro-Chetnik exile government and the Soviets, whose support and sympathies obviously lay with the Communist-led Partisan resistance movement in Yugoslavia. The British tried to persuade the Soviet government to cooperate in helping to unite the two resistance groups under Mihailović. This effort failed, and as the months went on and the Partisans and Chetniks grew further apart, there was an increase in diplomatic tension between the Soviet and Yugoslav governments. But when the Soviets continued successfully to resist the German onslaught and seemed destined to play a leading role in winning the war and shaping the peace, the Yugoslav government saw the wisdom of making an effort to improve its relations with the mighty Slavic state. Early in 1942 the two governments worked out a treaty of friendship and mutual assistance. Final signature was postponed (permanently, as it turned out) on the advice of the British government, which maintained that the conclusion of so important a treaty was unwise in time of war.[78] By mid-summer of 1942, news of Chetnik-Axis collaboration had begun to reach the Soviets from Partisan sources, but even so, normal relations between the two governments continued without interruption.[79]

On several occasions during visits to Yugoslavia I have heard speculation by Yugoslav scholars about Mihailović's having maintained some contact with Soviet intelligence from very early in his resistance career. Those who think that he did base their contention on three points: (1) Mihailović was on friendly terms with the Soviet military attachés when he served as military attaché in Sofia and Prague in the mid-1930's and he probably continued some of these contacts; (2) an agent of the Comintern, Mustafa Golubić,[80] established contact in 1940 or 1941 in Belgrade with two men, Dragiša Vasić, who during part of the interwar period reportedly had some contacts with Soviet intelligence services, and Mladen Žujović, both of whom later, along with Dr. Stevan Mo-

---

[78] Fotić, *The War We Lost*, pp. 172–73.

[79] For some messages of the Yugoslav government-in-exile to the Soviet authorities with regard to the unification of the two resistance groups and later in denying that Mihailović was collaborating with the Axis powers and the puppet regimes see Živan L. Knežević, *General Mihailovich and U.S.S.R.*

[80] Golubić was a Moslem from Herzegovina, a member of the revolutionary society Young Bosnia who volunteered for the Serbian army during the Balkan Wars and the First World War and was jailed in connection with the Salonika Trial. He had good contacts with Serbian nationalist circles but in 1920 became a Communist and from 1927 to 1940 lived in the Soviet Union. He was employed by the Comintern or the Soviet secret police as an agent for international operations. In July 1941 he was caught by the Germans in Belgrade and executed. See Marjanović, *Srbija u narodnooslobodilačkoj borbi: Beograd*, p. 132.

ljević, became chief political advisers to Mihailović; and (3) statements said to have been made by Vasić during the war to a Chetnik officer who was also a Partisan agent, to the effect that he had sent reports on the Partisans to the Russians and had told them that Yugoslav Communists were Trotskyists.[81]

This is an interesting thesis, but conclusive evidence exists to contradict it. First, in a message of April 17, 1944, Ambassador Fotić in Washington advised Prime Minister Purić to cultivate relations with the Russians and asked him to urge Mihailović to establish direct contact with the U.S.S.R. in regard to the coordination of military operations. It seems logical to assume that if Mihailović had already had Soviet contacts, both Fotić and Purić would have known them and would not have needed to make a point of urging him to get them. Second, in a message of July 12, 1944, to Jovan Djonović, since early April 1944 Yugoslavia's representative with the Free French government in Algiers, Mihailović asked Djonović whether it would be opportune to establish direct contact with the Russians through the good offices of General de Gaulle. Mihailović explained that if he could establish such contact and present the British with a fait accompli, he might keep them from carrying out whatever plans they had in mind at the expense of the Serbian people; at the same time it would checkmate the Yugoslav Communists who were hand in hand with the British, a fact which surely was not pleasing to the Russians. Djonović seems not to have made any attempt to consult de Gaulle, but he directed Chetnik intelligence officers in Cairo to get in touch with the Russians there and to push the matter. An aide-mémoire which the Russians requested on the subject was delivered to them in August, but, according to Djonović, there was no reply from the Russians until February 1945, and it was an evasive one.[82] Obviously, if Mihailović had had direct contact with the Russians prior to July 1944, there would have been no need for the inquiry to Djonović. Finally, and perhaps most conclusive of all, there is a flat denial of such contact from the previously mentioned German agent who had close contacts at Mihailović's headquarters. According to a message that was sent to higher authorities by the *Abwehrstelle* Belgrade on August 5, 1943, the agent reported: "DM himself has definitely no contact with the Soviets."[83]

It is evident, therefore, that the only contacts the Chetniks had with the Soviet authorities and military were through the government-in-exile until this government ceased to be their exponent in May 1944—and it was after this time that the Chetniks most needed such contacts,

[81] Milovanović, "I Was in Draža's Supreme Command," in *NIN*, Dec. 15, 1968.
[82] See this correspondence as published by Jovan Djonović in "My Connections with Draža Mihailović from the Middle East," pp. 90, 92–93.
[83] Microcopy No. T-311, Roll 196, Frame 150.

being now without British support and, despite the presence of an American mission at their headquarters, having not the remotest chance of real support from the Americans. With the Red Army nearing Yugoslav frontiers, the Chetniks knew that they must try to reach a modus vivendi with the Russians. To this end, Fotić continued even after his dismissal to maintain contact with Andrei Gromyko, the Soviet Ambassador in Washington, and Djonović through his agents maintained contact with Soviet representatives in Cairo. Finally, early in September, after both Romania and Bulgaria had been knocked out of the war and had come under Soviet control, and with Soviet troops on the Yugoslav doorstep, Mihailović himself tried to establish direct contact with Soviet forces.[84]

Mihailović's principal objectives in respect to the Russians at this juncture, that is, once Soviet troops had entered Serbia from Romania and Bulgaria, were to secure for the Chetniks the status of an allied force, recouping from the Russians what they had lost so far as the Western Allies were concerned and strengthening thereby their position vis-à-vis the Partisans, and to secure the right as Russian allies to assume power in liberated Serbia.

Mihailović made his first move while the Russian forces were still preparing for their operations against the Germans in Serbia and Vojvodina. He sent a mission under Lt. Colonel Velimir Piletić, commander of northeastern Serbia, to the Russian forces in Romania with instructions to establish contact with them. Mihailović's written orders contained no detailed instructions, but his emissary who brought the orders to Piletić suggested that the mission should try to obtain Russian agreement on a series of proposals, all essentially political. According to Lt. Colonel Ratković, one of the participants in the mission, the following proposals were to be offered: (1) the Russians should mediate with the Partisans to bring an end to the civil war so that all domestic forces could be turned against the enemy; (2) after the war was over both Chetnik and Partisan forces should be withdrawn to the casernes while free elections were held by a neutral domestic government under supervision of the Big Three; and (3) all war crimes trials should be postponed until

[84] It should be noted, before we proceed, that the Chetniks were aware throughout the war years of the inherent pro-Russian sympathies of the peoples of Yugoslavia, amounting at least to a sense of pan-Slav solidarity in the face of the all-out German effort to rob all Slav peoples of their statehood and nationhood. These sympathies were especially strong in the Serbs and Montenegrins, who shared the same religion and had a strong tradition of friendship with the Russians. The Chetniks could not allow the Partisans to become the sole beneficiaries of this popular sympathy for Russia, but there was the complicating factor that Russia was a Communist country. Chetnik propaganda therefore tried to differentiate between the Russian people and their Communist government and tried to show that the great struggle which the Russians were waging against the Germans was the struggle of the Russian national forces rather than of Communists. They also portrayed the Yugoslav Communists as Trotskyists, quite different from Russian Communists. See Microcopy No. T-501, Roll 249, Frame 99. Also on April 1, 1942, Lt. Colonel Živan Knežević, chief of the Military Office of Prime Minister Jovanović, sent a letter to the Soviet military attaché Colonel Sizov, stating that some of the Partisan groups in Yugoslavia were Stalinist and other Trotskyist, and that the latter sometimes attacked and spied on the former. Knežević, *General Mihailovich and U.S.S.R.*, pp. 14–15.

after the elections and then be taken up by the civil courts.[85] The Chetnik mission crossed the Danube into Romania on September 10 and moved on to Craiova, where it established contacts with the Russians. These contacts were disappointing, however, and learning that British and American military missions were already in Bucharest, they decided to push on in order to establish contact with them. But while still at Craiova, Piletić's aide, a student with alleged Communist leanings, denounced the members of the mission to the Russians as British spies. Thus instead of going to a conference table with Soviet commanders preparing to enter Yugoslavia, the Chetniks were arrested on October 1 and flown to Moscow, where they were imprisoned and investigated by the Soviet police.[86]

The Chetniks' hope of ingratiating themselves with the Russians and being accepted as their allies while at the same time continuing to fight the Partisans was but another example of the naïveté they had so often displayed before. This was apparent to the Germans, as indicated in an intelligence report of October 19, 1944, on the conduct of Mihailović's forces in Serbia: "The Chetniks have never been prepared by Draža Mihailović through appropriate propaganda for a fighting encounter with the Russians. Draža Mihailović has on the contrary upheld the fiction that the Russians as allies of the Americans and the British will never act against the interests of the Serbian nationalists."[87] Mihailović had himself said much the same thing in a circular order of October 5: "We consider the Russians as our allies. The struggle against Tito's forces in Serbia will be continued."[88] What he did not seem to grasp was the reality of the cooperation between Tito and the Russians (which was to be greatly intensified after their agreement announced in Moscow on September 28 regulating the entry of Russian troops into Yugoslav territory in pursuit of the German troops), and also the effect upon the Russians not only of the Chetniks' loss of Allied support but also of the long-standing collaboration between the Chetniks and the Axis forces.

In fact, only two important Chetnik commanders cooperated, and they only briefly, with Soviet troops. These were Lt. Colonel Keserović, commander of a group of Shock Corps, and Captain Raković, com-

---

[85] The trouble with this rendition of the supposed Chetnik proposals to the Russians is that in their vital aspect—that is, the policy toward the Partisans—they differ from the policy line confirmed by wartime documentary evidence, which was to the effect (as will presently be shown) that the Chetniks wanted to be accepted by the Russians as allies while continuing to fight the Partisans.

[86] See Ratković, pp. 115–17. Piletić was kept in prison by the Russians until November 1945 and was then sent to Yugoslavia where he was to stand trial, but he managed to escape in Romania and later reached western Europe, Karapandžić, pp. 350–51. Karapandžić's account of the Piletić mission is somewhat different from Ratković's.

[87] Microcopy No. T-311, Roll 194, Frames 562–63.

[88] *Ibid.*, Roll 189, Frame 961. This and all other references in this section to materials from Microcopy No. T-311, Roll 189, relate to German intercepts of radio messages among the Chetnik commands.

mander of the Second Ravna Gora Corps. Keserović's troops met the Russians advancing from Bulgaria in central-eastern Serbia. According to a message from the Keserović Group of Shock Corps to the Second Shock Corps of October 16, Keserović's Chetniks and some Russian forces together occupied the town of Kruševac, and the Russians then delegated the command over the town to Keserović. But two days later Keserović informed Major Račić, commander of the Fourth Group of Shock Corps, who was considering cooperating with the Russians, that the Russian command posts cooperated only with the Communists (Partisans), and that they demanded the disarming of the Chetniks and refused to cooperate with them. He advised Račić to give up his plan of meeting the Russians because the Russian bureaucratic machine made all contacts hopeless, and because the Russians were operating "with a thousand tricks."[89] On October 19 Keserović informed the Supreme Command that his representative with the Russian division had returned with a Russian ultimatum directing all Chetniks under his command to lay down their arms by noon on October 18 and to be transported to a camp near the town of Paraćin where they would be reorganized into units of the Yugoslav National Liberation Army. If the ultimatum was refused, the Russians threatened to open hostilities. This change in Russian attitude was brought about by a protest of Marshal Tito to Marshal Feodor I. Tolbukhin, the commander of the Third Ukrainian Front, when Tito was informed about the Russian-Chetnik cooperation.[90] Keserović did refuse the ultimatum—presumably following an order of the Chetnik Supreme Command of October 14—and withdrew toward the Ibar River valley with a small force of five hundred men.[91] Some more of his men may have succeeded in following him to Sandjak, but two of his brigades were disarmed by the Russians, who promised that they would be issued new arms after they laid down the ones they had.[92] The American liaison officer at Keserović's staff headquarters, Lieutenant Kramer, was also taken by the Russians and shipped off to Bulgaria, but soon thereafter was released.

Captain Raković and his Second Ravna Gora Corps cooperated with the Russians in the capture of Čačak. Unlike Keserović, Raković apparently did not keep the Supreme Command informed about the develop-

[89] *Ibid.*, Frames 1029, 1048, 1102.

[90] Information received from Colonel Vojmir Kljaković of the Institute of Military History, Belgrade.

[91] Microcopy No. T-311, Roll 189, Frame 1233, which is a message of Oct. 19 from Keserović to the Supreme Command. At Keserović's trial in August 1945, his brief cooperation with the Red Army was not mentioned. Keserović's testimony on the strength of troops under his command both before and in the course of his withdrawal was inconsistent within itself as well as with other information. See *Sudjenje članovima rukovodstva organizacije Draže Mihailovića*, pp. 216–20. The principal Russian work on the operations of the Soviet forces in Yugoslavia in the autumn of 1944 makes no specific reference to Soviet cooperation with the Chetniks, but it does refer to cooperation with Yugoslav forces in operations around Gornji Milanovac, Kragujevac, and Kruševac, and at least some of these forces were Chetnik. See Bir'uzov, ed., p. 109.

[92] Microcopy No. T-311, Roll 189, Frames 1047, 1134.

ment of this cooperation. However, on November 11 it became known that he had to flee from the Russians toward Sandjak. It was only on November 16 and 17 that the Supreme Command circulated a report to all Chetnik commands and explained Raković's case. Raković apparently established satisfactory relations with the Russians and concluded a written agreement with them according to which he was obliged to cooperate with them in fighting the Germans in exchange for the promise that his units with their arms would remain under his command. It was also understood that these units belonged to General Mihailović's army. In the operations around Čačak the Chetniks fought well and captured 339 members of the German-organized Russian Protective Corps whom they turned over to the Russians. They also helped the Russian forces with scouting. While these operations were under way the Russians kept the Partisan units in the area from attacking the Chetniks. Raković visited the headquarters of one of the Russian units without incident, but shortly thereafter, obviously following Tito's protest to Tolbukhin, the Russian commander demanded that Raković and his units switch under Tito's command. When Raković refused to do so, the Partisans tried to disarm one of his brigades and the Russians gave him an ultimatum to lay down arms and move to a camp where his troops would be reorganized as units of the Yugoslav National Liberation Army. Seeing that the Russians had double-crossed him and that no prospect for satisfactory cooperation or negotiations with them existed, Raković ordered his troops toward Sandjak, but he himself remained in Serbia in hiding. This same report of the Supreme Command makes clear that the Russians had also disarmed Lt. Colonel Ocokoljić's Chetnik units in northeastern Serbia.[93]

Major Račić, who had long been one of the most determined foes of the Partisans in Serbia, apparently thought it necessary to open hostilities against the Germans in southwestern Serbia in order to improve his standing in the projected meeting with the Russians.[94] He engaged, it seems only for a day (October 16), in fighting against the Germans, but probably hearing bad news from Keserović's and Ocokoljić's camps, he changed his mind and in conformity with Mihailović's orders directed his troops southwestward toward Sandjak.[95] Certain other Chetnik units, for example the Zlatibor Corps, also decided to fight the Germans in southwestern Serbia, and did so with some success for a brief time,[96] and then they also withdrew southwestward toward Sandjak.

---

[93] *Ibid.*, Frames 1211, 1237–38.

[94] The consolidated report of the Kommandeur der Nachrichtenaufklärung 4 for October states: "In the hope of preventing, by coordinating their own operational plans with the Russian plans, the occupation of southwestern Serbia by the Russians, [the Chetniks] gave up their hitherto existing cooperation with the Germans. On October 16 the troops of Major Račić opened hostilities against the German forces in the valley of Western Morava." *Ibid.*, Frame 1135.

[95] *Ibid.*, Frames 1029, 1055, 1111.

[96] *Ibid.*, Frames 1061, 1068, 1111.

According to one of the participating Chetnik commanders, confirmed largely by German intercepts of messages among various Chetnik commands, a great number of Chetnik commanders and their troops were in full withdrawal by October 21 and on that day the commanders held a conference at the town of Ivanjica to discuss the situation. At this point they were beyond the reach of the Red Army and thought that they were going in a direction that would lead them to a linking with Allied troops after they landed on the Adriatic coast.[97]

Fortunately for the Chetniks, few of their troops were located in areas of the main Soviet drive; the forces of Keserović, Raković, and Račić were close, and they were only on the flanks of the main drive.[98] Even as these commanders were trying to deal with the Russians (or thinking of doing so in the case of Račić), Soviet and Partisan forces were fighting to free Belgrade from the Germans. The liberation of the city on October 20 spelled the end of the Chetnik cause in Serbia.[99]

News of the events in Serbia were variously interpreted by Chetnik commanders elsewhere in the country. Major Lukačević, then in Herzegovina but out of favor with Mihailović, proposed on October 19 that the position of the Chetnik movement should be redefined as follows: first, that the coming Russian forces be greeted as the "allied Russian liberation army," and second, that the Russians be asked to take the Chetniks under the command of a Russian general.[100] Lt. Colonel Ostojić, the area commander of eastern Bosnia, feared that the Russians intended to deliver the Chetniks to the Communists. On October 21 he requested a meeting with Colonel McDowell in order to propose to him that the Chetnik forces be put under the command of an American general, and if this move failed, that the Chetniks should try to make some arrangement with the Russians.[101] Finally there was Lt. Colonel Baćo-

---

[97] Milošević, pp. 217–19.

[98] See Map 2 in Bir'uzov, following p. 64. The primary objective of the Russian drive into the valley of the Western Morava River was to cut off the rail line through the Ibar River valley as an escape route for the German troops from Greece. See Microcopy No. T-501, Roll 257, Frame 210.

[99] During their brief period of cooperation with the Soviet forces the Chetniks discovered that the Soviets were using in the operations around Čačak the Yugoslav Legion which they had organized in Russia. Chetnik sources reported that the unit was a division of about three thousand men, led by a former Ustasha, Lt. Colonel Marko Mesić. See Microcopy No. T-311, Roll 189, Frame 1253. Bir'uzov (p. 107), who was one of the Soviet commanders in operations in Serbia, is full of praise for Mesić and another officer of the unit, Captain Milutin Perišić, a Serb. The Yugoslav Legion had an interesting history. It was formed partly of men who had belonged to the 369th Croatian Reinforced Regiment which was established in Pavelić's Croatia on July 16, 1941, with an original complement of 3,870 men and sent to the Russian front. Its members could be only Croats, Ukrainians, and (White) Russians. Approximately a third were Bosnian Moslems. Gradually the regiment was enlarged, and in August 1942 it had a complement, including reserves, of 6,300 men. As part of the Sixth Army of Field Marshal von Paulus it was crushed at Stalingrad. From its surviving prisoners and manpower from other sources the Russians established the Yugoslav Legion early in 1944. On April 16, 1944, it had a complement of 1,543 men, of whom 775 were Croats, 440 Slovenes, 293 Serbs, 14 Jews, 10 Slovaks, 5 Russians, 3 Ruthenians, 2 Hungarians, and 1 Montenegrin. (Data obtained from Colonel Vojmir Kljaković of the Institute of Military History, Belgrade.) It is possible, of course, that the legion was enlarged before it was sent to the Yugoslav front and that its composition then was different from that of April 1944.

[100] Microcopy No. T-311, Roll 189, Frame 1036.

[101] *Ibid.*, Frame 1043.

vić, another leading Chetnik commander, who said a few days later that he was convinced that the British had let the Chetnik movement down and that unless the Allies soon staged a mass landing on the Dalmatian coast, the Chetniks would be facing the life of outlaws.[102]

The Chetnik attempt to improve their fortunes by working out some sort of arrangement with the Russians while at the same time continuing to fight the Partisans could never have been successful. Up until the spring of 1943, at the latest, the Russians, for diplomatic reasons, might have had an interest in not antagonizing Mihailović and his forces, but after the Chetnik collaboration with the Italians and the Germans was proved and the British themselves withdrew their support, there was no reason whatsoever for the Russians to show any consideration for the Chetniks. Moreover, Tito was their man; though he displeased them occasionally by his independent actions, he and the Partisans were the Russians' best bet to acquire great if not controlling postwar influence in Yugoslavia.[103]

[102] *Ibid.*, Frame 1072.
[103] In a specific sense, too, Tito was the choice of the British and the Americans, who counted on his troops to help the Allied drive in Italy by tying up a large number of German troops in Yugoslavia and impeding the flow of German troops and supplies, especially of oil, to the German forces in Italy.

CHAPTER ELEVEN

The Loss of the Serbian Base

The collaboration between the Germans and the Chetniks in Serbia which was begun in November 1943 was dictated primarily by the prospect of increased Partisan operations designed to gain control of that area. In all areas of the country outside Serbia, the position of the Partisans was now relatively satisfactory. They had lost some of the territory they had liberated, but they were growing stronger in every way, politically and diplomatically as well as militarily, while the Chetniks, and the Germans also, were losing strength. For the Partisans, it was now possible to think about invading Serbia in strength and taking control. Up to this time Partisan activity had been limited in Serbia, the Chetnik's home base and main source of strength; the control of Serbia was, however, the key to control of Yugoslavia. In a message of December 6, 1943, to the commander of the 2nd Partisan Corps in Montenegro—the unit tentatively scheduled to lead the operation for the liberation of Serbia—Tito analyzed the importance of the undertaking.[1] Besides its importance for all Yugoslavia, he said, Serbia was also of fundamental significance to the military and political activities in other Balkan countries, especially Bulgaria. Even though Mihailović and his Chetniks were politically defeated already, their forces and their political organization in Serbia must also be liquidated. Not the least, Tito said, Serbia, along with Macedonia and the Kosovo region, represented important reservoirs of manpower for future Partisan military operations. Of course, the attack upon Serbia would require large forces. (He added that he had planned to order the attack before the onset of winter, but unfavorable conditions had forced postponement.)

The Partisan plan for operations in Serbia had two aspects: one, to strengthen their units already in Serbia and increase their military and

---

[1] Tito, *Vojna djela*, I, 208–9.

political activities,[2] and two, to penetrate into Serbia with large forces from the west and southwest, linking up with the Partisan Serbian forces for combined actions. On December 2 the Germans, acting on the reasonable assumption that Partisan forces being assembled in Montenegro, Sandjak, and eastern Bosnia were preparing for a drive on Serbia, made a move to trap and destroy the Partisans before the anticipated drive could be got under way. For this operation, called Kugelblitz, the Germans assembled a large force consisting of the 1st Mountain Division, the 7th SS Prinz Eugen Division, parts of the 369th Infantry Division (Croatian legionnaires), parts of the 187th Reserve Division, and several smaller units, assisted by the 24th Bulgarian Division from Serbia and some Chetnik units from Sandjak under Lukačević. The operation was directed by the commander of the Vth SS Mountain Corps, who also controlled those troops stationed in Serbia (the 24th Bulgarian Division) that were temporarily subordinated to him and had the task of defending the Serbian frontiers against the Partisans.

Operation Kugelblitz was directed primarily against four Partisan divisions—the 2nd, 5th, 17th, and 27th.[3] The plan was to surround the Partisan troops in a wide sweep and then tighten the ring as quickly as possible and destroy them. This was a tactic the Germans had used many times in the past, though as a rule unsuccessfully, and it was unsuccessful this time as well. As soon as the Partisans saw what was intended, Tito issued orders for his troops to spread out and move to the flanks and rear of the German forces to avoid a frontal attack.[4] This maneuver was successful. The bulk of the Partisan forces eluded the Germans altogether, and on December 18 the operation was halted. Almost at once, however, the same German divisions (minus the 24th Bulgarian Division, which was returned to the command of the Military Commander in Southeast Europe) were sent into a new action. Operation Schneesturm, against Partisan forces in the valley of the Krivaja River north of Sarajevo. But again the Partisans proved elusive.[5] At approximately

---

[2] Toward the end of 1943 the CPY Provincial Committee for Serbia sent a circular letter (No. 6) to all party organizations and party members in Serbia. The letter contained advice on how to infiltrate and serve in German, quisling, and Chetnik formations as a way of promoting Partisan objectives; it pointed out the necessity of blaming all attacks and sabotage acts on the Chetniks so that ensuing reprisals could also be blamed on them, told how to foment struggle between the Chetniks and the Serbian quisling formations in order to prevent their uniting against the Partisans, and so on. This letter has never been published in Yugoslavia, and when I tried in June 1972 to locate a copy of it in the Archives of the SR Serbia in a Belgrade suburb, where the files of the CPY Provincial Committee for Serbia are deposited, I was told that there was no copy of any such letter in the files. Long excerpts from it in German translation are contained in Microcopy No. T-313, Roll 488, Frames 863–65.

[3] For the order for Operation Kugelblitz see Microcopy No. T-313, Roll 189, Frames 7,449,037–45; see also Frames 7,449,062–80. For the significance of Operation Kugelblitz from the point of view of the Military Commander in Southeast Europe, who was also the chief of the occupation regime in Serbia, see Microcopy No. T-501, Roll 253, Frames 879–83 and 893–96. See also *Oslobodilački rat*, II, 11–12.

[4] *Oslobodilački rat*, II, 14.

[5] *Ibid.*, pp. 22–27; *KTB/OKW/WFSt*, Vol. III, Part 2, pp. 1372–73, 1396.

the same time, the three divisions and several smaller attached units forming the XVth Mountain Army Corps mounted a series of operations (Ziethen, Herbstgewitter, Panther, Delphin, Merkur, Waldrausch, Weihnachtsmann) against the Partisans in northern and western Bosnia, Dalmatia, and Croatia.[6]

All these operations were under the overall command of Colonel General Lothar Rendulic, commander of the Second Panzer Army, who had been transferred to Yugoslavia from the Russian front the preceding August for two specific tasks: to take over the Italian-occupied parts of Yugoslavia and Albania after the anticipated collapse of Italy, and to destroy Tito and his Partisans.[7] The operations in December were thus only the beginning of what proved to be a series of wide-ranging operations extending over a period of six months. The details of these operations are not our concern here. In some, the Germans and their allies inflicted heavy losses on the Partisans, and they retook a substantial part of the territory that had been liberated by them. But in the main objective—the destruction of the Partisans as an effective combat force—the Germans were unsuccessful.

THE CONGRESS AT BA

Not long after the turn of the new year, with the Partisan threat to Serbia in abeyance, the Chetniks, taking advantage of the relative security afforded them as a consequence of their armistice agreements with the Germans, convoked a congress in the village of Ba near Ravna Gora in western Serbia. This was by far the most important political manifestation of the Chetnik movement during the entire war—and since the Germans could easily have prevented it or dispersed it midway in its deliberations, it must be assumed that it was held with the tacit approval of the German occupation authorities. The congress met from the twenty-fifth to the twenty-eighth of January (the day of St. Sava, the patron saint of the Serbs, being January 27, it is also often called the Congress of St. Sava). It was attended by over three hundred delegates,[8] bringing together for the first and only time the principal Chetnik military commanders, the politicians who had sided with the Chetnik movement from the beginning such as Dragiša Vasić and Dr. Stevan Moljević, and a fair number of politicians of the old Serbian political parties who, somewhat belatedly, had decided to line up openly with

---

[6] For the times and areas of these operations see Microcopy No. T-314, Roll 554, Frames 75–126. See also *Oslobodilački rat*, II, 32–69.

[7] Rendulic, pp. 156 and *passim*.

[8] Also present was Lieutenant George Musulin, one of the American officers attached to the British military mission to Mihailović. Two other American officers, Lt. Colonel Seitz and Captain Mansfield, were at that time on their inspection trip in the interior of Serbia. So far as I have been able to establish, the members of the British military mission did not attend and apparently were not invited. But exhaustive reports on the congress exist in the Public Record Office in London.

the Chetniks—men such as Živko Topalović, Adam Pribićević, and others. At the congress were also some Croats (Vladimir Predavec, Djuro Vilović, and Niko Bartulović),[9] a Slovene (Anton Krejči, a refugee in Serbia), and a Bosnian Moslem (Mustafa Mulalić).[10] With the exception of Mulalić, these non-Serbian members were not politicians and represented only themselves. In its Serbian and Montenegrin participants, the Ba congress had a much broader representation than the earlier conference of Young Chetnik Intellectuals held in the village of Šahovići in Sandjak late in 1942.

Opinions on the character of the congress at Ba differ greatly among those who took part in it, the chief difference lying between the Chetniks of long standing, in both the military and the political branches of the movement, and the politicians who attended as representatives of the old parties. The two groups brought different assets to the new organization: the Chetniks brought the military organization and leadership, and the official standing as an arm of the government-in-exile, while the politicians brought at least a token of old popular democratic traditions of Serbia. And both groups wanted an equal say in the future state of Yugoslavia. Some of the politicians, particularly Topalović, head of the miniscule Socialist Party who was named chairman, later spoke of the congress as having been essentially a founding congress of the Yugoslav Democratic National Union, which he hailed as the bearer of all-Yugoslav, democratic, popular resistance against the occupying powers, and in which the political parties were equal partners with the Chetniks.[11] The Chetniks, in his view, became the military arm of the Union. The

---

[9] Bartulović and Vilović were both writers from the area of Split, who had been pro-Chetnik since early in the war. Neither one represented any political party. Predavec seems to have had some status in the Chetnik movement, partly because he was one of the first Croats to join the Chetniks, partly because he was the son of Josip Predavec, a former vice-president of the Croatian Peasant Party who was assassinated in 1931; he himself had no connection with the CPP, however. With a notable lack of success, he issued appeals to the Croats to join the Chetniks (see e.g. his appeal of September 1943 in Microcopy No. T-501, Roll 257, Frames 1030–31) and toward the end of the war tried to help establish contact between Mihailović and both Maček and Pavelić.

[10] See Microcopy No. T-311, Roll 196, Frames 244–49 for the letter sent by Mulalić to Husein Rovčanin, commander of the Moslem militia in Sandjak, on Dec. 28, 1943. This seems to have been a circular letter, which probably went to other Moslem leaders as well. In it, Mulalić, formerly a member of the Yugoslav parliament belonging to the Yugoslav National Party, argued against both the Ustashas and the Partisans and in favor of the Chetniks and urged the alignment of the Sandjak (and surely also of Bosnian) Moslems, especially the Moslem militia, behind Mihailović. For the Chetnik openings toward the Moslems from late 1943 onward and the efforts of a number of Moslem leaders, including Mulalić, to bring the Moslem leaders and armed groups behind the Chetniks see Hurem, "Conceptions of Some Moslem Bourgeois Politicians About the Situation of Bosnia and Herzegovina," esp. pp. 536–38, 542–45.

[11] For Chetnik views on the Ba congress see *Knjiga o Draži*, II, 1–32. For the views of the politicians as represented by Topalović, who besides being chairman of the congress was also chairman of the Organizational Committee of Three established by the congress, see Topalović's book, *Pokreti narodnog otpora*, pp. 80–94.

Dr. Topalović was given a leading role at the congress because Mihailović thought that he could be helpful to the Chetnik cause owing to his personal acquaintance with the Labor members of the British cabinet, Clement Atlee and Ernest Bevin, whom Topalović had met from time to time at international congresses of Socialist parties. Mihailović thought that the Partisans' close relations with the Soviet government were a tremendous asset to them, whereas the Yugoslav government-in-exile by being transferred to Cairo had been removed from the center of action and was now only a toy in the hands of the British—hence his hopes that Topalović's connections might serve to bring a better understanding of the Chetnik cause to some members of the British cabinet. See Topalović, *Borba za budućnost Jugoslavije*, pp. 97–98.

truth, more likely, was the opposite, that is, the Yugoslav Democratic National Union was to function as the political arm of the Chetniks, because Mihailović retained all military and political powers.[12]

It was quickly apparent to both the Chetnik spokesmen and the politicians at the congress that agreement even on procedural matters, as well as on decisions, would not be easy. Mihailović said later at his trial that the Central National Committee and the Chetnik Belgrade Committee had been opposed to any congress that would include representatives of the old political parties and that they were invited only at his insistence.[13] Mihailović, it seems, was opposed to allowing any major role to Vasić, with whom he was increasingly at odds, and gave way only at Topalović's insistence. And many of the younger Chetniks were antagonistic to the older group of party politicians, whom they scorned as both inferior and corrupt and therefore a hindrance to any real political, economic, or social advances after the war.[14]

The resolutions finally adopted after three days of debate encompassed both political and military decisions. First, the congress denounced the decisions of the second session of the Anti-Fascist Council of National Liberation of Yugoslavia (AVNOJ), which had met at Jajce in November 1943, as the work of the Ustasha-Communist minority. To counter AVNOJ's claims of being the sole representative of the sovereignty of Yugoslavia, the Ba congress expressed full support for the government-in-exile, the Yugoslav Army in the Homeland, and Mihailović's military leadership. It also reasserted Chetnik enmity toward the German occupation regime and all its allies and declared its resolve to mobilize all anti-Communist Serbs in the fight to save Serbdom. Finally, it announced its own plans for the future political and socioeconomic organization of Yugoslavia, reminding the Serbian people, in conformity with the existing Chetnik propaganda line, that the Partisans and the

[12] Nor is there validity, in my view, in Topalović's assertion (*Pokreti narodnog otpora*, pp. 92–95) that the chief aim of these united Chetnik and Serbian party political forces was to reach an agreement with the Partisans in order to end the civil war. It is true that during December 1943 and January 1944, Mihailović expressed to the British his readiness to enter into discussion with the Partisans, provided British officers would serve as mediators. But this undoubtedly was a tactical move on his part, or as the British said, a "death-bed repentance," at a time when, as we have already seen, the British had started to press King Peter for his removal from the cabinet. Thus the British declined to serve as mediators.

[13] *The Trial of Draža Mihailović*, p. 331. For more of Mihailović's views on the Ba congress see *ibid.*, pp. 320–24, 330–33. After the congress and the enlargement of the Central National Committee, Mihailović especially wanted the Chetniks to acquire a wider political base among the people, with the representatives of the old political parties bearing a share of the responsibility.

[14] As communicated by Dr. Milorad M. Drachkovitch of the Hoover Institution, Stanford University. See also the article by Drachkovitch and Lazitch, "Staff 501 of the Ravna Gora Youth," p. 104, where they say that the delegates of the youth organization as well as many other civilian and military delegates opposed the official line of the congress because it appeared to them that the "second-rate" politicians who up to that time had had only a symbolic connection with the Chetnik movement wanted to take over the leadership and give it a different line and content. Only their discipline and devotion to Mihailović, they say, kept them from protesting openly at the congress. For a discussion, from a pro-Mihailović point of view, of the relationship between the Serbian political parties (then operating illegally, of course) and the Chetnik movement see Lazitch, *La tragédie du Général Draja Mihailovitch*, pp. 50–61. For Vasić's opposition to the Serbian party politicians and to the convening of the Ba congress see also Milovanović, in *NIN*, March 2, 1969.

Ustashas had joined forces to exterminate them.[15] Point 1 of the resolution passed by the congress declared that the congress with "enthusiasm and special recognition salutes the Yugoslav national army which under the command of General Mihailović has been organized in the fatherland. This truly national army, under the command of national leaders and under the leadership of national officers, is the true defender of national liberties as well as being the guarantee of the future state of all Yugoslavs."[16]

For the first time, the Chetniks openly endorsed the principle of federalization as the basic idea of the future organization of the Yugoslav state.[17] Point 4 (*b*) of the congress resolution said: "Yugoslavia should be organized as a federal state, in the form of a constitutional and parliamentary succession monarchy, with the national dynasty of Karadjordjević and King Peter II at its helm." This constitutional principle was to be worked out and put into operation only after the war was over, and a strict constraint was placed on it: "The Congress considers that the solidarity of future Yugoslavia is conditioned by the creation, in a democratic way, of a Serbian unit in the state as a whole, which on a democratic basis would gather the whole Serbian people on its territory. The same principle ought to be valid for the Croats and the Slovenes." Although the implementation of the federalization was to be carried out in "a democratic way," one easily recognizes in this provision the ideas, somewhat modified, of Dr. Moljević and other Chetnik leaders about a Great Serbia. Had they been victorious, the Chetniks most probably would have carried out their earlier program—that is, they would have defined the frontiers of Serbia unilaterally and presented the Croats and Slovenes with a fait accompli in regard to the Serbian unit. Not only did the Ba congress not recognize the existence of Macedonia and Montenegro as separate nations, but also it implied that Croatia and Slovenia, in terms of territory and population, were to become mere appendages of Great Serbia. Thus, for the non-Serbs—mean-

[15] Similarly, the Ustashas referred to the Partisans as "Serbo-Communists" who were bent on destroying the Croats. There was, of course, neither an "Ustasha-Communist" nor a "Serbo-Communist" conspiracy; the Partisans simply pursued a truly Yugoslav program which worked as much against the Ustashas as against the Chetniks.

[16] For the text of the resolution see *Knjiga o Draži*, II, 10–15, esp. p. 13, and *Poruka*, No. 19, p. 18.

[17] The proposal for a federal organization of postwar Yugoslavia had appeared earlier in internal Chetnik documents, especially in Moljević's programmatic memorandum "Homogeneous Serbia" prepared in June 1941, but it was a federalism that rested on the terms of the Great Serbia forces, obviously unacceptable to the other nations of Yugoslavia. Later, in a message from London dated December 5, 1942, Prime Minister Jovanović informed Mihailović that the postwar organization of Yugoslavia would have to be based on federalization. The message read in part: "The internal organization of Yugoslavia after the war will not be, according to all signs, based on centralism. The reasons for this are: steady tendency of the Croats toward federation as well as the wish of the Serbs to protect themselves in the future from the horrible experiences sustained in the Pavelić state. The federation, which guarantees the unity of the state, would be most feasible to quiet down the Serbian sensitivities caused by the Ustasha massacres. The federation would take into account the specific interests of all three nations, and it would safeguard the future." Radoje L. Knežević, "The Yugoslav Government and Draža Mihailović," *Poruka*, No. 10, p. 13.

ing close to 60 percent of the population of the whole country—what the Chetniks envisioned in January 1944 for the postwar Yugoslav state, renewed and under their full control, would have been no improvement over the interwar period, would indeed have been much worse, especially for the Croats. Given the almost exclusively Serbian composition of the congress, however, it is hardly surprising that the spirit was one of saving Serbdom and safeguarding the Serbian predominance in the renewed state after the war, not one of creating a viable and strong Yugoslavia acceptable to all South Slav nations.

In a statement on socioeconomic affairs, the congress "expressed the desire" that in the process of re-creation of the new state preconditions should be set for thorough reforms in the economic, social, and general cultural fields, "which the spirit of the times imposed and which would correspond to the needs of the Serbian, Croatian, and Slovene peoples, in order that the basic democratic ideas could be realized not only on the political, but also on the economic, social, and cultural planes."[18] On the whole, the Chetnik political program as set forth in the resolution of the congress at Ba was a marked departure from Chetnik political goals as stated in 1941 and 1942, notably in its emphasis on democratic principles with some socialist features. The purpose of these avowals of democracy, however, seems to have been far more propagandistic than programmatic; there is no indication that they reflected a true change of heart among the Chetnik leaders and that they were going to be followed by a genuine effort to meet the needs of the majority of the people of Yugoslavia, and of some nations like the Croats and Macedonians in particular.

In practical terms, the establishment of the Yugoslav Democratic National Union was the most important outcome of the congress. Since all the various elements present declared themselves ready to forgo independent political action until the "establishment of normal conditions in Yugoslavia," they readily agreed that the existing Chetnik Central National Committee should be enlarged to include representatives of all forces participating in the new political organization. But owing to the considerable differences that existed between the Chetnik leaders and the party politicians, the actual selection of the central committee members was assigned to the Organizational Committee of Three (Topalović, Vasić, Moljević), with instructions for them to consult with the leaders of the various parties. The committee was chosen by the follow-

---

[18] The political and socioeconomic platform for the Chetnik congress apparently was written by Adam Pribićević, a member of a well-known political family and leader of the Independent Democratic Party. His draft was discussed at the congress and it appears that it influenced some of the wording of the resolution that was approved. The draft was then sent to the local Ravna Gora People's Committees, the local organs of the Union, for comments, but the revision was never completed. Later, in exile, Pribićević wrote from memory a version of the proposed platform; see his article "The Ideology of Draža's Movement."

ing June,[19] and included also men such as Konstantin Fotić and Jovan Djonović who had been active abroad on behalf of the Chetniks since the start of the Chetnik movement.

The German authorities were, naturally, interested in all that went on at the Ba congress, and through the Higher SS and Police Leader General Meyszner, who received detailed reports of the proceedings from his agents, they were aware of the frequent outbursts of anti-German sentiment that occurred.[20] One agent reported that General Mihailović had said that the German formula of killing one hundred Serbs for every German killed would be repaid, at the proper time, by killing one thousand Germans for every Serb killed.[21] This story was possibly a plant, since the agents, though Serbs, may have been pro-Nedić or pro-Ljotić and in that case opposed to the German-Chetnik agreements then in force and ready to malign Mihailović.[22] On the other hand, the agents may simply have been trying to cater to their employer General Meyszner, whom they knew to be opposed to the agreements. Or perhaps Mihailović did make the somewhat grandiose threat. Whatever the facts, reports of this nature certainly did nothing to ease the already strained relations between the Germans and the Chetniks in Serbia. As shown in Chapter 9, soon after the Ba congress all the Chetnik-German armistice agreements were terminated, but circumstances were continuing to force an informal intermittent kind of cooperation. The situation in Serbia, as in Europe generally, was, however, rapidly coming to a head.

By the beginning of the summer, the Germans, markedly weakened as a consequence of setbacks on the Russian front and facing whole Allied armies after D-Day, could no longer be certain of their ability to defend Serbia or for that matter any part of southeastern Europe. This meant that the Chetniks could no longer count on the security of the German occupation apparatus to keep the Partisans out of their home territory of Serbia. At the start of June the Chetniks were dealt a devastating political blow when the Purić cabinet was ousted and Mihailović was dropped as Minister of the Army, Navy, and Air Force. Though weak, the Purić government had at least provided Mihailović with legitimacy, an official status and an official representation abroad. Deprived of his cabinet rank and claim to legitimacy, Mihailović now looked upon the government-in-exile, formerly his tool, as his enemy. Furthermore,

---

[19] Topalović, *Pokreti narodnog otpora*, p. 89. For a list of committee members as of July 15, 1944, see Jovan Djonović, "My Connections with Draža Mihailović from the Middle East," p. 90.
[20] Microcopy No. T-311, Roll 286, Frames 181–84, 211–13.
[21] *Ibid.*, Frame 183.
[22] Nedić was much offended by the fact that there was a Chetnik congress at all. He told the Germans that for more than two years he had been trying to get permission from them to convene an assembly, and now the Chetniks, after only three months of collaboration, had been allowed to stage a congress, and it turned out to be anti-German in character. See Nedić's letter of Feb. 22, 1944, to General Felber, Military Commander in Southeast Europe, in Microcopy No. T-501, Roll 256, Frame 883.

the departure of the last members of the British military mission from Chetnik headquarters at the end of May had cut all remaining ties to the British and dashed all hopes of support from them. The only course now open was to try and go it alone.

The military actions in Serbia that began in the summer of 1944 were to assume foremost priority for all Chetniks. On June 30 Mihailović named a six-man Committee of Experts to act as an advisory body on nonmilitary matters, with one each of the six members to be responsible for foreign affairs, legislative affairs, economic and fiscal affairs, nationality questions and propaganda, social affairs, or economic reconstruction. One of the committee's first decisions was to condemn the new Šubašić government as a government of Croatian separatists and Communist friends and to name special representatives for the Chetnik movement abroad: Konstantin Fotić in the United States, Bogoljub Jevtić in the United Kingdom, Jovan Djonović in Algiers, General Petar Živković in Italy, and Mladen Žujović in Egypt[23]—all men who had lost their high positions in the government-in-exile or the diplomatic corps with the change in the nature of the exile government.

A plenary session of the Central National Committee which met July 20–23 also condemned the Šubašić government, declaring that because it did not include any representatives of the political parties associated in the Yugoslav Democratic National Union, it was unauthorized to speak or act in the name of Yugoslavia. The committee's resolution stated that the new government could not properly protect the interests of the country and the Crown, and reserved for itself the freedom of action toward it as well as "the freedom of undertaking measures [deemed necessary] for the protection of national and state interests."[24] In the months that followed, Mihailović and the Central National Committee with their friends among Yugoslav politicians in exile did all they could to work against the Šubašić government, apparently encouraged in their endeavor by a warning message from Purić of April 4, 1944, in which he reported on continuing British maneuvers to oust Mihailović by bringing down the Purić government and installing an interim government which would make an agreement with Tito. Purić had added: "The King and I are strongly opposed to this. Do not believe whatever you may hear over the radio. I am saying all this because there is a possibility that our communications may be interrupted. In case of any combination without you as Minister of the Army, the King and I

---

[23] Plenča, *Medjunarodni odnosi Jugoslavije*, p. 310. For the statute of the Committee of Experts see Archives of the Institute of Military History, Belgrade, Chetnik Documents, Reg. No. 28/2, Box 7. On this committee see also Milovanović, in *Borba*, Oct. 23 and 24, 1970.

[24] For the text of this resolution see Jovan Djonović, "The Connections with Draža Mihailović from the Middle East and North Africa," pp. 59–60. See also Plenča, *Medjunarodni odnosi Jugoslavije*, pp. 310–11.

think that you should continue [functioning] in the country as the only
free member of the government with the slogan: 'The King is captive,
long live the King.' "[25] Mihailović's determination to follow the advice
is apparent in a message of July 21, 1944, to Djonović and Žujović, answering Djonović's query as to what should be the (present) attitude of
Yugoslav government officials, soldiers, and civilians abroad:

(1) The Central National Committee expresses the unflinching will of the
people that together with their great allies they will continue the fight until
the liberation of the Yugoslav territory from the enemy.

(2) It expresses its loyalty to the Karadjordjević dynasty.

(3) It expresses its full confidence in General Draža Mihailović and salutes
all the representatives of the Serbian and Slovene political parties in exile for
their determined stand taken on the occasion of the formation of the Šubašić
government.

(4) It considers to be its duty to the country, in view of the circumstances under which the Šubašić government was formed, and its composition, to state
that the Central National Committee does not have the confidence that this
government will defend the legitimate interests of the Serbian and Slovene
peoples and of the Kingdom of Yugoslavia in a worthy manner.

(5) It takes full exception to all the future actions of the cabinet and assumes
full freedom toward it in regard to measures that it might deem necessary to
undertake.[26]

It was clear that Mihailović was not accepting the official loss of his
ministerial position. Nor did he seem to accept the loss, in August, of
his post as Chief of Staff of the Supreme Command. To the end of the
war, the Chetnik forces continued to call themselves the Yugoslav Army
in the Homeland, with Mihailović as head of that army.

The history of the political wing of the Chetnik movement for the
remainder of its existence can be briefly told. Between July 1944 and
March 1945 the Central National Committee met only twice.[27] Topalović had been sent to Italy at the end of May to represent Mihailović
and do what he could to promote the Chetnik cause with the Allied
military command and political representatives of the British and American governments attached to that command (Harold Macmillan for
the British and Robert D. Murphy followed by Alexander C. Kirk for
the Americans). In August several additional members of the CNC
(Adam Pribićević, Vladimir Belajčić, and Ivan Kovač) and one of Mihailović's top commanders, Major Vučković, were dispatched to join
him. The various memoranda they submitted to the Allied command
did nothing to help the Chetnik cause, however.[28]

[25] Jovan Djonović, "The Connections with General Mihailović from the Middle East," p. 24.

[26] Jovan Djonović, "My Connections with Draža Mihailović from the Middle East," pp. 90–91.

[27] At the trial of military and political leaders of the Draža Mihailović organization in July and
August 1945, among whom were nine members of the Central National Committee, very little
information was presented on the activities of the committee. See Sudjenje članovima rukovodstva
organizacije Draže Mihailovića, pp. 69–136 and passim.

[28] For a memorandum presented by this committee on September 3, 1944, to the Supreme Allied
Command, Mediterranean Theater, and to the representatives of the British and American governments see Topalović, Pokreti narodnog otpora, pp. 95–96.

Mihailović dissolved the Committee of Experts just before he was forced to withdraw from Serbia to northeastern Bosnia in mid-September, saying that he could take with him only fighting men.[29] Most of the members of the CNC, however, along with Moljević and the recently arrived American mission headed by Colonel McDowell, accompanied Mihailović in the withdrawal.

THE COMING BATTLE FOR SERBIA

With the approach of spring 1944, the Partisans had ventured a move: two of their divisions, the 2nd Proletarian and the 5th Shock, entered Serbia from Sandjak in mid-March. The objective was to cross the Ibar River and Kopaonik Mountain into southeastern Serbia where they would join other Partisan units, the largest and best organized of all the Partisan units in Serbia, and serve as a leavening agent for the intensification of the national liberation struggle in all of Serbia. The two units soon met stiff opposition from German, Bulgarian, Serbian quisling, and Chetnik forces (Operation Kammerjäger), and were deflected to the northwest. After some eight weeks of fighting, and heavy losses, the two Partisan divisions were obliged to retreat to Sandjak.

Thus thwarted in their first probing assault on the German and Chetnik stronghold of Serbia, the Partisans decided to try a somewhat different line of approach, based partly on strengthening their military and political organization in Serbia, and partly on using much stronger forces from the west and southwest. Between May 20 and June 21 Partisan brigades in southern Serbia were transformed into divisions (the 21st, 22nd, 23rd, 24th, and 25th Serbian divisions), and early in July General Koča Popović, who had been very successful as commander of the 1st Proletarian Division, arrived in southeastern Serbia to assume command of the Chief Headquarters of the Partisan Forces for Serbia, whose main units were those of the newly created Serbian divisions.[30]

Several events made it more urgent that the Partisans should enter Serbia, and the time seemed ripe at last. The Red Army was nearing Yugoslav territory from the northeast, and it was important that the Partisans should establish operational contact with it and join it in chasing the Germans out of Serbia. Bulgaria, about to switch sides in the war, was preparing to withdraw its troops from Serbia, leaving parts of the Serbian frontier in the west underprotected. Moreover, for Allied strategic needs as well as their own, and under prodding from the Allied command in Italy, the Partisans wanted to make it impossible for the German army in Greece to use as escape routes either the railroad line Salonika-Skopje-Niš-Belgrade—the most direct and fastest line—or the

---

[29] According to a personal communication from a former member of this committee.

[30] *Hronologija 1941–1945*, pp. 750, 779–81, 829. These divisions started out with perhaps 1,500 to 2,500 men each. Yugoslav writers estimate the total strength of Partisan divisions and detachments in southern and southeastern Serbia at that time at about 15,000. See Pantelić, p. 252.

Ibar Valley railroad to Kraljevo and then to Užice and Bosnia. The German withdrawal was imminent, and the Russians also wanted the Niš-Belgrade route blocked to the Germans so that they would not imperil their advance across the borders in northeastern Serbia and Vojvodina.

Mindful of the changed strategic situation in Serbia, the Partisans continued their buildup in Montenegro, Sandjak, and eastern Bosnia and the strengthening of their forces in southern Serbia, readying themselves for operations in Serbia. But in July the Germans set in motion a series of plans intended to foil the Partisans. First, they mounted Operation Trumpf against the Partisan forces in southern Serbia (the newly formed 21st, 22nd, 24th, and 25th Serbian divisions), in the area of Kapaonik Mountain, Jastrebac Mountain, and the valleys of the Toplica and Jablanica rivers, with the object of rendering them ineffective as part of any pincers operation against the Germans and their allies in central and northern Serbia.[31] This was a combined operation of German forces assisted by Bulgarian and Serbian quisling troops and elite Chetnik units under the command of Major Radoslav Račić. Besides Račić's own Fourth Group of Shock Corps which he brought from western Serbia, the Chetnik forces included the local Rasina-Kopaonik Group of Shock Corps headed by Lt. Colonel Dragutin Keserović, in total strength exceeding 10,000 men.[32] The coordination between the German command and the Chetnik forces was, as already stated, in the hands of German Major Weyel, and the Germans of course supplied the Chetniks with ammunition and some arms.[33]

On July 12 General Mihailović sent a message to Djonović in Algiers informing him of these operations: "We are carrying out operations against the Communists," the message said, "[but] at the same time other forces fight against them. To us the main thing is that these other forces do not interfere with us."[34] It would appear that General Mihailović knew exactly what was going on. After the conclusion of the operations in southern Serbia, which they expected to be crowned with success, the Chetniks were planning to mount large-scale operations against the Partisans in Sandjak and Montenegro, and their Supreme Command was making extensive plans for these operations calling for as many as 20,000 troops.[35] But the operations in southern Serbia were not crowned

[31] The Partisan 23rd Division had been sent into eastern Serbia against Chetnik and Bulgarian forces there. See Vojin Popović, "The Breakthrough of the Units of the Chief Headquarters of Serbia into Eastern Serbia in 1944," and Ratković, pp. 110–13, 116.

[32] See the report of July 15, 1944, of the Military Commander in Southeast Europe (Felber), who had overall command of Operation Trumpf, in Microcopy No. T-311, Roll 195, Frames 725–26. One of the principal Yugoslav studies of this operation, Višnjić's "The German Offensive Against Liberated Areas in Southern Serbia in Mid-1944," p. 122, gives somewhat larger figures.

[33] For Keserović's testimony on these operations see *Sudjenje članovima rukovodstva organizacije Draže Mihailovića*, pp. 242–44.

[34] Jovan Djonović, "The Connections with Draža Mihailović from the Middle East and North Africa," pp. 56–57. See also Mihailović's report of July 27 in *ibid.*, p. 61.

[35] *Ibid.*, pp. 56–57. For the centers of the domestic Partisans in Serbia and Partisan troop concentrations as well as the location of the chief Chetnik commanders and their units in Serbia and elsewhere as of July 23, 1944, see a German map in Microcopy No. T-311, Roll 196, Frame 617.

with success. Some of the Partisan divisions were seriously battered and all of them were chased around a great deal, but they were not knocked out for further action.[36] And meanwhile other developments were under way which not only would relieve the pressure on the Partisan divisions in southern Serbia but would soon compel the Germans and the Chetniks to shift their forces to the southwest and west to meet the incoming Partisan divisions from Sandjak and Bosnia.

Parallel with Operation Trumpf in southern Serbia the Germans undertook another action for the purpose of knocking out the main body of Partisan forces that were being readied in Montenegro, Sandjak, and Bosnia. Early in July, Operation Draufgänger (or what Yugoslav historians call Operation Andrijevica) was launched against Partisan troops in Montenegro. This operation delayed by some days the entry of the first three Partisan divisions into Serbia, but it did not stop it.[37] Nor did it have fateful consequences for the four Serbian Partisan divisions that were the object of Operation Trumpf, although Tito did acknowledge that the endangering of these units was due in part at least to the delayed entry into Serbia of the divisions from Montenegro and Sandjak. In Tito's order of July 25 to the group of divisions scheduled for operations against southern Serbia, he told them to advance at once in the planned direction.[38] Two days later, the 2nd Proletarian Division and the 5th Shock Division—the two divisions that had failed to penetrate into southeastern Serbia in the spring—and the 17th Division were moving toward Serbia, and by August 2 they were crossing the Ibar River on the sector between Kosovska Mitrovica and Raška.[39] The Germans and the Chetniks, in an effort to stem the advance of the Partisans, shifted part of their forces westward, away from the action in southern and southeastern Serbia. But this maneuver only lightened the pressure on the Serbian divisions and did nothing to halt the entry of the Partisan divisions from Montenegro. It was only a matter of time before these divisions linked with the Partisan Serbian divisions and the entire force was ready for further operations.[40]

Operation Draufgänger having failed to block the Partisan advance toward southern Serbia, the Germans (in accordance with an order issued on July 29 by the Commander in Chief in Southeast Europe) turned their attention to the Partisan forces still waiting in Montenegro, consisting of the 1st Proletarian Division, the 3rd Shock Division, and the 37th Division, hoping to keep them from pushing toward southwestern Serbia. This task they assigned to the bulk of the forces of the Vth SS Mountain Corps, which had been greatly strengthened by the arrival

[36] *Oslobodilački rat*, II, 253–57.
[37] *Ibid.*, pp. 257–59; *KTB/OKW/WFSt*, Vol. IV, Part 1 (1944), pp. 672–74, 681.
[38] Tito, *Vojna djela*, I, 251.
[39] *Oslobodilački rat*, II, 259–60; *KTB/OKW/WFSt*, Vol. IV, Part 1, pp. 682–83.
[40] *Oslobodilački rat*, II, 260–62.

of the German 1st Mountain Division from Greece, an elite unit that had had fighting experience in Montenegro in May and June 1943 in Operation Schwarz.[41] The plan was to bottle up the Partisan divisions on the plateau between the Piva and Tara rivers and destroy them. But these divisions were under strict orders from Tito to avoid this encounter and to proceed toward southwestern Serbia.[42] Other divisions, from eastern Bosnia, were also under orders to cross the Drina River and coordinate their actions with those of the divisions coming from Montenegro. But the divisions in Montenegro, hampered in part by the necessity of safeguarding the evacuation of about one thousand of their sick and wounded by air to Italy,[43] were caught by the Germans in an attack begun on August 12. At the end of some two weeks of fighting, in what Yugoslav historians call Operation Durmitor (otherwise the Montenegrin phase of the German Operation Rübezahl), the Partisan divisions extricated themselves, and after a brief delay they resumed their march toward southwestern Serbia. Again the Germans had succeeded in inflicting considerable losses on the Partisans and causing some delay in their plans, but had failed to prevent their breakthrough into southwestern Serbia. Thus in the last week of August, the second group of three divisions from Montenegro, forming the 1st Corps, penetrated into southwestern Serbia, due southwest of the town of Užice.[44]

Part of Operation Rübezahl had been carried out by the German 7th SS Prinz Eugen Division and the 13th SS Division "Handschar" in central and eastern Bosnia against the divisions of the Partisan 3rd and 12th corps which in the area of Šekovići southeast of Tuzla were preparing to cooperate with or support the Partisan divisions from Montenegro in the invasion of Serbia. The German objective was to push the 3rd and 12th corps as far west and away from the Drina River as possible. Under heavy fighting during most of August the two Partisan corps moved first southwestward to the area of the Konjuh, Zvijezda, and Javor mountains, and then, to force a spreading of the German units, the 12th Corps moved still further south to the area of Foča. Both Partisan corps sustained heavy losses and were forced to abandon their original favorable staging areas for operations against Serbia. The three divisions forming the 12th Corps—the 6th, 16th, and 36th—were not able to cross the Drina until September 5 and 6, and the crossing, at

[41] See *KTB/OKW/WFSt*, Vol. IV, Part 1, p. 682. These forces included also the SS Division "Skanderbeg," composed of Albanian soldiers and German officers and specialists (which was the main force used in Operation Draufgänger), and, according to Yugoslav sources, also some of Djurišić's Montenegrin Volunteer Corps units.

[42] *Oslobodilački rat*, II, 268.

[43] *Ibid.*, p. 271.

[44] *Ibid.*, pp. 272–73; *KTB/OKW/WFSt*, Vol. IV, Part 1, pp. 683–84. For a report of Aug. 22, 1944, from the Staff of the Commander in Chief in Southeastern Europe on Operations Trumpf, Draufgänger, and Rübezahl, in which Partisan successes are conceded, see Microcopy No. T-311, Roll 195, Frames 956–59.

Stari Brod north of Višegrad, took place about sixty kilometers further south than originally planned. Once inside Serbia, the units of the 12th Corps cooperated with the units of the 1st Corps that were already there. In northeastern Bosnia the Partisans were even more delayed in their plans: because of German action, the 11th Division did not cross the Drina River until September 18. But here again, though the Bosnian phase of Operation Rübezahl delayed the Partisans, it did not stop them.[45]

Matters elsewhere, however, were assuming priority, for the Germans were facing a new and truly overwhelming threat in eastern and northeastern Yugoslavia—the approach of the Soviet armies. On August 30 Operation Rübezahl was cut short. The 1st Mountain Division in Montenegro was transferred to northeastern Serbia and the 7th SS Prinz Eugen Division was transferred from Bosnia to eastern Serbia,[46] and most of the German troops in western and southwestern Serbia were moved to northeastern Serbia or the Banat to strengthen defenses against the Soviet forces. At the same time, the Bulgarians withdrew their 24th Division from southwestern and western Serbia to Bulgaria. The German defenses in southwestern and western Serbia were thus left in the hands of small German contingents, some units of the Serbian Volunteer Corps, and the Russian Protective Corps, and above all the Chetniks. The whole area of northwestern Serbia between the Kolubara and Drina rivers was under the command of Colonel von Jungenfeld.[47]

COLLAPSE OF GERMAN-CHETNIK DEFENSES IN WESTERN SERBIA

Tito's strategy for operations in Serbia, as communicated on August 28, 1944, to the commander of the Operational Group of Divisions, was that one section of his forces was to link up with the Partisan Serbian divisions in southeastern Serbia, thus enabling some of these Serbian divisions to move northward toward the Danube River and meet the Red Army, while other divisions moved into central Serbia to cooperate with the incoming Red Army in the liberation of Belgrade.[48] The Partisan divisions that entered southwestern Serbia from Montenegro late in August and those scheduled to enter western Serbia early in September from Bosnia were to move in a northerly direction, systematically working toward control of the various mountains in their paths, until they reached the plain of Mačva and the Sava River. There, they were to turn east toward Belgrade, synchronizing their operations with those of other Partisan forces and with the Russians. Since Tito expected the

---

[45] *Oslobodilački rat*, II, 263, 267; *KTB/OKW/WFSt*, Vol. IV, Part 1, p. 684.
[46] *KTB/OKW/WFSt*, Vol. IV, Part 1, pp. 684–85; *Oslobodilački rat*, II, 271.
[47] Microcopy No. T-501, Roll 257, Frames 157 and 173.
[48] I provide here only a sketchy analysis of the liberation of Serbia. My primary concern is to show how the Chetniks lost their main base of strength.

Germans to put up a vigorous defense of the valley of the Western Morava River, which was the secondary line of communications with Greece through the Ibar River valley, he thought this area should be bypassed at first.[49] With a few deviations, these directives of Tito were followed by his commanders.[50]

Underlying the entire operation was, of course, the fundamental objective of crushing the Chetnik military forces and political organization in Serbia. Tito made this clear in an order of September 5 to the "Operational Group for the Speeding of Movement [in Serbia] and for the Liquidation of the Chetniks": "Keep in mind that the basic aim of this whole operation is to liquidate the Chetniks of Draža Mihailović and the Nedić forces, as well as their [political and administrative] apparatus. Do not allow Mihailović to carry out mobilization and to take people with him. Arrest Chetnik headmen in the villages, because they are the chief pillar of Mihailović's strength among the people."[51] On September 1 Mihailović called for a general mobilization in Serbia. How many young people responded to his call is not known; owing to the lack of arms and other supplies, many of those who responded were sent home, or left on their own initiative. It was hardly a propitious moment for a general mobilization, since the odds against the Chetniks were extremely great and there was very little time for carrying out such an undertaking. Without the proper organization and sufficient supplies of weapons and ammunition it was a futile gesture. Even the existing Chetnik forces were short of arms and ammunition, Mihailović's pleas to the Germans in August having been largely in vain; and psychologically many of the units were close to disintegration, sorely tempted by Tito's proclamation on August 17 of a general amnesty for the fighters in the Chetnik ranks and in various quisling formations in Yugoslavia, provided they transferred to the Partisans by September 15.[52] Tito had also ordered his forces breaking into Serbia from the southwest and west to prevent the Chetnik mobilization.

The total number of Chetnik forces in Serbia at the end of August 1944 (prior to Mihailović's call for a general mobilization) can only be estimated approximately. Von Weichs's estimate for mid-August, contained in materials which he as Commander in Chief in Southeast Europe presented to Hitler on August 22, was a total of about 25,000 Chetniks under arms in Serbia, divided as follows: northwestern Serbia, 2,500; southwestern Serbia, 3,000; southeastern Serbia, 1,500; northeastern Ser-

[49] *Oslobodilački rat*, II, 276–77.

[50] Tito strongly criticized these deviations in a message of September 18. *Vojna djela*, I, 285.

[51] *Ibid.*, p. 273.

[52] In accordance with a subsequent order by Tito of September 18, even those members of the Chetnik and various quisling forces who shifted to the Partisans after the amnesty date expired were treated rather liberally. Whole units that shifted were not kept intact, however, but were broken up, with their manpower spread among the existing Partisan units, and their specialists sent to various Partisan training centers. *Ibid.*, pp. 284–85.

bia, 5,500; and central Serbia, 12,500.[53] Since the Chetniks made strenuous efforts to increase their effectives during the second part of August
and called for a general mobilization on September 1, it is reasonable
to assume (even allowing for the only partial success of the mobilization) that in September the total number of armed Chetniks in Serbia
was somewhere between 30,000 and 40,000 men.

The large agglomeration of Chetnik forces in central Serbia in mid-
August had resulted partly from the shift of the Chetnik forces under
Major Račić and Captain Kalabić from western Serbia for the operations against the Partisans in the Toplica-Jablanica area in the south
in July and early August. When it became evident that Partisan forces
from Montenegro, Sandjak, and Bosnia were about to move against
southwestern and western Serbia, the Račić and Kalabić forces were
ordered to western Serbia, where they were reinforced by additional
units, and later used as the chief Chetnik defenders of Serbia against
the oncoming Partisans.

As we have seen, one of the principal organizational characteristics of
the Chetnik forces in Serbia until June 1944 was their distribution
throughout the country in relatively small and medium-sized units—
brigades and corps, a corps consisting usually of two to five brigades and
varying from 500 to at the most 2,000 men. According to German sources,
as of March 31, 1944, occupied Serbia was blanketed by not less than
thirty-four Chetnik corps; there were in addition nine corps in Macedonia and Bulgarian-occupied southeastern Serbia, three in Sandjak,
and eighteen in Montenegro, Bosnia and Herzegovina, Dalmatia, and
Croatia.[54] This type of military organization had certain advantages,
but mobility was hardly one of them, nor was efficiency of tactical use
of troops or strict execution of orders of the Chetnik Supreme Command. And Mihailović needed both of these things in the summer of
1944.

After the expulsion of the 2nd and 5th Partisan divisions which had
penetrated from Sandjak into Serbia in the spring, Mihailović and his
Supreme Command had somewhat belatedly decided to organize a
higher category of command—the Groups of Corps and the Groups of
Shock Corps, which consisted of several corps under one commander.
The foremost and only well-known unit of this higher order was the
Fourth Group of Shock Corps, established in June 1944, and consisting
of the two Mountain Guards corps, the First and Second Ravna Gora
corps, the Zlatibor, and the Javor corps—in other words, the leading
Chetnik corps from southwestern Serbia. The units included in these

---

[53] Microcopy No. T-311, Roll 195, Frame 973. A year earlier (Sept. 22, 1943), the Germans
estimated the number of Chetnik forces in Serbia at only 16,500 men. See Microcopy No. T-501,
Roll 253, Frame 355.

[54] See the detailed map prepared by the Commander of the Security Police and the SD
(*Sicherheitsdienst*) in Belgrade in Microcopy No. T-311, Roll 286, Frames 316–17.

corps consisted of elite troops (unmarried men), and they were further strengthened by the inclusion of the so-called flying brigades from some other corps. The Fourth Group of Shock Corps was put under the command of Major Račić, with Captain Neško Nedić as chief of staff. Nikola Kalabić as the commander of the Guards Corps and Predrag Raković as the commander of the Second Ravna Gora Corps were the other leading commanders in the new Fourth Group of Shock Corps. According to Mihailović's own testimony, he organized the groups of corps both to have a mobile and true army and to bring in line or to dismiss various Chetnik commanders over whom he apparently could not exercise full control.[55]

The Fourth Group of Shock Corps had a complement of between 8,000 and 9,000 men, or in August approximately a third of all Chetnik troops in Serbia. Its first important assignment was in Operation Trumpf against the Partisans in the Jablanica and Toplica valleys in July and August, joined by the troops of Keserović (who was not happy at the arrangement). When the Partisan troops from Sandjak and Bosnia began entering Serbia at the beginning of August, the Fourth Group of Shock Corps was quickly shifted more to the west to try to stop them, and later it was used against other Partisan divisions penetrating from Sandjak and Bosnia. Other groups of corps, including one under Keserović's command, were organized along the same lines as the Račić group, but Mihailović's plans for a thorough reorganization of his forces were only partially fulfilled; possibly a half of the Chetnik forces in Serbia still operated, as they always had, as territorial militia.

With the arrival of the three Partisan divisions from Montenegro at the beginning of August, the Partisans had in Serbia eight divisions and a number of detachments. During the last days of August and the early part of September six additional divisions entered from Montenegro, Sandjak, and Bosnia, and two more divisions (the 11th and the 28th) also entered from Bosnia later in September and at the beginning of October. Also, the Partisan forces that had reached the Sava River in northwestern Serbia were further reinforced by manpower from Srijem.[56] The five Serbian divisions, which had been growing rapidly especially during the summer, now totaled about 15,000 men. The eleven divisions that arrived in August, September, and October had complements of 1,000 to 3,000 men each. However, with volunteers, shifting from Chetnik units, and stepped-up compulsory recruiting within Serbia, in some cases their complements more than tripled within a few weeks.[57] Most importantly, they all had a large core of battle-tested men, led by

[55] *The Trial of Draža Mihailović*, pp. 245–54; see also Milošević, pp. 207–8.
[56] *Oslobodilački rat*, II, 294, 313.
[57] *Ibid.*, pp. 275, 295, 303, 325.

battle-tested and confident officers. They were well equipped with light arms, and to some extent continued to be supplied by Allied air drops (and after they linked with the Soviets they obtained arms and ammunition also from them). And unlike the Chetniks, they had a high morale which was improving daily.

Tito's orders to his forces in Serbia were to proceed against any Chetnik troops, and any German and Serbian quisling forces, that might be in their path, and push on to establish contact with the Soviet forces as soon as possible and cooperate with them in the liberation of Serbia and Belgrade. Belgrade, besides having great strategic value as the main transportation center in southeastern Europe, had for the Partisans an extraordinary political and psychological significance, especially in the Serbian context, so it was doubly important to reach the city with the Russians at the earliest possible date.

On September 5 the Chetnik Fourth Group of Shock Corps under Račić attacked the Partisan troops penetrating from Sandjak, with the objective of "beating the Communists in the area of Požega and Užice, to be followed by a concentration of forces for further annihilation of the Reds in the territory of Serbia."[58] The initial onslaught was successful, and the Partisans were thrown back south and west of Užice; but "three days later, after regrouping its forces, the 1st Proletarian Corps inflicted such a defeat to this group of Chetniks at Jelova Gora (northwest of Užice) that they were never able to recover."[59] The Partisans resumed their advance northward and on September 11 just failed to complete the encirclement and capture of General Mihailović and the Chetnik Supreme Command, as well as the members of the Central National Committee and the American military mission headed by Colonel McDowell. Mihailović and his entourage were rescued by a unit of the Serbian Volunteer Corps, but they were compelled to retreat through northwestern Serbia and cross the Drina River into northeastern Bosnia.[60] In this retreat Mihailović had with him only about four hundred troops.[61]

At this crucial point for the Chetniks in Serbia—after defeat in battle at Jelova Gora on September 9, and Mihailović's near capture two days later, King Peter's speech over the BBC came as a stunning blow to all their hopes. The king's appeal to all Serbs, Croats, and Slovenes to unite

[58] Bir'uzov and Hamović, eds., p. 112, quoting from Directive No. 6 of Sept. 4, 1944, issued by the Staff of the Fourth Group of Shock Corps.
[59] *Ibid.*, p. 113.
[60] *Oslobodilački rat*, II, 274–309; *Karapandžić*, pp. 356–58; *The Trial of Draža Mihailović*, pp. 258–60, 263–65. Mihailović stated at his trial (p. 259) that the suggestion to move to Bosnia came to him from Račić, who informed him that he could no longer hold out against the Communists. A very confused Chetnik account of the battle at Jelova Gora can be found in Milošević, pp. 211–12.
[61] Banović and Stepanović, in *Politika*, Aug. 9, 1962. McDowell in our interview at Stanford University on March 19, 1968, confirmed their figure.

under the command of Marshal Tito was directed also to Croats and Slovenes in quisling formations, but there was no doubt of its being aimed mainly at the Chetniks, whose commander in chief he was and with whom both the king and the dynasty stood in high esteem. Those who did not obey, the king warned, would be branded traitors both by their people and by history. The political and psychological effects of the king's speech on the Chetniks were devastating, and in some cases immediate. According to a message of the Area Staff of Southern Serbia to the Chetnik Supreme Command on September 13, Peter's speech contributed to the disintegration of numerous Chetnik units in the Nišava Group of Corps and also hastened the collapse of the Chetnik forces in eastern Serbia.[62] Mihailović's reaction to the speech is seen from his letter to Fotić of November 18, 1944: "The King dealt us a terrible blow. His speech affected especially a certain number of vacillating officers, but on the population it had a contrary effect. The people have started to grumble against the King and dynasty; the protests were general and in public."[63]

During the second half of September the main Chetnik units under Major Račić in western and northwestern Serbia suffered further defeats at the hands of the Partisans, and the same was true of Chetnik units in other parts of Serbia wherever they did battle with the Partisans. Since there was no hope of substantial additional support from the Germans, who were themselves sustaining repeated setbacks at the hands of the Soviets and the Partisans, the Chetniks had no choice but to retreat on all fronts. Račić's forces, by arrangement, fought along with German forces under Colonel von Jungenfeld, who also had command over some units of the Serbian Volunteer Corps and the Russian Protective Corps. Two daily reports from the Military Commander in Southeast Europe, General Felber, to the Commander in Chief in Southeast Europe refer to this collaboration in von Jungenfeld's area: on September 26, "Planned attack with the Chetniks postponed for September 27," and on September 28, "Chetnik formations have been moved to the area east-southeast of Šabac for a rest; allegedly will be again at the disposal of Group Jungenfeld from October 1 on."[64]

[62] Microcopy No. T-311, Roll 189, Frame 1210.

[63] *Knjiga o Draži*, II, 172–73. More than a year ealier, on October 20, 1943, Mihailović said in a message to the government-in-exile that in view of the existing popular notions and feelings, King Peter should not make any statements about the Communists and indeed should not even mention them. See Jovan Djonović, "Mihailović's Telegrams About British Missions," *Glasnik SIKD 'Njegoš'*, June 1960, p. 34. Fotić's reaction to the speech is seen from his letter of September 18, 1944, to Jovan Djonović, in which he refers to the king as "that young unfortunate," and says that later, when the people in the country know the true position, both Draža and the C.N. Committee should take a "different attitude" and that neither his youth nor pressure exercised upon the king "will help him as an excuse." F.O. 371/44326, R16741/850/92.

The confusion that the king's speech produced among the Serbian peasantry is vividly indicated in a sarcastic popular rhyme that circulated shortly afterward: *"Mi za kralja, kralj za Tita/Šta će biti, Bog te pita."* ("We're for the king, and the king is for Tito./What will happen, only God knows.) See Topalović, *Kako su komunisti dograbili vlast u Jugoslaviji*, p. 111.

[64] Microcopy No. T-501, Roll 257, Frames 157 and 160.

The Germans were especially worried that the Partisans might cross into Srijem, where they would be in a position to cut off the vital communications between Belgrade and the west, and they feared that what appeared to be a move toward Šabac might be part of a Russian-Partisan tactical maneuver to isolate the vital transportation and defense center of Belgrade. No such joint maneuver seems to have existed, but the Germans, with the Chetniks helping, made it their immediate objective to keep the Partisans from entering the Mačva Plain and endangering the town of Šabac with its bridge over the Sava River and immediate connection with the area of Srijem, and the communications leading to Belgrade.[65] The key to possession of the area was Cer Mountain, situated due south of Šabac. This was defended by the Chetniks, and on September 26 they lost possession of it to the Partisan 12th Corps and the way was open for the Partisans to move onto the Mačva Plain and to Šabac.[66] The German report of September 27 summarized the action and its consequences thus: "The enemy 12th Corps in the attack toward Šabac forced the Chetnik troops of Račić onto the Mačva Plain. . . . It appears that after the confirmed crossing of Mihailović over the Drina River these Chetnik forces also intend to withdraw into Bosnia. Thereby our own position is greatly worsened."[67]

A few days after this action, on October 2, Račić's Fourth Group of Shock Corps, or what still remained of it, was in the area between the towns of Šabac and Obrenovac on the Sava River. Mihailović had moved into eastern Bosnia somewhere in the area of Majevica Mountain and established headquarters there. Račić reported to the Majevica Corps that the Communists had taken the towns of Valjevo, Loznica, Lazarevac, and Ljig in western Serbia and had surrounded the town of Šabac.[68] Realizing the hopelessness of the Chetnik-German position in northwestern Serbia, Račić decided to pull out of the Chetnik arrangement with von Jungenfeld. His forces had sustained heavy losses, and he wanted not only to save the remnants from destruction but also to put himself in a better position for future maneuvers. But instead of moving toward Bosnia to join Mihailović, he broke his forces into small groups and on October 3 or 4 ordered them to head south to the valleys of the Western Morava and Djetinja, where they could join other Chetnik groups and await further developments.

SOVIET FORCES ENTER SERBIA

On September 22 the first units of the Red Army—the 113th Division of the Second Ukrainian Front—crossed the Danube River from Ro-

---

[65] Microcopy No. T-311, Roll 194, Frame 105.
[66] *Oslobodilački rat*, II, 293–95.
[67] Microcopy No. T-501, Roll 257, Frames 158–59.
[68] Microcopy No. T-311, Roll 189, Frame 984.

mania into northeastern Serbia. Six days later forces of the Third Ukrainian Front entered from Bulgarian territory to begin their attack against German forces in northeastern Serbia, and on October 2 the main forces of the Second Ukrainian Front crossed from Romania to attack German forces in the Banat.[69]

The German forces facing the Russians in the Banat and Serbia (organized as Army Group Felber from October 1 on) included the 1st Mountain Division, two regiments of the Brandenburg Division, the 117th Light Infantry Division, the 7th SS Prinz Eugen Division in the area of Niš far to the south, and about ten other units, some of brigade strength and others much smaller.[70] Against them the Soviets threw a massive invasion force. The units of the Third Ukrainian Front alone used 2,200 artillery pieces and mortars and 358 tanks and motorized artillery pieces. The Red Army also had at its disposal 1,292 airplanes and 80 armed river vessels. Sizable additions to heavy arms of these units were made in late September and early October, and the units were replenished with new manpower.[71]

In this battle of foreign armies on Yugoslav soil, the two rival Yugoslav forces, far outnumbered in manpower and weaponry, necessarily played a subsidiary role. But the Partisans, well though not heavily armed, and well trained for their tasks, were of great help to the Russians. Prior to the Soviet entry, they carried out preparatory demolition work to impede German forces defending the frontier toward Bulgaria, and after the Soviets arrived they cooperated with them in all parts of Serbia, partly in independent actions and partly in joint actions. In the west, they alone successfully cleared the area of the few German troops, Serbian quisling forces, and the main Chetnik force, and in central and eastern Serbia where they cooperated closely with the Soviet forces their share in operations was invaluable. For the first time, they engaged in regular frontal operations with large units. They were especially important in the battle for the liberation of the city of Belgrade. Although their entry into Belgrade at the head of the liberating columns was due in part to prior arrangements between Tito and Tolbukhin, the casualty figures in the liberation of the city alone—2,953 Partisans killed, as against some 1,000 Russians killed—prove that they more than held their own in the joint undertaking.[72] Some Russian writers as well as pro-Chetnik writers have made light of the Partisans' role in the liberation of Serbia as a whole, and of Belgrade in particular, but in view of the facts such interpretations are patently unfair.[73]

[69] Bir'uzov, ed., p. 62; *Oslobodilački rat*, II, 298.
[70] Microcopy No. T-501, Roll 257, Frame 175.
[71] Bir'uzov and Hamović, eds., pp. 91–93.
[72] *Ibid.*, p. 260. Bir'uzov, p. 71, says, however, that Marshal Tito requested from Marshal Tolbukhin on October 13 that Yugoslav forces be given an opportunity to enter Belgrade first and that the Russians give them support with tanks and artillery.
[73] See e.g. Bosnitch, who, defending the Chetniks, says (pp. 705–6): "Thus the Partisans won

To prevent the Germans from withdrawing their forces of over 300,-000 men rapidly and without great losses from Greece and putting them to use on other fronts against the Western Allies or the Russians, the Allied command in Italy together with the Partisans in the first week of September launched a heavy air-ground attack on railroad and road communications throughout Yugoslavia, the already mentioned Operation Ratweek. The plans designated the targets and precise times of attack by both the Allied air forces and the Partisans, and with but a few exceptions the combined operations went smoothly. The main targets were the communications in the valleys of the Vardar and Morava rivers in Macedonia and Serbia. In the course of the operation the Allied air forces sent over Yugoslavia 1,973 aircraft (all but 600 of them from the American Fifteenth Air Force), which discharged over 3,000 tons of bombs. These air sorties did a great deal to raise Partisan morale, besides being of great military and political value.[74] In Serbia the chief objective was to disrupt the communications on the Skopje-Niš-Belgrade railroad line, rendering it inoperative either as a withdrawal route for German troops from Greece or as a troop transport and supply line in the defense of Serbia.

In eastern and southeastern Serbia (the Southern Morava valley) and in the Vardar River valley, the troops of the new Bulgarian regime, which by a special agreement with Tito were allowed to operate on Yugoslav soil, cooperated with the Partisans in preventing German troops from Macedonia and Greece from continuing their withdrawal toward Belgrade to strengthen German defenses there, or, alternatively, heading to outflank the Soviet armies advancing toward the capital. By the middle of October the Partisans and the Bulgarians, working with the Soviets, had succeeded in forcing the Prinz Eugen Division out of the area of Niš. Other Soviet forces advancing from the northeast toward the towns of Kruševac, Kraljevo, and Čačak, in the Western Morava valley, and assisted by the Partisans and Bulgarians coming from the direction of Niš, were used to deflect the Germans westward off their route north to Belgrade.[75] It was these Soviet forces which encountered and briefly cooperated with the Chetniks of Keserović and Raković, as described in Chapter 10.

---

control of Serbia without having defeated their rivals in a decisive military or political contest"— a statement which ignores the Partisan victories over the principal Chetnik forces in western and northwestern Serbia as well as their major contribution in the liberation of Belgrade. The anti-Partisan slant of the volume edited by Bir'uzov aroused so much adverse criticism that a new study was prepared jointly by Soviet and Yugoslav writers and published under the joint editorship of Bir'uzov and Hamović (the already cited *Beogradska operacija*).

[74] See Maclean, *Eastern Approaches*, pp. 470–90. The most complete and best Yugoslav study of the operation is Dželebdžić, esp. pp. 7–14, 22, 47–57. Schmidt-Richberg, p. 7, says that the German forces in Greece numbered over 300,000, but Dželebdžić, p. 9, puts them at over 400,000.

[75] *Oslobodilački rat*, II, 303–9; Bir'uzov, Map 2, facing p. 64; Schmidt-Richberg, pp. 43–54. One of the main targets of Allied bombers during Operation Ratweek was the town of Leskovac, about forty miles south of Niš, where there was a large German garrison with sizable armored units, Maclean, *Eastern Approaches*, pp. 486–87.

Russian-Partisan operations aiming directly at the liberation of Belgrade began on October 11, and on October 20 the city was liberated.[76] As early as October 2 the Germans were preparing to give up Belgrade, realizing that their defenses were bound to crumble under the Soviet-Partisan assault.[77] Giving up Belgrade meant scrapping part of the plans for evacuating troops. Some of the German forces defending Serbia had already been withdrawn through Belgrade, but part of them also withdrew through Šabac, and part through the valley of the Western Morava to Bosnia, and that was the route used after the Germans lost Belgrade to the Soviets and Partisans. It appears that the last German troops of any sort left Serbian soil at the end of December.

For a time, at least, the Chetniks seem to have entertained thoughts of trying to take control of Belgrade themselves, before the Germans pulled out. On July 25, evidently in reply to a suggestion to that effect from Jovan Djonović in Algiers, Mihailović wired him as follows (No. 538):

Reference to your Nos. 71 and 72. Thanks for your suggestions which are always welcome. We have [already] organized Belgrade. There we have our commander who has organized five corps. The corps have their arms which are continuously augmented. The corps now operate in a secret manner. Otherwise, the commander of Belgrade works on mobilizing the population of the city for our organization. We have developed strong propaganda. We have foreseen that in the case of need all more important governmental offices and all important public utilities such as the city water supply, the electric power plant, and the radio station and similar installations will be taken over by our forces.

It is also planned that other forces from Serbia will immediately enter various sectors of the city. The commander of Belgrade often comes [to me] to report. We are paying great attention to Belgrade.[78]

The strength of the Chetnik forces in Belgrade, as well as their fate, is something of a mystery. They are not mentioned in Chetnik, German, or Partisan sources dealing with the battle for Belgrade. The Chetnik commander of Belgrade, Captain Saša Mihajlović, had moved out late in July, perhaps to have easier access to Mihailović. A pro-Ljotić source states that the Chetnik troops started withdrawing from the capital toward the interior on October 5 with the State Guard, to move later toward Sandjak and Bosnia. The same source also states (and I was able to confirm) that some of the leaders of the Chetnik Youth Staff 501 had arranged to be evacuated from Belgrade to Austria by the Germans.[79] Two of the Chetnik Belgrade commanders, Majors Ivan Pavlović and Jovan Navelić, went to Vienna and along with Milan Aćimović served

[76] Bir'uzov and Hamović, eds., pp. 189–264.
[77] See the directive on the evacuation of Belgrade by the Commander in Chief in Southeast Europe in Microcopy No. T-311, Roll 194, Frames 153–54.
[78] Jovan Djonović, "The Connections with Draža Mihailović from the Middle East and North Africa," p. 61.
[79] Karapandžić, pp. 381–83, 385–86.

as liaison officers between Mihailović and Envoy Neubacher during the remaining months of the war.

THE CHETNIKS WITHDRAW FROM SERBIA

By the time the Russian and Partisan forces entered Belgrade, all the Chetnik forces in Serbia, including the elite Fourth Group of Shock Corps, had been decisively beaten or greatly weakened. Unless they were to be totally destroyed, they had to withdraw from Serbia. On October 14 the Supreme Command had issued an order forbidding the laying down of arms, stating that the people would need arms after the end of the war.[80] This was followed within a week by the forcible disarming of two of Keserović's brigades and the Ocokoljić forces by the Russians, as explained in Chapter 10. Nor were Keserović or Raković working out a satisfactory cooperation with the Russians. Thus by October 20 practically all Chetnik units in Serbia were in the process of withdrawal toward Sandjak or the Western Morava valley on the way to Sandjak. On October 21 the commanders of these withdrawing units, including Vasić (who, though no longer totally in sympathy with Mihailović, was still one of his political advisers), held a conference in the small town of Ivanjica, about forty kilometers south of the Čačak-Užice railroad line, to decide what to do. Mihailović's intentions for the withdrawal of all troops from Serbia (confirmed by an order four days later) were clearly understood, and that was the decision that prevailed, although the commanders also considered Djurišić's invitation to move to Montenegro.[81]

The Chetniks were accompanied in the general withdrawal toward Sandjak, and later to northeastern Bosnia, by the remaining units of the former Serbian State Guard, which lately had allied themselves with Mihailović. On October 6 the command of the Serbian State and Frontier Guards was given to General Damjanović, Nedić's *chef de cabinet,* by order of General Felber. Damjanović also happened to be Mihailović's principal confidant in the Nedić administration, and he and the Guards commanders promptly put themselves under Mihailović's command. These units, renamed the Serbian Shock Corps of the Yugoslav Army in the Homeland, thus joined the withdrawal toward Sandjak with the other Chetniks. Their alliance was an uneasy one, however, and as will be shown in the following chapter, soon fell apart.[82]

During the last weeks of the German presence in Serbia the German commanders and political and police authorities were analyzing the

[80] Microcopy No. T-311, Roll 189, Frames 1025, 1030.
[81] For the order of the Supreme Command of Oct. 25 see *ibid.,* Frames 1106, 1139.
[82] Microcopy No. T-501, Roll 256, Frame 871; *ibid.,* Roll 257, Frame 187. A good description of the Chetniks-Guardists relationship from the beginning of October 1944 in Serbia to their separation at the beginning of January 1945 in northeastern Bosnia and the ultimate fate of the Guards is Solarić's "The Other Side of the 'Bosnian Golgotha.'"

performance of the Chetniks against the Partisans, and as German allies, and to what extent they might still be useful in the future. At a conference on October 8 attended by the Commander in Chief in Southeast Europe Field Marshal von Weichs, General Hermann Behrends, the Higher SS and Police Leader in Serbia, Envoy Neubacher, and the SS Commander in Croatia General Kammerhofer, it was decided that the Germans would use any group—Chetniks included—that continued to fight against the Communists; possibly the Chetniks could be used as vanguard against the Partisans in areas through which the German forces were withdrawing. Two additional points were discussed. One was the political problem that would arise with the Croatian government when the Serbian Chetniks moved, as they were expected to do, into its territory. It was first decided that the Commander in Chief in Southeast Europe would inform the Armed Forces High Command and Envoy Neubacher would inform the Foreign Ministry about the expected difficulties, implying that these top Reich authorities would take up the matter with the Croatian government; later this idea was given up, because it was thought that if and when the German-Russian military operations moved to the territory of the Croatian state the Chetnik problem would have only minor and purely military significance and could be handled easily by the Commander in Chief in Southeast Europe himself.[83] The second problem was to find a more effective technique for further control over and command of the Chetniks. Since sometime in August, the Chetniks in northwestern Serbia had been under the command of German Colonel von Jungenfeld and those in northeastern and eastern Serbia under General Artur Müller, who had under him both the 1st Mountain Division and the 7th SS Prinz Eugen Division and smaller units grouped around these two divisions. Von Weichs was of the opinion that the Higher SS and Police Leader in Serbia (Behrends) was the most suitable person for this function; the minutes of the meeting state that "In conclusion General Behrends remarked that he had already included [*eingebaut*] sufficiently strong *Sicherheitsdienst*-Commandos in the Chetnik [units] which will remain with the Chetniks. Thereupon the Commander in Chief stated that this fact alone ensures further direction of the Chetnik formations by the Higher SS and Police Leader."[84] Who these SD Commandos were and how they were recruited is not clear, nor is it clear whether General Mihailović and the Chetnik commanders were aware of their presence and their function in the Chetnik units. These detachments may have helped in keeping the Chetniks in line as long as the Germans were strong in Serbia and could enforce their policies in regard to various Chetnik com-

[83] Microcopy No. T-311, Roll 194, Frames 45–47.
[84] *Ibid.*, Frame 46. Behrends had replaced Meyszner in the spring of 1944.

manders. But the necessity of making large and rapid shifts in their forces to meet the danger from the Russians led to a breakdown in the mechanism of the German control over the Chetniks,[85] and the Germans were unable to keep several important Chetnik commanders, such as Keserović and Raković, from trying to reach an accommodation with the Russians after they pushed deep into Serbia. Neither is it known whether these *Sicherheitsdienst* Commandos remained attached to the Chetnik units after they withdrew from Serbia. Unlike some of the Bosnian, Herzegovinian, and Sandjak Chetniks, however, and even some Chetniks in Montenegro, who engaged in sporadic clashes with the Germans, the Serbian Chetniks (aside from Keserović and Raković and, very briefly, Račić) never took up arms against the Germans during the remaining months of the war but, on the contrary, continued to maintain contacts with them, occasionally fought with them against the Partisans, and received from them at least some arms and ammunition.

For reasons of his own, General Mihailović in dispatches sent to his representatives abroad in the autumn of 1944 did not mention the Chetnik rout in Serbia. The following spring, in a communication to Fotić dated April 14, 1945, but dealing mostly with the events in Serbia the previous September and October, he offered his own interpretation of the withdrawal:

> In order to avoid the inevitable collision with Soviet troops, to which we would have inevitably come because of such actions [he had previously reported their unfriendly treatment of Chetnik troops and the disarming of some of them by the Soviet forces], the Supreme Command of the Yugoslav Army in the Homeland ordered the withdrawal of the fighting units from Serbia, and this alone made it possible for the Partisans to impose their rule in Serbia after the withdrawal of the occupying forces from the land.[86]

Even at that late date, Mihailović was not willing to admit to his friends abroad what really happened, fearing perhaps that such knowledge might still further impair their effectiveness with the British and American authorities, and with the general public, in generating support for the Chetnik cause.

One cannot be certain to what extent Mihailović, though still commander in chief, exerted direct control over Chetnik forces in Serbia opposing the Partisan attack at the beginning of September. His near capture by the Partisans on September 11 and ensuing separation from the main body of his troops in Serbia, and his withdrawal to Bosnia at a time when other Chetnik commanders and their troops were still in Serbia fighting for survival, hardly improved his stature or lifted the morale of his troops. There is indeed abundant evidence that confidence

---

[85] *Ibid.*, Frame 562.
[86] Jovan Djonović, "The Reports of General Mihailović from the End of 1943 and 1944," p. 76.

between Mihailović and his commanders was seriously undermined and that there was much disappointment on both sides.[87] But it was a combination of setbacks that forced Mihailović and his Chetniks out of Serbia: the defeats at the hands of the Partisans, the disarming of some of the Chetniks by the Russians and the impossibility of establishing a modus vivendi with them, and the defeats of the Germans in Serbia and their consequent inability to aid the Chetniks. A revealing statement on the Chetnik situation in Serbia at that time is contained in a German intelligence report of October 19, 1944:

> The feeling of inferiority on the part of the Chetniks was obviously increased by the military successes of Tito and his capable moves in foreign political matters. In the present conditions Tito must really appear to the Serbs as the mainstay of Yugoslav unity. Under these conditions, Tito, who always has been politically adroit especially on the lower levels of the administration, and has consciously played down Communist slogans, has undoubtedly acquired many new followers also in Serbia. The numerical shrinkage of the Chetnik forces which are still in Serbia is therefore a result not only of the undoubtedly heavy losses in the fight with the Tito Partisans during the last weeks, but also of a growing desertion movement. But precise figures in this regard are not available.[88]

By the end of October practically all the Chetnik units that had managed to extricate themselves were on their way toward Sandjak. The only exception was the units of Captain Raković, which for a period of two weeks or so had cooperated with the Russians and fought the Germans in the area of Čačak. But after considering the Russian ultimatum to lay down their arms or shift to the command of Marshal Tito, by mid-November these units had also decided to move toward Sandjak.[89]

The loss of Serbia was irreparable, for the Chetnik movement and for Mihailović personally. Serbia was the place where, under Mihailović's leadership, the Chetniks had originally started as an organized, armed group with grandiose expectations; where, in the autumn of 1941, they were reorganized as the official army of the government-in-exile and acquired the enthusiastic support of the British, with the ensuing rise of Mihailović as a world figure; where they first formulated their military and political strategy toward the occupation powers and quisling regimes and toward their rivals the Partisans; where they had their

---

[87] See especially Mihailović's statements at his trial, particularly with regard to Major Račić and Captain Neško Nedić. *The Trial of Draža Mihailović*, pp. 252, 258–59. See also Banović and Stepanović, in *Politika*, Aug. 8 and 9, 1962.

[88] Microcopy No. T-311, Roll 194, Frame 563. The phrase "capable moves in foreign political matters" is undoubtedly an allusion to Tito's agreement with the Soviet Command regarding the entry of Soviet forces into Yugoslav territory for operations against the Germans, an agreement which the Partisans interpreted as the first formal recognition of their regime by one of the Great Allies. The Partisan leadership hoped that this recognition by the Soviet Union would help them to resist British pressure for permission to land troops on the Yugoslav coast, at least to the extent of making the British ask their permission first. See e.g. Čolaković, *Zapisi iz oslobodilačkog rata*, V, 302.

[89] Microcopy No. T-311, Roll 189, Frames 1116, 1201–11, 1303–4.

strongest political organization and, in fact, after the middle of 1943 had organized and maintained a sort of shadow government under the occupation regime;[90] where they had their main forces in August 1944; and where, even in the summer of 1944, they still had the overwhelming support of the people.[91]

But the Serbian population, a people known for political shrewdness and perspicacity and strong anti-German attitude, were increasingly being drawn to the Partisan side, partly because of what the Partisans stood for and the way they fought and partly because they represented the only alternative. No doubt the Chetnik defeats in September and October 1944 convinced many more people in Serbia that the Partisans were the winning side. The Chetniks, it now seemed clear, were inferior to the Partisans in numbers, arms, leadership, connections with the Great Allies, and fighting ability. The difference between the two in regard to fighting ability was neatly summed up by General August Winter, Chief of Staff to the Commander in Chief in Southeast Europe, in a message to the Second Panzer Army dated October 2, 1944: "The DM formations, according to experience up to now, have never shown themselves as effective counterweights against Tito's forces."[92]

Curiously, neither Mihailović nor the commanders and the Chetnik troops in Serbia seem to have realized the magnitude and implications of their defeat. In moving toward Sandjak they apparently believed that they were moving in the direction in which they would, in time, meet the Western Allied troops coming from the landing beaches on the Dalmatian or Montenegrin coast and would return with them victoriously to Serbia. Such a landing never, of course, materialized, and the exodus from Serbia was in fact the first phase on the Chetnik road to complete destruction.

LUKAČEVIĆ SPLITS OFF FROM MIHAILOVIĆ

The ouster of the Purić cabinet in May 1944 and with it the removal of General Mihailović from the post of Minister of the Army, Navy, and Air Force was bound to have an effect on the future military conduct and alignments of Chetnik forces outside Serbia that were not directly concerned in the coming battle for the main Chetnik stronghold. Major

---

[90] The German military authorities recognized in some of their reports that Mihailović's Chetniks were maintaining what in effect amounted to a shadow government in Serbia. See e.g. the report of the Chief of Staff of the Commander in Chief in Southeast Europe, General Winter, of July 5, 1944, in *ibid.*, Roll 195, Frames 788–91; and the comments of the former Chief of Staff of the Military Commander in Serbia, General von Geidtner, of March 1945, on the Concluding Report on the German Military Administration in Serbia in Microcopy No. T-501, Roll 260, Frame 424.

[91] A German intelligence report of July 11, 1944, said that the Chetniks in Serbia were backed by about 90 percent of the population; the same figure was used by von Weichs in his report to Hitler on August 22, 1944. In October 1944 Captain Raković claimed in his conversations with Soviet commanders in Serbia that the Chetniks had 80 percent of the Serbian people behind them. See Microcopy No. T-311, Roll 195, Frames 733, 961, and Roll 189, Frame 1237.

[92] *Ibid.*, Roll 194, Frame 149.

Lukačević, commander of the Chetnik forces in Sandjak, Lt. Colonel Ostojić, commander of the Chetnik forces in eastern Bosnia, Lt. Colonel Baćović, commander of the Chetnik forces in Herzegovina, as well as Lt. Colonel Pavle Novaković and Captain Krivošić made attempts on their own to get in touch by radio with the Allied forces in Italy. When these efforts failed, they addressed on August 12 a letter to Brigadier Maclean, the chief of the British military mission with the Partisans, requesting that they be put in contact with the Supreme Allied Commander in the Mediterranean for the purpose of reaching an understanding on the common fight against the enemy. Specifically, they were asking for a temporary nonaggression pact to be concluded between them and the Yugoslav Army of National Liberation until their arrangements with the Allied Supreme Command had been made. They asked that a copy of their letter be sent to King Peter and that they be put in contact with the Yugoslav government-in-exile.

After due consideration, British authorities in Italy informed Marshal Tito of the proposal. Tito did not reject the Chetnik proposal, but he insisted that the Chetnik commanders would have to come under his command and that they should initiate direct talks with the commander of the Partisan First Corps.[93] It appears, however, that neither the British military authorities nor the Yugoslav government-in-exile sent an answer to Lukačević's letter, or if the British did answer, that the answer was noncommittal. In the first days of September Lukačević, Ostojić, and Baćović apparently agreed to issue a proclamation to the people explaining the reasons why they planned to begin an active fight against the enemy. It seems that Lukačević alone composed the proclamation and issued it in the name of all three commanders, only to find that Ostojić and Baćović had had second thoughts and reneged on their agreement, although it appears that at least Baćović directed some of his troops to join Lukačević.[94]

For Lukačević the die was cast. He decided to go ahead even without an arrangement with the British or contact with the Yugoslav government-in-exile or a temporary truce with the Partisans, and without the support of Ostojić and Baćović. He ordered the troops under his command, numbering about 4,500, toward southern Herzegovina, and on September 22 attacked the units of the German 369th Infantry Division (Croatian legionnaires). He took some localities and captured a few

[93] A series of British documents dealing with this matter, including a copy of the Chetnik commanders' letter, can be found under number F.O. 371/44262, R13201/8/92. On September 24, 1944, Captain Krivošić reached Bari with a group of companions in a small boat. He was interrogated by Allied military authorities and pleaded for help for the Lukačević group, but his mission remained without any practical results. See F.O. 371/44280, R18689/11/92.

[94] A full discussion of Lukačević's attempt to act independently is contained in an article by Pajović, "The Formation of the Chetnik Independent Group of National Resistance." One of the special sources of information used by Pajović was the transcripts of interrogation of Lukačević by the Partisan police authorities after his capture, although, as Pajović says, the source had to be used with reserve since Lukačević tried to defend himself rather than tell the truth.

hundred prisoners.[95] Mihailović, lost no time in stripping Lukačević of his command, and he asked his other commanders to suppress Lukačević's activity.[96] But the Partisans, suspecting that Lukačević might be trying to establish a strong foothold in southern Herzegovina and on the coast in order to be in a position to get in touch with the hoped-for British expeditionary forces, decided that they must attack. Any such linkage between Lukačević and the British—whom the Partisans, despite close cooperation, still did not fully trust—could mean unpleasant political and military difficulties for the Partisans. The Partisans attacked Lukačević's forces on September 25 from the interior, and within a few days took the Chetnik stronghold of Bileća and then advanced toward southern Herzegovina where they roundly defeated Lukačević's forces. Lukačević, with the few hundred battered troops that still remained to him, withdrew first toward the interior of Herzegovina, and finally into the area of Foča in southeastern Bosnia.[97]

In the last days of October, following an agreement with Tito, some detachments of British troops landed in the Dubrovnik area and were soon afterward deployed in Montenegro with the Partisans against the German XXIst Mountain Corps which was withdrawing from Albania and parts of Montenegro. Early in December one of the British units penetrated deep into Herzegovina and reached the town of Bileća. Lukačević's opportunity to contact the British had come at last, but his attempt to do so failed, and Lukačević himself was taken prisoner by the Partisans.[98]

Baćović and Ostojić not only took no part in Lukačević's action against the Germans in September but made no attempt to contact the British forces at Dubrovnik and elsewhere. They made a few ineffectual gestures toward getting out of the hopeless situation in which they, like Chetnik commanders everywhere, found themselves at this time but in the end stayed where they were.[99]

All semblance of unity among the Chetnik forces, which had never

[95] *Ibid.*, pp. 62–64, 67–68.

[96] *Ibid.*, pp. 60–62; Microcopy No. T-311, Roll 189, Frame 1137. A German intelligence report of Oct. 2, 1944, using what it called a reliable source, said "Draža Mihailović expressly disapproves the hostile attitude of these Chetniks against the Germans." See Microcopy No. T-311, Roll 194, Frames 105–6.

[97] Microcopy No. T-311, Roll 189, Frames 1139, 1305.

[98] Pajović, "The Formation of the Chetnik Independent Group of National Resistance," p. 70. Lukačević was tried along with a group of other Chetnik military and political leaders by the Superior Military Court in Belgrade between July 28 and August 9, 1945, and found guilty of being one of the leading military commanders of the Chetnik movement, of conducting military operations against the National Liberation Army, of collaborating with the enemy, and of various other war crimes. He was sentenced to death and was executed on August 14, 1945. See *Sudjenje članovima rukovodstva organizacije Draže Mihailovića*, pp. 25–27, 136–38, 549–51, 562–64.

[99] According to Lt. Lalich, the chief of the air crew rescue unit with the Chetniks, Baćović told Mihailović that he had been called to Bari by General Masterson (of the SOE), but Lalich checked with Bari and found Baćović's assertion to be false. Baćović, also according to Lalich, wanted to stow away on one of the flights of the air crew rescue unit. Lalich also reported that Lt. Colonel Ostojić wanted to establish direct contact with the British in Italy and even gave Lalich a special code for that purpose, but after a few days changed his mind and withdrew it. RG 226, OSS–File No. XL5727, p. 6.

been remarkable for their unity, was fast disappearing, and the commanders tended to act more and more on their own as circumstances and their own judgment dictated. Some troops, notably those under Djujić and Jevdjević as well as a large part of the forces in eastern Bosnia, continued to collaborate with the Germans against the Partisans. Others merely waited, kept on the move mostly in eastern Bosnia, uncertain what to do or what to expect next. The fissures that appeared within the commanding cadres continued to widen under the stress of one discouraging development after another. Only Mihailović, it seems, still believed that in the end salvation would come from the West. He clung to this belief partly because of his conviction that there would have to be a falling out between the Western Allies and the Soviet Union in the final stages of the war when their opposing long-term political objectives and interests collided, and partly because of the counsel given him by Colonel McDowell, who remained at Chetnik headquarters until November 1. In the meantime he knew that he must hold on to as much as he could of the territory still under Chetnik control. It was for that reason that he ordered a withdrawal to northeastern Bosnia, an area where the Chetniks were still quite strong and where the food supply was relatively abundant—an important consideration with another winter approaching. But the worst was yet to come, as events reached their resolution in the months of March, April, and May, 1945.

CHAPTER TWELVE

The Final Months

Mihailović's position as the autumn of 1944 drew to a close was very serious indeed. He and a few of his troops had made a hasty exit from Serbia, and now the last of his Serbian forces had withdrawn under orders to Sandjak. Sandjak was a good place to be in that it was centrally located for shifts in several directions, but for other reasons it was most unsuitable as a stopping place. For one thing, the Chetniks had been withdrawing along with or on the flanks of German forces, some from Serbia and some en route from Greece, Albania, and Montenegro, and after the Germans had moved on the Chetniks would be extremely vulnerable to attacks from the Partisans. Moreover, Allied bombers were making frequent attacks on the towns along the important communication lines leading through Sandjak, and although their targets were the withdrawing German troops, Chetnik troops were also being hit. Mihailović issued orders that the larger towns should be avoided, but according to an agreement that had been concluded recently with the Germans, the Chetniks were supposed to assist the withdrawing German troops until they reached Sarajevo.

Another consideration of great importance was the approach of winter and the problem of provisioning the Chetnik troops. Sandjak was a food-deficit area. Montenegro, to which Lt. Colonel Djurišić had invited the Serbian Chetniks, was even more so. Northeastern Bosnia, on the other hand, was a fertile area, which presumably could provide food for the Chetniks. Mihailović testified at his trial that provisioning was an important consideration when he issued orders for his troops to move from Sandjak toward northeastern Bosnia.[1]

As we have seen, it had been strongly suggested to Mihailović by his representative in Cairo, Mladen Žujović, that he concentrate his troops in one or two areas considered safe and then hold them there while awaiting the expected shift in Western Allied policy in favor of the

---

[1] *The Trial of Draža Mihailović*, pp. 260–61.

Chetniks, a change supposedly contingent to a large degree on the ability of the Chetniks to hold out in the interim. It would seem that Mihailović was also interested in concentrating his forces in northeastern and north-central Bosnia for purposes of easier control and probably also in order to have a large force at his disposal for whatever maneuvers he might wish to make later. Therefore, early in October, he also ordered the Chetnik forces under Major Vranješević, estimated at about ten thousand men, to move from northwestern Bosnia and the Vrbas River valley to north-central Bosnia, that is, to the valley of the Bosna River.[2] Later he ordered the Montenegrin Chetniks (the Montenegrin Volunteer Corps), under Djurišić's command, to join him in northeastern Bosnia.

Another reason apparently important to Mihailović in issuing orders for the concentration of all Chetniks in northeastern Bosnia was that the local Chetniks had good relations with the Germans and, to some extent, even with Croatian quisling forces. Mihailović would have had no wish to make trouble with the Germans at that stage but rather preferred to continue to cooperate with them in order to obtain arms and ammunition for use against the Partisans. It was in the German interest, too, to continue the cooperation, partly for the help they might get from the Chetniks against the Partisans, who were becoming increasingly dangerous to the Germans as they acquired strength, and partly for the Chetniks' help in maintaining control of the communication lines along the withdrawal route between Sarajevo and Bosanski Brod, paralleling most of the way the Bosna River. Nearly all the German troops withdrawn from Greece, Albania, Yugoslav Macedonia, and Montenegro during the autumn and winter of 1944–45, up until April, were funneled through the communications hub of Sarajevo and northward to Bosanski Brod.

Thus, during this period of waiting for the arrival of his troops in northeastern Bosnia, Mihailović maintained his contacts with the Germans, both indirectly through some of his commanders and sometimes directly, obtaining some arms and ammunition from them, and his units continued to fight the Partisans, either in combination with the Germans or independently. At the same time, however, he also pursued a second policy, that of trying to regain recognition by the Western Allies so that he could transfer his forces under their command, obtain their military and political support, and begin to fight the Germans.

FURTHER OVERTURES TO THE ALLIES

In a message of November 13, 1944, delivered through Dr. Živko Topalović, Mihailović's representative in Italy, to General Wilson, Su-

[2] Microcopy No. T-311, Roll 189, Frames 991, 1141.

preme Allied Commander Mediterranean, Mihailović offered to bring all his troops—which he claimed to be about 50,000 strong—under General Wilson's command, and expressed his willingness to undertake any task assigned to him in the Balkans or in any other theater of war. The timing of this appeal—coming less than two weeks after Colonel McDowell had left Chetnik headquarters for Italy—suggests that Mihailović, who had put great hopes in McDowell, was assuming that McDowell had successfully launched his plan for a change in Western Allied policy toward substantial aid to the Chetniks. Mihailović probably hoped to strengthen McDowell's effort by his own message. In this he was disappointed; but when very shortly thereafter Wilson was replaced by Field Marshal Harold Alexander, Mihailović was encouraged to try again. According to Topalović, Mihailović considered Alexander his friend. At Mihailović's orders Topalović sent a memorandum to Alexander on November 29, asking that Mihailović's troops—estimated in this letter at about 55,000 to 57,000 men—be put under Allied command and used for bottling up and annihilating some 40,000 German troops that were withdrawing from Greece and Albania and were massed in the area of Lake Scutari in northern Albania.[3] But Alexander, like his predecessor, did not even bother to acknowledge Mihailović's message. Under the now clear policy of the Great Allies which supported Tito and his Partisans, any form of cooperation with the Chetniks was quite out of the question. Only Mihailović seems to have persisted in the hope that this Allied policy would be reconsidered.

Under the existing conditions, the Allies were little interested in what happened to the German troops in the area of Lake Scutari. And in areas that counted, Mihailović was in no position to help. Alexander still nursed a vague hope of getting through the Po Valley and northern Italy rapidly enough to reach Vienna, by way of the Ljubljana Gap, ahead of the Russians.[4] But the German defenses in Italy were proving very tough, and help in Yugoslav territory once the Allied forces reached the Ljubljana Gap area could come only from Tito—not from Mihailović, the bulk of whose forces was in Sandjak and Montenegro, some 450 kilometers to the southeast.[5]

In view of the Chetniks' position, it is no wonder that Mihailović's optimism was beginning to waver. The utter failure of his appeals to Wilson and Alexander and McDowell's inability to produce any results in Washington seem to be reflected in a message from Mihailović of December 5, 1944, to his representatives abroad. "Among the people

[3] For the texts of Mihailović's appeals through Topalović to General Wilson and Field Marshal Alexander see Topalović, "The Last Attempt."

[4] Alexander, pp. 138, 151.

[5] Moreover, Mihailović himself had been told by General Trifunović, who was in command of the Serbian Chetniks who had moved to Sandjak: "These are fugitives, one can do nothing with them." *The Trial of Draža Mihailović*, p. 260.

there is a great fear that the Communists are going to acquire power in all Yugoslavia," the message said. "The only salvation is expected from the Americans and the British. However, their troops are not landing and this causes great depression among the people."[6] From Fotić in Washington came a reply (dated December 15, 1944) that was both discouraging and intended to encourage:

> In these difficult moments, the happiest solution for you and your courageous fighters would be to be placed under the Allied Command so that you could join them in the final struggle for the liberation of the fatherland. This, unfortunately, seems impossible of achievement. Therefore, I consider that it would be of decisive importance for you to remain in the country to adjust your activity to the circumstances, and that you avoid any conflict with the Russians. Your possible departure from the country would be immediately utilized to the limit by your enemies, who in their propaganda would represent your departure as proof of your treason. The Serbian people would feel that you deserted them and without you would remain leaderless, whereas your remaining in the country would represent the symbol of their unbreakable will to resist the imposed rule of the Partisans and their undesirable leaders. This would act as an incentive to the people to resist until the end for their right to make their own decisions about their existence and fate. It would be very useful if you could arrange that a group of intellectuals be pulled out of the country in order to help us in our activity among our friends.[7]

It is another of the numerous ironies of the Second World War in Yugoslavia that Fotić, one of Mihailović's most devoted followers and after the ouster of the Purić cabinet the most important and most able representative of Mihailović and the Great Serbia forces abroad, was at that time, with the best of motives, advising Mihailović to do exactly what, surreptitiously, and of course for quite different motives, Tito's security forces began advising him to do a little later on—that is, remain in the country.

CONTINUED COLLABORATION WITH THE GERMANS

Undoubtedly, the Chetniks would have been extremely glad to have dropped their collaboration with the Germans if they could have made a satisfactory arrangement with the Western Allies, or even with the Russians. Since neither of these options was open, collaboration with the Germans continued. Two Chetnik officers have been specifically identified as having maintained some contacts or having made arrangements with the Germans late in 1944: Colonel Gojko Borota, the commander of a Chetnik corps in the area of Sarajevo, and a Major Jevdjenijević from the Chetnik Supreme Command. Certain Chetnik units have been identified as having obtained ammunition from the Germans and others as having fought the Partisans under the orders of the Ger-

---

[6] Jovan Djonović, "The Reports of General Mihailović from the End of 1943 and 1944," p. 66.
[7] *Ibid.*, pp. 66–67.

mans. In the last weeks before the Germans withdrew from Yugoslavia altogether, other Chetnik-German contacts took place. In a radio message of October 13, 1944, intercepted by the German monitoring services, the Chetnik Area Command of East Bosnia informed Borota that its units were getting ammunition from the Germans.[8] Another German-intercepted message of the East Bosnia Area Command to the Supreme Command, dated October 28, stated that Colonel Borota, his ammunition reserves exhausted, had obtained permission to get in touch with the Germans and that the Germans had promised larger arms and ammunition deliveries if the Chetnik Supreme Command would send one of its delegates to arrange the conditions.[9] The Supreme Command followed this suggestion immediately; a report of the Command of the German Army Group F of November 3 stated that Major Jevdjenijević from the Chetnik Supreme Command had engaged in negotiations with the officers of Army Group F and that an agreement had been reached on the following points: (1) The Chetniks would accompany and help the German troops then withdrawing from Greece toward Sarajevo. (2) In the event that Yugoslavia was left to the Russians, the Chetniks would continue to march with the Germans. If, on the other hand, the Western Allies intervened in Yugoslavia, the Chetniks, who because of short supplies would depend on the Germans for supplies, promised not to move toward the coast but to remain in the area of Sarajevo and fight the Partisans. (3) Acceding to a German condition for the negotiations, the Chetniks promised the Germans that they would release all members of the German armed forces whom they held as prisoners. (These numbered 20 officers and about 300 noncommissioned officers and men, probably men belonging to the 369th Infantry Division captured by units of Major Lukačević in September 1944.) The report concludes by saying: "The command posts at Sarajevo will have to employ the utmost skill in negotiations and the strongest military pressure to prevent the veering away [*Abschwenken*] of Draža Mihailović."[10]

Several considerations seem to have prompted the German eagerness to make this agreement with the Chetniks. One of these was the recent anti-German activity of Chetnik forces under Keserović, Raković, and (to a very small extent) Račić in Serbia, who not only had briefly turned their arms against the Germans but had tried, though unsuccessfully, to arrive at some arrangement with the Soviet forces. Outside Serbia, other Chetnik commanders such as Lukačević had fought the Germans briefly in Herzegovina in September, and the Germans also knew from radio messages intercepted in October that Lukačević, and also Dju-

[8] Microcopy No. T-311, Roll 189, Frame 1033.
[9] *Ibid.*, Frame 1109; *The Trial of Draža Mihailović*, pp. 266–67, 280–81, 299–300.
[10] Microcopy No. T-311, Roll 196, Frames 264–65.

rišić in Montenegro, were urging the Chetniks to start fighting the Germans as a way of influencing "public opinion in England and the United States in favor of the Chetniks."[11] But since the Germans needed whatever help the Chetniks could give them against the Partisans, or, at the least, wanted to assure their neutrality until the forces of Army Group E withdrawing from Greece and forces from other areas of the Balkans had reached the area of Sarajevo, they were willing to pay the Chetniks to a limited extent in the form of arms and ammunition. At approximately the same time, the Germans dispatched their agent Stärker to see Mihailović, no doubt for the same objective—keeping Mihailović and his Chetniks from turning against the Germans.[12] Thus, because no other course was open to them, and because they were dependent upon them for military supplies, the Chetniks continued to collaborate with the Germans up until the first part of April 1945.

Other German sources besides those referring to intercepted messages among the Chetnik command posts provide information on German-Chetnik collaboration in Bosnia during the last months of 1944. A Situation Report on southeast Europe of October 26, 1944, states that the German 1st Mountain Division (which after the loss of Serbia had been moved to northeastern Bosnia, with its headquarters in Bijeljina) had established preliminary contacts with the Chetnik forces in the area.[13] On November 29 the German Battle Group Brčko reported (following some protests by the local Ustasha authorities) that up to that time it was delivering to the Chetniks only as much ammunition as they reasonably could use in combined operations (meaning, that is, against the Partisans).[14] A report of the *Einsatzgruppe* of the *Sicherheitspolizei* and of the SD in Croatia a month later said that the Chetnik groups that had withdrawn from Serbia by way of Sandjak were presently located mostly between the towns of Višegrad and Zvornik in eastern Bosnia and were fighting the local Communist bands, partly on their own and partly "by being put into action by the Wehrmacht." The same report (of December 28) said that Mihailović had given his approval for the use of Chetnik troops on the Serbian side of the Drina River, but that the problems of maintenance and supply with arms and ammunition presented great difficulties.[15] This very likely referred to commando groups that were being trained by the Chetniks—one of which included a Serb named Gašparović (known also as Gara), who was a Gestapo agent.[16] Most of the commandos were apprehended by the Communist

[11] *Ibid.*, Roll 189, Frame 1302.
[12] *The Trial of Draža Mihailović*, pp. 265–66.
[13] Microcopy No. T-501, Roll 257, Frame 235.
[14] *Ibid.*, Frame 1076.
[15] Microcopy o. T-311, Roll 196, Frame 491; see also *Oslobodilački rat.* II, 444–48.
[16] The Chetnik Supreme Command was at this time seriously thinking also about total reorganization of the Chetnik underground in Serbia. A long memorandum entitled "Project for

police soon after they crossed the Drina into Serbia, for the police used a supposed Chetnik radio station—of which more will be said below—in communicating with at least one group to "help" it plan the entry into Serbia. Only a few Chetnik commandos reached their destination, and they were later caught and killed. Among them was the former Chetnik commander of Belgrade, Saša Mihajlović.[17]

Even while trying to get back into the good graces of the Western Allies and carrying on intermittent collaboration with the Germans, Mihailović was busy planning operations of his own, and executing a few of them. One plan, which never materialized but was talked about from the end of September 1944 on for quite some time, was to use the local Chetnik forces in northeastern Bosnia, under Mihailović's direct command, to win that area from the units of the Partisan 3rd Corps.[18] Another plan, which was attempted, was to take the principal town in northeastern Bosnia, Tuzla, which in mid-September 1944 had been captured by the Partisans from Croatian quisling forces. For this operation, undertaken in the last days of December, the Chetniks also used the First Serbian Shock Corps (the former Serbian State and Frontier Guards), which had come under Chetnik command at the beginning of October. The capture of Tuzla would have ensured the Chetniks of food, salt, ammunition, and housing for the winter months, and, no less important, would have been a great psychological boost for the demoralized troops and could have paid propaganda dividends both at home and in the West.[19] The attack failed, and the failure was followed by mutual accusations between the Chetnik regulars and the former Guardists, each side blaming the other for not having fought well.[20]

As a result of this quarrel, the Guardists left the Chetniks and returned to the Germans. By January 10, 1945, about 3,000 of them were already at Slavonski Brod awaiting transportation, and another 2,000 followed less than a week later.[21] The Germans transported most of them to Austria and put them to work as labor battalions assigned to Organization Todt. But since the Germans also needed auxiliary forces, they allowed some scores of officers and about 1,500 men from these formations to shift to the Ljubljana Gap area, where they were free to join either the Serbian Volunteer Corps or the Chetnik units of Djujić and Jevdjević.[22] It appears that Mihailović, who later described the

Action in Serbia" (undated, but apparently written in November 1944) gives interesting details. See Archives of the Institute of Military History, Belgrade, Chetnik Documents, Reg. No. 11/2–1, Box 11. The pressure of more immediate problems made it impossible even to attempt the implementation of these plans.

[17] *The Trial of Draža Mihailović*, pp. 270–82; Banović and Stepanović, in *Politica*, Aug. 20–22, 1962. See also *Sudjenje članovima rukovodstva organizacije Draže Mihailovića*, pp. 246–49.

[18] Microcopy No. T-311, Roll 189, Frames 931, 1141.

[19] *Oslobodilački rat*, II, 448–50; Banović and Stepanović, in *Politika*, Aug. 16, 1962.

[20] Solarić, pp. 32–35.

[21] *Ibid.*, pp. 35–38; Microcopy No. T-501, Roll 266, Frames 537, 575.

[22] Karapandžić, pp. 400–401.

units formed from the State Guards as the "worst troops in the world," was not sorry to see them leave.[23] According to Communist sources, Mihailović was very depressed by the defeat at Tuzla, which aggravated the tensions within the Chetnik military and political leadership, and it apparently had the effect of making him more receptive to some of the plans that the Partisan security services were hatching for dealing with him and his troops.[24]

Despite the hopelessness of his military and political position, Mihailović spent some time in January 1945 drafting a plan for the reorganization of the Yugoslav Army in the Homeland along the lines of a plan that he had first worked out early in 1939 (and submitted to his army superiors), by which there would be separate national armies united under a single command as the Yugoslav Army. This new plan (which existed mainly on paper, or at best only in the naming of small staffs) called for the organization of separate Croatian and Slovene armies and a group of Moslem corps. The commanders were designated by nationally symbolic names: "General Gubec" for the Croatian army, "General Andrej" for the Slovene army, and "General Djerdjelez" for the Moslem corps. "General Gubec" was in reality Colonel Matija Parac, a Croat, suited for the position by reason of nationality but not, it seems, particularly by reason of any earlier distinction either in the Yugoslav military establishment or during his short stint with Mihailović's Chetniks. "General Andrej" was in reality Colonel Ivan Prezelj, commander of the few Chetniks who still remained in Slovenia. Both Parac and Prezelj were promoted to the rank of general, but they were generals without troops.[25] It seems, however, that the commander of the Slovene Domobrans, General Leon Rupnik, who after the Axis invasion had collaborated first with the Italians and then with the Germans, was willing to put his forces, numbering ten to twelve thousand, under Prezelj's command in case the Western Allies entered Slovene territory.[26] "General Djerdjelez" I have not been able to identify, and perhaps no one was ever selected for the job, since the Chetniks in January 1945 seem to have had only one Moslem corps in all of northeastern Bosnia, in the Majevica Mountain area.[27] Mihailović's Moslem corps, just as the Croatian and Slovene armies, was but a vision and a dream.

[23] The Trial of Draža Mihailović, p. 262.

[24] Banović and Stepanović, in Politika, Aug. 16 and 17, 1962.

[25] The staff and the few troops that Parac had were those Croats who earlier served in the Serbian Volunteer Corps and whom Ljotić shifted to Parac. Karapandžić, pp. 235–36; Kostić, p. 240. Kostić (p. 216) says that Parac and his forces were fully armed and supplied by Ljotić's Serbian Volunteer Corps. (The latter were, of course, completely maintained by the German SS forces.)

[26] Karapandžić, pp. 402–3.

[27] Microcopy No. T-501, Roll 266, Frames 554–55.

COMMUNIST PLANS TO TRAP MIHAILOVIĆ

While Mihailović was thus occupied, and while his Chetnik forces were growing steadily weaker both in fighting strength and in fighting spirit because of poor food supply and lack of housing, typhus and other sickness, and internal dissension over what to do next in the hopeless situation, the Partisans maintained a certain amount of military pressure on Chetnik forces wherever they were located. They engaged in systematic propaganda campaigns designed to undercut Chetnik morale and the morale of other anti-Communist forces, repeatedly extending the dates of the amnesty and promising those who shifted to Partisan units that they would be allowed to keep their rank. And all the time they were devising ways of bringing about the final destruction of all their opponents. Mihailović was, of course, the special prize, and the plans for him and his Chetniks were not necessarily the same as those for other domestic anti-Communist forces. At a meeting held in Belgrade at the end of 1944, the directors of the security forces of Communist Yugoslavia had, it seems, decided literally to destroy all their internal enemies in the concluding stages of the war. In the last weeks of the war, the difficulties with the Western Allies, especially the British, over Istria and Trieste, and the danger that the anti-Communist forces, should they escape, might be used in the future against the new Yugoslavia, undoubtedly strengthened that resolve. Banović and Stepanović, writing in the already quoted series of articles on the capture of Mihailović, summarize the decisions this way:

Toward the end of December 1944, while the fiercest battles were being fought on the Srijem front, there was held in Belgrade a conference of the directors of OZNA from the entire country. At this conference, which was chaired by Aleksandar Ranković, as a member of the Supreme Headquarters of the National Liberation Army of Yugoslavia, the principal topic of discussion was the elaboration of a plan for further struggle against the quisling forces and their remnants in Yugoslavia. "The occupier is finished," said Aleksandar Ranković. "Today or tomorrow not one member of the armed forces of the occupying powers will remain on the territory of our country. Peace is very near, but for the officers of OZNA there remains the difficult and persistent struggle against domestic traitors. In this struggle, we are going to have, as we have had up to now, the unstinting aid of our people, the people's government, our army, and especially of the Corps of National Defense, and the People's Militia."

One part of the renegade bands, it was stressed by Ranković, would try to reach the frontiers and foreign territory. From there in different ways they would act against Yugoslavia, while the other part would try to remain in the country, where they would attempt by other means to hinder its development. The bands in the country must be broken up and destroyed in armed actions, he said.

On the other hand, in the quisling units that were withdrawing [toward the frontiers] there were also many innocent people, who were mobilized or misled, who actually should not be fleeing from their homeland to flounder or to languish elsewhere in the world; nor should they be called upon to answer for their wartime aberrations. But as for the criminals, whether they were made prisoners in the concluding operations, on the roads of their withdrawal, or after the war, they would receive the treatment they deserved.

The discussion about the withdrawal of the quisling units in general showed that some of them were withdrawing with the Germans and that it would be impossible to hold them back. Among the larger groups, which remained within the reach of the army and OZNA, were also the Chetniks of Draža Mihailović. About the liquidation of the Chetnik units a special discussion was held.[28]

The decision to destroy all domestic enemies of the Communists made in December 1944 by Ranković and the directors of the security services is one of those things that the Yugoslavs do not write about. Politically, it was one of the most important decisions of the entire war period, and it cost a great deal of blood. It is hardly likely that it was a decision made by the security forces on their own: a decision of such magnitude must have been arrived at in consultation with the Party-Army leadership—that is, with Tito and other top leaders. Probably what happened was that when Ranković went to the meeting of the OZNA directors, he had prior instructions from the top Party-Army leadership and transmitted them to the lower echelons. Svetozar Vukmanović Tempo, who was the top political officer, or political commissar, of the CPY in the Yugoslav army from October 1944 until 1952, does not discuss these matters in his memoirs published in 1971.[29]

But however vague the circumstances of the decision, the results are amply attested to: on the specific measures employed in carrying out this policy of destroying internal enemies—in this case General Mihailović and his Chetniks—there exists a large body of evidence from which we can draw a fairly complete picture of the whole process.

Although the Partisans had soundly defeated the Chetniks when they tried to take Tuzla from them in the last week of December, it appears that they were unable and unwilling to launch an all-out drive against the Chetniks at the beginning of 1945. This was due in part to the fact that the bulk of the Partisan forces were engaged in fighting elsewhere against the withdrawing Germans, mainly on the Srijem front and in Herzegovina and southeastern Bosnia, but also they were cautious about undertaking operations in the area of Sarajevo and

---

[28] Banović and Stepanović, in *Politika*, Aug. 5, 1962. OZNA stands for *Odjeljenje za zaštitu naroda*, or Department for the Protection of the People, the name then applied to the Yugoslav police.

[29] He does briefly mention that his brother Luka, an Orthodox priest and ideological adversary of the Communists, was caught with some other Djurišić men in Slovenia, and that he was informed of it but did not want to do anything about it. Shortly after that Luka was shot. The destruction by Yugoslav forces of a large part of the Croatian quisling army in May 1945, along with some thousands of civilian refugees, is a matter about which the Yugoslav government and historians prefer to remain silent. This will be fully discussed in a later volume.

along the Bosna River toward Bosanski Brod, where strong German forces guarding the withdrawal of their troops from the Balkans also served as a protection for the Chetniks. In addition, the Partisans seem to have wanted to lull the Chetniks into a feeling of relative security and to keep them in northeastern and north-central Bosnia. Therefore the Partisans worked out a long-range operation for dealing with Mihailović, at a time of their own choosing and at the least cost in blood and effort. The whole plan was calculated to take several months, and it had some of the qualities of fiction.

Toward the end of December the Yugoslav police began to set an ingenious trap for Mihailović. Instead of pushing him and his troops toward the frontier in Slovenia or contributing to his deciding to accept evacuation by air to the West, they would lure him into remaining somewhere in the center of the country. Then, in time, he could be destroyed, or captured alive to stand trial. The plan, which seems to have been under Ranković's direct supervision, was carefully conceived and developed, and as carefully implemented.

Late in December the Yugoslav militia entrapped in a village in western Serbia Captain Predrag Raković, one of the leading Chetnik commanders, who had remained in Serbia after the Chetnik withdrawal to Sandjak and eastern Bosnia, with a few of his men. By means of a trick, his men were induced to surrender, but Raković committed suicide. On his body the militia found the code and next to him the unit that he used in his radio communications with Mihailović. The security forces already had in their hands two former Chetnik radio operators, as well as a former Chetnik officer, Major Trifun Ćosić, and the police, using promises and pressure, persuaded one of the operators to establish radio contact with Mihailović. The operator pretended that the messages were coming from a small Chetnik unit under Major Ćosić, which was still at large and operating in Serbia. By this method, early in January 1945, the security services began sending Mihailović false information on general conditions in Serbia and what were said to be operations of a Chetnik group headed by Ćosić. Mihailović, who as an experienced intelligence officer was always suspicious of everyone, took pains to check his new contact, but in time he was convinced that he was communicating with a bona fide Chetnik group and radio station, and from then on the security forces were in control. The hook continued to hold until the German surrender, and even beyond. The whole ploy was designed to feed Mihailović bogus information suggesting, in increasingly encouraging terms, that there was a strong underground swell against the new Communist regime in Serbia. Major Ćosić's supposed Chetnik unit was described as being engaged in small operations against the Partisan militia and in sabotaging the lines of communications; many soldiers from Partisan units were said to be deserting and joining the Chetniks. There was, the broadcasts said, a real chance of organizing an anti-Communist revolt in Serbia, because the new regime's mistakes and acts of terror had strengthened the old hostilities and had created many new enemies, but the Chetnik forces, in order to suceed, were in need of strong and experienced leadership. In return, Mihailović gave "Major Ćosić" various points of advice, and several other Chetnik military leaders also sent messages to Serbia by the same radio connection.[30] In view of later developments, it is clear that between January and mid-April of 1945, these messages from Serbia turned out to be of great importance in influencing Mihailović's decisions.[31]

RETURN TO SERBIA OR GO TO SLOVENIA?

Around the middle of January, Mihailović and his troops had moved from the Majevica Mountain area northwest to the area of Trebava Mountain. There they remained for about two months—joined in the latter part of February by some seven to eight thousand Chetniks of the Montenegrin Volunteer Corps, accompanied by about three thousand civilian refugees, all under the command of Lt. Colonel Pavle Djurišić.[32] The Montenegrin Volunteer Corps, as explained in the previous chapter, was the special military formation established as an instrument of Neubacher's policy for combating the Partisans in Sandjak and Montenegro, and it was fully in German service. But it also owed allegiance to Mihailović, as evidenced by the fact that Djurišić, who would much have preferred to withdraw through Albania to Greece, followed Mihailović's orders to join him in northeastern Bosnia. The Djurišić Chetniks had, of course, withdrawn from Montenegro intermixed with or closely following the withdrawing German troops.[33] According to Yugoslav Communist sources, the Montenegrin Chetniks were better outfitted and better trained than any other Chetnik troops, and had absolute and first allegiance to their leader, Djurišić.[34] As soon as he joined Mihailović, Djurišić realized that he had made a serious mistake, for the General had no solution whatsoever for the Chetnik predicament.

[30] For this story see Banović and Stepanović, in *Politika*, Aug. 5, 16, 21, 22, 1962.

[31] The supposed information received by Mihailović in these messages is reflected in his communications to his representatives abroad and to Ljotić. See e.g. his message of March 21, 1945, to his representatives abroad in Jovan Djonović, "The Reports of General Mihailović from the End of 1943 and 1944," p. 71, and his messages to Ljotić of April 1 and 11 in Kostić, pp. 237–39.

[32] Cemović, p. 55. Banović and Stepanović, in *Politika*, Aug. 18, 1962, give the figure of about 7,000 for refugees, but the figure of 3,000 as given by Cemović, one of the survivors of the Djurišić group, seems to me more realistic.

[33] The crew of an American bomber who bailed out over Djurišić-controlled territory in Montenegro made the trek into eastern Bosnia with the Djurišić forces and accompanying refugees. They later separated from them and established contact with the Partisans, who took them to Belgrade, from where they were subsequently evacuated. The experience is described by Major James M. Inks, one of the participants, in an account (in diary form) published in 1954; see the Bibliography.

[34] Banović and Stepanović, in *Politika*, Aug. 19 and 22, 1962. In a message of April 8, 1945, to Ljotić, Mihailović said that these troops were of "low fighting quality"—but this was after Djurišić had left Mihailović. See Karapandžić, p. 414.

Whereas he might have had a chance to save his troops by going through Albania to Greece or, alternatively, following Djujić's and Jevdjević's example and taking the coastal route up to the Ljubljana Gap, he was stuck with a commander who seemed bent on returning to Serbia.[35]

Sometime in the middle of March these various Chetnik forces of General Mihailović moved across the Bosna River to the area of Vučjak Mountain (see Map 7). In all these moves, the Chetniks reacted to two basic considerations: the actual and potential operations of the Partisans, and the moves of the German forces, who, still in firm control of the area encompassing the communication line between Sarajevo and Bosanski Brod, thus continued to serve as a protection for the Chetniks against the Partisans.[36]

Even in this situation, Mihailović still held on to his belief that salvation would come from the West.[37] But as the days passed and such aid did not materialize, Mihailović knew that he had to come to some decision about his next move. Each day, the Chetnik position in north-central Bosnia was becoming more untenable. Two possibilities were open to Mihailović.

One was to try to return to Serbia, the terrain that the Chetniks believed to be still friendly to them, where, so they were being led to think, there was a chance to start a new resistance to the Communist rule that had been established there in October 1944. Mihailović was the chief, and the most determined, proponent of this alternative. Obviously under the influence of the Ćosić messages, he had the idea that the population in Serbia was only awaiting the arrival of spring to rise en masse and that all he had to do was to return and give them leadership. But no matter how Mihailović may have interpreted the perspective of a popular uprising in support of the Chetnik cause or what hopes he may have had regarding Western intervention if the Chetniks should start an anti-Communist uprising, it was necessary first for the Chetnik forces to get back to Serbia.

The other alternative was to push to the west, to the area of the Ljubljana Gap, through the territory still held in part by German and Croatian puppet state forces and in part by Partisan forces. There they could join the Serbian quisling and Chetnik forces that were already in

[35] Since Djurišić's Montenegrin Volunteer Corps was formally a part of the Serbian Volunteer Corps, Ljotić had for some months been hoping to get Djurišić to move his forces to Slovenia. In September he called Parežanin to Belgrade from Pljevlja, where he was a liaison officer with Djurišić's forces, for the specific purpose of instructing him to persuade Djurišić to do just that. When Parežanin's efforts failed and Djurišić followed Mihailović's orders to go to eastern Bosnia, Parežanin left Djurišić at Prijepolje in Sandjak during the last days of December and, accompanied by a group of about thirty men that he brought with him from Serbia, went to Slovenia. See Parežanin, pp. 494–98. Kostić, p. 202, quoting from Parežanin's report on his mission to Montenegro, shows that Parežanin returned to Slovenia by way of Slavonski Brod, which means that he traveled by German- and Ustasha-controlled railroads.

[36] Banović and Stepanović, in *Politika*, Aug. 17 and 22, 1962.

[37] This is what Djurišić told Kostić at the time of his visit with the Chetniks in mid-March 1945. See Kostić, p. 231.

the area, and eventually, no doubt, make contact with American and British forces coming from Italy, or if that were not possible, with Allied troops moving into Austria through southern Germany. This course of action was particularly attractive inasmuch as Jevdjević's Chetnik detachments from Lika had been in the Ljubljana Gap area since the beginning of November, and Djujić's detachments from northern Dalmatia, western Bosnia, and southern Lika moved to the area early in January. These detachments, numbering together perhaps as many as eight or nine thousand men, joined the troops of the Serbian Volunteer Corps, whom the Germans had pulled out of Serbia in October and transported to that area for use against the Partisans. With these troops was also the Serbian fascist leader, Dimitrije Ljotić.[38] Furthermore, throughout Slovenia there were the Slovene Domobrans (the White Guards) under the leadership of General Rupnik, and also a few Slovene Chetniks under General Prezelj. Moreover, a portion of the Serbian State Guards shifted from Austria to the Ljubljana Gap and joined the Serbian Volunteer Corps, and a small number of other Chetniks and some released prisoners of war from Germany also came to this area. In all, these troops, according to pro-Ljotić sources, amounted to perhaps thirty-five thousand men.[39]

Although all these Serbian and Slovene quisling forces, as well as the Chetnik troops of Djujić and Jevdjević, still hoped to be accepted as allies by the Western Allied forces, they must have realized that their known collaboration with the enemy made their chances of such an eventuality very remote. Mihailović, on the other hand, despite his marred record, still had many friends and supporters in the West; certainly he was the only man who would probably be accepted as supreme commander of the motley assortment of Serbian and Slovene anti-Communist forces. The driving political force behind the schemes for the concentration of all Serbian and Slovene anti-Communist forces in the Ljubljana Gap area was Ljotić. It seems that Ljotić's efforts to induce Mihailović to move to Slovenia were first conveyed to him through Jevdjević and Djujić, who were in regular radio communication with Mihailović, and they culminated, as will presently be shown, in the sending of a special emissary to Mihailović in mid-March.

The details of events and decisions in the Chetnik camp in north-

[38] The movement of Djujić troops was arranged by a German-Croatian agreement. According to an order issued on December 21, 1944, by Pavelić to all military and concerned civilian authorities, Croatian troops in conjunction with German troops were to ensure "an orderly and unimpeded passage of the [Djujić] group." Archives of the Institute of Military History, Belgrade, Independent State of Croatia Documents, Reg. No. 48/1–2, Box 233a. Djujić had at the most about 6,000 troops (Microcopy No. T-501, Roll 266, Frame 524); Jevdjević seems to have had only about 3,000 men. Both Ljotić and Jevdjević were helpful in getting the Germans' permission to move the Djujić Chetniks to the Ljubljana Gap area. See Kostić, p. 185, and Karapandžić, pp. 396–99.

[39] Kostić, p. 211. This estimate seems to me to be too high by perhaps as much as 20 to 25 percent.

eastern and north-central Bosnia from January 1945 on, and especially from the beginning of March on, were not completely cleared up either at the trial of the political and military leaders of the Mihailović organization in 1945 or at Mihailović's trial in 1946. Certain documents and writings, however, are helpful in expanding the testimony given at these trials: the various German and Chetnik documents, the writings of several Chetnik survivors who succeeded in coming to the West, such as Milošević, Vučetić, and Cemović, the writings of such other Serbian exiles as Kostić, Karapandžić, and Topalović, and especially the already mentioned series of articles in the Belgrade *Politika* of August and September 1962 dealing with the capture of Mihailović. From the testimony at these trials and these other sources we can draw a fairly clear picture of the final period of the wartime Chetnik movement. The materials presented in the articles in *Politika*, though carefully screened by the Yugoslav security services, are undoubtedly based on the interrogations of Mihailović himself, of his political coworkers who were active with him in Bosnia (Stevan Moljević, Aleksandar Aksentijević, and Mustafa Mulalić), of such military commanders as Nikola Kalabić and Dragutin Keserović, and also on the reports of police officers who participated in the capture of Mihailović. According to my sources, the articles are essentially true.

Two important events occurred during March 1945 that profoundly affected the fate of the Chetniks: (1) the formation of the unified Yugoslav government in Belgrade on March 7, through the fusion of Tito's National Committee of Liberation of Yugoslavia and Šubašić's Yugoslav government-in-exile, and (2) the arrival at Chetnik headquarters of Boško N. Kostić, an emissary of Dimitrije Ljotić, to urge the Chetniks to join the anti-Communist Serbian and Slovene forces in the Ljubljana Gap.

Since the unified government, with Marshal Tito as Prime Minister and Minister of National Defense and Dr. Šubašić as Foreign Minister, had been formed in pursuance of the decisions of the Yalta Conference, and had been almost immediately recognized by the Big Three, the Partisans had acquired full domestic and international legitimacy. For most Chetniks, this must have ended all hope of regaining the favor of the Western Allies. Only Mihailović and a few of his commanders continued to believe that the Grand Alliance would crack and they would be rescued. Sometime in the early part of March, the members of the Central National Committee, who apparently realized that all was lost, held a meeting (probably their last official one) in the village of Kožuhe near the town of Doboj in north-central Bosnia. Mihailović turned down their invitation to attend, so the committee went to him with the suggestion that he end the collaboration with the Germans and try to reach some arrangements with the new Communist government whereby the Chetniks would start cooperating with the regime and their forces would join the National Liberation Army. Mihailović refused to consider either part of the suggestion: he would not end the collaboration because he was "using" the Germans to advantage, and he flatly rejected any idea of trying to work with the Communists and reproached the committee members for even suggesting such an idea. Instead, he proposed that the Chetniks should return to Serbia, where, he believed, the people awaited an opportune moment to rise against the Communist regime. If an uprising occurred, he argued, Western intervention would follow, and the Chetniks would gain the upper hand. Mihailović succeeded in persuading all but one member of the committee. The one exception was Mustafa Mulalić, the Moslem Vice-Chairman of the committee, who immediately after the meeting with Mihailović went to the nearest Partisan outpost and surrendered.[40]

The alternative proposed by Ljotić—moving to the Ljubljana Gap area—was still open, and in pursuance of his suggestion Ljotić arranged to send a mission to the Chetnik headquarters consisting of his confidant Boško Kostić, two officers representing the Chetnik commanders Djujić and Jevdjević, and General Matija Parac, whom Mihailović had made head of the "Croatian Army" within the Yugoslav Army in the Homeland. Clearance had to come from Envoy Neubacher, however, and because Neubacher was in favor of sending Mihailović the Chetnik liaison group in Vienna, in the persons of Milan Aćimović and Majors Ivan Pavlović and Jovan Navelić, in the end the only member of the entire Ljotić-designated delegation included was Kostić.[41]

The group arrived at Chetnik headquarters near Vučjak Mountain on March 15. Kostić brought Mihailović messages from Ljotić and from the Chetnik groups already in Slovenia, and he did all he could to persuade Mihailović to move with his troops to Slovenia in order to concentrate all Serbian and Slovene anti-Communist forces there. Ljotić shared Mihailović's belief that, sooner or later, there would have to be a parting of the ways between the Western Allies and the Russians and their new satellites, and he thought that if all the anti-Communist troops joined forces under Mihailović's command and then made contact with the Anglo-American forces that were supposed to come from northern Italy, they could launch a military campaign against the Partisans. With Allied support, the Mihailović forces could annihilate the

[40] Banović and Stepanović, in *Politika*, Aug. 19, 1962. Some weeks before this meeting, an American diplomat, after a fortnight in Belgrade, submitted to the State Department a report composed on the basis of unofficial contacts which contained also the following appraisal: "Draza's stock lowering unsavory reputation his associates and his own lack of political acumen and military strength. It is generally admitted Draza would have been worse than Tito." *FRUS 1945*, V, 1212.

[41] Kostić, pp. 206–7; Karapandžić, pp. 401–5.

Partisans and establish a Yugoslav government of their own choosing.[42]
This scheme was dependent, first of all, upon the willingness and ability
of General Mihailović and his Chetniks to fight their way from north-
central Bosnia to Slovenia. It also depended upon a break in the Allied-
Soviet alliance of such seriousness that the Allies actually would take
arms against the Soviet Union immediately after, or even before, the
final defeat of Germany, and at that time would accept the Chetniks
and other Serbian and Slovene anti-Communist forces as allies.

Nearly all the important Chetnik political and military staff in northeastern and north-central Bosnia found Ljotić's proposal to their liking.
Only Mihailović was definitely opposed to it.[43] To Kostić's argument
that by remaining in Bosnia the General and his troops, in the case of
sudden German collapse, might find themselves in a very difficult situation, Mihailović is reported to have replied: "I think that the Germans can hold out like this for another year. Therefore, I still have
time to come to you."[44] Unlike the politician Ljotić, who interpreted
the existing military situation quite realistically, both in its general and
in its specific Yugoslav aspects, it appears that Mihailović was completely
misreading, or ignoring, the situation in Yugoslavia and elsewhere. By
March 1945, the military position clearly showed that the days of the
German forces on all fronts were numbered. If Mihailović wanted to
save himself and his troops by going to Slovenia, he could not afford a
moment's delay. His gross miscalculation of the military situation in

---

[42] Kostić, pp. 211–12, 235, 241–43, quoting various messages of Ljotić to Mihailović and a proclamation of General Damjanović.

One curious plan of Mihailović's, mentioned as early as February 1943, was to have the Yugoslav prisoners of war in Germany and Italy (about 90 percent of them Serbs) organized at the end
of the war as a special army under his command. After being supplied and transported to the
western parts of Yugoslavia by the Western Allies, this army was to help Mihailović seal off the
Yugoslav borders in Slovenia and Croatia and then was to occupy areas populated by Croats and
Slovenes but still under foreign sovereignty (i.e. Istria, the Slovene Littoral, and parts of Carinthia) and also disarm and guard the Croatian quisling forces of Pavelić and the Partisans, while
the Chetnik forces were establishing the Chetnik regime in the country. Later on, the special force
would be absorbed by the Yugoslav Army in the Homeland. For the text of Mihailović's order of
Feb. 5, 1943, on the organization of this army see Topalović, "Unfulfilled Hopes." It seems that
during the last few months of the war the Germans tried to induce some of the Serbian prisoners
of war to join the Serbian Volunteer Corps located in the Ljubljana Gap area, but the pro-Mihailović officers in captivity urged these prisoners to refuse. Mihailović, when informed of this,
considered this attitude of the officers a mistake and on March 16, 1945, through Kostić he addressed
a message to the prisoners of war in Germany asking their support and help. Kostić, pp. 222–26.

[43] Ljotić and others must have assumed that Mihailović and his troops would be able to fight
their way through to the west, or have the good luck to move without being attacked. It was by
no means a realistic assumption. Passage through Partisan-controlled territories would have meant
bitter fighting, for Mihailović's capture was much desired by the Partisans. As for passage through
Croatian quisling territory, it is true that the passage of the Djujić and Jevdjević troops had been
easy, but some parts of Ljotić's Serbian Volunteer Corps withdrawing to the west and under German protection through Ustasha territory in October and November 1944 had run into serious
trouble, even though Ljotić's troops had never fought the Ustashas and had an excellent record as
a German-maintained military force. Some thirty or forty officers of a small contingent of these
troops passing through Zagreb were taken from the transport by the Ustashas and summarily executed. The Ustashas also killed a group of about 120 Chetnik soldiers, including some sick and
wounded, who were being transported westward through their territory and whom they caught in
Kostajnica on December 17, 1944. Kostić, pp. 186–89. These and some other shows of force are
pointed out by Ustasha General Luburić as expressions of the Ustasha independence of the Germans. See Luburić [General Drinjanin, pseud.], p. 21.

[44] Kostić, pp. 229–30.

his own vicinity is clear from these statements contained in a dispatch to Ljotić dated April 1, 1945: "For the present we do not see any moves of German withdrawal from Yugoslavia. On the contrary, they are now undertaking a very strong offensive against the Partisans in the areas of Sarajevo and Tuzla. We are even in a position to believe from certain signs and from this kind of action by the Germans in Yugoslavia, that they even might have some agreement with the Anglo-Saxons." The same message also said: "We expect that you will move with all your forces here" and "actions in our area are developing very favorably for us."[45] But the German actions that Mihailović was talking about were in fact only delaying actions to keep the Sarajevo communications hub open. Only five days after Mihailović's message, following unfavorable developments for the Germans in western Hungary and under increasing Partisan pressure but with the last troop transports successfully moved, the German and Croatian quisling troops pulled out of Sarajevo.[46]

DJURIŠIĆ'S ILL-FATED MOVE

From the time of his arrival in north-central Bosnia, Pavle Djurišić had been very critical of Mihailović's leadership, and he was the chief proponent of moving to Slovenia. Djurišić's firm hold over the Montenegrin Chetniks and good military record were respected by the other Chetnik commanders, and most of them agreed with him about moving to Slovenia. When Mihailović remained unconvinced, Djurišić decided that he would take his Montenegrin troops and leave. He implored Ljotić to help by sending some of his troops to meet him halfway, and this Ljotić willingly agreed to do; but Djurišić still had to reach the area of Bihać in western Bosnia on his own.[47] Djurišić then arranged what he understood to be a safe-conduct agreement with the Croatian Ustasha authorities and representatives of the Montenegrin separatist, Dr. Sekula Drljević. Drljević had spent most of the war years in the puppet state of Croatia, first in Zemun and from the spring of 1944 in Zagreb, and in the summer of 1944 he set up a Montenegrin State Council, which amounted to a sort of Montenegrin government-in-exile. The idea was to establish a Montenegrin state with German and Croatian help, and he wanted to establish his own Montenegrin army. Thus when

---

[45] *Ibid.*, pp. 237–38.

[46] The holding of Sarajevo was also to some extent conditioned on the progress of the German offensive in western Hungary. That offensive fizzled out in mid-March, and on March 20 Hitler gave permission for Sarajevo to be evacuated, an operation which from "an operational point of view was unavoidable for a long time." Schmidt-Richberg, pp. 98–108, esp. p. 107. See also *Hronologija 1941–1945*, p. 1094. It might be noted in passing that for the protection of the Sarajevo-Bosanski Brod communication line, the Germans used in certain sections the Russian Protective Corps which they organized and had used in Serbia. Later they evacuated it to Germany. See Vertepov, ed., pp. 316–25.

[47] Karapandžić, pp. 405–17; Kostić, pp. 230–32.

Djurišić's representatives negotiated with his representatives for safe-conduct, Drljević saw a chance to appropriate the Djurišić Chetnik forces for his own ends. It was after the conclusion of this safe-conduct agreement with Ustasha authorities and Drljević that Djurišić and his troops, accompanied by a large group of civilian refugees including several scores of Montenegrin Orthodox priests, set out on March 18 from Vučjak Mountain toward Slovenia (see Map 7).[48]

How deep the split among the Chetniks had become was indicated not only by Djurišić's breaking away from Mihailović, but even more so by the fact that Mihailović's original titular deputy and chief political adviser, Dragiša Vasić, joined Djurišić for the trek westward. So did many of Mihailović's leading commanders, among them Zaharije Ostojić, the chief of the East Bosnia Area Command, Petar Baćović, commander of the Herzegovinian Chetniks, Mirko Lalatović, one of the leading Chetnik staff officers, Luka Baletić, and Pavle Novaković.[49] The principal Chetnik commanders from Serbia, Dragoslav Račić and Nikola Kalabić, also favored the march westward and did their best to persuade Mihailović to make it, but when he refused to move, they stayed with him.[50] The bulk of the Bosnian Chetniks (excepting those under Ostojić) joined neither Djurišić nor Mihailović but simply disbanded, most of them to slip back into the mass of the Serbian Orthodox population of Bosnia whence they had come, others to go into the deep forests of Bosnia, where they remained for many months after the end of the war. Thus there were at the beginning of April four distinct groups of Chetniks, each pursuing its own way in the hope of escaping the impending disaster: the group that remained true to Mihailović, the group that sided with Djurišić, the Bosnian Chetniks who stayed back, and the Chetniks of Djujić and Jevdjević, who were already in the Ljubljana Gap area.

The details of the agreement that Djurišić made with the Ustashas and the representatives of Drljević are not known, but it appears that Djurišić and his troops were supposed to cross the Sava River into Slavonia. There they would align themselves with Drljević under the name "Montenegrin National Army," with Djurišić retaining operational command, and would be moved west by rail transport. Chetnik sources indicate that Djurišić intended to follow this agreement only to the point where he could rid himself of the sick and wounded among his troops and following, so that he could achieve greater mobility and opera-

[48] Metropolitan Joanikije was not among the priests. He apparently went from eastern Bosnia to Serbia, where he is reported to have died later in 1945.

[49] Banović and Stepanović, in *Politika*, Aug. 22 and 23, 1962. The Sandjak Chetnik leader Vuk Kalaitović also started out with Djurišić, but after a time changed his mind and struck off toward Sandjak with about 200 of his men. Apparently they reached Sandjak successfully. On the last phase of the ill-fated trek of the Djurišić group see Cemović, pp. 68–88.

[50] Kostić, p. 229; Banović and Stepanović, in *Politika*, Aug. 22, 1962.

tional freedom.[51] With that intention, he sent about eight hundred of his sick and wounded across the Sava River to the Ustashas and Drljević. Then with his troops and other refugees, and reinforced by the detachments of Baćović and Ostojić, he moved westward somewhat south of the right bank of the Sava River. It is more than likely that Drljević and the Ustashas had from the outset intended the agreement as a trap for Djurišić; when Djurišić tried to outsmart them, they abandoned all pretense of good faith. Both the Ustashas and Drljević had specific reasons to want to ensnare Djurišić—the Ustashas because Djurišić had been one of the most active practitioners of mass terror over the Moslem population in Sandjak and southeastern Bosnia, and Drljević because Djurišić was one of the strongest exponents of complete union between Montenegro and Serbia, and thus opposed to Drljević's separatism.

Almost from the beginning of their move westward, Djurišić and his troops had to fight off intermittent Ustasha attacks and occasionally attacks by Partisans, but they reached the Vrbas River, and most of the troops crossed it and reached the Lijevče Polje plain, north of Banja Luka. But at that point they were attacked by strong Ustasha forces. Djurišić's forces were badly beaten, and as a consequence of the defeat representatives of Drljević and the Ustashas succeeded in inducing Djurišić's first regiment to switch to Drljević's leadership.[52] Djurišić and a part of his remaining troops tried to make a roundabout turn south of Banja Luka, intending to continue on in a westerly direction, but again they encountered Croatian quisling forces. Djurišić was contacted by Ustasha officers and he at last agreed to undertake direct negotiations with the Ustasha authorities and Drljević's representatives about further movement of his troops westward. This talk of new negotiations proved to be only a snare. On his way to the meeting place Djurišić was attacked and captured by the Ustashas, along with many of his followers, including some political leaders and priests. There are several versions of what happened next. What is definite is that Djurišić and several other Chetnik commanders, including Ostojić and Baćović, Vasić and some other political leaders, and also a number of Orthodox priests were all killed. Some of the troops and refugees who were accompanying Djurišić were killed also. A small part of Djurišić's troops managed to escape and pushed their way west; but a larger part of them, left leaderless, were integrated into Drljević's forces and dispatched

---

[51] Cemović, p. 65; Zečević, pp. 87–91. Zečević, like Cemović, was a survivor of the Djurišić troops, but he belonged to a unit that rather early shifted to Drljević. See also Vučetić, pp. 139–40.

[52] Cemović, pp. 71–80; Banović and Stepanović, in *Politika*, Aug. 22–25, 1962. For the Ustasha view of this engagement see Luburić [Domangoj, pseud.], "The Battle at Lijevče Polje." Luburić's thesis seems to be (p. 78) that Djurišić's march westward was part of a grand Chetnik plan intended to establish a link with the Serbian forces in the Ljubljana Gap area, then to destroy the Independent State of Croatia, and to bring back King Peter. Luburić mentions (p. 89) that the Ustashas captured on that occasion about 7,000 men, but he says nothing about the fate of Djurišić and his troops after their capture.

toward the Austrian border. A portion of both these groups were later caught by the Partisans in Slovenia. Most of those who succeeded in crossing into Austria were returned by the Partisans to Slovenia, where, with various other collaborationist forces, they met their doom in the second half of May. Of the entire force that started with Djurišić in Montenegro and those other Chetniks who joined him for the trek westward, perhaps less than a fourth survived. Drljević himself, like his Ustasha friends, was forced by the advancing Partisans to flee to Austria in the last days of the war. There he and his wife were discovered a few weeks later and killed by some followers of Djurišić.[53] It should be noted that on April 11 three regiments of the Serbian Volunteer Corps and a contingent of Jevdjević Chetniks had been sent into southwestern Croatia to meet Djurišić forces, which of course never appeared. These units were later directed northward toward Ljubljana where they fought against the Partisans. In the closing days of the war they succeeded in crossing into Austria, but they were later returned to Slovenia with Slovene quisling forces and there liquidated by the Partisans.[54]

THE LAST DAYS AT VUČJAK MOUNTAIN

Although Mihailović had firmly made up his mind to return to Serbia with his Serbian Chetniks, he had nonetheless dispatched to Slovenia General Damjanović (formerly an aide of General Nedić and in October 1944 for a brief time commander of the Serbian State Guards), appointing him commander of the Forward Headquarters of the Supreme Command. On March 27 Damjanović took command of the Chetnik and Serbian Volunteer Corps troops situated in the Ljubljana Gap area, and thus according to an agreement worked out during Kostić's visit to Mihailović, the latter troops became also part of the Yugoslav Army in the Homeland. All these units were serving under and were maintained by the Higher SS and Police Leader General Odilo Globocnik in Trieste.[55]

Obviously, Mihailović was trying to maintain some hold over the troops in Slovenia, even though he was dead set against going there himself. Going to Serbia was what he wanted to do, especially now that he had the impression (from the bogus messages that he was receiving from his supposed Chetnik commander Major Ćosić) that there was great potential for an uprising against the new Communist regime. Mihailović thought of himself as a leader and fighter for his people, and this image had to be fulfilled by returning to his people in their

---

[53] Cemović, pp. 80–88; Karapandžić, pp. 416–19; Banović and Stepanović, in *Politika*, Aug. 25, 1962. On the safe-conduct agreement, Drljević's efforts to organize a Montenegrin army, and the fate of these forces after the disaster on Lijevče Polje, see also Pajović, "Political Action of Sekula Drljević," pp. 79–89.

[54] Kostić, p. 247.

[55] *Ibid.*, pp. 222, 233–34, 240–43. See also Tomac, ed., p. 142.

hour of need. In a message to Ljotić of April 1 he said: "We have to develop the strongest possible guerrilla activity in our entire sector of Yugoslavia. Among the Communists there is great distintegration, especially in Serbia. The population in Serbia is eagerly waiting for us, and when spring arrives they will fill the forests and mountains." In another message to Ljotić, of April 11, he said: "As far as the uprising in Serbia is concerned, it is the people who are rising and this cannot be stopped. I only take advantage of the situation which is thereby created."[56] But Mihailović had other reasons for not going to Slovenia. For him to have joined the Serbian Volunteer Corps and the Chetniks of Jevdjević and Djujić in the Ljubljana Gap area would have meant that he and his troops would have come under the direct command of General Globocnik. Mihailović, who had consistently maintained that he was not collaborating with the Germans but was resisting them, could not willingly have placed himself in a position of open personal collaboration with a German SS general in these closing days of the war. The alternative—returning to Serbia—was worth the risk if it could fulfill his hopes of successfully organizing an uprising against the new regime and thereby inducing the Western Allies to intervene and come to his and his troops' assistance.

One of Mihailović's last messages to Fotić, dated April 2, 1945, shows how far he had gone in his dreams about the eventual Western intervention. In this message, Mihailović gave Fotić certain instructions, to be carried out "in a manner he thought most suitable and at the appropriate places." (a) He was to ask that Allied commissions be sent to Yugoslavia to investigate the political situation in the country and to see for themselves that the Chetniks were engaging in civil war not in order to seize power, but rather for the protection of democratic freedoms and the introduction of a democratic administration. (b) He was to emphasize that it was necessary to rely on the democratic political parties in the country and their participation in the provisional government and urge that the interim government in Belgrade be replaced by one in which the democratic parties, including the [Chetnik-controlled] Yugoslav National Democratic Union, would take part. (c) It was "urgently necessary that the Allied American forces occupy the whole territory of Yugoslavia and thereby prevent the civil war and make possible the introduction of a democratic rule in the country. Our Supreme Command and the Yugoslav Army in the Homeland, which is under it, would greet this move and would join them."[57] The last point was, of course, the most important one, in that it was meant not only to prevent the establishment of Communist rule in Yugoslavia

---

[56] Kostić, pp. 238–39.
[57] Jovan Djonović, "The Reports of General Mihailović from the End of 1943 and 1944," p. 74.

but at the same time to enable the Chetniks to establish their rule in Yugoslavia. Fotić did submit a memorandum to the founding meeting of the United Nations which convened at San Francisco on April 25, but not for purposes requested by Mihailović, because after the formation of the unified government in Belgrade on March 7 and its speedy recognition by the Big Three, such a request would have been ludicrous. Rather, he asked for an international commission to supervise and guarantee free elections and for a truly democratic implementation of the decisions of the Yalta Conference as far as they pertained to Yugoslavia.[58]

It may be noted that there were others besides Mihailović who wanted Western occupation of parts of Yugoslavia in the closing weeks of the war. Dr. Gregorij Rožman, Bishop of Ljubljana, and one of the outstanding leaders of the anti-Communist political forces in Slovenia, sent a message to Pope Pius XII for transmittal to the Allied Command at Caserta asking them to occupy Slovenia in order to prevent the establishment of Communist rule.[59] And Pavelić, the head of the collapsing puppet state of Croatia, dispatched a special envoy, Dr. Vjekoslav Vrančić, to the Allied Command in Italy to ask the Western Allies to come to the aid of the Croatian people and to safeguard its core and many thousands of internal refugees from the Partisans. The Pavelić government asked for a speedy dispatch of an Allied mission to ascertain the facts and requested that the Allied armies "come to our state territory to relieve this difficult and dangerous situation."[60] Both Rožman's and Pavelić's pleas were unavailing.

As the situation developed, the Chetniks and other Serbian forces which were assembled in the Ljubljana Gap area, seeing that the Germans were losing on all fronts and were drawing in from the south and southeast toward Austria and southern Germany, and seeing no sign of an entry of Allied troops from Italy, had to come to a decision about where to move to save themselves from annihilation at the hands of the advancing Partisans. In the midst of this crisis of decision, on April 23, Ljotić, the political leader of the Serbian Volunteer Corps, was killed in an automobile accident.[61] Six days later Damjanović issued orders to all troops under his command to cross the Soča (Izonco) River further into Italian territory. On May 4 these forces reached Palmanova, a town about fifty kilometers northwest of Trieste, and on May 5, by order of the British forces there, they surrendered their arms and became British prisoners of war.[62] General Kosta Mušicki, the commander of the

---

[58] Fotić, *The Political Situation in Yugoslavia Today*, pp. 17–18.

[59] For the text of Bishop Rožman's message see Clissold, p. 223.

[60] Instead of being ushered to the conference table with Field Marshal Alexander, Vrančić was taken to a prisoner-of-war camp. About his mission see his *S bielom zastavom preko Alpa*. The text of the memorandum of the Pavelić government may be found in Stanić, ed., pp. 46–48.

[61] Kostić, p. 250.

[62] *Ibid.*, pp. 259–67.

former Serbian Volunteer Corps, was later turned over to the Yugoslavs, but the other officers and the rank and file of these troops remained for some time in British prisoner-of-war camps in Italy and after their release gradually scattered throughout the world. General Damjanović died in Hannover in August 1956; *vojvoda* Jevdjević died in Rome in October 1962; and *vojvoda* Djujić, as of 1973, was living in the United States.

For some months Mihailović had been eager to cooperate with the forces of the Croatian puppet state "because the common goal was the annihilation of the Communists."[63] He sent his own emissary, a lawyer named Dr. Ranko Brašić, not only to Dr. Pavelić, the head of the Croatian puppet state, but also to the head of the Catholic Church in Croatia, Archbishop Alojzije Stepinac, and also to Dr. Maček, the head of the Croatian Peasant Party, who had passively opposed the quisling government.[64] Pavelić gave Brašić a supply of medicines for the treatment of typhus, which was widespread among the Chetnik troops in Bosnia. Besides Dr. Brašić, Chetnik Major Žika Andrić seems to have been a sort of steady contact with the Croatian military authorities in Zagreb during the last few months of the war.[65] Finally, in mid-April 1945, Mihailović sent General Svetomir Djukić supposedly on a mission to establish contact with the advancing Allied armies in northern Italy, but at the same time, while passing through Zagreb, to see Pavelić and discuss with him the possibility of cooperation between the Chetniks and Croatian troops and to obtain from him a series of concessions. To assist Djukić in his efforts in Zagreb, Mihailović sent with him

---

[63] See the report of the German Plenipotentiary General in Croatia of Dec. 24, 1944, referring to the statement of one of his reliable agents. Microcopy No. T-311, Roll 196, Frame 427.

[64] Although Mihailović stated at his trial that Brašić was only empowered to contact representatives of the Croatian Peasant Party, it has been well established that Brašić saw Pavelić and Stepinac as well. See *The Trial of Draža Mihailović*, pp. 289–96, 453–56. In a letter of April 26, 1972, to Dr. Brašić, who was then living in New York, I asked him whether he had written anything on his activities as a contact man between Mihailović and Pavelić, and if he had not, whether he would be kind enough to answer a series of questions pertaining to these matters. Dr. Brašić in his reply of May 5, 1972, said that so far he had written nothing meritorious about his "national-political activities during the Second World War" because he believed in the principle that memoirs and similar writings should be published only fifty years after the events they describe took place. For that reason, he was also unwilling to answer any questions referring to his activities during the war. Dr. Brašić died the following November 22.

It should be noted that as early as 1943 representatives of Mihailović and of the Croatian Peasant Party (to which in time many of the Domobran officers gave their support) had some discussions about the future of Yugoslavia. No agreements were reached, however, because the CPP would not recognize Mihailović as commander in chief of all Yugoslav forces including the Domobrans, and Mihailović would not agree to disown the Chetnik groups that had been responsible for mass terror against the Croatian population. This information originates with the Domobran colonel Ivan Babić, who in January 1944 was helped by high Croatian army authorities to escape to Italy for the purpose of establishing contact with the Allied forces on behalf of the Croatian army and the CPP. See F.O. 371/44245, R1040/8/92 and F.O. 371/44249, R3364/8/92. Also, late in 1944, some Domobran units in Bosnia, specifically those located in the towns of Vareš and Zenica, apparently made overtures of some sort to Mihailović with a view toward recognizing his supreme command. See e.g. Mihailović's letter of Nov. 29, 1944, to the Croatian commander of Vareš, Mate Matićević, in *The Trial of Draža Mihailović*, p. 218, and Microcopy No. T-501, Roll 257, Frames 1077–78. See also the quite improbable story related by Lieutenant Lalich in his already cited report to his OSS superiors.

[65] Karapandžić, p. 438.

Vladimir Predavec, who had been for a long time a member of the Chetnik Central National Committee. Djukić, accompanied by Predavec and also Brašić and Andrić, had two conferences with Pavelić, on April 17 and 22. In them, he asked for the following: release of a Chetnik hospital and its inmates captured by the Ustashas on Vučjak Mountain; release of 1,200 Serb civilians captured by the Ustashas and held in the town of Šamac; medical supplies, ammunition, and food for the Chetniks; and free passage of Chetnik troops through Croatia on their way to Slovenia (but without Mihailović, who would stay behind in the mountains).[66] The last-named request, for free passage through Croatian territory, was apparently intended to mislead the Ustasha authorities (and even more the Partisans, whose Zagreb intelligence sources were sure to be working efficiently) into thinking that Mihailović planned to send his forces into Slovenia rather than to Serbia.

Also, in the first days of April, the German intelligence agent Stärker paid a last visit to Mihailović to bring him Colonel General Löhr's offer of surrender to the Western Allies, along with the request that Mihailović submit it to them. Mihailović testified at his trial that he did this, and that two of his important commanders, Major Račić and Captain Nedić, went to Zagreb (presumably before April 12) to ask Löhr to surrender, but, of course, without success.[67] This was probably a follow-up to Stärker's visit to Mihailović.

TOWARD SERBIA AND FINAL DISASTER

On April 13 Mihailović and his remaining Serbian Chetniks, numbering about twelve thousand men, left Vučjak Mountain in north-central Bosnia to begin the long trek to Serbia.[68] Instead of heading for the lower reaches of the Drina River, where at that time of year because of the spring runoff a crossing would be impossible without special equipment, they took a westerly route along the right bank of the Sava River until they were near the junction with the Vrbas River. (This route was intended to suggest to the Partisans that they were heading toward Slovenia.) The approximate route, as Map 7 shows, then veered sharply south and southeast through the mountains to a point somewhat east of Konjic on the Neretva River, then southeast in the direction of Kali-

---

[66] A series of articles by General Djukić about his mission to Pavelić appeared in the monthly newspaper *Srpska zastava* (Buenos Aires) between December 1954 and May 1955 under the title "From the Forests into Emigration." Djukić was answered by Ustasha General Luburić in an "Open Letter to the Serbian General Svetomir Djukić," in *Drina* (Madrid) in December 1955. Pavelić also, in 1949, published his recollections of these conferences. Karapandžić, pp. 436–39, quotes extensively from Djukić's articles, and on pp. 439–44 quotes in full Pavelić's statement regarding the same matter.

[67] *The Trial of Draža Mihailović*, pp. 270–71, 291–92.

[68] Banović and Stepanović, in *Politika*, Aug. 26, 1962. Mihailović also gives a figure of 12,000 in his message of Feb. 28, 1945, to his representatives abroad (he actually talks of 20,000 Chetnik fighters from Serbia and Montenegro). See Jovan Djonović, "The Reports of General Mihailović from the End of 1943 and 1944," p. 71.

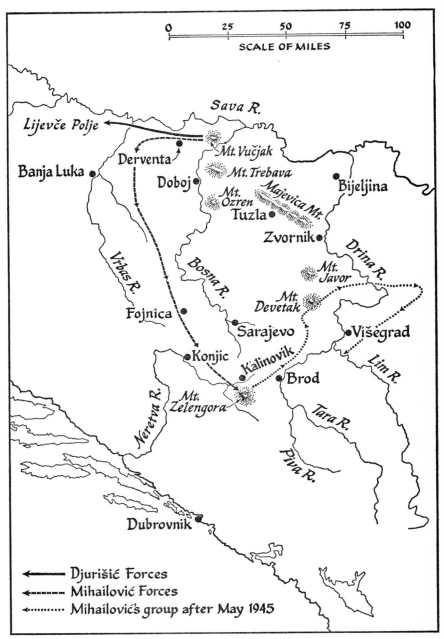

SCALE OF MILES

0   25   50   75   100

Sava R.

Lijevče Polje

Mt. Vučjak

Derventa

Mt. Trebava

Banja Luka

Doboj

Mt. Ozren

Majevica Mt.

Bijeljina

Tuzla

Zvornik

Drina R.

Vrbas R.

Bosna R.

Mt. Javor

Mt. Devetak

Fojnica

Sarajevo

Višegrad

Konjic

Kalinovik

Lim R.

Mt. Zelengora

Brod

Neretva R.

Tara R.

Piva R.

Dubrovnik

Djurišić Forces

Mihailović Forces

Mihailović's group after May 1945

Map 7. Mihailović's and Djurišić's roads to disaster

novik and Zelengora Mountain, and further east again to the Drina at a point around Brod where it could be crossed without difficulty.[69]

The Chetnik forces on this march of two hundred eighty kilometers were the remnants of an army whose cause was lost and whose forces had been decimated by military reverses and typhus and weakened by internal dissension. It was an army that lacked military supplies and medicines as well as means of transport, and it was burdened by sick and wounded soldiers. At the start, these discouraged troops had to contend with intermittent but unrelated harassment by both Ustashas and Partisans; then it became only the Partisans, operating both as local detachments and as regular army units, who kept up a steady, though not overwhelming, pressure, seemingly designed to hinder but not halt the progress of the Chetniks. After about two-thirds of the way, the Partisan air force became the Chetniks' daily follower, sometimes attacking, sometimes not, but reporting their movement to the Partisan command posts.

Mihailović, all the while, was still getting messages from "Major Ćosić" painting an enticing picture of conditions in Serbia, and so the Chetniks pressed on, enduring bad weather conditions along with Partisan harassment, toward what they thought would be a safe haven. After about four weeks of marching they were nearing the point where they planned to cross the Drina River. Then, on May 10, a concentrated Partisan attack forced them into a position of real peril on the bank of the small right tributary of the Neretva, the Jezerica River, west of Kalinovik. The bank of the Jezerica at that point is a sheer, high cliff, and descent to the river is extremely difficult. Thus halted, the Chetniks were at the mercy of combined aerial and ground attack by Partisan forces. In the process of the descent and crossing (though the Jezerica is here little more than a stream), the Chetniks lost all their heavy equipment, all their radio equipment, all their horses, and a large number of men.[70] Two days later, the weakened Chetnik columns were concentrically attacked again by Partisan forces, the Third Shock Corps of the Yugoslav People's Army and the Third Division of the Corps of National Defense of Yugoslavia (*Korpus narodne odbrane Jugoslavije*).[71] The official *Chronology* of the War of National Liberation notes under the events of May 12, 1945, in the section on Bosnia and Herzegovina:

In the area of the Sutjeska River and the village of Zakmur the units of the Third Shock Corps of the Yugoslav Army and of the Third Division of the

---

[69] The most complete Chetnik account of this trek, by a survivor who managed to escape abroad, is to be found in Milošević, pp. 228–44. At his trial in August 1945, Keserović stated that Mihailović selected "the longest and the most difficult route" for the journey back to Serbia. *Sudjenje članovima rukovodstva organizacije Draže Mihailovića*, p. 219.

[70] Banović and Stepanović, in *Politika*, Aug. 26, 1962; Milošević, pp. 238–39.

[71] The latter, known as KNOJ, were special troops on the Russian model, whose first units were established in August 1944. They were especially used for mopping up and destroying the remnants of the opposing internal forces.

KNOJ started with the annihilation of a strong Chetnik group. (The Chetniks were mostly made prisoners and annihilated, except for 300 to 400 Chetniks dispersed in the area from Zelengora Mountain to the Prača River, with whom were also Draža Mihailović and the members of the Chetnik Supreme Command.)[72]

With these Partisan forces was also a detachment of the OZNA under Lt. Colonel Djordje Lazić, whose special task was to catch Mihailović alive. But his prize eluded him. In the state of confusion that prevailed among the Chetniks, the three leading Chetnik commanders—Dragoslav Račić, Dragutin Keserović, and Nikola Kalabić—succeeded in breaking away with some of their troops, and escaped separately toward Serbia. Two other leading Chetnik commanders, General Trifunović and Captain Neško Nedić, were killed. Ironically, in the four days May 10–13, the overwhelming portion of the Serbian Chetnik forces met their doom close to the spot where the Partisans' main forces and their military and political leadership had barely escaped total destruction in June 1943, in the closing phases of Operation Schwarz (the Fifth Enemy Offensive). During the weeks following the Chetnik disaster, the remaining Chetniks, with the exception of those who attempted to reach Serbia on their own, were hunted down by the Partisan forces. Perhaps the largest group of these, among whom was General Mihailović, was surrounded on the night of May 21–22 by the Third Proletarian Brigade near the village of Bulozi in southeastern Bosnia and almost completely wiped out. Mihailović and seventeen others managed to escape. According to a detailed Communist account, between May 1 and May 18, the Chetnik losses in killed and captured amounted to 9,235 men, including over 300 officers.[73]

The freedom of the three Chetnik commanders who successfully escaped the Partisan attack near the village of Zakmur was short lived. Keserović was caught by the Partisans immediately after crossing the Drina River into Serbia, was tried and sentenced to death, and in August was executed. Račić was located by Communist security forces in a village in western Serbia the following November and was immediately killed. Kalabić, who reached Serbia with perhaps as many as one hundred fifty men, managed to evade the security forces until December, when he was captured by an ingenious ruse.[74] As will be shown, he played an important role in the capture of Mihailović a few months later.

[72] Hronologija 1941–1945, p. 1107.

[73] For a full account of the final Partisan attack on the Chetniks and the fate of some of the commanders see Banović and Stepanović, in Politika, Aug. 26 and 27, 1962.

[74] Ibid., Sept. 6–8, 1962. After learning by pure chance of Kalabić's whereabouts, agents of the Yugoslav police, posing as Chetniks, established contact with a junior Chetnik officer, Milić Bošković, whom Kalabić after his return to Serbia had appointed commander of the Valjevo district, and through him made contact with Kalabić. They told Kalabić that they had connections with an American intelligence agent who was in Yugoslavia and was eager to help Kalabić escape abroad. When Kalabić insisted on seeing the American agent, a man posing as an American was brought to him; Kalabić was convinced, and disregarding the advice of some of his officers, agreed

Mihailović, miraculously still free with a handful of his men despite the disaster that had overtaken the bulk of his troops, managed remarkably to continue on his way. With his small entourage, he cleverly outmaneuvered his pursuers by moving from mountain to mountain, backtracking when necessary to throw off pursuit, and after a time reached the area of the Devetak and Javor mountains in eastern Bosnia. There the small party ran into some Bosnian Chetniks who were hiding in the forests and joined forces with them. The group around Mihailović who were directly supplying him with food, lodging, and information numbered at that point about sixty men, including Major Dragiša Vasiljević, Borko Radović, and several other Chetnik commanders. The Yugoslav security forces, never far behind, soon discovered their general whereabouts, and in July they got from one of Mihailović's former companions who was captured full data on his exact location, the number of men with him, and so on.[75] In August and September, OZNA made its first determined attempt to capture Mihailović. It assigned this task to one of its operatives, a man known as Major Ljubo Popović. After growing a beard in the manner of the Chetniks, Popović, with several similarly disguised assistants, went to eastern Bosnia; there, in Chetnik attire, they entered the forests in the suspected area in order to seek out Mihailović's group. It was a fruitless search. Either Mihailović slipped away at the last moment, or there was no way to penetrate the protective cordon built around him by his men and his sympathizers in the villages. Major Popović was withdrawn to Belgrade, but security forces kept a steady watch in the area.[76]

Mihailović had had no contact with "Major Ćosić" since losing his radio equipment at the Jezerica River, but he still had faith in Ćosić's messages and was eager to continue on to Serbia. On the night of September 20–21, by a bold attack on a rather disorganized Partisan guards outpost, the Chetniks secured a boat and put Mihailović safely on the right bank of the Drina. After resting for a few days in the vicinity of the river, Mihailović and a small group of men made their way into Serbia. They managed to penetrate to the neighborhood of the little town of Kosjerići, about twenty kilometers northeast of Užice, but were disappointed to find no Chetnik detachments there and apparently no inclination on the part of the peasants to help. According to Yugoslav Communist sources, it was only then that Mihailović began to grasp the truth about "Major Ćosić" and the messages that had lured him back

to accompany the agents to Belgrade in order, supposedly, to make contact with Chetniks there who were underground. Kalabić and his bodyguard went to Belgrade with the supposed Chetniks and the "American" agent and were hidden in a house there. But after a meal accompanied by much drinking, Kalabić and his guard were separated and overpowered and taken off to prison.

[75] *Ibid.*, Aug. 28 and 29, 1962. Mihailović seems to have had his first contact with eastern Bosnian Chetniks on June 18 and soon thereafter he even held a conference with several Bosnian Chetnik commanders still at large, including Colonel Borota. After the conference he sent them back to their areas, promising that after he returned to Serbia the signal would be given for a new revolt.

[76] *Ibid.*, Aug. 29–31, 1962.

into Serbia. Instead of trying to penetrate further into Serbia, he and his group returned to Bosnia, to somewhere in the area of Višegrad, and went into hiding behind a wall of trusted Chetniks and Chetnik sympathizers. The Communist security forces, meanwhile, having come to the conclusion that the simple pursuit of Mihailović from one place to another was going to achieve nothing, were devising a completely new plan for capturing him.[77]

MIHAILOVIĆ IS CAUGHT

Kalabić, who had by this time (December 1945) been trapped by security forces, was the key figure in the new plan for Mihailović's capture. Kalabić knew that he had forfeited his life by falling into the hands of the Communist authorities, but he was willing to do almost anything to try to save his skin. His first service to the police was to aid in the apprehension of the fifteen members of his own former staff.[78] Then he tried to bargain with the security services: if they would apply a policy of generosity, he would attempt to influence the pro-Chetnik population in Serbia to accept the new regime; in return, he wanted his captors to let him go abroad or else allow him to live under an assumed name in some small town in Serbia, renouncing all political activity against the regime. The police refused this offer, but they appealed to Kalabić to help them net Mihailović, and after thinking the matter over (and refusing at first), Kalabić agreed to cooperate. The police were alert to the possibility that at the last moment Kalabić might back out or might contrive to give a sign to Mihailović and his men that they were being trapped, and they realized that in such circumstances some of their men, and Mihailović as well, might be killed. They had no desire to see Mihailović killed, since only with a live Mihailović could the Communist regime stage a full-scale political trial, needed for political reasons, both domestic and international. But time was of the essence: the longer Mihailović managed to stay free, the better were his chances of eluding them altogether, for once spring came and the weather improved, he could maneuver much more successfully.

For sixteen years, the Yugoslav authorities kept secret the circumstances surrounding the capture of Mihailović. An inkling of what happened was published as early as 1948 in the West by Monty Radulovic, who was the Belgrade correspondent of Reuter's before the war.[79] Radulovic heard the story from an OZNA major, who was under the influence of alcohol at the time. Not until 1962 did a full, semiofficial account of the capture appear, in the previously quoted series of articles

[77] *Ibid.*, Sept. 1–3, 1962.
[78] *Ibid.*, Sept. 10, 1962.
[79] See his book, *Tito's Republic*, pp. 186–88.

by Gojko Banović and Kosta Stepanović in the Belgrade daily *Politika* between August 5 and September 17, 1962.[80]

Apparently what happened was as follows. Around the twentieth of January, 1946, after appropriate planning and preparation, a group of security officers, disguised as Chetniks, went with Kalabić to the area of Višegrad and began inquiring among the peasants in certain villages, specifically questioning a number of them who were suspected of having knowledge of Chetnik activity in the area or of having members of their families among the Chetniks who were hiding Mihailović. Then Kalabić, acting in his capacity as deputy commander of the Chetniks in Serbia (OZNA had already sent a letter in Kalabić's name to Mihailović through known Chetnik contacts), ordered these peasants to arrange a meeting with one of the local Bosnian Chetniks, a man named Budimir Gajić, who was thought to be intimately involved in hiding Mihailović. Gajić was suspicious of the authenticity of the message that was brought to him by one of the villagers and directed him to return to Kalabić and say that Gajić could not be found. When Kalabić and the security officers made two more attempts to get a letter delivered to Gajić by the same peasant contact, Gajić, more and more suspicious that OZNA was behind the whole thing, advised the contact not to return to Kalabić. The contact sent word to Kalabić by a relative that he could not find Gajić, whereupon Kalabić dispatched still another letter to Gajić informing him that he was returning to Serbia but would come back to Bosnia later on.

All this maneuvering took several weeks, and finally, sometime early in March, owing to a lack of coordination between Belgrade and the local OZNA, the local officials made an attempt to apprehend Mihailović on their own. The attempt failed, and Mihailović and his companions, realizing that their hideout had been discovered, quickly fled to a new hideout. It appears, however, that Kalabić's second and third letters to Gajić came into Mihailović's hands. Because they included

---

[80] This series of articles (which would amount to perhaps 200 pages in book form) is a rather curious blend of fact and fictionalized narrative. There are imaginary dialogues between Mihailović and various members of his staff, and Mihailović's thoughts and reflections are described. There are also accounts of many specific terrorist acts which, though committed by the Chetniks or ascribed to them, are totally unrelated to the capture of Mihailović, and in many places the authors engage in subjective interpretation instead of giving documentary evidence. Nevertheless, according to a number of well-informed persons with whom I have discussed the matter, this account does, on the whole, present the main facts accurately. The articles were to have been issued later in book form, along with additional documentary materials: the final installment carried an announcement that the volume would be forthcoming soon. But the intense interest aroused by the articles throughout Serbia, and no doubt in other parts of Yugoslavia as well, apparently created a political problem for the League of Communists of Yugoslavia. A special Party committee that was appointed to look into the matter subsequently recommended against publication in book form. For comments on the *Politika* articles made by a Chetnik, or Chetnik sympathizer, in exile, see Nenad Petrović's article in *Naša Reč*, June–July 1966, pp. 20–23. Late in 1971, the security agent known as Ljubo Popović published in Belgrade a book entitled *Velika igra sa Dražom Mihailovićem* (The Great Game with Draža Mihailović), dealing with the capture of General Mihailović. His narrative, which begins in October 1945, is very similar to the account by Banović and Stepanović on which I have based my description.

photographs of Kalabić, signed by him, Mihailović decided that the messages were bona fide. His stay in the area of Višegrad was becoming precarious anyway, so he urged his guards to get in touch with Kalabić.[81] Thus on the third try, which the security agents with Kalabić in tow had initiated on March 6, both Kalabić and Mihailović were eager to get together. The Chetniks were still reasonably cautious, and it was only after going through several Chetnik contacts, and after being repeatedly scrutinized, that Kalabić and his "officers" were accepted as genuine, but at last, on March 12, still in the area of Višegrad, they established direct contact with Mihailović and were admitted to his hideout.

Kalabić had little difficulty persuading the apparently unsuspecting Mihailović to return with him and his "Chetniks" to Serbia, and it was agreed that they would set out on the journey that very night. Mihailović also readily assented to Kalabić's suggestion that a dozen or so of his guards—roughly half of them—should be sent on an assignment toward Višegrad, in the opposite direction from the route that Mihailović and Kalabić and the others would be taking. This was a precaution that the security officers had been particularly anxious about, since otherwise they would have been outnumbered.

The group of guards, led by Gajić, left on their assignment, and that night the rest of the party—the agents, Kalabić, Mihailović, and about a dozen of Mihailović's guards—started for Serbia. It was a moonlight night, and the small party moved through the woods in single file. At the head of the column was a Chetnik guard; behind every Chetnik was one of the security agents in disguise. Two agents were assigned to Mihailović (they even carried him over a creek so that he would not wet his feet). Apparently some misunderstanding delayed the springing of the trap, but when the signal that had been agreed upon was called, the agents leaped into action. Each agent killed the Chetnik guard in front of him—Kalabić excepted. Mihailović was thrown to the ground and manacled. Only the lead Chetnik, although wounded, managed to escape. Thus Mihailović was outfoxed, and was finally the prisoner of his archenemies, the Communists.

The next day (March 13) Mihailović was taken to Belgrade. To Marshal Tito, away on a state visit to Poland, Aleksandar Ranković, Minister of the Interior and thus head of the security forces, sent a triumphant message announcing the capture.[82] A few days later Ranković informed the National Assembly about the action. Furthermore, he told the Assembly, "numerous other Chetnik commanders . . . will not menace our peaceful villages and inhabitants any more" (obviously implying that they had been either killed or imprisoned). Among these, in addi-

[81] Banović and Stepanović, in *Politika*, Sept. 7, 11–14, 1962.
[82] *Ibid.*, Sept. 15–17, 1962.

tion to Kalabić, Račić, and Raković, were the following Serbian and Bosnian Chetnik commanders: Captain Vasić, Captain Vasiljević, *vojvoda* Voja Tribrodjanin, Lieutenant Mišić, *vojvoda* Borivoje Kerović, Captain Medić, Lieutenant Filip Ajdačić, *vojvoda* Guda Bosiljčić, Lieutenant Milić Bošković, Lieutenant Marko Kotarac, Lieutenant Matić, Captain Boroš, Lieutenant Mirko Tomašević, Captain Leka Damjanović, Captain Miloš Erić, Captain Bora Mitranović, Colonel Gojko Borota, Major Slavoljub Vranješević, and *vojvoda* Radoslav Radić.[83]

Kalabić's life was spared and he was allowed to withdraw under an assumed name to a small Serbian town. But he tended to get drunk often and in that state talked too much. This became known in Belgrade, and because some of the things he said apparently proved embarrassing to the authorities, it was found necessary quietly to liquidate him.

On June 10, 1946, after nearly three months of interrogation, Mihailović went on trial for high treason and war crimes. The trial, highly staged and much publicized, lasted until July 15. The verdict was "guilty," the sentence, death. Mihailović's appeal for mercy was quickly rejected by the Presidium of the People's Assembly of the Federative People's Republic of Yugoslavia, and on July 17 he was executed by a firing squad.[84] His place of burial has never been revealed to the public.

In addition to Mihailović, twenty-three other persons were also tried at the same time. These were Mihailović's close political collaborators (Dr. Stevan Moljević, Dr. Mladen Žujović, Dr. Živko Topalović, Djuro Vilović), Chetnik officers (*vojvoda* Radoslav Radić, Major Slavoljub Vranješević, Captain Miloš Glišić), former leaders of the government-in-exile and Yugoslav diplomats (Slobodan Jovanović, Dr. Božidar Purić, Dr. Momčilo Ninčić, General Petar Živković, Radoje Knežević, Dr. Milan Gavrilović, Lt. Colonel Živan Knežević, Ambassador Konstantin Fotić—all these tried in absentia), military commanders and political functionaries of the Nedić government and Ljotić forces (Dragomir-

[83] Yugoslavia, Ministry of Information, *The Debate on the Budget for 1946* (Belgrade, April 1946), pp. 37–40.

[84] The official record of Mihailović's indictment, trial, sentencing, and execution is the often cited *Trial of Dragoljub-Draža Mihailović*, published in 1946. The trial stimulated a great deal of protest on the part of Mihailović's friends abroad, especially in the United States, and a special publication was issued by them—*The Report of Commission of Inquiry of the Committee for a Fair Trial for Draja Mihailovich* (1946). In the years since, Chetniks in exile, helped somewhat by their friends in Great Britain and the United States especially, have expended a great deal of time and effort perpetuating and defending the legend of General Mihailović. Of the major Chetnik exile efforts in this regard, in addition to the two-volume *Knjiga o Draži*, the studies by Branko Lazitch (*La tragédie du Général Draja Mihailovitch*), Evgueniyé Yourichitch (*Le procès Tito-Mihailovitch*), and Radoje Vukčević (*Na strašnom sudu*) are especially worthwhile. Avakumović's *Mihailović prema nemačkim dokumentima* may be noted as an extremely biased interpretation of German documents to sustain the idea that Mihailović's Chetniks were a genuine resistance movement against the Axis powers. It is nothing but a political pamphlet which tries to promote and defend an untenable thesis.

There are at least two selections of statements in support of Mihailović prior to, during, and after his trial: *General Mihailovich—The World's Verdict* (1947), and *Tributes to General Mihailovich* (1966).

Dragi Jovanović, Tanasije Dinić, Velibor Jonić, General Djuro Dokić, General Kosta Mušicki, Boško Pavlović), and two old Serbian politicians who had no official functions during the war but did engage in some anti-Partisan activity (Dr. Lazar Marković and Dr. Kosta Kumanudi).[85] Of these, seven were sentenced to death and executed: Radoslav Radić, one of the Bosnian Chetnik leaders; Miloš Glišić, a Serbian Chetnik officer; Dragomir-Dragi Jovanović, mayor of Belgrade and chief of the Belgrade police under the Nedić regime; Tanasije Dinić, a colonel and Nedić minister; Velibor Jonić, a Nedić minister; Kosta Mušicki, the former commander of the Serbian Volunteer Corps; and Boško Pavlović, deputy commander of Nedić's State Guard. Žujović and Živković were sentenced to death in absentia. The other seven who stood trial in Belgrade received prison terms ranging from a minimum of two to a maximum of twenty years. In addition to the two great trials of Chetnik and other anti-Communist leaders in Serbia, the new Yugoslav authorities apprehended, interrogated, tried, and sentenced to prison terms of various duration (or simply released after investigation) many thousands of other people who had been associated with and supported the Chetnik cause or the Serbian quisling authorities.

The government plan in the trial of Mihailović and his codefendants of using Mihailović to discredit himself and his cause, and to discredit his domestic coworkers and followers and former Yugoslav officials abroad, appears to have been largely successful. The trial also was used to castigate, for political and propaganda purposes, the Chetniks' Western friends, even though many of them (as well as their governments) had jettisoned Mihailović and the Chetniks during 1943 and 1944, shifting their support to Tito and the Partisans and in that way helping them rise to power.[86] During Mihailović's trial in 1946, as during the trial of the other political and military leaders of the Chetnik movement in August 1945, there was a great deal of mutual recrimination among the accused. Again and again Mihailović tried to evade the questioning of the prosecutor by accusing his commanders, charging them with collaboration, disregard of his orders, professional incompetence, willful behavior, and so on.[87] In the same way, his commanders, particularly Keserović and Lukačević, during their trial in August 1945, blamed the Supreme Command for most of the actions that they were charged with,

---

[85] General Nedić was apprehended in Austria by the Allied forces sometime in early autumn of 1945 and delivered to the Yugoslav authorities. He is said to have committed suicide in October 1945 by jumping from a window in a corridor of the prison in which he was incarcerated.

[86] See e.g. references to the British liaison officers with the Chetniks, Colonels Bailey and Hudson, and the chief of the American military mission at Mihailović's headquarters, Colonel McDowell, in the *Trial of Draža Mihailović*, pp. 123–24, 158–59, 184–85, 191–95, 199–203, 304–9, 465–67; and Ziherl, "The Epilogue of an Anti-People Conspiracy."

[87] *The Trial of Draža Mihailović*, pp. 162, 249–50, 252, 254, 258–59, 262, 270, 283–89, 296–97, 304, 334, 351, 358, 377–78, 384.

using the familiar response that they had simply carried out orders.[88] The testimony at the trials shows that Mihailović never had full and firm control over most of his commanders, and that most of the time the commanders did not receive from him clear and precise orders but instead had to work with orders of a general nature. They were to carry these orders according to their own judgment and specific conditions under which they operated and they were not strictly accountable for their actions. Under such conditions it was natural for many Chetnik commanders to follow their own special personal and area interests rather than to act as parts of a well-coordinated military organization.

Lack of strong and appropriate direction from the center in military affairs, lack of growth in the personal capacities of General Mihailović required by the times, and the absence of a viable political program and the necessary political organization, all prevented the development of proper cohesion in the Chetnik movement and inhibited its capacity to grow as time advanced. These weaknesses, together with persistent collaboration with the enemy against their domestic foes and the inability to handle successfully the international problems that faced them, made inevitable the disaster that in the end befell the Chetnik movement and its leaders.

[88] *Sudjenje članovima rukovodstva organizacije Draže Mihailovića*, pp. 144, 146, 149–50, 157, 161–63, 166, 209–10, 213, 221–23, 233–36, 245, 248.

Conclusion

For all practical purposes, the wartime Chetnik movement was finished as a fighting force in mid-October 1944, when Mihailović, after his earlier hasty retreat from Serbia to northeastern Bosnia, ordered the rest of his troops in Serbia to follow him. After these troops withdrew, first to Sandjak and then slowly to northeastern Bosnia, the fate of the Chetniks was sealed. In the months that remained until the war came to an end, the Chetniks were a force in limbo, waiting, hoping, making a few ineffectual attempts to save themselves, and finally following Mihailović and Djurišić, respectively, in their last ventures to what proved to be their doom.

In the preceding pages we have traced the story of Draža Mihailović from the collapse of the country in mid-April 1941, when he refused to surrender to the invader, through the formative stages of his movement, his days of international glory, the collaboration of his Chetnik forces with the enemy, his falling out with the Western Allies, and the declining fortunes of his movement, to the destruction of the remnants of his forces by the Partisans in May 1945, and thence to his capture, trial, and execution in July 1946. It remains to offer a final assessment of Mihailović as a wartime military and political leader, and to summarize the effects of the Chetnik defeat on the interwar Serbian ruling groups that he represented.

GENERAL MIHAILOVIĆ: A PORTRAIT

What sort of man was Mihailović, and how was the conduct of the Chetnik movement influenced by his personality and character? Mihailović's character, like most men's, was a mixture of strengths and weaknesses. He had the virtues of courage and loyalty, he could hold a steady course, and he had a certain native cunning. He had, as we have seen, respectable military training. But for all his cunning he was not shrewd, and he lacked the broadness of vision, the military and organizational capacities, and the energy that might have made him successful. The failure of the Chetnik movement was thus to a certain extent a consequence of the limitations of his outlook and personality.

First, and in some ways worst, Mihailović was a naïve and incorrigible optimist. Until the last stages, he seems never to have doubted the ultimate success of his movement. The odds against his success were enormous: Hitler, his war machine, and his allies and satellites threatened from the right; Tito, his well-organized revolutionary movement, and his powerful political and social ideology from the left. Undaunted by these odds, Mihailović held fast to his faith in the strength and loyalty of his following among the Serbs. He never stopped believing that in time the Soviet-Western alliance would come apart and he and his cause would be saved by the West.

Again and again his optimism betrayed him. Thus he persistently overrated his own forces and underrated Tito's, and thus also his initial realization of the dangers of the Chetniks' collaborating with the Axis forces gave way to a foolish belief that he and his troops could escape the onus of collaboration by denying the fact. In the end, a groundless optimism was responsible for his ill-fated attempt to lead his ragged troops back to Serbia in April 1945.

Besides being naïve and overoptimistic, Mihailović was strikingly unconcerned about the practical implementation of his grand designs. Some of his plans, of course, were simply chimerical; others depended wholly on an Allied landing in Yugoslavia that was never seriously contemplated. Still others, more realistic, failed because they were not carefully worked out or were too complicated to be carried out successfully. Generally speaking, Mihailović seems not to have realized how complex an undertaking he was engaged in. Recent history has shown that successful resistance movements require a theoretical foundation, compelling ideology, good staff work, all-out political and military organization efforts, and steady attention to the manifold aspects of the whole undertaking so that no part of it gets out of control. The old-fashioned, strictly military approach, even when, as in Mihailović's case, it is in the service of a well-defined political program, is insufficient.

Overoptimistic in the large, Mihailović tended to rely on guile in the particular instance. Intent on preserving Serbian lives, he favored a minimum of fighting against the forces of occupation until after the Allies landed in Yugoslavia or the Balkans. While he waited, he sought to liquidate his rivals the Communists. This decision led inevitably to a complex policy of cooperation with friend and foe alike—with the Italians and the Germans, the Nedić forces and the Pavelić forces, the

British, the Americans, and even the Russians—that would have tested the ingenuity of a military and political genius. For Mihailović, a man of average capabilities and provincial outlook, it was sheer folly. His streak of peasant cunning was not sufficient to carry him through, and in the end he became hopelessly entangled.

Mihailović was a poor organizer, and his inability to exert strong control over his scattered troops had much to do with their ineffectiveness. The Chetnik forces were for the most part tied to specific areas in the manner of a territorial militia; in the absence of strict central leadership and control, they owed their highest loyalty to local commanders, many of whom were by nature independent and bent on mantaining their independence. Mihailović seems to have had no serious concern about this situation, or indeed about the poor discipline of his troops and commanders generally. Not until June 1944 did he start organizing mobile forces not tied to specific areas; and these forces, the Groups of Shock Corps, were formed too late to change the course of events.

Moreover, unlike the Partisans, the Chetniks had no ideology worth the name and no program of troop indoctrination. One reason why the Partisans were so effective was that they had a tested theoretical model for their military and political actions and knew how to adapt it to the specific Yugoslav conditions. Their political line, a new synthesis of Yugoslav nationalism, and their excellent leadership not only brought them new adherents and new popular support, but imparted to their fighting men the strength of dedication to a cause.

Mihailović had a purely Great Serbian view of the Yugoslav problem, and his movement suffered for it. Bound by his overriding commitment to Serbian hegemony, he could not comprehend the extent to which the old order had been demolished, not merely by defeat and occupation but by the rise of the Partisan movement. He had only a very limited comprehension of the intense desire of all South Slav nations and national minorities for political, economic, and social reform. Chetnik programmatic statements since late 1941 included promises of some cooperativist and socialist changes in the postwar Yugoslav economy, and from the congress of Ba in January 1944 the Chetnik movement was officially committed to the federalization of the country, but only under the aegis of the Great Serbia forces. The Chetniks were successful in acquiring a political base in Serbia, Montenegro, Bosnia and Herzegovina, and parts of Dalmatia, and they also had a tenuous political arrangement with the anti-Communist forces in Slovenia. But Mihailović's attempted negotiations with Croatian anti-Communist leaders were dictated solely by political expediency and not directed toward finding a viable solution to the issues dividing the Serbian and Croatian nations. The fear of Chetnik postwar retribution in Croatia was so great that even so strong an anti-Communist as Archbishop Stepinac preferred a Partisan victory as the lesser of two evils.[1]

Mihailović's dislike of politics and politicians contributed to the political failure of his movement. He liked to say that he was himself only a soldier carrying out his duties toward King and Fatherland; but the circumstances of the war forced upon him also the role of political leadership. His political advice, such as it was, came from a small group of inconsequential Serbian politicians, organized as the Central National Committee with an Executive Council, whose ideas were completely outdated. As one of the former Chetnik commanders wrote in 1966, "The political committee, created in the summer of 1941, failed in its principal task—the creation of a national policy to which the entire guerrilla activity should have been subordinated. And without fresh ideas and with a very limited provincial mentality, we failed to find our way in the struggle between the two worlds, and time rolled past us mercilessly."[2]

Just as the political wing of the Chetnik movement was limited by the mediocrity of its political staff, so the military wing was handicapped by the mediocrity of its military staff; and for this, too, Mihailović must bear the blame.[3] He put his earliest supporters—mostly lower- and middle-ranking officers of the old Yugoslav army and the gendarmerie—in positions of responsibility, and for the most part kept them there. These men were loyal, and most of them stayed with him to the end—partly, to be sure, because they had little choice. But their horizons were as narrow as his, their Great Serbian nationalism as unquestioned, their ideas as outdated. Thus Mihailović remained a professional soldier surrounded by other professional soldiers like himself, inaccessible to politicians and intellectuals with a better grasp of the realities of a changing world.[4]

Mihailović's direct and open manner, unencumbered by urban polish or intellectual superiority, appealed genuinely to the rank and file of the Serbian people, particularly the peasantry, the great majority of whom gave him their loyalty wholeheartedly until the late summer of 1944. To them he was simply Draža, or "Čiča"—the Old Man. Some of

---

[1] See Vukina, "Last Visit to Archbishop Stepinac." Vukina was a parish priest in Croatia who in 1945 went into exile.

[2] See Vučković, "Away with Apologies," p. 17.

[3] In his report after the tour of duty in Yugoslavia, Captain Mansfield, the OSS operative, expressed these views: "Most troop commanders impress me as capable soldiers. Mihailovic himself, while in good health and obviously having considerable ability as a leader, has surrounded himself with a second-rate General Staff, with a political adviser, Dr. Moljevic, who is an extreme Pan-Serb. Mihailovic lacks ability to delegate." F.O. 371/44271, R7885/11/92.

[4] Not all Chetniks in exile view the matter in this light. See, for example, the reaction of Radoje L. Knežević in *Poruka*, No. 46 (London, Nov. 1957), pp. 15–16, to an editorial in the Chetnik émigré paper *Ravnogorski borac*, No. 104, for August 1957, in which it is stated that Mihailović could not rely on politicians and intellectuals and that a relatively very small number of them rallied to his flag.

the propagandists spoke of the Chetnik uprising as the Third Serbian Revolution, thus ranking Mihailović implicitly with Karageorge and Prince Miloš, the heroes of the earlier two. His decision to adopt peasant dress and grow a beard, and to have his troops affect these and other superficial characteristics of the pre-1912 Chetniks, was to some extent an effort to build up the legend, although in his own case there were also security advantages. Yet even this minor move, much as it pleased his Serbian supporters, must be seen as politically questionable, since the very term Chetnik was anathema to non-Serbs.

A key weakness in the long run was Mihailović's inability to work with the Western Allies when by his own reckoning his best hope for success lay in their support. He was not alone responsible for the steady deterioration in relations between the Chetniks and the British from late 1942 on: he was ill-served by the government-in-exile in London, for one thing, and the British were by no means easy to work with. But at the crucial point in Chetnik-British relations, when the right move by Mihailović might have turned the balance, he did nothing to show his good faith or to prove his usefulness.

One of the principal characteristics of Mihailović's personality was that he was not a creative leader. Except for his decision to fight the Partisans as the chief enemy in the autumn of 1941 in Serbia—a policy from which he never swerved—his military and political conduct mostly followed the familiar patterns established during the interwar period by Serbian-dominated governments in Belgrade, or else was simply a reaction to the actions of others, notably his rival Tito. Perhaps worst of all, Mihailović did not grow in a professional, political, or ideological sense as his responsibilities grew. His promotions from colonel to general of the army within a period of six months and his appointment as both Minister of the Army, Navy, and Air Force and Chief of Staff of the Supreme Command were no doubt sufficient to satisfy an ego that had little tendency toward questioning and self-doubt. But his background, his professional training as an officer, and his average intellectual capacities prevented him from growing into his historical role, and as a result he became daily less capable of successfully handling the ever more difficult and complex problems that arose for the Chetniks. The discrepancy in this respect between Tito and Mihailović is one of the most important differences between the two leaders and goes a long way to explain the one's success and the other's failure.

Owing to his background and professional training, Mihailović had no real understanding of the appeal of a Yugoslavia in which all South Slav nations enjoyed freedom and equality. His Yugoslavism, like that of the interwar Belgrade governments, was a veneer over his Great Serbianism, and thus constrained by Serbian interests whose satisfaction in any large-scale manner would have been unacceptable to other South Slav nations. Tito, by contrast, was working out a new formulation of Yugoslavism which, by combining the elements of nationalism of various South Slav nations and an overall Yugoslav nationalism, was destined to become a truly formidable ideological and political weapon.

In sum, Mihailović's no more than average intelligence, shaped by a limited and purely military training, was inadequate to deal with the complex military conditions of war and occupation in Yugoslavia and the even more complex political conditions at home and in the international sphere. Some of his staunchest defenders have noted that he was a top student in his military class and had a successful army career during the interwar period. This may be true, but it tells us only that success at this level in peacetime is no predictor of success in the convulsions of war and revolution. Tito's evaluation of Mihailović is worth quoting, for it is succinct and accurate: "I saw as early as our second [and last] meeting that Draža was just an average officer (*običan oficir*)."[5] In short, if Mihailović is judged by his military ideas, by his record as a military organizer, and above all by his performance on the battlefield, the conclusion is inescapable that of generalship in the general there was precious little. And of political leadership even less.

The final months of the Chetnik movement, after the withdrawal from Serbia, have a certain tragic quality. Seeing himself as the savior of the Serbian dynasty and the Serbian people, the defender of King and Fatherland, he chose to return to Serbia rather than be evacuated, there to make a new effort to defeat the Communist enemy; yet in military and political terms this move proved his most foolish. Tragic also, in its way, was his treatment—in fact betrayal, in his and other Chetniks' eyes—at the hands of those he most counted on: King Peter, and the British and American governments.[6] To be rejected by the King himself, after three years of supporting the King personally and his government-in-exile and a lifetime of service and devotion to the dynasty, was perhaps the most terrible blow of all. One can imagine Mihailović's bitterness in September 1944, when King Peter, under intense British pressure, appealed over the London radio to all Serbs, Croats, and Slovenes to shift their allegiance to Marshal Tito.

One can imagine also the misery of Mihailović's last months in Bosnia

---

[5] From my interview with Marshal Tito. In the same interview, Tito repeated to me the well-known story that because of his accent he had been taken by Mihailović for a Russian officer in disguise, and that this in fact had saved his life.

[6] Mihailović's friends point out with pride that President Truman, in an act of March 29, 1948, posthumously awarded Mihailović the medal of the Legion of Merit in recognition of the help of his troops in evacuating American airmen from Yugoslavia and for his contribution to the Allied victory. The decoration was classified until 1967, when Congressman Edward J. Derwinski of Illinois made it public. *Naša reč*, No. 186 (Oct. 1967), p. 6.

before his capture. Even his own children had turned against his cause.[7]
A passage from his final statement to the court that tried him in July
1946 is illuminating: "Destiny was merciless towards me when it threw
me into the most difficult whirlwinds. I wanted much, I began much,
but the whirlwind, the world whirlwind, carried me and my work
away."[8] Among many of the Serbian people at home and in exile, and
among some others as well, Mihailović still lives in legend. For them
his cause was just, his wartime record attests to his valor in no way
inferior to that of the Great Serbian heroes of the past, and his capture
and execution have made him a martyr.

THE CONSEQUENCES OF DEFEAT

In losing the civil war, the Chetniks and the Serbian ruling groups
lost not only the main prize, the control of postwar Yugoslavia, but
also a great many specific political institutions and political, economic,
and ecclesiastical positions of power. Further, as a result first of the
sequestration and nationalization of the property of collaborators and
of many Chetnik supporters, and later of general nationalization, the
Serbian ruling groups (together with the remainder of Yugoslavia's
bourgeoisie) lost the economic base they had developed during the
interwar period. We shall conclude by enumerating a few basic effects
of these losses as a consequence of war and revolution.

First and most obviously, the Serbs lost their dynasty and the monarchic system of government. Unlike the imported and imposed dynas-
ties in the other Balkan countries, the Serbian ruling house was a domestic dynasty with roots in the Serbian peasantry, and thus a strong
Serbian national institution. Since in interwar Yugoslavia the Crown
rather than the parliament held the political initiative, with the Chetnik defeat the Serbian ruling groups in fact lost the country's principal
political decision-making institution. To make things even worse, the
first head of the postwar Yugoslav state was—and still is—not only a
professional Communist revolutionary but a Croat.

Second, the Partisan triumph brought an end to the great power of
the Serbian Orthodox Church, which between the wars had been in
effect, if not formally, a state church, and which was a bulwark of the
Serbian ruling groups, especially in areas outside Serbia. In Communist
Yugoslavia all churches are excluded from educational, social, and political functions; most of their property has been nationalized, and
their state subsidies have been eliminated. Though most churches in

---

[7] Mihailović's son and daughter joined the Partisans after the liberation of Serbia. According
to Radulovic, pp. 196–97, Mihailović's divorced wife believed in him, and a stepson by his second
wife's first marriage stayed with him to the end and was killed in Bosnia.
[8] *The Trial of Draža Mihailović*, p. 499.

Yugoslavia seem to be holding their own remarkably well,[9] they are clearly unlikely to regain anything like their former influence. Two specific and tremendously painful consequences of Communist victory for the Serbian Orthodox Church are the creation of a separate Macedonian Orthodox Church and the schism among its members outside Yugoslavia.

Third, the Serbs are today masters only in the pre-1912 territory of Serbia. The Socialist Republic of Serbia in present-day Yugoslavia does include, as autonomous regions, Vojvodina and Kosovo, but the Serbs have to share power in the first with the Hungarians and the Croats and in the second with the Albanians. Traditionally the Great Serbia forces have considered "Serbian lands" to include Yugoslav Macedonia, Kosovo, Montenegro, Bosnia and Herzegovina, Vojvodina, and large parts of Croatia-Slavonia and Dalmatia. Since 1945, the possibility of the Serbs' ever getting these areas under their exclusive control seems to have vanished.

Fourth, the structure of the Yugoslav army has been radically altered. As we have seen, the army of the interwar period was in effect a continuation of the pre-1918 Serbian army; and so was General Mihailović's Yugoslav Army in the Homeland. Not so the wartime Army of the Partisans, which was made up of men from all parts of Yugoslavia and dedicated to a state of free and equal South Slav nations, to the Communist ideology, and to its creator and leader, Marshal Tito. The Partisans' officer corps was truly Yugoslav in composition. At the end of the war, of some sixty-six Partisan generals (including three who were killed in action), seven were Serbs from Serbia, thirteen were Serbs from outside Serbia, twenty-three were Montenegrins, eleven were Croats, ten were Slovenes, one was Macedonian, and one, Feodor Mahin, was a former Russian Tsarist officer and émigré who had joined the Yugoslav Communist Party in 1939.[10]

Fifth, as in the army, so too in civil affairs the Serbs no longer occupy most of the positions of control at all levels. In interwar Yugoslavia, with only brief exceptions, the key ministries (premiership, interior, foreign affairs, army, finance) were always held by Serbs; ministers from other nations were mainly part of a political façade. The Serbs

---

[9] On the rise of the influence of the Serbian Orthodox Church, see *Borba*, Dec. 12, 1970. Note also the reestablishment of diplomatic relations between Yugoslavia and the Vatican, the greatly strengthened Catholic press, and Tito's visit to Pope Paul VI in March 1971.

[10] Compiled on the basis of *Bilten Vrhovnog štaba Narodnooslobodilačke vojske Jugoslavije*, as reprinted in *Zbornik DNOR*, Tome II, Vol. 1 (Belgrade, 1949), pp. 256, 282, and *passim*. Tito, a Croat, is the only one holding the rank of marshal. Of the sixty-six Partisan generals no fewer than fifteen were veterans of the Spanish Civil War. Some of the generals were actually political functionaries who had both political and military functions during the war but immediately afterward reverted to civilian status, e.g. Milovan Djilas, Aleksandar Ranković, Sreten Žujović, Vladimir Velebit. Many other Partisan generals reverted to civilian status a few years after the war.

For the composition of the officer corps in Yugoslavia as of early 1972, see Antic, pp. 3–5.

controlled the army, the gendarmerie, the police, and the foreign service. They held almost all the top posts in the state-owned financial and economic enterprises, and as a result of rampant nepotism most lesser posts as well. Now all this has changed. Great inequalities in the distribution of federal jobs still exist, but owing in part to a system of national quotas, the Serbs no longer have the lion's share of government patronage.

Chetnik writers in exile and their friends never tire of criticizing the treatment of Mihailović and the Chetniks by the Western Allies, and by Prime Minister Churchill in particular. They argue that in jettisoning Mihailović and switching their support to Tito, the Allies not only betrayed a loyal ally who had done more than his duty, but made possible the establishment of a Communist state against their own better interests.

In the last analysis, the Serbian interwar ruling groups could not accept their defeat as a consequence of their own shortsightedness and lack of political and military leadership capacities. Power elites never do; instead they find someone else to blame, and by so doing justify their own policies and actions. Inside Yugoslavia, of course, the surviving members of the old Serbian ruling groups are silent. But the Chetnik and pro-Chetnik writers in the Western world who act as their spokesmen gloss over the failures of the Yugoslav interwar and wartime governments and the wartime Chetniks alike; nor do they question the rightness of the Great Serbia policy that made these failures inevitable. They say little about the Chetniks' record of collaboration with the enemy, little about the ineptness of their political, diplomatic, and military leadership, and little indeed about the victorious Partisans and their leader. Blind to the end, they blame everyone but themselves for their downfall.

Bibliography

UNPUBLISHED MATERIALS

Among the unpublished primary materials used in the preparation of this study, the most important were the captured German and Italian wartime documents available on microfilm at the United States National Archives and to some extent at other depositories. These materials are organized in a large number of groups, but with a great deal of duplication: many of the documents appear in more than one group, or in more than one roll within the same group. The groups of materials and their designations, as well as the microfilm rolls of different groups used, were the following:

Microcopy No. T-501. Records of German Field Commands: Rear Areas, Occupied Territories, and Others. Rolls 246, 247, 249, 250, 251, 253, 256, 257, 258, 260, 264, 265, 266, 267, 268, 351, 352.

Microcopy No. T-311. Records of German Field Commands: Army Groups. Rolls 189, 192, 194, 196, 286.

Microcopy No. T-312. Records of German Field Commands: Armies. Roll 470.

Microcopy No. T-313. Records of German Field Commands: Panzer Armies. Rolls 151, 189, 488.

Microcopy No. T-314. Records of German Field Commands: Corps. Rolls 554, 559, 561, 566, 1457.

Microcopy No. T-315. Records of German Field Commands: Divisions. Rolls 64, 66.

Microcopy No. T-77. Records of Headquarters, German Armed Forces High Command (OKW). Rolls 883, 895, 1295 (the last contains documents of the Military Economics and Armaments Office).

Microcopy No. T-78. Records of Headquarters, German Army High Command (OKH). Rolls 329, 332.

Microcopy No. T-84. Miscellaneous German Records Collection. Rolls 103, 104, 105.

Microcopy No. T-120. Records of the German Ministry of Foreign Affairs. Rolls 753, 1025. I have also used microfilm Serial 9771 supplied by the British Foreign Office, containing documents originating with the German Foreign Ministry.

Of the microfilmed German wartime documents deposited in the National Archives in Washington I have used many documents of Record Group 238: World War II Crimes Records. From the same group of documents I have used a report prepared by Ernst Wisshaupt, which I obtained from another source (see below under Wisshaupt).

Of the Italian microfilmed wartime documents I have used the following series:

Microcopy No. T-821. Collection of Italian Military Records, 1935–1943. Rolls 21, 31, 53, 55, 60, 65, 125, 247, 248, 252, 356.

Microcopy No. T-586. Italian Ministry of the Interior—Office III, and Italian Ministry of Popular Culture. Rolls 366, 424, 426.

I have also consulted at the Archives of the Hoover Institution at Stanford University a series of mimeographed reports prepared by various German officers after they became prisoners of war of the American armed forces. As a rule, these studies, written from memory and giving personal recollections and impressions, are of limited value as source material, but I have found some of them worthwhile and have cited them in appropriate places.

I have used a series of the R and A (Research and Analysis) reports of the United States Office of Strategic Services (OSS) which are declassified and deposited with the National Archives in Washington under the designation Record Group 226. The reports of the field operatives of the same service are still classified. I have also used a number of Foreign Office documents pertaining to Yugoslav affairs during the Second World War, and quotations of Crown-copyright records in the Public Record Office appear by permission of the controller of H.M. Stationery Office.

Finally, I have used a series of unpublished Chetnik and Yugoslav government-in-exile documents deposited in the Archives of the Institute of Military History (Vojnoistorijski institut) in Belgrade, Xerox copies of which are in my files.

PUBLISHED MATERIALS

Names beginning with Č, Ć, Š, and Ž in Serbo-Croatian form are listed following the entries for C, S, and Z, respectively. In cases where authors have published both under their name as originally spelled in Serbo-Croatian and under the Americanized form, only the latter is used (except in the case of Konstantin Fotić, where only the Serbo-Croatian form is used).

Adamic, Louis. "Mikhailovitch: Balkan Mystery Man," *Saturday Evening Post*, December 19, 1942, pp. 20–21, 84, 86.
———. *My Native Land*. New York, 1943.
Adamich, Zenon V. "The Royal Yugoslav Navy in World War II." In United States Naval Institute, *Proceedings*, April 1963, pp. 138–41.
Alexander, Field Marshal Harold. *The Alexander Memoirs, 1940–1945*. London, 1962.
Allied Force, Mediterranean Headquarters. *The Četniks: A Survey of Četnik Activity in Yugoslavia, April 1941–July 1944*. Bari [?], September 1944.
Allied Force Headquarters, Mediterranean Branch. *Handbook of Jugoslav Personalities*. [Bari, 1944.] Copy in the Library of the British Museum. Material ordered alphabetically, no pagination.
[Anti-Communist Forces in Slovenia.] *Črne bukve o delu komunističke Osvobodilne fronte proti slovenskemu narodu* (The Black Book About the Activities of the Communist Liberation Front Against the Slovene People). Ljubljana, 1944.
Antic, Zdenko. "National Structure of the Yugoslav Army Leadership." In

Radio Free Europe Research, Communist Area, pp. 1–5. New York, April 12, 1972.

"The April War, April 6–18, 1941." *Vojna enciklopedija*, I, 185–89. Belgrade, 1958. (All references to articles in *Vojna enciklopedija*, if not otherwise indicated, are to the first edition.)

Arnez, John A. *Slovenia in European Affairs*. New York, 1958.

Assmann, Kurt. "The Battle of Moscow, Turning Point of the War," *Foreign Affairs*, January 1950, pp. 409–26.

————. *Deutsche Schicksalsjahre*. Wiesbaden, 1950.

Auty, Phyllis. "Some Aspects of British-Yugoslav Relations in 1941." Unpublished paper read at a symposium at Belgrade, November 1971.

Avakumović, Ivan. *Mihailović prema nemačkim dokumentima* (Mihailović in the Light of German Documents). London, 1969.

Bagdolio, Pietro. *Italy in the Second World War*. London, 1948.

Bajić, Nevenka. "The June 1941 Uprising in Herzegovina." In *Godišnjak Istoriskog društva Bosne i Hercegovine*, VIII, 225–44. Sarajevo, 1956.

Bandović, Milan. "On Deceiving History," *Naša reč* (London), No. 172–73 (June–July 1966), pp. 18–19.

Banović, Gojko, and Kosta Stepanović. "How Was Draža Mihailović Captured?" Published in serialized form in *Politika* (Belgrade, daily), August 5–September 17, 1962.

Bathe, Rolf, and Erich Glodschey. *Der Kampf um den Balkan*. Oldenburg and Berlin, 1942.

Biber, Dušan. "Open Secret Archives of British Diplomacy." Published in serialized form in *Vijesnik u srijedu* (*VUS*; Zagreb, weekly), June 7–October 26, 1972.

Bir'uzov, S. S., ed. *Sovetskie vooruzhennie silli v borbe za osvobozhdenie narodov Iugoslavii* (Soviet Armed Forces in the Struggle for the Liberation of the Peoples of Yugoslavia). Moscow, 1960.

Bir'uzov, S. S., and Rade Hamović, eds. *Beogradska operacija* (The Belgrade Operation). Belgrade, 1964.

Boban, Ljubo. *Sporazum Cvetković-Maček* (The Cvetković-Maček Agreement). Belgrade, 1965.

Bojić, Alija. "German Preparations for Operation 'Schwarz' and Their Estimates of Possible Allied Landings in the Balkans During the First Half of 1943." In *Neretva-Sutjeska 1943*, pp. 125–34. Belgrade, 1969.

Borković, Milan. "The United Communist Youth of Yugoslavia and the Youth Movement in Serbia in 1942." In Slavko Odić, ed., *Prvo zasjedanje AVNOJ-a* (The First Session of AVNOJ), pp. 299–310. Bihać, 1967.

Bosnitch, Sava D. "The Significance of the Soviet Military Intervention in Yugoslavia, 1944–1945," *Review* (London), No. 8 (1969), pp. 695–710.

Broz, Josip. See Tito, Josip Broz.

Cavallero, Ugo. *Comando Supremo*. Bologna, 1948.

Cemović, Predrag Lj. "From Podgorica to Gradiška," *Glasnik SIKD 'Njegoš'* (Chicago), June 1961, pp. 44–88.

Cervi, Mario. *Storia della guerra di Grecia*. 3rd ed. Milan, 1966. English edition: *The Hollow Legions*, with an introduction by F. W. Deakin. New York, 1971.

Churchill, Winston S. *The Second World War*. 6 vols. Boston, 1948–53. Vol. III, *The Grand Alliance*, 1950; Vol. V, *Closing the Ring*, 1951; Vol. VI, *Triumph and Tragedy*, 1953.

Ciano, Galeazzo. *Ciano's Diary 1939–43.* London, 1947.

Clissold, Stephen. *Whirlwind.* London, 1949.

Committee for a Fair Trial for Draja Mihailovich. *Report of Commission of Inquiry.* New York, 1946.

Communist Party of Yugoslavia (since 1952, League of Communists of Yugoslavia). "Conclusions of the April [*sic*] 1941 Consultation of the Communist Party of Yugoslavia in Zagreb," *Zbornik DNOR,* Tome II, Vol. 2, pp. 7–23.

———. *Istorijski arhiv Komunističke partije Jugoslavije* (Historical Archives of the Communist Party of Yugoslavia). 7 vols. Belgrade, 1949–51.

———. *VII kongres Saveza komunista Jugoslavije* (The Seventh Congress of the League of Communists of Yugoslavia). Belgrade, 1958.

Cvetković, Dragiša. "Conversations at Berchtesgaden." In *Dokumenti o Jugoslaviji,* No. 8, pp. 7–17. Paris, 1956.

———. "The Meaning, Character, and Consequences of the Serbo-Croatian Agreement," *Glasnik SIKD 'Njegoš',* December 1962, pp. 8–27.

———. "The 'Proofs' of Radoje Knežević." In *Dokumenti o Jugoslaviji,* No. 2, pp. 14–22. Paris, 1951.

———. "Regarding the Article of Radoje Knežević About the 25th and 27th of March." In *Dokumenti o Jugoslaviji,* No. 1, pp. 11–22. Paris, 1951.

———. "Yugoslavia and the Development of the International Situation Between the Wars," *Glasnik SIKD 'Njegoš',* December 1960, pp. 1–32.

Čolaković, Rodoljub. *Zapisi iz oslobodilačkog rata* (Memoirs from the Liberation War). 5 vols. Sarajevo, 1945–55.

Čolaković, Rodoljub, et al., eds. *Pregled istorije Saveza komunista Jugoslavije* (A Survey of the History of the League of Communists of Yugoslavia). Belgrade, 1963.

Čubrilović, Branko. *Zapisi iz tudjine* (Notes from Abroad). Sarajevo, 1946.

Čulinović, Ferdo. *Dvadeset sedmi mart* (The Twenty-seventh of March). Zagreb, 1965.

———. *Jugoslavija izmedju dva rata* (Yugoslavia Between the Two Wars). 2 vols. Zagreb, 1961.

———. *Okupatorska podjela Jugoslavije* (The Partition of Yugoslavia Among the Occupying Powers). Belgrade, 1970.

———. *Slom stare Jugoslavije* (The Collapse of Old Yugoslavia). Zagreb, 1958.

Ćorović, Vladimir. *Istorija Jugoslavije* (History of Yugoslavia). Belgrade, 1933.

Dalton, Hugh. *The Fateful Years—Memoirs 1931–1945.* London, 1957.

Danilović, Uglješa. "The Conference in Ivančići." In *Istočna Bosna u NOB-u 1941–1945* (Eastern Bosnia in the National Liberation Struggle, 1941–1945), I, 467–79. Belgrade, 1971.

———. "The Crisis in the Uprising in Eastern Bosnia in the Spring of 1942." In *Istočna Bosna u NOB-u 1941–1945,* I, 383–421. Belgrade, 1971.

Deakin, F. W. D. *The Embattled Mountain.* New York, 1971.

———. "The First British Military Mission to Tito." In *Neretva-Sutjeska 1943,* pp. 184–95. Belgrade, 1969.

———. "Great Britain and Yugoslavia, 1941–1945," *Jugoslovenski istorijski časopis* (Belgrade), 1963, No. 2, pp. 43–58. Serbo-Croatian translation of a revised version of a paper read at a Conference on Britain and European Resistance, 1939–1945, St. Antony's College, Oxford, December 1962.

———. Untitled paper, in St. Antony's College, Oxford University, *Proceedings of a Conference on Britain and European Resistance 1939–45* (December 10–16, 1962), pp. 1–16. Also remarks in the discussion on Yugoslav matters, pp. 1–9, 12, 19–22.

Dedijer, Vladimir. *Dnevnik* (Journal). 3 vols. Belgrade, 1945–50.

———. *Josip Broz Tito.* Belgrade, 1953.

———. *On Military Conventions.* Lund, 1961.

———. "Sur l'armistice 'germano-yougoslave'," *Revue d'histoire de la deux-ième guerre mondiale* (Paris), July 1956, pp. 1–9.

Djelević, Jakša V. "The First Months [of the Chetnik Movement]." In *Knjiga o Draži*, I, 177–89.

Djilas, Milovan. *Conversations with Stalin.* New York, 1962.

Djonlagić, Ahmet, and Mišo Leković. *Njemačka ofanziva na istočnu Bosnu—januar–februar 1942* (The German Offensive on Eastern Bosnia—January–February 1942). Belgrade, 1962.

Djonović, Dušan J. "Aid in Money Sent by the Yugoslav Government to General Mihailović," *Glasnik SIKD 'Njegoš',* December 1960, pp. 98–105, and December 1961, pp. 55–65.

———. [D., pseud.]. "Aid Sent by Great Britain [to General Mihailović], *Glasnik SIKD 'Njegoš',* December 1959, pp. 90–95.

Djonović, Jovan. "The Connections with Draža Mihailović from the Middle East and North Africa," *Glasnik SIKD 'Njegoš',* July 1958, pp. 41–65.

———. "The Connections with General Mihailović from the Middle East," *Glasnik SIKD 'Njegoš',* December 1959, pp. 17–25.

———. "From the Wailing Wall to the Land of the Pharaohs," *Glasnik SIKD 'Njegoš',* December 1962, pp. 28–42.

———. "Mihailović's Telegrams About British Missions at His Headquarters and British Policy in the Country," *Glasnik SIKD 'Njegoš',* June 1960, pp. 24–35; December 1960, pp. 53–57; June 1961, pp. 33–38.

———. "My Connections with Draža Mihailović from the Middle East," *Glasnik SIKD 'Njegoš',* December 1958, pp. 82–89.

———. "The Reports of General Mihailović from the End of 1943 and 1944," *Glasnik SIKD 'Njegoš',* June 1959, pp. 63–80.

Djordjević, Boško. *Pregled ugovorne trgovinske politike of osnivanja države Srba, Hrvata i Slovenaca do rata 1941 godine* (A Survey of Treaty-Regulated Commercial Policy from the Establishment of the State of the Serbs, Croats, and Slovenes Until the War of 1941). Zagreb, 1960.

Djukić, Svetomir. "From the Forests into Emigration." Series of articles in *Srpska zastava* (Buenos Aires, monthly), between December 1954 and May 1955.

Drachkovitch, Milorad M., and Branko Lazitch. "Staff 501 of the Ravna Gora Youth," *Glasnik SIKD 'Njegoš',* December 1962, pp. 91–105.

Drainac, Rade. *Crni dani* (Black Days). Belgrade, 1963.

Dudić, Dragojlo. *Dnevnik 1941* (Journal, 1941). Belgrade, 1945.

Dželebdžić, Milovan. "The Attack on Communications in Yugoslavia from September 1 to 7, 1944—Operation 'Ratweek'," *Vojnoistorijski glasnik* (Belgrade), 1970, No. 3, pp. 7–61.

Eden, Anthony, Earl of Avon. *The Reckoning.* Boston, 1965.

Ehrman, John. *Grand Strategy.* Vol. V, *August 1943–September 1944.* History of the Second World War, United Kingdom Military Series. London, 1956.

Fotić, Konstantin. *The Political Situation in Yugoslavia Today.* Washington, D.C., April 1945.

———. *The War We Lost.* New York, 1948.

General Mihailovich—The World's Verdict. Gloucester, England, 1947.

Germany, Auswärtiges Amt. *Documents relatifs au conflit germano-yougoslave et germanoc-grec.* Berlin, 1941.

————. Länderrat des Amerikanischen Besatzungsgebiets. *Statistisches Handbuch von Deutschland, 1928–1944.* Munich, 1949.

————, Wehrmacht, Oberkommando. *Der Feldzug auf dem Balkan und die Rückeroberung der Cyrenaika.* Berlin, 1941[?].

————. *Kriegstagebuch des Oberkommandos der Wehrmacht (Wehrmachtführungsstab).* 4 vols., of which II-IV are in two parts each. Frankfurt am Main, 1963–65.

Gizdić, Drago. *Dalmacija 1942.* Zagreb, 1959.

Glišić, Venceslav. *Teror i zločini nacističke Nemačke u Srbiji 1941–1944* (Terror and Crimes of Nazi Germany in Serbia, 1941–1944). Belgrade, 1970.

Görlitz, Walter. *Der Zweite Weltkrieg 1939–1945.* 2 vols. Stuttgart, 1951–52.

Görlitz, Walter, ed. *General Feldmarschall Keitel: Verbrecher oder Offizier?* Göttingen, 1961.

Grafenauer, Bogo, et al. *Istorija naroda Jugoslavije* (History of the Peoples of Yugoslavia). 2 vols. Belgrade, 1953, 1960.

Gregorić, Danilo. *So endete Jugoslawien.* Leipzig, 1943.

Grdjić, Radmilo. "The Contribution of the Croats from the Adriatic Littoral." In *Knjiga o Draži,* II, 262–68.

Grdjić, Risto. "The General Renewal of Church Life and Organization." In Serbian Orthodox Church, The Holy Synod, ed., *Srpska pravoslavna crkva 1920–1970* (The Serbian Orthodox Church, 1920–1970), pp. 239–52. Belgrade, 1971.

Great Britain. *Documents Relating to the Conditions of an Armistice with Italy (September–November 1943).* Cmd. 6693. London, 1945.

————. *Parliamentary Debates.* Session 1943–44. Vol. 400.

————, Foreign Office. "Relations Between General Mihailovic and His Majesty's Government." Report of July 27, 1944. F.O. 371/44–276.

Greiner, Helmuth. *Die Oberste Wehrmachtführung 1939–1943.* Wiesbaden, 1951.

Grum, France, and Stane Pleško. *Svoboda v razvalinah* (Liberty in Ruins). Cleveland, 1961.

Hadri, Ali. "The Occupation System in Kosovo and Metohia, 1941–1944," *Jugoslovenski istorijski časopis,* 1965, No. 2, pp. 39–60.

Hagen, Walter. *Die geheime Front.* Zurich, 1950.

Harriman, Helga H. "Slovenia as an Outpost of the Third Reich," *East European Quarterly,* June 1971, pp. 222–31.

Hasanagić, Edib, ed. *Komunistička partija Jugoslavije 1919–1941* (The Communist Party of Yugoslavia, 1919–1941). Zagreb, 1959.

Hassell, Ulrich von. *The von Hassell Diaries, 1938–1944.* London, 1948.

Herzog, Robert. *Grundzüge der deutschen Besatzungsverwaltung in den ost- und südosteuropäischen Ländern während des zweiten Weltkrieges,* Tübingen, 1955.

Hitler e Mussolini, letere e documenti. Milan, 1946.

Hoptner, Jacob B. *Yugoslavia in Crisis, 1934–1941.* New York, 1962.

Hory, Ladislaus, and Martin Broszat. *Der kroatische Ustascha-Staat 1941–45.* Stuttgart, 1964.

Howard, Michael. *Grand Strategy,* Vol. IV, *August 1942–September 1943.* History of the Second World War, United Kingdom Military Series. London, 1972.

————. *The Mediterranean Strategy in the Second World War.* New York, 1968.

Hubatsch, Walther, ed. *Hitlers Weisungen für die Kriegführung 1939–1945.* Frankfurt am Main, 1962.

Hudson, Duane T. Remarks in the discussion on Yugoslav matters, in St. Antony's College, Oxford University, *Proceedings of a Conference on Britain and European Resistance 1939–45* (December 10–16, 1962), Yugoslav discussion, pp. 11–13, 17–18.

Hurem, Rasim. "The Attempt of Some Moslem Bourgeois Politicians to Separate Bosnia and Herzegovina from the Independent State of Croatia." In *Godišnjak Društva istoričara Bosne i Hercegovine*, XVI, 191–221. Sarajevo, 1965.

———. "The Collaboration Agreements Between the Authorities of the Independent State of Croatia and Some Chetnik Detachments in Eastern Bosnia in 1942." Institut za istoriju radničkog pokreta, Sarajevo, *Prilozi*, II (1966), 285–325.

———. "Conceptions of Some Moslem Bourgeois Politicians About the Situation of Bosnia and Herzegovina During the Period from the Middle of 1943 to the End of 1944." Institut za istoriju radničkog pokreta, Sarajevo, *Prilozi*, IV (1968), 533–48.

Independent State of Croatia. *Brzopisni zapisnici Prvog zasjedanja Hrvatskog državnog sabora u Nezavisnoj Državi Hrvatskoj godine 1942* (Stenographic Minutes of the First Session of the Croatian State Diet in the Independent State of Croatia in 1941). Zagreb, 1942.

———, Ministry of Foreign Affairs. *Medjunarodni ugovori 1941* (International Treaties, 1941). Zagreb, n.d.

———, Ministry of Justice and Religion. *Zbornik zakona i naredaba Nezavisne Države Hrvatske* (A Collection of Laws and Decrees of the Independent State of Croatia). Zagreb, annually, 1941–45.

Inks, James M. *Eight Bailed Out.* New York, 1954.

Italy, Stato Maggiore del R. Esercito. *Bollettini della guerra.* Rome, 1941.

International Military Tribunal. *Trial of the Major War Criminals Before the International Military Tribunal, Nuremberg, 14 November 1945–1 October 1946.* Vols. XXV, XXVII, XXXIV, XXXIX. Nuremberg, 1948, 1949.

Janeković, Slavko. "On the Operations of the Italian Intelligence Service Against the National Liberation Movement of Yugoslavia," *Vojnoistorijski glasnik*, 1965, No. 2, pp. 27–46.

Jareb, Jere. *Pola stoljeća hrvatske politike* (A Half-Century of Croatian Politics). Buenos Aires, 1960.

Jovanović, Batrić. *Crna Gora u NOR i socijalističkoj revoluciji* (Montenegro in the National Liberation War and Socialist Revolution). Vol. I. Belgrade, 1960.

Jukić, Ilija. *Pogledi na prošlost, sadašnjost i budućnost hrvatskog naroda* (Reflections on the Past, Present, and Future of the Croatian People). London, 1965.

Kačavenda, Petar. "The Collaboration of the Chetniks and the Ustashas in Bosnia During 1942," *Vojnoistorijski glasnik*, 1966, No. 5, pp. 37–67.

Karapandžić, Bor. M. *Gradjanski rat u Srbiji 1941–1945* (Civil War in Serbia, 1941–1945). Cleveland, 1958.

Kardelj, Edvard. "Ten Years of People's Revolution," *Komunist* (Belgrade), March–May 1951, pp. 49–136.

——— [Sperans, pseud.]. *Razvoj slovenskega narodnega vprašanja* (The Development of the Slovene National Question). Ljubljana, 1939.

Kašić, Dušan. "The Serbian Church in the So-Called Independent State of Croatia." In Serbian Orthodox Church, The Holy Synod, ed., *Srpska pravoslavna crkva 1920–1970* (The Serbian Orthodox Church, 1920–1970), pp. 183–204. Belgrade, 1971.

———. "The Serbian Church Under German Occupation." In Serbian Orthodox Church, The Holy Synod, ed., *Srpska pravoslavna crkva 1920–1970* (The Serbian Orthodox Church, 1920–1970), pp. 225–36. Belgrade, 1971.

Kladarin, Djuro. *Slom Četvrte i Pete okupatorsko-kvislinške ofanzive* (The Debacle of the Fourth and Fifth Offensives of the Occupation and Quisling Forces). Zagreb, 1954.

Kljaković, Vojmir. "About the Elements of Socialist Revolution in the Liberation War of the Peoples of Yugoslavia." Unpublished paper read at a symposium at Ljubljana, January 1972.

———. "The Change in the Policy of Great Britain Toward Yugoslavia in the First Half of 1943," *Jugoslovenski istorijski časopis*, 1969, No. 3, pp. 25–57.

———. "Dalmatia in Perception and Action of the Government-in-Exile and the Western Allies During 1941–1942." Unpublished manuscript.

———. "Enemy Preparations for the Fourth Offensive According to Foreign Sources and Enemy Documents," *Vojnoistorijski glasnik*, 1952, No. 2, pp. 65–82.

———. "Great Britain, the Soviet Union, and the Uprising in Yugoslavia in 1941," *Vojnoistorijski glasnik*, 1970, No. 2, pp. 69–103.

———. "Memoirs of General Simović and Documents, 1939–1942." Published in 96 installments in *Politika* (Belgrade, daily), August 21–November 24, 1970.

———. "The Yugoslav Government-in-Exile and the Allies in Relation to the Problem of Croatia, 1941–1944," *Časopis za suvremenu povijest* (Zagreb), 1971, No. II-III, pp. 97–138; 1973, No. I, pp. 5–31.

Knežević, Radoje L. "The Beginnings of the Resistance Movement." In *Knjiga o Draži*, I, 7–14.

———. "The Letter Z." In *Knjiga o Draži*, I, 250–63.

———. "On the Occasion of the Tenth Anniversary of the Death [of Draža Mihailović]. In *Knjiga o Draži*, II, 336–41.

———. "Prince Paul, Hitler, and Salonika," *International Affairs* (London), January 1951, pp. 38–44. Reprinted in *Poruka* (London), No. 2–3 (March 1951), pp. 3–6.

———. "Slobodan Jovanović in Politics," *Poruka* (London), No. 53–54 (January-March 1959), pp. 26–41.

———. The "Yugoslav Government and Draža Mihailović," *Poruka* (London), No. 8 (November 1, 1952), pp. 5–14; No. 10 (February 1, 1953), pp. 5–13; No. 13 (June 16, 1953), pp. 9–19; No. 18 (February 1, 1954), pp. 5–15; No. 23 (October 16, 1954), pp. 5–15; No. 24 (November 1, 1954), pp. 11–15.

Knežević, Radoje L., ed. *Knjiga o Draži* (The Book About Draža). 2 vols. Windsor, Ont., 1956.

Knežević, Živan L. *General Mihailovich and U.S.S.R.: With Official Memoranda and Documents*. Washington, D.C., 1945.

———. "The Soviet Invasion of Serbia in 1944." In *Knjiga o Draži*, II, 147–70.

———. *Why the Allies Abandoned the Yugoslav Army of General Mihailovich: With Official Memoranda and Documents*. Washington, D.C., April 25, 1945.

Knjiga o Draži. See Knežević, Radoje L., ed., *Knjiga o Draži*.

Kosanović, Sava N. *Šta se moglo videti iz emigracije* (What Could Be Seen from Emigration). Belgrade, 1945.

Kostić, Boško N. *Za istoriju naših dana* (Contributions to the History of Our Days). Lille, 1949.
Kovačević, Branko, and Savo Skoko. "The Uprising in Herzegovina in June 1941." In *Istorija radničkog pokreta—Zbornik radova I* (History of the Workers' Movement—Symposium I), pp. 89–168. Belgrade, 1965.
Krakov, Stanislav. *General Milan Nedić*. 2 vols. Munich, 1963, 1968.
Kriegsheim, Herbert. *Getarnt, Getäuscht und doch Getreu—Die geheimnisvollen "Brandenburger."* Berlin, 1958.
Krizman, Bogdan. *Hitlerov "Pothvat 25" protiv Jugoslavije* (Hitler's "Operation 25" Against Yugoslavia). Zagreb, 1953.
Kukoleča, Stevan. *Analiza privrede Jugoslavije pred Drugi svetski rat* (An Analysis of the Economy of Yugoslavia on the Eve of the Second World War). Belgrade, 1956.
Lawrence, Christie. *Irregular Adventure*. London, 1946.
Lazitch, Branko. "From the History of Ravna Gora." In *Knjiga o Draži*, I, 167–72.
——. *La tragédie du Général Draja Mihailovitch*. Paris, 1946.
——. *Osnovne istine o radu i ciljevima Tita i komunista* (Fundamental Truths About the Activity and Goals of Tito and the Communists). Free Serbian Mountains, Staff 501, August 1944. Published anonymously.
——. *Titov pokret i režim u Jugoslaviji 1941–1946* (Tito's Movement and Rule in Yugoslavia, 1941–1946). N.p., 1946.
Lederer, Ivo J. *Yugoslavia at the Paris Peace Conference: A Study in Frontiermaking*. New Haven, 1963.
Leighton, Richard M. "OVERLORD Revisited: An Interpretation of American Strategy in the European War, 1942–1944," *American Historical Review*, July 1963, pp. 919–37.
Leković, Mišo. "Mihailović's Plans for the Destruction of the 'Partisan State' in Western Bosnia in the Second Half of 1942," *Jugoslovenski istorijski časopis*, 1966, No. 1–2, 79–100.
——. *Ofanziva proleterskih brigada u leto 1942* (The Offensive of the Proletarian Brigades in the Summer of 1942). Belgrade, 1965.
——. "The Sojourn of the British Military Mission in the Liberated Territory of Montenegro and Southeastern Bosnia," *Istorijski zapisi* (Titograd), 1971, No. 1–2, pp. 301–28.
——. "Some Aspects of Italian-Ustasha Relations and Their Reflection on the Operations of the National Liberation Army and Partisan Detachments of Yugosalvia," *Jugoslovenski istorijski časopis*, 1965, No. 4, pp. 83–95.
Lockhart, R. H. Bruce. *Comes the Reckoning*. London, 1947.
Lojen, Stjepan. *Uspomene jednog iseljenika* (Reminiscences of an Emigrant). Zagreb, 1963.
Luburić, Vjekoslav. "Open Letter to the Serbian General Svetomir Djukić," *Drina* (Madrid), No. 8–12 (December 1955), pp. 217–32.
—— [Domagoj, pseud.]. "The Battle at Lijevče Polje," *Drina* (Madrid), No. 1–3 (February 1955), pp. 75–92.
—— [General Drinjanin, pseud.]. "The Ustashas as a State-building and Anti-Communist Military Factor," *Drina* (Madrid), No. 10–12 (December 1954), pp. 3–27.
Maclean, Fitzroy. *Eastern Approaches*. London, 1949.
——. *The Heretic*. New York, 1957.
Macura, Miloš. *Stanovništvo i radna snaga kao činioci privrednog razvoja Jugo-*

slavije (Population and Labor Force as Factors in the Economic Development of Yugoslavia). Belgrade, 1958.

Maček, Vladko. *In the Struggle for Freedom.* New York, 1957.

Mansfield, Walter R. "Marine with the Chetniks," *Marine Corps Gazette,* January 1946, pp. 3–9, and February 1946, pp. 15–20.

———. "Mihailović and Tito." In *Knjiga o Draži,* II, 345–56.

Marić, Mihailo. *Kralj i vlada u emigraciji* (The King and the Government in Exile). Zagreb, 1966.

Marjanović, Jovan. "Contributions to the History of the Conflict Between the National Liberation Movement and the Chetniks of Draža Mihailović in Serbia in 1941." In Institut društvenih nauka, *Istorija XX veka—Zbornik radova I,* pp. 153–233. Belgrade, 1959.

———. "Great Britain and the National Liberation Movement in Yugoslavia, 1941–1945," *Jugoslovenski istorijski časopis,* 1963, No. 2, pp. 31–42. This is a revised version of a paper read at a Conference on Britain and European Resistance, 1939–1945, at St. Antony's College, Oxford University, December 1962.

———. *Srbija u narodnooslobodilačkoj borbi: Beograd* (Serbia in the National Liberation Struggle: Belgrade). Belgrade, 1964.

———. *Ustanak i narodnooslobodilački pokret u Srbiji 1941* (The Uprising and the National Liberation Movement in Serbia in 1941). Belgrade, 1963.

Martin, David. *Ally Betrayed.* New York, 1946.

Martinović, Milan. "The Painstaking Labors of Dr. Krnjević in London During the War." In *Kalendar Hrvatski glas 1955* (Croatian Almanac, 1955), pp. 66–79. Winnipeg, 1955.

Martinović-Bajica, Petar. *Milan Nedić.* Chicago, 1956.

Matl, Josef. "Between Collaboration and Resistance." In Institut für Zeitgeschichte, *Das Dritte Reich und Europa,* pp. 152–63. Munich, 1957.

Matloff, Maurice, *United States Army in World War II. The War Department: Strategic Planning for Coalition Warfare, 1943–1944.* Washington, D.C., 1959.

Mellenthin, F. W. von. *Panzer Battles.* Norman, Okla., 1956.

Mešković, Pavle. "At Ravna Gora." In *Knjiga o Draži,* I, 53–70.

———. "From Bosnia to Ravna Gora." In *Knjiga o Draži,* I, 28–33.

Mi. Mić. [Miloš Minić]. "The Chetniks During the Second World War." In *Enciklopedija Jugoslavije,* II, 572–87. Zagreb, 1956.

Mićanović, Slavko. "The Attack of the Chetniks on the Partisans at the Majevica Mountain." In *Godišnjak Društva istoričara Bosne i Hercegovine,* XII, pp. 165–81. Sarajevo, 1961.

Mikuž, Metod. *Pregled razvoja NOB u Sloveniji* (A Review of the Development of the National Liberation Struggle in Slovenia). Vol. I. Belgrade, 1956.

Miletić, Antun. "The Collaboration of Jezdimir Dangić, Commander of Chetnik Detachments of Eastern Bosnia, with the Germans," *Vojnoistorijski glasnik,* 1972, No. 2, pp. 135–47.

Milićević, Todor. "The Causes of Our Military Debacle in 1941," *Glasnik SIKD 'Njegoš',* December 1961, pp. 5–49.

Milićević, Vladeta. *Der Königsmord von Marseille,* Bad Godesberg, 1959.

Milosavljević, Dragoslav V. "Mihailović Before Ravna Gora." In *Knjiga o Draži,* I, 44–52.

Milošević, Aleksandar. "Golgotha." In *Knjiga o Draži,* II, 207–44.

Milovanović, Nikola. "The Conspiracy Against Revolution," installments 14 and 15 of a series of articles in *Borba* (Belgrade), October 23 and 24, 1970.

————. "I Was in Draža's Supreme Command." A series of articles in *NIN* (Belgrade, weekly), between October 20, 1968, and March 2, 1969.

————. *Vojni puč i 27 mart* (Military Putsch and the 27th of March). Belgrade, 1960.

Minić, Mihailo P. *Rasute kosti (1941–1945)* (The Scattered Bones, 1941–1945). Detroit, 1965.

Moore, Wilbert E. *Economic Demography of Eastern and Southern Europe.* Geneva, 1945.

Morača, Pero. "The Communist Party of Yugoslavia in the Period of the National Liberation War and Revolution, April 1941–May 1945." In Rodoljub Čolaković et al., eds., *Pregled istorije Saveza komunista Jugoslavije* (A Survey of the History of the League of Communists of Yugoslavia), pp. 293–422. Belgrade, 1963.

————. *Prelomna godina narodnooslobodilačkog rata* (The Critical Year of the National Liberation War). Belgrade, 1957.

Mueller-Hillebrand, Hermann Burkhart. *The German Campaign in the Balkans, 1941—A Model of Crisis Planning.* Foreign Military Studies, No. 1. Office of the Chief of Military History, United States Army, 1950.

————. *Der Zusammenhang zwischen dem deutschen Balkanfeldzug und der Invasion in Russland.* German Report Series, M.S. No. C-101. Office of the Chief of Military History, United States Army, 1941.

Neretva-Sutjeska 1943. See Yugoslavia, Vojnoistorijski institut, *Neretva-Sutjeska 1943.*

Neretva—Zbornik radova (Neretva—A Symposium). 3 vols. Belgrade, 1965.

Neubacher, Hermann. *Sonderauftrag Südost 1940–1945.* Göttingen, 1956.

Novak, Karlo. "The Resistance Movement in Slovenia." In *Knjiga o Draži,* I, 317–32.

Odić, Slavko F. *Neostvareni planovi* (Unfulfilled Plans). Zagreb, 1961.

Omrčanin, Ivo. *Istina o Draži Mihailoviću* (The Truth About Draža Mihailović). Munich and New York, 1957.

Oppenheim, L., and H. Lauterpacht. *International Law.* 7th ed. Vol. II. London, 1952.

Ostović, P. D. *The Truth About Yugoslavia.* New York, 1952.

Pajović, Radoje. "The Chetnik Movement and the National Liberation Movement in Montenegro During the Battle at the Sutjeska River." In *Neretva-Sutjeska 1943,* pp. 395–403. Belgrade, 1969.

————. "The Formation of the Chetnik Independent Group of National Resistance," *Jugoslovenski istorijski časopis,* 1964, No. 4, pp. 53–72.

————. "The Liquidation of the Chetnik Leadership in Ostrog in October 1943 with a Review of the Chetnik Movement in Montenegro After the Battle of the Neretva River," *Istorijski zapisi,* 1965, No. 2, pp. 278–303.

————. "The Massacre of Moslems in Sandjak and Part of Eastern Bosnia in January and February 1943." In *Neretva-Sutjeska 1943,* pp. 510–19. Belgrade, 1969.

————. "Political Action of Sekula Drljević and His Collaboration with the Ustasha Leadership and the German Legation in Zagreb (1943–1945)," *Časopis za suvremenu povijest* (Zagreb), 1971, No. I, pp. 75–89.

Pantelić, Milojica. "The Twenty-fifth Division in the Toplica-Jablanica Operation," *Vojnoistorijski glasnik,* 1969, No. 1, pp. 251–66.

Papagos, Alexander. *The Battle of Greece, 1940–1941.* Athens, 1949.

Parežanin, Ratko. *Drugi svetski rat i Dimitrije V. Ljotić* (The Second World War and Dimitrije V. Ljotić). Munich, 1971.

Paris, Edmond. *Genocide in Satellite Croatia, 1941–1945.* Chicago, n.d.

Pavelić, Ante Smith. "The British and Draža Mihailović," *Hrvatska revija* (Buenos Aires), September 1957, pp. 235–53.

————. *Dr. Ante Trumbić: Problemi hrvatsko-srpskih odnosa* (Dr. Ante Trumbić: The Problems of Croato-Serbian Relations). Munich, 1959.

————. *Kairska afera* (The Scandal of Cairo). Paris, 1961.

————. "Yugoslavia and the Tripartite Pact," *Hrvatska revija* (Buenos Aires), June 1956, pp. 65–108.

Pavlović, Kosta St. "The Fall of the Jovanović Cabinet," *Glasnik SIKD 'Njegoš'*, December 1959, pp. 1–16.

————. "The Fall of the Purić Cabinet," *Glasnik SIKD 'Njegoš'*, June 1961, pp. 7–32.

————. "The Fall of the Simović Cabinet," *Glasnik SIKD 'Njegoš'*, December 1958, pp. 67–81.

————. "The Fall of the Trifunović Cabinet," *Glasnik SIKD 'Njegoš'*, December 1960, pp. 58–70.

————. *Jovan Dučić.* Milan, 1967.

Perović, Puniša. "The End of the Two Greatest Montenegrin Traitors," *Stvaranje* (Cetinje), April–May 1947, pp. 185–200.

Perović, Vukašin. "What Preceded the Civil War," *Glasnik SIKD 'Njegoš'*, July 1958, pp. 66–76.

Petelin, Stanko. "The Defeat of the Slovene Part of Mihailović's 'Yugoslav Army in the Homeland' at Grčarice and Turjak," *Vojnoistorijski glasnik*, 1962, No. 6, pp. 3–25.

————. *Izmedju Triglava i Trsta* (Between Mount Triglav and Trieste). Belgrade, 1967.

Peter II of Yugoslavia. *A King's Heritage.* London, 1955.

Petković, Dušan. "The Chetnik Radio Station Karadjordje," *Glasnik SIKD 'Njegoš'*, June 1959, pp. 43–48.

————. "How the Contact with General Mihailović from Istanbul Was Established," *Glasnik SIKD 'Njegoš'*, June 1960, pp. 49–55.

Petrović, Dragoljub. "The Chetnik Organization of Kosta Pećanac in Occupied Serbia Until the Beginning of October 1941," *Vojnoistorijski glasnik*, 1968, No. 2, pp. 173–203.

Piljević, Djordje. "Some Specific Characteristics of the Uprising in Herzegovina in 1941," *Jugoslovenski istorijski časopis*, 1968, No. 3–4, pp. 147–56.

Playfair, I. S. O., et al. *The Mediterranean and Middle East.* 4 vols. History of the Second World War, United Kingdom Military Series. London, 1954–66.

Plećaš, Nedjeljko B. "From the Sea and by Air into the Occupied Homeland," *Glasnik SIKD 'Njegoš'*, June 1960, pp. 36–48.

Plenča, Dušan. *Medjunarodni odnosi Jugoslavije u toku Drugog svjetskog rata* (International Relations of Yugoslavia During the Second World War). Belgrade, 1962.

————. "On Nationalist Manifestations and Deformations in the Historiography of the War of National Liberation and Revolution," *Gledišta* (Belgrade), January 1965, pp. 29–50.

Poole, DeWitt C. "Light on Nazi Foreign Policy," *Foreign Affairs*, October 1946, pp. 130–54.

Popović, Ljubo. *Velika igra sa Dražom Mihailovićem* (The Great Game with Draža Mihailović). Belgrade, 1971.

Popović, Vojin. "The Breakthrough of the Units of the Chief Headquarters of Serbia into Eastern Serbia in 1944," *Vojnoistorijski glasnik*, 1956, No. 4, pp. 20–52.

————. "The Bulgarian Army in Occupied Serbia, 1941–1944," *Vojnoistorijski glasnik*, 1952, No. 3, pp. 22–57, and No. 4, pp. 37–74.

Pribićević, Adam. "The Ideology of Draža's Movement." In *Knjiga o Draži*, II, 33–55.

Purković, M. A. "Dragoljub Mihailović—A Short Biography." In *Knjiga o Draži*, I, 1–5.

Putnik, Dimitrije R. "Radio Connections with the Country in the Course of the Second World War," *Glasnik SIKD 'Njegoš'*, June 1961, pp. 39–43.

Raditsa, Bogdan. "The Plot Against Yugoslavia," *The Nation*, January 29, 1944, pp. 118–22, 138–42.

Radulovic, Monty. *Tito's Republic*. London, 1948.

Radulović, Borivoje. "The Battle of the Neretva River," *Glasnik SIKD 'Njegoš'*, December 1960, pp. 78–92.

Raičević, Pero. "The Fight for Prozor in February 1943." In *Godišnjak Istoriskog društva Bosne i Hercegovine*, III, 169–80. Sarajevo, 1951.

Ratković, Miodrag. "The Organization of Eastern Serbia." In *Knjiga o Draži*, II, 99–117.

Rendel, George. *The Sword and the Olive*. London, 1957.

Rendulic, Lothar. *Gekämpft, Gesiegt, Geschlagen*. Wels-Heidelberg, 1952.

Ribar, Ivan. *Stara Jugoslavija i komunizam* (Old Yugoslavia and Communism). Zagreb, 1967.

Richards, Denis. *Royal Air Force, 1939–1945*, Vol I, *The Fight at Odds*. History of the Second World War, United Kingdom Military Series. London, 1953.

Rintelen, Enno von. *Mussolini als Bundesgenosse*. Tübingen, 1951.

Ristić, Dragiša N. *Yugoslavia's Revolution of 1941*. University Park, Pa., 1966.

Roatta, Mario. *Otto milioni di baionette*. Milan, 1946.

Roberts, Walter R. *Tito, Mihailović and the Allies, 1941–1945*. New Brunswick, 1973.

Rootham, Jasper. *Miss Fire*. London, 1946.

Rossi, Francesco. *Mussolini e lo Stato Maggiore*. Rome, 1951.

Rozenberg, V. V., and J. Lj. Kostić, *Ko financira jugoslovensku privredu?* (Who Is Financing the Yugoslav Economy?). Belgrade, 1940.

St. Antony's College, Oxford University. "Proceedings of a Conference on Britain and European Resistance 1939–45." Mimeographed. Oxford, 1962.

Saje, Franček. *Belogardizem* (White Guardism). Ljubljana, 1951.

Saunders, H. St. George. *Royal Air Force, 1935–1945*, Vol. III, *The Fight Is Won*. History of the Second World War, United Kingdom Military Series. London, 1954.

Schmidt-Richberg, Erich. *Der Endkampf auf dem Balkan*. Heidelberg, 1955.

Seitz, Albert B. *Mihailović: Hoax or Hero?* Columbus, 1953.

Sekulić, Miloš. *Izveštaj o stanju u Jugoslaviji od aprila do septembra meseca [1941] zaključno i poruke naroda i vojske koja se bori* (A Report on Conditions in Yugoslavia from April to the End of September [1941] and Messages from the People and the Army That Is Fighting). September 1941. Mimeographed copy in Archives of the Institute of Military History, Belgrade, Chetnik Documents, Reg. No. 12/2, Box 20.

Serbian Orthodox Church, The Holy Synod, ed. *Srpska pravoslavna crkva 1920–1970* (The Serbian Orthodox Church, 1920–1970). Belgrade, 1971.

Simović, Dušan T. "Explanation of the Role of Leading Personalities in the

488   Bibliography

coup d'état of March 27, 1941," *Glasnik SIKD 'Njegoš'*, December 1962, pp. 76–78.

————. *Memoirs* . . . . See Kljaković, Vojmir, *Memoirs of General Simović* . . . .

Smiljanić, Milan, et al. *Spomenica pravoslavnih sveštenika—žrtava fašističkog terora i palih u narodnooslobodilačkoj borbi* (The Jubilee Memorial of Orthodox Priests—Victims of Fascist Terror and Those Killed in the National Liberation Struggle). Belgrade, 1960.

Solarić, Milenko. "The Other Side of the 'Bosnian Golgotha,' or How I Became a Member of the Serbian Volunteer Corps," *Zapisi iz dobrovoljačke borbe* (Munich), 1955, No. II, pp. 15–38.

Sperans. See Kardelj, Edvard.

Stajić, Stevan. *Nacionalni dohodak Jugoslavije 1923–1939 u stalnim i tekućim cenama* (National Income of Yugoslavia 1923–1939 in Constant and in Current Prices). Belgrade, 1959.

————. "Real National Income of Yugoslavia During the Periods 1926–1939 and 1947–1956." In Yugoslavia, Economic Institute, *Ekonomski problemi— Zbornik radova* (Economic Problems—A Symposium), pp. 7–58. Belgrade, 1957.

Stakić, Vladislav D. *Moji razgovori sa Musolinijem* (My Conversations with Mussolini). Munich, 1967.

Stambolić, Slobodan. "The Occupation of Serbia in 1941," *Vojnoistorijski glasnik*, 1953, No. 4, pp. 49–67.

Stanić, Milan, ed. *Sudjenje Lisaku, Stepincu, Šaliću, i družini* . . . (The Trial of Lisak, Stepinac, Šalić, and Others . . .). Zagreb, 1946.

Stanisavljević, Djuro. "The Beginning and the Development of the Chetnik Movement in Croatia, 1941–1942." In *Istorija XX veka—Zbornik radova IV*, pp. 5–137. Belgrade, 1962.

Stettinius, Edward R. Jr. *Lend-Lease—Weapon for Victory*. New York, 1944.

Stimson, Henry L., and McGeorge Bundy. *On Active Service in Peace and War*. New York, 1947.

Stojadinović, Milan. *Ni rat ni pakt: Jugoslavija izmedju dva rata* (Neither War Nor Pact: Yugoslavia Between the Wars). Yugoslav edition. Rijeka, 1970.

Stojanović, M. K. "How Draža Mihailović Was Punished," *Glasnik SIKD 'Njegoš'*, June 1962, pp. 61–65.

Sutjeska. 5 vols. Belgrade, 1959–61.

Sweet-Escott, Bickham. *Baker Street Irregular*. London, 1965.

Šehić, Nusret. *Četništvo u Bosni i Hercegovini (1918–1941)* (The Chetniks in Bosnia and Herzegovina, 1918–1941). Sarajevo, 1971.

Šidak, Jaroslav, et al. *Povijest hrvatskog naroda g. 1860–1914* (History of the Croatian People, 1860–1914). Zagreb, 1968.

Škerl, France. "Political Currents in the Slovene Liberation Front During the First Year of Its Existence," *Zgodovinski časopis* (Ljubljana), V (1951), pp. 7–86.

Šubašić, Ivan. "Yugoslavia and the World," *Yugoslavia* (Ridgefield, Conn.), Vol. II (1943), No. 1, pp. 5–8.

Terzić, Velimir. *Jugoslavija u Aprilskom ratu 1941* (Yugoslavia in the April War of 1941). Titograd, 1963.

Tito, Josip Broz. *Borba za oslobodjenje Jugoslavije 1941–1945* (The Struggle for the Liberation of Yugoslavia, 1941–1945). Belgrade, 1947.

————. *Political Report of the Central Committee of the Communist Party of Yugoslavia*. Report delivered at the Fifth Congress. Belgrade, 1948.

———. "The Previous Work and the Tasks of the Party" [report to the Fifth Conference of the Communist Party of Yugoslavia at Zagreb, October 1940], *Communist* (Belgrade, English edition), No. 1 (October 1946), pp. 49–89.

———. *Stvaranje i razvoj Jugoslovenske armije* (The Creation and Development of the Yugoslav Army). Belgrade, 1949.

———. "Tito vous parle" [interview with Raymond Tournoux], *Paris Match*, November 16, 1968.

———. *Vojna djela* (Military Works). 3 vols. Belgrade, 1961. One-volume English-language edition: *Selected Military Works*. Belgrade, 1966.

———. "War Memoirs" [excerpts from the manuscript under the same name], *Socialist Thought and Practice* (Belgrade), June-July 1972, pp. 45–86.

Todorović, Borislav J. "Notes of a Liaison Officer." In *Knjiga o Draži*, I, 372–412.

Tomac, Petar. *Četvrta neprijateljska ofanziva* (The Fourth Enemy Offensive). Belgrade, 1951.

Tomac, Petar, ed. *Oslobodilački pohod na Trst Četvrte jugoslovenske armije* (The Operation of the Fourth Yugoslav Army for the Liberation of Trieste). Belgrade, 1952.

Tomasevich, Jozo. *Financijska politika Jugoslavije 1929–1934* (Fiscal Policy of Yugoslavia, 1929–1934). Zagreb, 1935.

———. "Foreign Economic Relations, 1918–1941." In Robert J. Kerner, ed., *Yugoslavia*, pp. 169–214. Berkeley and Los Angeles, 1949.

———. *Peasants, Politics, and Economic Change in Yugoslavia*. Stanford, 1955.

———. "Yugoslavia During the Second World War." In Wayne S. Vucinich, ed., *Contemporary Yugoslavia*, pp. 59–118. Berkeley and Los Angeles, 1969.

Topalović, Živko. "The Attempts to Oust Mihailović." In *Knjiga o Draži*, II, 120–35.

———. *Borba za budućnost Jugoslavije* (The Struggle for the Future of Yugoslavia), London, 1967.

———. "The Departure from the Country." In *Knjiga o Draži*, II, 56–65.

———. *Kako su komunisti dograbili vlast u Jugoslaviji* (How the Communists Seized Power in Yugoslavia). London, 1964.

———. "The Last Attempt." In *Knjiga o Draži*, II, 177–80.

———. *Pokreti narodnog otpora u Jugoslaviji 1941–1945* (The Movements of Popular Resistance in Yugoslavia, 1941–1945). Paris, 1958.

———. *Srbija pod Dražom* (Serbia Under Draža). London, 1968.

———. "Unfulfilled Hopes," *Poruka* (London), No. 33 (December 16, 1955), pp. 6–10.

Toynbee, Arnold, and Veronica Toynbee, eds. *Survey of International Affairs, 1939–1946: The Initial Triumph of the Axis*. London, 1958.

Trgo, Fabijan. "The Communist Party of Yugoslavia and the Defense of the Country." Unpublished paper read at a symposium at Split, October 1969.

———. *Četvrta i Peta neprijateljska ofanziva* (The Fourth and Fifth Enemy Offensives). Belgrade, 1968.

Trial of Draža Mihailović, see under Yugoslavia, Federal People's Republic of, Union of the Journalists' Associations.

Trials of War Criminals Before the Nuernberg Military Tribunals Under Control Council Law No. 10, Nuernberg, October 1946–April 1949. Vol. XI. Washington, D.C., 1950.

Tributes to General Mihailovich. Windsor, Ont., 1966.

Trišić, Jovan P. *O Milanu Nediću* (About Milan Nedić). Windsor, Ont. 1960.
Trojanović, Radmilo S. "The Negotiations for an Armistice with Germany on April 16 and 17, 1941," *Glasnik SIKD 'Njegoš'*, June 1972, pp. 9–17.
Tudjman, Franjo. *Okupacija i revolucija* (Occupation and Revolution). Zagreb, 1963.
————. *Rat protiv rata* (War Against the War). 2nd ed. Zagreb, 1970.
T. Z. "Vojislav Lukačević," *Glasnik SIKD 'Njegoš'*, June 1962, pp. 93–100.
United States, Department of the Army. *The German Campaigns in the Balkans (Spring 1941)*. Department of the Army Pamphlet No. 20–260. Washington, D.C., November 1953.
————, Department of State. *Documents on German Foreign Policy, 1918–1945*. Washington, D.C., Series D., Vol. XI, 1960; Vol. XII, 1962; Vol. XIII, 1964.
————. *Foreign Relations of the United States—Diplomatic Papers*. Washington, D.C. Volumes for 1941–45.
————. *Foreign Relations of the United States, Diplomatic Papers: The Conferences at Cairo and Tehran, 1943*. Washington, D.C., 1961.
Valev, L. B., H. M. Slavin, and I. I. Udaljcov, eds. *Istoriia Iugoslavii* (History of Yugoslavia). II, 7–184. Moscow, 1963.
Vauhnik, Vladimir. "Ten Years Since the Dismemberment of Yugoslavia." In *Dokumenti o Jugoslaviji*, No. 2, pp. 23–26. Paris, 1951. Partial reprint of the original from *Svobodna Slovenija* (Buenos Aires).
Vertepov, D. P., ed. *Russkii Korpus na Balkanah vo vremia II Velikoi voini 1941–1945 g.g.* (The Russian Corps in the Balkans During the Second World War, 1941–1945). New York, 1963.
Vinaver, Vuk. "The Yugoslav-British Agreement on Arms Deliveries in 1940," *Vojnoistorijski glasnik*, 1966, No. 5, pp. 77–92.
Vinski, Ivo. "National Product and Fixed Assets in the Territory of Yugoslavia, 1909–1959." In International Association for Research in Income and Wealth, *Income and Wealth*, Series IX, pp. 206–33. Chicago, 1961.
————. *Procjena nacionalnog bogatstva po područjima Jugoslavije* (An Estimate of the National Wealth of Yugoslavia by Regions). Zagreb, 1959.
Višnjić, Petar. "The German Occupation System in Serbia in 1941," *Istoriski glasnik* (Belgrade), 1956, No. 3–4, pp. 84–92.
————. "The German Offensive Against Liberated Areas in Southern Serbia in Mid-1944," *Vojnoistorijski glasnik*, 1970, No. 2, pp. 105–67.
————. "The Offensive of Occupation and Quisling Forces in Western Serbia in 1941," *Vojnoistorijski glasnik*, 1966, No. 4, pp. 19–57.
Vrančić, Vjekoslav. *S bielom zastavom preko Alpa* (With a White Flag over the Alps). Buenos Aires, 1953.
Vučetić, Stevan J. *Gradjanski rat u Crnoj Gori 1941–1945* (Civil War in Montenegro, 1941–1945). Detroit, 1947.
Vucinich, Wayne S. "Interwar Yugoslavia." In Wayne S. Vucinich, ed., *Contemporary Yugoslavia*, pp. 3–58. Berkeley and Los Angeles, 1969.
————. "Nationalism and Communism." In Wayne S. Vucinich, ed., *Contemporary Yugoslavia*, pp. 236–84. Berkeley and Los Angeles, 1969.
Vučković, Zvonimir. "The Attack on Serbia in the Spring of 1944." In *Knjiga o Draži*, II, 76–79.
————. "Away with Apologies," *Naša reč* (London), No. 172–73 (June–July 1966), pp. 17–18.
————. "Guerrilla Formation of the Yugoslav Army in the Homeland." In *Knjiga o Draži*, I, 71–73.

————. "The Rescue of American Fliers." In *Knjiga o Draži*, II, 85–90.

————. "The Uprising in Western Serbia." In *Knjiga o Draži*, I, 127–40.

Vujasinović, Todor. *Ozrenski partizanski odred* (The Ozren Mountain Partisan Detachment). Sarajevo, 1950.

Vujošević, Jovan. "German-Italian Relations and the Chetniks in Operation 'Schwarz'." In *Neretva-Sutjeska 1943*, pp. 143–50. Belgrade, 1969.

Vujović, Djuro. "The Situation in the Quisling Formations in Old Montenegro in the Middle of 1944," *Istorijski zapisi*, 1965, No. 3–4, pp. 491–505.

Vukčević, Radoje. "The Americans at Ravna Gora," *Glasnik SIKD 'Njegoš'*, June 1959, pp. 81–93.

————. "From Tehran to the Establishment of the Šubašić Government," *Glasnik SIKD 'Njegoš'*, December 1962, pp. 43–72.

————. "In Regard to the Book of Dr. Ž. Topalović, *The Movements of Popular Resistance in Yugoslavia, 1941–1945*," *Glasnik SIKD 'Njegoš'*, December 1958, pp. 113–25.

————. *Na strašnom sudu* (Before the Dreadful Court). Chicago, 1968.

Vukina, Ivo. "Last Visit to Archbishop Stepinac," *Hrvatski glas* (Winnipeg), February 20, 1945.

Vukmanović Tempo, Svetozar. "In Sarajevo and Eastern Bosnia in 1941 and Early 1942: The Conference at Ivančići." Institut za istoriju radničkog pokreta, Sarajevo, *Prilozi*, IV (1968), 651–61.

Warlimont, Walter. *Im Hauptquartier der deutschen Wehrmacht 1939–1945.* Frankfurt am Main, 1962.

Wedemeyer, Albert C. *Wedemeyer Reports.* New York, 1958.

Wilson, Henry M. W. (Field Marshal Lord Wilson). *Eight Years Overseas 1939–1947.* London, 1950.

Wiskemann, Elizabeth. "The Subjugation of South-eastern Europe, June 1940 to June 1941." In Arnold Toynbee and Veronica Toynbee, eds., *Survey of International Affairs 1939–1946: The Initial Triumph of the Axis*, pp. 319–63. London, 1958.

Wisshaupt, Ernst. "Die Bekämpfung der Aufstandsbewegung im Südostraum." Report prepared by Higher Army Archivist Wisshaupt for the Chief of Staff of the Commander in Chief in Southeast Europe (Army Group F), dated February 1, 1944 (covering the period June 1941–August 1942). Available, in somewhat abbreviated form, as Document No. NOKW-1898, Office of Chief of Counsel (Nuremberg). Mimeographed, 190 pp. A microfilm copy of this report was made available to me by courtesy of Rodoljub Čolaković, Belgrade.

Woodward, Ernest Llewellyn. *British Foreign Policy in the Second World War.* History of the Second World War Series. London, 1962.

————. *British Foreign Policy in the Second World War.* 3 vols. History of the Second World War Series. London, 1970–71.

Yourichitch, Evgueniyé. *Le procès Tito-Mihailovitch.* Paris, 1950.

"Yugoslav Army [Old Yugoslavia]." *Vojna enciklopedija*, IV, 235–55. Belgrade, 1961.

Yugoslavia, Federal People's Republic of. *Statistički godišnjak FNRJ* (Statistical Yearbook of the FPR Yugoslavia), volumes for 1954 and 1956. Belgrade, 1954, 1956.

————. *Sudjenje članovima političkog i vojnog rukovodstva organizacije Draže Mihailovića* (The Trial of the Political Military Leaders of the Organization of Draža Mihailović). Belgrade, 1945.

————, Federal Statistical Office. *Nacionalni sastav stanovništva po opštinama*

(National Composition of Population by Communes). Statistical Bulletin No. 727. Belgrade, 1972.

————. *Narodni dohodak 1952–1956* (National Income, 1952–1956). Statistical Bulletin No. 115. Belgrade, 1958.

————, Information Service. *The Church in the Federal People's Republic of Yugoslavia*. Belgrade, 1959.

————, [People's Republic of Slovenia]. *Proces proti vojnim zločincem in izdajalcem Rupniku, Rösenerju, Rožmanu, Kreku, Vizjaku, in Hacinu* (The Trial of War Criminals and Traitors Rupnik, Rösener, Rožman, Krek, Vizjak, and Hacin). Ljubljana, 1946.

————, State Commission on Ascertainment of Crimes Committed by Occupying Powers and Their Helpers. *Dokumenti o izdajstvu Draže Mihailovića* (Documents on the Treason of Draža Mihailović). Vol. I. Belgrade, 1945.

————, Union of the Journalists' Associations of the FPRY. *The Trial of Dragoljub-Draža Mihailović*. Belgrade, 1946.

Yugoslavia, Kingdom of. *Službene novine Kraljevine Jugoslavije* (Official Gazette of the Kingdom of Yugoslavia). Belgrade, 1921–41; London, 1941–44.

————, Ministry of Finance, Customs Section. *Statistique du commerce extérieur*. Belgrade, annually, 1931–35.

————, National Bank. *L'activité économique en Yougoslavie*. Belgrade, monthly until January 1941.

Yugoslavia, Vojnoistorijski institut. *Aprilski rat 1941—Zbornik dokumenata* (The War of April 1941—A Collection of Documents). Belgrade, 1969.

————. *Drugi svetski rat (Pregled ratnih operacija)* (The Second World War—Review of Military Operations). 4 vols. Belgrade, 1957, 1961, 1964, 1967.

————. *Hronologija oslobodilačke borbe naroda Jugoslavije 1941–1945* (Chronology of the Liberation War of the Peoples of Yugoslavia, 1941–1945). Belgrade, 1964.

————. *Neretva-Sutjeska 1943*. Belgrade, 1969.

————. *Oslobodilački rat naroda Jugoslavije 1941–1945* (Liberation War of the Peoples of Yugoslavia, 1941–1945). 2nd ed. 2 vols. Belgrade, 1963, 1965.

————. *Zbornik dokumenata i podataka o narodnooslobodilačkom ratu jugoslovenskih naroda* (Collection of Documents and Information on the National Liberation War of the Peoples of Yugoslavia). Belgrade, 1949————. Thus far published, 13 tomes in over 150 volumes.

Zanussi, Giacomo. *Guerra e catastrofe d'Italia*. 2 vols. Rome, 1945.

Zečević, Vasilije. " 'From Podgorica to Gradiška'," *Glasnik SIKD 'Njegoš'*, December 1961, pp. 87–91.

Zelenika, Milan. "About Military Operations in Yugoslavia in April 1941," *Vojnoistorijski glasnik*, 1951, No. 4, pp. 198–227.

Ziherl, Boris. "The Epilogue of an Anti-People Conspiracy." In his *Članci i rasprave* (Articles and Studies), pp. 98–115. Belgrade, 1948.

Živanović, Milan Ž. *Solunski proces hiljadu devetsto sedamnaeste* (The Salonika Trial of 1917). Belgrade, 1955.

Živanović, Sergije M. *Djeneral Mihailović i njegovo delo* (General Mihailović and His Deeds). 3 vols. Chicago, 1962, 1966.

Žujović, Mladen J. *Dragiša Vasić*. Pittsburgh, 1948[?].

Žurić, Neva Scotti. "Cooperation Between Serbian Bourgeois Politicians and the Italians with a View to Expanding the Area Under Occupation in Dalmatia, 1941–1942," *Vojnoistorijski glasnik*, 1969, No. 2, pp. 195–211.

Index

Names beginning with Č, Ć, Š, and Ž in Serbo-Croatian form are listed following the entries for C, S, and Z, respectively. Because of the large number and changes in names of individual military units and command posts of various warring nations and groups, these are not indexed.